AN AUTOBIOGRAPHY OR
THE STORY OF MY
EXPERIMENTS WITH TRUTH

An Autobiography
or The Story of My Experiments with Truth

M.K. GANDHI

A CRITICAL EDITION

Translated from the original
in Gujarati by Mahadev Desai

Introduced with Notes by Tridip Suhrud

Foreword by Ashis Nandy

Yale

UNIVERSITY PRESS

New Haven and London

This critical edition of *An Autobiography or The Story of My Experiments With Truth* by M.K. Gandhi, translated by Mahadev Desai and edited by Tridip Suhrud, first published in India in Penguin Books by Penguin Random House India 2018.
First published in the United States in 2018 by Yale University Press.
Introduction and Notes copyright © Tridip Suhrud 2018.
All photographs courtesy the Sabarmati Ashram Preservation and Memorial Trust.

Yale University Press books may be purchased in quantity for educational, business, or promotional use. For information, please e-mail sales.press@yale.edu (U.S. office) or sales@yaleup.co.uk (U.K. office).

Typeset in Bembo Std by Manipal Digital Systems, Manipal.
Printed in the United States of America.

Library of Congress Control Number: 2017963810
ISBN 978-0-300-23407-7 (hardcover : alk. paper)

A catalogue record for this book is available from the British Library.

This paper meets the requirements of ANSI/NISO Z39.48-1992 (Permanence of Paper).

10 9 8 7 6 5 4 3 2 1

CONTENTS

PART II

PART III

FOREWORD

A DESANCTIFIED, USABLE GANDHI

During the last two decades, Tridip Suhrud has emerged as a vital bridge between the late-nineteenth- and early-twentieth-century world of Gujarati literature and culture—from within which Mohandas Karamchand Gandhi emerged—and the global fraternity of scholars who find in Gandhi a voice that defies the seductive mix of the Enlightenment values and a utopic, urban-industrial world to project an altogether different vision of a desirable society.

In that alternative vision, there is a built-in admission that the Enlightenment might have made some significant contributions to human civilization but the utopic vision, which the Enlightenment projects, has little or nothing to say about the central problem humanity faces today—massive, organized, structural and, one might add, 'scientized' violence—towards fellow humans, living nature and future generations that are supposed to inherit the earth.

That quasi-nihilistic violence, which in the twentieth century took a toll of roughly 225 million lives in only genocides, has two crucial components. First, the brutalization that in many societies have taken an epidemic form and, second, the cultivation of political terror without which—one of the protagonists of the French Revolution, Maximilien Robespierre, believed—virtue was helpless.

Like many others, Suhrud rediscovered Gandhi after the Emergency and the suspension of civil rights in India in the 1970s. That discovery is part of a larger movement that sees Gandhi as a serious thinker, whose heritage can no longer be left at the mercy of two kinds of admirers who have played an important role in retailing Gandhi earlier. The first kind venerates him as a saint who must be shelved, because it will be unfair to drag him into the dirty, violent, corrupt world of everyday politics. Talking of this Gandhi, poet Umashankar Joshi once rather sharply reminded philosopher and thinker Ramchandra Gandhi at a seminar that saints in India were a dime a dozen; Gandhi was unique in that he was one saint who was willing to live in the 'slum of politics'. Joshi added that he had borrowed his words from historian Arnold Toynbee who, after the assassination of Gandhi, had said in an homage, 'Henceforth mankind will ask its prophets, "Are you willing to live in the slum of politics?"'

Second, there are those who see Gandhi as only a practical visionary whose political and social interventions were either from Indian traditions or *ex nihilo*, that is, from nowhere. Hence, these admirers consider any serious intellectual engagement with him either a waste of time or an attempt to mislead the present generation of Indians away from the real Gandhi. There is a touch of vulgarity in this stereotype of Gandhi, and it has become now a political ploy to say that Gandhi was all about doing, not thinking or researching. Such a stance has helped the likes of Vinayak Damodar Savarkar to claim that not only was Gandhi anti-science and superstitious, but ignorant of modern European political theory.

My sporadic encounters with Gandhi over the last fifty years prompts me to propose that, among the great freedom fighters and political and social reformers of twentieth-century India, Gandhi was arguably the best acquainted with the dissenting political thinkers and scholars of the West who tried to break radically with the Dionysian self of the European civilization. The three persons Gandhi called his intellectual gurus were all Western—Leo Tolstoy, Henry David Thoreau, John Ruskin—and, perhaps we may now add, Ralph Waldo Emerson as the fourth. And Gandhi was in excellent touch with movements that were fighting racism, colonialism and for what we now might call feminism, human-scale technology and environmental justice in other parts of the world.

Not surprisingly, the Sri Lankan Gandhian, T.K. Mahadevan, whose book *Dvija* was rediscovered during the Emergency, claimed that Gandhi seriously took to the street only twice in his life; the rest of the time he was thinking and writing. Gandhi's ninety-seven-volume *Collected Works* endorses Mahadevan, not his critics.

~

It is in this context that we must judge Tridip Suhrud's efforts to bring the power and the complexity of Gandhi's thought to this generation of Indian intellectuals. Probably Suhrud's first majestic effort along these lines was his much-acclaimed, four-volume English translation of Narayan Desai's massive four-volume Gujarati biography of Gandhi, *My Life Is My Message*, later to become the basis of Desai's moving series of storytelling, *Gandhikatha*, in riot-ravaged Gujarat in the first decade of this century. Desai took *Gandhikatha* not only to small towns and villages of Gujarat but to different parts of India and even to the United States and was invited to take it to Bangladesh when death intervened.

Suhrud's second major venture was the translation of Chandulal Bhagubhai Dalal's perhaps unintentionally moving biography of Harilal, Gandhi's prodigal eldest son. It was published as *Harilal Gandhi: A Life*, with a marvellous brief foreword by Ramchandra Gandhi, which in two pages provides a brilliant, refreshingly new perspective on the critical role Harilal unwittingly played in his father's life as both a seductive anti-self and an unacknowledged critical-moral presence. This book and its suggestive foreword must be read by anyone trying to enter the inner life of Mohandas Gandhi.

The predecessor of the present book was a joint venture of Suresh Sharma and Tridip Suhrud—an annotated, critical edition of *Hind Swaraj*. It can be considered a companion volume to this, an annotated, critical edition of Gandhi's autobiography. The reader will be able to read the autobiography not only as it stands in English but also get some flavour of the Gujarati version and should be able to make a fair guess about the author's intentions, the translator's hesitations and ambivalences and, perhaps, even about the tonal differences between the Gujarati and English versions. Suhrud is an excellent, non-intrusive guide, but he also keeps more than enough space for you to draw your own conclusions and differ violently with his version of truth. (Indeed, this foreword, too, differs at some points from Suhrud's more diffident reading of his own project, as reflected in his less-known book, *Reading Gandhi in Two Tongues and Other Essays*.)

On second thoughts, the present book is one that mediates between not merely Gandhi's time and ours, but also indirectly between Gandhi's global vision and an over-Indianized, venerated but de-radicalized Gandhi—caught in a spider's net called Indian politics.

New Delhi   Ashis Nandy
11 September 2017

A NOTE ON THE ANNOTATIONS

There are two kinds of annotations in this Critical Edition. The notes on the margins of the page, denoted by 'M' before the reference number, offer alternative translations to certain words, phrases and sentences, which have been marked in italics in Gandhi's text. These alternative renderings intend to bring readers closer to the original Gujarati and to enable them to discover some more instances of Gandhi's unique use of language.

The footnotes, numbered by section, contextualize the *Autobiography* by providing details of the persons, institutions or organizations, dates, places and events mentioned by Gandhi. There are also explanations and comments on the text itself, corrections of some inadvertent errors, as well as a comparison between the two editions of the *Autobiography*.

EDITOR'S INTRODUCTION

On 23 November 1925, after two days of agony M.K. Gandhi decided to go on a fast for seven days. There was a 'moral lapse' among the young boys and some girls at the Satyagraha Ashram at Sabarmati. This fast was to commence on 24 November and last up to the 30th.

On the day of the decision Gandhi had a talk with the boys and girls of the Ashram and had told them, rather ominously, 'Do not become the cause of my death.'[1] This had led to a series of confessions—not private but public confessions. Two of the principal ashramites, Mahadev Desai and Kishorelal Mashruwala, objected to the public nature of these confessions and argued that they and by extension none of the other ashramites, with the exception of the founder of the ashramic community, Gandhi, had a right and more crucially the necessary spiritual attainment to hear the confessions. Gandhi argued and demonstrated the inherent beauty in the act of confession, but did not insist upon the public admission of wrongdoing and attendant guilt, nor did he share with anyone that which was shared with him. Gandhi, even if he wanted, could not have fasted for more than seven days. Maganlal Gandhi, the person who held the ashramic routine and organization together during Gandhi's long absences—sometimes enforced by a prison sentence—from the Ashram at Sabarmati, had bound Gandhi to a promise that in the event of a fast he would not undertake one that exceeded seven days.

This decision was taken neither in haste nor without the awareness of its consequences, both on his body and on the boys and girls whose moral lapse had prompted it. It would have reminded Gandhi and many of his associates from South Africa of a similar incident. In July 1913, a moral lapse involving his son Manilal

---

[1] Mahadev Desai, *Mahadevbhai Ni Diary*, vol. 8, edited by C.B. Dalal (Ahmedabad: Sabarmati Ashram Preservation and Memorial Trust, 1966), p. 372. All translations from original Gujarati by Tridip Suhrud (henceforth TS), unless stated otherwise.

1

and Jaykuvar Doctor, the daughter of his close associate Dr. Pranjivandas Mehta had prompted Gandhi to go on a fast for seven days and a vow to have one meal a day for a period of four and a half months. Gandhi later said that he was moved by 'the purest pity for them'. And yet, there was a reoccurrence of the lapse that had forced him to undertake a fourteen-day fast and continue with one meal a day vow till June 1914. In effect, Gandhi had fasted from 12 July 1913 till 26 June 1914, which involved both complete fast and the one-meal-a-day observance. This prolonged fast and his ignorance about the method of resting the body during and immediately after the fast broke his general health, otherwise described as 'excellent'. He recalled this at the conclusion of the 1926 fast. 'It was as a result of the strain I ignorantly put upon my body that I had to suffer from a violent attack of pleurisy which permanently injured a constitution that was fairly sound.'[2]

The Phoenix Settlement in South Africa had an 'ashramic character' especially after the advent of satyagraha in 1906. The community at Sabarmati was ashramic, in the full sense. That is, each member was aware of the Ashram observances and the ideal conduct that they were expected to strive towards, if not attain in every instance.

What was it about this community that its moral lapse prompted Gandhi on several occasions to undertake a purificatory penance? In his account of the lapse at the Phoenix Settlement, Gandhi said, 'News of an apparent failure in the great satyagraha struggle never shocked me, but this incident came upon me like a thunderbolt. I was wounded.'[3]

The Ashram and its community were Gandhi's greatest experiment and also the site for his experiments. It was a community that had its foundations in Truth. Truth is not merely that which we are expected to speak and follow. It is that which alone is, it is that of which all things are made, it is that which subsists by its own power, which alone is eternal. Gandhi's intense yearning was that such Truth should illuminate his heart. In the absence of Truth, or even in case of violation of it, the Ashram could not be. It was simultaneously a community that aspired to ahimsa, not only as a negation, as non-violence, but as an active working of love. This community sought

---

[2] *The Collected Works of Mahatma Gandhi* (New Delhi: Publications Division), vol. 29, p. 316. The project known as the *CWMG* commenced in September 1956 and concluded with the publication of 100 volumes in 1994, of these ninety-seven volumes contain Gandhi's writings and volumes 98 and 99 contains subject index and index of names respectively, while the last volume is a compilation of the editorial prefaces of the preceding volumes. Henceforth cited as *CWMG*; year of publication of each individual volume is not necessary in the customary citation of the *CWMG*.

[3] TS's translation, Chapter XXXVI, Part IV, see n. 1.

to lead a life of 'non-stealing', which included in its understanding 'bread-labour' and non-acquisition. This community sought to cultivate equability or *samabhava*, with regard to religion and on the practice of untouchability. Samabhava, Gandhi knew, is possible only when the sense of *mamabhava*, of 'mine-ness', of possession, disappears. Gandhi had hoped that his Ashram would be like the *sthitaprajna*, a person of 'equi-poise', a person whose intellect is 'secure'—both lodged firmly and unwavering in its processes—as described in the Bhagvad Gita. 'When it is night for all other beings, the disciplined soul is awake! When all other beings are awake it is the night for the seeing ascetic.'[4] Such an Ashram Gandhi believed was his only creation, the only measure by which he would be judged and would like to be judged. Writing at the conclusion of the 1925 fast he said of the Ashram, 'It is my best and only creation. The world will judge me by its results.'[5]

For Gandhi, the purity or the impurity of the principal worker affected the community. If he were free from fault, the atmosphere would be affected by his innocence. Thus untruth in the Ashram was a symptom of a deep failing, a failing which could only be attributed to himself. It was a sign that the light with which he aspired to lead his life still eluded him. What he was required to do was to reach deep within and seek to dispel the darkness. Reaching deep within himself necessitated for Gandhi a combination of a set of self-practices, silence, prayer, self-search, fidelity to Truth and *brahmacharya*. These are also the Ashram observances. The mode by which Gandhi sought to reach within himself and the observances that made him an ashramite are the same. To be an ashramite is to acquire the capacity for self-search and only by acquiring this capacity could he be an ashramite. This he hoped and believed would purify himself and those around him. He wrote on the steps to be taken on the emergence of untruth: 'The first thing attended to was the purity of the principal workers in charge, the idea being that if they were free from fault, the atmosphere about them was bound to be affected by their innocence.'[6] The second mode was confession by the wrongdoer. This confession had to be judiciously adopted. The confession should not be tainted by force and the confession should not lead to the person confessing taking leave of shame. It would also require the community to not castigate the wrongdoer as unworthy of

---

[4] Bhagvad Gita, Verse 69, Discourse II. *The Gospel of Selfless Action or the Gita According to Gandhi*, (trans.) Mahadev Desai (Ahmedabad: Navajivan, 1946), p. 166.

[5] *CWMG*, vol. 29, p. 291.

[6] M.K. Gandhi, *Ashram Observances in Action*, translated from the Gujarati by Valji Govindji Desai (Ahmedabad, Navajivan, 1955), p. 13.

being part of the ashramic community. The third measure was a fast, both by the
principal worker of the Ashram and by the wrongdoer. For the latter, as it was a
matter of self-violation, s/he was free to decide if such a fast should be undertaken.
Such bodily penance had, according to Gandhi, a threefold influence: 'First over
the penitent, secondly over the wrongdoer and thirdly over the congregation. The
penitent becomes more alert, examines the innermost recesses of his own heart
and takes steps to deal with any personal weakness that he may discover. If the
wrongdoer has any pity, he becomes conscious of his own faults, is ashamed of it
and resolves never to sin any more in the future. The congregation takes a course
of self introspection.'[7]

This moral lapse and the attendant fast came to Gandhi at a time when he
had begun to write his autobiography. The awareness that there was darkness and
untruth within and around him at the very instance of commencement of the
narrative devoted to the search for Truth could only have made Gandhi more alert
and humble about both the endeavours—that of being an ashramite and a seeker
after Truth about to narrate the journey of his striving.

Gandhi commenced his fast on 24 November 1925 and the first chapter of his
autobiography, *Satya Na Prayogo* (My Experiments with Truth), was published in
Navajivan on 25 November. The coming together of the autobiographical act and
fasting might suggest serendipity to some but to Gandhi it would have appeared as a
sign—not from above, not from without and beyond but from within, from a voice
which he described as 'a small, still voice'—that he was ready to lay bare what was
hitherto known only to him and his God, Satyanarayan, God as Truth.

If the *Autobiography* required him to dwell within himself, fasting was *upvas*, to
dwell closer to Him, to be closer to Truth. Both the autobiographical act and the
upvas were modes by which Gandhi dwelled closer to Truth. This in-dwelling had
a physicality, not grossly in his body but within the Ashram and with the Ashram
community.

The Ashram or 'a community of men of religion'[8] is central to Gandhi's striving.
He was to later claim, 'Ashram was a necessity of life for me'.[9] The Ashram is a
community of co-religionists, co-practitioners, bound together by a shared quest
and a set of obligatory observances. The Ashram, therefore, is where the ashramites

---

[7] Ibid., pp. 15–16.

[8] Ibid., p. 4.

[9] Ibid.

are. Thus the Yeravada prison—*mandir*, or temple, as he called it—the Agakhan Palace prison were as much an Ashram as the Satyagraha Ashram at Sabarmati and Sevagram at Wardha. But the Ashram for Gandhi, more than anything else, eventually came to signify the ashramic observances. In his need and quest to inhabit the Ashram, the Ashram found a space within him. The Ashram went with him on his lonely pilgrimage to Noakhali and to Bihar that was his Karbala.

Before establishing the Satyagraha Ashram first at Kochrab and later at Sabarmati, Gandhi had established two Ashram-like communities in South Africa. Ashram-like, as he steadfastly refused to describe them as an Ashram. One was merely a settlement, at Phoenix, and the other a farm, the Tolstoy Farm. The Phoenix Settlement was established in 1904 under the 'Magic spell' of John Ruskin's *Unto This Last* but acquired an Ashram-like character only after 1906. It was in 1906 that Gandhi took the vow of brahmacharya, initially in the limited sense of chastity and celibacy. Gandhi says, 'From this time onward I looked upon Phoenix deliberately as a religious institution.'[10] The observance of a *vrata*, often inadequately translated as a vow, too was a defining characteristic of the Ashram.[11] It was only through these observances that a community became a congregation of co-religionists and a settlement, a place for experiments with Truth.

The year 1906 was also the year of the advent of satyagraha. Its origin was in a pledge, a pledge that was different from a normal, deliberate oath; as the pledge was taken in the name of God and with God as witness, it was based on religion and implied an unshakeable faith in Satyanarayan. Such a pledge was not externally administered. Phoenix and later Tolstoy Farm, established in 1911, became places where personal spiritual quest and the community's search for dignity and self-respect were combined in and through satyagraha. When Gandhi established the Ashram at a hired bungalow at Kochrab village, Ahmedabad, he was conscious of setting it up as an Ashram, Satyagraha Ashram.

Satyagraha was to be the chosen mode of experiments with Truth. Satyagraha is not only a method based on the moral superiority of self-suffering and the recognition of the humanity of others—especially those we seek to oppose—but is a mode of conduct that leads to self-knowledge. Without self-knowledge Satyagraha is not possible as it is based upon an inviolable relationship between the means and ends, and its essence is in the purity of means. Pure means are not only non-violent means

---

[10] Ibid., pp. v–vi.

[11] *Vrata* is a rite, a resolute observance that necessarily involves the acceptance of a higher power, and has within it an element of devotion.

but means adopted by a pure person—a person who through a constant process of self-examination cleanses and purifies the self; whose only aim is to be a seeker after Truth. Gandhi posits an immutable relationship between satyagraha, pure means and the purity of the practitioner. In the absence of the latter, true satyagraha is not possible. Satyagraha is fundamentally an experiment with Truth in the sense that it allows those who practise it to know themselves.

Satyagraha as a mode of self-recognition is directly linked to Swaraj. 'It is Swaraj when we learn to rule ourselves.'[12] This idea of ruling the self was fundamentally different from self-rule or Home Rule. To rule ourselves means to be devoted to Truth, to be moral and to have control over our senses. His idea of civilization is based on this possibility of rule over the self. He says, 'Civilization is that mode of conduct which points out to man the path of duty. Performance of duty and observance of morality are convertible terms. To observe morality is to attain mastery over our mind and our passions. So doing, we know ourselves.'[13]

In this, we have an understanding of Gandhi's quest. His quest is to know himself, to attain moksha, that is, to see God (Truth) face-to-face. In order to fulfil this quest, he must be an ashramite, a satyagrahi and a seeker after Swaraj.

This quest is made possible by Ashram observances. Satyagraha and Swaraj as modes of self-knowledge are based on Truth because without Truth there can be no knowledge. That is why the term *chit*, or knowledge, is associated with *sat*, that is, Truth. Hence, Truth becomes a primary observance; it constitutes the root of the Ashram. What can be known by Truth is knowledge. What is excluded from it is not Truth, not true knowledge. Steadfastness to Truth, even unto death, requires immense and inexhaustible faith in God as Truth. Yet, Gandhi would confess that such perfect knowledge, realization of perfect Truth, might not be possible so long as we are imprisoned in a mortal body.

This impossibility leads the seeker to ahimsa, or love. Violence and the quest for Truth cannot exist together. Gandhi said, 'Hence, the more he took to violence, the more he receded from Truth.'[14] If violence makes a person recede from Truth, it also makes a person recede from the self. Violence leads to self-forgetfulness, and amnesia about the self makes both satyagraha and Swaraj impossible, as they are

---

[12] *M.K. Gandhi's Hind Swaraj: A Critical Edition*, annotated, translated and edited by Suresh Sharma and Tridip Suhrud (New Delhi: Orient Blackswan, 2010), pp. 59–60.

[13] Ibid., p. 56.

[14] M.K. Gandhi, *From Yeravda Mandir*, translated from the original Gujarati by Valji Govindji Desai (Ahmedabad: Navajivan, 1935, second edition), p. 5.

based on the capacity for self-realization. Thus, Truth is the end and ahimsa, the means to it.

A person whose only object is Truth, his method satyagraha, cannot be faithful to anything but Truth. 'The man, who is wedded to Truth and worships faith alone, proves unfaithful to her if he applies his talents to anything else.'[15] This leads him and us to brahmacharya. For Gandhi, the realization of Truth and self-gratification appear a contradiction in terms. From this emanates not only brahmacharya but also three other observances: control of the palate, *aparigraha* (non-possession) and *asteya* (non-stealing).

Brahmacharya came to Gandhi as a necessary observance at the time he organized an ambulance corps during the Zulu rebellion in South Africa. He realized that service of the community was not possible without celibacy. At the age of thirty-seven, in 1906 Gandhi took the vow of brahmacharya.

He had begun to experiment with food and diet as a student in Rajkot and later in England. It was much later that he was to comprehend the relationship between brahmacharya and the control of the palate. Brahmacharya is not possible when other senses are allowed free play. It requires not the suppression of one sense and the unbridled expression of all the others. Brahmacharya is a mode by which the sense organs are withdrawn from the objects of the senses. A *brahmachari*, like the sthitaprajna of the Gita is one who puts away 'all the cravings that arise in the mind and finds comfort for himself only from the *Atman*'[16] and one 'whose senses are reined in on all sides from their objects' (verse 68) so that the mind is 'untroubled in sorrows and longeth not for joys, who is free from passion, fear and wrath; who knows attachment nowhere' (verse 56); only such a brahmachari can be in the world, 'moving among sense objects with the senses weaned from likes and dislikes and brought under the control of the *Atman*' (verse 64).

For Gandhi, the twin concepts of non-possession and non-stealing were suggestive of a mental state as the body itself is a possession and the effort to sustain it brings other possessions in its train. Non-stealing is not only a prohibition against theft, of taking something that belongs to someone else, but to take something that someone else might need, to take, possess and consume more than the minimum necessary as 'God never creates more than what is strictly needed for the moment'.[17]

---

[15] Ibid., p. 8.

[16] Gita, Verse 55, Discourse II, *The Gospel of Selfless Action or the Gita According to Gandhi*, translated from the original Gujarati by Mahadev Desai (Ahmedabad: Navajivan, 1946).

[17] *Ashram Observances in Action*, p. 58.

The twin concepts, with deep ecological significance, are linked to the idea of 'trusteeship', so that we act not only as trustees of our wealth, but that of the earth and the futures to come. Non-stealing and non-possession, for Gandhi, inculcate a spirit of detachment in the ashramites and prepares them to give up all possessions, including the body.

These observances and strivings, Gandhi was later to feel, were 'secretly preparing' him for satyagraha.[18] It would take him several decades, but through his observances, his experiments, Gandhi developed insights into the interrelatedness of Truth, ahimsa and brahmacharya. This understanding allowed him to expand the idea of brahmacharya itself. He began with a popular and limited notion of chastity and celibacy, including celibacy in marriage. He expanded this to mean observance in thought, word and deed. However, it is only when he began to recognize the deeper and fundamental relationship that brahmacharya shared with satyagraha, ahimsa and Swaraj that Gandhi could go to the root of the term 'brahmacharya'. *Charya*, or conduct, adopted in search of Brahma, that is Truth, is brahmacharya. In this sense, brahmacharya is not denial or control over one sense, but an attempt to bring all senses in harmony with each other. Brahmacharya so conceived and practised becomes the mode of conduct that leads to Truth, knowledge and hence moksha. An experiment in Truth is an experiment in brahmacharya. An experiment with Truth cannot have any possibility of secrecy. As an experiment, it was important and imperative, Gandhi felt, to record the unusual, uncontrolled occurrences. It was essential to speak of the darkness within. To speak of the darkness within required a sense of detachment and equanimity with regard to the self. This sense occupies a ground philosophically different from objectivity or distance. In objectivity and distance, a divide of the observer and the observed is implied; it is the objectivity that a scientist cultivates. The equanimity of a seeker is with regard to the self, where the observer and the observed is the self. Gandhi used two terms from the Gita to describe such a philosophical disposition with regard to the self: sthitaprajna and non-attachment, or *nishkama*. A sthitaprajna is a yogi who acts without attachment either to the action or the fruits thereof. Nishkama does not imply absence of purpose or action; as the supreme purpose, moksha remains even in a state of renunciation. It is for the purpose of self-realization that the fruits of all action and the desire for action itself have to be abandoned. It is, therefore, not surprising that Gandhi sought to cultivate the state of equipoise, of sthitaprajna.

~

---

[18] See, *Autobiography*, Chapter XXVI, Part IV.

As Gandhi found himself face-to-face with the autobiographical act and the penitent, purificatory fast that had come upon him, he must have reflected on the necessity of two other kinds of observances, two kinds of in-dwelling that were required for him to attempt the story of his soul in the quest for Truth and brahmacharya.

These were the necessity of being an ashramite and the other to reflect deeply on the meaning of the Bhagvad Gita.

Gandhi had one deeply felt need, desire, want and aspiration: to be an ashramite in the sense of living for a length of time in the communities that he had created. His oft-repeated lament was that his work and obligation to myriad causes made him an itinerant ashramite. The Ashram observances went with him, but the community of co-religionists could not. This was true not only of the Ashram at Sabarmati, but also of the Phoenix Settlement and the Tolstoy Farm.

The day the Ashram at Sabarmati was founded—17 June 1917—Gandhi was far away in Motihari for his work on the Agrarian Inquiry Commission. From 17 June 1917 to 12 March 1930, when he left the Ashram for the coastal village of Dandi, never to return, Gandhi spent a total of 1520 days at the Ashram. On 3 January 1928, in an article in *Navajivan*, and on 7 January 1926 in a longer one in *Young India*, Gandhi announced his decision to suspend all engagements, including previously fixed tours and spend the year (the date fixed for this sabbatical was 20 December 1926) at the Ashram and at Ahmedabad. 'It is not without sorrow that I have to announce to the numerous co-workers the suspension of my touring programme for about one year. At least up to 20th December meet, I am not to stir out of the Ashram, certainly not out of Ahmedabad, except for imperative reasons of health or some unforeseen event.'[19] Gandhi described this year of in-dwelling at the Ashram: 'For me this year of grace is both an indulgence and self-denial.'[20] 'Grace' clearly because it had come upon him like a shower of mercy, unsought, unbeckoned but deeply longed for. He had waited for this patiently, preparing himself and the decision had come to him at perhaps the most propitious moment. 'It is an indulgence because I hope to fulfil the long-cherished desire of being in the midst of the boys and girls and the fellow-workers of the Ashram. It is self-denial because it was a pleasure to me to be with so many friends in the different provinces and be the recipient of the affection of the masses between whom and myself there is a bond which defies description but is nevertheless is felt alike by them and me.'[21]

---

[19] *CWMG,* vol. 29, p. 318.

[20] *CWMG,* vol. 29, p. 382.

[21] Ibid.

Gandhi's in-dwelling at the Ashram during the period of writing the *Autobiography* was the most sustained and intense ever. In his declaration of suspension of public work, Gandhi had said that he would not stir out of the Ashram, certainly not Ahmedabad. Within a week he amended the condition and excluded even Ahmedabad, the city within which the Ashram was located, from his notion of in-dwelling. He wrote, 'When I decided on voluntary retirement from active work, I excluded, whether out of ignorant attachment or fear, from the scope of my decision though I personally wished for it, a visit to Ahmedabad . . . if I really wished to have peace, my retirement from public life should mean retirement to the Ashram. I cannot, therefore, leave the Ashram to attend any function or participate in any activity outside it, even in Ahmedabad.'[22]

From 25 November 1925 to 3 February 1929, the period during which the *Autobiography* was written and published, Gandhi spent 685 days at the Ashram. The *Autobiography*, in that sense, was written during his period of in-dwelling at the Ashram.

Gandhi's in-dwelling at the Ashram and within himself began with a series of lectures that Vinoba Bhave gave between 4 and 16 January 1926. These lectures delivered each morning and evening to the Ashram congregation at prayer time were on the *Kenopanishad* and the Gita.

Gandhi first read the Gita as a student in London with theosophist friends— Bertram and Archibald Keightley—in Sir Edwin Arnold's translation, *The Song Celestial*. Gandhi recalled in the *Autobiography* that he was captured by Verses 62 and 63 of the second discourse.

> 'If one
> Ponders on object of the sense, there springs
> Attraction; from attraction grows desire,
> Desire flames to fierce passion, passion breeds
> Recklessness; then the memory – all betrayed-
> Lets noble purpose go, and saps the mind,
> Till purpose, mind, and man are all undone.'

The verses describe the state that is the opposite of brahmacharya. In 1888–89, young Gandhi was far from making brahmacharya, even in a limited sense of chastity and celibacy, a quest of his life. But what awakened in Gandhi a religious quest and

---

[22] *CWMG,* vol. 29, pp. 390–91.

longing that was to govern his entire life henceforth was the message contained in these two verses. That the only way to be in the world was to strive to reach the state of brahmacharya. This reading produced a keen desire in him to read the Gita in the original Sanskrit and in various Gujarati translations. The Gita became a lifelong companion and a spiritual guide. As his engagement with it deepened, he 'by-hearted' it in South Africa. By-hearted because its verses were not only committed to memory but they came to be etched on his heart.

During his imprisonment in 1922 Gandhi composed a lexicographic dictionary and a concordance of each term in the Gita and its various meanings in the poem. This was published in 1936 as *Gita Padarthkosha*.[23] The Gita was not only central to his life but several Ashram associates too wrote commentaries on and translated the Gita. The most celebrated among them are Vinoba Bhave, Kishorelal Mashruwala and Mahadev Desai. The text came to occupy a role of a guide not only to philosophical reflection but also for conduct. Gandhi said 'The *Gita* has for years been an authoritative guide to belief and conduct for Satyagraha Ashram. It has provided us with a test with which to determine the corrections or otherwise of our conduct in question.'[24] It became a measure of the 'truth' of their actions. 'The Gita for me is a perennial guide to conduct. From it I seek support for all my actions and if, in a particular case, I don't find the needed support, I would refrain from the proposed action or at any rate feel uncertain about it.'[25]

In order that the Gita become the spiritual guide book for the ashramites, it was necessary that it be ever present as an object of contemplation; each ashramite was urged to commit the Gita to memory. It became an essential part of the Ashram prayers, both in the morning and the evening. The day at the Ashram began with the congregational morning prayer at 4.20 a.m., a time when the tiller of the soil and a true devotee of God woke up. The Ashram's congregational activities ceased with the evening prayer at 7 p.m. So central was this prayer to the life of the Ashram community that Gandhi could claim, 'Ever since the Ashram was founded, not a single day has passed to my knowledge without this worship.'[26] During the morning prayers the recitation of the Gita was so arranged that the entire text was recited every fourteen days; later this was changed so that the recitation was completed in

---

[23] M.K. Gandhi, *Gita Padarthkosha*, edited by Kakasaheb Kalelkar (Ahmedabad: Navajivan, 1936).

[24] *CWMG*, vol. 56, p. 156.

[25] *CWMG*, vol. 84, p. 71.

[26] *CWMG*, vol. 56, p. 152.

seven days.[27] The eighteen verses of the second discourse of the Gita that describe
the characteristics of sthitaprajna became part of the daily evening prayers. But the
recitation of the Gita and committing it to memory hardly constitute following the
truth of the Gita. The framework for conduct was provided by the Ashram vows.
Gandhi said, 'The Ashram life is conceived in the light of comprehensive and non-
formal sanyasa of the Bhagvad Gita.'[28]

As Gandhi dwelled in the Ashram and reflected on this journey in pursuit of
Truth and brahmacharya, he was increasingly drawn to the Gita as a philosophical
text. He decided to give a daily discourse on the Gita, hoping to elaborate on the
incessant striving to lead his life by its ideals. The morning prayer provided the
occasion. On 24 February 1926 Gandhi gave the first discourse; by the time he
concluded the lecture series on 23 November 1926 he had given 218 discourses
on the Gita. Gandhi had been commenting on stray verses and deducing his own
meaning from them, often leaving his co-workers confounded by his interpretation.
Not satisfied with his discourses they demanded that Gandhi also translate the Gita
into Guajarati with notes. The year-long in-dwelling at the Ashram afforded the
opportunity. Thus, along with his autobiographical narrative and daily discourses,
Gandhi began the translation of the Gita so that the meaning he derived from it could
be fully comprehended. Gandhi's Gujarati translation of the Gita was published on
the day that Gandhi, along with chosen satyagrahis, began his march to Dandi on
12 March 1930.

Gandhi rarely made a claim to originality and even rarer it was for him to claim
literary merit for his writings. But while presenting his translation he made a claim
that no translation had made thus far. 'This desire does not mean much disrespect
to other renderings. They have their own place. But I am not aware of the claim
made by the translators of enforcing their meaning of the Gita in their own lives. At
the back of my reading there is the claim of an endeavour to enforce the meaning
in my own conduct for an unbroken period of 40 years. For this reason I do indeed
harbour the wish that all Gujarati men or women wishing to shape their conduct
according to their faith should digest and derive strength from the translations
here presented.'[29] The path of the Gita, Gandhi said, was neither contemplation,

---

[27] The recitations of various Discourses of the Gita were distributed among the days as follows: Friday
      1 & 2, Saturday 3, 4 & 5, Sunday 6, 7 and 8; Monday 9, 10, 11 & 12; Tuesday 13, 14 & 15;
      Wednesday 16 &17; Thursday 18.

[28] *CWMG*, vol. 40, p.110.

[29] *Gita According to Gandhi*, p. 123.

nor devotion; the ideal was sthitaprajna. Gandhi adopted, and wanted the Ashram community to adopt, a mode of conduct, a self practice to attain a state where one acts and yet does not act. This mode, this disposition was *yajna*, sacrifice. The Gita declared that 'together with the sacrifice did the Lord of beings create'[30] and the world would sustain so long as there was sacrifice, as 'sacrifice produced rain'.[31] Gandhi found the word yajna full of beauty and power. He saw this ideal of sacrifice as the basis of all religions. Gandhi emphasized the aspect of cultivating the disposition of a yogi, and his exemplar was Jesus Christ. It was he who had shown the path. Gandhi said that the term yajna had to be understood in the way 'Jesus put on a crown of thorns to win salvation for his people, allowed his hands and feet to be nailed and suffered agonies before he gave up the ghost. This has been the law of *Yajna*. From immemorial times without *Yajna* the earth cannot exist even for a moment.'[32]

For Gandhi, an act of service was sacrifice, or yajna. But how does one perform sacrifice in daily life?

His response was twofold; for one, he turned to the Bible and other was uniquely his own.

'Earn thy bread by the sweat of thy brow', says the Bible. Gandhi made this central to the life of the Ashram and borrowed the term 'bread labour' from Tolstoy to describe the nature of work. This was an eternal principal; it was dharma, duty, to perform bread labour, and those who did not perform this yajna, ate, according to the Gita, 'stolen' food. The other form of yajna was that which is peculiar to one's times, as every age may and should have its own yajna, known as *Yug-dharma*, duty entailed upon one by the particular age. For Gandhi, the yajna of his times was spinning, his Yug-dharma. Spinning was an obligatory Ashram observance; each member was required to spin 140 threads daily, each thread measuring four feet. This spinning was called *sutra-yajna*, sacrificial spinning. One of the reasons for his decision to spend the year at the Ashram was to devote more attention to spinning and to resolving the organizational issues of the body that he had created, the All India Spinners Association.

During the same year, students of the Gujarat Vidyapith that he had founded in 1920, and whose chancellor he was, invited him to give lectures. They wanted him to reflect on the life of Christ. The lectures on the Bible, specifically the Sermon on

---

[30] Verse 10, Discourse III.

[31] Verse 14, Discourse III.

[32] *CWMG*, vol. 20, p. 404.

the Mount, began on 24 July 1926. The plan was to conduct these classes on each Saturday thereafter. But as soon as Gandhi began teaching the New Testament, he was 'taken to task' for reading it to the students. One correspondent asked, 'Will you please say why you are reading the Bible to the students of the Gujarat National College? Is there nothing useful in our literature? Is the Gita less to you than the Bible? You are never tired of saying that you are a staunch *Sanatani*. Have you not now been found as a Christian in secret? You may say that a man does not become a Christian by reading the Bible. But is not reading the Bible to the boys a way of converting them to Christianity? Can the boys remain uninfluenced by the Bible reading? Are they not likely to become Christians by reading the Bible? What is there specifically in the Bible that is not to be found in our sacred books? I do hope you will give an adequate reply and give preference to the Vedas over the Bible.'[33]

Gandhi saw this hyper sensitivity as an indication of the intensity of 'the wave of intoleration that is sweeping through this unhappy land'[34] and refused the correspondent's request to give preference to the Vedas over the Bible. To him, his study and reverence for the Bible and other scriptures was wholly consistent with his claim to be a Hindu. 'He is no *Sanatani* Hindu who is narrow, bigoted and considers evil to be good if it has the sanction of antiquity and is to be found supported in any Sanskrit book.'[35]

The charge of being a Christian in secret was not new. He found it both a libel and a compliment. It was a libel because there were still people in the world, especially at a time when he was writing and publishing the *Autobiography*, who believed that he was capable of being anything in secret, for the fear of being that openly. He declared, 'There is nothing in the world that would keep me from professing Christianity or any other faith the moment I felt the truth of and the need for it.'[36] This was a compliment, because therein Gandhi felt an acknowledgement, however reluctant, of his capacity for appreciating the beauties of Christianity. He wished to own up to that charge and the compliment.

~

---

[33] *Young India*, vol. VIII, no. 35, p. 308.

[34] *CWMG*, vol. 31, p. 351.

[35] Ibid.

[36] Ibid.

The *Autobiography* had to be written in Gujarati. This was not just a gesture, though Gandhi understood the importance of gestures in political life. The choice was also not made because he had hoped to serve the country through the mother tongue.

If the Ashram, with its observances and the ashramic community that affirmed Gandhi's experiments and quest, was one form of in-dwelling, the other form of dwelling within was through the Gujarati language. This in-dwelling was not only with the language of experiences and memory, but for Gandhi it was also about the very form that he wished to give to his autobiography. Just as he was urged by his associates to write the autobiography, 'a God-fearing friend had his doubts, which he shared with me on my day of silence. "What has set you on these adventures?" he asked, "Writing an autobiography is a practice peculiar to the West. I know of nobody in the east having written one, except among those who have come under Western influence."'[37]

Gandhi was being reminded—if he needed to be so reminded—of the autobiography's roots in early Christianity, and the emergence of the practice of writing the story of one's life in nineteenth-century India. The autobiography had emerged along with the novel and the practice of writing history, principally amongst those who had acquired education of the English type and sought to reform, literally re-form themselves and their cultural milieu.

There were two significant autobiographies written and published in Gujarati before Gandhi's *Atmakatha*. Poet, lexicographer, reformer, historian and pioneering journalist Narmadashanker Lalshanker Dave (1833–1886) wrote in 1866, at the age of thirty-three, his autobiography, *Mari Hakikat* (My Factual Account). Narmad was the first one to write and publish an autobiographical account in Gujarati. 'For someone like me to write his own story and moreover print and publish it during my lifetime itself may appear disrespectful to our people. I am not a learned man, nor a warrior, nor a religious leader, nor am I a wealthy philanthropist.'[38] Narmad chose to introduce a self-conscious break with the past not 'Either to be famous (I am already famous) or to amass wealth or position'[39] but this act, he hoped, would allow him 'to institute the practice of writing the autobiography which does not exist among us'.[40] This impulse to modernize the literary culture is evident in many

---

[37] *Autobiography*, Introduction.

[38] Narmad, *Mari Hakikat*, edited by Ramesh Shukla (Surat: Kavi Narmad Yugavrat Trust, 1994), p. 21; translated here from the Gujarati by TS.

[39] Ibid.

[40] Ibid.

pioneering efforts at writing the autobiography in various Indian languages from mid- to late nineteenth century.

The other published autobiography in Gujarati was that of Narayan Hemchandra. There is no written evidence that Gandhi had read these two autobiographies but he had read the writings of Narmad and was acquainted with Narayan Hemchandra to whom Gandhi devoted a chapter in the *Autobiography*. It is possible that Gandhi was not unfamiliar with their autobiographical narratives.

Both these narratives are chronicles of the lives of the two authors. The lives of interiority, of their intellectual, spiritual or social strivings do not move the narrative.

The God-fearing friend who cautioned Gandhi had these examples of the modernizing impulse before him when he cautioned Gandhi.

Gandhi records that this argument had some effect on him. In one of the most creative transpositions of literary forms in Gujarati, Gandhi differentiated 'a real autobiography' and the story he would write. He wrote, 'But it is not a real autobiography. I simply want to tell the story of my numerous experiments with truth, and as my life consists of nothing but these experiments, it is true that the story will take the shape of the autobiography.'[41] In the original Gujarati, Gandhi introduced this difference through two forms, *jivan vrutant* (autobiography or the chronicle of life) and *atmakatha* (the story of a soul). What Gandhi wanted to write was an *atmakatha* and not a *jivan vrutant*. This distinction gets blurred in the English rendering, 'autobiography'. The *atmakatha*, Gandhi knew, would only be written in Gujarati, the language in which he communicated with the self and also the language in which he heard the 'small, still voice' speaking from within.

The response that Gandhi gave to the friend who cautioned him also provides primacy to his experiments with Truth and not to the narration of his life story. This emphasis is captured in the Gujarati, where the title *Satya Na Prayogo athva Atmakatha* foregrounds the experiments with Truth. The order is reversed in the English translation, where 'An Autobiography' has primacy.

Gandhi wrote the *Autobiography* in 166 instalments, which were serially published in *Navajivan* and its English translation followed in *Young India*, which was also republished in *Indian Opinion* and the American journal *Unity*. In January 1926, John Haynes Holmes, a minister of the community church wrote to Gandhi, 'I am writing at this time not merely to state my gratitude for this forthcoming story of your immortal life but also to state my intention of publishing it in my

---

[41] *Autobiography*, Introduction.

paper, *Unity*, as it comes to me from week to week through the medium of your Journal.'[42]

We should remind ourselves that the *Autobiography* was neither written nor placed before the readers as a 'book'. The readers had the opportunity, while the *Autobiography* was being written, to respond to it. Gandhi confessed that he did not have a plan before him as he wrote the story of his experiments with Truth week after week for 166 weeks.

Even after almost a year and a half into the exercise Gandhi wrote to Haynes, 'I am unable to tell you when the autobiography will be finished. I have to write from day to day. I have mapped out no fixed plan. I write every week as past events develop in my mind.'[43]

Gandhi claimed that he wrote at the prompting of the 'dweller within'—'Spirit', as Mahadev Desai translated the term *antaryami*.

On 24 July 1927 the chapter on 'Intimate European Contacts' (Chapter XI, Part IV) was published in *Navajivan*. In this chapter he felt it necessary to explain to the reader how the story was being written from week to week, an exercise that had begun in the December of 1925. He told them, 'When I began writing it, I had no definite plan before me. I have no diary or documents on which to base the story of my experiments. I write first as the Spirit moves me at the time of writing. I do not claim to know definitely that all conscious thought and actions on my part is directed by the Spirit . . . I think it will not be improper to say that all of them were directed by the Spirit'.[44] This claim of writing at the prompting of the antaryami, the dweller within, distinguishes an *atmakatha* from a *jivan vrutant*. Gandhi suggests that an *atmakatha* is not only the story of the soul in its quest for Truth, but it is written through a process which reveals that which was hitherto known only to the self and had come to subside in the self.

And it is for this reason that Gandhi is aware of the inadequacy of the autobiography as history. 'I know that I do not set down in this story all that I remember, who can say how much I must give and how much omit in the interest of truth? And what would be the value in a court of law of the inadequate *ex parte* evidence being tendered by me of certain events in my life? If some busybody were to cross examine me on the chapters already written, he could probably shed much

---

[42] Sabarmati Nidhi 32215 (Sabarmati Nidhi followed by a number refers to the accession number in the archives of the Sabarmati Ashram Preservation and Memorial Trust; henceforth SN).

[43] *CWMG*, vol. 33, p. 299.

[44] Chapter XI, Part IV.

more light on them, and if it were a hostile critic's cross-examination, he might even flatter himself for having shown up the hollowness of many of my pretentions.'[45] Mahadev Desai also confirmed Gandhi's doubts about the autobiography as history. He admitted that Gandhi wished to rewrite some parts. In a letter to G.A. Natesan, Gandhi's long-time publisher in Madras, Mahadev Desai wrote, 'Bapu has decided not to allow anyone to publish the Autobiography in Book form as it will have to be entirely revised after it is once finished in *Young India*, and it might have to be rewritten in parts if necessary in light of the criticism that appears and will appear in the press.'[46]

Some of the criticism and responses that came were about the accuracy of Gandhi's memory while recounting his life. In his recollection of his childhood in Rajkot in a chapter 'Glimpses of Religion', Gandhi wrote about the early grounding in a sense of equability with regard to all branches of Hinduism and its sister religions.[47] He said therein that Christianity was an exception, for which he had developed a dislike. This dislike he attributed to the conduct of Christian missionaries who 'used to stand in a corner near the high school and hold forth, pouring abuse on Hindus and their gods'.[48] Conversion to Christianity required, according to Gandhi, consumption of beef and liquor and adoption of European costume.

Rev. S.R. Scott[49] wrote a repudiation in response. Gandhi and Rev. Scott, at that time serving in Surat, had earlier corresponded. Rev. Scott wrote to Gandhi, challenging his account, and said that he was the only Christian missionary serving in Rajkot during the years Gandhi referred to. Rev. Scott contended that he had never preached standing near the gates of the High School and 'pouring abuse' on Hindus gods was not his way of converting the hearts and minds of Hindus to Christianity. He wrote, 'as a sincere lover of truth you cannot wish to lend the great weight of your authority to perpetuate such a wilfully malicious misrepresentation of Christian Missionaries'.[50] Gandhi published this letter along with his response in the *Young India* of 4 March 1926. In his response, Gandhi declined to accept Rev. Scott's version, claiming that though it took place forty years ago 'the painful memory

---

[45] Ibid.

[46] SN 32234, letter of 27 February 1926.

[47] Chapter X, Part I.

[48] Ibid.

[49] Erroneously identified as H.R. Scott in *CWMG*.

[50] *Young India*, 4 March 1926. Vol. viii, no. 9, p. 82.

of it is still vivid before me'.[51] On the question of beef eating and liquor drinking, Gandhi claimed to have written what he had heard; while accepting that he had no personal knowledge of that particular incident, Gandhi did not refrain from stating that this experience pointed to the contrary. 'I have mixed freely among thousands of Christian Indians, I know very few who have scruples about eating beef or other flesh meats and drinking intoxicating liquors.'[52]

His description of Sonja Schlesin, one of his closest co-workers in South Africa invited sharp rebuke from her. Gandhi, in his laudatory recollection, described her as 'head of a girls' school in the Transvaal'. In a letter dated 2 June 1928, she wrote, 'Dear Mr. Gandhi, Time for just a line by this mail to ask you *on no account* to publish the allusions to myself in your wretched autobiography in a book from until I send you a revised copy which I shall do by next mail. You say that I am at the head of a girls' school. I have never had anything to do with a girls' school and it would take many more years of experience than I possess to attain the principalship at a high school, even if I desired such a position, which I don't.' She wrote further, 'The whole thing is simply a fabrication of your own fancy. Your brain is so tired that you have just the haziest recollection of things, you jumble up facts and you unconsciously invent. I therefore seriously think you should cease writing until you are in a normal state again . . . In fact so far as your allusions to me are concerned, at any rate, the autobiography should indeed be entitled not "The Story of My Experiments with Truth" but *Illustrations of My Experiments with Untruth*.'[53]

Gandhi issued a correction in *Young India* of 28 June 1928, adding that 'The error has given her pain for which I am sorry. I may at once say that she is in no way responsible for the error.'[54] In the subsequent book edition the line was changed to 'She is at present a teacher in one of the high schools in the Transvaal.'

Gandhi was not always willing to make changes, albeit he was ever willing to publish challenges to his narrative and his response publicly. In the English translation Mahadev Desai had chosen the adjective 'volatile' to translate the Gujarati term '*tej*' used by Gandhi to describe Sister Nivedita. Gandhi wrote also that he was 'taken aback by the splendour that surrounded her'.

---

[51] *CWMG,* vol. 30, p. 70.

[52] Ibid., pp. 70–71.

[53] SN 15040, emphasis in the original.

[54] *CWMG,* vol. 36, p. 468. See, n. 137 in Chapter XII, Part IV, for more details.

The *Modern Review* of July 1927 took exception to the adjective 'volatile' and the description of 'splendour', pointing out that at the time of Gandhi's meeting with her, Sister Nivedita was a guest at the American Consulate in Calcutta and not responsible for the splendour. It also said that the term 'volatile' wronged her memory. Gandhi 'gladly' published this in *Young India* but stated that 'such references should be regarded merely as impressions left upon my mind at the time to which they may relate'.[55] As to the choice of the adjective 'volatile', Gandhi recalled the discussion with Mahadev Desai at the time of translation. 'We both had doubts about the use of the adjective being correct. The choice lay between volatile, violent and fantastical. The last two were considered to be too strong. Mahadev had chosen volatile and I passed it.'[56]

Even when suggested by close associates Gandhi was reluctant to carry out changes in the *Autobiography*. In 1928, clearly wanting to verify incidents and impressions pertaining to Gandhi's life in South Africa, Mahadev Desai sent proofs of the first editions of the *Autobiography* to H.S.L. Polak, who along with Hermann Kallenbach was Gandhi's closest associate, having—like Kallenbach—lived with Gandhi in his house in Johannesburg and at the Phoenix Settlement.

Polak pointed out several inaccuracies. 'In Chapter 13, he refers to Mansukhlal Nazar's editorship of the paper. I do not think that he is quite fair to Nazar, whose critical faculty and sense of humour during the time upto the beginning of 1906 when he died, very often saved Gandhiji from indiscretions due to misplaced enthusiasm and inexperience.'[57] Polak further wrote, 'He is slightly inaccurate . . . as to the exact circumstances in which I made his acquaintance. The proprietress of one of those restaurants, who was a mutual friend, had asked me whether I would care to attend one of her "At Home's". If so, I should probably meet Mr. Gandhi, whom I ought to know. I jumped at the opportunity and attended the "At Home," which was just a pleasant private affair. Gandhiji and I at once became intimate by reason of the fact that I was almost the only other person that he had met in Johannesburg who had read a certain book entitled *Return to Nature* (dealing with earth treatment and other forms of nature cure) by Adolf Just.'[58]

He also pointed out that Gandhi had been unfair to Millie Polak. 'He does Mrs. Polak an injustice. She and Mrs. Gandhi never had any difference. Indeed it often

---

[55] *CWMG*, vol. 34, p. 80.

[56] Ibid., pp. 80–81.

[57] SN 13590, letter of 19 March 1928.

[58] Ibid.

fell to her lot to make representations to Gandhiji in respect of various domestic matters about which Mrs. Gandhi hesitated to approach him.'[59]

Gandhi did not take any of these suggestions and make any corrections in the text, either in the first editions or the subsequent revised edition.

Gandhi's reluctance to make changes even while admitting to inaccuracies is perplexing; more so in case of H.S.L. Polak who was invited by Mahadev Desai to provide critical feedback. He had shown similar reluctance to make any changes in *Hind Swaraj*. He admitted that his characterization of the English parliament as a 'prostitute' and 'a sterile woman' had hurt sensibilities, and had promised to remove the offending term in future editions. The change was never made. The reluctance to change the impressions or even correct factual errors may have its roots in Gandhi's belief that he was not writing an autobiographical narrative, a *jivan vrutant*. A *jivan vrutant* would be required to show greater fidelity to facts. He was probably governed by a belief that facts were not of material significance to him.

Not all responses were about factual inaccuracies or impressions. An acquaintance from Pretoria, Jane Howard, wrote in response to the chapter 'A Sacred Recollection and Penance': 'When I read my *Young India* of July 21st I wished you had not given us that picture of yourself. The Mr. Gandhi I have known is much nicer. I wonder that Mrs. Gandhi did not smack you in the face when you talked about "Your House".'[60]

A member of the Psychological Society of Calcutta asked him to dwell deeper into the psychological factors for the benefit of the discipline: 'Here you have touched a psychological factor of great importance and will it be asking too much to an introspective great mind like you, to elucidate the matter further for the benefit of Psychological Science.'[61] Gandhi in his response hoped that the correspondent did not 'want me to develop further the theme of the chanting of Ramanama and the so-called autobiographical chapters I am writing'.[62]

~

Gandhi wrote and published the *Autobiography* from week to week. Many responded to him with criticisms, suggestions, requests and corrections, while Gandhi admitted

---

[59] Ibid.

[60] SN 11966, letter of 13 February 1928. See Chapter X, Part IV.

[61] SN 13002, letter of 19 November 1928.

[62] *CWMG*, vol. 38, p. 112.

to his errors and responded both publicly and privately through letters. And yet, he did not allow those exchanges to shape his narrative. This unwillingness to allow the narrative to be shaped by his readers and interlocutions has its roots in his conviction that the story of the strivings of his soul was being written at the urging of his 'antaryami', the 'dweller within' or the 'spirit'. It was not given to Gandhi to modify what came to him from the antaryami.

Gandhi's desire at the time of writing the *Atmakatha* is expressed by his location within the Ashram, his lectures on and translation of the Gita, the choice of the Gujarati language, his attempt to reflect on the life of Christ. But, in the final instance, Gandhi's notion of in-dwelling is the antaryami who spoke to him in a 'small, still voice' and whose exhortations Gandhi submitted to. It is in this that Gandhi's conviction that he was writing an '*atmakatha*' inheres. The *atmakatha* is not only the story of the soul in search of Truth; it is a story that is shaped by the antaryami.

Let us consider this possibility. If the *Atmakatha* is being written at the prompting of the 'dweller within', is it possible for Gandhi to communicate all his strivings?

In his 'Introduction' to the *Autobiography* Gandhi writes, 'What I want to achieve—what I have been striving and pining to achieve these thirty years—is self-realization, to see God face to face, to attain *moksha*. I live and move and have my being in pursuit of this goal.'[63]

The *Atmakatha* is the story of Gandhi's attempts to achieve his objective. It also promises to tell the reader how such a seeker lives and moves, very much like the question posed by Arjuna to Sri Krishna in the Gita.[64] Given Gandhi's admission that it was his 'antaryami' which was urging the narration of his quest, nothing of this quest should have been beyond his capacity to communicate. Were there aspects of his quest that were known only to him and his antaryami?

Gandhi answered this question. 'There are some things which are known only to oneself and one's Maker. They are clearly incommunicable. The experiments I am about to relate are not such.'[65]

The Gujarati original is more opaque. The term 'oneself' translates 'atma' (soul, self) and enigmatically the term 'one's maker' also translates 'atma'. A literal translation of the Gujarati sentence would be: 'There are certainly some things that arise and find repose in the soul, it is beyond my capacity to write about them.' If

---

[63] *Autobiography*, Introduction.

[64] 'What o Keshava is the mark of the man whose understanding is secure, whose mind is fixed in concentration? How move?' Verse 54, Discourse II, *The Gospel of Selfless Action*, p. 11.

[65] *Autobiography*, Introduction.

this is true, is it given to us as readers of Gandhi's quest to get a glimpse of them or will they remain hidden by the golden orb?

There is one instance when Gandhi tried to communicate the incommunicable. If we read along with Gandhi his attempt to describe something that arose and found repose in his soul, we understand his struggle to listen to and submit to the promptings of the antaryami.

On 30 April 1933 Gandhi decided to undertake a twenty-one-day fast for self-purification as a prisoner in the Yeravada jail. Just seven months ago he had fasted against some specific provisions of the Communal Award. This fast had lasted merely six days from 20 to 26 September 1932.

He could not reveal the reason for his resolve to undertake a fiery ordeal for self-purification. He said to Sardar Vallabhbhai Patel, his fellow prisoner, 'After all, does one express, can one express, all one's thoughts to others?'[66] He described to Sardar his sudden resolve to fast. He said he had been feeling restless for the past three days. He could not sleep but did not feel tired as a result of lack of sleep. This unease of spirit had gone unnoticed by his fellow prisoner Sardar and even Mahadev Desai, a man who could anticipate many of Gandhi's spiritual crises. Gandhi said, 'As if for the last three days I were preparing myself for the great deluge!'[67] He did not know what agitated his mind and when the 'excitement' started. However, the thought of the fast came to him repeatedly, a thought he tried to drive away and shut out. He described the moment when he heard the voice: 'In the night when I retired I had no idea that something was coming up today. But after eleven I woke up, I watched the stars, repeated Ramanama but the same thought would persistently come to my mind: "If you have grown so restless, why don't you undertake the fast? Do it?" The inner dialogue went on for quite some time. At half past twelve came the clear, unmistakable voice. "You must undertake the fast." That was all.'[68]

In a public statement issued on the same day, he spoke of the unease and his struggle against the persistent voice that told him to fast. The struggle was in vain and he had resolved to go on an unconditional and irrevocable fast for twenty-one days.

Gandhi gave some vital clues to the working of his soul before he heard the voice. Gandhi would often describe the state before the communion with his inner voice as a state of darkness, of groping.

---

[66] *CWMG*, vol. 55, p.76.

[67] Ibid.

[68] Ibid.

In 1918, between 15 and 18 March, Gandhi undertook his first public fast since his return to India from South Africa in 1915. In the *Autobiography* he has described his groping and the sudden light that came to him. 'One morning—it was at the mill-hands' meeting—while I was still groping and unable to see my way clearly, the light came to me. Unbidden and all by themselves the words came to my lips: "Unless the strikers rally," I declared to the meeting, "and continue the strike till a settlement is reached or till they leave the mills altogether, I will not touch any food."'[69]

Similarly, on 12 January 1948 Gandhi in his prayer speech that was read out by Sushila Nayar—it was Monday, his day of silence—he announced a fast in almost similar terms. He spoke of his agony, his brooding, and the persistent thought of a fast that he tried to shut out and the final moment of clarity, a moment when he saw light.[70]

Gandhi was often asked as to what enabled him to heat the voice of conscience, his antaryami? He described a conscientious man as a man who hesitated to assert himself, was humble, never boisterous, always ready to listen, ever willing and anxious to admit his mistakes.[71] Gandhi described conscience as something acquired after the strictest training. He said, 'Wilfulness is not conscience; conscience is the ripe fruit of strictest discipline.'[72] Gandhi says that it is not possible to hear the inner voice without the necessary effort and training. This training and effort was in self-restraint, in other words, in brahmacharya. He described the training in the following words: 'a conscious practice of self-restraint and ever-increasing effort implicitly to obey the will of God speaking within and then known as the inner voice.'[73] Gandhi claimed that it was his observances in Truth, non-violence and brahmacharya, along with non-possession and non-stealing, that allowed him to know his conscience and hear the unmistakable inner voice. The capacity to hear the antaryami came to Gandhi through the Ashram observances and for this reason too his in-dwelling at the Ashram at the time of writing the *Autobiography* was an imperative.

This clear voice that he heard did not go unchallenged. When he announced his fast in April 1933, even his closest associates like C. Rajagopalachari and his

---

[69] *Autobiography*.

[70] *CWMG*, vol. 90, p. 408.

[71] *CWMG*, vol. 25, pp. 23-24.

[72] Ibid.

[73] *CWMG*, vol. 54, p. 114.

youngest son, Devadas, did not believe that he had been prompted by God to fast. Their doubt was fundamental. They doubted the very basis of the fast. Gandhi dealt with this publicly: 'They believe me under self-delusion—a prey to my own heated imagination made hotter by the suffocation produced by the cramping walls of a prison.'[74] The voice of conscience that he had heard was so direct and powerful that he was not swayed in the least by the doubts of a scholar of Rajagopalachari's calibre. Gandhi argued that his claim to hear the voice of God was not new. The voice had been increasingly audible to him. He could give no proof; as a human it was not given to him to prove the existence of God. The only way he knew of proving his claim—not of the existence of God—was the outcome of his fast. If he survived the ordeal, he would be right in claiming that he had been prompted by his inner voice. He said, 'God will not be God if he allowed himself to be an object of proof by his creatures. But he does give his willing slave the power to pass through the fiercest of ordeals.'[75] Gandhi spoke of his submission to God: 'He had left me not a vestige of independence.'[76] Gandhi described the nature of his experience. 'I saw no form. I have never tried, for I have always believed God to be without form.'[77] He further explained the nature of the divine inspiration. 'The night I got the inspiration, I had a terrible inner struggle. My mind was restless. I could see no way. The burden of my responsibility was crushing me. But what I did hear was like a voice from afar and yet quite near. It was as unmistakable as some human voice definitely speaking to me, and irresistible. I was not dreaming at the time when I heard the voice. The hearing of the voice was preceded by a terrific struggle within me. Suddenly the voice came upon me. I listened, made certain that it was the voice, and the struggle ceased. I was calm.'[78]

He felt that his submission to God as Truth was so complete, at least in that particular act of fasting, that he had no autonomy left. He wrote in a letter, 'Of course, for me personally it transcends reason, because I feel it to be a clear will from God. My position is that there is nothing just now that I am doing on my own accord. He guides me from moment to moment.'[79]

---

[74] *CWMG*, vol. 55, p. 120.

[75] Ibid., p. 121.

[76] Ibid.

[77] Ibid. p. 255.

[78] *CWMG*, vol. 55, p. 225.

[79] *CWMG*, vol. 52, p. 244.

Gandhi's claim to hear the inner voice was neither unique nor exclusive. The validity and legitimacy of such a claim is recognized in the spiritual realm. The idea of perfect surrender is integral to and consistent with religious life. Although Gandhi never claimed to have attained self-realization, of having seen God face-to-face, he said, 'The inner voice is the voice of the Lord.'[80]

This is the closest that Gandhi came to declaring his communion with God. In this we have an understanding of what he called, variously, antaryami, spirit, the dweller within, the inner voice or the 'small, still voice'. This voice came to him not from a force outside of him. Gandhi made a distinction between 'an outer force' and 'a power beyond us'. A power beyond us has its locus within us. It is superior to us, not subject to our command or wilful action but it is still located within us. He explained it thus: '"Beyond us" means "the power which is beyond our ego".'[81] According to Gandhi one acquires this capacity when the 'ego is reduced to zero'.[82] Reducing the ego to zero meant for him total surrender to God as Truth. A person who has cultivated such ever wakefulness that reminds them at all moments of the subjugation of the will to God acquires the capacity to distinguish between the voice of the ego and the call of the antaryami. This capacity for discernment is vital to any act of hearing and submission as 'One cannot always recognize whether it is the voice of Rama or Ravana'.[83] For Gandhi, Rama is the antaryami, the spirit from which Shri Ramchandra gets his name. Ravana embodies ego, falsehood and, for that reason, the denial of God as Truth.

The ever wakefulness was acquired through prayer and Ashram observances, which he likened to an attempt to empty the sea with a drainer small as a blade of grass and yet natural as life itself. A person, who lives constantly in the sight of God, when he or she regards each thought with God as witness and its master, could feel Rama, Truth, dwelling in the heart. Gandhi meditated upon and strove towards the ideal of sthitaprajna as described in the Gita. As he sought to cultivate this equipoise, his capacity to hear the antaryami and to surrender to that voice increased. He said, 'I have been a willing slave to this most exacting master for more than half a century. His voice has been increasingly audible as years have rolled by. He has never forsaken

---

[80] *CWMG*, vol. 53, p. 483.

[81] Ibid.

[82] Ibid.

[83] *CWMG*, vol. 52, p. 130.

me even in my darkest hour. He has saved me often against myself . . . The greater the surrender to him, the greater has been my joy.'[84]

This provides us an insight into Gandhi's experiments and his quest, which is to know himself, to see God face-to-face and attain moksha. The experiments with truth are a means to this quest. Means to be means have to be within reach, communicable and ever replicable. The experiments narrated in the *Atmakatha*, Gandhi claimed, were of that kind. But the antaryami speaking in a 'small, still voice' from within and pointing out to him the path of duty remained incommunicable.

~

Mahadev Haribhai Desai (1892–1942), trained in philosophy and law from the University of Bombay, joined Gandhi in November 1917. Prior to this he had worked in the Oriental Translator's office in Bombay, learning the art and craft of translation that he would eventually master. He made his mark as a translator early, having been chosen from a competitive process by the Forbes Gujarati Sabha to translate Lord Morley's *On Compromise*. Before joining Gandhi, as he struggled, like many others, to establish his legal practice in Ahmedabad, Mahadev and his friend, fellow lawyer and soon to be ashramite Narhari Parikh co-translated Rabindranath Tagore's *Chitrangada* and *Bidai Abhishap* and *Prachin Sahitya* from Bengali into Gujarati. Both Narhari Parikh and Mahadev Desai in a joint letter responded to the draft rules of the Satyagraha Ashram that Gandhi had founded in Ahmedabad. Narhari was the first to take the plunge and join the Ashram. It appears that the first serious discussion between Gandhi and Mahadev was about translation. Gandhi had written a pamphlet on the nature of satyagraha in Gujarati which was given to the teachers of the Rashtriya Shala (National School) for translation into English. Narhari Parikh, who had joined the Rashtriya Shala in May 1917, gave the pamphlet to his friend Mahadev, then visiting him at the Ashram, to translate. Mahadev was at that time was employed in the Bombay Central Cooperative Bank. Mahadev's translation was reviewed by Gandhi in the presence of the teachers of the Rashtriya Shala. Narhari recounts the incident: 'Mahadev had a long discussion with Gandhiji as the latter went on suggesting changes in the translation. The translation by Mahadev and discussion over it raised Mahadev in Gandhiji's esteem.'[85]

---

[84] *CWMG*, vol. 55, p. 121.

[85] Narayan Desai, *Fire and the Rose*, translated from the original Gujarati by Chitra Desai (Ahmedabad: Navajivan, 1995), p. 59.

By 31 August 1917 Mahadev was 'love-struck' and pondering over a possible future by Gandhi's side. By 19 September 1917, Gandhi had begun to treat Mahadev as his secretary; a letter of Gandhi's bearing that date to Satyendranath Bose is in Mahadev's hand. Mahadev was twenty-five then. He spent the next twenty-five years by Gandhi's side, as a constant companion, following him even to prison on several occasions. Mahadev's ambition was not only to serve Gandhi as his secretary or even as 'servant and porter', as he liked to describe himself. Mahadev's aspiration was to capture something of Gandhi's tryst with Truth. His diaries, published posthumously as *Mahadevbhai Ni Diary*, are a record of each day that he spent with Gandhi. The twenty-two published and three unpublished volumes of the diary is one of the most outstanding examples of the aspiration to capture the unfolding of the practice of Truth. Mahadev was chosen as the translator of Gandhi's *Autobiography*.

Prior to the writing of the *Autobiography*, Gandhi had written *Hind Swaraj* in 1909 and *Dakshin Africa Na Satyagraha No Itihas* as a prisoner in Yeravada. Gandhi translated or, as he liked to call it, 'paraphrased' *Hind Swaraj* into English. The word 'written' is an inexact description for *Dakshin Africa Na Satyagraha No Itihas*. He began to dictate this account to his fellow prisoner Indulal Yagnik in the Yeravada Central Prison on 26 November 1923. By the time he was released, due to ill-health, on 5 February 1924—earlier than his stipulated term of six years—he had completed thirty chapters, which appeared serially in *Navajivan* from 13 April 1924 to 22 November 1925. The remaining twenty chapters were written after his release. They appeared in a book form in two parts, in 1924 and 1925. The English translation, *Satyagraha in South Africa*, was done by Valji Govindji Desai, fellow ashramite and teacher at the Ashram School. It was seen and approved by Gandhi, and published in 1928 by S. Ganesan, Madras. A second revised edition was published by Navajivan Press in December 1950.

Neither Gandhi nor Mahadev Desai has left any record of the discussion about the possible translators for the *Autobiography*. There is no record perhaps because there was no discussion. Mahadev was not only the closest companion of Gandhi but also one who bore witness, like no one else, to Gandhi's experiment with Truth and brahmacharya. Mahadev can be said to have had unique access to Gandhi's antaryami, if it was possible for a person other than Gandhi to have access to the workings of his conscience. The original Gujarati manuscript of the *Atmakatha* in Gandhi's hand does not survive. But the archives of the Sabarmati Ashram have thirty-nine chapters (totalling to 450 handwritten pages) of Mahadev's translation.

Mahadev's translation of the *Autobiography* commenced with the 3 December 1925 issue of *Young India* and continued till the issue of 3 February 1929. With the exception of Chapters XXIX–XLIII of Part V, all other chapters were translated by Mahadev. These chapters were translated by Pyarelal Nayar during Mahadev's absence from the Ashram at the time of the Bardoli Agrarians Inquiry by the Broomfield Committee in 1928–29. The translation, according to Mahadev, had the benefit of Gandhi's revision and Mirabehn's (Madeline Slade) careful reading. In the 'Translator's Preface' Mahadev wrote, 'No one, perhaps, is more conscious of the blemishes in the translation than myself. But it might be some comfort for the reader to know, that the volume, in the form in which it now appears, has had, so far as the meaning of the author is concerned, the benefit of his own careful revision, and so far as the language is concerned, the advantage of equally careful revision by Shrimati Miraben (Miss Madeline Slade), who cast in her lot with us at the Ashram a year and a half ago.'[86] The first edition was published in two volumes. The first, containing three parts, was issued in 1927 and the second, containing parts IV and V, in 1929.

The second volume does not contain any 'preface' by the translator. It carries, however, the names of two translators: Mahadev Haribhai Desai and Pyarelal Nair (not the more prevalent and correct 'Nayar'). This edition priced at Rupee 1 sold more than 50,000 copies and ran through five reprints. The price was seen to be 'prohibitive for the Indian reader' and the need for 'a cheap edition' was long felt. It was decided to publish the book in a single volume.[87]

The second 'revised' edition of *The Story of My Experiments with Truth* appeared in May 1940. In the 'Translator's Preface' to this edition Mahadev Desai wrote, 'The translation as it appeared serially in *Young India* had it may be noted, the benefit of Gandhiji's revision. It has now undergone careful revision, and from the point of view of language, it has had the benefit of careful revision by a revered friend, who among many other things has the reputation of being an eminent English scholar. Before undertaking the task, he made a condition that his name should on no account be given out. I accept the condition. It is needless to say it heightens my sense of gratitude to him.'[88] It was clear from Mahadev's remarks that Gandhi had not made any changes to the facts. The changes were from the point of view of language. This gives rise to two questions. One, regarding the identity of the 'revered friend' who was eminent English 'scholar', and the second and more significant question about

---

[86] 'Translator's Preface', 1927 edition.

[87] 'Translator's Preface', second revised edition.

[88] Ibid.

the extent and nature of the changes suggested and made. A causal glance at the title page of the second revised edition shows two significant changes.

The title of the book now read *An Autobiography or The Story of My Experiments with Truth*.

The words 'An Autobiography or' do not appear in either the *Young India* or in the two volumes of the first edition. This change was clearly in keeping with the original Gujarati title, which has the word '*atmakatha*' in it. The second and equally significant change was that Pyarelal's name was removed from the title page as one of the translators. Nevertheless, in his preface, Mahadev did mention that chapters XXIX–XLIII of Part V were translated by Pyarelal. Apart from these, it was not obvious as to the nature and extent of changes in the text itself.

The 'revered friend' who had suggested the changes from the point of language was the great liberal statesman Right Honourable Sir V.S. Srinivas Sastri. The letters between Mahadev Desai and Srinivas Sastri suggest that the work of revisions was assigned to Sastri sometime in early 1935. In a letter of 12 March 1935, Sastri wrote to Mahadev, 'I'll remember the Auto. I ought not to have lost the sight of it.'[89]

The letters suggest that Sastri's first concern was the improvements in punctuation. 'When I write next, I shall give you two or three instances of how I should like the punctuations improved.'[90]

Sastri knew that Mahadev, ever so polite and humble, would not ask him for reasons for the suggested changes. He wrote, 'Please ask without hesitation why certain changes have been suggested, if the reasons are not apparent. You have been very deferential, in fact excessively so, and I should feel guilty indeed if I had taken advantage of it and become a fault-finder for the fun of it.'[91]

Commas were Mahadev's bugbear and Sastri made it bold to suggest that Mahadev read two or three great classics with special attention to punctuations. He also suggested that Mahadev read journals like the *Times* or *The Manchester Guardian*. He considered Mahadev somewhat of a beginner in the art of English composition and said that he would send him a treatise on it. 'Another knotty point as to which you seem innocent is the distinction between restrictive adjectival clauses and coordinating adjectival clauses. . . . This distinction is somewhat hard

---

[89] Tridip Suhrud, *An Autobiography or The Story of My Experiments with Truth: A Table of Concordance* (New Delhi: Routledge, 2010), p. 212. Henceforth *A Table of Concordance*.

[90] Ibid.

[91] Ibid.

for the beginner. You won't find it difficult at all, though for a long time individual cases will worry you, especially when a doubt assails you.'[92]

In two days of writing this, he sent Mahadev a treatise: 'I spent some time yesterday looking into grammar and composition treatise before I chose Fowler's book. In its field it's a nonpareil.'[93] The revisions were completed in July of 1939. In a letter of 7 July, Sastri informed him, 'While you are immersed in Frontier problems, a registered book pocket will reach you. You will find with immense relief that it is the Autobiography.'[94]

In the same letter he forbade Mahadev from disclosing his name, 'So let me take leave for the moment with the reminder that my name should never be disclosed in the preface or introduction or press notices. The fewer the people that are let into the secret the better.'[95]

The archives and library of Sabarmati Ashram Preservation and Memorial Trust houses a part of Mahadev Desai's personal collection of books. In this collection are two volumes of the first edition of the *Autobiography* with both volumes carrying a note in Mahadev's unmistakable hand: 'Corrections in this book are made by the Honourable Shrinivas Shastri.' Both volumes are profusely marked in blue ink, with suggested changes and corrections. With a help of this a table of concordance between the first and the revised edition was prepared. Srinivas Sastri had suggested 1740 changes.

A bilingual reader commented to Gandhi that Mahadev's translation did not capture the arresting cadence of Gandhi's Gujarati prose and suggested that the task be given to Valji Govindji Desai. Gandhi replied, 'If you find Gujarati interesting enough, take it from me that Mahadev's English rendering is highly spoken of by many who know English well.'[96] Bhikhu Parekh's essay 'Gandhi and his Translators'[97] brought the question of the English translations of Gandhi's works to scholastic scrutiny. Since Gandhi wrote all his important works in Gujarati, Parekh argued that close attention ought to be paid to the relationship between the original and

---

[92] Ibid., p. 213.

[93] *A Table of Concordance*, p. 214. The reference is to *A Dictionary of Modern English Language* (1926) by Henry Watson Fowler (1858–1933).

[94] Ibid., p. 220.

[95] Ibid.

[96] *CWMG*, vol. 31, p. 124.

[97] *Gandhi Marg*, June 1986.

the translation. 'Barring a very few, most of Gandhi's commentators lack knowledge of Gujarati and thus they never refer to the Gujarati texts, take issues with the translations or locate his writings within the Gujarati literary tradition. As a result, nuances of Gandhi's thought often elude them.'[98] Parekh's comments were not confined to the translation and interpretation of his principal books and pamphlets but to the monumental *Collected Works of Mahatma Gandhi* project, which sought to provide in three languages (Gujarati, Hindi and English) all of Gandhi's writings. Parekh says, '. . . *Collected Works* leave a good deal more to be desired. They miss out important phrases and sentences, distort Gandhi's meaning, overlook crucial distinctions and inaccurately interpret some of his basic ideas. They also fail to give a full flavor of Gandhi's distinctive style of writing.'[99] He showed by comparing the original and the English rendering that the translation of the *Autobiography* was 'unsatisfactory'. '*Prima Facie* this is puzzling, especially because Gandhi's translators were all able and conscientious men—one of them, Mahadev Desai, was not only his secretary for many years but personally also he was very close to him. And Gandhi took care to ensure that the translations of his work did not misrepresent his thought.'[100] Parekh attributes the unsatisfactory translations to three sources. 'First, they were sometimes done in a great hurry and could not be given enough attention that they deserved.'[101] In the case of the *Autobiography* Mahadev had to translate the instalment within a few days of its publication. The second reason according to Parekh is that 'in some cases the English translations were subsequently revised by men and women with no knowledge of Gujarati and whose sole qualification for doing the revision was their allegedly superior command of English'.[102] This comment does apply to both Madeline Slade and V.S. Srinivas Sastri. But to be more precise, Sastri's changes were largely confined to grammar and punctuations. In the absence of the complete manuscript of Mahadev's English translation, we are unable to ascertain the nature and extent of the changes made by Miss Slade. Notwithstanding this, the argument made by Parekh remains valid.

The third is a more important and complex argument. According to Parekh Gandhi's attitude to Hindu religious tradition was very complex; while being in

---

[98] Ibid., p. 163.

[99] Ibid., p. 164.

[100] Ibid., p. 169.

[101] Ibid.

[102] Ibid.

broad sympathy with it, Gandhi disapproved of some of its institutions and practices. 'Gandhi had therefore to deploy several extremely subtle and complex intellectual maneuvers and evolve a somewhat elusive and ambiguous mode of discourse that sent out different and even contradictory messages to different communities.'[103]

He further argues that sometimes Gandhi's translators failed to capture his meaning and 'when they did grasp the meaning, they seem to have been worried by its harshness and morality and tried to soften it'.[104] In light of his arguments he advanced three suggestions. First, that Gandhi's key works be translated anew. Two, the task of preparing authentic editions of Gandhi's texts should be undertaken and three, for 'better understanding of his intellectual evolution'[105] a close reading of Gandhi's texts should be done.

In his 'Foreword' to the concordance table that compared the first and the revised editions of the *Autobiography*, Gopalkrishna Gandhi faced the question of Mahadev's translation and Bhikhu Parekh's criticism of it. He began by offering his 'salutations' to Mahadev Desai and 'profound admiration' for all the translators of Gandhi. Gopalkrishna Gandhi proposed a possible mode of reading of the translation. 'The text in Gujarati, and Desai's English translation of it should be seen as twins (or can we say, should be seen as the reverse and obverse of one coin). They came almost in tandem; intense political and public activity surrounded their appearance.'[106] Unlike Parekh, Gopalkrishna Gandhi believes that M.K. Gandhi participated actively in the translation exercise itself. There is at least one instance where Gandhi admits to have chosen a particular word in the English translation, that is, in the case of Sister Nivedita discussed earlier. The surviving pages of Mahadev's translation also suggest that apart from Mirabehn, Gandhi also read and corrected the translation at some places. Gopalkrishna Gandhi concludes, 'The English *Autobiography* therefore stands beside the original work not just as an authorised and outstanding translation but also as its first recension, prepared under the author's direct guidance by one who was his *alter ego*, whose mother-tongue was the same as his, and who was, like him, perfectly at home in English.'[107] He admits, however that he finds in some instances the Gujarati description 'visually valuable'. Gopalkrishna Gandhi

---

[103] Ibid., p. 170.

[104] Ibid.

[105] Ibid.

[106] *A Table of Concordance*, p. ix.

[107] Ibid., p. x.

suggests that the usage of Gujarati colloquialisms, alliteration available in Gujarati, is consciously and deliberately dropped in the English rendering. 'It seems to me that Gandhi and Mahadev Desai wanted to make the English version leaner than the Gujarati one, and to remove from it embellishment, metaphors, proverbs and the like which though appealing to the Indian reader would not make immediate sense to the English-reading world.'[108] Gopalkrishna Gandhi, while in disagreement with Parekh's criticism of the translation/translators, found 'merit and value' in the suggestion that textual studies be undertaken of the Gujarati original and its various translations.

If one were to take Gopalkrishna Gandhi's suggestion of reading the Gujarati original and the English translation as 'twins' and the English as the first *recension* of the Gujarati, as well as Bhikhu Parekh's caution about textual studies of Gandhi's writing, a method of reading the *Autobiography* could possibly emerge.

A textual reading and viewing the 'recension' as a 'twin' of the original are to me suggestive of a method that has informed this work. The method necessarily involves placing the original Gujarati and the English side by side. It would involve admitting the possibility that the English translation could also have informed the Gujarati, that terms and descriptions or explanations that were added in the English may have been included in the later editions of the Gujarati *Atmakatha*. It would also involve an exercise in doing a close textual reading of both the texts and to mark the differences, additions, deletion and changes in the meaning introduced in the act of translation, as well as the attempt to capture something of what Gopalkrishna Gandhi calls 'visually valuable' and the cadence of the colloquial. An ideal mode would be to prepare a bilingual edition, but pragmatic considerations suggested otherwise. Instead, an interwoven exercise has been attempted, that is, to prepare two separate and yet in some fundamental way connected editions: one in Gujarati and the other in English. Both moved by the conviction that to read the *Autobiography* is to read it in two tongues, Gujarati and English. The Gujarati edition, to be published almost simultaneous to the present work by Navajivan, a publishing trust established by Gandhi, treats the English as a 'recension' and marks all those instances where the English translation found its way into the subsequent editions of the *Atmakatha* and are now taken as 'authentic'—for that text is included as an authoritative text in the Gujarati *Akshardeha*, a companion set to the English *Collected Works*.

The present works takes the second revised edition of 1940 as published in volume 39 of the *CWMG* as the authoritative text.

---

[108] Ibid., p. xii.

This work does not mark the changes between the first and the revised edition, except where the revision is of the kind that has altered the structure of meaning.

There are two types of annotations that mark this exercise. The first, printed on the margins of the body text. These are by way of alternative translation to the translation of Mahadev Desai. The attempt is to take the reader as close to the original as possible and not necessarily to provide stylistic or literary improvement. At times these are almost literal, disregarding the literary merit of Mahadev's rendering. Gujarati sayings, metaphors and colloquial terms are indicated in complementary footnotes to provide the reader access to the original.

The second kind of annotations are footnotes. These include words, sentences, phrases added or deleted in the English translation, bibliographic details about books mentioned in the *Autobiography*, biographical notes on persons, expository notes on institutions or organizations mentioned, details about dates, places, events and persons that abound in the *Autobiography*, and some of these notes are by way of supplying corrections to the details provided in the text, which escaped even Mahadev's scrutiny.

The scope of the present work is in this sense limited. It is not an attempt to provide a new, improved translation. It is an exercise in close reading of two intertwined texts of M.K. Gandhi's *Atmakatha*.

A question could be asked, why not attempt a new translation? It certainly can and should be attempted, as each generation contends with Gandhi and his quest to remove the golden lid that covers Truth, his desire to see God face-to-face and his pining to know himself. But I find myself unequal to the task, not only in the sense of literary ability but, more fundamentally, a moral lack. My moral universe remains too opaque to receive a glimpse of Bapu's antaryami. Also, Mahadev is in exemplar for me. My journey to Gandhi has been through him and other ashramites. His translation of the *Atmakatha* has illuminated my life and I hope my thought.

This work was done during my own period of in-dwelling at the Sabarmati Ashram. It could not have been otherwise. The last five years as a caretaker of the Sabarmati Ashram have been deeply fulfilling and life-altering. And yet, as I write this, I am aware, with deep and abiding sadness, my period of grace, of in-dwelling at the Ashram, is over.

Sabarmati Ashram, Ahmedabad   Tridip Suhrud
29 August 2017

An Autobiography or
The Story of My Experiments with Truth[1]

By

M.K. Gandhi

Translated from the original in Gujarati by
Mahadev Desai[2]

---

[1] In the Gujarati original the title is *Satyana Prayogo Athva Atmakatha*. The translation in English as it began to appear in *Young India* (vol. VII, no. 49) was published under the title: *The Story of My Experiments with Truth*. The first edition, published in two volumes (1927, 1929) had the same title as in *Young India*. In the second edition of 1940, the cover page carried the title as in the first edition, but on the half-title page 'An Autobiography' was introduced. The title page of this edition carried the title *An Autobiography or The Story of My Experiments with Truth*. This is closer to the Gujarati original, although there is a reversal of order in the English title; in Gujarati the word *Atmakatha* appears after *Satyana Prayogo*.

[2] *Young India* carried the translation credit as 'Translated from *Navajivan* by Mahadeo Desai'. The first edition, vol. 1 (1927), said 'Translated from the original in Gujarati by Mahadev Desai', while in vol. 2 (1929), the translators' names appeared as Mahadev Haribhai Desai and Pyarelal Nair. The second edition mentioned only one translator, Mahadev Desai. Pyarelal had translated chapters XXIV–XLIII of Part V of the *Autobiography* during Mahadev Desai's absence at the time of the Bardoli Agrarian Inquiry by the Broomfield Committee in 1928–29.

TRANSLATOR'S PREFACE[1]

It was by a fortunate accident that the privilege of translating into English, for *Young India*, the *Story of My Experiments with Truth* or Gandhiji's Autobiography, as it was being published in *Navajivan* from week to week, fell to me. No one, perhaps, is more conscious of the blemishes, in the translation than myself. But it might be some comfort to the reader to know, that the volume, in the form in which it now appears, has had, so far as the meaning of the author is concerned, the benefit of his own careful revision, and so far as the language is concerned, the advantage of equally careful revision by Shrimati Miraben (Miss Madeleine Slade), who cast in her lot with us at the Ashram a year and a half ago.

Satyagrahashram   M.D.
1 August 1927

---

[1] To the first edition.

TRANSLATOR'S PREFACE[2]

The first edition of Gandhiji's Autobiography was published in two volumes, Vol. I in 1927 and Vol. II in 1929. The original in Gujarati which was priced at Rs. 1/- has run through five editions, nearly 50,000 copies having been sold. The price of the English translation (only issued in library edition) was prohibitive for the Indian reader, and a cheap edition has long been needed. It is now being issued in one volume. The translation, as it appeared serially in *Young India*, had, it may be noted, the benefit of Gandhiji's revision. It has now undergone careful revision, and from the point of view of language, it has had the benefit of careful revision by a revered friend, who, among many other things, has the reputation of being an eminent English scholar. Before undertaking the task, he made it a condition that his name should on no account be given out. I accept the condition. It is needless to say it heightens my sense of gratitude to him. Chapters XXIX–XLIII of Part V were translated by my friend and colleague Pyarelal during my absence in Bardoli at the time of the Bardoli Agrarian Inquiry by the Broomfield Committee in 1928–29.

A few photographs (some of them by Kanu Gandhi) add, I am sure, to the value of this edition.

Mahadev Desai

---

[2] To the second revised edition.

INTRODUCTION

Four or five years ago, at the instance of some of my nearest co-workers, I agreed to write my autobiography. I made the start, but scarcely had I *turned over the first sheet*[M1] when *riots*[M2] broke out in Bombay[1] and *the work remained at a standstill. Then followed a series of events which culminated in my imprisonment at Yeravda.*[2] *Sjt.*[M3] Jairamdas[3] who was one of my fellow-prisoners there, asked me to put everything else on one side and finish writing the autobiography. I *replied*[M4] that I had already framed a programme of study[4] for myself, and that I could not *think*

[M1] completed one foolscap sheet

[M2] conflagration

[M3] what I began remained incomplete. Then I got involved, one after another, in such affairs which ultimately gave me my place in Yeravda. Bhai

[M4] sent him a reply

---

[1] The conflagration in Bombay started on 17 November 1921. MKG commenced a fast against the disturbances on 19 November and broke it after peace was restored on 22 November. As a consequence of the Bombay disturbances, MKG decided to observe a fast every Monday till Swaraj was obtained. He commenced the practice of Monday fast from 27 November 1921.

[2] MKG was arrested on 10 March 1922 and charged with sedition on 11 March. He was tried on 18 March and awarded a prison sentence of six years. He was shifted from Sabarmati Jail in Ahmedabad and confined at the Yeravada Central Prison, Poona, on 21 March 1922. He was released unconditionally on 5 February 1924, while he was admitted to the Sassoon Hospital after an appendicitis operation.

[3] Jairamdas Doulatram (1892–1979), general secretary, Indian National Congress (1931–34), served as Governor of Bihar and Assam and as Union Minister for food supply in post-Independence India, first editor of *The Collected Works of Mahatma Gandhi*.

[4] MKG wrote to Hakim Ajmal Khan on 14 April 1922 that he devotes six hours daily to literary studies and four hours to hand-spinning

M5 commence the autobiography

M6 I would have certainly written the autobiography there had I the good fortune to go through my full term of imprisonment at Yeravda. But I still had one year before I could reach there. Before that, no way could I have commenced the autobiography, hence it remained unattempted.

M7 demand

M8 I do not have that much time all at once. If I write, I can only write for *Navajivan*.

M9 decision and now I have the opportunity to write the autobiography

M10 As I arrived at this decision, a pure and unsullied associate gently spoke thus to me on Monday, my day of silence: 'Why do you intend writing an autobiography?'

of doing anything else[M5] until this course was complete. *I should indeed have finished the autobiography had I gone through my full term of imprisonment at Yeravda for there was still a year left to complete*[5] *the task, when I was discharged.*[M6] Swami Anand[6] has now repeated the *proposal,*[M7] and as I have finished the history of Satyagraha in South Africa[7] I am tempted to undertake the autobiography for *Navajivan.*[8] The Swami wanted me to write it separately for publication as a book. *But I have no spare time. I could only write a chapter week by week.*[M8] Something has to be written for *Navajivan* every week. Why should it not be the autobiography? The Swami agreed to the *proposal, and here am I hard at work.*[M9]

But a God-fearing friend had his doubts, which he shared with me on my day of silence. 'What has set you on this adventure?'[M10] he asked. 'Writing an autobiography is a practice peculiar to the West. I know of nobody in the East having written one, except amongst those who

and carding. His studies began at 6.30 a.m. and he worked till 7 p.m.; he could not work before or after these times as no artificial light was allowed in the prison. To see the list of books that he read during the prison term, see his Jail Diary, 1922 (*CWMG*, vol. 23, pp. 144–53) and Jail Diary, 1923 (ibid., pp. 178–88).

5 In the first edition 'reach', changed in the 1940 edition. In the present critical edition, all changes made in the revised edition of 1940 have been enumerated. These are based on a previous work, Tridip Suhrud, *An Autobiography or The Story of My Experiments with Truth: A Table of Concordance* (New Delhi: Routledge, 2010).

6 Swami Anandanand (1887–1976), monk of the Ramakrishna Mission, worked as the manager of *Navajivan* for a decade after 1919 and edited it for some time while MKG was in prison during 1922–24. He was conferred the Sahitya Akademi Award for his Gujarati work *Kulkathao* in 1969.

7 *Dakshin Africa Na Satyagraha No Itihas* was written partly in prison and the rest after his premature release. It was published by *Navajivan* in 1924 and its English translation by Valji Govindji Desai was published as *Satyagraha in South Africa* in 1928 by G. Ganesan, Madras.

8 'for *Navajivan*' added in the English translation.

have come under Western influence.[9] And what will
you write? Supposing you reject tomorrow the things
you hold as principles today or supposing you revise in
the future *your plans of today,*[M11] is it not likely that the
men who shape their conduct on the authority of your
word, spoken or[10] written, may be misled? Don't you
think it would be better[11] not to write anything like an
autobiography, at any rate just yet?'

   This argument had some effect on me. *But it is
not my purpose to attempt a real autobiography.*[M12] I simply
want to tell the story of my numerous experiments
with truth, and as my life consists of nothing but those
experiments, it is true that the story will take the shape
of an autobiography. *But I shall not mind,*[M13] if every
page of it speaks only of my experiments. I believe, or at
any rate flatter myself with the belief, that a connected
account of all these experiments will not be without
benefit to the *reader.*[M14] My experiments in the political
field are now known, not only to India, but to a certain
extent to the 'civilized' world. For me, they have not
much value; and the title of 'Mahatma' that they have
won for me has, therefore, even less. Often the title has
deeply pained me; and there is not a moment I can recall
when it may be said to have tickled me. But I should
certainly like to narrate my experiments in the spiritual
field which are known only to myself, and from which
I have derived such power as I possess for working in
the political field. If the experiments are really spiritual,
then there can be no room for self-praise. They can only
add to my humility. The more I reflect and look back
on the past, the more vividly do I feel my limitations.

[M11] your activities in pursuance of these principles?

[M12] But, do I intend to write an autobiography?

[M13] I would consider that narration faultless

[M14] people

---

[9] 'except amongst those who have come under Western influence'
   added in the English translation.

[10] 'spoken or' added in the English translation. The original reads:
   'shape their conduct on the authority of your written word'.

[11] 'to be cautious and' to add.

What I want to achieve—what I have been striving and pining to achieve these thirty years—is self-realization, to see God face to face, to attain *moksha*.[12] I live and move and have my being in pursuit of this goal. All that I do by way of speaking and writing, and all my ventures in the political field, are directed to this same end. But as I have all along believed that what is possible for one is possible for all, my experiments have not been conducted in the closet, but in the open; and I do not think that *this fact*[M15] detracts from their spiritual value. *There are some things which are known only to oneself and one's Maker. These are clearly incommunicable. The experiments I am about to relate are not such.*[13] *But they are spiritual, or rather moral; for the essence of religion is morality.*[M16]

Only those matters of religion[14] that can be comprehended as much by children as by older people, will be included in this story. If I can narrate them in a dispassionate and humble spirit, many other experimenters will find in them provision for their onward march. Far be it from me to claim any degree of perfection for these experiments. I claim for them nothing more than does a scientist who, though he conducts his experiments with the utmost accuracy, forethought and minuteness, never claims any finality about his conclusions, *but keeps an open mind regarding them*.[M17] I have gone through deep self-introspection, searched myself through and through, and examined and analysed every psychological situation. *Yet I am far from claiming any finality or infallibility about my conclusions.*[M18] One claim I do indeed make and it is this. For me they

M15 because they are seen by all

M16 There are certainly some things that arise and find repose in the soul, it is beyond my capacity to write about them. In my experiments the spiritual is moral, religion is morality; morality observed from the perspective of the soul is religion.

M17 or remains dispassionate, if not doubtful, about the truth of his own conclusions. Such is my claim with regard to my experiments.

M18 But I do not ever wish to make a claim that conclusions thus arrived at are final for all, that they are true or only they are true.

---

[12] MD's footnote: Lit. Freedom from birth and death. The nearest English equivalent is salvation.

[13] 'The experiments I am about to relate are not such.' Added in the English translation.

[14] 'of religion' added in the English translation.

appear to be absolutely correct, and seem for the time being to be final. For if they were not, I should base no action on them. But at every step I have carried out the process of acceptance or rejection and acted accordingly. And so long as my acts satisfy[15] my reason and my heart, I must firmly adhere to my original conclusions.

If I had only to discuss academic principles, I should clearly not attempt an autobiography. But my purpose being to give an account of various practical applications of these principles, *I have given the chapters I propose to write the title of The Story of My Experiments with Truth.*[M19] These will of course include experiments with non-violence, celibacy and other principles of conduct believed to be distinct from truth. But for me, truth is the sovereign principle, which includes numerous other principles. This truth is not only truthfulness in word, but truthfulness in thought also, and not only the relative truth of our conception, but the Absolute Truth, the Eternal Principle, that is God. There are innumerable definitions of God, because His manifestations are innumerable. They overwhelm me with wonder and awe and for a moment stun me. But I worship God as Truth only.[16] I have not yet found Him, but I am seeking after Him. I am prepared to sacrifice the things dearest to me in pursuit of this quest. Even if the sacrifice demanded be my very life, I hope I may be prepared to give it. But as long as I have not realized this Absolute Truth, so long must I hold by the relative truth as I have conceived it. That relative truth must, meanwhile, be my beacon, my shield and buckler. Though this path is straight and narrow and sharp as the razor's edge, for me it has been the quickest and[17] easiest.

[M19] I have given the primary title 'Experiments with Truth' to this endeavour

---

[15] 'me' to add.

[16] 'He alone is True, all else is unreal.' To add.

[17] 'quickest and' added in the English translation.

M20 terrible

M21 the readers of *Navajivan*, etc., who constitute my world

M22 means

M23 a little soul

Even my *Himalayan*M20 blunders have seemed trifling to me because I have kept strictly to this path. For the path has saved me from coming to grief,[18] and I have gone forward according to my light. Often in my progress I have had faint glimpses of the Absolute Truth, God, and daily the conviction is growing upon me that He alone is real and all else is unreal. Let *those*,M21 who wish, realize how the conviction has grown upon me; let them share my experiments and share also my conviction if they can. The further conviction has been growing upon me that whatever is possible for me is possible even for a child, and I have sound reasons for saying so. The *instruments*M22 for the quest of truth are as simple as they are difficult. They may appear quite impossible to an arrogant person, and quite possible to an innocent child. The seeker after truth should be humbler than the dust. The world crushes the dust under its feet, but the seeker after truth should so humble himself that even the dust could crush him. Only then, and not till then, will he have a glimpse of truth. The dialogue between Vasishtha and Vishwamitra[19] makes this abundantly clear. Christianity and Islam also amply bear it out.

If anything that I write in these pages should[20] strike the reader as being touched with pride, then he must take it that there is something wrong with my quest, and that my glimpses are no more than mirage. Let hundreds like me perish, but let truth prevail. Let us not reduce the standard of truth even by a hair's breadth for judging *erring mortals*[21] M23 like myself.

I hope and pray that no one will regard the advice interspersed in the following chapters as authoritative.

---

[18] 'in spite of my errors' to add.

[19] Ramayana, 'Balakanda'.

[20] 'may' in the first edition, changed in the 1940 edition.

[21] '*Alpatma*' in the original, the opposite of 'mahatma'.

The experiments narrated should be regarded as illustrations, in the light of which everyone may carry on his own experiments according to his own inclinations and capacity. I trust that to this limited extent the *illustrations*[M24] will be really helpful; because I am not going either to conceal or understate any ugly[22] things that must be told. I hope to acquaint the reader fully with all my faults and errors. My purpose is to describe experiments in the science of satyagraha, not to say how *good*[M25] I am. *In judging myself I shall try to be as harsh as truth, as I want others also to be. Measuring myself by that standard*[M26] I must exclaim with Surdas:

> Where is there a wretch
> So wicked and loathsome as I?
> I have forsaken my Maker,
> So faithless have I been.[23]

For it is an unbroken torture to me that I am still so far from Him, Who as I fully know, governs every breath of my life, and *Whose offspring I am.*[M27] I know that it is the evil passions within that keep me so far from Him, and yet I cannot get away from them.

But I must close.[24] I can only take up the actual story in the next chapter.

The Ashram, Sabarmati,　　　　　　　M.K. Gandhi
November 26, 1925[25]

[M24] autobiographical writings

[M25] attractive

[M26] According to the measure that I wish to use for judging myself, the standard that all of us should use to measure ourselves,

[M27] Whom I look upon as the provider of my salt

---

[22] 'ugly' added in the English translation.

[23] MKG's prose translation of the verse reads: 'Who can be so crooked, bad or dissolute as I? I am so faithless that I have forgotten the very God who gave me this body.' See *CWMG*, vol. 44, p. 415.

[24] 'I cannot begin the narration of experiments in the introduction.' To add.

[25] In Gujarati original, the date is given as Magsar Sud 11, 1982.

PART I

I

BIRTH AND PARENTAGE[1]

The Gandhis belong to the Bania caste and[2] seem to
have been originally grocers. But for three generations,
from my grandfather, they have been Prime Ministers
in several Kathiawad States.[3] Uttamchand Gandhi, alias
Ota Gandhi, my grandfather,[4] must have been a man
of principle. State intrigues compelled him to leave
Porbandar, where he was Diwan,[5] and to seek refuge
in Junagadh. There he saluted the Nawab with the left
hand. Someone,[6] noticing the apparent discourtesy,
asked for an explanation,[7] which was given thus: 'The
right hand is already pledged to Porbandar.'

Ota Gandhi married *a second time,*[8] *having lost his first
wife.*[9] [M1] He had four sons by his first wife[10] and two by   [M1] twice in succession

---

[1] 'and Parentage' added in the English translation.

[2] 'belong to the Bania caste and' added in the English translation.

[3] 'in several Kathiawad States' added in the English translation.

[4] 'my grandfather' added in the English translation.

[5] 'where he was Diwan' added in the English translation.

[6] Comma (,) added in the 1940 edition.

[7] Comma (,) added in the 1940 edition.

[8] Comma (,) added in the 1940 edition.

[9] His two wives were Kadvi Bai and Lakshmi Bai, respectively.

[10] Vallabhji, Pitambar, Ratanji, Jiwanlal.

his second wife.[11] I do not think that in my childhood I ever felt or knew that these sons of Ota Gandhi were not all of the same mother. The fifth of these six brothers was Karamchand Gandhi, alias Kaba Gandhi, and the sixth was Tulsidas Gandhi. Both these brothers were Prime Ministers in Porbandar,[12] one after the other. Kaba Gandhi was my father. *He was*[M2] member of the Rajasthanik Court. It is now extinct,[13] but in those days it was a very influential body for settling disputes between the chiefs and their fellow-clansmen.[14] He was for some time Prime Minister in Rajkot and then in Vankaner. He was a pensioner of the Rajkot State when he died.

Kaba Gandhi married four times in succession,[15] having lost his wife each time by death.[16] He had two daughters by his first and second marriages.[17] His last wife, Putlibai, bore him a daughter and three sons,[18] I being the youngest.

My father was a lover of his clan, truthful, brave and generous, but short-tempered. To a certain extent he might[19] have been given to carnal pleasures. For he married for the fourth time when he was over forty. But he was incorruptible and had earned a name for strict impartiality in his family as well as outside. His loyalty

[M2] After ceasing to be the Prime Minister of Porbandar he became

---

[11] Karamchand, Tulsidas.

[12] Comma (,) added in the 1940 edition.

[13] The first edition read, 'Rajasthanik Court now extinct'.

[14] 'It is now extinct . . . fellow-clansmen.' Line added in the English translation.

[15] Comma (,) added in the 1940 edition.

[16] 'having lost his wife each time by death' added in the English translation.

[17] Mulibehn, Pankuvarbehn.

[18] Raliatbehn (Gokibehn), Lakshmidas, Karsandas, Mohandas.

[19] 'may' in the first edition.

to the State was well known. An Assistant Political Agent spoke insultingly of the Rajkot Thakore Saheb, his chief,[20] and he stood up to the insult. The *Agent*[M3]   [M3] Sahib
was angry and asked Kaba Gandhi to apologize. This he refused to do and was therefore kept under detention for a few hours. But when the *Agent*[M4] saw that Kaba   [M4] Sahib
Gandhi was adamant,[21] he ordered him to be released.

My father never had any ambition to accumulate riches and left us[22] very little property.

He had no education, save that of experience. At best, he might[23] be said to have read up to the fifth Gujarati standard. Of history and geography he was innocent. But his rich experience of practical affairs stood him in good stead in the solution of the most intricate questions and in managing *hundreds of*[M5] men.   [M5] a thousand
Of religious training he had very little, but he had had that kind of religious culture which frequent visits to temples and listening to religious discourses make available to many Hindus. In his last days he began reading the Gita at the instance of a learned Brahmin friend of the family, and he used to repeat aloud some verses every day at the time of worship.

The outstanding impression my mother has left on my memory is that of saintliness.[24] She was deeply

---

[20] 'his chief' added in the English translation.

[21] Comma (,) added in the 1940 edition.

[22] 'the brothers' to add.

[23] 'may' in the first edition.

[24] Mahadev Desai has reported the following conversation with MKG in Yeravada Prison in 1932: 'In the morning while examining the proofs of the abridged edition of *An Autobiography*, I asked Bapu: 'You have spoken of your mother's austere vows such as *ekadashi, chaturmas, chandrayana,* etc., but you have used the word saintliness. Do you not wish to say penance instead of saintliness here? Cannot the word austerity be put in?'
BAPU: 'No. I have used the word saintliness deliberately. In penance there may be external renunciation, endurance and even

^{M6} worship and prayers

religious. She would not think of taking her meals without her daily *prayers*.^{M6} Going to *Haveli*—the Vaishnava temple[25]—was one of her daily duties. As far as my memory can go back, I do not remember her having ever missed the *Chaturmas*.[26] She would take the hardest vows and keep them without flinching. Illness was no excuse for relaxing them. I can recall her once falling ill when she was observing the *Chandrayana*[27] vow, but the illness was not allowed to interrupt the observance. To keep two or three consecutive fasts was nothing to her. Living on one meal a day during *Chaturmas* was a habit with her. Not content with that, she fasted every alternate day during one *Chaturmas*. During another *Chaturmas* she vowed not to have food without seeing the sun. We children on those days would stand, staring at the sky, waiting to announce the appearance of the sun to our mother. Everyone knows that at the height of the rainy season the sun often does not condescend to show his face. And I remember days when,[28] *at his sudden appearance, we*

---

hypocrisy. But saintliness is an inner quality. My mother's inner life would reflect itself in her austerity. If you notice any purity in me, that is not my father's but my mother's. My mother died at the age of forty, so I have seen her in the prime of life, but I have never seen in her any frivolity, recourse to beauty aids or interest in the pleasures of life or hypocrisy. The one lasting impression she left on my mind is that of saintliness.' *Mahadevbhai Ni Diary I*, p. 67. Reproduced from *CWMG*, vol. 39, p. 8.

[25] 'the Vaishnava temple' added in the English translation.

[26] MD's footnote: literally, a period of four months. A vow of fasting and semi-fasting during the four months of the rains. The period is a sort of long Lent.

[27] MD's footnote: a sort of fast in which the daily quantity of food is increased or diminished according as to the moon waxes or wanes. (However, in *Young India* the footnote reads: 'An expiatory vow regulated by the waxing and waning of the moon.' *Young India*, vol. VII, no. 50.)

[28] Comma (,) added in the 1940 edition.

would rush and announce it to her. She would run out to see with her own eyes, but by that time the fugitive sun would be gone, thus depriving her of her meal.[M7] 'That does not matter,' she would say cheerfully, 'God did not want me to eat today.' And then she would return to her round of duties.

My mother had strong common sense. She was well informed about all *matters of State,*[M8] and ladies of the *court*[M9] thought highly of her intelligence. Often I would accompany her, exercising the privilege of childhood, and I still remember many lively discussions she had with the widowed mother of the Thakore Saheb.[29] Of these parents I was born at Porbandar, otherwise known as Sudamapuri, on[30] the 2nd October, 1869. I passed my childhood in Porbandar. I recollect having been put to school.[31] It was with some difficulty that I got through the multiplication tables. The fact that I recollect nothing more of those days than having[32] learnt, in company with other boys, *to call our teacher all kinds of names,*[M10] would strongly suggest that my intellect must have been sluggish, and my memory raw.[33]

[M7] we would see the Sun and exclaim, 'Ba, Ba, the Sun can be seen'; and Ba would come out hurriedly but by then the Sun would have disappeared

[M8] courtly matters

[M9] Queens' quarters

[M10] to abuse our teacher

---

[29] 'Bama Saheb' in the original.

[30] 'Bhadarva Vad 12, in the Samvat 1925' to add.

[31] Luliya Master's school (literally, 'lame teacher's school'). The teacher's name was Virji Kamdar. It was a private school. See J.M. Upadhyaya, *Mahatma Gandhi: A Teacher's Discovery* (Vallabh Vidyanagar: Sardar Patel University, Undated), p. 3.

[32] 'of having' in the first edition.

[33] The original reads: 'my memory raw like the half-baked *papad* in the rhyme that we boys used to sing. I must give those lines. "One is one, bake the *papad,* the *papad* is unbaked, . . . is my . . .!" The first blank would have the teacher's name. I do not wish to immortalize that. The second blank would have an abuse, which I have omitted and need not be filled.'

II

CHILDHOOD

I must have been about seven when my father left Porbandar for Rajkot to become a member of the Rajasthanik Court. There I was put into[34] a *primary*[35] [M1] school, and I can well recollect those days, including the names and other particulars of the teachers who taught me. As at Porbandar, so here, there is hardly anything to note about my studies. I could only have been a mediocre student. From this[36] school I went to the suburban school[37] and thence to the high school,[38] having already reached my twelfth year. I do not remember having ever told a lie during this short *period, either to my teachers or to my school-mates*.[M2] I used to be very shy and avoided all company.[39] My books and my lessons were my sole companions. To be at school at the stroke of the hour and to run back home as soon as the school closed—that was my daily habit. I literally ran back, because I could not bear to talk to anybody. I was even afraid lest anyone should poke fun at me.

There is an incident which occurred at the examination during my first year at the high school and which[40] is worth recording. Mr. Giles, the Educational Inspector, had come on a visit of inspection. He had set us[41] five words to write as a spelling exercise. One of the

[M1] village

[M2] period to my teachers or having made any friends

---

[34] 'put to' in the first edition.

[35] MKG was in this so-called 'Branch school' in 1877 and 1888, and studied Gujarati standard 1 and 2.

[36] 'village' to add.

[37] MKG studied Gujarati standards 3 and 4 in this school from 21 January 1879 to 2 October 1880.

[38] MKG was admitted to Kattywar High School on 1 December 1880.

[39] 'and avoided all company' added in the English translation.

[40] 'at the High School which' in the first edition.

[41] 'the first standard boys' to add. (First standard here refers to English First Standard, equal to class six.)

words was 'kettle'. I had misspelt it. The teacher[42] tried to prompt me with the point of his boot, but I would not be prompted. It was beyond me to see that he wanted me to copy the spelling from my neighbour's slate, for I had thought that the teacher was there to supervise us against copying. The result was that all the boys, except myself, were found to have spelt every[43] word correctly. Only I had been stupid. The teacher tried later to bring this stupidity home to me, but without effect. I never could learn the art of 'copying'.

Yet the incident did not in the least diminish my respect for my teacher. I was by nature, blind to the faults of elders. Later I came to know of many other failings of this teacher, but my regard for him remained the same. For I had learnt to carry out the orders of elders, not to *scan their actions*.[M3]

[M3] be their judge

Two other incidents belonging to the same period have always clung to my memory. As a rule I had *a distaste for*[M4] any reading[44] beyond my school books. The daily lessons had to be done, because I disliked being taken to task by my teacher as much as I disliked deceiving him. Therefore I would do the lessons, but often without my mind in them. Thus when even the lessons could not be done properly, there was of course no question of any extra reading. But somehow my eyes fell on a book purchased by my father. It was *Shravana Pitribhakti Nataka* (a play about Shravana's devotion to his parents[45]). I read it with intense interest. There came to our place about the same time itinerant showmen.[46]

[M4] no fondness for

---

[42] Nathu Nagji Ganatra.

[43] 'each' in the first edition.

[44] Comma (,) in the first edition: 'reading, beyond'.

[45] Added in the translation. This three act play written by Ganapatram Jethabhai Bhatt later came to be published as 'Pitrubhakta Shravan: Natak No Opera.'

[46] 'show-men' in the first edition; 'who showed pictures on a bioscope' to add.

One of the pictures I was shown was of Shravana carrying, by means of slings fitted for his shoulders, his blind parents on a pilgrimage. The book and the picture left an indelible impression on my mind. 'Here is an example for you to copy,' I said to myself. The agonized lament of the parents over Shravana's death is still fresh in my memory. *The melting tune*[47] *moved me deeply,*[48] *and I played it on a concertina*[M5] which my father had purchased for me.

M5 I played that melting tune on a concertina. I had a fondness for playing the concertina

There was a similar incident connected with another play. Just about this time, I had secured my father's[49] permission to see a play performed by a certain dramatic company. This play-*Harishchandra*[50]-captured my heart. I could never be tired of seeing it. But how often should I be permitted to go? It haunted me and I must have acted *Harishchandra to myself times without number.*[M6] 'Why should not all be truthful like Harishchandra?' was the question I asked myself day and night. To follow truth and to go through all the ordeals Harishchandra went through was the one ideal it inspired in me. I literally believed in the *story*[M7] of Harishchandra. The thought of it all often made me weep. My common sense tells me today that Harishchandra could not have been a historical character. Still both Harishchandra and Shravana are living realities

M6 this play in my mind hundreds of times

M7 ordeal

---

[47] The term in the original is 'Lalit Chand', a poetic meter as also a melting tune.

[48] Comma (,) added in the 1940 edition.

[49] 'my father's' added in the English translation.

[50] The legend of King Harishchandra appears in several classical Sanskrit texts such as *Aitereya Brahmana*, the Mahabharata, the *Markandeya Purana* and the *Devi Bhagvata Purana*. It is the story of his sacrifice and steadfastness to truth as narrated in the *Markandeya Purana* that has captured popular imagination. The first full-length feature film made in India was *Raja Harishchandra* (1914) by Dada Saheb Phalke. The Gujarati play *Harishchandra* written by Ranchhodbhai Udayram Dave(1837-1923) was an adaption from an English translation of a Tamil play. The play was usually performed by Parsi Natak Mandali.

for me,[51] and I am sure I should be moved[52] as before if I were to read those plays again[53] today.

III

CHILD MARRIAGE

Much as I wish that I had not[54] to write this chapter, I know that I shall have to swallow many such bitter draughts in the course of this narrative. And I cannot do otherwise, if I claim to be a worshipper of Truth. It is my painful duty to have to record here my marriage at the age of thirteen.[55] As I see *the youngsters of the same age*[M1] about me who are under my care, and think of my own marriage, I am inclined to pity myself and to congratulate them on having escaped my lot. I can see no moral argument in support of *such a preposterously early marriage.*[M2]

Let the reader make no mistake. I was married, not betrothed. For in Kathiawad there are two distinct rites—betrothal and marriage. Betrothal is a preliminary promise on the part of the parents of the boy and the girl to join them in marriage, and it is not inviolable. The death of the boy entails no widowhood on the girl.

[M1] children of twelve to thirteen

[M2] my marriage at the age of thirteen

---

[51] 'But for me both Harishchandra and Shravana are living realities,' in the first edition.

[52] 'touched' in the first edition; 'to tears' to add.

[53] 'read again those plays' in the first edition.

[54] 'might not have to' in the first edition.

[55] The year and month of marriage remain uncertain. MKG states that he was married at the age of 13, which would make the year 1882. According to Chandubhai Bhagubhai Dalal, *Gandhiji Ni Dinvari* (Ahmedabad: Sabarmati Ashram Preservation and Memorial Trust, 1976), vol. 1, p. 3, footnote 2 (1), the marriage took place in the month of May of 1881. *CWMG*, vol. 1, p. 343, gives the year of marriage as 1881. J.M. Upadhyaya, *Mahatma Gandhi—A Teacher's Discovery* (Vallabh Vidyanagar: Sardar Patel University, 1969) gives the month as May (p. 44) and also as December (p. 143) of 1881.

It is an agreement purely between the parents, and the children have no concern with it. Often they are not even informed of it. It appears that[56] I was betrothed thrice, though without my knowledge. I was told that two girls chosen for me had died in turn, and therefore I infer that I was betrothed three times. I have a faint recollection, however, that the third betrothal took place in my seventh year. But I do not recollect having been informed about it.[57] In the present chapter I am talking about my marriage, of which I have the clearest recollection.

It will be remembered that we were three brothers. The first was already married. The elders decided to marry my second brother, who was two or three years my senior, a cousin,[58] possibly a year older, and me, all at the same time. In doing so there was no thought of our welfare, much less our wishes. It was purely a question of their own convenience and economy.

Marriage among Hindus is no simple matter. The parents of the bride and the bridegroom often bring themselves to ruin over it. They waste their substance, they waste their time. Months are taken up over the preparations—in making clothes and ornaments and in preparing budgets for *dinners*.[M3] Each tries to outdo the other in the number and variety of courses to be prepared. Women, whether they have a voice or no, sing themselves hoarse, even get ill, and disturb the peace of their neighbours. These in their turn quietly put up with all the turmoil and bustle, all the dirt and filth, representing the remains of the feasts, because they know that a time will come when they also will be behaving in the same manner.

[M3] the community feast

---

[56] 'It appears that' added in the English translation.

[57] 'Marriage requires the presence of the groom and the bride, it entails rituals.' To add.

[58] Motilal Tulsidas.

It would be better, thought my elders, to have all this bother over at one and the same time.[M4] Less expense and greater *éclat*.[M5] For money could be freely spent if *it had only to be spent once instead of thrice.*[M6] My father and my uncle were both old, and we were the last children they had to marry. It is likely that they wanted to have the last best time of their lives. In view of all these considerations, a triple wedding was decided upon, and as I have said before, months were taken up in preparation for it.

It was only through these preparations that we got *warning of the coming event.*[M7] I do not think it meant to me anything more than the prospect of good clothes to wear, drum beating, marriage processions, rich dinners and a strange girl to play with. The carnal desire came later.[59] I propose to draw the curtain over my shame, except for a few details worth recording. To these I shall come later. But even *they*[M8] have little to do with the central idea I have kept before me in writing this story.

So my brother and I were both taken to Porbandar from Rajkot. There are some amusing details of the preliminaries to the final drama—e.g., smearing our bodies all over with turmeric paste—but I must omit them.

My father was a Diwan, but nevertheless a servant, *and all the more so because he was in favour with the Thakore Saheb.*[M9] The latter would not let him go until the last moment. And when he did so, he ordered for my father special stage-coaches, reducing the journey by two days. But the fates had willed otherwise. Porbandar is 120 miles from Rajkot—a cart journey of five days. My father did the distance in three, but the coach toppled over in the third stage, and he sustained severe

[M4] Won't it be better to have such flurry and bustle once instead of three times?

[M5] marriage would shine forth

[M6] three marriages were held together

[M7] got to know that marriages were to be held

[M8] these details

[M9] a favourite of the ruler, hence more in bondage

---

[59] 'I can describe how it came, but let the reader not be curious about it.' To add.

M10 Bandages on the hands, bandages on the back.

M11 Father. But was I any less devoted to the passions? Passions here does not mean only sexual desire but all cravings.

injuries. *He arrived bandaged all over.*M10 Both his and our interest in the coming event was half destroyed, but the ceremony had to be gone through. For how could the marriage dates be changed? However, I forgot my grief over my father's injuries in the childish amusement of the wedding.

I was devoted to *my parents. But no less was I devoted to the passions that flesh is heir to.*M11 I had yet to learn that all happiness and pleasure should be sacrificed in devoted service to my parents. And yet, as though by way of punishment for my desire for pleasures, an incident happened, which has ever since rankled in my mind and which[60] I will relate later.[61] Nishkulanand[62] sings: 'Renunciation of objects, without the renunciation of desires, is short-lived, however hard you may try.' Whenever I sing this song or hear it sung, this bitter untoward incident rushes to my memory and fills me with shame.

My father put on a brave face in spite of his injuries, and took full part in the wedding. As I think of it, I can even today call before my mind's eye the places where he sat as he went through the different details of the ceremony. Little did I dream then that one day I should severely criticize my father for having married me as a child. Everything on that day seemed to me right and proper and pleasing. There was also my own eagerness to get married. And as everything that my father did then struck me as beyond reproach, the recollection of those things is fresh in my memory. I can picture to myself, even today, how we sat on our wedding dais,

---

[60] 'which I will relate later, that has ever since rankled in my mind' in the first edition.

[61] 'and which I will relate later' added in the English translation.

[62] (1766–1848), an ascetic and poet of the Swaminarayan sect, composed *Bhaktachintamani*, his poetic compositions have been compiled as *Nishkulanand Kavya*.

how we performed the *Saptapadi*,[63] how we,[64] the newly
wedded husband and wife, put the sweet *kansar*[65] into
each other's mouth, and how we began to live together,
and oh! that first night. Two innocent children all
unwittingly hurled themselves into the ocean of life.
My brother's wife had thoroughly coached me about
my behaviour on the first night. *I do not know who had
coached my wife.*[66] *I have never asked her about it, nor am I
inclined to do so now.*[M12] The reader may *be sure that we
were too nervous to face each other.*[M13] We were certainly
too shy. How was I to talk to her, and what was I to say?
The coaching could not carry me far. *But no coaching is
really necessary in such matters.*[M14] The impressions of the
former birth are potent enough to make all coaching
superfluous. We gradually began to know each other,
and to speak freely together. We *were*[M15] the same age.
But I *took no time in assuming the authority of a husband.*[M16]

IV

PLAYING THE HUSBAND

About the time of my marriage, little pamphlets costing
a pice, or a pie (I now forget how much), used to be
issued, in which conjugal love, thrift, child marriages,
and other such subjects were discussed. Whenever I

[M12] I do not remember having asked my wife as to who had coached her. I can still ask her. But, I have not the least desire to do so.

[M13] know that I have a hazy recollection of being afraid of each other

[M14] But is coaching really necessary?

[M15] are

[M16] played the husband

---

[63] MD's footnote: *Saptapadi* are seven steps a Hindu bride and bridegroom walk together, making at the same time promises of mutual fidelity and devotion, after which the marriage becomes irrevocable.

[64] 'we' added in the 1940 edition.

[65] MD's footnote: *Kansar* is a preparation of wheat which the pair partake together after the completion of the ceremony.

[66] Kastur Bai (1869–1943), daughter of Vrajkunwarba and Gokuldas Makanji Kapadia.

came across any of these, I used to go through them cover to cover, and it was a habit with me to forget what I did not like, and to carry out in practice whatever I liked. Lifelong faithfulness to the wife, inculcated in these booklets as the duty of the husband, remained permanently imprinted on my heart. Furthermore, *the passion for truth was innate in me,*[M1] and to be false to her was therefore out of the question.[67] And then there was very little chance of my being faithless at that tender age.

But *the lesson of faithfulness*[M2] had also an untoward effect. *'If I should be pledged to be faithful to my wife, she also should be pledged to be faithful to me,' I said to myself.*[M3] The thought made me a jealous husband. *Her duty was easily converted into my right to exact faithfulness from her, and if it had to be exacted, I should be watchfully tenacious of the right.*[M4] I had absolutely no reason to suspect my wife's fidelity, but jealousy does not wait for reasons. I must needs be forever on the look-out regarding her movements, and therefore she could not go anywhere without my permission. This sowed the seeds of a bitter quarrel between us. The restraint was virtually a sort of imprisonment. And Kasturbai was not the girl to brook *any such thing.*[M5] She made it a point to go out whenever and wherever she liked.[68] *More restraint on my part resulted in more liberty being taken by her*[M6] and in my getting more and more cross. Refusal to speak to one another thus became the order of the day with us, married children. I think it was quite innocent of Kasturbai to have taken those liberties with my restrictions. How could a guileless girl brook any restraint on going to the temple or on going on visits to friends? If I had the right to impose restrictions on her, had not she also a similar

<hr />

[67] 'I had also understood that one cannot have relationship with any other woman.' To add.

[68] 'without having sought my permission' to add.

Margin notes:

[M1] I had passion for truth

[M2] these good thoughts

[M3] 'If I should observe the vow of being faithful to my wife, so should the wife pledge to be faithful to me.'

[M4] From 'to observe' I deduced 'to enforce observation'. And if I had to enforce observation, I should keep a watch as well.

[M5] such imprisonment

[M6] The more restraints I placed on her, the more liberties she took right? All this is clear to me today. But at that time I had to make good my authority as a husband!

Let not the reader think, however, that ours was a life of unrelieved bitterness. For my severities were all based on love. I wanted to *make* my wife an ideal wife. My *ambition*[M7] was to *make*[69] her live a pure life, learn what I learnt, and *identify her life and thought with mine*.[M8]

I do not know whether Kasturbai had any such *ambition*.[M9] She was illiterate. By nature she was simple, independent, persevering and, with me at least, reticent. She was not *impatient of*[M10] her ignorance and I do not recollect my studies having ever spurred her to go in for a similar adventure. I fancy, therefore, that my *ambition*[M11] was all one-sided. My passion was entirely centred on one woman, and I wanted it to be reciprocated. But even if there were no reciprocity, it could not be all unrelieved misery because there was active love on one side at least.

I must say I was passionately fond of her. Even at school I used to think of her, and the thought of nightfall and our subsequent meeting was ever haunting me. Separation was unbearable. I used to keep her awake till late in the night with my *idle talk*.[M12] If with this devouring passion there had not been in me a burning attachment to duty, I should either have fallen a prey to disease and premature death, or have sunk into a burdensome existence. But the appointed tasks had to be gone through every morning, and lying to anyone was out of the question. It *was this last thing*[M13] that saved me from many a pitfall.

I have already said that Kasturbai was illiterate. I was very anxious to teach her, but *lustful love left me no time*.[M14] For one thing the teaching had to be done against her will, and that too at night. I dared not *meet*[M15] her in the presence of the elders, *much less talk to her*.[M16] Kathiawad

[M7] sentiment

[M8] that we wholly merge with one another

[M9] sentiment

[M10] discontented with

[M11] sentiment

[M12] sweet, childish prattle

[M13] were these ideas of mine

[M14] how was my lustful love to allow me to teach?

[M15] even look at

[M16] how was one to talk to her?

---

[69] Emphasis in the original.

had then, and to a certain extent has even today, its own peculiar, useless and barbarous *purdah*. Circumstances were thus unfavourable.[70] I must therefore confess that most of my efforts to instruct Kasturbai in our youth were unsuccessful. And when I awoke from the sleep of lust, I had already launched forth into public life, which did not leave me much spare time. I failed likewise to instruct her through private tutors. As a result, Kasturbai can now with difficulty write simple letters and understand simple Gujarati. I am sure that, had my love for her been absolutely untainted with lust, she would be[71] a learned lady today; for I could then have conquered her dislike for studies. I know that nothing is impossible for pure love.

I have mentioned one circumstance that more or less saved me from the disasters of lustful love. There is another worth noting. Numerous examples have convinced me that God ultimately saves him whose motive is pure. Along with the cruel custom of child marriages, Hindu society has another custom which to a certain extent diminishes the evils of the former. Parents do not allow *young*[M17] couples to stay together long. The child-wife spends more than half her time at her father's place. Such was the case with us. That is to say, *during the first five years of our married life (from the age of 13 to 18)*,[M18] we could not[72] have lived together longer than an aggregate period of three years. We would hardly have spent six[73] months together, when there would be a call to my wife from her parents. Such calls were very unwelcome[74] in those days, but they saved us both. At

[M17] child

[M18] from the age of thirteen to nineteen

---

[70] 'for me to teach her.' To add.

[71] 'would have been' in the first edition.

[72] 'cannot' in the first edition.

[73] 'to eight' to add.

[74] 'unpleasant' in the first edition.

the age of eighteen I went to England, and this meant a long and healthy spell of separation. Even after my return from England we hardly stayed together longer than six months. For I had to run up and down between Rajkot and Bombay.[75] Then came the call from South Africa, and *that found me already fairly free from the*[76] *carnal appetite.*[M19]

[M19] meanwhile, I had fairly awakened

V

AT THE HIGH SCHOOL

I have already said that I was learning at the high school when I was married. We three brothers were learning at the same school. The eldest brother was in a much higher class, and the brother who was married at the same time as I was, only one class ahead of me. Marriage resulted in both of us wasting a year. Indeed the result was even worse for my brother, for he gave up studies altogether.[77] Heaven knows how many youths are in[78] the same plight as he. Only in our present[79] Hindu society do studies and marriage go thus hand in hand.

My studies were continued. I was not regarded as a dunce at the high school. I always enjoyed the affection of my teachers. Certificates of progress and character used to be sent to the parents every year. *I never had a bad certificate.*[M1] In fact I even won prizes after I passed out of the second standard. In the fifth and sixth I obtained

[M1] My conduct or studies were never criticized in them.

---

[75] 'from Rajkot to Bombay' in the first edition.

[76] 'the' added in the 1940 edition.

[77] 'after the marriage' to add.

[78] 'suffer' in the first edition.

[79] 'present' added in the English translation.

scholarships of rupees four and ten respectively, an
achievement for which I have to thank good luck more
than my merit. For the scholarships were not open to
all, but reserved for the best boys amongst those coming
from the Sorath Division of Kathiawad.[80] And in those
days there could not have been many boys from Sorath
in a class of forty to fifty.

My own recollection is that I had not any high
regard for my ability. I used to be astonished whenever
I won prizes and scholarships. But I very jealously
guarded my character. *The least little*[M2] blemish drew
tears from my eyes. When I merited, or seemed to the
teacher to merit, a rebuke, it was unbearable for me. I
remember having once received corporal punishment.
I did not so much mind the punishment, as the fact that
it was considered my desert.[M3] I wept piteously. That was
when I was in the first or second standard. There was
another such incident during the time when I was in
the seventh standard. Dorabji Edulji Gimi was the head
master then.[81] He was popular among boys, as he was a
disciplinarian, a man of method and a good teacher. He
had made gymnastics and cricket compulsory for boys
of the upper standards. I disliked both. I never took
part in any exercise, cricket or football, before they
were made compulsory. My shyness was one of the
reasons for this aloofness, *which I now see was wrong.*[M4] I
then had the false notion that gymnastics had nothing
to do with education. Today I know that physical
training should have as much place in the curriculum
as mental training.

I may mention, however, that I was none the
worse for abstaining from exercise. That was because
I had read in books about the benefits of long

M2 Any

M3 I was considered deserving of
punishment

M4 my dislike was wrong

---

[80] 'of Kathiawad' added in the English translation.

[81] Gimi was the headmaster of the Kattywar High School from 1882
to 1896.

walks in the open air, and having liked the advice, I had[82] formed a habit of taking walks, which has still remained with me. These walks gave me a fairly hardy constitution.

The[M5] reason of my dislike for gymnastics was my keen desire to serve as nurse to[83] my father. As soon as the school closed, I would hurry home and begin serving him. Compulsory exercise came directly in the way of this service. *I requested Mr. Gimi to exempt me from gymnastics so that I might be free to serve my father.*[M6] But *he*[M7] would not listen to me. Now it so happened that one Saturday, when we had school in the morning, I had to go from home to the school for gymnastics at 4 o'clock in the afternoon. I had no watch, and the clouds deceived me. Before I reached the school the boys had all left. The next day Mr. Gimi, examining the roll, found me marked absent. Being asked the reason for absence, I told him what had happened. He refused to believe me and ordered me to pay a fine of one or two annas (I cannot now recall how much).

I was convicted of lying! That deeply pained me. How was I to prove my innocence? There was no way.[84] I cried in deep anguish. I saw that a man of truth must also be a man of care. This was the first and last instance of my carelessness in school. I have a faint recollection that I finally succeeded in getting the fine remitted. The exemption from exercise was of course obtained, as my father wrote himself to the head master saying that he wanted me at home after school.[85]

M5 Another

M6 I requested to be exempted from exercise so as to serve my father.

M7 Gimi Sahib

---

[82] 'while in the upper classes at the high school' to add.

[83] 'as nurse to' added in the English translation.

[84] 'I seethed inside me.' To add.

[85] 'so that I could serve him' to add.

M8 I chose to walk instead of doing gymnastics and for that reason perhaps I have not paid penalty of not exercising the body, but

M9 pearl-like

M10 can one add a rim to a perfectly baked clay pot?

M11 Then his handwriting would be like a printed letter.

But though I was none the worse for having neglected exercise,[86] M8 I am still paying the penalty of another neglect. I do not know whence I got the[87] notion that good handwriting was not a necessary part of education, but I retained it until I went to England. When later, especially in South Africa, I saw the *beautiful*M9 handwriting of lawyers and young men born and educated in South Africa, I was ashamed of myself and repented of my neglect. I saw that bad handwriting should be regarded as a sign of an imperfect education. I tried later to improve mine, but *it was too late.*M10 I could never repair the neglect of my youth. Let every young man and woman be warned by my example, and understand that good handwriting is a necessary part of education.[88] I am now of opinion that children should first be taught the art of drawing before learning how to write.[89] Let the child learn his letters by observation as he does different objects, such as flowers, birds, etc., and let him learn handwriting only after he has learnt to draw objects. *He will then write a beautifully formed hand.*M11

Two more reminiscences of my school days[90] are worth recording. I had lost one year because of my marriage, and the teacher wanted me to make good the loss by skipping a class—a privilege usually allowed to industrious boys. I therefore had only six months in

---

[86] 'But though I was none the worse for having neglected exercise'—this line is not in the Gujarati original as published in *Navajivan* of 3 January 1926. It was probably introduced by Mahadev Desai in his translation and later incorporated in the subsequent Gujarati editions.

[87] 'wrong' to add.

[88] 'Skill in drawing is necessary for cultivating good handwriting.' To add.

[89] 'before learning how to write' added in the English translation.

[90] 'concerning my studies' to add.

the third standard and was promoted to the fourth after the examinations which are followed by the summer vacation. English became the medium of instruction in *most*[M12] subjects from the fourth standard. I found myself completely at sea. Geometry was a new subject in which I was not particularly strong, and the English medium made it still more difficult for me. The teacher taught the subject very well, but I could not follow him. Often I would lose heart and *think of going back to the third standard, feeling that the packing of two years' studies into a single year was too ambitious.*[M13] But this would discredit not only me,[91] but also the teacher; because, counting on my industry, he had recommended my promotion. So the fear of the double[92] discredit kept me at my post. When, however, with much effort I reached the thirteenth proposition of Euclid, the utter simplicity of the subject was suddenly revealed to me. A subject which only required a pure and simple use of one's reasoning powers could not be difficult. Ever since that time geometry has been both easy and interesting for me.

Samskrit, however, proved a harder task.[93] In geometry there was nothing to memorize, whereas in Samskrit, I thought, everything had to be learnt by heart. This subject also was commenced from the fourth standard. As soon as I entered the sixth I became disheartened. The teacher was a hard taskmaster, anxious, as I thought, to force the boys. There was a sort of rivalry going on between the Samskrit and the Persian teachers. The Persian teacher was lenient. The boys used to talk among themselves that Persian was very easy and the Persian teacher very good and

[M12] some

[M13] would feel that I should give up trying to do two standards in one year and revert to third standard

---

[91] 'Yet this would not only discredit me,' in the first edition.

[92] 'double' added in the English translation.

[93] 'then geometry.' To add.

M14 tolerated whatever the
students did

M15 'At least consider whose son
you are.

M16 I was ashamed.

M17 Sanskrit scriptures that I do

M18 child

*considerate to the students.*M14 The 'easiness' tempted me
and one day I sat in the Persian class. The Samskrit
teacher was grieved. He called me to his side and said:
*'How can you forget that you are the son of a Vaishnava
father?*M15 Won't you learn the language of your own
religion? If you have any difficulty, why not come to
me? I want to teach you students Samskrit to the best of
my ability. As you proceed further, you will find in it
things of absorbing interest. You should not lose heart.
Come and sit again in the Samskrit class.'

*This kindness put me to shame.*M16 I could not disregard
my teacher's affection. Today I cannot but think with
gratitude of Krishnashankar Pandya.[94] For if I had not
acquired the little Samskrit that I learnt then, I should
have found it difficult to take any interest in our *sacred
books.*M17 In fact I deeply regret that I was not able to
acquire a more thorough knowledge of the language,
because I have since realized that every Hindu *boy and
girl*M18 should possess sound Samskrit learning.

It is now my opinion that in all Indian curricula of
higher education there should be a place for[95] Hindi,
Samskrit, Persian, Arabic and English, besides of course
the vernacular. This big list[96] need not frighten anyone.
If our[97] education were more systematic, and the boys
free from the burden of having to learn their subjects
through a foreign medium, I am sure learning all these
languages would not be an irksome task, but a perfect
pleasure. A scientific knowledge of one language makes
a knowledge of other languages comparatively easy.

In reality, Hindi, Gujarati and Samskrit may be
regarded as one language, and Persian and Arabic also as

---

[94] 'Pandya' added in the English translation; in the original:
'Krishnashankar master'.

[95] 'the national language' to add.

[96] 'of languages' to add.

[97] 'language' to add.

one. Though Persian belongs to the Aryan, and Arabic to the Semitic family of languages, there is a close relationship between Persian and Arabic, because both claim their full growth through the rise of Islam. Urdu I have not regarded as a distinct language, because it has adopted the Hindi grammar and its vocabulary is mainly Persian and Arabic, and he who would learn good Urdu must learn Persian and Arabic, as one who would learn good Gujarati, Hindi, Bengali or Marathi must learn Samskrit.

VI

A TRAGEDY[98]

Amongst my few friends at the high school[M1] I had, at different times, two who might be called intimate. One of these friendships did not last long, though I never forsook my friend. He forsook me, because I made friends with the other. This latter friendship I regard as a tragedy in my life.[99] It lasted long. I formed it in the spirit of a reformer.

This companion was originally my elder brother's friend. They were classmates.[100] I knew his weaknesses,

[M1] I have already said that I had few intimate friends in the high school.

---

[98] 'A Tragedy (1)' in the original.

[99] This friend was Sheikh Mehtab. Mehtab went to Natal and lived in MKG's house. Chapter 23, part 2, 'As a Householder', of the *Autobiography* describes the incident of their life together in South Africa. Mehtab and his wife Fatima Bai took part in the satyagraha campaign in South Africa. His poems on the satyagraha were published in MKG's *Indian Opinion* and have been collected and translated in Surendra Bhana and Neelima Shukla-Bhatt, *A Fire that Blazed in the Ocean: Gandhi and the Poems of Satyagraha in South Africa, 1909–1911* (Promila and Co., New Delhi, in association with Bibliophile South Asia, Chicago, 2011). Also see *CWMG*, vol. 1, p. 4.

[100] The first edition has 'classmates together'.

but I regarded him as a faithful friend. My mother, my eldest brother, and my *wife warned me that I was in bad company. I was too proud*[101] *to heed my wife's warning. But I dared not go against the opinion of my mother and my eldest brother.*[M2] Nevertheless I pleaded with them saying, 'I know he has the weaknesses you attribute to him, but you do not know his virtues. He cannot lead me astray, as my association with him is meant to reform him. For I am sure that if he reforms his ways, he will be a splendid man. I beg you not to be anxious on my account.'

I do not think this satisfied them, but they accepted my explanation and let me go my way.

I have seen since that I had calculated wrongly.[102] A reformer cannot afford to have close intimacy with him whom he seeks to reform. True friendship is an identity of souls rarely to be found in this world. Only between like natures can friendship be altogether worthy and enduring. Friends react on one another. Hence in friendship there is very little scope for reform. I am of opinion that all *exclusive intimacies*[M3] are to be avoided; for man takes in vice far more readily than virtue.[103] And he who would be friends[104] with God must remain alone, or make the whole world his friend. I may be wrong, but my effort to cultivate an intimate friendship proved a failure.

M2 wife, all three, found this companionship disagreeable. How was I, a proud husband, to heed my wife's warning? I would not disobey my mother. I would certainly listen to my eldest brother.

M3 intimate friendships

---

[101] 'I was too proud a husband' in the first edition, changed in the 1940 edition. Srinivas Sastri, while suggesting the change, remarked, 'The expression "proud husband" means the party was proud of his wife. It is best to omit them.' This is on page 52 of the first edition, preserved in the archives of the Sabarmati Ashram Preservation and Memorial Trust, Ahmedabad.

[102] 'One should not venture into deep waters even for the sake of reform.' To add.

[103] 'than virtue' added in the English translation. 'Acquisition of virtue involves an effort.' To add. The first edition reads, 'for a man far more readily takes in vice than virtue'.

[104] 'with the *Atman*' to add.

A wave of 'reform' was sweeping over Rajkot at the time when I first came across this friend. He informed me that many of our[105] teachers were secretly taking meat and wine. He also named many well-known people of Rajkot as belonging to the same company. There were also, I was told, some high-school boys among them.

I was surprised and pained. I asked my friend the reason and he explained it thus: 'We are a weak people because we do not eat meat. The English are able to rule over us, because they are meat-eaters. You know how hardy I am, and how great a runner[106] too. It is because I am a meat-eater. Meat-eaters do not have boils or tumours,[107] and even if they sometimes happen to have any, these[108] heal quickly. *Our teachers and other distinguished people who eat meat are no fools.*[M4] They know its virtues.[109] You should do likewise. There is nothing like trying. Try, and see what strength it gives.'

All these pleas on behalf of meat-eating[110] were not advanced at a single sitting. *They represent the substance of a long and elaborate argument which my friend was trying to impress upon me from time to time.*[M5] My elder brother had already *fallen.*[M6] He therefore supported my friend's argument. I certainly looked feeble-bodied by the side of my brother and this friend. They were both hardier, physically stronger, and more daring. This friend's exploits cast a spell over me. He could run long distances and extraordinarily fast. He was an adept in high and

M4 Do our teachers and other distinguished people who eat meat do so without awareness?

M5 Such arguments, adorned with many examples, were presented to me many a time.

M6 been polluted.

---

[105] 'Hindu' to add.

[106] 'a great runner' in the first edition.

[107] 'or tumours' added in the English translation.

[108] 'they' in the first edition.

[109] 'They know its virtues.' Added in the English translation.

[110] 'on behalf of meat-eating' added in the English translation.

long jumping. He could put up with any amount of corporal punishment. He would often display his exploits to me and, as one is always dazzled when he sees in others the qualities that he lacks himself, I was[111] dazzled by this friend's exploits. This was followed by a strong desire to be like him. I could hardly jump or run. Why should not I also be as strong as he?

Moreover,[112] I was a coward. I used to be haunted by the fear of thieves, ghosts and serpents.[113] I did not dare to stir out of doors at night. *Darkness was a terror to me.*[M7] It was almost impossible for me to sleep in the dark, as I would imagine ghosts coming from one direction, thieves from another and serpents from a third. I could not therefore bear to sleep without a light in the room. How could I disclose my fears to my wife, no child, but already at the threshold of youth, sleeping by my side?[114] I knew that she had more courage than I, and I felt ashamed of myself. She knew no fear of serpents and ghosts. She could go out anywhere in the dark. My friend knew all these weaknesses of mine. He would tell me that he could hold in his hand live serpents, could defy thieves and did not believe in ghosts. And all this was, of course, the result of eating meat.

A doggerel of the Gujarati poet Narmad[115] was in vogue amongst us schoolboys, as follows:

> Behold the mighty Englishman
> He rules the Indian small,

---

[111] 'also dazzled' in the first edition.

[112] 'Again' in the first edition.

[113] 'I was tormented by these fears.' To add.

[114] The first edition reads: 'How could I disclose my fears to the wife sleeping by my side, now at the threshold of youth?'

[115] This was composed by not poet Narmad but by Navalram. It is part of his *Bal Lagna Batrsi*, poem 23, *Naval Granthavali* (first edition, 1891), part 1, p. 248.

Because being a meat-eater
He is five cubits tall.[116]

All this had its due effect on me. I *was beaten*.[M8] It   ^{M8} melted.
began to grow on me that meat-eating was good, that
it would make me strong and daring, and that, if the
whole country took to meat-eating, the English could
be overcome.

A day was thereupon fixed for beginning the
experiment. *It had to be conducted in secret*.[M9] The Gandhis   ^{M9} Not all readers would
were Vaishnavas. My parents were particularly staunch   comprehend the meaning of
Vaishnavas. They would regularly visit the *Haveli*. The   this decision—of this venture.
family had even its own temples. Jainism was strong
in Gujarat, and its influence was felt everywhere and
on all occasions. The opposition to and abhorrence of
meat-eating that existed in Gujarat among the Jains and
Vaishnavas were[117] to be seen nowhere else in India
or outside in such strength. These were the traditions
in which I was born and bred. And I was extremely
devoted to my parents. I knew that the moment they
came to know of my having eaten meat, they would
be shocked to death. Moreover, *my love of truth made
me extra cautious*.[M10] I cannot say that I did not know   ^{M10} by conscious effort or
then that I should have to deceive my parents if I began   otherwise, I was a servant of
Truth

---

[116] A literal prose translation of the Gujarati original would be:
'The Englishmen rule, the natives are suppressed. Compare
the two bodies. He is five cubits tall and a match for five
hundred.'
Gopalkrishna Gandhi has translated the verse thus:

> The Englishman rules, and the ruled the Indian is;
> Ruled the Indian is, just look at their frames!
> On one stands five hands tall,
> He can make five hundred of us fall.

From the Foreword to *An Autobiography or The Story of My
Experiments with Truth: A Table of Concordance*, by Tridip Suhrud
(New Delhi: Routledge, 2010).

[117] 'was' in the first edition.

eating meat.[118] But my mind was bent on the 'reform'. It was not a question of pleasing the palate. I did not know that it had a particularly good relish. I wished to be strong and daring and wanted my countrymen also to be such, so that we might defeat the English and make India free. The word 'swaraj' I had not yet heard. But I knew what freedom meant. The frenzy of the 'reform' blinded me. And having ensured secrecy, I persuaded myself that mere hiding the deed from parents was no departure from truth.[119]

VII

A TRAGEDY (CONTD.)[120]

So the day came. It is difficult fully to describe my condition. There were, on the one hand, the zeal for 'reform' and the novelty of making a momentous departure in life. There was, on the other, the shame of hiding like a thief to do this very thing. I cannot say which of the two swayed me more. We went in search of a lonely spot by the river, and there I saw, for the first time in my life—meat. There was baker's bread also. I relished neither. The goat's meat was as tough as leather. I simply could not eat it. I was sick and had to leave off eating.

I had a very bad night afterwards.[121] A horrible nightmare haunted me. Every time I dropped off

---

[118] 'Under the circumstances, my decision to eat meat was for me a serious and a terrible thing.' To add.

[119] 'And having ensured secrecy, I persuaded myself that mere hiding of the deed from parents was no departure from truth.' Added in the English translation.

[120] 'A Tragedy (2)' in the original.

[121] 'Sleep eluded me.' To add.

to sleep,[122] it would seem as though a live goat were bleating inside me, and I would jump up full of remorse. But then I would remind myself that meat-eating was a duty and *so become more cheerful*.[M1]

M1 I must not lose courage

My friend was not a man to give in easily. He now began to cook various delicacies with meat, and dress them neatly. And for dining, no longer was the secluded spot on the river[123] chosen, but a State house, with its[124] dining-hall, and tables and chairs, about which my friend had made arrangements in collusion with the chief cook there.

This bait[125] had its effect. I got over my dislike for bread, forswore my compassion for the goats, and became a relisher of meat-dishes, if not of meat itself. This went on for about a year. But not more than half a dozen meat-feasts were enjoyed in all; because the State house was not available every day, and there was the obvious difficulty about frequently preparing *expensive*[126] *savoury*[M2] meat-dishes. *I had no money to pay for this 'reform'.*[M3] My friend had therefore always to find the wherewithal. *I had no knowledge where he found it.*[M4] But find it he did, because he was bent on turning me into a meat-eater.[127] But even his means must have been limited, and hence these feasts had necessarily to be few and far between.

M2 tasty

M3 Moreover, such meals cost money. I did not have even a bad coin, hence could pay nothing.

M4 I have, to this day, no knowledge of where he found it.

Whenever I had occasion to indulge in these surreptitious[128] feasts, dinner at home was out of the question. My mother would naturally ask me to come

---

[122] 'Every time I dropped off to sleep,' added in the English translation.

[123] 'river was chosen' in the first edition.

[124] 'allurements of' to add.

[125] 'bait' added in the English translation.

[126] 'expensive' added in the English translation.

[127] 'and polluting me' to add.

[128] 'surreptitious' added in the English translation.

M5 lie

M6 Each time I said so, it pained me.

M7 their sons

M8 meat-eaters, lightning would fall over them

and take my food and want to know the reason why I did not wish to eat. I would *say*M5 to her, 'I have no appetite today; there is something wrong with my digestion.' *It was not without compunction that I devised these pretexts.*M6 I knew I was lying, and lying to my mother. I also knew that, if my mother and father came to know of *my*M7 having become *a meat-eater, they would be deeply shocked.*M8 This knowledge was gnawing at my heart.

Therefore I said to myself: 'Though it is essential to eat meat, and also essential to take up food reform in the country yet deceiving and lying to one's father and mother is worse than not[129] eating meat. In their lifetime, therefore, meat-eating must be out of the question. When they are no more and[130] I have found my freedom, I will eat meat openly, but until that moment arrives I will abstain from it.'

This decision I communicated to my friend, and I have never since gone back to meat. My parents never knew that two of their sons had become meat-eaters.

I abjured meat out of the purity of my desire not to lie to my parents, but I did not abjure the company of my friend. My zeal for reforming him had *proved disastrous for*M9 me, and all the time I was completely unconscious of *the fact.*M10

M9 polluted

M10 my pollution

M11 debauched conduct

The same company would have led me into *faithlessness to my wife.*M11 But I was saved by the skin of my teeth.[131] My friend once took me to a brothel. He sent me in with the necessary instructions. It was all pre-arranged. The bill had already been paid.[132] *I went*

---

[129] 'abstinence from' in the first edition.

[130] 'when' in the first edition.

[131] 'But I was saved by the skin of my teeth.' Added in the English translation.

[132] 'I had only to amuse myself.' To add.

into the jaws of sin, but God in His infinite mercy protected me against myself.[M12] I was almost struck blind and dumb[133] in this *den of vice. I sat near the woman on her bed, but I was tongue-tied.*[M13] She naturally lost patience with me, and showed me the door, with abuses and insults. I then felt as though my manhood had been injured, and wished to sink into the ground for shame. But I have ever since given thanks to God for having saved me. I can recall four more similar incidents in my life, and in most of them *my good fortune,*[M14] rather than any effort on my part, saved me.[134] From a strictly ethical point of view, all these occasions must be regarded as moral lapses; for the carnal desire was there, and it was as good as the act. But from the ordinary point of view, a man who is saved from physically committing sin is regarded as saved. And I was saved only in that sense.[135] There are some actions from which an escape is a godsend both for the man who escapes and for those about him. Man, as soon as he gets back his consciousness of right, is thankful to the Divine mercy for the escape. As we know that a man often succumbs to temptation, however much he may resist it, we also know *that Providence often intercedes and saves him*[M15] in spite of himself. How all this happens—how far a man is free and how far a creature of circumstances—how far free will comes into play and where fate enters on the scene—all this is a mystery *and will remain a mystery.*[M16]

But to go on with the story. Even this was far from opening my eyes to the viciousness of my friend's company. I therefore had many more bitter draughts in store for me, until my eyes were actually opened

[M12] I imprisoned myself in that house. But he whom God wishes to save remains pure in spite of his desire for a fall.

[M13] room. I lost speech. Deep in shame, I sat stunned with the woman on her bed, but remained tongue-tied.

[M14] circumstances

[M15] from experience that many circumstances intercede and he is saved

[M16] these have hitherto not been resolved and it is difficult to say if they can be resolved with any finality

---

[133] 'and dumb' added in the English translation.

[134] On 17 May 1925, writing in *Navajivan* in response to questions posed by a correspondent about the attributes of Ramanama, MKG recalled these instances. See *CWMG*, vol. 27, pp. 107–11.

[135] 'and only to that extent' to add.

by an ocular demonstration of some of his lapses quite unexpected by me. But of them later, as we are proceeding chronologically.[136]

One thing, however, I must mention now, as it pertains to the same period. One of the reasons of my differences with my wife was undoubtedly the company of this friend. I was both a devoted and a jealous husband, and this friend fanned the flame of my suspicions about my wife. I never could doubt his veracity. And I never have forgiven myself the violence of which I have been guilty in often having pained my wife by *acting on his information*.[M17] Perhaps[137] only a Hindu wife would tolerate these hardships, and that is why I have regarded woman as an incarnation of tolerance. A servant wrongly suspected may throw up his job, a son in the same case may leave his father's roof, and a friend may put an end to the friendship. The wife, if she suspects her husband, will keep quiet,[138] but if the husband suspects her, she is ruined. Where is she to go? A Hindu wife[139] may not seek divorce in a law-court. *Law has no remedy for her*.[140] [M18] And I can never forget or forgive myself for having *driven my wife to that desperation*.[M19]

The canker of suspicion was rooted out only when I understood ahimsa[141] in all its bearings. I saw then the glory of *brahmacharya*[142] and realized that the wife

M17 believing his stories

M18 Such is the one-sided justice available to her.

M19 dealt such justice to her

---

136 'as far as possible' to add.

137 'Perhaps' added in the 1940 edition.

138 'and suffer in silence' to add.

139 'of the so-called high castes' to add.

140 Emphasis in the original.

141 MD's footnote: *Ahimsa* means literally innocence, not hurting, non-violence.

142 MD's footnote: *Brahmacharya* means literally conduct that leads one to God. Its technical meaning is self-restraint, particularly mastery over the sexual organ.

is not the husband's bondslave, but his companion and his helpmate, and an equal partner in all his joys and sorrows—as free as the husband to choose her own path.[143] Whenever I think of those dark[144] days of doubts and suspicions, I am filled with loathing of[145] my folly and my lustful cruelty, and I *deplore*[M20] my blind devotion to my friend.

[M20] pity myself for

VIII

STEALING AND ATONEMENT

I have still to relate some of my failings during this meat-eating period and also previous to it, which date from before my marriage or soon after.

A relative and I became fond of smoking.[146] Not that we saw any good in smoking, or were enamoured of the smell of a cigarette.[147] We simply imagined a sort of pleasure in emitting clouds of smoke from our mouths. My uncle had the habit, and when we saw him smoking, we thought we should copy his example. But we had no money. So we began pilfering stumps of cigarettes thrown away by my uncle.

The stumps, however, were not always available, and could not emit much smoke either. So we began to steal coppers from the servant's pocket-money in order to purchase Indian cigarettes. But the question was where to keep them. We could not of course smoke

---

[143] 'good or bad' to add.

[144] 'dark' added in the English translation.

[145] 'at' in the first edition.

[146] 'We had no money.' To add.

[147] Throughout this chapter the original word 'bidi' has been translated as 'cigarette' or as 'Indian cigarette'.

in the presence of elders.[148] We managed somehow for a few weeks on these stolen coppers. In the mean time we heard that the stalks of a certain plant[149] were porous and could be smoked like cigarettes. We got them and began this kind of smoking.

But we were far from being satisfied with such things as these. Our want of independence began to smart. It was unbearable that we should be unable to do anything without the elders' permission. At last, in sheer disgust, we decided to commit suicide!

But how were we to do it? From where were we to get the poison? We heard that dhatura[150] seeds were an effective poison. Off we went to the jungle in search of these seeds, and got them. *Evening was thought to be the auspicious hour.*[M1] We went to Kedarji Mandir, put ghee in the temple-lamp, had the *darshan* and then looked for a lonely corner. But *our courage failed us.*[M2] Supposing we were not instantly killed? And what was the good of killing ourselves? Why not rather put up with the lack of independence? But we swallowed two or three seeds nevertheless. We dared not take more. Both of us fought shy of death, and decided to go to Ramji Mandir to compose ourselves, and to dismiss the thought of suicide.

I realized that it was not as easy to commit suicide as to contemplate it. And since then, whenever I have heard of someone threatening to commit suicide, it has had little or no effect on me.

The thought of suicide ultimately resulted in both of us bidding good-bye to the habit of smoking stumps of cigarettes and of stealing the servant's coppers for the purpose of smoking.

[M1] We sought the evening hour.

[M2] we lacked the courage to eat the poison

---

[148] 'that we knew' to add.

[149] '(whose name I have forgotten)' to add.

[150] A poisonous vespertine flowering plant.

Ever since I have been grown up, I have never desired to smoke and have always regarded the habit of smoking as barbarous, dirty and harmful.[151] I have never understood why there is such a rage for smoking throughout the world. I cannot bear[152] to travel in a compartment full of people smoking. I become choked.

But much more serious than *this theft was the one*[M3] I was guilty of a little later. *I pilfered the coppers when*[M4] I was twelve or thirteen, possibly less. The other theft was committed when I was fifteen. In this case I stole a bit of gold out of my meat-eating brother's armlet. This brother had run into a[153] debt of about twenty-five rupees.[154] He had on his arm an armlet of solid gold. It was not difficult to clip a bit[155] out of it.

Well, it was done,[M5] and the debt cleared. But this became more than I could bear. I resolved never to steal again. I also made up my mind to confess it to my father. But I did not dare to speak. Not that I was afraid of my father beating me. No. I do not recall his ever having beaten any of us. I was afraid *of the pain that I should cause him.*[M6] But I felt the risk should be taken; that there could not be a cleansing without a clean confession.

I decided at last to write out the confession, to submit it to my father, and ask his forgiveness. I wrote it on a slip of paper and handed it to him myself. In this note not only did I confess my guilt, but I asked

M3 the stealing of cigarette stumps and the servant's coppers was what

M4 At the time of the failing with regard to smoking

M5 The armlet was cut

M6 lest he should be pained and strike his head in anguish

---

[151] In his 'Guide to London' MKG citing the authority of Count Leo Tolstoy describes tobacco as 'acrid poison' and advises abstinence from it, whether smoked, chewed or snuffed. See *CWMG*, vol. 1, p. 89.

[152] 'It is unbearable to me' in the first edition.

[153] 'small' to add.

[154] 'We, the brothers, thought of ways of paying it off.' To add.

[155] 'One *tola*' in the original. 'Tola' in Gujarat measures about 10 grams.

adequate punishment for it, and closed with a request to him not to punish himself for my offence. I also pledged myself never to steal in future.

I was trembling as I handed the confession to my father. He was then suffering from a[156] fistula and was confined to bed. His bed was a plain wooden plank. I handed him the note and sat opposite the plank.[157]

He read it through, and pearl-drops trickled down his cheeks, wetting the paper. For a moment he closed his eyes in thought and then tore up the note. He had sat up to read it. He again lay down. I also cried. I could see my father's agony. If I were a painter I could draw a picture of the whole scene today. It is still so vivid in my mind.

Those *pearl-drops of love cleansed my heart, and washed my sin away.*[M7] Only he who has experienced such love can know what it is. As the hymn says:

> 'Only he
> Who is smitten with the arrows of *love*,[M8]
> Knows its power.'

This was, for me, an object-lesson in ahimsa. Then I could read in it nothing more than a father's love, but today I know that it was pure ahimsa. When such ahimsa becomes all-embracing, it transforms everything it touches. *There is no limit to its power.*[M9]

This sort of sublime forgiveness was not natural to my father. I had thought that he would be angry, say hard things, and strike his forehead. But he was so wonderfully peaceful, and I believe this was due to my clean confession. A clean confession, combined with a promise never to commit the sin again, when offered

[M7] pearl-drops, like shafts of love, pierced me. I was purified

[M8] Rama

[M9] It is impossible to measure the power of such all-embracing ahimsa.

---

[156] 'a' added in the 1940 edition.

[157] In the Gujarati original this line comes after 'I handed the confession to my father.'

before one who has the right to receive it, is the purest type of repentance. I know that my confession made my father feel absolutely safe about me, and increased his[158] affection for me beyond measure.[159]

IX

MY FATHER'S DEATH AND
MY DOUBLE[160] SHAME

The time of which I am now speaking is my sixteenth year. My father, as we have seen, was bed-ridden, suffering from a[161] fistula. My mother, an old servant of the house, and I were his principal attendants. I had the duties of a nurse,[162] which mainly consisted in dressing the wound, giving my father his medicine, and compounding drugs whenever they had to be made up at home. Every night I massaged his legs and retired only when he asked me to do so or after he had fallen asleep. I loved to do this service.[163] I do not remember ever having neglected it.[164] All the time at my disposal, after the performance of the daily duties, was divided between school and attending *on*[M1] my father. I would only go out for an evening walk either when he permitted me or when he was feeling well.

[M1] to

---

[158] 'great' to add.

[159] 'beyond measure' added in the English translation.

[160] 'Double' added in the English translation.

[161] 'a' added in the 1940 edition.

[162] The English word 'nurse' used in the Gujarati original.

[163] On 25 March 1909 MKG wrote to his son Manilal; 'Let me tell you that when I was younger than you are, my keenest enjoyment was to nurse my father.' *CWMG*, vol. 9, p. 205.

[164] 'These were the days of my high school.' To add.

This was also the time when my wife was expecting a baby,—a circumstance which, as I can see today, meant a double shame for me. For one thing I did not restrain myself, as I should have done, whilst I was yet a student. And secondly, this carnal lust got the better of what I regarded as my duty to study, and of what was even a greater duty, my devotion to my parents, Shravana having been my ideal since childhood. Every night whilst my hands were busy massaging my father's legs, my mind was hovering about the bed-room— and that too at a time when religion, medical science and common sense alike forbade sexual intercourse. I was always glad to be relieved from my duty, and went straight to the bed-room after doing obeisance to my father.

At the same time my father was getting worse every day. Ayurvedic physicians[165] had tried all their ointments, hakims their plasters, and local *quacks*[M2] their nostrums. An English *surgeon*[M3] had also used his skill. *As the last and only resort he had re-commended a surgical operation.*[M4] But the family physician came in the way. He disapproved of an operation being performed[166] at such an advanced age. The physician was competent and well known, and his advice prevailed. The operation was abandoned, and various *medicines*[M5] purchased for the purpose were of[167] no account. I have an impression that, if the physician had allowed the operation, the wound would have been easily healed. The operation also was to have been performed by a surgeon who was then well known in Bombay. But God had willed otherwise.[168] When death is imminent, who can think

[M2] barbers, etc.

[M3] doctor

[M4] At last, the English doctor recommended a surgical operation as the only remedy.

[M5] bottles

---

[165] 'Vaidya' in the original.

[166] 'on my father' to add.

[167] 'went to' in the first edition.

[168] 'But God had willed otherwise.' Added in the English translation.

of the right remedy? My father returned from Bombay with all the paraphernalia of the operation, which were now useless.[169] He despaired of living any longer. He was getting weaker and weaker, until at last he had to be asked to perform the necessary functions in bed. But up to the last he refused to do anything of the kind, always insisting on going through the strain of leaving his bed. The Vaishnavite rules about external cleanliness[170] are so inexorable.

Such[171] cleanliness is quite essential no doubt, but Western medical science has taught us that all the functions, including[172] a bath, can be done in bed with the strictest regard to cleanliness, and without the slightest discomfort to the patient, the bed always remaining spotlessly clean. I should regard such cleanliness as quite consistent with Vaishnavism. But my father's insistence on leaving the bed only struck me with wonder then, and I had nothing but admiration for it.

The dreadful night[173] came. My uncle was then in Rajkot. I have a faint recollection that he came to Rajkot having had news that my father was getting worse. The brothers were deeply attached to each other. My uncle would sit near my father's bed the whole day, and would insist on sleeping by his bedside after sending us all to sleep. No one had *dreamt*[M6] that this was to be the fateful night. The danger of course was there.

It was 10.30 or 11 p.m. I was giving the massage.[174] My uncle *offered to relieve me*.[M7] I was glad and went straight to the bed-room. My wife, poor thing, was

[M6] any inkling

[M7] told me, 'You go, now I will sit.'

---

[169] 'which were now useless' added in the English translation.

[170] 'about external cleanliness' added in the English translation.

[171] 'external' to add.

[172] 'defecation and' to add.

[173] 'of death' to add.

[174] 'to his feet' to add.

fast asleep. But how could she sleep when I was there?
I woke her up. In five or six minutes, however, the
servant[175] knocked at the door. I started with alarm.
'Get up,' he said, 'Father is very ill.' I knew of course
that he was very ill, and so I guessed what 'very ill'
meant at that moment. I sprang out of bed.

'What is the matter? Do tell me!'
'Father is no more.'[176]

[M8] What was the use of my
remorse now.

So all was over! I had but to wring my hands.[M8] I felt deeply
ashamed and miserable. I ran to my father's room. I
saw that, if animal passion had not blinded me, I should
have been spared the torture of separation from my
father during his last moments. I should have been
massaging *him and he would have died in my arms. But now
it was my uncle who had had this privilege.*[177] [M9] He was so
deeply devoted to his elder brother that he had earned
the honour of doing him the last services! My father
had forebodings of the coming event. He had made a
sign for pen and paper, and written: *'Prepare for the last
rites.'*[M10] He had then snapped the amulet off his arm and
also his gold necklace of *tulasi* beads[178] and flung them
aside. A moment after this he was no more.

[M9] his feet, but, instead I had to
hear from my uncle, 'Bapu has
left us.'

[M10] 'Make preparations.'

The shame, to which I have referred in a foregoing
chapter, was this shame of my carnal desire *even at the
critical hour of my father's death, which demanded wakeful
service.*[M11] It is a blot I have never been able to efface
or forget, and I have always thought that, although my
devotion to my parents knew no bounds and I would

[M11] at the hour of service

---

[175] 'whom I have mentioned earlier' to add.

[176] The date was 16 November 1885. J.M. Upadhyaya, *Mahatma
Gandhi: A Teacher's Discovery* (Vallabh Vidyanagar: Sardar Patel
University, 1969), p. 76.

[177] 'honour' in the first edition.

[178] 'of *tulasi* beads' added in the English translation.

have given up anything for it, yet it was weighed and found unpardonably wanting because my mind was at the same moment in the grip of lust. I have therefore always regarded myself as a lustful, though a faithful, husband. It took me long to get free from the shackles of lust,[179] and I had to pass through many ordeals before I could overcome it.

Before I close this chapter of my double shame, I may mention that the *poor mite*[M12] that was born[180] to my wife scarcely breathed for more than three or four days. *Nothing else could be expected.*[M13] Let all *those who are married*[M14] be warned by my example.

[M12] child

[M13] What other outcome could there be?

[M14] parents or child couples

X

GLIMPSES OF RELIGION

From my sixth or seventh year up to my sixteenth I was at school, *being taught all sorts of things except religion.*[M1] I may say that I failed to get from the teachers what they could have given me without any effort on their part. And yet I kept on picking up things here and there[181] from my surroundings. The term 'religion' I am using in its *broadest*[M2] sense, meaning thereby self-realization or knowledge of self.

[M1] but did not receive education of religion

[M2] liberal

Being born in the Vaishnava faith, I had often to go to the *Haveli*. But it *never appealed to me.*[M3] I did not like its glitter and pomp. Also I heard rumours of immorality being practised there, and lost all interest in it. Hence I could gain nothing from the *Haveli*.

[M3] did not induce faith in me

---

[179] 'of lust' added in the English translation.

[180] The child, whose gender remains unknown, was born on 20 November 1885. Upadhyay, *A Teacher's Discovery*, p. 76.

[181] In the first edition, 'And yet things here and there I kept picking up.'

But what I failed to get there I obtained from my nurse, an old servant of the family, whose affection for me I still recall. I have said before that there was in me a fear of ghosts and spirits. Rambha, for that was her name,[182] suggested, as a remedy for this fear, the repetition of Ramanama. I had more faith in her than in *her remedy*,[M4] and so at a tender age I began repeating Ramanama to cure my fear of ghosts and spirits. This was of course short-lived, but the good seed sown in childhood was not sown in vain. I think it is due to the seed sown by that good woman Rambha that today Ramanama is an infallible *remedy*[M5] for me.

Just about this time, a cousin of mine[183] who was a devotee of the *Ramayana* arranged for my second brother and me to learn *Rama Raksha*.[184] We got it by heart, and made it a rule to recite it every morning after the bath. The practice was kept up as long as we were in Porbandar. *As soon as we reached*[M6] Rajkot, it was forgotten. For I had not much belief in it. I recited it partly because[185] of my pride in being able to recite *Rama Raksha* with correct pronunciation.

What, however, left a deep impression on me was the reading of the *Ramayana* before my father. During part of his illness my father was in Porbandar. There every evening he used to listen to the *Ramayana*.[186] The reader was a great devotee of Rama-Ladha Maharaj of Bileshwar. It was said of him that he cured himself of his *leprosy*[M7] not by any medicine, but by applying to the

M4 Ramanama

M5 power

M6 In the atmosphere of

M7 leucoderma

---

[182] 'for that was her name' added in the English translation.

[183] Amritlal Tulsidas.

[184] A Sanskrit hymn in praise of Rama, recited as prayer for protection, composed by Budha Kaushika. They were taught by Anandji Tulsi Adhyaru. J.M. Upadhyaya, *Mahatma Gandhi: As a Student* (New Delhi: Publications Division, 1965), p. 12.

[185] 'of my respect for the elder cousin and partly because' to add.

[186] 'in the Ramji Mandir' to add.

affected parts *bilva* leaves which had been cast away after being offered to the image of Mahadeva in Bileshwar temple, and by the regular repetition of Ramanama. His faith, it was said, had *made him whole*.[M8] This may or may not be true. We at any rate believed the story. And it is a fact that when Ladha Maharaj began his reading of the *Ramayana* his body was entirely free from *leprosy*.[M9] He had a melodious voice. He would sing the *dohas* (couplets) and *chopais* (quatrains), and explain them, losing himself in the discourse and carrying his listeners along with him. I must have been thirteen at that time, but I quite remember being enraptured by his reading. That laid the foundation of my deep devotion to the *Ramayana*. Today I regard the *Ramayana* of Tulasidas as the greatest book in all devotional literature.

A few months after this we came to Rajkot. There was no *Ramayana* reading there. The *Bhagavata*, however, used to be read on every *Ekadashi*[187] day. Sometimes I attended the reading, but the reciter was uninspiring. Today I see that the *Bhagavata* is a book which can[188] evoke religious fervour. I have read it in Gujarati with intense interest. But when I heard portions of the original read by Pandit Madan Mohan Malaviya[189] during my twenty-one days' fast,[190] I wished I had heard it in my childhood from such a devotee as he is, so that I could have formed a liking for it at an

[M8] eradicated his leucoderma, root and branch

[M9] any disease

---

[187] MD's footnote: Eleventh day of the bright and the dark half of a lunar month.

[188] 'be so read as to' to add.

[189] 1861–1946. Twice president, Indian National Congress (1909, 1918), later member, Hindu Mahasabha, and president of its two special sessions (1921, 1923), founder Banaras Hindu University (1916), founder English newspaper *The Leader* (1909) and chairman, *Hindustan Times* (1924–46.)

[190] From 17 September to 8 October 1924, at Delhi for Hindu–Muslim unity.

early age. Impressions[191] formed at that age strike roots deep down into one's nature, and it is my perpetual regret that I was not fortunate enough to hear more good books of this kind read during that period.

In Rajkot, however, *I got an early grounding in toleration for all branches of Hinduism and sister religions.*[M10] For my father and mother would visit the *Haveli* as also Shiva's and Rama's temples, and would take or send us youngsters there. Jain monks also would pay frequent visits to my father, and *would even go out of their way to accept food from us—non-Jains.*[M11] They would have talks with my father on subjects religious and mundane.

He had, besides, Mussalman and Parsi friends, who would talk to him about their own faiths, and he would listen to them always with respect, and often with interest. Being his nurse,[192] I often had a chance to be present at these talks. These many things combined to inculcate in me a *toleration*[M12] for all faiths.

Only Christianity was at the time an exception. I developed a sort of dislike for it. And for a reason.[193] In those days *Christian missionaries*[M13] used to stand in a corner near the high school and hold forth, pouring abuse on Hindus and their gods. I could not endure[194] this. I must have stood there to hear *them*[M14] once only, but that was enough to dissuade me from repeating the experiment. About the same time, I heard of a well-known Hindu having been converted to Christianity. It was the talk of the town that, when he was baptized, he had to eat beef and drink liquor,[195] that he also had

M10 quite without any effort, I received training in equability towards all sects. I learnt to respect all sects of Hindu religion

M11 he would even invite them to receive offering of food from us

M12 sense of equability

M13 a Christian missionary

M14 the preaching

---

[191] 'I deeply feel that' to add at the beginning of this sentence.

[192] 'nurse' in the Gujarati original.

[193] 'And for a reason.' Added in the English translation.

[194] In the first edition, 'stomach'.

[195] Rev. H.R. Scott after reading the *Autobiography* wrote a letter to MKG. 'I was the only missionary in Rajkot during those

to change his clothes, and that thence-forth he began to go about in *European costume including a hat.*[M15] These things got on my nerves. Surely, thought I, a religion that compelled one to eat beef, drink liquor, and change one's own clothes did not deserve the name. I also heard that the new convert had already begun abusing the religion of his ancestors, their customs and their country. All these things created in me a dislike for Christianity.

[M15] a coat, pantaloons and an English hat

But the fact that I had learnt *to be tolerant to*[M16] other religions did not mean that I had any living faith in God. I happened, about this time, to come across

[M16] equability towards

---

years (from 1833 to 1897), and what you say about Christian Missionaries in Rajkot standing at a corner near the High School and pouring abuse on Hindus and their gods fills me with a painful wonder. I certainly never preached "at a corner near the High School"; my regular preaching station was under a banyan tree in the Para Bazar; and I certainly never "poured abuse on Hindus and their gods." That would be a strange way to win a hearing from Hindus. Then you say that a well-known Hindu was baptised at that time, and that "he had to eat beef and drink liquor, and to change his clothes and go about in European costume, including a hat." . . . I have been over 42 years in India, and I have never heard of such a thing happening; and indeed I know it to be quite contrary to what all missionaries with whom I am acquainted teach and believe and practice . . . But surely you must have had many opportunities since then of discovering that that particular libel is without foundation, and as a sincere lover of truth you cannot wish to lend the great weight of your authority to perpetuate such a wilfully malicious misrepresentation of Christian Missionaries.' *Young India*, 4 March 1926, vol. VIII, no. 9.
MKG's response was:

'Though the preaching took place over forty years ago the painful memory of it is still vivid before me. What I have heard and read since has confirmed that first impression . . . And whilst I accept Mr. Scott's repudiation I want to say that though I have mixed freely among thousands of Christian Indians, I know very few who have scruples about eating beef or other flesh meats and drinking intoxicating substances.' *CWMG*, vol. 30, pp. 70–71. *CWMG* identifies Rev. Scott both as H.R. Scott and S.R. Scott. The *Young* India has H.R. Scott.

Manusmriti[196] which was amongst my father's collection. The story of the creation and similar things in it did not impress me very much, but on the contrary made me incline somewhat towards atheism.

There was a cousin[197] of mine,[198] still alive, for whose intellect I had great regard. To him I turned with my doubts. But he could not resolve them. He sent me away with this answer: 'When you grow up, you will be able to solve these doubts yourself. These questions ought not to be raised at your age.' I was silenced, but was not comforted. Chapters about diet and the like in *Manusmriti* seemed to me to run contrary to daily practice. To my doubts as to this also, I got the same answer. 'With intellect more developed and with more reading I shall understand it better,' I said to myself.

Manusmriti at any rate did not then teach me ahimsa. I have told the story of my meat-eating. *Manusmriti* seemed to support it. I also felt that it was quite moral to kill serpents, bugs and the like. I remember to have killed at that age bugs and such other insects, regarding it as a duty.

But one thing took deep root in me—the conviction that morality is the basis of things, and that *truth is the substance of all morality*.[M17] Truth became my sole objective. It began to grow in magnitude every day, and my definition of it also has been ever widening.

M17 all morality is contained by Truth.

A Gujarati didactic stanza likewise gripped my mind and heart. Its precept—return good for evil—became my guiding principle. It became such a passion with me

---

196   MD's footnote: Laws of Manu. A Hindu law-giver. They have the sanction of religion.

197   Khushalchand, son of Jivanchand.

198   In the Gujarati original: 'My second uncle's son'.

that I began numerous experiments in it. Here are those (for me)[199] wonderful lines:

> For a bowl of water give a goodly meal;
> For a kindly greeting bow thou down with zeal;
> For a simple penny pay thou back with gold;
> If thy life be rescued, life do not withhold.
> Thus the words and actions of the wise regard;
> Every little service tenfold they reward.
> But the truly noble know all men as one,
> And return with gladness good for evil done.[200]

XI

PREPARATION FOR ENGLAND

I passed the matriculation examination in 1887.[201] It then used to be held at two centres, Ahmedabad and Bombay. The general poverty of the country[202] naturally led Kathiawad students to prefer the nearer and the cheaper centre. *The poverty of my family likewise dictated to me the same choice.*[M1] This was my first journey from Rajkot to Ahmedabad and that too without a companion.

[M1] The same was my lot.

My elders wanted me to pursue my studies at college after the matriculation. There was a college in Bhavnagar

---

[199] '(for me)' added in the English translation.

[200] By Shamal Bhatt (1718–65), a Gujarati poet.

[201] MKG's marks in the matriculation examination were: English 89/200, Second Language (Gujarati) 45.5/100, Mathematics 59/175, General Knowledge (which included History and Science) 54/150; total 247.5/625= 39.5%, see *Mahatma Gandhi as a Student*, p. 56. MKG's seat number for the examination was 2275. Of the total 3067 candidates enrolled for the examination, 799 were declared successful. His rank in the list of successful candidates was 404.

[202] 'and of the Gandhi family' to add.

M2 I did not know anything there.

as well as in Bombay, and as the former was cheaper, I decided to go there and join the Samaldas College. *I went, but found myself entirely at sea.*[M2] Everything was difficult. I could not follow, let alone taking[203] interest in, the professors' lectures. It was no fault of theirs. The professors in that College were regarded as first-rate.[204] But I was so raw. At the end of the first term, I returned home.

We had in Mavji Dave,[205] who was a shrewd and learned Brahmin, an old friend and adviser of the family. He had kept up his connection with the family even after my father's death. He happened to visit us during my vacation. In conversation with my mother and elder brother, he inquired about my studies. Learning that I was at Samaldas College, he said: 'The times are changed. *And none of you can expect to succeed to your father's gadi without having had a proper education.*[M3]

M3 If anyone amongst you brothers wishes to keep Kaba Gandhi's *gadi*, it cannot be had without education.

M4 he should be made to bear the burden of keeping the gadi

Now as this boy is still pursuing his studies, *you should all look to him to keep the gadi.*[M4] It will take him four or five years to get his B.A. degree, which will at best qualify him for a sixty rupees' post, not for a Diwanship. If like my son he went in for law[206] it would take him

---

203 'take' in the first edition.

204 The year MKG enrolled in the college the professors were: R.N. Gurion, principal and professor of English literature and history, J.N. Unawala, vice-principal and professor of physics, Fardunji M. Dastur (mathematics and natural philosophy), Manibhai Nabhubhai Dwivedi (philosophy, Sanskrit), B.A. Ente, (logic and political economy), B.H. Munshi (Sanskrit), Sheik Mohmad Isphani (Persian). He was required to study the following subjects: English, history, second language, algebra, Euclid, logic and physics. Established in 1885 by the then Maharaja Sir Takthasinhji of Bhavnagar and named Samaldas College in memory of his Diwan Samaldas Mehta.

205 Alias Mavji Joshi, a leading lawyer of Kathiawar; for another account of the decision to go to England, see *CWMG*, vol. 1, pp. 2–15.

206 'after that' to add.

still longer, by which time there would be a host of
lawyers, aspiring for a Diwan's post. I would far rather
that you sent him to England. My son Kevalram says *it
is very easy to become*[207] *a barrister.*[M5] In three years' time
he will[208] return. Also expenses will not exceed four to
five thousand rupees. Think of that barrister who has
just come back from England. How stylishly he lives!
He could get the Diwanship for the asking. I would
strongly advise you to send Mohandas to England this
very year. Kevalram has numerous friends in England.
He will give notes of introduction to them, and
Mohandas will have *an easy time of it*[M6] there.'

M5 education there is easy

M6 no difficulty

Joshiji—that is how we used to call old Mavji
Dave—turned to me with complete assurance,[209] and
asked: 'Would you not rather go to England than study
here?' Nothing could have been more welcome to me.
*I was fighting shy of my difficult studies. So I jumped at the
proposal and said that the sooner I was sent the better. It was
no easy business to pass examinations quickly.*[M7] Could I not
be sent to qualify for the medical profession?

M7 I was scared of the difficulties
of the college. I said, 'It would
be very good if I were sent to
England. It does not seem that I
would pass the college quickly.'

My brother interrupted me: 'Father never liked it.
He had you in mind when he said that we Vaishnavas
should have nothing to do with dissection of dead
bodies. Father intended you for the bar.'

Joshiji chimed in: 'I am not opposed to the medical
profession as was Gandhiji. Our Shastras are not against
it. But a medical degree will not make a Diwan of you,
and I want you to be Diwan, or if possible something
better. Only in that way could you take under your
protecting care your large family. The times are fast
changing and getting harder every day. It is the wisest
thing therefore to become a barrister.' Turning to my

---

[207] 'be' in the first edition.

[208] 'would' in the first edition.

[209] 'about the acceptance of his advice' to add.

mother he said: 'Now, I must leave. Pray ponder over what I have said. When I come here next I shall expect to hear of preparations for England. Be sure to let me know if *I can assist in any way*.'[M8]

Joshiji went away, and I began building castles in the air.

My elder brother was greatly exercised in his mind. How was he to find the wherewithal to send me? *And was it proper to trust a young man like me to go abroad alone?*[M9]

My mother was sorely perplexed. She did not like the idea of parting with me. This is how she tried to put me off: 'Uncle,' she said, 'is now the eldest member of the family. He should first be consulted. If he consents we will consider the matter.'

My brother had another idea. He said to me: 'We have a certain claim on the Porbandar State. Mr. Lely is the Administrator. He thinks highly of our family and *uncle is in his good books*.[M10] It is just possible that he might recommend you for some State help for your education in England.'

I liked all this and got ready to start off for Porbandar. There was no railway in those days. It was a five days' bullock-cart journey. I have already said that I was a coward. But at that moment my cowardice vanished before the desire to go to England, which completely possessed me. I hired a bullock-cart as far as Dhoraji, and from Dhoraji I took a camel in order to get to Porbandar a day quicker. This was my first camel-ride.

I arrived at last, did obeisance to my uncle, and told him everything. He thought it over and said: 'I am not sure whether it is possible for one to stay in England without prejudice to one's own religion. From all I have heard, I have my doubts. When I meet these big barristers, I see no difference between their life and that of *Europeans*.[M11] They know no scruples regarding food. Cigars are never out of their mouths. *They dress as shamelessly as Englishmen.*[M12] All that would not be in keeping with our family tradition. I am shortly going on a pilgrimage and have not many years to live. At the threshold of death, how dare I give you permission to go to England, to cross the seas? But I will not stand in your way. It is your mother's permission which really matters. If she permits you, then *godspeed*![M13] Tell her I will not interfere. You will go with my blessings.'

'I could expect nothing more from you,' said I. 'I shall now try to win mother over. But would you not recommend me to Mr. Lely?'

'How can I do that?' said he. 'But he is a good man. You ask for an appointment telling him how you are connected. He will certainly give you one and may even help you.'[210]

I cannot say why my uncle did not give me a note of recommendation. I have a faint idea that he hesitated to co-operate directly in my going to England, which was in his opinion an irreligious act.

I wrote to Mr. Lely, who asked me to see him at his residence. He saw me as he was ascending the staircase; and saying curtly, 'Pass your B.A. first and then see me. No help can be given you now,' he hurried upstairs. I had made elaborate preparations to meet him. I had carefully learnt up a few sentences and had bowed low and saluted him with both hands. But all to no purpose!

I thought of[M14] my wife's ornaments. I thought of my elder brother, in whom I had the utmost faith. He was generous to a fault, and he loved me as his son.

I returned to Rajkot from Porbandar and reported all that had happened. I consulted Joshiji, who of course advised even incurring a debt if necessary. I suggested the disposal of my wife's ornaments, which could

[M12] They are almost naked in their dress.

[M13] go happily!

[M14] My eyes fell on

---

[210] 'if he so pleases.' To add.

fetch about two to three thousand rupees. My brother promised to find the money somehow.

My mother, however, was still unwilling. She had begun making minute inquiries. Someone had told her that young men got lost in England. Someone else had said that they took to meat; and yet another that they could not live there without liquor. 'How about all this?' she asked me. I said: 'Will you not trust me? I shall not lie to you, I swear that I shall not touch any of those things. If there were any such danger, would Joshiji let me go?'

'I can trust you,' she said. 'But how can I trust you in a distant land? I am dazed and know not what to do. I will ask Becharji Swami.'

Becharji Swami was originally a Modh Bania, but had now become a Jain monk. He too was a family adviser like Joshiji. He came to my help, and said: 'I shall get the boy solemnly to take the three vows, and then he can be allowed to go.' He ad-ministered the oath and I vowed not to touch wine, woman and meat. This done, my mother gave her permission.

The high school had a send-off in my honour. It was an uncommon thing for a young man of Rajkot to go to England. I had written out a few words of thanks. But I could scarcely stammer them out. I remember how my head reeled and how my whole frame shook as I stood up to read them.[211]

With the blessings of my elders, I started for Bombay. This was my first journey from Rajkot to Bombay. My brother accompanied me. *But there is many a slip, 'twixt the cup and the lip. There were difficulties to be faced in Bombay.*[M15]

[M15] But a hundred obstacles arise before a worthwhile task is accomplished. I could not leave the port of Bombay so easily.

---

[211] The send-off was on 4 July 1888. MKG said, 'I hope some of you will follow in my footsteps, and after you return from England you will work wholeheartedly for big reforms in India.' *CWMG*, vol. 1, p. 1.

XII

OUTCASTE

With my mother's permission and blessings, I set off exultantly for Bombay,[212] leaving my wife with a baby of a few months.[213] But on arrival there friends told my brother that the Indian Ocean was rough in June and July, and as this was my first voyage, I should not be allowed to sail until[214] November. Someone also reported that a steamer had just been sunk in a gale. This made my brother uneasy, and he refused to take the risk of allowing me to sail immediately. Leaving me with a friend in Bombay, he returned to Rajkot to resume his duty. He put the money for my travelling expenses in the keeping of a brother-in-law, and left word with some friends to give me whatever help I might need.

Time hung heavily on my hands in Bombay. I dreamt continually of going to[215] England.

Meanwhile my caste people were agitated over my going abroad.[216] No Modh Bania had been to England up to now, and if I dared to do so, I ought to be *brought to book!*[M1] A general meeting of the caste was called and I was summoned to appear before it. I went. How I suddenly managed to muster up courage I do not know.

[M1] answerable to them

---

[212] MKG left Rajkot on 10 August 1888, reaching Bombay on 12 August.

[213] Harilal Gandhi (1888–1948). For a biography of Harilal Gandhi, see C.B. Dalal, *Harilal Gandhi: A Life*, edited and translated from the original Gujarati by Tridip Suhrud (Chennai: Orient Longman, 2007).

[214] 'after Diwali that is in' to add.

[215] 'continually of going to' added in the English translation. The original reads: 'I dreamt of England.'

[216] 'over my going to England' added in the English translation.

Nothing daunted, and without the slightest hesitation, I came before the meeting. The Sheth—the headman of the community—who was distantly related to me and had been on very good terms with my father, thus accosted me:

'In the opinion of the caste, your proposal to go to England is not proper. Our religion forbids *voyage abroad.*[M2] We have also heard that it is not possible to live there without compromising our religion. One is obliged to eat and drink with *Europeans!*'[M3]

To which I replied: 'I do not think it is at all against our religion to go to England. I intend going there for further studies. And I have already solemnly promised to my mother to abstain from three[217] things you fear most. I am sure the vow will keep me safe.'

'But we tell you,' rejoined the Sheth, 'that it is not possible to keep our religion there. You know my relations with your father and you ought to listen to my advice.'

'I know those relations,' said I. 'And you are as an elder to me. But I am helpless in this matter. I cannot alter my resolve to go to England. My father's friend and adviser, who is a learned Brahmin, sees no objection to my going to England, and my mother and brother have also given me their permission.'

'But will you disregard the orders of the caste?'

'I am really helpless. I think the caste should not interfere in the matter.'

This incensed the Sheth. He swore at me. I sat unmoved. So the Sheth pronounced his order: 'This boy shall be treated as an outcaste from today. Whoever helps him or goes to see him off at the dock[218] shall be punishable with a fine of one rupee four annas.'

M2 crossing the seas

M3 Sahibs

---

[217] 'three' added in the English translation.

[218] 'at the dock' added in the English translation.

The order had no effect on me, and I took my leave of the Sheth. But I wondered how my brother would take it.[219] Fortunately he remained firm and wrote to assure me that *I had his permission to go, the Sheth's order notwithstanding.*[M4]

The incident, however, made me more anxious than ever to sail.[220] What would happen if they succeeded in bringing pressure to bear on my brother? Supposing something unforeseen happened? As I was thus worrying over my predicament, I heard that a Junagadh vakil was going to England, for being called to the bar, by a boat sailing on the 4th of September. I met the friends to whose care my brother had commended me. They also agreed that I should not let go the opportunity of going in such company. There was no time to be lost. I wired to my brother for permission, which he granted. I asked my brother-in-law to give me the money. But he referred to the order of the Sheth and said that he could not afford to lose caste. I then sought a friend of the family and requested him to accommodate me to the extent of my passage and sundries, and to recover the loan from my brother. The friend was not only good enough to accede to my request, but he cheered me up as well. I was so thankful. With part of the money I at once purchased the passage. Then I had to equip myself for the voyage. There was another friend who had experience in the matter. He got clothes and other things ready.[221] Some of the clothes I liked and some I did not like at all. The necktie,[222] which I delighted in wearing later, I then abhorred. The short jacket I looked upon as immodest. But this dislike was nothing before

[M4] notwithstanding the decree of the caste, he would not prevent me from going to England

---

[219] 'What if he were to lose courage?' to add.

[220] 'to sail' added in the English translation.

[221] 'I found them quite strange.' To add.

[222] 'necktie', English word in the Gujarati original.

the desire to go to England, which was uppermost in me.[223] Of provisions also I had enough and to spare for the voyage. A berth was reserved for me by my friends in the same cabin as that of Sjt. Tryambakrai Mazmudar,[224] the Junagadh vakil. They also commended me to him. He was an experienced man of mature age and knew the world.[225] I was yet a stripling of eighteen without any experience of the world. Sjt. Mazmudar told my friends not to worry about me.

I sailed at last from Bombay on the 4th of September.[226]

XIII

IN *LONDON*[M1] AT LAST

[M1] England

[M2] In the steamer I did not experience the sea in the least.

I did not feel at all sea-sick.[M2] But as the days passed, I became fidgety. I felt shy even in[227] speaking to the steward.[228] I was quite unaccustomed to talking English, and except for Sjt. Mazmudar all the other passengers in the second saloon[229] were English. I could not speak to

---

[223] 'which was uppermost in me' added in the English translation.

[224] He enrolled at the Middle Temple on 1 November 1888 was called to the Bar on 10 June 1891. The Inns of Courts are unincorporated associations which have existed since the fourteenth century. The Inns of Courts hold an exclusive right to call candidates to practise law at the Bar of England and Wales and during the colonial period to the British colonies. They consist of Honourable Societies of the Inner Temple (1388), the Middle Temple (1388), Lincoln's Inn (1422) and Gray's Inn (1388).

[225] 'and knew the world' added in the English translation.

[226] In *S.S. Clyde*. She sailed at 5 p.m.

[227] 'in' added in the 1940 edition.

[228] 'steward' English word in the Gujarati original.

[229] 'in the second saloon' added in the English translation.

them. For I could rarely follow their remarks when they came up to speak to me, and even when I understood I could not reply. I had to frame every sentence in my mind, before I could bring it out. I was innocent of the use of knives and forks and had not the boldness to inquire what dishes on the menu were free of meat. I therefore never took meals at table but always had them in my cabin, and they consisted principally of sweets and fruits[230] which I had brought with me. Sjt. Mazmudar had no difficulty, and he mixed with everybody. He would move about freely on deck, while I hid myself in the cabin the whole day, only venturing up on deck when there were but few people. Sjt. Mazmudar kept pleading with me to associate with the passengers and to talk with them freely. He told me that lawyers should have a long tongue, and related to me his legal experiences. *He advised me to take every possible opportunity of talking English, and not to mind making mistakes which were obviously unavoidable with a foreign tongue.*[M3] But nothing could make me conquer my shyness.

An English passenger,[231] taking kindly to me, drew me into conversation. He was older than I. He asked me what I ate, what I was, where I was going, why I was shy, and so on. He also advised me to come to table. He laughed at my insistence on abjuring meat, and said *in a friendly way*[M4] when we were in the Red Sea:[232] 'It is all very well so far[233] but you will have to revise your decision in the Bay of Biscay. And it is so cold in England that one cannot possibly live there without meat.'

M3 'English cannot be considered our language, and there are bound to be mistakes, yet one should speak it freely,' he would say.

M4 compassionately

---

[230] 'and fruits' added in the English translation. The original has 'sweets etc.'

[231] Mr. Jeffery. See 'London Diary', *CWMG*, vol. 1, p. 12.

[232] 'when we were in the Red Sea' added in the English translation.

[233] 'before we reached Port Said,' to add.

'But I have heard that people can live there without eating meat,' I said.

'Rest assured it is a fib,' said he. 'No one, to my knowledge, lives there without being a meat-eater. Don't you see that I am not asking you to take liquor, though I do so? But I do think you should eat meat, for you cannot live without it.'[234]

'I thank you for your kind advice, but I have solemnly promised to my mother not to touch meat, and therefore I cannot think of taking it. If it be found impossible to get on without it, I will far rather go back to India than eat meat in order to remain there.'[235]

We entered the Bay of Biscay, but I did not begin to feel the need either of meat or liquor. I had been advised to collect certificates of my having abstained from meat, and I asked the English friend to give me one. He gladly gave it and I treasured it for some time. But when I saw later that one could get such a certificate in spite of being a meat-eater, it lost all its charm for me. If my word was not to be trusted, where was the use of possessing a certificate in the matter?

[M5] We completed the voyage somehow and

However, we[M5] reached Southampton,[236] as far as I remember, on a Saturday. On the boat I had worn *a*

---

[234] 'for you cannot live without it' added in the English translation.

[235] 'in order to remain there' added in the English translation.

[236] The passengers disembarked at the new docks at Tilbury, 20 miles down the Thames from London, on Saturday, 29 September 1888. Most biographers give an inaccurate date for arrival of the *S.S. Clyde* at London and also the wrong port of entry. The original source of these errors is MKG himself. We owe it to James Hunt for having provided the accurate date and port of entry. MKG in his 'London Diary' (*CWMG*, vol. 1, p. 15) states that he reached London on 27 October 1888; while in the *Autobiography* he states that he reached London 'in last days of September'. Hunt shows that the October date would make it a fifty-three-day voyage, instead of the normal twenty-two days. Hunt confirms the date on the evidence of *The Times*,

black suit,[M6] the white flannel one, which my friends had
got me, having been kept especially for wearing when I
landed. I had thought that white clothes would suit me
better when I stepped ashore, and therefore I did so in
white flannels. Those were the last days of September,
and I found I was the only person wearing such clothes.
I left in charge of an agent of Grindlay and Co. all my
kit, including the keys, seeing that many others had
done the same and I must follow suit.

I had four notes of introduction: to Dr. P.J. Mehta,[237]
to Sjt. Dalpatram Shukla,[238] to Prince Ranjitsinhji[239] and

[M6] black attire

---

1 October 1888, p. 10, which reported the arrival of *S.S. Clyde*
on 29 September at London.

The *Autobiography* twice mentions Southampton, on the south
coast of England, as the port of entry; but MKG in his 'London
Diary' (*CWMG*, vol. 1, p. 15) states that he and his fellow
companions 'reached Victoria Hotel via Tilbury station'. James
D. Hunt, *Gandhi in London* (New Delhi: Promila and Co.;
second revised edition), pp. 7–8, footnote 10, provides extensive
evidence for this.

[237] Dr. Pranjivandas Jagjivandas Mehta (1864–1932) received
his Licentiate in Medicine and Surgery from Grant Medical
College, Bombay, in 1886, acquired an MD from Université
libre de Bruxelles, Belgium, in 1889 and enrolled at the
Middle Temple on 7 May 1887. While still studying for his
MD, he was called to the Bar on 21 June 1889. He and MKG
became lifelong friends and collaborators. Dr. Mehta, a wealthy
diamond merchant, provided generous financial help to MKG
both in South Africa and in India. For a detailed account of their
relationship, see S.R. Mehrotra, *The Mahatma and the Doctor:
The Untold Story of Dr. Pranjivan Mehta, Gandhi's Greatest Friend
and Benefactor (1864–1932)* (Mumbai: Vakils, Feffer and Simon
Pvt. Ltd 2014).

[238] Dalpatram Bhagwanji Shukla, a Brahmin from Morvi, enrolled
at the Inner Temple on 13 November 1886, and was called to
the Bar on 3 July 1889.

[239] Ranjitsinhji (1872–1933), ruler of the Indian princely state of
Navanagar (1907–33), noted test cricketer who played for
University of Cambridge and the English cricket team. The
first-class cricket tournament in India, the Ranji Trophy, was so
named in his honour. He had reached England in March 1888.

to Dadabhai Naoroji.[240] Someone on board had advised us to put up at the Victoria Hotel[241] in London. Sjt. Mazmudar and I accordingly went there. The shame of being the only person in white clothes was already too much for me. And when at the Hotel I was told that I should not get my things from Grindlay's the next day, it being a Sunday, I was *exasperated*.[M7]

M7 confounded

Dr. Mehta, to whom I had wired from Southampton,[242] called at about eight o'clock the same evening. *He gave me a hearty greeting*.[M8] He smiled at my being in flannels.[243] As we were talking,[244] I casually picked up his top-hat, and trying to see how smooth it was, passed my hand over it the wrong way and disturbed the fur. Dr. Mehta looked somewhat angrily[245] at what I was doing and stopped me. But the mischief had been[246] done. The incident was a warning for the future. This was my first lesson in European etiquette, into the details of which Dr. Mehta humorously initiated me. 'Do not touch other people's things,' he said. 'Do not ask questions as we usually do in India on first acquaintance; do not talk loudly; *never address people as 'sir'*[247] *whilst speaking to them as we do in India;*[M9] only

M8 He teased me affectionately.

M9 in India it is customary to address Sahibs as 'Sir', which is unnecessary

---

[240] Dadabhai Naoroji (1825–1917), also called the 'Grand Old Man of India', nationalist leader, Liberal member of parliament in the UK House of Commons (1892–95), provided an economic critique of the colonial rule through his *Poverty and Un-British Rule in India* (1901).

[241] Victoria Hotel, located on Northumberland Street, near Trafalgar Square.

[242] 'to whom I had wired from Southampton' added in the English translation.

[243] 'He smiled at my being in flannels.' Added in the English translation.

[244] 'As we were talking' added in the English translation.

[245] 'somewhat angrily' added in the English translation.

[246] 'was' in the first edition.

[247] 'sir' English word in the Gujarati original.

servants and sub-ordinates address their masters[248] *that way*.'[M10] And so on and so forth.[249] He also told me that it was very expensive to live in a hotel and recommended that I should live with a private family. We deferred consideration of the matter until Monday.[250]

Sjt. Mazmudar and I found the hotel to be a trying affair. It was also very expensive. There was, however, a Sindhi fellow-passenger from Malta who had become friends with Sjt. Mazmudar, and as he was not a stranger to London, he offered to find rooms for us. We agreed, and on Monday, as soon as we got our baggage, we paid up our bills and went to the rooms rented for us by the Sindhi friend. I remember my hotel bill came to £3, an amount which shocked me. And I had practically starved in spite of this heavy bill! For I could relish nothing. When I did not like one thing, I asked for another, but had to pay for both just the same. The fact is that all this while I had depended on the provisions which I had brought with me from Bombay.

I was very uneasy even in the new rooms. I would continually think of my home and[251] country. My mother's love always haunted me. At night the tears would stream down my cheeks and home memories of all sorts made sleep out of the question. It was impossible to share my misery with anyone. And even if I could have done so, where was the use? I knew of nothing that would soothe me. Everything was strange—the people, their ways, and even their dwellings.[252] *I was a complete novice in the matters of English etiquette and continually had to be on my guard. There was the additional inconvenience of the vegetarian vow.*[M11] Even the dishes that I could eat

[M10] as 'Sir'

[M11] I had little knowledge as to what speech and action would cause a possible breach of etiquette. Moreover, there were restrictions on food and drink.

---

[248] 'master' in the first edition.

[249] 'And so on and so forth.' Added in the English translation.

[250] 'Dr. Mehta left after giving some advice.' To add.

[251] 'home and' added in the English translation.

[252] 'Strange were to ways of living in the home.' To add.

were tasteless and insipid. I thus found myself between Scylla and Charybdis.[253] England I could not bear, but to return to India was not to be thought of. Now that I had come, I must finish the three years, said the inner voice.[254]

XIV

MY CHOICE

Dr. Mehta went on Monday to the Victoria Hotel expecting to find me there. He discovered that we had left,[255] got our new address, and met me at our rooms. Through sheer folly I had managed to get ringworm on the boat. For washing and[256] bathing we used to have sea-water, in which soap is not soluble. I, however, used soap, taking its use to be a sign of *civilization*,[M1] with the result that instead of cleaning the skin it made it greasy. This gave me ringworm. I showed it to Dr. Mehta,[257] who told me to apply acetic acid. I remember how the burning acid made me cry. Dr. Mehta inspected my room and its appointments[258] and shook his head in disapproval. 'This place won't do,' he said. 'We come to England not so much for the purpose of studies as for gaining experience of English life and customs.[259] And for this you need to live with

[M1] good conduct

---

[253] Literal translation of the Gujarati proverb would be 'like a nut being sliced by a nutcracker'.

[254] 'said the inner voice' added in the English translation.

[255] 'discovered that we had left' added in the English translation.

[256] 'washing and' added in the English translation.

[257] 'Doctor' in the original. Dr. Mehta is implied.

[258] 'and its appointments' added. In the original, 'room etc.'

[259] 'of English life and customs' added in the English translation.

a family. But before you do so, I think you had better serve a period of apprenticeship with ———.[260] I will take you there.'

I gratefully accepted the suggestion and removed to the friend's rooms.[261] He was all kindness and attention. He treated me as his own brother, initiated me into English ways and manners,[262] and accustomed me to talking the language. My food, however, became a serious question. I could not relish boiled vegetables[263] cooked without salt or condiments. The landlady was at a loss to know what to prepare for me. We had oatmeal porridge for breakfast, which was fairly filling, but I always starved at lunch and dinner. The friend continually reasoned with me to eat meat, but I always pleaded my vow and then remained silent.[264] Both for luncheon and dinner we had spinach and bread and jam too. I was a good eater and had a capacious stomach; but I was ashamed to ask for more than two or three slices of bread, as it did not seem correct to do so. Added to this, there was no milk either for lunch or dinner. The friend once got disgusted with this state of things, and said: 'Had you been my own brother, I would have sent you packing. What is the value of a vow made before an illiterate mother, and in ignorance of conditions here? It is no vow at all. It would not be regarded as a vow in law. It is pure superstition to stick to such a promise. And I tell you this persistence

---

[260] Dalpatram Shukla.

[261] MKG moved into these rooms with Shukla on his nineteenth birthday on 2 October 1888 and spent the month of October in these lodgings in Richmond.

[262] In his 'Guide to London' MKG wrote that the friend 'treated me very kindly and taught me how to behave and how to use the fork and the spoons'. *CWMG*, vol. 1, p. 115.

[263] 'vegetable' in the first edition.

[264] 'I could not match his arguments.' To add.

will not help you to gain anything here.[265] You confess
to having eaten and relished meat. You took it where
it was absolutely unnecessary, and will not where it is
quite essential. *What a pity!*[M2]

M2 How astonishing!

But I was adamant.

Day in and day out the friend would argue, but I
had an eternal negative[266] to face him with. The more
he argued, the more uncompromising I became. Daily
I would pray for God's protection and get it. Not that
I had any idea of God. It was faith that was at work—
faith of which the seed had been[267] sown by the good
nurse[268] Rambha.

One day the friend began to read to me Bentham's
Theory of Utility. I was at my wit's end. The language
was too difficult for me to understand. He began to
expound it. I said: 'Pray excuse me. These *abstruse*[M3]
things are beyond me. I admit it is necessary to eat meat.
But I cannot break my vow. I cannot argue about it. I
am sure I cannot meet you in argument. But please give
me up as foolish or obstinate. I appreciate your love
for me[269] and I know you to be my well-wisher. I also
know that you are telling me again and again about this
because you feel for me. But I am helpless. A vow is a
vow. It cannot be broken.'

M3 fine

The friend looked at me in surprise.[270] He closed
the book and said: 'All right. I will not argue anymore.'
I was glad. He never discussed the subject again. But
he did not cease to worry about me. He smoked and
drank, but he never asked me to do so. In fact he asked

---

[265] 'that you can take back to the country' to add.

[266] Literal translation of the Gujarati proverb from the original
would be: 'a no that cures thirty-six diseases'.

[267] 'was' in the first edition.

[268] 'the good nurse' added in the English translation.

[269] 'I understand your intent' to add.

[270] 'in surprise' added in the English translation.

me to remain away from both. His one anxiety was lest I should[271] become very weak without meat, and thus be un-able to *feel at home*[M4] in England.

M4 live freely

That is how I served my apprenticeship for a month. The friend's house was in Richmond, and it was not possible to go to London more than once or twice a week. Dr. Mehta and Sjt. Dalpatram Shukla therefore decided that I should be put with some family. Sjt. Shukla hit upon an Anglo-Indian's[272] house in West Kensington[273] and placed me there. The landlady was a widow. I told her about my vow. The old lady promised to look after me properly, and I took up my residence in her house. Here too I practically had to starve. I had sent for sweets and other eatables from home, but nothing had yet come. Everything was insipid. Every day the old lady asked me whether I liked the food,[274] but what could she do? I was still as shy as ever and dared not ask for more than was put before me.[275] She had two daughters. They insisted on serving me with an extra slice or two of[276] bread. But little did they know that nothing less than a loaf would have filled me.

But I had *found my feet*[M5] now. I had not yet started upon my regular studies. I had just begun reading newspapers, thanks to Sjt. Shukla. In India I had never read a newspaper. But here I succeeded in cultivating a liking for them by regular reading. I always glanced over *The Daily News*, *The Daily Telegraph*, and *The Pall*

M5 sprouted wings

---

[271] 'might' in the first edition.

[272] An English family that had lived in India; not of a mixed racial parentage as the term suggests at present.

[273] This Victorian-terraced house, four storeys high, was at 20, Baron's Court Road. MKG spent the winter of 1888 and spring of 1889 in this house.

[274] 'whether I liked the food' added in the English translation.

[275] 'and dared not ask for more than was put before me' added in the English translation.

[276] 'slice or two of' added in the English translation.

Mall Gazette.[277] This took me hardly an hour. I therefore began to wander about. I launched out in search of a vegetarian[278] restaurant. The landlady had told me that there were such places in the city. I would trot ten or twelve miles each day, go into a cheap restaurant and eat my fill of bread, but would never be satisfied. During these wanderings I once hit on a vegetarian restaurant in Farringdon Street.[279] The sight of it filled me with the same joy that a child feels on getting a thing after its own heart. Before I entered I noticed books for sale exhibited under a glass window near the door. I saw among them Salt's *Plea for Vegetarianism.*[280] This I purchased for a shilling and went straight to the dining-room. This was my first hearty meal since my arrival in England. God *had come to my aid.*[M6]

[M6] assuaged my hunger

I read Salt's book from cover to cover[281] and was very much impressed by it. From the date of reading

---

[277] *The Daily News* founded in 1846 by Charles Dickens, who also served as its first editor. During the period in which MKG read it John Robinson was its editor.

　The Daily Telegraph was founded in 1855 by Arthur B. Sleigh; among its editors was Edwin Arnold (1873–88).

　The Pall Mall Gazette founded in 1865 by George Murray Smith took its name from a fictional newspaper conceived by William Mackpeace Thackeray.

[278] In *Navajivan* of 7 March 1926 two terms 'niramishahar' and 'annahar' are used.

[279] This was 'The Central' at 16, Saint Bride Street. The date was probably Monday, 22 October 1888. In his 'Guide to London' MKG included the whole menu of a vegetarian restaurant including soups, porridge, savouries, vegetarian pies, extra vegetables, sweet puddings, pastry, stewed fruit and sundries. The menu bears this date.

[280] Henry Stephens Salt (1851–1939), noted ethical vegetarian, anti-vivisectionist, socialist, pacifist and naturalist. He also wrote a biography of Henry David Thoreau and introduced MKG to Thoreau's ideas. *Plea for Vegetarianism* was first published in 1886.

[281] 'from cover to cover' added in the English translation.

this book, I may claim to have become a vegetarian[282] by choice. I blessed the day on which I had taken the vow before my mother. I had *all along*[M7] abstained from meat in the interests of truth and[283] of the vow I had taken, but had wished at the same time that *every Indian should be a meat-eater,*[M8] and had looked forward to being one myself freely and openly someday, and to enlisting others in the cause. *The choice was now made in favour of vegetarianism, the spread of which henceforward became my mission.*[M9]

[M7] hitherto

[M8] all should be meat-eaters

[M9] Now I was eager to remain a vegetarian and make others do likewise.

XV

PLAYING THE ENGLISH GENTLEMAN[M1]

[M1] In 'Civilized' Attire

My faith in vegetarianism grew on me from day to day. Salt's book whetted my appetite for dietetic studies. I went in for all books available on vegetarianism and read them. One of these, Howard Williams's[284] *The Ethics of Diet*[285] was a 'biographical history of the literature of humane dietetics from the earliest period to the present day'. It tried to make out, that all philosophers and prophets from Pythagoras and Jesus down to those of the present age were vegetarians.*[M2]

[M2] described the dietary practices and ideas of learned persons, incarnations and prophets from different ages. He also tried to prove that Pythagoras, Jesus, etc., were vegetarians.

---

[282] In the original Gujarati the term is 'annahar', literally, eater of grains. In *Navajivan* of 7 March 1926 MKG used the term 'niramishahar', literally, non-eater of meat, and added a footnote: 'The more prevalent term for vegetarian is Shakahari (literally, eater of vegetables). This is closer to the root of the English term but does not indicate real substance. Hence I have used Niramishahari, though the term is abstruse. I would use another term, if I were to find it, that is closer to the meaning and simple. Will someone come to my aid?'

[283] 'subsequently' to add.

[284] Howard Williams (1837–1931), English humanitarian and vegetarian. MKG met him at Ventnor.

[285] First published in 1883. Leo Tolstoy wrote an introduction to the Russian translation of this work in 1892.

Dr. Anna Kingsford's[286] *The Perfect Way in Diet* was also an attractive book. Dr. Allinson's[287] writings on health and hygiene were likewise very helpful. He advocated a curative system based on regulation of the dietary of patients. Himself a vegetarian, he prescribed for his patients also a strictly vegetarian diet. The result of reading all this literature was that dietetic experiments came to take an important place in my life. Health was the principal consideration of these experiments to begin with. But later on *religion became the supreme motive*.[M3]

Meanwhile my friend had not ceased to worry about me. His love for me led him to think that, if I persisted in my objections to meat-eating, I should not only develop a weak constitution, but should remain a duffer, because I should never *feel at home in*[M4] English society. When he came to know that I had begun to interest myself in books on vegetarianism, he was afraid lest these studies should muddle my head; that I should fritter my life away in experiments, forgetting my own work, and become a crank. He therefore made one last effort to reform me. He one day invited me to go to the theatre. Before the play we were to dine together at the Holborn Restaurant,[288] to me a palatial place and the first big restaurant I had been to since leaving the Victoria Hotel. The stay at that hotel had scarcely been a helpful experience, for I had not lived there with my wits about me. The friend had planned to take me to this restaurant

M3 religious motive became supreme

M4 mingle with

---

[286] Anna Kingsford (1846–88), one of the first English women to obtain a degree of medicine. She was a passionate anti-vivisection advocate and a campaigner for vegetarianism. *The Perfect Way in Diet* was published in 1881. She was interested in theosophy and esoteric Christianity. She wrote with Edward Maitland *The Perfect Way or The Finding of Christ* and *Clothed with the Sun*.

[287] Dr. Thomas Allinson (1858–1918), trained in Edinburgh, was a voluminous scholar. His best-known work is *A System of Hygienic Medicine* (1886). A passionate vegetarian, he wrote on the advantages of nutritious whole foods in *The Advantage of Wholemeal Bread*.

[288] At No. 252, High Holborn.

evidently imagining that modesty would forbid any questions.[289] And *it was a very big company of diners in the midst of which*[M5] my friend and I sat sharing a table between us. The first course was soup.[290] I wondered what it might be made of, but durst not ask the friend about it. I therefore summoned the waiter. *My friend saw the movement and sternly asked across the table what was the matter. With considerable hesitation I told him that I wanted to inquire if the soup was a vegetable soup. 'You are too clumsy for decent society,' he passionately exclaimed. 'If you cannot behave yourself,*[M6] you had better go. Feed in some *other*[M7] restaurant and await me outside.' This delighted me. Out I went. There was a vegetarian restaurant close by, but it was closed.[291] So I went without food that night. I accompanied my friend to the theatre, but he never said a word about *the scene I had created.*[M8] On my part of course there was nothing to say.

That was the last friendly tussle we had. *It did not affect our relations in the least.*[M9] I could see and appreciate the love by[292] which all my friend's efforts were actuated, and my respect for him was all the greater on account of our differences in thought and action.

But I decided that I should put him at ease, that I should assure him that I would be *clumsy*[M10] no more, *but try to become polished and make up for my vegetarianism by cultivating other accomplishments which fitted one for polite society. And for this purpose I undertook the all too impossible task of becoming an English gentleman.*[M11]

The[293] clothes after the Bombay cut that I was wearing were, I thought, unsuitable for English society,

[M5] in the midst of hundreds of diners

[M6] The friend understood. He asked me in irritation, 'What is it?'
I replied softly and with hesitation: 'I wish to inquire, is there meat in this?'
'This kind of barbarism will not do in such a restaurant. If you still wish to quibble and cavil

[M7] smaller

[M8] that incident

[M9] It neither caused a breach in our relations, nor caused any bitterness.

[M10] barbaric

[M11] would cultivate civilized conduct and equip myself through other means of mingling with society and thus cover up the oddity of my vegetarianism. For this I took the course which was beyond my capacity and was superficial, of cultivating civilized conduct

---

[289] 'The friend had planned . . . forbid any questions.' Added in the English translation.

[290] 'soup' English word in the original.

[291] 'What was I to do, I did not know.' To add.

[292] 'with' in the first edition.

[293] 'English-style' to add.

and I got new ones at the Army and Navy Stores.[294] I also went in for a chimney-pot[295] hat costing nineteen shillings—an excessive price in those days. Not content with this, I *wasted ten pounds on*[M12] an evening suit made in Bond Street, *the centre of fashionable life in London;*[M13] and got my good and noble-hearted brother to send me a double watch-chain of gold. It was not correct[296] to wear a ready-made tie and I learnt the art of tying one for myself. While in India, *the mirror had been a luxury permitted on the days when the family barber gave me a shave.*[M14] Here I wasted ten minutes every day before a huge mirror, watching myself arranging my tie and parting my hair in the correct fashion. My hair was by no means soft, and every day it meant a regular struggle with the brush[297] to keep it in position. Each time the hat was put on and off, the hand would automatically move towards the head to adjust the[298] hair, not to mention the other civilized habit of the hand every now and then operating for the same purpose when sitting in polished society.

As if all this were not enough to make me look the thing, I directed my attention to other details that were supposed to go towards the making of an English gentleman. I was told it was necessary for me to take lessons in dancing, French and elocution. French was not only the language of neighbouring France, but it was the lingua franca of the Continent over which I had a desire to travel.[M15] I decided to take dancing lessons at a class and paid down £3 as fees for a term. I must have taken about six lessons in three weeks. But it was beyond

---

[294] 'Army and Navy Stores' English phrase in the original. The Army & Navy Co-operative Society was incorporated in 1871, with an aim to supply its members goods at lowest possible rates.

[295] 'chimney hat' in the original.

[296] 'etiquette' to add. First recorded usage of the word dates back to 1850–55.

[297] '(akin to a broomstick, isn't it?)' to add.

[298] 'parting in the' to add.

[M12] kindled ten pounds for

[M13] where fashionable people get their clothes tailored

[M14] one got to see a mirror on the day one got a shave

[M15] But this dandyism was not enough. Does civilized attire make of us a civilized person? I had learnt of other outward charms of civilized conduct, which I wished to cultivate. A civilized man must know dancing. He must know passable French because French was the language of England's neighbour France. It was also the national language of all Europe where I desired to study. Moreover, a civilized man must know how to make eloquent public speech.

me to achieve anything like rhythmic motion. I could not follow the piano and hence found it impossible to keep time.[299] What then was I to do?[300] The recluse in the fable kept a cat to keep off the rats, and then a cow to feed the cat with milk, and a man to keep the cow and so on. My ambitions also grew like the family of the recluse. I thought I should learn to play the violin in order to cultivate an ear for *Western music*.[M16] So I *invested*[M17] £3 in a violin and something more in fees. I sought a third teacher to give me lessons in elocution and paid him a preliminary fee of a guinea. He recommended Bell's *Standard Elocutionist*[301] as the text-book, which I purchased. And I began with a speech of Pitt's.[302]

But *Mr. Bell* [M18] rang the bell of alarm in my ear and I awoke.

I had not to spend a lifetime in England, I said to myself. What then was the use of learning elocution? And how could dancing make *a gentleman of me*?[M19] The violin I could learn even in India. I was a student and ought to go on with my studies. I should *qualify myself to join the Inns of Court*.[M20] If my character made *a gentleman of me*,[M21] so much the better. Otherwise I should forgo the ambition.

These and similar thoughts possessed me, and I expressed them in a letter which I addressed to the elocution teacher, requesting him to excuse me from further lessons. I had taken only two or three. I wrote

[M16] melody and rhythm

[M17] consigned

[M18] Bell Sahib

[M19] me civilized

[M20] prepare myself to join the profession

[M21] me civilized

---

[299] 'One, two, three would go on, but the intervals between them were indicated by the piano, which I could not follow.' To add.

[300] 'My lot was akin to the story of the mendicant and the cat.' To add.

[301] David Charles Bell and Alexander Melville Bell, *Bell's Standard Elocutionist, Principles and exercises followed by a copious selection of Extracts in prose and poetry, classified for reading and recitation* (William Mullon & Son, 1878; rev. ed.).

[302] Pitt's speech. On pages 131–32 of the *Standard Elocutionist* 'The Retort to Walpole' (1741) by William Pitt, Earl of Chatham.

a similar letter to the dancing teacher,[303] and went personally to the violin teacher with a request to dispose of the violin for any price it might fetch. *She was rather friendly to me, so I told her how I had discovered that I was pursuing a false idea.*[M22] She encouraged me in the determination to *make a complete change.*[M23]

This infatuation must have lasted about three months. The *punctiliousness*[M24] in dress persisted for years. But henceforward I became a student.

[M22] We had become somewhat friendly. I spoke to her about my insensate condition

[M23] free myself from the snare of dance, etc.

[M24] dandy-ness

XVI

CHANGES

Let no one imagine that my experiments in dancing and the like marked a stage of indulgence in my life. The reader will have noticed that even then I had my wits about me. That period of infatuation was not unrelieved by a certain amount of self-introspection on my part. I kept account of every farthing I spent, and my expenses were carefully calculated.[304] Every little item, such as omnibus fares or postage or a couple of coppers spent on news-papers,[305] would be entered, and the balance struck every evening before going to bed. That habit has stayed with me ever since, and I know that as a result, though I have had to handle *public funds*[M1] amounting

[M1] in public life funds

---

[303] This was a woman teacher. The gendered term in the Gujarati original indicates this.

[304] 'I had decided not to spend more than £15 a month.' To add.

[305] 'or a couple of coppers spent on news-papers' added in the English translation. In his 'Guide to London' MKG describes newspapers to be a daily requirement. 'In above estimates no mention is made of expenses on account of newspapers which are found to be an absolute necessity, a daily food as it were . . . The London newspapers are very cheap. An evening newspaper can be had for one half penny.' *CWMG*, vol. 1, pp. 100–01.

to lakhs, I have succeeded in exercising strict economy in their disbursement and, instead of outstanding debts, have had invariably a surplus balance in respect of all the movements I have led. *Let every youth take a leaf out of my book and make it a point to account for everything that comes into and goes out of his pocket, and like me he is sure to be a gainer in the end.*[M2]

As I kept strict watch over my way of living,[306] I could see *that it was necessary to economize.*[M3] I therefore decided to reduce my expenses by half. My accounts showed numerous items spent on fares. Again my living with a family meant the payment of a regular weekly bill. It also included the courtesy of occasionally taking members of the family out to dinner, and likewise attending parties with them. *All this involved heavy items for conveyances, especially as, if the friend was a lady, custom required that the man should pay all the expenses.*[M4] Also dining out meant extra cost, as no deduction could be made from the regular weekly bill for meals not taken. It seemed to me that all these items could be saved, as likewise the drain on my purse caused through a false sense of propriety.

So I decided to take rooms on my own account, instead of living any longer in a family, and also *to remove from place to place*[M5] according to the work I had to do, thus gaining experience at the same time. The rooms were so selected as to enable me to reach the place of business on foot in half an hour, and so save fares. Before this I had always *taken some kind of*[M6] conveyance whenever I went anywhere, and had to find extra time for walks. The new arrangement combined walks and

[M2] Let every youth keep a careful account of the little money he has and he would, like me, experience in the future its benefit for himself and the public.

[M3] how much money I should spend

[M4] Which involved expenses on carriage. If there were a lady companion, she could not be allowed to pay for the expenses.

[M5] change lodging in different suburbs

[M6] had to spend on

---

[306] In his 'Guide to London' MKG devoted a chapter on the cost of living, in which he cited examples of sparse but noble lives, including those of Charles Bradlaugh and Cardinal Manning. He also cited guides that could help an aspirant to model his finances: Dr. T.L. Nichols, *How to live on six pence a day* and *How to live on one pound a week.* See *CWMG*, vol. 1, pp. 82–101.

economy, as it meant a saving of fares and gave me walks of eight or ten miles a day. It was mainly this habit of long walks that kept me practically free from illness throughout my stay in England and gave me a fairly strong body.

Thus I rented a suite of rooms; one for a sitting-room and another for a bedroom.[307] This was the second stage. The third was yet to come.

These changes saved me half the expense. But how was I to utilize the time? I knew that Bar examinations did not require much study, and I therefore did not feel pressed for time. My weak English was a perpetual worry to me. Mr. (afterwards Sir Frederic)[308] Lely's words, 'Graduate first and then come to me,' still rang in my ears. I should, I thought, not only be called to the Bar, but *have some literary degree as well.*[M7] I inquired about the Oxford and Cambridge University courses, consulted a few friends, and found that, if I elected to go to either of these places, that would mean greater *expense and a much longer stay in England than I was prepared for.*[M8] A friend suggested that, if I really wanted to have the satisfaction of taking a difficult examination, I should pass the London Matriculation. It meant a good deal of labour and much addition to my stock of general knowledge, without any extra expense worth the name. I welcomed the suggestion. But the syllabus frightened me. Latin and a *modern*[M9] language were compulsory! How was I to manage Latin? But the friend entered a strong plea for it: 'Latin is very valuable to lawyers. Knowledge of Latin is very useful in understanding law-books. And one *paper*[M10] in Roman Law is entirely in Latin. Besides, a knowledge of Latin

[M7] study something else as well

[M8] expense. The course there was long. I could not stay longer than three years

[M9] second

[M10] question

---

[307] According to James Hunt this suite of rooms were on Store Street, close to the British Museum and the University of London. *Gandhi in London,* p. 221.

[308] '(afterwards Sir Frederic)' added in the English translation. The original has 'Lely Sahib.'

means greater command over the English language.'
It went home and I decided to learn Latin, no matter
how difficult it might be. French I had already begun,[309]
so I thought that should be the *modern*[M11] language. I   M11 second
joined a private Matriculation class. Examinations were
held every six months and I had only five months at my
disposal. It was an almost impossible task for me. But
the aspirant after being *an English gentleman*[M12] chose to   M12 civilized
convert himself into a serious student. I framed my own
time-table to the minute; but neither my intelligence
nor memory promised to enable me to tackle Latin and
French besides other subjects within the given period.[310]
The result was that I was ploughed in Latin.[311] I was sorry
but did not lose heart. I had acquired a taste for Latin, also
I thought my French would be all the better for another
trial and I would select a new subject in the science
group. Chemistry which was my subject in science had
no attraction for want of experiments, *whereas*[M13] it ought   M13 though I see it now
to have been a deeply interesting study. It was one of the
compulsory subjects in India and so I had selected it for
the London Matriculation. This time, however, I chose
Heat and Light instead of Chemistry. It was said to be
easy and I found it to be so.

With my preparation for another trial, I made an
effort to simplify my life still further. I felt that my way
of living did not yet befit[312] the *modest means*[M14] of my   M14 poverty
family. The thought of *my struggling brother, who nobly
responded to my regular calls for monetary help,*[M15] deeply   M15 the strained circumstances
pained me. I saw that most of those who were spending   and generosity of my brother
from eight to fifteen pounds monthly had the advantage
of scholarships. I had before me examples of much

---

[309] 'which I decided to complete' to add.

[310] 'within the given period' added in the English translation.

[311] In January 1890.

[312] 'become' in the first edition.

simpler living. I came across a fair number of poor students living more humbly than I. One of them was staying in the slums in a room at two shillings a week and living on two pence worth of cocoa and bread per meal from Lockhart's cheap Cocoa Rooms.[313] *It was far from me to think of emulating him,*[M16] but I felt I could surely have one room instead of two and cook some of my meals at home.[314] *That would be a saving of four to five pounds each month.*[M17] I also came across books on simple living. I gave up the suite of rooms and rented one[315] instead,[316] invested in a stove, and began cooking my breakfast at home. The process scarcely took me more than twenty minutes, for *there was only oatmeal porridge*[317]

[M16] I lacked the capacity to compete with him

[M17] Thus I could live within four or five pounds a month.

---

[313] '*Cocoa Rooms,* and especially Lockhart's cocoa rooms, have become an important factor in the life of the people. At first cocoa rooms, or coffee palaces as they were then called, were the result of philanthropic or religious effort. They were to pay their way; but they did not do it. They were to provide good refreshments; but tea, coffee, cocoa and cakes were alike bad. It was not till the work was taken up as a business that any good was done with it. Now it strides forward, and though Lockhart's are the best and the most numerous, others are following and are bound to come up to, or excel, the standard so established. Very soon we shall have no length of principal street without such a place, and we shall wonder how we ever got on without them. In their rules they are wisely liberal: those who drink the cocoa may sit at the tables to eat the dinner or breakfast they have brought from home, or bringing the bread and butter from home they can add the sausage or whatever completes the meal.'
Charles Booth *Life and Labour of the People in London,* 'Pubs and Cocoa Rooms,' in Peter Keating (edited), *Into Unknown England: 1866-1913 Selections from the social explorers.* Manchester University Press, 1976. pp. 130-31.

[314] In 'Guide to London', MKG provided menus, including recipes of three vegetarian meals which could be cooked in the rooms at a total cost of 11 dimes or 1 shilling per day.

[315] 'for eight shillings a week' to add.

[316] On Tavistock Street.

[317] MKG describes oatmeal porridge as 'a splendid dish especially in winter'. *CWMG*, vol. 1, p. 96.

to cook and water to boil for cocoa.[M18] I had lunch out and for dinner bread and cocoa at home. Thus I managed to live on a shilling and three pence a day. This was also a period of intensive study. Plain living saved me plenty of time and I passed my examination.[318]

[M18] how long would it take to cook oatmeal porridge and boil water for cocoa?

Let not the reader think that this living made my life by any means a dreary affair. On the contrary the change harmonized my inward and outward life. It was also more in keeping with the means of my family. My life was certainly more *truthful*[M19] and my soul knew no bounds of joy.

[M19] meaningful

XVII

EXPERIMENTS IN DIETETICS

As I searched myself deeper, the necessity for changes both internal and external began to grow on me. *As soon as, or even before, I made alterations in my expenses and my way of living, I began to make changes in my diet.*[M1] I saw that the writers on vegetarianism had examined the question very minutely, attacking it in its religious, scientific, practical and medical aspects. Ethically they had arrived at the conclusion that man's supremacy over the *lower*[M2] animals meant not that the former should prey upon the latter, but that the higher should protect the lower, and that there should be mutual aid between the two as between man and man. They had also brought out the truth that man eats not for enjoyment but to live. And some of them accordingly suggested and effected in their *lives*[M3] abstention not only from fleshmeat but from eggs and milk. Scientifically some had concluded that man's physical structure showed that he was not meant to be

[M1] The speed with which changes took place in my way of living and expenses, with the same speed, or perhaps at an even faster pace, I began changes in my diet.

[M2] birds and

[M3] diet

---

[318] June 1890.

a cooking but a frugivorous animal, that he could take only his mother's milk and, as soon as he had teeth, should begin to take solid foods. Medically they had suggested the rejection of all spices and condiments. According to the practical and economic argument they had demonstrated that a vegetarian diet was the least expensive. All these[319] considerations had their effect on me, and I came across vegetarians of all these types in vegetarian restaurants. There was a Vegetarian Society[320] in England with a weekly journal[321] of its own. I subscribed to the weekly, joined the Society and very shortly found myself on the Executive[322] Committee.[323] Here I came in contact with those who were regarded as pillars of vegetarianism, and began my own experiments in dietetics.

I stopped taking the sweets and condiments I had got from home. The mind having taken a different turn, the fondness for condiments wore away, and I now relished the boiled spinach, which in Richmond *tasted*[M4] insipid, cooked without condiments. Many such experiments

[M4] had tasted

---

[319] 'four' to add.

[320] The Vegetarian Society was established on 30 September 1848, with James Simpson as its president and William Horsell as its secretary.

[321] *The Vegetarian* commenced publication in January 1888, and became the London Vegetarian Society's (LVS) official organ. Its masthead announced 'A Paper for the Promotion of Humanity, Purity, Temperance, Health, Wealth and Happiness'. The office of the LVS was initially next door to the Central Restaurant in London where MKG discovered the Vegetarian movement and had his first satisfactory meal in London. In South Africa MKG became an 'agent' of the LVS and included this fact on his letterhead.

[322] 'Executive' added in the English translation.

[323] 'Committee' English word in the original. MKG became member of the Executive Committee of the LVS on 19 September 1890 and attended its meetings regularly till his departure in June of the following year.

taught me that the real seat of taste was not the tongue but the mind.

The economic consideration was of course constantly before me. There was in those days a body of opinion which regarded tea and coffee as harmful and favoured cocoa.[324] And as I was convinced that one should eat only articles that sustained the body, I gave up tea and coffee as a rule, and substituted cocoa.

There were two divisions in the restaurants I used to visit. One division, which was patronized by fairly well-to-do people, provided any number of courses from which one chose and paid for *a la carte*, each dinner thus costing from one to two shillings. The other division provided six-penny dinners of three courses with a slice of bread.[325] In my days of strict frugality I usually dined in the second division.

There were many minor experiments going on along with the main one; as for example, giving up starchy[326] foods at one time, living on bread and fruit alone at another, and once living on cheese, milk and eggs. This last experiment is worth noting. It lasted not even a fortnight.[327] The reformer who advocated starchless food had spoken highly of eggs and held that

---

[324] In 'Guide to London' MKG quoted Dr. Nicholas on tea and coffee: 'Even the milder stimulants such as tea and coffee have no appreciable nutritional value . . . Tea and coffee are stimulants only and their influence upon the body is either inappreciable or hurtful.' *CWMG*, vol. 1, pp. 88–89.

[325] MKG described the six-penny dinners thus: 'You buy a ticket and, on presenting the ticket, you get a selection of 3 out of about 20 courses. The popularity of these dinners is immense. From 1 pm to 2 pm, very often it becomes very difficult to find a place owing to the large number of customers.' *CWMG*, vol. 1, p. 97.

[326] 'starch' English word in the original.

[327] In an essay, 'The Foods of India', that MKG read on Saturday, 2 May 1891, he said: 'I am sorry to say that I have been taking eggs for about a month and half.' *CWMG*, vol. 1, p. 36.

eggs were not meat. It was apparent that there was no injury done to living creatures in taking eggs. I was taken in by this plea and took eggs in spite of my vow.[328] But the lapse was momentary. I had no *business*[M5] to put a new interpretation on the vow. *The interpretation of my mother who administered the vow was there for me. I knew that her definition of meat included eggs.*[M6] And as soon as I saw the true import of the vow I gave up eggs and the experiment alike.

There is a nice point underlying the argument, and worth noting. I came across three definitions of meat in England. According to the first, meat denoted only the flesh of birds and beasts. Vegetarians who accepted that definition abjured the flesh of birds and beasts, but ate fish, not to mention eggs. According to the second definition, meat meant flesh of all living creatures. So fish was here out of the question, but eggs were allowed. The third definition included under meat the flesh of all living beings, as well as all their products, thus covering eggs and milk alike. If I accepted the first definition, I could take not only eggs, but[329] fish also. But I was convinced that my mother's definition was the definition binding on me. If, therefore, I would observe the vow I had taken, I must abjure eggs. I therefore did so. This was a hardship inasmuch as inquiry showed that even in vegetarian restaurants many courses used to contain eggs. This meant that *unless*[M7] I knew what was what, I had to go through the awkward[330] process of ascertaining whether a particular course contained eggs or no, for many puddings[331] and cakes[332] were

[M5] authority

[M6] The interpretation of the person who administered the vow had to be accepted. I knew that my mother who gave me the pledge against meat could not have even thought of eggs.

[M7] until

---

[328] 'given to my mother' to add.

[329] 'not only eggs, but' added in the English translation.

[330] 'awkward' added in the English translation.

[331] English word in the original.

[332] English word in the original.

not free from them. But though the revelation of my duty caused this difficulty, it simplified my food. The simplification in its turn brought me annoyance in that I had to give up several dishes I had come to relish. These difficulties were only passing, for the strict observance of the vow produced an inward relish distinctly more healthy, delicate and permanent.[333]

The real ordeal, however, was still to come, and that was in respect of the other vow. But who dare harm whom God protects?

A few observations about the interpretation of vows or pledges may not be out of place here.[M8] Interpretation of *pledges*[M9] has been a fruitful source of strife all the world over. *No matter how explicit the pledge, people will turn and twist the text to suit their own purposes. They are to be met with among all classes of society, from the rich down to the poor, from the prince down to the peasant. Selfishness turns them blind, and by a use of the ambiguous middle they deceive themselves and seek to deceive the world and God.*[M10] One golden rule is to accept the interpretation honestly put on the *pledge*[M11] by the party administering it.[334] Another[335] is to accept the interpretation of the weaker party, where there are two interpretations possible. Rejection of these two rules gives rise to strife and *iniquity, which are rooted in*[M12] untruthfulness. He who seeks truth alone easily follows the golden rule. *He need not seek learned advice for interpretation.*[M13] My mother's interpretation of meat was, according to the golden rule,[336] the only true one for me, and not the one my wider experience or my pride of better knowledge might have taught me.

---

[333] 'compared to momentary taste.' To add.

[334] 'The meaning that we carry in our minds is either false or partial.' To add.

[335] 'golden rule' to add.

[336] 'according to the golden rule' added in the English translation.

[M8] It is necessary to say something about interpretation of vows before concluding this chapter. My vow was a contract entered into with my mother.

[M9] contracts

[M10] No matter how explicit the language of the contract, a master of language will turn a crow into a tiger. In this there is no distinction between the civil and the non-civil. Self-interest turns everyone blind. As a prince down to a pauper interpret contracts to suit themselves and deceive the world, themselves and god. This practice of parties to a contract putting convenient interpretation to words or sentences is known in logic as the fallacy of the ambiguous middle.

[M11] word

[M12] immorality. And injustice is rooted in

[M13] He does not need to search scriptures for that.

M15 It had not assumed a
religious dimension in England.
My strenuous experiments
from a religious perspective
were carried out in South Africa

My experiments *in England*[M14] were conducted from the point of view of economy and hygiene. *The religious aspect of the question was not considered until I went to South Africa where I undertook strenuous experiments*[M15] which will be narrated later. The seed, however, for all of them was sown in England.

A convert's enthusiasm for[337] his new religion is greater than that of a person who is born in it. Vegetarianism was then a new cult in England, and likewise for me, because, as we have seen, I had gone there a convinced meat-eater, and was intellectually converted to vegetarianism later.[338] Full of the neophyte's zeal for vegetarianism, I decided to start a vegetarian club in my locality, Bayswater.[339] I invited Sir Edwin Arnold,[340] who lived there, to be Vice-President. Dr. Oldfield[341] who was Editor of *The Vegetarian* became President. I myself became the Secretary. The club went well for a while, but came to an end in the course of a few months. For I left the locality, according to my custom of moving from place to place periodically. But this brief and modest experience gave me some little training in organizing and conducting institutions.

---

[337] 'and propagation of' to add.

[338] 'For me it was akin to conversion to a new religion.' To add.

[339] MKG lived at 52, St Stephens's Gardens, Bayswater, where he shared rooms with Josiah Oldfield.

[340] Sir Edwin Arnold (1832–1904), wrote a life of Buddha in verse, *The Light of Asia*, and translated the Gita as *Song Celestial*. MKG's first acquaintance with the Gita was through Sir Edwin's translation.

[341] Dr. Josiah Oldfield (1863–1953), theologian, barrister and physician. Perhaps the only Englishman with whom MKG lived as a friend and an equal during his student days. For Oldfield's reminiscences of MKG, see 'My Friend Gandhi', in Chandrashankar Shukla (ed.), *Reminiscences of Gandhiji* (Bombay: Vora & Co., 1951), pp. 187–90.

XVIII

SHYNESS MY SHIELD

I was elected to the Executive Committee of the Vegetarian Society, and made it a point to attend every one of its meetings, but I always felt tongue-tied. Dr. Oldfield once said to me, 'You talk to me quite all right, but why is it that you never open your lips at a committee meeting? You are a drone.' I appreciated the banter. The bees are ever busy, the drone is a thorough idler. And it was not a little curious that whilst others expressed their opinions at these meetings, I sat quite silent. Not that I never felt tempted to speak. But I was at a loss to know how to express myself. All the rest of the members appeared to me to be better informed than I. Then it often happened that just when I had mustered up courage to speak, a fresh subject would be started. This went on for a long time.

Meantime a serious question came up for discussion. *I thought it wrong to be absent,*[M1] and felt it cowardice to register a silent vote. The discussion arose somewhat in this wise.[342] The President of the Society was Mr. Hills,[343] proprietor of the Thames Iron Works. He was a puritan. It may[344] be said that the existence of the Society depended practically on his financial assistance. Many members of the Committee were more or less his proteges. Dr. Allinson of vegetarian fame[345] was also

[M1] I thought that to refrain from participating would be equal to acquiescing to injustice

---

[342] 'The discussion arose somewhat in this wise.' Added in the English translation.

[343] Arnold F. Hills (1857–1927), a wealthy industrialist and chairman of Thames Iron Works, a shipyard that built battleships and other large vessels.

[344] 'my' in the first edition.

[345] 'of vegetarian fame' added in the English translation.

a member of the Committee.[346] He was an advocate of the then new birth-control movement, and preached its methods among the working classes.[347] Mr. Hills regarded these methods as cutting at the root of morals. He thought that the Vegetarian Society had for its object not only dietetic but also moral reform, and that a man *of Dr. Allinson's anti-puritanic views*[M2] should not be allowed to remain in the Society. A motion was therefore brought for his removal. The question deeply interested me. I considered Dr. Allinson's views regarding artificial methods of birth control as dangerous, and *I believed that Mr. Hills was entitled, as a puritan, to oppose him.*[M3] I had also a high regard for Mr. Hills and his generosity. *But I thought it was quite improper to exclude a man from a vegetarian society simply because he refused to regard puritan morals as one of the objects of the Society. Mr. Hills's view regarding the exclusion of anti-puritans from the Society was personal to himself,*[M4] and it had nothing to do with the declared object of the Society, which was simply the promotion of vegetarianism and not of any system of morality. *I therefore held that any vegetarian could be a member of the Society irrespective of his views on other morals.*[M5]

There were in the Committee others also who shared my view, but I felt myself personally called upon to express my own. How to do it was the question. I had not the courage to speak and I therefore decided to set down my thoughts in writing.[348] I went to the meeting with the document in my pocket.[349] So far as I recollect, I did not find myself equal even to reading

[M2] like Dr. Allinson, whose views were detrimental to the Society,

[M3] considered Mr. Hills's opposition to them pure morality.

[M4] But it appeared to me that to disqualify a person from this Society for his lack of faith in and refusal to believe in puritanical morals was sheer injustice. I felt that Mr. Hills's views with regard to woman–man relationship were his personal views

[M5] Therefore I held the view that a person who had disregard for many other forms of morality had a place in the Society.

---

[346] 'There was then a movement for birth-control through artificial means.' To add.

[347] Dr. Allinson wrote *A Book for Married Women* that advocated artificial birth control.

[348] 'to the President' to add.

[349] 'in my pocket' added in the English translation.

it, and the President had it read by someone else. Dr. Allinson[350] lost the day.[351] Thus in the very first battle of the kind I found myself siding with the losing party. But I had comfort in the thought that the cause was right. I have a faint recollection that, after this incident, I resigned from the Committee.[352]

This shyness I retained throughout my stay in England. Even when I paid a social call the presence of *half a dozen or more*[M6] people would strike me dumb.

> [M6] five or seven

I once went to Ventnor with Sjt. Mazmudar. We stayed there with a vegetarian family.[353] Mr. Howard,[354] the author of *The Ethics of Diet*, was also staying at the same *watering-place*.[M7] We met him, and he invited us to speak at a meeting for the promotion of vegetarianism.[355] I had ascertained that it was not considered incorrect to read one's speech. I knew that many did so to express themselves coherently and briefly. To speak extempore would have been out of the question for me.[356] I had therefore written down my speech. I stood up to read it, but could not. My vision became blurred and I trembled, though the speech hardly covered a sheet of foolscap.[357] Sjt. Mazmudar had to read it for me. His

> [M7] port

---

[350] 'Dr. Allinson's faction' in the original.

[351] This meeting was held on 20 February 1891. Hills and Allinson debated 'The Meaning of Sexual Morality' with Oldfield in the chair.

[352] According to James Hunt, MKG continued to be the member of the Committee till June 1891, that is, till his departure for India.

[353] At the Osborne House.

[354] Howard Williams. The original Gujarati does not mention the name of the author.

[355] The meeting took place on 11 May 1891.

[356] 'To speak extempore would have been out of the question for me.' Added in the English translation.

[357] 'foolscap' English word in the original.

own speech was of course excellent and was received
with applause. I was ashamed of myself and sad at heart
for my incapacity.[358]

My last effort to make a public speech in England
was on the eve of my departure for home.[359] But
this time too I only succeeded in making myself
ridiculous.[360] I invited my vegetarian friends to dinner in
the Holborn Restaurant referred to in these chapters.[361]
'A vegetarian dinner could be had,' I said to myself, 'in
vegetarian restaurants as a matter of course. But why
should it not be possible in a non-vegetarian restaurant
too?' And I arranged with the manager of the Holborn
Restaurant to provide a strictly vegetarian meal. The
vegetarians hailed the new experiment with delight.[362]
All dinners are meant for enjoyment, but the West has
developed the thing into an art. They are celebrated
with great *éclat*, music and speeches. And the little
dinner party that I gave was also not unaccompanied
by some such display. Speeches, therefore, there had
to be.[363] When my turn for speaking came, I stood
up to make a speech. I had with great care thought
out one which would consist of a very few sentences.
But I could not proceed beyond the first sentence. I
had read of Addison that he began his maiden speech

---

[358] 'to speak' to add.

[359] According to Pyarelal, *Mahatma Gandhi: The Early Phase*
(Ahmedabad: Navajivan, 1965, 1986 reprint), p. 267, the dinner
was held on Saturday, 5 June 1891. *CWMG* puts the date of the
dinner as 11 June 1891, which is literally the eve of his departure
from England.

[360] 'But this time too I only succeeded in making myself ridiculous.'
Added in the English translation.

[361] 'referred to in these chapters' added in the English translation.

[362] 'but I ridiculed myself' to add.

[363] 'Speeches, therefore, there had to be.' Added in the English
translation.

in the House of Commons, repeating 'I conceive' three times, and when he could proceed no further, a wag stood up and said, 'The gentleman conceived thrice but brought forth nothing.' I had thought of making a humorous speech taking this anecdote as the text. I therefore began with it and stuck there. My memory entirely failed me and in attempting a humorous[364] speech I made myself ridiculous. 'I thank you, gentlemen, for having kindly responded to my invitation,' I said abruptly, and sat down.[365]

It was only in South Africa that I got over this *shyness, though I never completely overcame it. It was impossible for me to speak impromptu.*[M8] I hesitated whenever I had to face strange audiences and avoided making a speech whenever I could. Even today I do not think I could or would even be inclined to keep a meeting of friends engaged in idle talk.

I must say that, beyond occasionally exposing me to laughter, my constitutional shyness has been no disadvantage whatever. In fact I can see that, on the contrary, it has been all to my ad-vantage. My hesitancy in speech, which was once an annoyance, is now a pleasure. Its greatest benefit has been that it has taught me the economy of words. I have naturally formed the habit of restraining my thoughts. And I can now give myself the[366] certificate that *a thoughtless*[M9] word hardly ever escapes my tongue or pen. I do not recollect

[M8] shyness. It cannot be said that even now I have completely overcome it. I always consider before speaking.

[M9] an unconsidered or unmeasured

---

[364] 'and meaningful' to add.

[365] *The Vegetarian*, 13 June 1891, reported: 'At the close of the function, Mr. Gandhi, in a very graceful though somewhat nervous speech, welcomed all present, spoke of the pleasure it gave him to see the habit of abstinence from flesh progressing in England, related the manner in which his connection with the London Vegetarian Society arose, and in so doing took occasion to speak in a touching way of what he owed to Mr. Oldfield.' *CWMG*, vol. 1, p. 14.

[366] 'the' added in the 1940 edition.

ever having had to[367] regret anything in my speech or writing. I have thus been spared many a mishap and waste of time. Experience has taught me that silence is part of the spiritual discipline of a votary of truth. Proneness to exaggerate, to suppress or modify the truth, wittingly or unwittingly, is a natural weakness of man, and silence is necessary in order to surmount it.[368] A man of few words will rarely be thoughtless in his speech; he will measure every word. We find so many people impatient to talk. There is no chairman of a meeting who is not pestered with notes for permission to speak. And whenever the permission is given the speaker generally exceeds the time-limit, asks for more time, and keeps on talking without permission. All this talking can hardly be said to be of any benefit to the world. It is so much waste of time.[369] My shyness has been in reality my shield and buckler. It has allowed

M10 mature

me to *grow*.M10 It has helped me in my *discernment*M11 of truth.

M11 worship

XIX

M1 Poison

THE *CANKER*M1 OF UNTRUTH

M2 who travelled to

There were comparatively few *Indian students in*M2 England forty years ago. It was a practice with them to affect the bachelor even though they might be married. School or college students in England are all bachelors, studies being regarded as incompatible with married life. We had that tradition in the good old days, a student

---

[367] 'be ashamed of or' to add.

[368] 'Economy of words is necessary to overcome such dangers.' To add.

[369] 'My shyness that pinched me earlier, its memory gives me joy today.' To add.

then being invariably known as a *brahmachari*.[370] But in
these days we have child-marriages, *a thing*[M3] practically   M3 which are
unknown in England. Indian youths in England,[371]
therefore, felt ashamed to confess that they were married.
There was also another reason for dissembling,[372] namely
that in the event of the fact being known it would
be impossible for the young man to go about or flirt
with the young girls of the family in which they lived.
The flirting was more or less innocent. Parents even
encouraged *it*;[M4] and that sort of association between   M4 such friendship
young men and young women *may even be*[M5] a necessity   M5 is even considered
there, in view of the fact that every young man has to
choose his mate. If, however, Indian youths on arrival
in England indulge in these relations, quite natural to
English youths, the result is likely to be disastrous, as has
often been found. I saw that our youths had succumbed
to the temptation and chosen a life of untruth for the
sake of companionships which, however innocent in
the case of English youths, were for them undesirable.
I too *caught the contagion*.[M6] I did not hesitate to pass   M6 was caught in the snare
myself off as a bachelor though I was married[373] and
the father of a son. But I *was none the happier for being a
dissembler*.[M7] Only[374] my *reserve*[M8] and my reticence saved   M7 had little taste for such
me from going into deeper waters.[375] *If I did not talk, no*   deceit
girl would think it worth her while to enter into conversation   M8 shyness
with me or to go out with me.[M9]
                                                              M9 If I could not talk, which girl
My cowardice was on a par with my *reserve*.[M10] It   would be willing to go out with
was customary in families like the one in which I was   me? Rarely would a girl go out
                                                              with me.

---

370 MD's note: 'One who observes *brahmacharya*, i.e., complete self-   M10 shyness
restraint.'

371 'in England' added in the English translation.

372 'the fact of marriage' to add.

373 'for five–six years' to add.

374 'Only' added in English translation.

375 'from going into deeper waters.' Added in English translation.

staying at Ventnor[376] for the daughter of the landlady to take out guests for a walk.[377] My landlady's daughter[378] took me one day to the lovely hills round Ventnor. I was no slow walker, but my companion walked even faster, dragging me after her and chattering away all the while. I responded to her chatter sometimes with a whispered 'yes' or 'no', or at the most 'yes, how beautiful!' She was flying like a bird whilst I was wondering when I should get back home.[379] We thus reached the top of a hill. How to get down again was the question. In spite of her high-heeled boots this sprightly young lady of twenty-five darted down the hill like *an arrow*.[M11] I was shamefacedly *struggling to*[M12] get down. She stood at the foot smiling and cheering me and offering to come and drag me. How could I be *so chicken-hearted*?[M13] With the greatest difficulty, and crawling at intervals, I somehow managed to scramble to the bottom. She loudly laughed 'bravo' and shamed me all the more, as well she might.[380]

But I could not escape scatheless everywhere. For God wanted to rid me of the *canker*[M14] of untruth. I once went to Brighton,[381] another watering-place like

^{M11} lightning

^{M12} still thinking how to

^{M13} such a coward

^{M14} poison

---

[376] MKG stayed at this seaside resort on the Isle of Wight from 7 to 23 May 1891.

[377] 'at least as a matter of courtesy' to add.

[378] Mrs. Shelton was the landlady. Pyarelal, in *Early Phase*, p. 770, footnote 32, suggests a 'slim possibility' that the young lady might have been Mrs. Shelton's stepdaughter.

[379] 'I lacked the courage to say, "Let us return."' To add.

[380] Based on this episode Keith Heller wrote a novel, *The Woman Who knew Gandhi* (Houghton Mifflin Harcourt, 2004).

[381] The precise dates are not known. He went after giving his matriculation examinations between 9 and 13 June 1890 and spent four weeks here. He described the experience of his holiday in Brighton in detail in 'Guide to London', *CWMG*, vol.1, pp. 118-20. It was in Brighton that he learnt to cook with facility. His four-week-long holiday cost him £3-10-0 for board and lodging and £4-8-5 for fares.

Ventnor. This was before the Ventnor visit.[382] *I met there at a hotel an old widow of moderate means.*[M15] This was my first year in England.[383] The courses on the *menu* were all described in French, which I did not understand. I sat at the same table as the old lady. She saw that I was a stranger and puzzled, and *immediately came to my aid.*[M16] 'You seem to be a stranger,' she said, 'and look perplexed. Why have you not ordered anything?' I was spelling through the *menu* and preparing to ascertain the ingredients of the courses from the waiter, when the good lady thus intervened. I thanked her, *and explaining my difficulty told her that I was at a loss to know which of the courses were vegetarian as I did not understand French.*[M17]

'Let me help you,' she said. 'I shall explain the card to you and show you what you may eat.' I gratefully availed of her help. This was the beginning of an acquaintance that ripened into friendship and was kept up all through my stay in England and long after. She gave me her London address and invited me to dine at her house every Sunday. On special occasions also she would invite me, help me to conquer my bashfulness and introduce me to young ladies and draw me into conversation with them. Particularly marked out for these conversations was a young lady who stayed with her, and often we would be left entirely alone together.

I found all this very trying at first. I could not start a conversation nor could I indulge in any jokes. But she put me in the way. I began to learn; and in course of time looked forward to every Sunday and came to like the conversations with the young friend.

The old lady went on *spreading her net wider every day.*[M18] She felt interested in our meetings. Possibly she had her own plans about us.

[M15] At the same hotel was a widow of moderate means who had also come for a change of air.

[M16] she began a conversation

[M17] said, ' I do not understand this *menu* and being a vegetarian I must ascertain as to which items are un-sullied.'

[M18] enticing me

---

[382] 'This was before the Ventnor visit.' Added in the English translation.

[383] 'before I went to Ventnor' to add.

I was in a quandary. 'How I wished I had told the good lady that I was married!' I said to myself. 'She would then have not *thought of an engagement between us.*[M19] It is, however, never too late to mend. If I declare the truth, I might yet be saved more misery.' With these thoughts in my mind, I wrote a letter to her somewhat to this effect:

M19 desired to marry me to anyone

'Ever since we met at Brighton you have been kind to me. You have taken care of me even as a mother of her son. You also think that I should get married and with that view you have been introducing me to young ladies. Rather than allow matters to go further, I must confess to you that I have been unworthy of your affection. I should have told you when I began my visits to you that I was married. I knew that Indian students in England dissembled the fact of their marriage and I followed suit. I now see that I should not have done so. I must also add that I was married while yet a boy, and am the father of a son. I am pained that I should have kept this knowledge from you so long. But I am glad God has now given me the courage to speak out the truth. Will you forgive me? I assure you I have taken no improper liberties with the *young lady*[M20] you were good enough to introduce to me. I knew my limits. *You, not knowing that I was married, naturally desired that we should be engaged. In order that things should not go beyond the present stage, I must tell you the truth.*[M21]

M20 sister

M21 But your natural desire was that I be engaged with somebody. I must declare the truth to you so that this thing does not grow in your mind.

'If on receipt of this, you feel that I have been unworthy of your hospitality, I assure you I shall not take it amiss. You have laid me under an everlasting debt of gratitude by your kindness and solicitude. If, after this, you do not reject me but continue to regard me as worthy of your hospitality, which I will spare no pains to deserve, I shall naturally be happy and count it a further token of your kindness.'

Let the reader know that I could not have written such a letter in a moment. I must have drafted and redrafted it many times over. But it lifted a burden that was weighing me down. Almost by return post came her reply somewhat as follows:

'I have your frank letter. We were both very glad and had a hearty laugh over it. The untruth you say you have been guilty of is pardonable. But it is well that you have acquainted us with the real state of things. My invitation still stands and we shall certainly expect you next Sunday and look forward to hearing all about your child-marriage and to the pleasure of laughing at your expense. Need I assure you that our friendship is not in the least affected by this incident?'

I thus purged myself of the *canker*[M22] of untruth, and I never thenceforward hesitated to talk of my married state wherever necessary.

[M22] poison

XX

ACQUAINTANCE WITH RELIGIONS

Towards the end of my second year[M1] in England I came across two Theosophists,[384] brothers,[385] and both unmarried. They talked to me about the Gita. They were reading Sir Edwin Arnold's translation—*The Song Celestial*[386]—

[M1] After I had been a year or so

---

[384] The Theosophical Society was founded in New York on 17 November 1875 by Madam H.P. Blavatsky. Colonel Henry Steel Olcott gave the inaugural address.

[385] James Hunt writes: 'He calls them "brothers" but they have been tentatively identified as Bertram and Archibald Keightley, actually uncle and nephew, wealthy theosophists whose home at 17, Lansdowne Road, Notting Hill had been placed at Mme. Blavatsky's disposal.' *Gandhi in London*, p. 27. The identification of the Keightley 'brothers' was first done by Chandran D.S. Devanesan, *The Making of the Mahatma* (Madras: 1969), p. 202. Hunt surmises that they were probably vegetarians, which brought them in touch with MKG.

[386] *The Song Celestial* added in the English translation. Sir Edwin Arnold (1832–1904), English poet and journalist, came to India (1856–61) as principal of Government Sanskrit College, Poona.

M2 Sanskrit

M3 Gita

M4 Prakrit

and they invited me to read the *original*M2 with them. I felt ashamed, as I had read the *divine poem*M3 neither in Samskrit nor in *Gujarati*.M4 I was constrained to tell them that I had not read the Gita,[387] but that I would gladly read it with them, and that though my knowledge of Samskrit was meagre, still I hoped to be able to understand the original to the extent of telling where the translation failed to bring out the meaning. I began reading the Gita

M5 the brothers

M6 towards the end of

with *them*.M5 The verses *in*M6 the second chapter

> If one
> Ponders on objects of the sense, there springs
> Attraction; from attraction grows desire,
> Desire flames to fierce passion, passion breeds
> Recklessness; then the memory — all betrayed —
> Lets noble purpose go, and saps the mind,
> Till purpose, mind, and man are all undone.[388]

M7 Bhagvad Gita

M8 Philosophy

M9 retained the spirit of the original

made a deep impression on my mind, and they still ring in my ears. The *book*M7 struck me as one of priceless worth. The impression has ever since been growing on me with the result that I regard it today as the book *par excellence* for the knowledge of *Truth*.M8 It has afforded me invaluable help in my moments of gloom. I have read almost all the English translations of it, and I regard Sir Edwin Arnold's as the best. He has *been faithful to the text,*M9 and yet it does not read like a translation.

His other well-known poetic work is the life of Buddha, *The Light Of Asia: The Great Renunciation* (1879). *The Song Celestial* was published in 1885.

[387] MKG's first biographer Rev. Joseph Doke, however, writes: 'When he commenced, he was ashamed to find that, although he was familiar with the Sanskrit language and had frequently read the poem as a lesson, he was utterly unable to explain its subtle meanings.' Joseph Doke, *Gandhi: A Patriot in South Africa* (New Delhi: Publications Division, 1994), p. 39. It was first published in *The London Indian Chronicle* in 1909, and the first Indian edition came out in 1919.

[388] Verses 62, 63, Discourse II.

Though I read the Gita with these friends,[389] I cannot pretend to have studied it then. It was only after some years that it became a book of daily reading.[390]

The brothers also recommended *The Light of Asia*[391] by Sir Edwin Arnold, whom I *knew till then as the author only of The Song Celestial,*[M10] and I read it with even greater interest than I did the Bhagavad Gita. Once I had begun it I could not leave off. They also took me on one occasion to the Blavatsky Lodge[392] and *introduced me to*[M11] Madame Blavatsky[393] and Mrs. Besant.[394] The

[M10] had hitherto associated only with a translation of the Gita

[M11] presented me before

---

[389] 'Though I read the Gita with these friends' added in English translation.

[390] MKG's engagement with the Gita continued to deepen over the years. In 1926–27 he translated the Gita as *Anasakti Yoga* in Gujarati (published on 12 March 1930, the day he commenced the Salt March to Dandi). During his imprisonment in 1922 he wrote a lexicographic commentary on the text, published as *Gita Padarthkosha* in 1936. During his year-long stay at the Satyagraha Ashram at Ahmedabad, MKG gave, between 24 February and 27 November 1926, 218 discourses on the Gita. The imprisonments in 1930 and 1932 provided another occasion to discourse on the Gita, when he wrote a series of letters, called 'Letters on the Gita', to the inmates of his ashram, which were read out during the morning prayers. He also composed a primer on the Gita, called *Ram Gita* as it was composed for his son Ramdas. The recitation of the Gita was obligatory in the ashram prayers, both morning and evening. During the morning prayers the recitation was so arranged that the entire Gita was recited every fourteen days; later it was changed so as to complete it in seven days. The nineteen verses of Discourse II that describe the characteristics of a *Sthitaprajna* were recited daily during evening prayers.

[391] *Buddha Charitra* in the original.

[392] The Blavatsky Lodge was founded in 1887, which was the second theosophical lodge in England after the London Lodge. Archibald and Bertram Keightley were among the fourteen members who had founded the lodge, which was attended every Thursday by Mme. Blavatsky. The lodge was at 19, Avenue Road, North of Regents' Park.

[393] Helena Petrovna Blavatsky (1831–91). Among her books are *Isis Unveiled* (1877), *The Secret Doctrine* (1888), *The Voice of Silence* (1889).

[394] Mrs. Annie Besant (1847–1933), second president of the Theosophical Society (1907–33), founder of the Home Rule

M12 about

M13 sect

M14 Christianity

latter had just then joined the Theosophical Society,[395] and I was following with great interest the controversy about her conversion. The friends advised me to join the Society, but I politely declined saying, 'With my meagre knowledge *of my own*[M12] religion I do not want to belong to any religious *body*.'[M13] I recall having read, at the brothers' instance, Madame Blavatsky's *Key to Theosophy*.[396] This book stimulated in me the desire to read books on Hinduism, and disabused me of the notion fostered by the missionaries that Hinduism was rife with superstition.

About the same time I met a good Christian from Manchester in a vegetarian boarding house. He talked to me about Christianity. I narrated to him my Rajkot recollections. He was pained to hear them. He said, 'I am a vegetarian. I do not drink. Many Christians are meat-eaters and drink, no doubt; but neither meat-eating nor drinking is enjoined by *Scripture*.[M14] Do please read the Bible.' I accepted his advice, and he got me a copy. I have a faint recollection that he himself used to sell copies of the Bible, and I purchased from him an edition containing maps, concordance, and other aids. I began reading it, but I could not possibly read through

---

Movement and president, Indian National Congress (1917). In 1919, the editor of *New India* asked MKG for a birthday message to Mrs. Besant. He, in the message, recalled his first meeting with her in London and went on to add: 'I have sharp differences of opinion with her as to the methods of work. I have also been hurt to feel at times that she has lost her robust independence of 1888 and her uncompromising search after and adherence to truth at all cost. But in the midst of my doubts I have never wavered in my belief in her great devotion to India.' *CWMG*, vol. 16, p. 202.

[395] In May 1889.

[396] *The Key to Theosophy*. Being A CLEAR EXPOSITION, IN THE FORM OF QUESTION AND ANSWER, OF THE ETHICS, SCIENCE, AND PHILOSOPHY FOR THE STUDY OF WHICH THE THEOSOPHICAL SOCIETY HAS BEEN FOUNDED, first published in 1889.

the Old Testament. I read the Book of Genesis,[397] and the chapters that followed invariably sent me to sleep. But just for the sake of being able to say that I had read it, I plodded through the other books with much difficulty and without the least interest or understanding. I disliked reading the Book of Numbers.[398]

But the New Testament produced a different impression, especially the Sermon on the Mount which went straight to my heart. I[M15] compared it with the Gita. The verses, 'But I say unto you, that ye resist not evil: but whosoever shall smite thee on thy right cheek, turn to him the other also. And if any man take away thy coat let him have thy cloak too,' delighted me beyond measure and put me in mind of Shamal Bhatt's[399] 'For a bowl of water, give a goodly meal', etc.[400] My young mind tried to unify the teaching of the Gita, *The Light of Asia* and the Sermon on the Mount. That *renunciation was the highest form of religion*[M16] appealed to me greatly.

This reading whetted my appetite for studying the lives of other religious teachers. A friend recommended Carlyle's *Heroes and Hero-worship*.[401] I read the chapter on the Hero as a prophet and learnt of the Prophet's greatness and bravery and austere living.

Beyond this acquaintance with religion[402] I could not go at the moment, as reading for the examination left me scarcely any time for outside subjects. But I took

[M15] My intellect

[M16] religion inheres in renunciation

---

[397] 'Genesis' in the original. It has an explanatory phrase: 'the origin of the universe'.

[398] 'Numbers' in the original.

[399] See n. 200 in Chapter XI, Part I.

[400] '"For a bowl of water, give a goodly meal", etc.' added in the English translation. The original has 'Shamal Bhatt's verse.'

[401] Thomas Carlyle (1795–1881). *Heroes and Hero-worship and the Heroic in History* was first published in 1841.

[402] 'with religion' added in the English translation.

mental note of the fact that I should read more religious books and acquaint myself with all the principal religions.

And how could I help knowing something of atheism too? Every Indian knew Bradlaugh's[403] name and his so-called atheism. I read some book about it, the name of which I forget. It had no effect on me, for I had already crossed the Sahara of atheism. Mrs. Besant who was then very much in the limelight, had turned to theism from atheism, and that fact also strengthened my aversion to atheism. I had read her *book*[M17] *How I Became a Theosophist*.

^{M17} pamphlet

It was about this time that Bradlaugh died. He was buried in the Woking Cemetery.[404] I attended the funeral, as I believe every Indian residing in London did. A few clergymen also were present to do him the last honours. On our way back from the funeral we had to wait at the station for our train. A *champion*[M18] atheist from the crowd heckled one of these clergymen. 'Well, Sir, you believe in the existence of God?'

^{M18} wrestler

'I do,' said the good man in a low tone.

'You also agree that the circumference of the Earth is 28,000 miles, don't you?' said the atheist with a smile of self-assurance.

'Indeed.'

'Pray tell me then the size of your God and where he may be?'

'Well, if we but knew, He resides in the hearts of us both.'

'Now, now, don't take me to be a child,' said the *champion*[M19] with a triumphant look at us. The clergyman assumed a humble silence. This talk still further increased my prejudice against atheism.

^{M19} warrior

---

[403] Charles Bradlaugh (1833–91), Liberal member of the British parliament, founder of the National Secular Society (1866).

[404] Bradlaugh was cremated at the Brookwood Cemetery; Mme. Blavatsky was cremated at the Woking Cemetery.

XXI

निर्बल के बल राम[405]

Though I had acquired a nodding acquaintance with Hinduism[406] and other religions of the world, *I should have known that it would not be enough to save me in my trials.*[M1] Of the thing that sustains him through trials man has no inkling, much less knowledge, at the time. If an unbeliever, he will attribute his safety to chance. If a believer, he will say God saved him. He will conclude as well he may, that his religious study or spiritual discipline *was at the back of the state of grace within him.*[M2] But in the hour of his deliverance he does not know whether his spiritual discipline or something[407] else saves him. Who that has prided himself on his spiritual strength has not seen it humbled to the dust? A knowledge of *religion, as distinguished from experience, seems but chaff in such moments of trial.*[M3]

It was in England that I first discovered the futility of mere religious knowledge. How I was saved on previous occasions is more than I can say, for I was very young then;[408] but now I was twenty and had gained some experience as *husband and father.*[M4]

During the last year, as far as I can remember, of my stay in England, that is in 1890,[409] there was a Vegetarian

[M1] such knowledge is not sufficient to save a human being

[M2] was the reason for God's presence in his heart. He has a right to make this assumption.

[M3] scriptures at such moments seems worthless

[M4] a householder

---

[405] MD's footnote: '*Nirbal ke Bal Rama*—The refrain of one of Surdas's famous hymns. Its meaning is, "He is the help of the helpless, the strength of the weak."'

[406] '*Dharmashastra*' in the original; ancient body of jurisprudence in India, composed in Sanskrit and divided in three categories: (a) *Sutras* (maxims), (b) *Smriti* (treatise in stanza) and (c) *Nibandha* (compendium of Smriti verses) and *Vrittis* (commentaries on Smriti). In this context, Principles of Religion.

[407] 'what' in the first edition.

[408] See *CWMG*, vol. 27, p. 109.

[409] The year was 1891.

Conference at Portsmouth[410] to which an Indian friend[411] and I were invited.[412] Portsmouth is a sea-port with a large *naval population*.[M5] It has many houses with women of ill fame, women not actually prostitutes, but at the same time, not *very scrupulous about their morals*.[M6] We were put up in one of these houses. *Needless to say, the Reception Committee did not know anything about it*.[M7] It would have been difficult in a town like Portsmouth to find out which were good lodgings and which were bad for occasional travellers like us.[413]

We returned from the Conference in the evening. After dinner we sat down to play *a rubber of bridge, in which our landlady joined, as is customary in England even in respectable households*.[M8] Every player indulges in innocent jokes as a matter of course, but here my companion and our hostess began to make indecent ones as well. I did not know that my friend was an adept in the art. It captured me and I also joined in. Just when I was about to go *beyond the limit*,[M9] leaving the cards and the game to themselves, God through the good companion uttered the blessed warning: *'Whence this devil in you, my boy? Be off, quick!'*[M10]

I was ashamed. I took the warning and expressed within myself gratefulness to my friend. Remembering the vow I had taken before my mother, I fled from the scene. To my room I went quaking, trembling, and with beating heart, like a quarry escaped from its pursuer.

I recall this as the first occasion on which a woman, other than my wife, moved me to lust.[414] I passed that

---

[M5] population of sailors

[M6] unsullied either

[M7] I do not intend to say that the Reception Committee had intentionally sought such houses.

[M8] cards. In England even in respectable households, the lady of the house would play cards with the guests.

[M9] from word to deed

[M10] 'Whence this darkness in you? This is not for you. Run along now.'

---

[410] This was the Vegetarian Federal Union Conference held on 5 and 6 June 1891. MKG was appointed a delegate of the London Vegetarian Society and read out his essay, 'The Foods of India'.

[411] His sailing companion T.T. Majumdar.

[412] 'Both of us went. We were provided lodgings in a house of a woman.' To add.

[413] 'ourselves' in the first edition.

[414] 'and I desired to play games with her.' To add.

night sleeplessly, all kinds of thoughts assailing me. Should I leave this house? Should I run away from the place? Where was I? What would happen to me if I had not my wits about me? I decided to act thenceforth with great caution; not to leave the house, but somehow leave Portsmouth.[415] The Conference was not to go on for more than two days, and I remember I left Portsmouth the next evening, my companion staying there some time longer.

I did not then know the essence of religion or of God, and how He works in us. Only vaguely I understood that God had saved me on that occasion. *On all occasions of trial He has saved me.*[M11] I know that the phrase 'God saved me' has a deeper meaning for me today, and still I feel that I have not yet grasped its entire meaning. Only richer experience can help me to a fuller understanding. But in *all*[M12] my trials—of a spiritual nature, as a lawyer, in conducting institutions, and in politics—I can say that God saved me. When every hope is gone, *'when helpers fail and comforts flee'*,[416] [M13] I find[417] that help arrives somehow, from I know not where. Supplication, worship, prayer are no superstition; they are acts more real than the acts of eating, drinking, sitting or walking. It is no exaggeration to say that they alone are real, all else is unreal.

Such worship or prayer is no flight of eloquence; *it is no lip-homage. It springs from the heart.*[M14] If, therefore, we achieve that purity of the heart when it is 'emptied

[M11] I have had similar experiences in other spheres.

[M12] many of

[M13] when actions become futile,

[M14] its source is not in speech but in the heart

---

[415] 'soon.' To add.

[416] From 'Abide with Me', a hymn by Henry Francis Lyte:

'Abide with me, fast falls the eventide;
The darkness deepens, Lord with me abide.
When other helpers fail and comforts flee,
Help of the helpless, O abide with me.'

[417] 'experience' in the first edition.

M15 its music reaches the heavens

M16 It is by its very nature a mysterious thing.

M17 But to deserve such grace one must have perfect humility.

of all but love',[418] if we keep all the chords in proper tune, *they 'trembling pass in music out of sight'.*[419] M15 Prayer needs no speech. *It is in itself independent of any sensuous effort.*M16 I have not the slightest doubt that[420] prayer is an unfailing means of cleansing the heart of passions. *But it must be combined with the utmost humility.*M17

XXII

NARAYAN HEMCHANDRA[421]

Just about this time[422] Narayan Hemchandra[423] came to England. I had heard of him as a writer.[424] We met at

---

[418] 'emptied of all but love' added in the English translation. The phrase is from a hymn by Charles Wesley:

'He left his father's throne above,
So free, so infinite his grace,
Emptied himself of all but love,
And bled for Adam's helpless race.'

[419] The line is from Alfred Tennyson's 'Locksley Hall':

'Love took up the harp of Life, and smote on all the chords with might;
Smote the chord of Self, that, trembling, pass'd in music out of sight.'

[420] 'heartfelt' to add.

[421] This chapter was first published, without a title, in Gujarati in *Navajivan*, vol. VII, no. 47, 25 July 1926, after Chapter XI of Part II. In *Young India* it was published in vol. VIII, no. 40, 7 October 1926, after Chapter XXI of Part II under the title 'Narayan Hemchandra' with a footnote by MD: 'This is one of the two chapters newly added to the "Story of My Experiments with Truth," Part I. It will follow Chapter XXI, Part I.'

[422] 'Late' to add.

[423] Narayan Hemchandra (1855–1904) in 1900 published his autobiography *Hu, Pote* (lit., I, Myself). In his 'Guide to London' MKG wrote of him, 'Sadhu Narayan Hemchandra has been living on one pound a week. He has a room for 6s a week. He spends 3 or 4d for washing and 7s for food per week.' *CWMG*, vol. 1, p. 8.

[424] 'I know of a biography of the Prophet [that] was written by Narayan Hemchandra.' *CWMG*, vol. 11, p. 154.

the house of Miss Manning[425] of the National Indian Association.[426] Miss Manning knew that I could not make myself sociable. When I went to her place[427] I used to sit tongue-tied, never speaking except when spoken to. She introduced me to Narayan Hemchandra. He did not know English. His dress was queer—a clumsy pair of trousers, a wrinkled, dirty,[428] brown coat after the Parsi fashion, no necktie or collar,[429] and a tasselled woollen cap. He grew a long beard.

He was lightly built and short of stature. His round face was scarred with small-pox, and had a nose which was neither pointed nor blunt. With his hand he was constantly turning over his beard.

Such a queer-looking and queerly dressed person was bound to be singled out in fashionable society.[M1]

'I have heard a good deal about you,' I said to him. 'I have also read some of your writings. I should be very pleased if you were kind enough to come to my place.'

Narayan Hemchandra had a rather hoarse voice. With a smile on his face he replied:

'Yes, where do you stay?'
    'In Store Street.'

[M1] Among fashionable people Narayan Hemchandra seemed queer and stood out.

---

[425] Elizabeth Adelaide Manning (1828–1905), secretary, Frobel Society, honorary secretary, National Indian Association (1887–1905), and editor, *The Indian Magazine and Review*. Writing her obituary in 1905, MKG said: 'She was a true friend of Indians who went to England to study. Her house was ever open to receive them. Her guidance was always at their disposal.' *CWMG*, vol. 5, p. 62.

[426] National Indian Association (1870–1948), founded by Mary Carpenter in Bristol with assistance of Keshub Chunder Sen. It was originally called National Indian Association in Aid of Social Progress in India. In 1871, Elizabeth Manning and her stepmother Mrs. Charlotte Manning started the London branch. Its initial aim was to encourage female education in India. As the number of Indians in Britain grew, it sought to facilitate social intercourse between visiting Indians and the British.

[427] Her house was at Pembridge Crescent in Notting Hill.

[428] 'at the collars' to add.

[429] 'coat', 'necktie', 'collar' English words in the original.

'Then we are neighbours. I want to learn English. Will you teach me?'

'I shall be happy to teach you anything I can, and will try my best. If you like, I will go to your place.'

'Oh, no. I shall come to you. I shall also bring with me a *Translation Exercise Book*.'[M2] So we made an appointment. Soon we were close friends.

Narayan Hemchandra was innocent of grammar. 'Horse' was a verb with him and 'run' a noun. I remember many such funny instances. *But he was not to be baffled by his ignorance.*[M3] My little knowledge of grammar could make no impression on him. Certainly he never regarded his ignorance of grammar as a matter for shame.

With perfect nonchalance he said:[430] 'I have never been to school like you. I have never felt the need of grammar in expressing my thoughts. Well, do you know Bengali? I know it. I have travelled in Bengal. It is I who have given Maharshi Devendranath Tagore's[431] works to the Gujarati-speaking world. And I wish to translate into Gujarati the treasures of many other languages. And you know I am never literal in my translations. I always content myself with bringing out the spirit. *Others, with their better knowledge, may be able to do more in future.*[M4] But I am quite satisfied with what I have achieved without the help of grammar.[432] I know Marathi, Hindi, Bengali,[433] and now I have begun to know English.[434] What I want is a copious vocabulary.

M2 text-book

M3 But Narayan Hemchandra would have made a drink out of me.

M4 Let others dwell deeper after me.

---

[430] 'With perfect nonchalance he said:' added in the English translation.

[431] Maharshi Devendranath Tagore (1817–1905), son of Prince Dwarkanath Tagore, one of the founders of the Brahmo Samaj (1848), large landowner, father of poet Rabindranath Tagore.

[432] 'But I am quite satisfied with what I have achieved without the help of grammar.' Added in the English translation.

[433] 'Bengali' added in the English translation.

[434] 'without knowledge of grammar' to add.

And do you think my ambition ends here? No fear.[M5] I want to go to France and learn French. I am told that language has an extensive literature. I shall go to Germany also, if possible, and there learn German.' And thus he would talk on unceasingly. He had a boundless ambition for learning languages and for foreign travel.

'Then you will go to America also?'

'Certainly. How can I return to India without having seen the New World?'

'But where will you find the money?'

'What do I need money for? I am not a fashionable fellow like you. *The minimum amount of food and the minimum amount of clothing suffice for me.*[M6] And for this what little I get out of my books and from my friends is enough. I always travel third class. While going to America also I shall travel on deck.'

Narayan Hemchandra's simplicity was all his own, and his frankness was on a par with it. Of pride he had not the slightest trace, excepting, of course, a rather undue regard for his own capacity as a writer.

We met daily. There was a considerable amount of similarity between our thoughts and actions. Both of us were vegetarians. We would often have our lunch together. This was the time when I lived on 17s. a week and cooked for myself. Sometimes I would go to his room, and sometimes he would come to mine. I cooked in the English style. Nothing but Indian style would satisfy him. He could not do without dal. I would make soup[435] of carrots, etc., and he would pity me for my taste. Once he somehow hunted out *mung*,[436] cooked it and brought it to my place. I ate it with delight. This led on to a regular system of exchange between us. I would take my delicacies to him and he would bring his to me.

M5 And do not think I would be content with knowing only English.

M6 How much do I need to eat and wear?

---

[435] 'soup' English word in the original.

[436] MD's footnote: 'An Indian pulse.'

Cardinal Manning's[437] name was then on every lip. The dock labourers' strike[438] had come to an early termination owing to the efforts of John Burns[439] and Cardinal Manning. I told Narayan Hemchandra of Disraeli's[440] tribute[441] to the Cardinal's simplicity. 'Then I must see the sage,' said he.

'He is a big man. How do you expect to meet him?'

'Why? I know how. I must get you to write to him in my name. Tell him I am an author and that I want to congratulate him personally on his humanitarian work, and also say that I shall have to take you as interpreter as I do not know English.'

I wrote a letter to that effect. In two or three days came Cardinal Manning's card in reply giving us an appointment. So we both called on the Cardinal.[442] I put on the *usual visiting suit*.[M7] Narayan Hemchandra

[M7] customary clothes for calling on people

---

[437] Henry Edward Manning (1808–92), Cardinal Manning, was Roman Catholic Archbishop of Westminster (appointed 1865).

[438] The London Dock Strike of 1889 involved 1,00,000 dock workers. The strike began on 14 August 1889 over a dispute of payment of 'plus money' or bonus for speedy completion of work. It led to the establishment of trade unions among dock workers.

[439] John Elliot Burns (1858–1943), trade unionist, Liberal member of the British parliament.

[440] Benjamin Disraeli (1804–1881), twice served as the prime minister of the UK, his novel *Lothair* was published in 1870.

[441] In 'Guide to London' MKG wrote about Cardinal Manning: 'There are, to take a noted and living example, few harder working men in England than Archbishop Manning, a man full of cares and labours, yet I am assured by those who have had the most intimate personal relations with him that Mr. Disraeli in "Lothair" has not in the least exaggerated his habitual abstinence and that his ordinary meal, in public or private, is a biscuit or a bit of bread and a glass of water.' *CWMG*, vol. 1, p. 87.

[442] Cardinal Manning's residence was at Carlisle Place, Vauxhall Bridge Road, near Westminster Cathedral.

was the same as ever, in the same coat and the same trousers. I tried to make fun of this, but he laughed me out and said:

'You civilized fellows are all cowards. Great men never look at *a person's exterior.*[M8] They think of his heart.'

[M8] anyone's clothes

We entered the Cardinal's mansion.[443] As soon as we were seated, a thin, tall, old gentleman made his appearance, and shook hands with us. *Narayan Hemchandra thus gave his greetings:* [M9]

[M9] He welcomed Narayan Hemchandra.

'I do not want to take up your time. I had heard a lot about you and I felt I should come and thank you for the good work you have done for the strikers. It has been my custom to visit the sages of the world and that is why I have put you to this trouble.'

This was of course my translation of what he spoke in Gujarati.[M10] 'I am glad you have come. I hope your stay in London will agree with you and that you will get in touch with people here. God bless you.'

[M10] Narayan Hemchandra directed me to translate these lines.

With these words the Cardinal stood up and said good-bye.

Once Narayan Hemchandra came to my place in a shirt and dhoti. The good landlady opened the door, came running to me in a fright—*this was a new landlady who did not know Narayan Hemchandra*[M11]—and said: 'A sort of a madcap wants to see you.' I went to the door and to my surprise found Narayan Hemchandra. I was shocked. His face, however, showed nothing but his usual smile.

[M11] the reader will recall that I kept changing my lodging

'But did not the children in the street rag you?'

'Well, they ran after me, but I did not mind them and they were quiet.'

---

[443] 'The house was indeed a mansion.' To add.

Narayan Hemchandra went to Paris after a few months' stay in London. He began studying French and also translating French books. I knew enough French to revise his translation, so he gave it to me to read. It was not a translation, it was the[444] substance.

Finally he carried out his determination to visit America. It was with great difficulty that he succeeded in securing a deck ticket. While in the United States he was *prosecuted*[M12] for 'being indecently dressed', as he once went out in a shirt and dhoti. I have a recollection that he was discharged.

M12 arrested

XXIII

THE GREAT EXHIBITION[445]

There was a great Exhibition at Paris in 1890.[446] I had read about its elaborate preparations, and I also had a keen desire to see Paris. So I thought I had better combine two things in one and go there at this juncture. A particular attraction of the Exhibition was the Eiffel Tower, constructed entirely of iron, and nearly 1,000 feet high. *There were of course many other things of interest, but the Tower was the chief one, inasmuch as it had been supposed till then that a structure of that height could not safely stand.*[M1]

M1 Before this there was a supposition that a building one thousand feet high cannot stand. Apart from this, there was much else on display.

---

[444] 'a' in the first edition.

[445] This chapter was first published, without a title, in *Navajivan*, vol. 7, no. 49 of 8 August 1926, after Chapter XIII of Part II. In *Young India* it was published in vol. VIII, no. 41, after Chapter XXII of Part II dated 14 October 1926, under the title 'The Great Exhibition', which was later adapted for Gujarati as well. It carried a footnote by MD: 'This is the second of the two chapters newly added to the "Story of My Experiments with Truth", Part I. It will follow chapter XXII.'

[446] The Great Exhibition opened in Paris on 5 May 1889.

I had *heard of*[M2] a vegetarian restaurant in Paris. I engaged a room there and stayed seven days.[447] I managed everything very economically, both the journey to Paris and the sightseeing there. This I did mostly on foot and with the help of a map of Paris, as also a map of and guide to the Exhibition. These were enough to direct one to the main streets and chief places of interest.

I remember nothing of the Exhibition excepting its magnitude and variety. I have fair recollection of the Eiffel Tower as I ascended it twice or thrice. There was a restaurant on the first platform, and just for the satisfaction of being able to say that I had had my lunch at a great height, I *threw away seven shillings on*[M3] it.

The ancient churches of Paris are still in my memory. Their grandeur and their peacefulness are unforgettable. The wonderful construction of Notre Dame and the elaborate decoration of the interior with its beautiful sculptures cannot be forgotten. I felt then that those who expended millions on such divine cathedrals could not but have the love of God in their hearts.

I had read a lot about the fashions and frivolity[448] of Paris. These were in evidence in every street, but the churches stood noticeably apart from these scenes. A man would forget the outside noise and bustle as soon as he entered one of these churches. His manner would change, he would behave with dignity and reverence[449] *as he passed*[M4] someone kneeling before the image of the Virgin. The feeling I had then has since been growing on me, that all this kneeling and prayer could not be

[M2] read about

[M3] burnt seven shillings for

[M4] There was no noise and there was always

---

[447] According to James Hunt, this was probably the hotel of Madam T. Walker at 21, Avenue Carnot, l'Arc de Triomphe, which was advertised in *The Vegetarian Messenger* of this period. 'Gandhi in London', p. 223.

[448] 'and debauchery' to add.

[449] 'and reverence' added in the English translation.

M5 power of imagination that it was imbued with

M6 few words

M7 So long as we are ensnared by temptation, we too are children. This tower is good proof of this, and this may be considered its usefulness.

mere superstition; the devout souls kneeling before the Virgin could not be worshipping mere marble. They were fired with genuine devotion and they worshipped not stone, but the *divinity of which it was symbolic*.M5 I have an impression that I felt then that by this worship they were not detracting from, but increasing, the glory of God.

I must say *a word*M6 about the Eiffel Tower. I do not know what purpose it serves today.[450] But I then heard it greatly disparaged as well as praised. I remember that Tolstoy[451] was the chief among those who disparaged it. He said that the Eiffel Tower was a monument of man's folly, not of his wisdom. Tobacco, he argued, was the worst of all intoxicants, inasmuch as a man addicted to it was tempted to commit crimes which a drunkard never dared to do; liquor made a man mad, but tobacco clouded his intellect and made him build castles in the air.[452] The Eiffel Tower was one of the[453] creations of a man under such influence.

There is[454] no art about the Eiffel Tower. In no way can it be said to have contributed to the real beauty of the Exhibition. Men flocked to see it and ascended it as it was a novelty and of unique dimensions. It was the toy of the Exhibition. *So long as we are children we are attracted by toys, and the Tower was a good demonstration of the fact that we are all children attracted by trinkets.*M7 That may be claimed to be the purpose served by the Eiffel Tower.

---

[450] 'Having visited an exhibition, one also reads accounts of it.' To add.

[451] Count Leo Nikolayevich Tolstoy (1828–1910). The specific reference is to his essay 'Why do Men Stupefy Themselves?'

[452] 'Tolstoy declared that' to add.

[453] 'these' in the first edition.

[454] 'certainly' to add.

XXIV

'CALLED'—BUT THEN?

I have deferred saying anything up to now about the purpose for which I went to England, viz., being called to the bar.[455] It is time to advert to it briefly.

There were two conditions which had to be fulfilled before a student was formally called to the bar: 'keeping terms', *twelve terms equivalent to about three years;*[M1] and passing examinations. 'Keeping terms' meant eating one's terms, i.e., attending at least six out of about twenty-four dinners in a term.[456] Eating did not mean actually partaking of the dinner, it meant reporting oneself at the fixed hours and remaining present throughout the dinner. Usually of course everyone ate and drank the good commons and choice wines provided.[457] A dinner cost from two and six to three and six, that is from two to three rupees. This was considered moderate, inasmuch as one had to pay that same amount for wines alone if one dined at a hotel. To us in India it is a matter for surprise, if we are not 'civilized',[458] that the cost of drink

M1 —there are four terms a year, twelve such terms had to be kept—

---

[455] There are two classes of lawyers in England: solicitors and barristers. All barristers are members of one of the four societies called the Inns of Court. They are the Inner Temple (1388), the Middle Temple (1388), Lincoln's Inn (1422) and Gray's Inn (1388). In his 'Guide to London' MKG does not recommend, from the point of view of economy, his own inn, the Inner Temple, the most prestigious and the most expensive of the four. He says, 'From an economic point of view, the Lincoln's Inn is the best Inn, which boasts also of the best library.' *CWMG*, vol. 1, p. 108.

[456] A pupil at the Inner Temple was required to attend seventy-two dinners, called 'keeping terms' to qualify for being called to the Bar. English word 'term' in the original.

[457] 'Of course, they had to be paid for.' To add.

[458] The word in the original is 'sudhriya', from 'sudhar'. Generally translated as 'reform'; MKG consistently writes of sudhar

should exceed the cost of food. The first revelation gave
me a great shock, and I wondered how people had the
heart to throw away so much money on drink. Later I
came to understand. I often ate nothing at these dinners,
for the things that I might eat were only bread, boiled
potato and cabbage. In the beginning I did not eat these,
as I did not like them; and later, when I began to relish
them, I also gained the courage to ask for other dishes.

The dinner provided for the benchers[459] used to be
better than that for the students. A Parsi student, who
was also a vegetarian, and I applied, in the interests of
vegetarianism, for the vegetarian courses which were
served to the benchers. The application was granted,
and we began to get fruits and other vegetables from the
benchers' table.[460]

Two bottles of wine were allowed to each group of
four, and as I did not touch them, I was ever in demand
to form a quartet, so that three might empty two
bottles. And there was a 'grand night'[461] in each term
when extra wines, like champagne, in addition to port
and sherry,[462] were served.[463] I was therefore specially
requested to attend and was in great demand on that
'grand night'.

I could not see then, nor have I seen since, how these
dinners qualified the students better for the bar. There
was once a time when only a few students used to attend

---

as civilization, not just in the *Autobiography* but also in his
philosophical text, *Hind Swaraj*.

[459] 'benchers' English word in the original. The Gujarati has an
explanation of the word within parenthesis, which literally
translates into 'elders of the temple of learning'.

[460] 'table' English word in the original.

[461] In the original 'grand night' is in parenthesis. The term used
literally means 'heavy night'.

[462] 'champagne', 'port', 'sherry', in the original.

[463] 'The taste of champagne is considered a class by itself.' To add.

these dinners and thus there were opportunities for talks between them and the benchers, and speeches were also made. These occasions helped to give them knowledge of the world with a sort of polish and refinement, and also improved their power of speaking. No such thing was possible in my time, as the benchers *had a table all to themselves.*[464] M2 The institution had gradually lost all its meaning, but conservative[465] England retained it nevertheless.

M2 sat at a distance like untouchables

The curriculum of study was easy, barristers being humorously known as 'dinner barristers'.[466] Everyone knew that the examinations had practically no value. In my time there were two, one in Roman Law and the other in Common Law.[467] There were regular text-books prescribed for these examinations which could be taken in compartments,[468] but scarcely anyone read them. I have known many to pass the Roman Law examination by scrambling through[469] notes on Roman Law in a couple of weeks, and the Common Law examination by reading notes on the subject in two or three months. Question papers were easy and examiners were generous. The percentage of passes in the Roman Law examination used to be 95 to 99 and of those in the final examination 75 or even more. There was thus

---

[464] 'the benchers always sitting at a respectable distance from the students.' In the first edition.

[465] 'slow-changing' to add.

[466] 'dinner barristers' in the original. The Gujarati has in parenthesis the word 'khana', literally, 'meals'.

[467] In the original 'Laws of England'.

[468] The examination in Roman Law could be taken after keeping four terms and the one in Common Law required the eligibility of nine terms. MKG took his Roman Law examinations from 25–28 March 1890, in the Easter Term, and the Common Law examination from 15–20 December 1890.

[469] 'brief' to add.

M3 Examinations with such
facilities

little fear of being plucked, and examinations were held
not once but four times in the year. *They*[470] M3 could not
be felt as a difficulty.

But I succeeded in turning them into one. I felt
that I should read all the text-books. It was a fraud,
I thought, not to read these books. I invested much
money in them.[471] I decided to read Roman Law in
Latin. The Latin which I had acquired in the London
Matriculation stood me in good stead. And all this
reading was not without its value later on in South
Africa, where Roman Dutch is the common law. The
reading of Justinian,[472] therefore, helped me a great deal
in understanding the South African law.

It took me nine months of fairly hard labour to read
through the Common Law of England. For Broom's
Common Law,[473] a big but interesting volume, took up
a good deal of time. Snell's *Equity*[474] was full of interest,
but a bit hard to understand. White and Tudor's *Leading
Cases*,[475] from which certain cases were prescribed,
was full of interest and instruction. I read also with
interest Williams'[476] and Edwards'[477] *Real Property*, and

---

[470] 'These convenient examinations' in the first edition.

[471] MKG would have spent £10 for the books. In his 'Guide to
London' he gave a list of books required, with their prices after
a 20 per cent discount, which the booksellers offered on law
books. *CWMG*, vol. 1, p. 111.

[472] Thomas Collett Saunders, *The Institutes of Justinian; with English
Introduction, Translation and Notes* (1859).

[473] Herbert Broom, *Commentaries on Common Law, Designed as
Introductory to its Study*, eighth edition (1888).

[474] Edmund H.T. Snell, *The Principles of Equity, Intended for the Use of
Students and the Profession*, eighth edition (1887).

[475] Frederick T. White and Owen D. Tudor, *Leading Cases in
Equity*, sixth edition (1886).

[476] Joshua Williams, *Principles of the Law of Real Property, Intended as a
first book for the use of students in conveyancing*, sixteenth edition (1887).

[477] William Douglas Edwards, *A Compendium of the Law of Property
in Land* (1888).

Goodeve's *Personal Property*.[478] Williams' book read like a novel. The one book I remember to have read on my return to India, with the same unflagging interest, was Mayne's *Hindu Law*.[479] But it is out of place to talk here of Indian law-books.

I passed my examinations,[480] was called to the bar on the 10th of June 1891, and enrolled in the High Court on the 11th.[481] On the 12th I sailed for home.

But notwithstanding my study there was no end to my helplessness and fear. I did not feel myself qualified to practise law.

But a separate chapter is needed to describe this *helplessness*[M4] of mine.

[M4] agony

XXV

MY HELPLESSNESS[482]

It was easy[483] to be called, but it was difficult to practise at the bar. I had read the laws, but not learnt how to practise law. I had read with interest *'Legal Maxims'*,[M1] but did not know how to apply them in my profession. *'Sic utere tuo ut alienum non laedas'*[484] (Use your property

[M1] 'Moral Maxims in Law'

---

[478] Two volumes by Louis A. Goodeve, *The Modern Law of Real Property, with an Introduction for the Student,* second edition (1885), and *The Modern Law of Personal Property* (1887).

[479] John D. Mayne, *A Treatise on Hindu Law and Usage* (1876).

[480] He passed it on 12 January 1891. He was 34th in the field of 109 of whom 77 passed.

[481] 'by paying two and a half shillings' to add.

[482] In *Navajivan* the title is 'Mari Pamarta', literally, 'My Timidity'. The word 'pamarta' was changed to 'munjvan', which would translate as predicament, dilemma, quandary, plight.

[483] 'easy enough to be called' in the first edition.

[484] In the original the maxim in Latin is not given. MKG called it a 'grand doctrine of life' and added, 'It is the key to a proper practice of ahimsa or love.' *CWMG*, vol. 13, p. 224.

M2 is a moral injunction

M3 in the laws that I had read,
there was not even the name of
Indian law

in such a way as not to damage that of others) *was one of them*,[M2] but I was at a loss to know how one could employ this maxim for the benefit of one's client.[485] I had read all the leading cases on this maxim, but they gave me no confidence in the application of it in the practice of law.

Besides, *I had learnt nothing at all of Indian law.*[M3] I had not the slightest idea of Hindu and Mahomedan Law. I had not even learnt how to draft a plaint, and felt completely at sea. I had heard of Sir Pherozeshah Mehta[486] as one who roared like a lion in law-courts. How, I wondered, could he have learnt the art in England? It was out of the question for me[487] ever to acquire his legal acumen, but I had serious misgivings as to whether I should be able even to earn a living by the profession.

I was torn with these doubts and anxieties whilst I was studying law. I confided my difficulties to some of my friends. One of them suggested that I should seek Dadabhai Naoroji's advice. I have already said that, when I went to England, I possessed a note of introduction to Dadabhai. I availed myself of it very late. I thought I had no right to trouble such a great man for an interview. Whenever an address by him was announced, I would attend it, listen to him from a corner of the hall and go away after having feasted my eyes and ears. In order to come in close touch with the students

---

[485] 'case' to add. 'case' English word in the original.

[486] Sir Pherozeshah Mehta (1845–1915), drew up the Municipal Act of 1872. He was of the Bombay Legislative Council, elected to the Governor General's Supreme Legislative Council in 1893. President, Indian National Congress (1890), knighted in 1904, vice-chancellor, University of Bombay (1911), founded *Bombay Chronicle* (1910) and helped found the Central Bank of India.

[487] 'in this life' to add.

he had founded an association.[488] I used to attend its
meetings, and rejoiced at Dadabhai's solicitude for the
students, and the latter's respect for him. In course of
time I mustered up courage to present to him the note
of introduction. He[489] said: 'You can come and have
my advice whenever you like.' But I never availed
myself of his offer. I thought it wrong to trouble him
without the most pressing necessity. Therefore I dared
not venture to accept my friend's advice to submit
my difficulties to Dadabhai at that time. I forget now
whether it was the same friend or someone else who
recommended me to meet Mr. Frederick Pincott.[490]
He was a Conservative, but his affection for Indian
students was pure and unselfish. Many students sought
his advice and I also applied to him for an appointment,
which he granted. I can never forget that interview. He
greeted me as a friend. He laughed away my pessimism.
'Do you think,' he said, 'that everyone must be a
Pherozeshah Mehta? Pherozeshahs and Badruddins[491]
are rare. Rest assured it takes no unusual skill to be
an ordinary lawyer. Common honesty and industry are
enough to enable him to make a living. All cases are
not complicated. Well, let me know the extent of your
general reading.'

When I acquainted him with my little stock of
reading, he was, as I could see, rather disappointed.
But it was only for a moment. Soon his face beamed

---

[488] East India Association, founded in 1867. The meetings took
place at the Westminster Town Hall.

[489] 'had' to add.

[490] Frederick Pincott, also the translator of 'Chaturbhujmasa' of
Lallu Lal Kavi as *Prem Sagara or the Ocean of Love* (1897).

[491] Sir Badruddin Tyabji (1844–1906), called to the Bar in April
1867 from the Middle Temple, third president of the Indian
National Congress, appointed judge, High Court of Bombay,
1895.

with a pleasing smile and he said, 'I understand your trouble. Your general reading is meagre. You have no knowledge of the world, a *sine qua non* for a *vakil*. You have not even read the history of India. A *vakil* should know human nature. He should be able to read a man's character from his face. And every Indian ought to know Indian history. This has no connection with the practice of law, but you ought to have that knowledge. I see that you have not even read Kaye and Malleson's history of the Mutiny of 1857.[492] Get hold of that at once and also read two more books to understand human nature.' These were Lavator's[493] and Shemmelpennick's[494] books on physiognomy.

I was extremely grateful to this venerable friend. In his presence I found all my fear gone, but as soon as I left him I began to worry again. 'To know a man from his face' was the *question that haunted me*,[M4] as I thought of the two books on my way home. The next day I purchased Lavator's book. Shemmelpennick's was not available at the shop. I read Lavator's book and found it more difficult than Snell's *Equity*, and scarcely interesting. I studied Shakespeare's physiognomy, but did not acquire the knack of finding out the Shakespeares walking up and down the streets of London.

Lavator's book did not add to my knowledge. Mr. Pincott's advice did me very little direct service, but his kindness[495] stood me in good stead. His smiling open face stayed in my memory, and I trusted his advice that Pherozeshah Mehta's acumen, memory and ability were not essential to the making of a successful lawyer;

[M4] sentence I memorized

---

[492] Sir John William Kaye (1814–76) and George Bruce Malleson (1825–1898), *History of the Indian Mutiny of 1857–58* (1889).

[493] Johann Kasper Lavater (1741–1801), *Essays on Physiognomy*.

[494] Mary Anne Shemmelpennick (1778–1856), *Theory on the Classification of Beauty and Deformity* (1815).

[495] 'affection' in the first edition.

honesty and industry were enough. And as I had a fair share of these last I felt somewhat reassured.

I could not read Kaye and Malleson's volumes in England, but I did so in South Africa as I had made a point of reading them at the first opportunity.

Thus with just a little leaven of hope mixed with my despair, I landed at Bombay from *s.s. Assam*.[496] The sea was rough in the harbour, and I had to reach the quay in a launch.[497]

[496] He sailed from London on 12 June 1891, by *S.S Oceania*. At Aden the passengers for Bombay were transferred to *S.S Assam* on 30 June 1891 and reached Bombay on 5 July 1891.

[497] 'launch' English word in the original.

PART II

I

RAYCHANDBHAI

I said in the last chapter that the sea was rough in Bombay harbour, not an unusual thing in the Arabian Sea in June and July. It had been choppy all the way from Aden. Almost every passenger was sick; I alone was in perfect form, staying on deck to see the stormy surge, and enjoying the splash of the waves. At breakfast there would be just one or two people besides myself, eating their oatmeal porridge from plates carefully held in their laps, lest the porridge itself find its place there.

The outer storm was to me a symbol of the inner. But even as the former left me unperturbed, I think I can say the same thing about the latter. *There was the trouble with the caste[1] that was to confront me.*[M1] I have already adverted to my *helplessness in starting on my profession.*[M2] And then, as I was a reformer, I was taxing myself as to *how best to begin certain reforms. But there was even more in store for me than I knew.*[M3]

My elder brother had come to meet me at the dock. He had already made the acquaintance of Dr. Mehta and his elder brother,[2] and as Dr. Mehta insisted on putting me up at his house, we went there. Thus the acquaintance

[M1] There was of course the question of the caste.

[M2] concerns about my profession

[M3] certain reforms that I had conceived. Others arose unexpectedly

---

[1] The Modh Bania caste of Porbandar, at the request of the Gandhi family, had resolved on 2 July 1891 to take MKG back into the caste fold, provided he performed purification rites.

[2] Revashankar Jagjivan.

175

begun in England continued in India and ripened into a permanent friendship between the two families.

I was pining to see my mother.[3] I did not know that she was no more[4] in the flesh to receive me back into her bosom.[5] The sad news was now given me, and I underwent the usual ablution. My brother had kept me ignorant of her death, which took place whilst I was still in England. He wanted to spare me the blow in a foreign land. *The news, however, was none the less a severe shock to me. But I must not dwell upon it.*[M4] My grief was even greater than over my father's death. Most of my cherished hopes were shattered. But I remember that *I did not give myself up to any wild expression of grief.*[M5] I could even check the tears, and took to life just as though nothing had happened.

Dr. Mehta introduced me to several friends, one of them being his brother Shri Revashankar Jagjivan,[6] with whom there grew up a lifelong friendship. But the introduction that I need particularly take note of was the one to the poet Raychand or Rajchandra,[7] the son-in-law of an elder brother of Dr. Mehta, and partner[8] of the firm of jewellers conducted in the name of Revashankar Jagjivan. He was not above twenty-five then, but my

[M4] And I wish to draw a veil over my grief.

[M5] on hearing the news I did not wail inconsolably

---

[3] 'I was pining to see my mother.' Added in the English translation.

[4] Putlibai passed away probably around 12 June 1891.

[5] 'in the flesh to receive me back into her bosom' added in the English translation.

[6] His house 'Mani Bhavan' on 19, Laburnum Road, Bombay, hosted MKG on numerous occasions and is now a memorial museum and a library.

[7] Raychandbhai Ravjibhai Mehta (1867–1901), born at Vavania village, died at Rajkot. He was married to Jhabakbehn, daughter of Revashankar Mehta. On his passing MKG wrote: 'It was hard to believe the news. I can't put it out of my mind.' *CWMG*, vol. 3, pp. 230–31. MKG wrote five chapters towards a biography of Raychandbhai—*CWMG*, vol. 32, pp. 1–13—and referred to him as Kavi, poet, a title he later used for Rabindranath Tagore.

[8] 'and manager' to add.

first meeting with him convinced me that he was a man of great character and learning. He was also known as *shatavadhani* (one having the faculty of remembering or attending to a hundred things simultaneously),[9] and Dr. Mehta recommended me to see some of his memory feats. I exhausted my vocabulary of all the European tongues I knew,[10] and asked the poet to repeat the words. He did so in the precise order in which I had given them. I envied his gift without, however, coming under its spell. The thing that did cast its spell over me I came to know afterwards. This was his wide knowledge of the scriptures, his spotless character, and his burning passion for self-realization. I saw later that *this last*[M6] was the only thing for which he lived. The following lines of Muktanand[11] were always on his lips and engraved on the tablets of his heart:

M6 self-realization

> 'I shall think myself blessed only when I see Him
> In every one of my daily acts;
> Verily he is the thread,
> Which supports Muktanand's life.'

Raychandbhai's commercial transactions covered hundreds of thousands. He was a connoisseur of pearls and diamonds. No knotty business problem was too difficult for him. But all these things were not the centre round which his life revolved. That[12] centre was the passion[13]

---

[9] The explanation '(one having the faculty of remembering or attending to a hundred things simultaneously)' added in the English translation. In 1887 Raychandbhai is said to have given a demonstration in Bombay before an audience which included Sir Charles Sargent, the chief justice, Bombay High Court.

[10] 'of all the European tongues I knew' added in the English translation.

[11] Muktanand (1758–1830), a poet of the Swaminarayan sect.

[12] 'The' in the first edition.

[13] 'the endeavour' to add.

to see God face to face.[14] Amongst the[15] things on his business table there were invariably to be found some religious book and his diary. The moment he finished his business he opened the religious book or the diary. Much of his published writings is a reproduction from this diary.[16] The man who, immediately on finishing his talk about weighty business transactions, began to write about the hidden things of the spirit could evidently not be a businessman at all, but a real seeker after Truth. And I saw him thus absorbed in godly pursuits in the midst of business, not once or twice,[17] but very often. I never saw him *lose his state of equipoise.*[M7] There was no business or other selfish tie that bound him to me, and yet I enjoyed the closest association with him. I was but a *briefless*[M8] barrister then, and yet whenever I saw him he would engage me in conversation of a seriously religious nature. Though I was then groping and could not be said to have any serious interest in religious discussion, still I found his talk of absorbing interest. I have since met many a religious leader or teacher. I have tried to meet the heads of various faiths, and I must say that no one else has ever made on me the impression that Raychandbhai did. His words went straight home to me. His intellect compelled as great a regard from me as his moral earnestness, and deep down in me was the conviction that he would never willingly lead me astray and would always *confide to me his innermost thoughts.*[M9] In my moments of spiritual crisis, therefore, he was my refuge.

[M7] in a state of stupefaction

[M8] pauper

[M9] tell me what was on his mind

---

[14] 'to attain self-realization'. To add.

[15] 'other' in the first edition.

[16] In 1951, all his writings were published in a single volume, *Srimad Rajchandra* (Srimad Rajchandra Ashram, Agas). MKG quite often quoted two lines from Raychandbhai's poem: 'When shall I know the state supreme, when will the knots, outer and inner, snap?' *CWMG*, vol. 32, p. 6.

[17] 'or twice' added in the English translation.

And yet in spite of this regard for him I could not enthrone him in my heart as my[18] Guru. The throne has remained vacant and[19] my search still continues.

I believe in the Hindu theory of Guru and his importance in spiritual realization. I think there is a great deal of truth in the doctrine that true knowledge is impossible without a Guru. An imperfect teacher may be tolerable in *mundane matters*,[M10] but not in spiritual matters.[20] Only a perfect *Jnani*[21] deserves to be enthroned as Guru. *There must, therefore, be ceaseless striving after perfection.*[M11] For one gets the Guru that one deserves. Infinite striving after perfection is one's right. It is its own reward. The rest is in the hands of God.

Thus, though I could not place Raychandbhai on the throne of my heart as[22] Guru, we shall see how he was, on many occasions, my *guide and helper*.[23][M12] Three moderns have left a deep impress on my life, and captivated me: Raychandbhai by his living contact; Tolstoy by his book, *The Kingdom of God Is within You*;[24] and Ruskin[25] by his *Unto This Last*. But of these more in their proper place.

M10 knowledge of letters

M11 Success lies in finding a Guru.

M12 refuge

---

[18] 'religious' to add.

[19] 'The throne has remained vacant' added in English translation.

[20] In the first edition: 'An imperfect teacher in mundane matters may be tolerable but not so an imperfect one in spiritual matters.'

[21] MD's footnote: 'A Knowing one, a seer.'

[22] 'my' in the first edition.

[23] 'It will suffice here to state that' to add.

[24] In an appendix to his *Hind Swaraj*, MKG cites the following books by Tolstoy as 'Some Authorities' which were recommended as a follow-up study of the ideas expressed in the text: *The Kingdom of God Is Within You, What is Art?, The Slavery of Our Times, The First Step, How Shall We Escape, Letter to a Hindoo.*

[25] John Ruskin (1819–1900). Chapter XVIII of Part IV of the *Autobiography* deals with the 'Magic Spell' of Ruskin's *Unto This Last*, which MKG translated into Gujarati as *Sarvodaya*. He cites, apart from *Unto This Last*, Ruskin's *A Joy For Ever* as an authority in the appendix to *Hind Swaraj*.

II

HOW I BEGAN LIFE[M1]

M1 Worldly Pursuits

M2 authority

M3 princely

M4 would earn a great deal

My elder brother had built high hopes on me. The desire for wealth and name and *fame*[M2] was great in him. He had a *big*[M3] heart, generous to a fault. This, combined with his simple nature, had attracted to him many friends, and through them he expected to get me briefs. He had also assumed that I *should have a swinging practice*[M4] and had, in that expectation, allowed the household expenses to become top-heavy. He had also left no stone unturned in preparing the field for my practice.

The storm in my caste over my foreign voyage was still brewing. It had divided the caste into two camps, one of which immediately readmitted me,[26] while the other was bent on keeping me out. To please the former my brother took me to Nasik[27] before going to Rajkot, gave me a bath in the sacred river[28] and, on reaching Rajkot, gave a caste dinner.[29] I did not like all this. But my brother's love for me was boundless, and[30] my devotion to him was in proportion to it, and so I mechanically acted as he wished, taking his will to be law. The trouble about readmission to the caste was thus practically over.

I never tried to seek admission to the section that had refused it.[31] Nor did I feel even mental resentment

---

[26] The first edition reads '. . . readmitted me to the caste'.

[27] MKG was in Nasik on 7 July 1891.

[28] The term in the original is 'Ganga Snan', or bath in the river Ganga, implying a purificatory bath in a sacred river.

[29] They reached Rajkot on 10 July 1891 and the caste dinner was organized on 17 July.

[30] 'I believe' to add.

[31] The first edition reads '. . . refused it to me'.

against any of the headmen of that section. Some of these regarded me with dislike, but I *scrupulously avoided hurting their feelings.*[M5] I fully respected the caste regulations about excommunication. *According to these, none of my relations, including my father-in-law and mother-in-law, and even my sister and brother-in-law, could entertain me; and I would not so much as drink water at their houses.*[M6] They were prepared secretly to evade the prohibition, but it went against the grain with me to do a thing in secret that I would not do in public.

The result of my scrupulous conduct was that I never had occasion to be troubled by the caste; nay, I have experienced nothing but affection and generosity from the general body of the section that still regards me as[32] excommunicated. They have even helped me in my work, without ever expecting me to do anything for the caste. It is my conviction that *all these good things are*[M7] due to my non-resistance. Had I agitated for being admitted to the caste, had I attempted to divide it into more camps, had I provoked the caste-men, they would surely have retaliated, and instead of steering clear of the storm, I should, on[33] arrival from England, have found myself in a whirlpool of agitation, and perhaps a[34] party to dissimulation.

My relations with my wife were still not as I desired. Even my stay in England had not cured me of[35] jealousy. I continued my squeamishness and suspiciousness in respect of every little thing, and hence all my cherished desires remained unfulfilled. I had decided that my wife should *learn reading and writing*[M8] and that I should help her in her studies, but my lust came in the way and *she*

[M5] continued to behave respectfully towards them

[M6] I would not so much as drink water at the house of my mother-in-law and father-in-law, as also at my sister's house.

[M7] this sweet outcome is

[M8] have knowledge of letters

---

[32] 'officially' to add.

[33] 'my' in the first edition.

[34] 'a' added in the 1940 edition.

[35] 'my' in the first edition.

had to suffer for^{M9} my own shortcoming. Once I went the
length of sending her away to her father's house, and
consented to receive her back only after I had made her
thoroughly miserable. I saw later that all this was pure
folly on my part.

I had planned reform in the education of children.
My brother had children, and my own child which I
had left at home when I went to England was now a
boy of nearly four. It was my desire to teach these little
ones physical exercise and make them hardy, and also
to give them the benefit of my personal guidance. In
this I had my brother's support and I succeeded in my
efforts more or less. I very much liked the company of
children, and the habit of playing and joking with them
has stayed with me till today. I have ever since thought
that I should make a good teacher of children.

The necessity for food 'reform' was obvious. Tea and
coffee³⁶ had already found their place in the house. My
brother had thought it fit to keep some sort of English
atmosphere ready for me on my return, and to that end,
crockery and such other things,³⁷ which used to be kept in
^{M10} use as medicine and for the house only for *special occasions*,^{M10} were now in general
use. My 'reforms' put the finishing touch. I introduced
oatmeal porridge,³⁸ and cocoa was to replace tea and
coffee. But in truth it became an addition to tea and
^{M11} socks coffee. Boots and *shoes*^{M11} were already there. *I completed
the Europeanization by adding the European dress.*^{M12}

Expenses thus went up. New things were added
every day.³⁹ We had succeeded in tying a white
elephant at our door. But how was the wherewithal

---

³⁶ 'coffee' in the original. Gujarati does not have a word for coffee.

³⁷ China crockery and tea and' to add.

³⁸ 'oatmeal porridge' in the original. It has explanatory term 'Ghens'
in parenthesis.

³⁹ 'every day' added in English translation.

to be found? To start practice in Rajkot would have meant sure ridicule. I had hardly the knowledge of *a qualified vakil*[M13] and yet I expected to be paid ten times his fee! No client would be fool enough to engage me. And even if such a one was to be found, should I add arrogance and fraud to my ignorance, and increase the burden of debt I owed to the world?

Friends advised me to go to Bombay for some time in order to gain experience of the High Court, to study Indian law and to try and get what briefs I could. *I took up the suggestion and went.*[M14]

In Bombay[40] *I started a household with a cook as incompetent as myself.*[M15] He was a Brahmin. I did not treat him as a servant but as a member of the household.[41] He would pour water over himself but never wash. His dhoti was dirty, as also his sacred thread, and he was completely innocent of the scriptures. But how was I to get a better cook?

'Well, Ravishankar,' (for that was his name), I would ask him, 'you may not know cooking, but surely you must know your *sandhya* (daily worship),[42] etc.'

'*Sandhya*, sir! The plough is our *sandhya* and the spade our daily ritual. That is the type of Brahmin I am. I must live on your mercy. Otherwise agriculture is of course there for me.'

So I had to be Ravishankar's teacher. Time I had enough. I began to do half the cooking myself and introduced the English experiments in vegetarian cookery. I invested in a stove, and with Ravishankar began to run the kitchen.[43] I had no scruples about

[M13] a *vakil* who had passed out from Rajkot

[M14] I set out for Bombay.

[M15] I set up a household. Kept a cook. The cook was just like me.

---

[40] MKG reached Bombay on 15 November 1891.

[41] 'but as a member of the household' added in the English translation.

[42] '(daily worship),' added in the English translation as explanation.

[43] 'and with Ravishankar began to run the kitchen' added in the English translation.

inter-dining, Ravishankar too came to have none, and so we went on merrily together. There was only one obstacle. Ravishankar had sworn to remain dirty and to keep the food unclean!

But it was impossible for me to get along in Bombay for more than four or five months, there being no income to square with the ever-increasing expenditure.

This was how I began life. I found the barrister's profession *a bad job*[M16]—much show and little knowledge. I felt a crushing sense of my responsibility.

[M16] disagreeable

III

THE FIRST CASE

Whilst in Bombay, I began, on the one hand, my study of Indian[44] law and, on the other, my experiments in dietetics in which Virchand Gandhi, a friend,[45] joined me. My brother, for his part, was trying his best to get me briefs.

The study of Indian[46] law was a tedious business. The Civil Procedure Code[47] I could in no way get on with. Not so, however, with the Evidence Act. Virchand Gandhi was reading for the Solicitor's Examination and would tell me all sorts of stories about barristers and *vakils*. 'Sir Pherozeshah's ability,' he would say, 'lies in his profound knowledge of law. He has the Evidence Act[48] by heart and knows all the cases on the thirty-

---

[44] 'Indian' added in the English translation.

[45] 'a friend' added in the English translation.

[46] 'Indian' added in the English translation.

[47] 'Civil Procedure Code' in English in the original.

[48] 'Evidence Act' in English in the original, while in the first instance he used a Gujarati equivalent.

second section.[49] Badruddin Tyabji's *wonderful power of argument inspires the judges with awe.*[M1]

The stories of stalwarts such as these would unnerve me.

'It is not unusual,' he would add, 'for a barrister to *vegetate*[M2] for five or seven years. That's why I have signed the articles for solicitorship. *You should count yourself lucky if you can paddle your own canoe in three years' time.*'[M3]

Expenses were mounting up every month. To have a barrister's board outside the house, whilst still preparing for the barrister's profession inside, was a thing to which I could not reconcile myself. *Hence I could not give undivided attention to my studies.*[50] [M4] I developed some liking for the Evidence Act and read Mayne's *Hindu Law* with deep interest, but I had not the courage to conduct a case. *I was helpless beyond words, even as*[M5] the bride come fresh to her father-in-law's house!

About this time, *I took up*[M6] the case of one Mamibai. It was a 'small cause'.[51] 'You will have to pay some commission to the tout,' I was told. I emphatically declined.

'But even that great criminal lawyer Mr. So-and-So, who makes three to four thousand a month, pays commission!' 'I do not need to emulate him,' I rejoined. 'I should be content with Rs. 300 a month. Father did not get more.'

M1 acumen is such that judges are dazzled by it. His power of argumentation is wonderful

M2 belabour the dust in court

M3 You would have done well if after three years you earn enough to bear your own expenses.

M4 Hence I read with an agitated mind.

M5 With whom was I to share my agony? My condition was similar to

M6 as fate would have it, I chanced to get

---

[49] Section 32 of Indian Evidence Act, 1872, deals with statements, written or verbal, of relevant facts made by a person who is dead, or who cannot be found, or who has become incapable of giving evidence, or whose attendance cannot be procured without an amount of delay or expense which, under the circumstances of the case, appears to the court unreasonable, which are themselves considered relevant facts in specified cases. This section in lay terms refers to the 'Dying Declaration'.

[50] 'As I have said earlier' to add.

[51] 'small cause' English phrase in the original.

'But those days are gone. *Expenses in Bombay have gone up frightfully. You must be business-like.*'[M7]

I was adamant. I gave no commission, but got Mamibai's case all the same. It was an easy case. I charged Rs. 30 for my fees. The case was not likely to last longer than a day.

This was my *debut* in the Small Causes Court. I appeared for the defendant and had thus to cross-examine the plaintiff's witnesses.[52] I stood up, but my *heart sank into my boots.*[M8] My head was reeling and I felt as though the whole court was doing like-wise. I could think of no question to ask. The judge must have laughed, and the *vakils* no doubt enjoyed the spectacle. But I was past seeing anything. I sat down and told the agent that I could not conduct the case, that he had better engage Patel and have the fee back from me. Mr. Patel was duly engaged for Rs. 51. To him, of course, the case was child's play.

I hastened from the Court,[M9] not knowing whether my client won or lost her case, but I was ashamed of myself, and decided not to take up any more cases until I had courage enough to conduct them. Indeed I did not go to Court again until I went to South Africa. There was no virtue in my decision. I had simply made a virtue of necessity.[53] There would be no one so foolish as to entrust his case to me, only to lose it!

But there *was* another case in store for me at Bombay. It was a memorial to be drafted. A poor Mussalman's land was confiscated in Porbandar. He approached me as the *worthy*[M10] son of a worthy father. His case appeared to be weak, but I consented to draft a memorial for him, the cost of printing to be borne by him. I drafted it and read it out to friends. They approved of it, and that to

---

[52] 'the plaintiff's witness' added in the English translation.

[53] 'I had simply made a virtue of necessity.' Added in the English translation.

some extent made me feel confident that I was qualified enough to draft a memorial, as indeed I really was.

My business could flourish if I drafted memorials without any fees.[54] But *that would bring no grist to the mill.*[M11] So I thought I might take up a teacher's job. My knowledge of English was good enough, and I should have loved to teach English to Matriculation boys in some school. In this way I could have met part at least of the expenses. I came across an advertisement in the papers: 'Wanted, an English teacher to teach one hour daily. Salary Rs. 75.' The advertisement was from a famous high school. I applied for the post and was called for an interview. I went there in high spirits, but when the principal found that I was not a graduate, he regretfully refused me.

[M11] would it bring enough silver for the boy's rattle?

'But I have passed the London Matriculation with Latin as my second language.'

'True, but we want a graduate.'

There was no help for it. I wrung my hands in despair. My brother also felt much worried. We both came to the conclusion that it was no use spending more time in Bombay. I should settle in Rajkot where my brother, himself a petty pleader, could give me some work in the shape of drafting applications and memorials. And then as there was already a household at Rajkot, the breaking up of the one at Bombay meant a considerable saving. I liked the suggestion. My little establishment was thus closed after a stay of six months in Bombay.[55]

I used to attend High Court daily whilst in Bombay, but I cannot say that I learnt anything there. I had not sufficient knowledge to learn much. Often I could not follow the cases and dozed off. There were others also who kept me company in this, and thus lightened my

---

[54] 'But my concerns increased.' To add at the beginning of this paragraph.

[55] He returned to Rajkot on 15 September 1892.

load of shame. After a time, I even lost the sense of shame, as I learnt to think that it was fashionable to doze in the High Court.

If the present generation has also its briefless barristers like me in Bombay, I would commend them a little practical precept about living. Although I lived in Girgaum I hardly ever took a carriage or a tramcar. I had made it a rule to walk to the High Court. It took me quite forty-five minutes, and of course I invariably returned home on foot. I had inured myself to the heat of the sun. This walk to and from the Court saved a fair amount of money, and when many of my friends in Bombay used to fall ill, I do not remember having once had an illness. Even when I began to earn money, I kept up the practice of walking to and from the office, and I am still reaping the benefits of that practice.

IV

THE FIRST SHOCK

Disappointed, I left Bombay and went to Rajkot where I set up my own office. Here I got along moderately well. Drafting applications and memorials brought me in, on an average, Rs. 300 a month. For this[56] work I had to thank influence rather than my own ability, for my brother's partner had a settled practice. All applications, etc., which were really or to his mind of an important character, he sent to big barristers. To my lot fell the applications to be drafted on behalf of his poor clients.

I must confess that[57] here I had to compromise the[58] principle of giving no commission, which in Bombay I

---

[56] 'drafting' to add.

[57] 'I must confess that' added in the English translation.

[58] 'my' in the first edition.

had so scrupulously observed. I was told that conditions in the two cases were different; that whilst in Bombay commissions had to be paid to touts, here they had to be paid to *vakils* who briefed you;[59] and that here as in Bombay all barristers, without exception, paid a percentage of their fees as commission. The argument of my brother was, for me, unanswerable. 'You see,' said he, 'that I am in partnership with another *vakil*. I shall always be inclined to make over to you all our cases with which you can possibly deal, and if you refuse to pay a commission to my partner, you are sure to embarrass me. As you and I have a joint establishment, your fee comes to our common purse,[60] and I automatically get a share. But what about my partner? Supposing he gave the same case to some other *barrister*,[M1] he would certainly get his commission from *him*.'[M2] I was taken in by this plea, and felt that, if I was to practise as a barrister, I could not press my principle regarding commission in such cases. That is how I argued with myself, or to put it bluntly, how I deceived myself. Let me add, however, that I do not remember ever to have given a commission in respect of any other case.

Though I thus began to make both ends meet, I got the first shock of my life about this time. I had heard what a British officer was like, but *up to now had never been*[M3] face to face with one.

My brother had been secretary and adviser to the late Ranasaheb of Porbandar[61] before he was installed on his gadi,[62] and hanging over his head at this time was the charge of having given wrong advice when

M1 place

M2 there

M3 now I came

---

[59] 'who briefed you' added in the English translation.

[60] 'your fee comes to our common purse,' added in the English translation.

[61] Rana Bhavsingh.

[62] MD's footnote: 'Throne.'

in that office.[63] The matter had gone to the Political
Agent[64] who was prejudiced against my brother. Now
I had known this officer when in England, and he may
be said to have been fairly friendly to me. My brother
thought that I should avail myself of the friendship and,
putting in a good word on his behalf, try to disabuse the
Political Agent of his prejudice. I did not at all like this
idea. I should not, I thought,[65] try to take advantage of
a trifling acquaintance in England. If my brother was
really at fault, what use was my recommendation? If
he was innocent, he should submit a petition in the
proper course and, confident of his innocence, *face*[M4]
the result. My brother did not relish this advice. 'You
do not know Kathiawad,' he said, 'and you have yet to
know the world. Only influence counts here. It is not
proper for you, a brother, to shirk your duty, when you
can clearly put in a good word about me to an officer
you know.'

I could not refuse him, so I went to the officer much
against my will. I knew I had no right to approach him
and was fully conscious that I was compromising my
self-respect. But I sought an appointment and got it. I
reminded him of the old acquaintance, but I immediately
saw that Kathiawad was different from England; that
an officer on leave was not the same as an officer on
duty. The Political Agent owned the acquaintance, but
the reminder seemed to stiffen him. 'Surely you have
not come here to abuse that acquaintance, have you?'
appeared to be the meaning of that stiffness, and seemed
to be written *on his brow*.[M5] Nevertheless I opened my case.
The sahib was impatient. 'Your brother is an intriguer. I

---

[63] It was alleged that the young prince had removed some jewels
from the State's treasury without authority. Lakshmidas's failure
to report this made him an accessory to the act.

[64] E.C.K. (afterwards Sir Charles) Ollivant.

[65] 'I thought' added in the English translation.

want to hear nothing more from you. I have no time. If
your brother has anything to say, let him apply through
the proper channel.' The answer was enough, *was perhaps
deserved. But selfishness is blind. I went on with my story.*[M6]
The sahib got up and said: 'You must go now.'

    'But please hear me out,' said I. That made him
more angry. *He called his peon and ordered him to show me
the door.*[66] [M7] I was still *hesitating*[M8] when the peon came
in, placed his hands on my shoulders and put me out of
the room.

    The sahib went away as also the peon, and I
departed fretting and fuming. I at once wrote out and
sent over a note to this effect: 'You have insulted me.
You have assaulted me through your peon. If you make
no amends, I shall have to proceed against you.'

    Quick came the answer through his *sowar.*[67]

    'You were rude to me. I asked you to go and you
would not. I had no option but to order my peon to
show you the door. Even after he asked you to leave
the office, you did not do so. He therefore had to use
just enough force to send you out. You are at liberty to
proceed as you wish.'

    With this answer in my pocket, I came home
crestfallen, and told my brother all that had happened.
He was grieved, but was at a loss as to how to console
me. He spoke to his *vakil* friends. For I did not know
how to proceed against the sahib. Sir Pherozeshah
Mehta happened to be in Rajkot at this time, having
come down from Bombay[68] for some case. But how
could a junior barrister like me dare to see him? So I sent
him the papers of my case, through the *vakil* who had
engaged him, and begged for his advice. 'Tell Gandhi,'

---

[66] This sentence is in Hindustani in the original.

[67] *Sowar* is a rider, a messenger on horseback.

[68] 'having come down from Bombay' added in the English translation.

[M6] and was correct. But how is the selfish to be discerning?

[M7] He said, 'Peon, show him the door.'

[M8] talking on

M9 and retains the pride of
England

he said, 'such things are the common experience of many *vakils* and barristers. He is still fresh *from England, and hot-blooded*.M9 He does not know British officers. If he would earn something and have an easy time here, let him tear up the note and pocket the insult. He will gain nothing by proceeding against the sahib, and on the contrary will very likely ruin himself. Tell him he has yet to know life.'[69]

M10 I could not forget the insult, but I made good use of it.

The advice was as bitter as poison to me, but I had to swallow it. *I pocketed the insult, but also profited by it*.M10 'Never again shall I place myself in such a false[70] position, never again shall I try to exploit friendship in this way,' said I to myself, and since then I have never been guilty of a breach of that determination. This shock changed the course of my life.

V

PREPARING FOR SOUTH AFRICA

I was no doubt at fault in having gone to that officer. But his impatience[71] and overbearing anger were out of all proportion to my mistake. It did not warrant expulsion. I can scarcely have taken up more than five minutes of his time. But he simply could not endure my talking. He could have politely asked me to go, but power had intoxicated him to an inordinate extent. Later I came to know that patience was not one of the virtues of this officer. It was usual for him to insult his visitors. The slightest unpleasantness was sure to put the sahib out.

---

[69] In 1921, while addressing the Council of the Parsi Central Association, MKG recalled the event and the advice. See *CWMG*, vol. 20, p. 238.

[70] 'false' added in the English translation.

[71] 'conceit' to add.

Now most of my work would naturally be in his court. It was beyond me to *conciliate him. I had no desire to curry favour with him. Indeed, having once threatened to proceed against him, I did not like to remain silent.*[M1]

Meanwhile I began to learn something of the petty politics of *the country.*[M2] Kathiawad, being a conglomeration of small States, naturally had its rich crop of politicals. Petty intrigues between States, and intrigues of officers for power were the order of the day. Princes were always at the mercy of others and ready to lend their ears to sycophants. Even the sahib's peon had to be cajoled, and the sahib's *shirastedar* was more than his master, as he was his eyes, his ears and his interpreter. The *shirastedar's* will was law, and his income was always reputed to be more than the sahib's. This may have been an exaggeration, but he certainly lived beyond his salary.

This atmosphere appeared to me to be poisonous, and how *to remain unscathed*[M3] was a perpetual problem for me.

I was thoroughly depressed and my brother clearly saw it. We both felt that, if I could secure some job, I should be free from this atmosphere of intrigue. But without intrigue a ministership or judgeship was out of the question. And the quarrel with the sahib stood in the way of practice.

Porbandar was then under administration,[72] and I had *some work there in the shape of securing*[M4] more powers for the Prince. Also I had to see the Administrator in respect of the heavy *vighoti* (land rent) exacted from the Mers. This officer, though an Indian,[73] was, I found,

[M1] flatter him. I did not wish to please this officer through incorrect means. I did not like that having threatened to complain, I neither lodged a complaint nor wrote to him.

[M2] Kathiawad

[M3] I would retain my autonomy

[M4] to try and secure some

---

[72] The ruler Rana Vikmatij was sent into exile for continued misrule and charge of murder. By 1891 the ruler was permitted in his territory but full powers were not restored. See Ramachandra Guha, *Gandhi Before India* (New Delhi: Allen Lane, 2013), pp. 57–58.

[73] Porbandar's administrator was S.P. Pundit.

one better than the sahib in arrogance. He was able, but the ryots appeared to me to be none the better off for his ability. I succeeded in securing a few more[74] powers for the Rana, but hardly any relief for the Mers. It struck me that their cause was not even carefully gone into.

So even in this mission I was comparatively disappointed. I thought justice was not done to my clients, but I had not the means to secure it. At the most I could have appealed to the *Political Agent or to the Governor*[M5] who would have dismissed the appeal saying, 'We decline to interfere.' If there had been any rule or regulation governing such decisions, it would have been something, but here the sahib's will was law.

I was exasperated.

In the meantime a Meman firm from Porbandar wrote to my brother making the following offer: 'We have business in South Africa. Ours is a big firm, and we have a big case there in the Court, our claim being £40,000. It has been going on for a long time. We have engaged the services of the best *vakils* and barristers. If you sent your brother there, he would be useful to us and also to himself. He would be able to instruct our counsel better than ourselves. And he would have the advantage of seeing a new part of the world, and of making new acquaintances.'

My brother discussed the proposition with me. I could not clearly make out whether I had simply to instruct the counsel or to appear in court. But I was tempted.

My brother introduced me to the late Sheth Abdul Karim Jhaveri,[75] a partner of Dada Abdulla & Co.,[76] the

M5 superior officer

---

[74] 'more' added in the English translation.

[75] Brother of Dada Abdullah and second president of the Natal Indian Congress.

[76] The company traded in the wide range of commodities through its fifteen branches in the Transvaal, the Natal and Portuguese

firm in question. 'It won't be a difficult job,' the Sheth
assured me. 'We have big Europeans as our friends,
whose acquaintance you will make. You can be useful to
us in our shop. Much of our correspondence is in English
and you can help us with that too. You will, of course,
be our guest[M6] and hence will have no expense whatever.'   [M6] stay at our bungalow

'How long do you require my services?' I asked.
'And what will be the payment?'

'Not more than a year. We will pay you a first class
return fare and a sum of £105, all found.'

This was hardly *going there as a barrister. It was going
as a servant of the firm.*[M7] But I wanted somehow to leave   [M7] advocacy. It was employment.
India. There was also the tempting opportunity of seeing
a new country and of having new experience. Also I
could send £105 to my brother and help in the expenses
of the household. I closed with the offer[77] without any
higgling and got ready to go to South Africa.

VI

ARRIVAL IN NATAL

When starting for South Africa I did not feel the wrench
of separation which I had experienced when leaving for
England. My mother was now no more. I had gained
some knowledge of the world and of travel abroad, and
going from Rajkot to Bombay was no unusual affair.

This time I only felt the pang of parting with
my wife. Another baby[78] had been born to us since

East Africa. It was the first Indian firm to own ships in South
Africa.

[77] 'made by Sheth Abdul Karim' to add.

[78] Son Manilal was born on 28 October 1892 (d. 1956). For his
biography, see Uma Dhupelia Mesthrie, *Gandhi's Prisoner? The
Life of Gandhi's Son Manilal* (New Delhi: Permanent Black, 2005).

my return from England. Our love could not yet be called free from lust, but it was getting gradually purer. Since my return from *Europe*,M1 we had lived very little together; and as I had now become her teacher, however indifferent, and helped her to make certain reforms, we both felt the necessity of being more together, if only to continue the reforms. But the attraction of South Africa rendered the separation bearable. 'We are bound to meet again in a year,' I said to her, by way of consolation, and left Rajkot for Bombay.[79]

Here I was to get my passage through the agent of Dada Abdulla and Company. But no *berth*M2 was available on the boat, and if I did not sail then, I should be stranded in Bombay.[80] 'We have tried our best,' said the agent, 'to secure a first-class[81] passage, but in vain—unless you are prepared to go on deck. Your meals can be arranged for in the saloon.' Those were the days of my first-class travelling, and how could a barrister travel as a deck passenger? So I refused the offer. I suspected the agent's veracity, for I could not believe that a first-class passage was not available. With the agent's consent I set about securing it myself. I went on board the boat and met the chief officer.[82] He said to me quite frankly, 'We do not usually have such a rush. But as the Governor-General of Mozambique[83] is going by this boat, all the berths are engaged.'

'Could you not possibly squeeze me in?' I asked.

---

[79] MKG left Rajkot on 22 April 1893, reaching Bombay on 23 April.

[80] 'for a month' to add.

[81] 'first-class' added in the English translation.

[82] Captain Asthausen.

[83] Francisco Teixeira da Silva.

He surveyed me from top to toe and smiled. 'There is just one way,' he said. 'There is *an extra berth*[M3] in my cabin, which is usually not available for passengers. But I am prepared to give it to you.'[84] I thanked him and got the agent to purchase the passage. In April 1893 I set forth full of zest to try my luck in South Africa.[85]

The first port of call was Lamu, which we reached in about thirteen days.[86] The Captain and I had become great friends by this time. He was fond of playing chess, but as he was quite a novice, he wanted one still more of a beginner for his partner, and so he invited me. I had heard a lot about the game but had never *tried my hand at*[M4] it. Players used to say that this was a game in which there was plenty of scope for the exercise of one's intelligence. The Captain offered to give me lessons, and he found me a good pupil as I had unlimited patience. Every time I was the loser, and that made him all the more eager to teach me. I liked the game, but never carried my liking beyond the boat or my knowledge beyond the moves of the *pieces*.[M5]

At Lamu the ship remained at anchor for some three to four hours, and I landed to see the port. The Captain had also gone ashore, but he had warned me that the harbour was treacherous and that I should return in good time.

It was a very small place. I went to the Post Office and was delighted to see the Indian clerks there, and had a talk with them. I also saw the Africans and tried to acquaint myself with their ways of life which interested me very much. This took up some time.

There were some deck passengers with whom I had made acquaintance, and who had landed with a view to

[M3] a hammock

[M4] seen

[M5] bishop and the queen, etc.

---

[84] 'I was happy.' To add.

[85] MKG sailed on 24 April 1893 by *S.S Safari*.

[86] *S.S Safari* reached Lamu on 7 May 1893.

cooking their food on shore and having a quiet meal.
I now found them preparing to return to the steamer,
so[87] we all got into the same boat. The tide was high in
the harbour and our boat had more than its proper load.
The current was so strong that it was impossible to hold
the boat to the ladder of the steamer. It would just touch
the ladder and be drawn away again by the current. The
first whistle to start had already gone. I was worried. The
Captain was witnessing our plight from the bridge. He
ordered the steamer to wait an extra five minutes. There
was another boat near the ship which a friend hired for
me for ten rupees. This boat picked me up from the
overloaded one. The ladder had already been raised. I
had therefore to be drawn up by means of a rope and the
steamer started immediately. The other passengers were
left behind. I now appreciated the Captain's warning.

After Lamu the next port was Mombasa and then
Zanzibar. The halt here was a long one—eight or ten
days—and we then changed to another boat.[88]

The Captain liked me much but the liking took
an undesirable turn. He invited an English friend and
me to accompany him on an outing, and we all went
ashore in his boat. I had not the least notion of what
the outing meant. And little did the Captain know
what an ignoramus I was in such matters. We were
taken to some Negro women's quarters by a tout. We
were each shown into a room. I simply stood there
dumb with shame. Heaven only knows what the poor
woman must have thought of me. When the Captain
called me I came out just as I had gone in. He saw my
innocence. At first I felt very much ashamed, but as I
could not think of the thing except with horror, the

---

[87] 'I now found them preparing to return to the steamer, so' added
in the English translation.

[88] MKG reached Zanzibar on 8 May 1893 and stayed there till 17
May. He sailed for Durban in *S.S Admiral*.

sense of shame wore away, and I thanked God that the
sight of *the woman*[M6] had not moved me in the least. I   [M6] that sister
was disgusted at my weakness and pitied myself for not
having had the courage to refuse to go into the room.

This in my life was the third trial of its kind.[89] Many
a youth, innocent at first, must have been drawn into
sin by a false sense of shame. I could claim no credit
for having come out unscathed. I could have credit if
I had refused to enter that room. I must entirely thank
the All-merciful[90] for having saved me. The incident
increased my faith in God and taught me, to a certain
extent, to cast off false shame.

As we had to remain in this port for a week, I took
rooms in the town and saw a good deal by wandering
about the neighbourhood. Only Malabar can give any
idea of the luxuriant vegetation of Zanzibar. I was
amazed at the gigantic trees and the size of the fruits.

The next call was at Mozambique and thence we
reached Natal towards the close of May.[91]

VII

SOME EXPERIENCES[92]

The port of Natal is Durban, also known as Port Natal.
Abdulla Sheth was there to receive me. As the ship

---

[89] MKG recalled this incident and attributed the fact of having
emerged unsullied to the power of Ramanama. See *CWMG*,
vol. 27, pp. 110–11.

[90] In Gujarati, *Ishvar*, God, the attribute of mercy, added in the
English translation.

[91] *S.S Admiral* reached Natal on 24 May 1893.

[92] The title in Gujarati is *Anubhavo Ni Vangi. Anubhav* translates
as experience, *vangi* as novelty. The title could be translated as
'Novel Experiences'.

arrived at the quay and I watched the people coming on board to meet their friends, I observed that the Indians were not held in much respect. I could not fail to notice a sort of snobbishness about the manner in which those who knew Abdulla Sheth behaved towards him, and it stung me. Abdulla Sheth had got used to it. Those who looked at me did so with a certain amount of curiosity. My dress marked me out from other Indians. I had a frock-coat[93] and a turban, an imitation of the Bengal pugree.

M1 home

I was taken *to the firm's quarters*[M1] [94] and shown into the room set apart for me, next to Abdulla Sheth's. He did not understand me. I could not understand him. He read the papers his brother had sent through me, and felt more *puzzled.*[M2] He thought his brother had sent him a white elephant. *My style of dress and living struck him as being expensive like that of the Europeans.*[M3] There was no particular work then which could be given me. Their case was going on in the Transvaal. There was no meaning in sending me there immediately. And how far could he trust my ability and honesty? He would not be in Pretoria to watch me.[95] The defendants were in Pretoria, and for aught he knew they might bring undue influence to bear on me. And if work in connection with the case in question was not to be entrusted to me, what work could I be given to do, as all other work could be done much better by his clerks? The clerks could be brought to book, if they did wrong. Could I be, if I also happened to err?[96] So if no work in connection

M2 worried

M3 My Sahib style of living struck him as being expensive.

---

[93] 'frock-coat' English word in the original.

[94] Located at 427, West Street, a lane off Grey Street in West Central Durban.

[95] 'to watch me' added in the English translation.

[96] 'There was no work other than related to the case or that of the clerks.' To add.

with the case could be given me, I should have to be kept *for nothing.*[M4]

M4 home and fed

Abdulla Sheth was practically unlettered, but he had a rich fund of experience. He had an acute intellect and was conscious of it. By practice he had picked up just sufficient English for conversational purposes, but that served him for carrying on all his business, whether it was dealing with Bank Managers[97] and European merchants or explaining his case to his counsel. The Indians held him in very high esteem. His firm was then the biggest, or at any rate one of the biggest, of the Indian firms. With all these advantages he had one disadvantage[98]—he was by nature suspicious.

He was proud of Islam and loved to discourse on Islamic[99] philosophy. Though he did not know Arabic, his acquaintance with the Holy Koran and Islamic literature in general was fairly good. Illustrations he had in plenty, always ready at hand. *Contact*[M5] with him gave me a fair amount of practical knowledge of Islam. When we came closer to each other, we had long discussions on religious topics.

M5 Living

On the second or third day[100] of my arrival, he took me to see the Durban court. There he introduced me to several people and seated me next to his attorney. The Magistrate kept staring at me and finally asked me to take off my turban. This[101] I refused to do and left the court.[102]

---

[97] 'Bank Managers' English in the original.

[98] 'With all these advantages he had one disadvantage—' added in the English translation.

[99] 'Islamic' added in the English translation.

[100] On 25 May 1893, the day after his arrival in Durban.

[101] 'which' in the first edition.

[102] This was reported in *The Natal Advertiser* of 26 May 1893 under the heading 'An Unwelcome Visitor'. 'An Indian entered

So here too there was fighting in store for me.

Abdulla Sheth explained to me why some Indians were required to take off their turbans. Those wearing the Mussalman costume might, he said, keep their turbans on, but the other Indians on entering a court had to take theirs off as a rule.

I must enter into some details to make this nice distinction intelligible. In the course of these two or three days I could see that the Indians were divided into different groups. One was that of Mussalman merchants, who would call themselves 'Arabs'. Another was that of Hindu, and yet another of Parsi clerks. The Hindu clerks were neither here nor there, unless they cast in their lot with the 'Arabs'. The Parsi clerks

---

the Court House yesterday afternoon and took a seat at the horseshoe. He was well-dressed, and it was understood that he was an English barrister, on his way to Pretoria, where he is reported to be engaged in an Indian case. He entered the court without removing his head-covering or salaaming, and the Magistrate looked at him with disapproval.' *CWMG*, vol. 1, p. 57, footnote 2.

MKG, 'startled' to read this report, wrote the same day to the editor of *The Natal Advertiser*. 'I am very sorry if His Worship the Magistrate looked at me with disapproval. It is true that on entering the court I neither removed my head-dress nor salammed, but in so doing I had not the slightest idea that I was offending His Worship, or meaning any disrespect to the court. Just as it is a mark of respect amongst the Europeans to take of their hats, in like manner it is in Indians to retain one's head-dress . . . as to bowing or salaaming as you would call it, I again followed the rule observed in the Bombay High Court.' *CWMG*, vol. 1, pp. 57–58. He took up this issue of immense emotive and symbolic significance to the Indian community a decade later. The issue arose from a query by Sir Henry Bale, the chief justice of Natal, in regard to the conduct of an Indian witness, Manorath. MKG stated that Sir Henry had made 'much ado about nothing' and the matter had been settled through a judicial pronouncement. 'He was then able to secure a dictum from the judge that the British Indians were not to be forced to either remove their head-dress or their boots, but they were to *Salaam* on entering the court.' *CWMG*, vol. 4, p. 26.

would call themselves Persians. These three classes had
some social relations with one another. But by far the
largest class was that composed of Tamil, Telugu and
North Indian indentured and freed labourers. The
indentured labourers were those who went to Natal on
an agreement to serve for five years, and came to be
known there as *girmitiyas* from *girmit*, which was the
corrupt form of the English word 'agreement'. The
other three classes had none but business relations with
this class. Englishmen called them 'coolies' and as the
majority of Indians belonged to the labouring class,
all Indians were called 'coolies', or '*samis*'. '*Sami*' is a
Tamil suffix occurring after many Tamil names, and it
is nothing else than the Samskrit[103] swami, meaning a
master. Whenever therefore, an Indian resented being
addressed as a '*sami*' and had enough *wit*[M6] in him, he   [M6] courage
would try to return the compliment in this wise: 'You
may call me *sami*, but *you forget*[M7] that *sami* means a   [M7] do you know
master. I am not your master!' Some Englishmen would
wince at this, while others would get angry, swear at the
Indian and, if there was a chance, would even belabour
him; for '*sami*' to him was nothing better than a term of
contempt. To interpret it to mean a master amounted
to an insult!

I was hence known as a 'coolie barrister'. The
merchants were known as 'coolie merchants'. The
original meaning of the word 'coolie' was thus forgotten,
and it became a common appellation for all Indians.[104]
The Mussalman[105] merchant would resent this and say:
'I am not a coolie, I am an Arab,' or 'I am a merchant,'
and the Englishman, if courteous, would apologize to
him.

---

[103] 'the Samskrit' added in the English translation.

[104] 'and it became a common appellation for all Indians' added in
the English translation.

[105] 'Mussalman' added in the English translation.

The question of wearing the turban had a great importance in this state of things. Being obliged to take off[106] one's Indian turban would be pocketing an insult. So I thought I had better bid good-bye to the Indian turban and begin wearing an English hat, which would save me from the insult and the unpleasant controversy.

But Abdulla Sheth disapproved of the idea. He said, 'If you do anything of the kind, it will have a very bad effect. You will compromise those insisting on wearing Indian turbans. And an Indian turban sits well on your head. If you wear an English hat, you will pass for a waiter.'[107]

There was practical wisdom, patriotism and a little bit of narrowness in this advice. The wisdom was apparent, and he would not have insisted on the Indian turban except out of patriotism; the slighting reference to the waiter betrayed a kind of narrowness. Amongst the indentured[108] Indians there were three classes— Hindus, Mussalmans and Christians. The last were the children of indentured Indians who became converts to Christianity. Even in 1893 their number was large. They wore the English costume, and the majority of them earned their living by service as waiters in hotels. Abdulla Sheth's criticism of the English hat was with reference to this class. It was considered degrading[109] to serve as a waiter in a hotel. The belief persists even today among many.

On the whole I liked Abdulla Sheth's advice. I wrote to the Press about the incident and defended the wearing of my turban in the court. The question was

---

[106] 'Being obliged to take off' changed in the revised edition; in the first edition 'Taking off'.

[107] 'waiter' English word in the original.

[108] 'girmitiya' in the original.

[109] 'demeaning' in the first edition.

very much discussed in the papers, which described me as an 'unwelcome visitor'. Thus the incident gave me an unexpected advertisement in South Africa within a few[M8] days of my arrival there. Some supported me while others severely criticized my temerity.

[M8] three–four

My turban stayed with me practically until the end of my stay in South Africa.[110] When and why I left off wearing any head-dress at all in South Africa,[111] we shall see later.

VIII

ON THE WAY TO PRETORIA

I soon came in contact with the Christian Indians living in Durban. The Court Interpreter, Mr. Paul, was a Roman Catholic. I made his acquaintance, as also that of the late Mr. Subhan Godfrey,[112] then a teacher under the Protestant Mission, and father of Mr. James Godfrey,[113] who, as a[114] member of the South African

---

[110] 'of my stay in South Africa' added in the English translation.

[111] 'at all in South Africa' added in the English translation.

[112] In 1899 MKG wrote about Subhan Godfrey: 'Though his own education is not very liberal, he is most anxious to bring up his children in the best possible way. All his children but one have been educated in the Government Schools. He sent his eldest son to Calcutta, gave him a university training there, and has now sent him to Glasgow to study medicine. His second son is the first Indian to have passed the competitive examination for the Civil Service of the Colony . . . It may be stated that his family has been living in the European style. All the children have been brought up from their infancy to speak English, and naturally they speak it very well.' *CWMG*, vol. 3, p. 98.

[113] The third son of Subhan Godfrey, called to the Bar in 1907. Appeared as an attorney for MKG in a trial in 1913.

[114] 'since has been' in the first edition.

Deputation, visited India in 1924.[115] I likewise met the late Parsi Rustomji[116] and the late Adamji Miyakhan[117] about the same time. All these friends, who up to then had never met one another except on business, came ultimately into close contact, as we shall see later.

Whilst I was thus widening the circle of my acquaintance, the firm received a letter from their lawyer saying that preparations should be made for the case, and that Abdulla Sheth should go to Pretoria himself or send a representative.

Abdulla Sheth gave me this letter to read, and asked me if I would go to Pretoria. 'I can only say after I have understood the case from you,' said I. 'At present I am at a loss to know what I have to do there.' He thereupon asked his clerks to explain the case to me.

As I began to study the case, I felt as though I ought to begin from ABC of the subject.[M1] During the few days I had at Zanzibar, I had been to the court to see the work there. A Parsi lawyer was examining a witness and asking him questions regarding credit and debit entries in account books. *It was all Greek to me.*[M2] Book-keeping I had learnt neither at school nor during my stay in England. And the case for which I had come to

[M1] I saw that I would have to begin from one, two, three.

[M2] I knew nothing of credit and debit entries.

---

[115] In the Gujarati original the year is not mentioned. It says 'last year', which would make the year of deputation 1925; the first edition has 'last year', changed to 1924 in the revised edition, which was the correct date.

[116] Rustomji Jivanji Ghorkhodu (1861–1924) arrived in Natal in 1880 and by 1893 was one of the wealthiest Indians there. He was founder member and vice-president of the Natal Indian Congress, active satyagrahi and repeatedly went to prison. Rustomji was an appointed trustee of the Phoenix Settlement in 1912. In his obituary MKG wrote, 'With the passing of Parsee Rustomjee . . . India has lost a true soldier. So far as I am concerned, I have lost a true friend.' *CWMG*, vol. 25, p. 372.

[117] Adamji Miyakhan, leading Indian businessman, vice-president of the Natal Indian Congress, died in India in 1907.

South Africa[118] was mainly about accounts. Only one[119] who knew accounts could understand and explain it. The clerk went on talking about this debited and that credited, and I felt more and more confused. I did not know what a P. Note meant. I failed to find the word in the dictionary. I revealed my ignorance to the clerk, and learnt from him that a P. Note meant a promissory note. I purchased a book on book-keeping and studied it. That gave me some confidence. I understood the case. I saw that Abdulla Sheth, who did not know how to keep accounts, had so much practical knowledge that he could quickly solve intricacies of book-keeping. I told him that I was prepared to go to Pretoria.

'Where will you put up?' asked the Sheth.

'Wherever you want me to,' said I.

'Then I shall write to our lawyer. He will arrange for your lodgings. I shall also write to my Meman friends there, but I would not advise you to stay with them. The other party has great influence in Pretoria. Should anyone of them manage to read our private correspondence, it might do us much harm. The more you avoid familiarity with them, the better for us.'

'I shall stay where your lawyer puts me up, or I shall find out independent lodgings. Pray don't worry. *Not a soul shall know anything that is confidential between us.*[M3] But I do intend cultivating the acquaintance of *the other party*.[M4] I should like to be friends with *them*.[M5] I would try, if possible, to settle the case *out of court*.[M6] After all Tyeb Sheth is a relative of yours.'

Sheth Tyeb Haji Khan Muhammad was a near relative of Abdulla Sheth.

The mention of a probable settlement somewhat startled the Sheth, I could see. But I had already been six or seven days in Durban, and we now knew and

[M3] None of your confidential matter will become public.

[M4] all the people

[M5] the other party

[M6] within the family

---

[118] 'for which I had come to South Africa' added in the English translation.

[119] 'he' in the first edition.

understood each other. I was no longer a 'white elephant'. So he said:

> 'Y . . . es, I see. There would be nothing better than a settlement out of court.[120] But we are all relatives and know one another very well indeed. Tyeb Sheth is not a man to consent to a settlement easily. With the slightest unwariness on our part, he would screw all sorts of things out of us, and do us down in the end. So please think twice before you do anything.'
>
> 'Don't be anxious about that,' said I. 'I need not talk to Tyeb Sheth, or for that matter to anyone else, about the case. I would only suggest to him to come to an understanding, *and so save a lot of unnecessary litigation.*'[M7]

[M7] in the family so that you need not fill the coffers of lawyers

On the seventh or eighth day after my arrival, I left Durban.[121] A first-class seat was booked for me. It was usual there to pay five shillings extra, if one needed a bedding.[122] Abdulla Sheth insisted that I should book one bedding but, out of obstinacy and pride and with a view to saving five shillings, I declined. Abdulla Sheth warned me. 'Look, now,' said he, 'this is a different country from India. Thank God, we have enough and to spare. Please do not stint yourself in anything that you may need.'

I thanked him and asked him not to be anxious.

The train reached Maritzburg, the capital of Natal, at about 9 p.m. Beddings used to be provided at this station. A railway servant came and asked me if I wanted one. 'No,' said I, 'I have one with me.' He went away. But a passenger came next, and looked me

---

[120] 'out of court' added in the English translation.

[121] MKG left Durban for Pretoria on 31 May 1893.

[122] 'beddings' in the first edition.

up and down. He saw that I was a 'coloured' man. This disturbed him. Out he went and came in again with one or two officials. They all kept quiet, when another official came to me and said, 'Come along, you must go to the van compartment.'

'But I have a first-class ticket,' said I.

'That doesn't matter,' rejoined the other. 'I tell you, you must go to the van compartment.'

'I tell you, I was *permitted to travel*[M8] in this compartment at Durban, and I insist on going on in it.'

'No, you won't,' said the official. 'You must leave this compartment, or else I shall have to call a police constable to push you out.'

'Yes, you may. I refuse to get out voluntarily.'

The constable came. He took me by the hand and pushed me out. My luggage was also taken out. I refused to go to the other compartment and the train steamed away. I went and sat in the waiting room,[123] keeping my hand-bag with me, and leaving the other luggage where it was. The railway authorities had *taken charge of it.*[M9]

It was winter, and winter in the higher regions of South Africa is severely cold. Maritzburg being at a high altitude, the cold was extremely bitter. My over-coat[124] was in my luggage, but I did not dare to ask for it lest I should[125] be insulted again, so I sat and shivered. There was no light in the room. A passenger came in at about midnight and possibly wanted to talk to me. But I was in no mood to talk.

I began to think of my duty. Should I fight for my rights or go back to India, or should I go on to Pretoria without minding the insults, and return to India after finishing the case? It would be cowardice to run back to

[M8] given a seat

[M9] kept it somewhere

---

[123] 'waiting room' English word in the original.

[124] 'over-coat' English word in the original.

[125] 'might' in the first edition.

M10 leaving the case

M11 have the capability

India *without fulfilling my obligation.*M10 The hardship to which I was subjected was superficial—only a symptom of the deep disease of colour prejudice. I should try, if *possible,*M11 to root out the disease and suffer hardships in the process. Redress for wrongs I should seek only to the extent that would be necessary for the removal of the colour prejudice.[126]

So I decided[127] to take the next available train to Pretoria.

The following morning I sent a long telegram to the General Manager of the Railway[128] and also informed Abdulla Sheth, who immediately met the General Manager. The Manager justified the conduct of the railway authorities, but informed him that he had already instructed the Station Master[129] to see that I reached my destination safely. Abdulla Sheth wired to the Indian merchants in Maritzburg and to friends in other places to meet me and look after me. The merchants came to see me at the station and tried to comfort me by narrating their own hardships and explaining that what had happened to me was nothing unusual. They also said that Indians travelling first or second class had to expect trouble from railway officials and white passengers. The day was thus spent in listening to these tales of woe. The evening train arrived. There was a reserved berth for me. I now purchased at Maritzburg the bedding ticket I had refused to book at Durban.

The train took me to Charlestown.

---

[126] In a discussion with an American missionary, John Mott, in December 1938 MKG described this as 'a creative experience', one that changed the course of his life. He said: 'My active non-violence began from that date.' *CWMG*, vol. 68, p. 171.

[127] 'somehow' to add.

[128] David Hunter was then the general manager of the Natal Government Railways.

[129] Edward Campbell was the station master at Pietermaritzburg.

IX

MORE HARDSHIPS

The train reached Charlestown in the morning. There was no railway, in those days, between Charlestown and Johannesburg, but only a stage-coach,[130] which halted at Standerton for the night *en route*. I possessed a ticket for the coach, which was not cancelled by the break of the journey at Maritzburg for a day; besides, Abdulla Sheth had sent a wire to the coach agent at Charlestown.

But the agent only needed a pretext for putting me off, and so, when he discovered me to be a stranger, he said, 'Your ticket is cancelled.' I gave him the proper reply. *The reason at the back of his mind was not want of accommodation, but quite another.*[M1] Passengers had to be accommodated inside the coach, but as I was regarded as a 'coolie' and looked a stranger, it would be proper, thought the 'leader', as the white man in charge of the coach was called,[131] not to seat me with the white passengers. There were seats on either side of the coachbox. The leader sat on one of these as a rule. Today he sat inside and gave me his seat. I knew it was sheer injustice and an insult, but I thought it better to *pocket*[M2] it. I could not have forced myself inside, and if I had raised a protest, the coach would have gone off without me. This would have meant the loss of another day, and Heaven only knows what would have happened the next day. So, much as I fretted within myself, I prudently sat next to the coachman.

[M1] The reason for saying that my ticket was cancelled was quite another.

[M2] swallow

---

[130] MKG reached Charlestown on 2 June 1893. The rails did not reach Johannesburg until 1895. The stage–coach was operated by George Heys & Co. The fare was £4, 10s.

[131] 'the "leader", as the white man in charge of the coach was called' added in the English translation. The original has 'coachman'.

At about three o'clock the coach reached Pardekoph. Now the leader desired to sit where I was seated, as he wanted to smoke and possibly to have some fresh air. So he took a piece of dirty sack-cloth from the driver, spread it on the footboard and, addressing me said, '*Sami*, you sit on this, I want to sit near the driver.' The insult was more than I could bear. In fear and trembling I said to him, 'It was you who seated me here, though I should have been accommodated inside. I put up with the insult. Now that you want to sit outside and smoke, you would have me sit at your feet. I will not *do so*,[M3] but I am prepared to sit inside.'

[M3] sit at your feet

As I was struggling through these sentences, the man came down upon[132] me and began heavily to box my ears. He seized me by the arm and tried to drag me down. I clung to the brass rails of the coach box[133] and was determined to keep my hold even at the risk of breaking my wristbones. The passengers were witnessing the scene—the man swearing at me, dragging and belabouring me, and I remaining still. He was strong and I was weak. Some of the passengers were moved to pity and[134] exclaimed: 'Man, let him alone. Don't beat him. He is not to blame. He is right. If he can't stay there, let him come and sit with us.' 'No *fear*,'[M4] cried the man, but he seemed somewhat crestfallen and stopped beating me. He let go my arm, swore at me a little more, and asking the Hottentot servant who was sitting on the other side of the coachbox to sit on the footboard, took the seat so vacated.

[M4] , never

The passengers took their seats and, the whistle given, the coach rattled away. My heart was beating fast within my breast, and I was wondering whether I should

---

[132] 'for' in the first edition.

[133] 'like an obstinate ghost' to add.

[134] 'and they' in the first edition.

ever reach my destination alive. The man cast an angry look at me now and then and, pointing his finger at me, growled: 'Take care, let me once get to Standerton and I shall show you what I do.' I sat speechless and prayed to God to help me.

After dark we reached Standerton and I heaved a sigh of relief on seeing some Indian faces. As soon as I got down, these friends said: 'We are here to receive you and take you to Isa Sheth's shop. We have had a telegram from Dada Abdulla.' I was very glad, and we went to Sheth Isa Haji Sumar's shop. The Sheth and his clerks gathered round me. I told them all that I had gone through. They were very sorry to hear it and comforted me by relating to me their own bitter experiences.[135]

I wanted to inform the agent of the Coach Company of the whole affair. So I wrote him a letter, narrating everything that had happened, and drawing his attention to the threat his man had held out. I also asked for an assurance that he would accommodate me with the other passengers inside the coach when we started the next morning. To which the agent replied to this effect: 'From Standerton we have a bigger coach with different men in charge. The man complained of will not be there tomorrow, and you will have a seat with the other passengers.' This somewhat relieved me. I had, of course, no intention of proceeding against the man who had assaulted me, and so the chapter of the assault closed there.

In the morning Isa Sheth's *man*[M5] took me to the coach, I got a good seat and reached Johannesburg quite safely that night.

Standerton is a small village and Johannesburg a big city. Abdulla Sheth had wired to Johannesburg also, and given me the name and address of Muhammad

M5 men

---

[135] 'experience' in the first edition.

Kasam Kamruddin's firm there. Their man had come to receive me at the stage, but neither did I see him nor did he recognize me. So I decided to go to a hotel. I knew the names of several. Taking a cab I asked to be driven to the Grand National Hotel.[136] I saw the Manager and asked for a room. He eyed me for a moment, and politely saying, 'I am very sorry, we are full up', bade me good-bye. So I asked the cabman to drive to Muhammad Kasam Kamruddin's shop. Here I found Abdul Gani Sheth[137] expecting me, and he gave me a cordial greeting. He had a hearty laugh over the story of my experience at the hotel. *'However did you expect to be admitted to a hotel?'*[M6] he said.

'Why not?' I asked.

'You will come to know after you have stayed here a few days,' said he. 'Only *we* can live in a land like this, because, for making money, we do not mind pocketing insults, and here we are.' With this he narrated to me the story of the hardships of Indians in *South Africa.*[M7]

Of Sheth Abdul Gani we shall know more as we proceed.

He said: 'This country is not for men like you. Look now, you have to go to Pretoria tomorrow. You will *have* to travel third class. Conditions in the Transvaal are worse than in Natal. First and second-class tickets are never issued to Indians.'

'You cannot have made persistent efforts[138] in this direction.'

M6 'Would they ever allow us to stay at a hotel?'

M7 the Transvaal.

---

[136] Then located at the corner of Rissik and Pritchard streets.

[137] Partner and manager of Muhammad Kasam Kamruddin's firm and first chairman of the British Indian Association of the Transvaal. Satyagrahi in the first phase, arrested on 22 January 1908 and remanded. Released after provisional settlement at the end of January 1908.

[138] 'effort' in the first edition.

'We have sent representations, but I confess our own men too do not want as a rule to travel first or second.'

I sent for the railway regulations and read them. There was a loophole. The language of the old Transvaal enactments was not very exact or precise; that of the railway regulations was even less so.

I said to the Sheth: 'I wish to go first class, and if I cannot, I shall prefer to take a cab to Pretoria, a matter of only thirty-seven miles.'

Sheth Abdul Gani drew my attention to the extra time and money this would mean, but agreed to my proposal to travel first, and accordingly we sent a note to the Station Master. I mentioned in my note that I was a barrister and that I always travelled first. I also stated in the letter that I needed to reach Pretoria as early as possible, that as there was no time to await his reply I would receive it in person at the station, and that I should expect to get a first-class ticket. There was of course a purpose behind asking for the reply in person. I[139] thought that if the Station Master gave a written reply, he would certainly say 'no', especially because he would have his own notion of a 'coolie' barrister. I would therefore appear before him in faultless English dress, talk to him and possibly persuade him to issue a first-class ticket. So I went to the station in a frock-coat and necktie,[140] placed a sovereign for my fare on the counter and asked for a first-class ticket.

'You sent me that note?' he asked.

'That is so. I shall be much obliged if you will give me a ticket. I must reach Pretoria today.'

He smiled and, moved to pity, said: 'I am not a Transvaaler. I am a Hollander. I appreciate your feelings, and you have my sympathy. I do want to give

---

[139] 'had' in the first edition.

[140] 'frock-coat' and 'necktie' in English in the original.

you a ticket—on one condition, however, that, if the guard should ask you to shift to the third class, you will not involve me in the affair, by which I mean that you should not proceed against the Railway Company. I wish you a safe journey. I can see you are a gentleman.'

With these words he booked the ticket. I thanked him and gave him the necessary assurance.

Sheth Abdul Gani had come to see me off at the station. The incident gave him an agreeable surprise, but he warned me saying: 'I shall be thankful if you reach Pretoria all right. I am afraid the guard will not leave you in peace in the first class and even if he does, the passengers will not.'

I took my seat in a first-class compartment and the train started. At Germiston the guard came to examine the tickets. He was angry to find me there, and signalled to me with his finger to go to the third class. I showed him my first-class ticket. 'That doesn't matter,' said he, 'remove to the third class.'

There was only one English passenger in the compartment. He took the guard to task. 'What do you mean by troubling the gentleman?' he said. 'Don't you see he has a first-class ticket? I do not mind in the least his travelling with me.' Addressing me, he said, 'You should make yourself comfortable where you are.'

The guard muttered: 'If you want to travel with a coolie, what do I care?' and went away.

At about eight o'clock in the evening the train reached Pretoria.

X

FIRST DAY IN PRETORIA

I had expected someone on behalf of Dada Abdulla's attorney to meet me at Pretoria station. I knew that no Indian would be there to receive me, since I had particularly promised not to put up at an Indian house. But the attorney had sent no one. I understood later that, as I had arrived on a Sunday,[141] he could not have sent anyone without inconvenience. I was perplexed, and wondered where to go, as I feared that no hotel would accept me.

Pretoria station in 1893 was quite different from what it was in 1914. The lights were burning dimly. The travellers were few.

I let all the other passengers go and thought that, as soon as the ticket collector was fairly free, I would hand him my ticket and ask him if he could direct me to some small hotel or any other such place where I might go; otherwise I would spend the night at the station. I must confess I shrank from asking him even this, for I was afraid of being insulted.

The station became clear of all passengers. I gave my ticket to the ticket collector and began my inquiries. He replied to me courteously, but I saw that he could not be of any considerable help. But an American Negro[142] who was standing near by broke into the conversation.

'I see,' said he, 'that you are an utter stranger here, without any friends. If you will come with me, I will take you to a small hotel, of which the proprietor is an American who is very well known to me. I think he will accept you.'

I had my own doubts about the offer, but I thanked him[M1] and accepted his suggestion. He took me to Johnston's Family Hotel.[143] He drew Mr. Johnston aside to speak to him, and the latter agreed to accommodate

M1 the gentleman

---

[141] 4 June 1893.

[142] 'gentleman' to add.

[143] 'Family Hotel' English in the original.

me for the night, on condition that I should have my dinner served in my room.

'I assure you,' said he, 'that I have no colour prejudice. But I have only European custom, and, if I allowed you to eat in the dining-room, my guests might be offended and even go away.'

'Thank you,' said I, 'even for accommodating me for the night. I am now more or less acquainted with the conditions here, and I understand your difficulty. I do not mind your serving the dinner in my room. I hope to be able to make some other arrangement tomorrow.'

I was shown into a room, where I now sat waiting for the dinner and musing, as I was quite alone. There were not many guests in the hotel, and I had expected the waiter[144] to come very shortly with the dinner. Instead Mr. Johnston appeared. He said: 'I was ashamed of having asked you to have your dinner here. So I spoke to the other guests about you, and asked them if they would mind your having your dinner in the dining-room. They said they had no objection, and that they did not mind your staying here as long as you liked. Please, therefore, come to the dining-room, if you will, and stay here as long as you wish.'

I thanked him again, went to the dining-room and had a hearty dinner. Next morning I called on the attorney, Mr. A.W. Baker.[145] Abdulla Sheth had given me some description of him; so *his cordial reception*[M2] did not surprise me. He *received me very warmly*[M3] and

[M2] our first meeting

[M3] embraced me with affection

---

[144] 'waiter' English in the original.

[145] Albert Weir Baker (1856–1939), carpenter, lawyer and lay preacher. In 1893 he was a member of the South African General Mission, which he parted with in 1896 and established his own work, the South African Compounds and Interior Mission. See his autobiography, *Grace Triumphant* (Glasgow: 1939) and James D. Hunt, *Gandhi and the Non-Conformists: Encounters in South Africa* (New Delhi: Promila and Co., 1986). The chambers of Baker and Lindsay were off Church Street.

made kind inquiries. I explained all about myself. Thereupon he said: 'We have no work for you here as barrister, for we have engaged the best counsel.[146] The case is a prolonged and complicated one, so I shall take your assistance only to the extent of getting necessary information. And of course you will make communication with my client easy for me, as I shall now ask for all the information I want from him through you. That is certainly an advantage. I have not yet found rooms for you. I thought I had better do so after having seen you. There is a fearful amount of colour prejudice here, and therefore it is not easy to find lodgings for such as you.[147] But I know a poor woman. She is the wife of a baker. I think she will take you and thus add to her income at the same time. Come, let us go to her place.'

So he took me to her house. He spoke with her privately about me, and she agreed to accept me as a boarder at 35 shillings a week.

Mr. Baker, besides being an attorney, was a staunch lay[148] preacher.[149] He is still alive and now engaged purely in missionary work, having given up the legal profession. He is quite well-to-do. He still corresponds with me.[150] In his letters he always dwells on the same theme. He upholds the excellence of Christianity from various points of view, and contends that it is impossible to find eternal peace, unless one accepts Jesus as the only son of God and the Saviour of mankind.

---

[146] Hendrick Cloete. Sheth Tyeb Haji Khan Muhammad's case was represented by Findlay and Rice.

[147] 'for such as you' added in the English translation.

[148] 'lay' added in the English translation.

[149] The original has 'Padri', literally a Christian priest.

[150] 'He has still kept up correspondence with me.' In the first edition.

During the very first interview Mr. Baker ascertained my[151] religious views. I said to him: 'I am a Hindu by birth. And yet I do not know much of Hinduism, and I know less of other religions. In fact I do not know where I am, and what is and what should be my belief. I intend to make a careful study of my own religion and, as far as I can, of other religions as well.'

Mr. Baker was glad to hear all this, and said: 'I am one of the Directors of the South Africa General Mission.[152] I have built a church at my own expense, and[153] deliver sermons in it regularly. I am free from colour prejudice. I have some co-workers, and we meet at one o'clock every day for a few minutes and pray for peace and light.[154] I shall be glad if you will join us there. I shall introduce you to my co-workers who will be happy to meet you, and I dare say you will also like their company. I shall give you, besides, some religious books to read, though of course the book of books is the Holy Bible, which I would specially recommend to you.'

I thanked Mr. Baker and agreed to attend the one o'clock prayers as regularly as possible.

'So I shall expect you here tomorrow at one o'clock, and we shall go together to pray,' added Mr. Baker, and we said goodbye.

I had little time for reflection just yet.

I went to Mr. Johnston, paid the bill and removed to the new lodgings, where I had my lunch. The landlady was a good woman. She had cooked a vegetarian meal

---

[151] 'from me my religious views' in the first edition.

[152] The South Africa General Mission was established in 1889 as Cape General Mission by W. Spencer Walton with support from Rev. Andrew Murray and Mrs. M.S. Osborne-Howe, who had established a series of institutions for missionary work in Cape Town.

[153] 'I deliver' in the first edition.

[154] In the original an explanation of the word 'light' is provided in parenthesis, which would translate as 'enlightenment of knowledge'.

for me. It was not long before I made myself quite at home with the family.

I next went to see the friend[155] to whom Dada Abdulla had given me a note. From him I learnt more about the hardships of Indians in South Africa. He insisted that I should stay with him. I thanked him, and told him that I had already made arrangements. He urged me not to hesitate to ask for anything I needed.

It was now dark. I returned home, had my dinner, went to my room and lay there absorbed in deep thought. There was not any immediate work for me. I informed Abdulla Sheth of it. What, I thought, can be the meaning of Mr. Baker's interest in me? What shall I gain from his religious co-workers? How far should I undertake the study of Christianity? How was I to obtain literature about Hinduism? And how was I to understand Christianity in its *proper perspective*[M4] without   [M4] intrinsic form
thoroughly knowing my own religion? I could come to only one conclusion: I should make a dispassionate study of all that came to me, and deal with Mr. Baker's group as God might guide me; I should not think of embracing another religion before I had fully understood my own.

Thus musing I fell asleep.

XI

CHRISTIAN CONTACTS

The next day at one o'clock I went to Mr. Baker's prayer-meeting. There I was introduced to Miss Harris, Miss Gabb, Mr. Coates[156] and others. Everyone kneeled

---

[155] Sheth Haji Muhammad Haji Jesoab.

[156] Clara Harris, Georgina Gabb and Michael Coates. Coates was about thirty years of age in 1893 and one of the earliest members of the South Africa General Mission.

down to pray, and I followed suit. The prayers were supplications to God for various things, according to each person's desire. Thus the usual forms were for the day to be passed peacefully, or for God to open the doors of the heart.

A prayer was now added for my welfare: 'Lord, show the path to the new brother who has come amongst us. Give him, Lord, the peace that Thou hast given us. May the Lord Jesus who has saved us save him too. We ask all this in the name of Jesus.' There was no singing of hymns or other music at these meetings. After the supplication for something special every day, we dispersed, each going to his lunch, that being the hour for it. The prayer did not take more than five minutes.

The Misses Harris and Gabb were both elderly maiden ladies. Mr. Coates was a Quaker. The two ladies lived together, and they gave me a standing invitation to four o'clock tea at their house every Sunday.

When we met on Sundays, I used to give Mr. Coates my religious diary for the week, and discuss with him the books I had read and the impression they had left on me. The ladies used to narrate their sweet experiences and talk about the peace they had found.

Mr. Coates was a frank-hearted staunch young man.[M1] We went out for walks together, and he also took me to other Christian friends.

[M1] Quaker

As we came closer to each other, he began to give me books of his own choice, until my shelf was filled with them.[157] He loaded me with books, as it were. In pure faith I consented to read all those books, and as I went on reading them we discussed them.

I read a number of such books in 1893. I do not remember the names of them all, but they included

---

[157] 'until my shelf was filled with them' added in the English translation.

the *Commentary* of Dr. Parker of the City Temple,[158] Pearson's *Many Infallible Proofs*[159] and Butler's *Analogy*.[160] Parts of these were unintelligible to me. I liked some things in them, while I did not like others.[161] *Many Infallible Proofs* were proofs in support of the religion of the Bible, as the author understood it. The book had no effect on me. Parker's *Commentary* was morally stimulating, but it could not be of any help to one who had no faith in the prevalent Christian beliefs. Butler's *Analogy* struck me to be a very profound and difficult book, which should be read four or five[162] times to be understood properly. It seemed to me to be written with a view to converting atheists to theism. The arguments advanced in it regarding the existence of God were unnecessary for me, as I had then passed the stage of unbelief but the arguments in proof of Jesus being the only incarnation of God and the Mediator between God and man left me unmoved.

But Mr. Coates was not the man easily to accept defeat. He had great affection for me. He saw, round my neck, the Vaishnava necklace of Tulasi-beads.[163] He thought it to be superstition and was pained by it. 'This superstition does not become you. Come, let me break the necklace.'

---

[158] Dr. Joseph Parker, *The People's Bible: Discourses Upon the Holy Scriptures* (London: 1889). According to James Hunt, MKG had attended Dr. Parker's weekday services in London. See *Gandhi and the Non-Conformists*, p. 31.

[159] Arthur T. Pierson, *Many Infallible Proofs: The Evidence of Christianity* (New York: 1886).

[160] Bishop Joseph Butler, *The Analogy of Religion, Natural and Revealed, to the Constitution and Course of Nature* (1736).

[161] 'I would narrate all these to Coates.' To add.

[162] 'five to seven' in the original.

[163] 'necklace of Tulasi-beads' translates *kanthi*, literally, one that is worn around the neck, usually made of tulsi (basil) beads.

'No, you will not. It is a sacred gift from my mother.'

'But do you believe in it?'

'I do not know its mysterious significance. I do not think I should come to harm if I did not wear it. But I cannot, without sufficient reason, give up a necklace that she put round my neck out of love and in the conviction that it would be conducive to my welfare. When, with the passage of time, it wears away and breaks of its own accord, I shall have no desire to get a new one. But this necklace cannot be broken.'

Mr. Coates could not appreciate my argument, as he had no regard for my religion. He was looking forward to delivering me from the abyss of ignorance. He wanted to convince me that, no matter whether there was some truth in other religions, salvation was impossible for me unless I accepted Christianity which represented the truth, and that my[164] sins would not be washed away except by the intercession of Jesus, and that all good works were useless.

Just as he introduced me to several books, he introduced me to several friends whom he regarded as staunch Christians. One of these introductions was to a family which belonged to the Plymouth Brethren, a Christian sect.

Many of the contacts for which Mr. Coates was responsible were good. Most struck me as being God-fearing. But during my contact with this family, one of the Plymouth Brethren confronted me with an argument for which I was not prepared:

'You cannot understand the beauty of our religion. From what you say it appears that you must be brooding over your transgressions every moment of your life, always mending them and atoning for them. How can this ceaseless cycle of action bring you redemption?

---

[164] 'my' added in the English translation.

You can never have peace. You admit that we are all sinners. Now look at the perfection of our belief. Our attempts at improvement and atonement are futile. And yet redemption we must have. How can we bear the burden of sin? We can but throw it on Jesus. He is the only sinless Son of God. It is His word that *those who believe in Him shall have everlasting life.*[M2] Therein lies God's infinite mercy. And as we believe in the atonement of Jesus, our own sins do not bind us. *Sin we must.*[M3] It is impossible to live in this world sinless. And therefore Jesus suffered and atoned for all the sins of mankind. Only he who accepts His *great redemption*[M4] can have eternal peace. Think what a life of restlessness is yours, and what a promise of peace we have.'

The argument utterly failed to convince me. I humbly replied:

'If this be the *Christianity acknowledged by all Christians,*[M5] I cannot accept it. I do not seek *redemption*[M6] from the consequences of my sin. I seek to be *redeemed*[M7] from sin itself, or rather from the very thought of sin. Until I have attained that end, I shall be content to be restless.'

To which the Plymouth Brother rejoined: 'I assure you, your attempt is fruitless. Think again over what I have said.'

And the Brother proved as good as his word. He knowingly[165] committed *transgressions,*[M8] and showed me that he was undisturbed by the thought of them.[166]

But I already knew before meeting with these friends that all Christians did not believe in such a theory of atonement.[167] Mr. Coates himself walked in the fear of *God.*[M9] His heart was pure, and he believed in

[M2] He washes away the sins of those who believe in Him

[M3] Sin is inescapable.

[M4] Supreme Sacrifice

[M5] accepted notion of Christianity

[M6] deliverance

[M7] freed

[M8] immoral acts

[M9] sin

---

[165] 'voluntarily' in the first edition.

[166] 'and showed me that he was undisturbed by the thought of them.' Added in English translation.

[167] 'of atonement' added in the English translation.

the possibility of *self-purification*.[M10] The two ladies also shared this belief. Some of the books that came into my hands were full of devotion. So, although Mr. Coates was very much disturbed by this latest experience of mine, I was able to reassure him and tell him that the distorted belief of a Plymouth Brother could not prejudice me against Christianity.

My difficulties lay elsewhere. They[168] were with regard to the Bible and its accepted interpretation.[169]

XII

SEEKING TOUCH[M1] WITH INDIANS

Before writing further about Christian contacts, I must record other experiences of the same period.

Sheth Tyeb Haji Khan Muhammad had in Pretoria the same position as was enjoyed by Dada Abdulla in Natal. There was no public movement that could be conducted without him. I made his acquaintance the very first week and told him of my intention to get in touch with every Indian in Pretoria. I expressed a desire to study the conditions of Indians there, and asked for his help in my work, which he gladly agreed to give.

My first step was to call a meeting of all the Indians in Pretoria[170] and to present to them a picture of their condition in the Transvaal.[171] The meeting was held at the house of Sheth Haji Muhammad Haji Joosab, to whom I had a letter of introduction. It was principally

---

[168] 'lay elsewhere. They' added in the English translation.

[169] In *Navajivan*, the chapter 'Narayan Hemchandra' was published along with this chapter, which was subsequently incorporated as Chapter XXII of Part I.

[170] 'in Pretoria' added in the English translation.

[171] 'in the Transvaal' added in the English translation.

attended by Meman merchants, though there was a sprinkling of Hindus as well. The Hindu population in Pretoria was, as a matter of fact,[172] very small.

My speech at this meeting may be said to have been the first public speech in my life. I went fairly prepared with my subject, *which was about observing truthfulness in business.*[M2] I had always heard the merchants say that truth was not possible in business. I did not think so then, nor do I now. Even today there are merchant friends who contend that truth is inconsistent with business. Business, they say, is a very practical affair, and truth a matter of religion; and they argue that practical affairs are one thing, while religion is quite another. Pure truth, they hold, is out of the question in business; one can speak[173] it only so far as is suitable. I strongly contested the position in my speech and awakened the merchants to a sense of their duty, which was twofold. Their responsibility to be truthful[174] was all the greater in a foreign land, because the conduct of a few Indians was the measure of that of the millions of their fellow-countrymen.

[M2] and I intended to speak about truth

I had found our people's habits to be insanitary, as compared with those of the Englishmen around them, and drew their attention to it. I laid stress on the necessity of forgetting all distinctions such as Hindus, Mussalmans, Parsis, Christians, Gujaratis, Madrasis, Punjabis, Sindhis, Kachchhis, Surtis and so on.

I suggested, in conclusion, the formation of an association to make representations to the authorities concerned in respect of the hardships of the Indian settlers, and offered to place at its disposal as much of my time and service as was possible.

---

[172] 'as a matter of fact' added in the English translation.

[173] 'and observe' to add.

[174] 'to be truthful' added in the English translation.

I saw that I made a considerable impression on the meeting.

My speech was followed by discussion. Some offered to supply me with facts. I felt encouraged. I saw that very few amongst my audience knew English. As I felt that knowledge of English would be useful in that country, I advised those who had leisure to learn English. I told them that it was possible to learn a language even at an advanced age, and cited cases of people who had done so. I undertook, besides, to teach a class, if one was started or personally to instruct individuals desiring to learn the language.

The class was not started, but three young men expressed their readiness to learn at their convenience, and on condition that I went to their places to teach them. Of these, two were Mussalmans—one of them a barber and the other a clerk—and the third was a Hindu, a petty shopkeeper. I agreed to suit them all. I had no misgivings regarding my capacity to teach. My pupils might become tired, but not I. Sometimes it happened that I would go to their places only to find them engaged in their business. But I did not lose patience. None of the three desired a deep study of English, but two may be said to have made fairly good progress in about eight months. Two learnt enough to keep accounts and write ordinary business[175] letters. The barber's ambition was confined to acquiring just enough English for dealing with his customers. As a result of their studies, two of the pupils were equipped for making a fair income.

I was satisfied with the result of the meeting. It was decided to hold such meetings, as far as I remember, once a week or, may be, once a month. These were held more or less regularly, and on these occasions there was a free exchange of ideas. The result was that there was now in Pretoria no[M3] Indian I did not know, or whose

[M3] a rare

---

[175] 'business' added in the English translation.

condition I was not acquainted with. This prompted me in turn to make the acquaintance of the British Agent in Pretoria, Mr. Jacobus de Wet. He had sympathy for the Indians, but he had very little influence. However, he agreed to help us as best he could, and invited me to meet him whenever I wished.

I now communicated with the railway authorities and told them that, even under their own regulations, the disabilities about travelling under which the Indians laboured could not be justified. I got a letter in reply to the effect that first and second class tickets would be issued to Indians who were properly dressed. This was far from giving adequate relief, as it rested with the Station Master to decide who was 'properly dressed'.

The British Agent showed me some papers dealing with Indian affairs. Tyeb Sheth had also given me similar papers. I learnt from them how cruelly the Indians were hounded out from the Orange Free State.

In short, my stay in Pretoria enabled me to make a deep study of the social, economic and political condition of the Indians in the Transvaal and the Orange Free State. I had no idea that this study was to be of invaluable service to me in the future. For I had thought of returning home by the end of the year, or even earlier, if the case was finished before the year was out.

But God[176] disposed otherwise.

XIII

WHAT IT IS TO BE A 'COOLIE'[M1]

M1 The Experience of Being a Coolie

It would be out of place here to describe fully the condition of Indians in the Transvaal and the Orange

---

[176] 'But God had' in the first edition.

Free State. I would suggest that those who wish to have a full idea of it may turn to my *History of Satyagraha in South Africa.*[177] It is, however, necessary to give here a brief outline.

In the Orange Free State the Indians were deprived of all their rights by a special law enacted in 1888 or even earlier.[178] If they chose to stay there, they could do so only to serve as waiters in hotels or to pursue some other such menial calling. The traders were driven away with a nominal compensation.[179] They made representations and petitions, but *in vain.*[M2]

A very stringent enactment was passed in the Transvaal in 1885.[180] It was slightly amended in 1886, and it was provided under the amended law that all Indians should pay a poll-tax of £3 as fee for entry into the Transvaal. They might not own land except in locations set apart for them, and in practice even that

[M2] who would listen to their feeble and lowly voice?

---

[177] On 23 November 1923 as a prisoner at the Yeravada Central Prison MKG commenced writing *Dakshin Africa Na Satyagraha No Itihas* in Gujarati, which appeared serially in *Navajivan* from 13 April 1924 to 22 November 1925. It was published as a book in two parts in 1924 and 1925. The authorized English translation, *Satyagraha In South Africa*, by Valji Govindji Desai was published by S. Ganesan, Madras in 1928. *CWMG*, vol. 29, pp. 1–269, carries the text of the third impression published by Navajivan in 1961.

[178] By Ordinance 1 of 1885.

[179] According to Maureen Swan, there were only nine Indian merchants in Orange Free State. See Maureen Swan, *Gandhi: The South African Experience* (Johannesburg: Raven Press, 1985), p. 38.

[180] The Transvaal was subject to British suzerainty under the Pretoria Convention of 1881, which allowed it to regulate the conditions regarding the presence of Indians. According to Law 3 of 1885, 'so-called Coolies, Arabs, Malays and Mahomedan subjects of the Turkish Empire' could not vote or acquire new land. Settlers were required to pay £25 registration fee within eight days of entry. See Burnett Britton, *Gandhi Arrives in South Africa* (Greenleaf Books: Canton, Maine, 1999), p. 29.

was not to be ownership. They had no franchise. All this was under the special law for Asiatics, to whom the laws for the coloured people were also applied. Under these latter, Indians might not walk on public footpaths, and might not move out of doors after 9 p.m. without a permit. The enforcement of this last regulation was elastic so far as the Indians were concerned. Those who passed as 'Arabs' were, as a matter of favour, exempted from it. The exemption thus naturally depended on the sweet will of the police.

I had to experience the effect of both these regulations. I often went out at night for a walk with Mr. Coates, and we rarely got back home much before ten o'clock. What if the police arrested me? Mr. Coates was more concerned about this than I. He had to issue passes to his Negro servants. But how could he give one to me? Only a master might issue a permit to a servant. If I had wanted one, and even if Mr. Coates had been ready to give it, he could not have done so, for it would have been fraud.

So Mr. Coates or some friend of his took me to the State Attorney, Dr. Krause.[181] We turned out to be barristers of the same Inn.[182] The fact that I needed a pass to enable me to be out of doors after 9 p.m. was *too much*M3 for him. He expressed sympathy for me. Instead of ordering for me a pass, he gave me a letter authorizing me to be out of doors at all hours without police interference. I always kept this letter on me whenever I went out. The fact that I never had to make use of it was a mere accident.

M3 unbearable

---

[181] Dr. Albert E.J. Krause was the attorney general. He obtained his law degree from Göttingen University where he wrote a dissertation titled 'Über die "Transmissio ex capite in integrum restitutionis"'. I am grateful to Andrew Mussell, the archivist of the Hon. Society of Gray's Inn, for this information.

[182] Dr. Krause was not called to the Bar from the Inns of Court in England.

Dr. Krause invited me to his place, and we may be said to have become friends.[183] I occasionally called on him, and it was through him that I was introduced to his more famous brother,[184] who was Public Prosecutor in Johannesburg. During the Boer War he was court-martialled for conspiring to murder an English officer, and was sentenced to imprisonment for seven years. He was also disbarred by the Benchers.[185] On the termination of hostilities he was released and, being honourably readmitted to the Transvaal bar, resumed practice.

These connections were useful to me later on in my public life, and simplified much of my work.

The consequences of the regulation regarding the use of footpaths were rather serious for me. I always went out for a walk through President Street to an open plain. President Kruger's house was in this street—a very modest, unostentatious building, without a garden, and not distinguishable from other houses in its neighbourhood. The houses of many of the millionaires in Pretoria were far[186] more pretentious, and were surrounded by gardens. Indeed President Kruger's simplicity was proverbial. Only the presence of a police patrol before the house indicated that it belonged to

---

[183] Dr. Krause's brother Hon'ble F.E.T. Krause recalled in 1948, 'I remember an incident which occurred when my brother had invited him to dinner one night. The natives serving at the table, protested at being called upon to attend to an Indian, and it had been explained to them that Gandhiji was a great man, just like a native chief, that they were prepared to continue their service.' In Chandrashankar Shukla (ed.), *Reminiscences of Gandhiji* (Bombay: Vora and Co., 1951), p. 160.

[184] Frederick Edward Trangott Krause of the Middle Temple, joined 5 June 1890, called to the Bar 14 June 1893, described in the Inn's records as '5th son of Dr. Carl Johann Gottlieb'.

[185] 'Benchers' English word in the original.

[186] 'larger,' to add.

some official. I nearly always went along the footpath past this patrol without the slightest hitch or hindrance.

Now the man on duty used to be changed from time to time. Once one of these men, without giving me the slightest warning, without even asking[187] me to leave the footpath, pushed and kicked me into the street. I was dismayed. Before I could question him as to his behaviour, Mr. Coates, who happened to be passing the spot on horseback, hailed me and said:

'Gandhi, I have seen everything. I shall gladly be your witness in court if you proceed against the man. I am very sorry you have been so rudely assaulted.'

'You need not be sorry,' I said. 'What does the poor man know? All coloured[188] people are the same to him. He no doubt *treats Negroes just as he has treated me*.[M4] I have made it a rule not to go to court in respect of any personal grievance. So I do not intend to proceed against him.'

[M4] pushes Negros off the footpath in the same way, and hence he did the same with me.

'That is just like you,' said Mr. Coates, 'but do think it over again. We must teach such men a lesson.' He then spoke to the policeman and reprimanded him. I could not follow their talk, as it was in Dutch, the policeman being a Boer. But he apologized to me, for which there was no need.[189] I had already forgiven him.

But I never again went through this street. *There would be other men coming in this man's place and, ignorant of the incident, they would behave likewise.*[M5] Why should I unnecessarily court another kick? I therefore selected a different walk.

[M5] How were other policemen to know of this incident?

The incident deepened my feeling for the Indian settlers. I discussed with them the advisability of making

---

[187] 'having asked' in the original.

[188] 'black' in the original.

[189] 'for which there was no need' added in the English translation.

a test case,[190] if it were found necessary to do so, after having seen the British Agent in the matter of these regulations.

I thus made an intimate study of the hard condition of the Indian settlers, not only by reading and hearing about it, but by personal experience. I saw that South Africa was no country for a self-respecting Indian, and my mind became more and more occupied with the question as to how this state of things might be improved.

But my principal duty for the moment was to attend to the case of Dada Abdulla.

XIV

PREPARATION FOR THE CASE

The year's stay in Pretoria was a most valuable experience[191] in my life. Here it was that I had opportunities of learning public work and acquired some measure of my capacity for it. Here it was that the religious spirit within me became *a living force*,[M1] and here too I acquired a true knowledge of legal practice. Here I learnt the things that a junior barrister learns in a senior barrister's chamber, and here I also[192] gained confidence that I should not after all fail as a lawyer. It was likewise here that I learnt the *secret of success as a lawyer*.[M2]

M1 acute

M2 key to be a lawyer

Dada Abdulla's was no small case. The suit was for £40,000.[193] Arising[194] out of business transactions,

---

[190] 'test case' in the original. It also provides an explanation in parenthesis which translates as 'as an example'.

[191] 'experience' added in the English translation.

[192] 'also I' in the first edition.

[193] 'that is six lakh rupees' to add.

[194] 'Arising as it did' in the first edition.

it was full of intricacies of accounts. Part of the claim was based on promissory notes,[195] and part on the specific performance of promise to deliver promissory notes. The defence was that the promissory notes were fraudulently taken and lacked sufficient consideration. There were numerous points of fact and law[196] in this intricate case.[197]

Both parties had engaged the best attorneys and counsel. I thus had a fine opportunity of studying their work. The preparation of the plaintiff's case for the attorney and the sifting of facts in support of his case had been entrusted to me. It was an education to see how much the attorney accepted, and how much he rejected from my preparation, as also to see how much use the counsel made of the brief prepared by the attorney. I saw that this preparation for the case would give me a fair measure of my powers of comprehension and my capacity for marshalling evidence.

I took the keenest interest in the case. Indeed I threw myself into it. I read all the papers pertaining to the transactions. My client was a man of great ability and reposed absolute confidence in me, and this rendered my work easy. I made a fair study of book-keeping.

---

[195] 'promissory notes' English term in the original.

[196] 'and of book-keeping' to add.

[197] *Dada Abdulla and Co. versus Tyeb Haji Khan Mahomed and Co. and Mossa Amod and Co.* On 31 July 1890 Dada Abdullah and Co., wishing to dispose of the Transvaal branch of business, entered into an agreement with Tyeb Haji Khan Mahomed and Co., whereby all of Abdullah's interests in the Transvaal, including stores in Johannesburg, Pretoria, Rustenburg and Heidelberg, were to be handed over to Mahomed and Co. at the price of £40,000. Dada Abdullah and Co. brought a suit for £18,000 against Mahomed and Co., for the balance alleged owing on the sale. See Charles DiSalvo, *M.K. Gandhi, Attorney at Law: The Man Before the Mahatma* (New Delhi: Random House, 2012), p. 47.

My capacity for translation was improved by having to translate the correspondence, which was for the most part in Gujarati.

Although,[198] as I have said before, I took a keen interest in religious communion and in public work and always gave some of my time to them, they were not then my primary interest. The preparation of the case was my primary interest. Reading of law and looking up law cases, when necessary, had always a prior claim on my time. As a result, I acquired such a grasp of the facts of the case as perhaps was not possessed even by the parties themselves, inasmuch as I had with me the papers of both the parties.

I recalled the late Mr. Pincott's[199] advice—facts are three-fourths of the law. At a later date it was amply borne out by that famous barrister of South Africa, the late Mr. Leonard.[200] In a certain case in my charge I saw that, though justice was on the side of my client, the law seemed to be against him. In despair I approached Mr. Leonard for help. He also felt that the facts of the case were very strong. He exclaimed, 'Gandhi, I have learnt one thing, and it is this, that if we take care of the facts of a case, the law will take care of itself. Let us dive deeper into the facts of this case.' With these words he asked me to study the case further and then see him again. On a re-examination of the facts I saw them in an entirely new light, and I also hit upon an old South African case bearing on the point. I was delighted and went to Mr. Leonard and told him everything. 'Right,' he said, 'we shall win the case. Only we must bear in mind which of the judges takes it.'

---

[198] To add at the beginning of the paragraph: 'I was very diligent.'

[199] Frederick Pincott, whom MKG met on being called to the Bar. See Chapter XXV: 'My Helplessness', Part I.

[200] J.W. Leonard.

When I was making preparation for Dada Abdulla's case, I had not fully realized this paramount importance of facts. Facts mean truth, and once we adhere to truth, the law comes to our aid naturally. I saw that the facts of Dada Abdulla's case made it very strong indeed, and that the law was bound to be on his side. But I also saw that the litigation, if it were persisted in, would ruin the plaintiff and the defendant, who were relatives and both belonged to the same city. *No one knew how long the case might go on. Should it be allowed to continue to be fought out in court, it might go on indefinitely and to no advantage of either party.*[M3] Both, therefore, desired an immediate termination of the case, if possible.

I approached Tyeb Sheth and requested and advised him to *go to arbitration.*[M4] I recommended him to see his counsel. I suggested to him that if an arbitrator commanding the confidence of both parties could be appointed, the case would be quickly finished. The lawyers' fees were so rapidly mounting up that they were enough to devour all the resources of the clients, big merchants as they were. The case occupied so much of their attention that they had no time left for any other work. In the meantime mutual ill-will was steadily increasing. I became disgusted with the profession. As lawyers the counsel on both sides were bound to rake up points of law in support of their own clients. I also saw for the first time that the winning party never recovers all the costs incurred. Under the Court Fees Regulation there was a fixed scale of costs to be allowed as between party and party, the actual costs as between attorney and client being very much higher. This was more than I could bear. I felt that my duty was to befriend both parties and bring *them*[M5] together. I *strained every nerve*[M6] to bring about a compromise. At last Tyeb Sheth agreed. An arbitrator[201] was appointed,

[M3] No one could see the end of the case. If it remained in the court, it could be prolonged as one wished. Neither of the two would benefit by prolonging it.

[M4] settle it in-house

[M5] the relatives

[M6] did heart-wrecking labour

---

[201] John Livingston of Durban.

the case was argued before him, and Dada Abdulla won.[202]

But that did not satisfy me. If my client were to seek immediate execution of the award, it would be impossible for Tyeb Sheth to meet the whole of the awarded amount, and there was an unwritten law among the Porbandar Memans living in South Africa that death should be preferred to bankruptcy. It was impossible for Tyeb Sheth to pay down the whole sum of about £37,000 and costs. He meant to pay not a pie less than the amount, and he did not want to be declared bankrupt. There was only one way, Dada Abdulla should allow him *to pay in moderate instalments.*[M7] He was equal to the occasion, and granted Tyeb Sheth instalments spread over a very long period. It was more difficult for me to secure this concession of payment by instalments than to get the parties to agree to arbitration. But both were happy over the result, and both rose in the public estimation. My joy was boundless. I had learnt the true practice of law. I had learnt to find out the better side of human nature and to enter men's hearts. I realized that the true function of a lawyer was to unite parties riven asunder. The lesson *was so indelibly burnt into*[M8] me that a large part of my time during the twenty years of my practice as a lawyer was occupied in bringing about private compromises of hundreds of cases. I lost nothing thereby—not even money, certainly not my soul.

M7 sufficient time

M8 took such firm root in

---

[202] The operative part of the arbitrator's award read: 'After carefully weighing the evidence given on oath and considering it in connection with the productions put in, I must say that I am far from satisfied with the evidence adduced by and given on behalf of Tyeb Haji Khan Mohammed and Co. The witness is in my opinion not only a very much biased witness, but his attitude and demeanour when giving evidence was anything but indicative of truth.' Burnett Britton, *Gandhi Arrives in South Africa*, p. 47.

XV

RELIGIOUS FERMENT

It is now time to turn again to my *experiences*[M1] with   [M1] relations
Christian friends.

Mr. Baker was getting anxious about my future.
He took me to the Wellington Convention.[203] The
Protestant Christians organize such gatherings every few
years for religious enlightenment or, in other words,
self-purification. One may call this religious restoration
or revival. The Wellington Convention was of this type.
The chairman was the famous divine of the place, the
Rev. Andrew Murray. Mr. Baker had hoped that the
atmosphere of religious exaltation at the Convention, and
the enthusiasm and earnestness of the people attending
it, would inevitably lead me to embrace Christianity.

But his final hope was the efficacy of prayer. He had
an abiding faith in prayer. It was his firm conviction that
God could not but listen to prayer fervently offered. He
would cite the instances of men like George Muller of
Bristol,[204] who depended entirely on prayer even for his
temporal needs. I listened to his discourse on the efficacy
of prayer with unbiased attention, and assured him that
nothing could prevent me from embracing Christianity,
should I feel the call. I had no hesitation in giving him
this assurance, as[205] I had long since taught myself to

---

[203] The Wellington Convention for the Deepening of Spiritual Life
was held at Huguenot College in Wellington, forty miles from
Cape Town. This was the fourth annual meeting since the first
held in 1889. It was held from Wednesday to Friday, 25 to 27
October 1893. For more details, see James Hunt, *Gandhi and the
Non-Conformists*, pp. 32–36.

[204] In the original 'Muller (a famous devout Christian)'.

[205] 'I had no hesitation in giving him this assurance, as' added in the
English Translation.

follow the inner voice. I delighted in submitting to it.[206]
To act against it would be difficult and painful to me.

So we went to Wellington. Mr. Baker was hard
put to it in having 'a coloured man' like me for his
companion. He had to suffer inconveniences on many
occasions entirely on account of me. We had to break
the journey on the way,[207] as one of the days happened
to be a Sunday, and Mr. Baker and his party would
not travel on the sabbath. Though the manager of the
station hotel agreed to take me in after much altercation,
he absolutely refused to admit me to the dining-room.
Mr. Baker was not the man to give way easily. He
stood by the rights of the guests of a hotel. But I could
see his difficulty. At Wellington also I stayed with Mr.
Baker.[208] In spite of his best efforts to conceal the little
inconveniences that he was put to, I could see them all.

This Convention was an assemblage of devout
Christians. I was delighted at their faith. I met the Rev.
Murray. I saw that many were praying for me. I liked
some of their hymns, they were very sweet.

The Convention lasted for three days. I could
understand and appreciate the devoutness of those
who attended it. But I saw no reason for changing
my belief—my religion.[209] It was impossible for me
to believe that I could go to heaven or attain salvation
only by *becoming*[M2] a Christian. When I frankly said so to

M2 calling myself

---

[206] 'submitting myself to it' in the first edition.

[207] The party halted at Colesburg, Cape Town.

[208] Baker recollected in his autobiography, 'My host, who was a
Dutch Salvationist, put a double-bedded room at our service,
and I had the great distinction of sleeping in the same bed with
the now so highly esteemed Indian philosopher.' Quoted in
James Hunt, *Gandhi and the Non-Conformists*, p. 35.

[209] MKG told his first biographer Rev. Joseph Doke with an 'amused
smile': 'These people loved me so well, that if they would have
influenced me to become a Christian, they would have become
vegetarians themselves!' Doke, *Gandhi: A Patriot in South Africa*, p. 46.

some of the good Christian friends, they were shocked. But there was no help for it.

My difficulties lay deeper. It was more than I could believe that Jesus was the only incarnate son of God, and that only he who believed in him would have everlasting life. If God could have sons, all of us were His sons. If Jesus was like God, or God Himself, then all men were like God and could be God Himself. My reason was not ready to believe literally that Jesus by his death and by his blood redeemed the sins of the world. Metaphorically there might be some truth in it. Again, according to *Christianity*[M3] only human beings had souls, and not other living beings, for whom death meant complete extinction; while I held a contrary belief. I could accept Jesus as a *martyr, an embodiment of sacrifice,*[M4] and a divine teacher, but not as the *most perfect man ever born.*[M5] His death on the Cross[210] was a great example to the world, but that there was anything like a mysterious or miraculous virtue in it my heart could not accept. The pious lives of Christians did not give me anything that the lives of men of other faiths had failed to give. I had seen in other lives just the same reformation that I had heard of among Christians. Philosophically there was nothing extraordinary in Christian principles. From the point of view of *sacrifice,*[M6] it seemed to me that the Hindus greatly surpassed the Christians. It was impossible for me to regard Christianity as a perfect religion or the greatest of all religions.

I shared this mental churning with my Christian friends whenever there was an opportunity, but their answers could not satisfy me.

Thus if I could not accept Christianity either as a perfect, or the greatest religion, neither was I then convinced of Hinduism being such. *Hindu defects*[M7] were pressingly visible to me. If untouchability could

[M3] Christian belief

[M4] renunciate, a great soul

[M5] man without a second

[M6] renunciation

[M7] The defects of Hindu religion

---

[210] 'on the Cross' added in the English translation.

M8 existence

be a part of Hinduism, it could but be a rotten part or an excrescence. I could not understand the *raison d'etre*[M8] of a multitude of sects and castes. What was the meaning of saying that[211] the Vedas were the inspired Word of God? If they were inspired, why not also the Bible and the Koran?

M9 influence

As Christian friends were endeavouring to *convert*[M9] me, even so were Mussalman friends. Abdulla Sheth had kept on inducing me to study Islam, and of course he had always something to say regarding its beauty.

I expressed my difficulties in a letter to Raychandbhai.[212] I also corresponded with other religious authorities in India and received answers from them. Raychandbhai's letter somewhat pacified me. He asked me to be patient and to study Hinduism more deeply. One of his sentences was to this effect: 'On a dispassionate view of the question I am convinced that no other religion has the subtle and profound thought

M10 compassion

of Hinduism, its vision of the soul, or its *charity*.'[M10]

I purchased Sale's translation of the Koran[213] and began reading it. I also obtained other books on Islam. I communicated with Christian friends in England. One of them introduced me to Edward Maitland,[214] with whom I opened correspondence.[215] He sent me *The*

---

[211] 'only' to add.

[212] For the text of the questions posed by MKG, see *CWMG*, vol. 1, pp. 127–28. For Raychandbhai's responses, *CWMG*, vol. 32, pp. 593–602.

[213] George Sale (1697–1736); the translation appeared in 1734.

[214] Edward Maitland (1824–97), a vegetarian, established the Esoteric Christian Union in 1891.

[215] Nothing of this correspondence survives. MKG became 'Agent of the Esoteric Christian Union and the London Vegetarian Society' and inserted a notice in *The Natal Mercury* of 28 November 1894 that books by Anna Kingsford and Edward Maitland could be obtained from him. See *CWMG*, vol. 1, p. 168.

Perfect Way,[216] a book he had written in collaboration with Anna Kingsford. The book was a repudiation of the current Christian belief. He also sent me another book, *The New Interpretation of the Bible*.[217] I liked both. They seemed to support Hinduism. Tolstoy's *The Kingdom of God Is within You* overwhelmed me. It left an abiding impression on me. Before the independent thinking, profound morality, and the truthfulness of this book, all the books given me by Mr. Coates seemed to pale into insignificance.

My studies thus carried me in a direction unthought of by the Christian friends. My correspondence with Edward Maitland was fairly prolonged, and that with Raychandbhai continued until his death. I read some of the books he sent me. These included *Panchikaran, Maniratnamala, Mumukshu Prakaran* of *Yogavasishtha*, Haribhadra Suri's *Shaddarshana Samuchchaya* and others.[218]

Though I took a path my Christian friends had not intended for me, I have remained forever indebted to them for the religious quest that they awakened in me. I shall always cherish the memory of their contact. The years that followed had more, not less, of such sweet and sacred contacts in store for me.

---

[216] *The Perfect Way: Or, The Finding of Christ*, published in 1882.

[217] *The New Gospel of Interpretation*, published in 1892. The title given in the text is a literal translation of the Gujarati original.

[218] *Panchikaran* was composed by Adi Shankara; *Maniratnamala*, by Manibhai Nabhubhai Dwivedi; *Mumukshu Prakaran* is attributed to Valmiki, the composer of the Ramayana. *Yogavasistha* has six chapters, in which *Mumukshu Prakaran* is the second, which describes the attributes to a seeker after freedom.

Haribhadra Suri was a Svetambara Jain monk; it is believed that he lived from AD 429 to 529, while some scholars believe that he was born after AD 650. *Shaddarshana Samuchchaya* is a comparative discussion of Jain philosophy with other branches of Hindu philosophies.

XVI

M1 Who Can Foretell Tomorrow?

MAN PROPOSES, GOD DISPOSES[219][M1]

The case having been concluded, I had no reason for staying in Pretoria. So I went back to Durban[220] and began to make preparations for my return home. But Abdulla Sheth was not the man to let me sail without a send-off. He gave a farewell party in my honour at Sydenham.[221]

It was proposed to spend the whole day there. Whilst I was turning over the sheets of some of the newspapers I found there, I chanced to see a paragraph in a corner of one of them under the caption 'Indian Franchise'.[222] It was with reference to the Bill then before the House of Legislature, which sought to deprive the Indians of their right to elect members of the Natal Legislative Assembly.[223] I was ignorant of

---

[219] To add:

> 'In this world,
> The next moment is unknown.
> Know this, o' mind. Who can
> Foretell tomorrow.'

In *Navajivan* of 29 August 1926 this couplet was the title of the chapter. The last line became the title when the first Gujarati edition was published.

[220] MKG returned to Durban on 16 May 1894.

[221] On Sunday, 24 June 1894. MKG noted in his diary, 'Went out for a picnic with Abdoola.' *CWMG*, vol. 91, p. 1.

[222] According to Burnett Britton, it was *The Natal Mercury* of Friday, 22 June 1894. The report 'Indians and the Franchise' was carried on page 4 of the newspaper. See Britton, *Gandhi Arrives in South Africa*, p. 48. In the original the word 'franchise' is explained by a sentence: 'It means the right to vote for the Indians.'

[223] The Bill to amend the franchise was first announced on 25 April 1894, which stated 'no persons belonging to Asiatic races not accustomed to the exercise of the franchise rights under

the Bill, and so were the rest of the guests who had assembled there.

I enquired of Abdulla Sheth about it. He said: 'What can we understand in these matters? We can only understand things that affect our trade. As you know all our trade in the Orange Free State has been swept away. We agitated about it, but in vain. We are after all lame men, being unlettered. *We generally take in newspapers simply to ascertain the daily market rates, etc.*[M2] What can we know of *legislation?*[M3] Our eyes and ears are *the European*[M4] attorneys here.'

'But,' said I, 'there are so many young Indians born and educated here. Do not they help you?'

'They!' exclaimed Abdulla Sheth *in despair.*[224] [M5] 'They never care to come to us, and to tell you the truth, we care less to recognize them. Being Christians, they are under the thumb of the white clergymen, who in their turn are subject to the Government.'

This opened my eyes. I felt that this class should be claimed as our own. Was this the meaning of Christianity? Did they cease to be Indians because they had become Christians?

But I was on the point of returning home and hesitated to express what was passing through my mind in this matter. I simply said to Abdulla Sheth: 'This Bill, if it passes into law, will make *our*[M6] lot extremely difficult. *It is the first nail into our coffin.*[M7] It strikes at the root of our self-respect.'

[M2] If we read newspapers, we comprehend only market rates.

[M3] legal matters

[M4] our white

[M5] touching his forehead

[M6] your

[M7] This is the first step towards obliterating the Indians.

---

parliamentary institutions' could in the future qualify to vote. This did not curtail the rights of those who were already eligible to vote. According to Maureen Swan, less than 300 Indians could exercise franchise in 1894. See Swan, *Gandhi: The South African Experience*, p. 45.

[224] 'What can we get from them? What do they understand of such matters?' To add.

'It may,' echoed Sheth Abdulla. 'I[225] will tell you the genesis of the franchise[226] question. We knew nothing about it. But Mr. Escombe,[227] one of our best attorneys, whom you know, put the idea into our heads. It happened thus. He is a great fighter, *and there being no love lost between him and the Wharf Engineer, he feared that the Engineer might deprive him of his votes and defeat him at the election.*[M8] So he acquainted us with our position, and at his instance we all registered ourselves as voters, and voted for him. You will now see how the franchise has not for us the value that you attach to it. But we understand what you say. Well, then, what is your advice?'

[M8] He and the wharf engineer are locked in a fierce battle, and this battle is an obstacle to Mr. Escombe's entry into the Legislature.

The other guests were listening to this conversation with attention. One of them said: 'Shall I tell you what should be done? You cancel your passage by this boat, stay here a month longer, and we will fight as you direct us.'

All the others chimed in: 'Indeed, indeed. Abdulla Sheth, you must detain Gandhibhai.'

The Sheth was a shrewd man. He said: 'I may not detain him now. Or rather, you have as much right as I to do so. But you are quite right. Let us *all* persuade him to stay on. But you should remember that he is a barrister. What about his fees?'

The mention of fees pained me, and I broke in: 'Abdulla Sheth, fees are out of the question. There can be no fees for public work. I can stay, if at all, as a servant. And as you know, I am not acquainted with all these friends. But if you believe that they will co-

---

225 'But I' in the first edition.

226 The original has the word franchise spelt as 'farenchise' in Gujarati; it further adds in parenthesis 'Many English words, thus corrupted, had taken root among the Indians. Nobody would understand the word "matadhikar", if used.'

227 Sir Harry Escombe (1833–99), advocate in Natal, later became the attorney general and premier of Natal (1897). He argued for MKG's admission to the Bar of the Natal Supreme Court on 3 September 1894.

operate, I am prepared to stay a month longer. There is one thing, however. Though you need not pay me anything, work of the nature we contemplate cannot be done without some funds to start with. Thus we may have to send telegrams, we may have to print some literature, some touring may have to be done, the local attorneys may have to be consulted, and as I am ignorant of your laws, I may need some law-books for reference. All this cannot be done without money.[228] And it is clear that one man is not enough for this work. Many must come forward to help him.'

And a chorus of voices was heard: 'Allah is great and merciful. Money will come in. Men there are, as many as you need.[229] You please consent to stay, and all will be well.'

The farewell party was thus turned into a working committee. I suggested finishing dinner, etc., quickly and getting back home. I worked out in my own mind an outline of the campaign. I ascertained the names of those who were on the list of voters, and made up my mind to stay on for a month.

Thus God laid the foundations of my *life*[M9] in South Africa and sowed the seed of the fight for national[230] self-respect.

M9 permanent residence

XVII

SETTLED IN NATAL[M1]

M1 Stayed

Sheth Haji Muhammad Haji Dada was regarded as the foremost leader of the Indian community in Natal in

---

[228] 'All this cannot be done without money.' Added in English translation.

[229] 'as many as you need' added in the English translation.

[230] 'national' added in the English translation.

1893. Financially Sheth Abdulla Haji Adam[231] was the chief among them, but he and others always gave the first place to Sheth Haji Muhammad in public affairs. A meeting was, therefore, held under his presidentship at the house of Abdulla Sheth, at which it was resolved to offer opposition to the Franchise Bill.[232]

Volunteers were enrolled. Natal-born Indians, that is, mostly Christian Indian youths, had been invited to attend this meeting. Mr. Paul,[233] the Durban Court Interpreter, and Mr. Subhan Godfrey, Head Master of a mission school, were present, and it was they who were responsible for bringing together at the meeting a good number of Christian youths. All these enrolled themselves as volunteers.

Many of the local[234] merchants were of course enrolled, noteworthy among them being Sheths Dawud Muhammad,[235] Muhammad Kasam Kamruddin,[236] Adamji Miyakhan,[237] A. Kolandavellu Pillai, C. Lachhiram, Rangasami Padiachi, and Amad Jiva. Parsi Rustomji was of course there. From among the clerks

---

[231] Founding member of the Natal Indian Congress, which was launched under his chairmanship. Died 1912.

[232] The meeting took place on Tuesday, 26 June 1894.

[233] H.L. Paul, also operated a small school in Durban in 1912.

[234] 'local' added in the English translation.

[235] One of the earliest Indian traders in South Africa, a principal contributor to public funds, and among the first to retain MKG as a lawyer. He was president, Natal Indian Congress (1906), and as a satyagrahi his longest prison sentence was six months. Early NIC meetings were held at his hall on Pine Street. His son Hoosen was among the first pupils at Phoenix School.

[236] Merchant from Johannesburg, among the first vice-presidents of NIC.

[237] Lace merchant, migrated to South Africa at the age of eighteen in 1884. Worked as the hon. secretary of the NIC during the period of MKG's absence. Died 20 July 1907 at the age of forty-one in Ahmedabad. For his obituary, see CWMG, vol. 7, pp.12–13.

were Messrs Manekji, Joshi,[238] Narsinhram and others, employees of Dada Abdulla and Co. and other big firms. They were all agreeably surprised to find themselves taking a share in public work. To be invited thus to take part was a new experience in their lives. In face of the calamity that had overtaken the community, all distinctions such as high and low, small and great, master and servant, Hindus, Mussalmans, Parsis, Christians, Gujaratis, Madrasis, Sindhis, etc., were forgotten. All were alike the children and servants of *the motherland*.[M2]   [M2] India

The Bill had already passed, or was about to pass, its second reading.[239] In the speeches on the occasion the fact that Indians had expressed no opposition to the stringent Bill was urged as proof of their[240] unfitness for the franchise.

I explained the situation to the meeting. The first thing we did was to despatch a telegram to the Speaker of the Assembly[241] requesting him to postpone further discussion of the Bill. A similar telegram was sent to the Premier, Sir John Robinson,[242] and another to Mr. Escombe, as a friend of Dada Abdulla's. The Speaker promptly replied that discussion of the Bill would be postponed for two days.[243] This gladdened our hearts.

---

[238] Probably Harishankar Ishwar Joshi, satyagrahi, sentenced six weeks in 1908; sergeant in the Stretcher Bearer Corps during the Zulu rebellion.

[239] The second reading of the Bill took place on Wednesday, 20 June 1894.

[240] 'indifference to and' to add.

[241] J.W. Leauchars. The telegram was sent on Wednesday, 27 June 1894.

[242] Sir John Robinson became the Premier on 10 October 1893, was also the first editor of *The Natal Mercury*, died 1903.

[243] Speaker Leauchars at first wired in reply that the measure was too late as the Bill was scheduled for the third reading that day.

The petition[244] to be presented to the Legislative Assembly was drawn up. Three copies had to be *prepared*[M3] and one extra was needed for the Press. It was also proposed to obtain as many signatures to it as possible, and all this work had to be done in the course of a night. The volunteers with a knowledge of English and several others sat up the whole night. Mr. Arthur, an old man, who was known for his calligraphy, wrote the principal copy. The rest were written by others to someone's dictation.[245] Five copies were thus got ready simultaneously. Merchant volunteers went out in their own carriages, or carriages whose hire they had paid, to obtain signatures to the petition. This was accomplished in quick time and[246] the petition was despatched. The newspapers published it with favourable comments. It likewise created an impression on the Assembly. It was discussed[247] in the House. Partisans of the Bill offered a defence, an admittedly lame one, in reply to the arguments advanced in the petition. The Bill, however, was passed.[248]

We all knew that this was a foregone conclusion, but the agitation had infused new life into the community and had brought home to them the conviction that the community was one and indivisible, and that it was as

MKG and the campaign committee sent another wire requesting postponement of the third reading, which was deferred for a day.

[244] See 'Petition to the Natal Legislative Assembly', *CWMG*, vol. 1, pp. 128–32. In the first instance the petition was addressed both to the Legislative Council and the Legislative Assembly, and thus not admissible in either of the houses. It was thus amended and a separate petition was addressed to the Legislative Council on 4 July 1894. See *CWMG*, vol. 1, pp. 138–39.

[245] 'One dictated which five others wrote.' To add.

[246] 'This was accomplished in quick time and' added in the English translation.

[247] 'at length' to add.

[248] It became Law 25 of 1894 on Friday, 6 July 1894.

M3 sent

much their duty to fight for its *political*[M4] rights as for its   [M4] community
trading rights.

Lord Ripon was at this time Secretary of State
for the Colonies.[249] It was decided to submit to him a
monster petition.[250] This was no small task and could
not be done in a day. Volunteers were enlisted, and all
did their due share of the work.

I took considerable pains over drawing up this
petition.

I read all the literature available on the subject. My
argument centred round a principle and an expedience.
I argued that we had a right to the franchise in Natal, as
we had a kind of franchise in India. I urged that it was
expedient to retain it, as the Indian population capable
of using the franchise was very small.

Ten thousand signatures were obtained in the course
of a fortnight. To secure this number of signatures from
the whole of the province was no light task, especially
when we consider that the men were perfect strangers
to the work. Specially competent volunteers had to
be selected for the work, as it had been decided not
to take a single signature without the signatory fully
understanding the petition. The villages were scattered
at long distances. The work could be done promptly
only if a number of workers put their whole heart into
it. And this they did. All carried out their allotted task
with enthusiasm. But as I am writing these lines, the
figures of Sheth Dawud Muhammad, Rustomji, Adamji
Miyakhan, and Amad Jiva rise clearly before my mind.
They brought in the largest number of signatures.
Dawud Sheth kept going about in his carriage the
whole day. And it was all a labour of love,[251] not one of

---

[249] Also the Viceroy of India, 1880–84.

[250] See *CWMG*, vol. 1, pp. 147–57.

[251] 'it was all a labour of love,' added in the English translation.

them asking for even his out-of-pocket expenses. Dada Abdulla's house became at once a caravanserai and a public office. A number of educated friends who helped me and many others had their food there. Thus every helper was put to considerable expense.

The petition was at last submitted. A thousand copies had been printed for circulation and distribution. It acquainted the Indian public for the first time with conditions in Natal. I sent copies to all the newspapers and *publicists*[M5] I knew.

The Times of India,[252] in a leading article on the petition, strongly supported the Indian demands. Copies were sent to *journals and publicists in England representing different parties*.[M6] *The London Times* supported our claims, and we began to entertain hopes of the Bill being vetoed.

It was now impossible for me to leave Natal. The Indian friends surrounded me on all sides and importuned me to remain there permanently. I expressed my difficulties. I had made up my mind not to stay at public expense. I felt it necessary to set up an independent household. I thought[253] that the house should be good and situated in a good locality. I also had the idea that I could not add to the credit of the community, unless I lived in a style usual for barristers. And it seemed to me to be impossible to run such a household with anything less than £300 a year. I therefore decided that I could stay only if the members of the community guaranteed legal work to the extent of that minimum, and I communicated my decision to them.

'But,' said they, 'we *should like you to draw*[M7] that amount for public work, and we can easily collect it.

[M5] public leaders

[M6] the leaders of all the parties in England

[M7] can afford to let you have

---

[252] Originally called *The Bombay Times and Journal of Commerce*. Founded in 1838, became a daily in 1851 and changed its name to *The Times of India* in 1861.

[253] 'at that time' to add.

Of course this is apart from the fees you must charge for private legal work.'

'No, I could not thus charge you for public work,' said I.[254] 'The work would not involve the exercise on my part of much skill as barrister. My work would be mainly to make you all work. And how could I charge you for that? And then I should have to appeal to you frequently for funds for the work, and if I were to draw my maintenance from you, I should find myself at a disadvantage in making an appeal for large amounts, and we should ultimately find *ourselves at a standstill.*[M8]   [M8] that our barge is stuck Besides I want the community to find more than £300 annually for public work.'

'But we have now known you for some time, and are sure you would not draw anything you do not need. And if we wanted you to stay here, should we not find your expenses?'

'It is your love and present enthusiasm that make you talk like this. How can we be sure that this love and enthusiasm will endure for ever? And as your friend and servant,[255] I should occasionally have to say hard things to you. Heaven only knows whether I should then retain your affection. But the fact is that I must not accept any salary for public work. It is enough for me that you should all agree to entrust me with your legal work. Even that may be hard for you. For one thing I am not a white barrister. How can I be sure that the court will respond to me? Nor can I be sure how I shall fare as a lawyer. So even in giving me retainers you may be running some risk. I should regard even the fact of your giving them to me as the reward of my public work.'

The upshot of this discussion was that about twenty merchants gave me retainers for one year for their legal work. Besides this, Dada Abdulla purchased me the

---

[254] 'I would not put such a price on my public service.' To add.

[255] 'And as your friend and servant,' added in the English translation.

necessary furniture[256] in lieu of a purse he had intended to give me on my departure.[257]

Thus I settled in Natal.

XVIII

M1 The Black Collar

COLOUR BAR[M1]

The symbol of a court of justice is a pair of scales held evenly by an impartial and blind but sagacious[258] woman. Fate has purposely made her blind, in order that she may not *judge a person from his exterior but from his intrinsic worth.*[M2] But the Law Society of Natal set out to persuade the *Supreme Court to act in contravention of this principle and to belie its symbol.*[M3]

M2 anoint a person by looking at his face, but anoint only the virtuous

M3 Court to judge on the basis of appearances. But, on this occasion, the Court proved worthy of the symbol.

I applied for admission as an advocate of the Supreme Court. I held a certificate of admission from the Bombay High Court. The English certificate I had to deposit with the Bombay High Court when I was enrolled there. It was necessary to attach two certificates of character to the application for admission, and thinking that these would carry more weight if given by Europeans, I secured them from two well-known European merchants[259] whom I

---

[256] 'furniture' English word in the original.

[257] Dada Abdullah paid for 'a lounge carpet, a sofa, two stuffed arm chairs, a round table covered with a cloth, a cupboard (for books), paraffin lamps and pantry ware. For dining room, he bought a long table, eight wicker chairs and a corner what-not.' Britton, *Gandhi Arrives in South Africa*, p. 130.

[258] 'old' to add.

[259] One was a German, Max Heilbut, and the other a Scot, Alexander McWilliam. Both the references were identical and read: 'This is to certify that I have known Mr. M.K. Gandhi for one year and I believe him to be a gentleman of good character and am unaware of any circumstances that should unfit him to be admitted to practice as an Advocate of the Supreme Court of the Colony of Natal.' Britton, *Gandhi Arrives in South Africa*, p. 136.

knew through Sheth Abdulla. The application had to be presented through a member of the bar, and as a rule the Attorney General presented such applications without fees. Mr. Escombe, who, as we have seen, was legal adviser to Messrs Dada Abdulla & Co., was the Attorney General. I called on him, and he willingly consented to present my application.

The Law Society now sprang a surprise on me by serving me with a notice opposing my application for admission.[260] One of their objections was that the original English certificate was not attached to my application. But the main objection was that, when the regulations regarding admission of advocates were made, the possibility of a *coloured*[M4] man applying could not have been contemplated.[261] Natal owed its growth to European enterprise, and therefore it was necessary that the European element should predominate in the bar. If coloured people were admitted, they might gradually outnumber the Europeans, and the bulwark of their protection would break down.

[M4] black or a yellow

The Law Society had engaged a distinguished lawyer[262] to support their opposition. As he too was connected with Dada Abdulla & Co., he sent me word through Sheth Abdulla to go and see him. He talked with me quite frankly, and inquired about my antecedents, which I gave. Then he said:

> 'I have nothing to say against you. I was only afraid lest you should[263] be some Colonial-born

---

[260] Henry Bale was the president of the Natal Law Society.

[261] The society had resolved to oppose the application on the grounds 'that it was never intended by the Rules of Court dated 2nd January 1893 to admit persons as advocates or attorneys of the Supreme Court other than those of European extraction'. Britton, *Gandhi Arrives in South Africa*, p. 136.

[262] Gustave Aristide de Roquefeuil Labistour.

[263] 'might' in the first edition.

adventurer. And the fact that your application
was unaccompanied by the original certificate
supported my suspicion. There have been men
who have made use of diplomas which did not
belong to them. The certificate of character from
European traders you have submitted have no
value for me. What do they know about you?
What can be the extent of their acquaintance
with you?'

'But', said I, 'everyone here is a stranger to me.
Even Sheth Abdulla first came to know me here.'

'But then you say he belongs to the same place as
you? If your father was Prime Minister there, Sheth
Abdulla is bound to know your family. If you were
to produce his affidavit, I should have absolutely
no objection. I would then gladly communicate
to the Law Society my inability to oppose your
application.'

This talk enraged me, but I restrained my feelings. 'If I
had attached Dada Abdulla's certificate,' said I to myself,
'it would have been rejected and they would have asked
for Europeans' certificates. And what has my admission
as advocate to do with my birth and my antecedents?
How could my birth, whether humble or objectionable,
be used against me?' But I contained myself and quietly
replied:

'Though I do not admit that the Law Society has
any authority to require all these details, I am quite
prepared to present the affidavit you desire.'

Sheth Abdulla's affidavit was prepared and duly
submitted to the counsel for the Law Society. He
said he was satisfied. But not so the Law Society.[264] It

---

[264] Labistour retired from the case. The Law Society then engaged
Edward Mackenzie Green to present its case.

opposed my application before the Supreme Court,
which ruled out the opposition without even calling
upon Mr. Escombe to reply.[265] The Chief Justice said
in effect:

> 'The objection that the applicant has not attached
> the original certificate has no substance. If he has
> made a false affidavit, he can be prosecuted, and
> his name can then be struck off the roll, if he is
> proved guilty. The *law makes*[M5] no distinction   ^{M5} rules of the Court make
> between white and coloured people. The Court
> has therefore no authority to prevent Mr. Gandhi
> from being enrolled as an advocate. We admit
> his application. Mr. Gandhi, you can now take
> the oath.'

I stood up and took the oath before the Registrar. As
soon as I was sworn in, the Chief Justice, addressing
me, said:

> 'You must now take off your turban, Mr. Gandhi.
> You must submit to the rules of the Court with
> regard to the dress to be worn by practising
> barristers.'

I saw my limitations. The turban that I had insisted on
wearing in the *District*[M6] Magistrate Court I took off in   ^{M6} Durban
obedience to the order of the Supreme Court. Not that,
if I had resisted the order, the resistance could not have

---

[265] The proceedings were held on Monday, 3 September 1894,
before a bench comprising Chief Justice Sir Michael Henry
Gallway, Justice John William Turnbull and Justice Sir Walter
Thomas Wragg. There were lengthy arguments in which both
Escombe and Green were required to present their respective
cases. For a detailed transcript of the proceedings, see Britton,
Gandhi Arrives in South Africa, pp. 137–38. DiSalvo, *M.K.
Gandhi, Attorney at Law*, pp. 56–57, provides a summary of the
proceedings.

been justified. But I wanted to reserve my strength for fighting bigger battles. I should not exhaust my skill as a fighter in insisting on retaining my turban. *It was worthy of a better cause.*[M7]

M7 Perhaps it would have been ignominious.

Sheth Abdulla and other friends did not like my submission (or was it weakness?). They felt that I should have stood by my right to wear the turban while practising in the Court. I tried to reason with them. I tried to press home to them the truth of the maxim, 'When at Rome do as the Romans do.'[266] 'It would be right,' I said, 'to refuse to obey, if in India an English officer or judge ordered you to take off your turban; but as an officer of the Court, it would have ill become me to disregard a custom of the Court in the province of Natal.'

I pacified the friends somewhat with these and similar arguments, but I do not think I convinced them completely, in this instance, of the applicability of the principle of looking at a thing from a different standpoint in different circumstances. But all my life through, *the very insistence on truth has taught me to appreciate the beauty of compromise.*[M8] I saw[267] in later life that this spirit was an essential part of satyagraha. It has often meant endangering my life and incurring the displeasure of friends. But truth is hard as adamant and tender as a *blossom.*[M9]

M8 resistance has always been accompanied by yielding

M9 lotus

The opposition of the Law Society gave me another advertisement in South Africa. Most of the newspapers condemned the opposition and accused the Law Society of jealousy. The advertisement, to some extent, simplified my work.

---

[266] The original has a Gujarati saying. Literally, 'Such is the country, so is the dress.'

[267] 'many a times' to add.

XIX

NATAL INDIAN CONGRESS

Practice as a lawyer was and remained for me a subordinate occupation. It was necessary that I should concentrate on public work to *justify my stay in Natal.*[M1] The despatch of the petition regarding the disfranchising bill was not sufficient in itself. Sustained agitation was essential for making an impression on the Secretary of State for the Colonies. For this purpose it was thought necessary to bring into being a permanent[268] organization. So I consulted Sheth Abdulla and other friends, and we all decided to have a public organization of a permanent character.[269]

[M1] make my stay in Natal meaningful

To find out a name to be given to the new organization *perplexed me sorely.*[270] [M2] It was not to identify itself with any particular party. The name 'Congress',[271] I knew, was in bad odour with the Conservatives[272] in England, and yet the Congress was the very life of India. I wanted *to popularize it in Natal.*[M3] It savoured of cowardice to hesitate to adopt the name. Therefore, with full explanation of my reasons, I recommended that the organization should be called the Natal Indian Congress, and on the 22nd May the Natal Indian Congress came into being.[273]

[M2] posed a moral dilemma

[M3] its strength to increase

---

[268] 'permanent' added in the English translation.

[269] 'of a permanent character' added in the English translation.

[270] The term in the original is 'dharma sankat', 'moral dilemma'.

[271] The term in the original is 'mahasabha', with 'Congress' in parenthesis.

[272] 'Conservative' in the original, followed by an explanation in parenthesis, 'prachin', literally, 'ancient'.

[273] The Natal Indian Congress was established on 22 August 1894, with Abdulla Haji Adam as its president, twenty-three vice-presidents and MKG as its honorary secretary. For its constitution, see *CWMG*, vol. 1, pp. 162–65.

M4 merchants

M5 like taking out an insurance

M6 Soon the folly of 'brave to begin with' became apparent.

Dada Abdulla's spacious room was packed to the full on that day. The Congress received the enthusiastic approval of all present. Its constitution was simple, the subscription was heavy. Only he who paid five shillings monthly could be a member. The well-to-do *classes*[M4] were persuaded to subscribe as much as they could. Abdulla Sheth headed the list with £2 per month. Two other friends also put down the same. I thought I should not stint my subscription, and put down a pound per month. This was for me *no small amount*.[M5] But I thought that it would not be beyond my means, if at all I was to pay my way. And God helped me. We thus got a considerable number of members who subscribed £1 per month. The number of those who put down 10s. was even larger. Besides this, there were donations which were gratefully accepted.[274]

Experience showed that no one paid his subscription for the mere asking. It was impossible to call frequently on members outside Durban. *The enthusiasm of one moment seemed to wear away the next.*[M6] Even the members in Durban had to be considerably dunned before they would pay in their subscriptions.

The task of collecting subscriptions lay with me, I being the secretary. And we came to a stage when I had to keep my clerk engaged all day long in the work of collection. The man got tired of the job, and I felt that, if the situation was to be improved, the subscriptions should be made payable annually and not monthly, and that too strictly in advance. So I called a meeting of the Congress. Everyone welcomed the proposal for making the subscription annual instead of monthly and for fixing the minimum at £3. Thus the work of collection was considerably facilitated.

I had learnt at the outset not to carry on public work with borrowed money. One could rely on people's

---

[274] 'from non-members' to add.

promises in most matters except in respect of money. I had never found people quick to pay the amounts they had undertaken to subscribe, and the Natal Indians were no exception to the rule. *As, therefore, no work was done unless there were funds on hand, the Natal Indian Congress has never been in debt.*[M7]

[M7] Therefore the Natal Indian Congress never undertook any activity with borrowed money.

My co-workers evinced extraordinary enthusiasm in canvassing members. It was work which interested them and was at the same time an invaluable experience. Large numbers of people gladly came forward with cash subscriptions. Work in the distant villages of the interior was rather difficult. People did not know the nature of public work. And yet we had invitations to visit far-away places, leading merchants of every place extending their hospitality.

On one occasion during this tour the situation was rather difficult. We expected our host to contribute £6, but he refused to give anything more than £3. If we had accepted that amount from him, others would have followed suit, and our collections would have been spoiled.[275] It was a late hour of the night, and we were all hungry. But how could we dine without having first obtained the amount we were bent on getting? All persuasion was[276] useless. The host seemed to be adamant. Other merchants in the town reasoned with him, and we all sat up throughout the night, he as well as we determined not to budge one inch. Most of my co-workers were burning with rage, but they *contained themselves.*[M8] At last, when day was already breaking, the host *yielded,*[M9] paid down £6 and feasted us. This happened at Tongaat, but the repercussion of the incident was felt as far as Stanger on the North Coast and Charlestown in the interior. It also hastened our work of collection.

[M8] remained courteous

[M9] melted

---

[275] 'We were to stay at his place.' To add.

[276] 'were' in the first edition.

But collecting funds was not the only thing to do. In fact I had long[277] learnt the principle of never having more money at one's disposal than necessary.

Meetings used to be held once a month or even once a week if required. Minutes of the proceedings of the preceding meeting would be read, and all sorts of questions would be discussed. People had no experience of taking part in public discussions or of speaking briefly and to the point. Everyone hesitated to stand up to speak. I explained to them the rules of procedure at meetings, and they respected them. They realized that it was *an education*[M10] for them, and many who had never been accustomed to speaking before an audience soon acquired the habit of thinking and speaking publicly about matters of public interest.

Knowing that in public work minor expenses at times absorb large amounts, I had decided not to have even the receipt books printed in the beginning. I had a cyclostyle[278] machine in my office, on which I took copies of receipts and reports.[279] Such things I began to get printed only when the Congress coffers were full, and when the number of members and work had increased. Such economy is essential for every organization, and yet I know that it is not always exercised. That is why I have thought it proper to enter into these little details of the beginnings of a small but growing organization.

People never cared to have receipts for the amounts they paid,[280] but we always insisted on the receipts being given. Every pie was thus clearly accounted for, and I dare say the account books for the year 1894

M10 beneficial

---

[277] 'long' added in the English translation.

[278] 'cyclostyle' English word in the original. The machine was invented by David Gestner in 1890.

[279] 'reports' in the original.

[280] 'for the amounts they paid' added in the English translation.

can be found intact even today in the records of Natal
Indian Congress. Carefully kept accounts are a *sine
qua non*[M11] for any organization. Without them it falls
into disrepute. Without properly kept accounts it is
impossible to *maintain*[M12] truth in its pristine purity.

M11 matter of prestige

M12 guard

Another feature of the Congress was service of
Colonial-born educated Indians. The Colonial-born
Indian Educational Association was founded under
the auspices of the Congress. The members consisted
mostly of these educated youths. They had to pay
a nominal subscription. The Association served to
ventilate their needs and grievances, to stimulate thought
amongst them, to bring them into touch with Indian
merchants and also to afford them scope for service of
the community. It was a sort of debating society. The
members met regularly and spoke or read papers on
different subjects. A small library was also opened in
connection with the Association.

The third feature of the Congress was propaganda.
This consisted in acquainting the English in South
Africa and England and people in India with the real
state of things in Natal. With that end in view I wrote
two pamphlets. The first was *An Appeal to Every Briton
in South Africa*.[281] It contained a statement, supported by
evidence, of the general condition of Natal Indians. The
other was entitled *The Indian Franchise—An Appeal*.[282] It
contained a brief history of the Indian franchise in Natal
with facts and figures. I had devoted considerable labour
and study to the preparation of these pamphlets, and the
result was quite commensurate with the trouble taken.
They were widely circulated.

All this activity resulted in winning the Indians
numerous friends in South Africa and in obtaining the

---

[281] See *CWMG*, vol. 1, pp. 170–88. It was sent on 19 December
1894.

[282] Ibid., pp. 266–90. It was sent on 16 December 1895.

active sympathy of all parties in India.[283] It also opened out and placed before the South African Indians[284] a definite line of action.

XX

BALASUNDARAM

The heart's earnest and pure desire is always fulfilled. In my own experience I have often seen this rule verified.[285] Service of the[286] poor has been my heart's desire, and it has always thrown me amongst the poor and enabled me to identify myself with them.

Although the members of the Natal Indian Congress included the Colonial-born Indians and the clerical class, the unskilled wage-earners, the indentured labourers were still outside its pale. The Congress was not yet theirs. They could not afford to belong to it by paying the subscription and becoming its members. The Congress could win their attachment only by serving them. An opportunity offered itself when neither the Congress nor I was really ready for it. I had put in scarcely three or four months' practice, and the Congress also was still in its infancy, when a Tamil man in tattered clothes, head-gear in hand, two front teeth broken and his mouth bleeding, stood before me trembling and weeping. He had been heavily belaboured by his master. I learnt all about him from my clerk,[287] who

---

[283] 'and in England' to add.

[284] 'and placed before the South African Indians' added in the English translation.

[285] 'being verified' in the first edition.

[286] 'people, that is, the' to add in the English translation.

[287] Vincent Lawrence. The other clerk was Joseph Royeppen.

was a Tamilian.[M1] Balasundaram, as that was the visitor's name,[288] was serving his indenture under a well-known European resident of Durban. The master, getting angry with him, had lost self-control, and had beaten Balasundaram severely, breaking two of his teeth.

I sent him to a doctor. In those days only white doctors were available. I wanted a certificate from the doctor about the nature of the injury Balasundaram had sustained. I secured the certificate, and straightway took the injured man to the magistrate,[289] to whom I submitted his affidavit. The magistrate was indignant when he read it, and issued a summons against the employer.

It was far from my desire to get the employer punished. I simply wanted Balasundaram to be released from him. I read the law about indentured labour. If an ordinary servant left service without giving notice, he was liable to be sued by his master in a civil court. With the indentured labourer the case was entirely different. He was liable, in similar circumstances, to be proceeded against in a criminal court and to be imprisoned on conviction.[290] That is why Sir William Hunter[291] called the indenture system almost as bad as slavery. Like the

[M1] knew Tamil

---

[288] 'as that was the visitor's name' added in the English translation.

[289] James Francis Dillon.

[290] According to Section 30, Law 25 of 1891, an indentured labourer found more than two miles from the place of his master without a written leave could be arrested, and under Section 31, be declared 'deserter'. In the first instance the punishment was 10s and seven days' imprisonment with hard labour, in the second instance a sentence of fourteen days and in the third instance he would serve thirty days' hard-labour sentence. The expenses incurred for his return to his employer were to be deducted from his wages.

[291] Sir William Wilson Hunter (1840–1900), Scottish historian, member of the Indian Civil Service, well known for his *The Imperial Gazetteer of India*, of which he compiled nine volumes by 1881.

slave the indentured labourer was the property of his master.

There were only two ways of releasing Balasundaram: either by getting the Protector of Indentured Labourers to cancel his indenture or transfer him to someone else, or by getting Balasundaram's employer to release him. I called on the latter and said to him: 'I do not want to proceed against you and get you punished. I think you realize that you have severely beaten the man. I shall be satisfied if you will transfer the indenture to someone else.' To this he readily agreed. I next saw the Protector.[292] He also agreed, on condition that I found a new employer.

So I went off in search of an employer. He had to be a European, as no Indians could employ indentured labour. At that time I knew very few Europeans. I met one of them.[293] He very kindly agreed to take on Balasundaram. I gratefully acknowledged his kindness. The magistrate convicted Balasundaram's employer, and recorded that he had undertaken to transfer the indenture to someone else.

Balasundaram's case reached the ears of every indentured labourer, and I came to be regarded as their friend. I hailed this connection with delight. A regular stream of indentured labourers began to pour into my office, and I got the best opportunity of learning their joys and sorrows.

The echoes of Balasundaram's case were heard in far off Madras.[294] Labourers from different parts of the province, who went to Natal on indenture, came to know of this case through their indentured brethren.

---

[292] Louis H. Mason.

[293] Oswald Askew, in Chapter XXII, Part II, MKG narrates his relations with the Askew family.

[294] In Chapter XXVIII, Part II, MKG records about the reception in Madras: 'It was wild with enthusiasm. The Balasundaram incident made a profound impression on the meeting.'

There was nothing extraordinary in the case itself, but the fact that there was someone in Natal[295] to espouse their cause and publicly work for them gave the indentured labourers a joyful surprise and *inspired them with hope.*[M2]

[M2] a sense of being cared for

I have said that Balasundaram entered my office, head-gear in hand. There was a peculiar pathos about the circumstance which also showed our humiliation. I have already narrated the incident when I was asked to take off my turban. A practice had been forced upon every indentured labourer and every Indian stranger to take off his head-gear when visiting a European, whether the head-gear were a cap, a turban or a scarf wrapped round the head. A salute even with both hands was not sufficient. Balasundaram thought that he should *follow the practice even with me.*[M3] This was the first case in my experience. I felt humiliated and asked him to tie up his scarf. He did so, not without a certain hesitation, but I could perceive the pleasure on his face.

[M3] approach me in the same manner as well

It has always been a mystery to me how men can feel themselves honored by the humiliation of their fellow-beings.

XXI

THE £3 TAX

Balasundaram's case brought me into touch with the indentured Indians. What impelled me, however, to make a deep study of their condition was the campaign for bringing them under special heavy taxation.

In the same year, 1894, the Natal Government *sought*[M1] to impose an annual tax of £25[296] on the

[M1] drafted a Bill

---

[295] 'in Natal' added in the English translation.

[296] 'that is, rupees 375' to add.

M2 Bill

indentured Indians. The *proposal*M2 astonished me. I put the matter before the Congress for discussion, and it was immediately resolved to organize the necessary opposition.

At the outset I must explain briefly the genesis of the tax.

M3 whites

About the year 1860 the *Europeans*M3 in Natal, finding that there was considerable scope for sugarcane cultivation, felt themselves in need of labour. Without outside labour the cultivation of cane and the manufacture of sugar were impossible, as the Natal Zulus were not suited to this form of work. The Natal Government therefore corresponded with the Indian Government, and secured their permission to recruit Indian labour.[297] These recruits were to sign an indenture to work in Natal for five years, and at the end of the term they were to be at liberty to settle there and to have full rights of ownership of land. Those were the inducements held out to them, for the whites then had looked forward to improving their agriculture by the industry of the Indian labourers after the term of their indentures had expired.

But the Indians gave more than had been expected of them. They grew large quantities of vegetables. They introduced a number of Indian varieties and made it possible to grow the local varieties cheaper. They also introduced the mango. Nor did their enterprise stop at agriculture. They entered trade.[298]

---

[297] Maureen Swan states that between 1860 and 1891, when the importation of Indian labour ceased, 1,52,184 indentured labourers were shipped to Natal out of Calcutta and Madras ports. Swan, *Gandhi: The South African Experience*, p. 19.

[298] At the peak of their commercial success formerly indentured Indians owned thirty out of thirty-seven retail shops licensed to Indians and in 1884, seventy-eight formerly indentured Indians owned ninety-eight properties valued at £17,605. Swan, *Gandhi: The South African Experience*, p. 4.

They purchased land for building, and many raised themselves from the status of labourers to that of owners of land and houses. Merchants from India followed them and settled there for trade.[299] The late Sheth Abubakar Amod was first among them. He soon built up an extensive business.

The white traders were alarmed. When they first welcomed the Indian labourers, they had not reckoned with their business skill. They might be tolerated as independent agriculturists, but their competition in trade could not be brooked.

This sowed the seed of the antagonism to Indians. Many other factors contributed to its growth. Our different ways of living, our simplicity, our contentment with small gains, our indifference to the laws of hygiene and sanitation, our slowness in keeping our surroundings clean and tidy, and our stinginess in keeping our houses in good repair—all these, combined with the difference in religion, contributed to fan the flame of antagonism. Through legislation this antagonism found its expression in the disfranchising bill and the bill to impose a tax on the indentured Indians. Independent of legislation a number of pinpricks had already been started.[300]

The first suggestion was that the Indian labourers should be forcibly repatriated, so that the term of their

---

[299] Those Indians who came for trade were called 'passenger Indians' to distinguish them from 'indentured labour'. In 1885, a decade after the arrival of first passenger Indians, they owned sixty stores in Durban with twenty branches across Natal, the Transvaal and Orange Free State. Swan, *Gandhi: The South African Experience*, p. 5.

[300] In 1885 the 'Indian Immigration Commission' was constituted under the chairmanship of Justice Walter Thomas Wragg and with James Renault Saunders, Dr. Robert Lewer and Henry Francis Richardson as members. The Wragg Commission (1885–87) found preponderance of European opinion in the Colony against 'the presence of free Indians as a rival or competitor, either in agriculture or commercial pursuits'.

indentures might expire in India. The Government of India was not likely to accept the suggestion. Another proposal was therefore made to the effect that

1. the indentured labourer should return to India on the expiry of his indenture; or that
2. he should sign a fresh indenture every two years, an increment being given at each renewal; and that
3. in the case of his refusal to return to India or renew the indenture he should pay an annual tax of £25.[301]

A deputation composed of Sir Henry Binns[302] and Mr. Mason[303] was sent to India to get the proposal approved by the Government there.[304] The Viceroy at that time was Lord Elgin.[305] He disapproved of the £25 tax, but agreed to a poll tax of £3. I thought then, as I do even now, that this was a serious blunder on the part of the Viceroy. In giving his approval he had in no way thought of the interests of India. It was no part of his duty thus to accommodate the Natal Europeans. In

---

[301] Maureen Swan suggests that the tax was linked to a Bill to remove an annual £10,000 grant paid out of general revenue for the cost of importing Indian labour. Swan, *Gandhi: The South African Experience*, p. 45. The chief proposer of this move was Sir Henry Binns.

[302] Sir Henry Binns (1837–99), chairman, Indian Immigration Trust Board, founder of the Umhlanga Valley Sugar Estate, was called 'split-pea' Binns as he was suspected of splitting peas before planting them. Britton, *Gandhi Arrives in South Africa*, p. 63.

[303] Louis H. Mason, mentioned earlier.

[304] The deputation stayed in India from December 1893 to March 1894. Their report was published in the *Natal Government Gazette* of April 1894.

[305] Victor Alexander Bruce, Ninth Earl of Elgin (1849–1917), Viceroy of India (11 October 1894–6 January 1899). The Viceroy at the time of the deputation's visit would have been the Marquees of Lansdowne who was in office from 10 December 1888 to 11 October 1894.

the course of three or four years an indentured labourer with his wife and each male child over 16 and female child over 13 came under the impost. To levy a yearly tax of £12[306] from a family of four—husband, wife and two children—when the average income of the husband was never more than 14s. a month, was atrocious and unknown anywhere else in the world.

We organized a fierce campaign against this tax.[307] If the Natal Indian Congress had remained silent on the subject, the Viceroy might have approved of even the £25 tax. The reduction from £25 to £3 was probably due solely to the Congress agitation. But I may be mistaken in thinking so. It may be possible that the Indian Government had disapproved of the £25 tax from the beginning and *reduced it to*[M4] £3, irrespective of the opposition from the Congress. In any case it was a *breach of trust on the part of the Indian Government.*[M5] As trustee of the welfare of India the Viceroy ought never to have approved of this inhuman tax.

The Congress could not regard it as any great achievement to have succeeded in getting the tax reduced from £25 to £3.[308] The regret was still there that it had not completely safeguarded the interests of the indentured Indians. It ever remained its determination to get the tax remitted, but it was twenty years before the determination was realized. And when it was realized, it came as a result of the labours of not only the Natal Indians but of all the Indians in South Africa. *The breach of faith with the late Mr. Gokhale became the*

[M4] would have accepted only

[M5] violation of the interests of India

---

[306] 'that is, rupees 180' to add.

[307] The Natal Indian Congress sent a petition to the Natal Legislative Council in June 1895, *CWMG*, vol. 1, pp. 229–31; to the Secretary of Colonies Joseph Chamberlain on 11 August 1895, *CWMG*, vol. 1, pp. 232–42; and to the Viceroy of India Lord Elgin on the same date, *CWMG*, vol. 1, pp. 242–44.

[308] 'that is, from rupees 375 to 45' to add.

M6 Gokhale became the cause for

M7 Truth became manifest in the penance of the Indians. It demanded

M1 I served India

M2 brothers had deepened my desire for spiritual knowledge

occasion of[M6] the final campaign, in which the indentured Indians took their full share, some of them losing their lives as a result of the firing that was resorted to, and over ten thousand suffering imprisonment.

But truth triumphed in the end. *The sufferings of the Indians were the expression of that truth. Yet it would not have triumphed except for*[M7] unflinching faith, great patience and incessant effort. Had the community given up the struggle, had the Congress abandoned the campaign and submitted to the tax as inevitable, the hated impost would have continued to be levied from the indentured Indians until this day, to the eternal shame of the Indians in South Africa and of the whole of India.

XXII

COMPARATIVE[309] STUDY OF RELIGIONS

If I found myself entirely absorbed in the service of the community, the reason behind it was my desire for self-realization. I had made the religion of service my own, as I felt that God could be realized only through service. *And service for me was the service of India,*[M1] because it came to me without my seeking, because I had an aptitude for it. I had gone to South Africa for travel, for finding an escape from Kathiawad intrigues and for gaining my own livelihood. But as I have said,[310] I found myself in search of God and striving for self-realization.

Christian *friends had whetted my appetite for knowledge,*[M2] which had become almost insatiable, and they would not leave me in peace, even if I desired

---

[309] 'Comparative' added in the English translation.

[310] 'But as I have said,' added in the English translation.

to be indifferent. In Durban Mr. Spencer Walton,[311] the head of the South Africa General Mission, found me out. I became almost a member of his family. At the back of this acquaintance was of course my contact with Christians in Pretoria. Mr. Walton had a manner all his own. I do not recollect his ever having invited me to embrace Christianity. But he placed his life as an open book[312] before me, and let me watch all his movements. Mrs. Walton was a very gentle and talented woman. I liked the attitude of this couple. We knew the fundamental differences between us. Any amount of discussion could not efface them. Yet even differences prove helpful, where there are[313] tolerance, *charity*[M3]   [M3] generosity
and truth. I liked Mr. and Mrs. Walton's humility, perseverance and devotion to work, and we met very frequently.

This friendship *kept alive my interest in religion.*[M4] It   [M4] awakened me
was impossible now to get the leisure that I used to have in Pretoria for my religious studies. But what little time I could spare I *turned to good account.*[M5] My religious   [M5] used it for reading such books
correspondence continued. Raychandbhai was guiding me. Some friend sent me Narmadashanker's book *Dharma Vichar.*[314] Its preface proved very helpful. I had heard about the *Bohemian*[M6] way in which the poet had   [M6] licentious
lived, and a description in the preface of the revolution effected[315] in his life by his religious studies[316] captivated

---

[311] W. Spencer Walton (1850–1906), founder of the South African General Mission, author of the hymn 'In Tenderness He Sought Me'.

[312] 'as an open book' added in the English translation.

[313] 'is' in the first edition.

[314] Narmadashanker Lalshankar Dave (1833–86), poet, reformer, lexicographer, historian, founder editor of Gujarati journal *Dandiyo*.

[315] 'effected' added in the English translation.

[316] 'by his religious studies' added in the English translation.

me.[317] I came to like the book, and read it from cover to cover[318] with attention. I read with interest Max Muller's book, *India—What Can It Teach Us?*[319] and the translation of the Upanishads published by the Theosophical Society.[320] All this enhanced my regard for Hinduism, and *its beauties began to grow upon me.*[M7] It did not, however, prejudice me against other religions. I read Washington Irving's *Life of Mahomet and His Successors*[321] and Carlyle's panegyric on the Prophet.[322] *These books raised Muhammad in my estimation.*[M8] I also read a book called *The Sayings of Zarathustra.*

Thus I gained more knowledge of the different religions. The study stimulated my self-introspection and fostered in me the habit of putting into practice whatever appealed to me in my studies. *Thus I began some of the Yogic practices, as well as I could understand them from a reading of the Hindu books.*[M9] But I could not get on very far, and decided to follow them with the help of some expert when I returned to India. The desire has never been fulfilled.

I made too an intensive study of Tolstoy's books. *The Gospels in Brief, What to Do?*[323] and other books

M7 I began to appreciate its uniqueness

M8 My regard for the Prophet increased.

M9 Thus I began certain practices like *pranayam* suggested in Hindu religion, as I understood them from the books.

---

[317] For an intellectual biography of Narmad, see Tridip Suhrud, *Writing Life: Three Gujarati Thinkers* (Delhi: Orient Blackswan: 2009).

[318] 'from cover to cover' added in the English translation.

[319] Friedrich Max Muller (1823–1900), *India—What Can It Teach Us?* is based on a course of lectures that he gave at the University of Cambridge and was published in 1882.

[320] Probably Alladi Mahadev Sastri's translation of *The Yoga Upanishada*.

[321] Washington Irving (1783–1859) published *Mahomet and His Successors* in 1849; best known for his short stories 'Rip Van Winkle' (1819) and 'The Legacy of Sleepy Hollow' (1820).

[322] Thomas Carlyle (1795–1881). 'The Hero as Prophet' lecture delivered on 8 May 1840, part of *On Heroes, Hero-worship and the Heroic in History* published in 1841.

[323] Sometimes called *What Is to be Done? Or What Then Must We Do?*

made a deep impression on me. I began to realize more and more *the infinite possibilities of universal love.*[M10]

    About the same time I came in contact with another Christian family.[324] At their suggestion I attended the Wesleyan church every Sunday. For these days I also had their standing invitation to dinner. The[325] church did not make a favourable impression on me. The sermons seemed to be uninspiring. The congregation did not strike me as being *particularly religious. They were not*[M11] an assembly of devout souls; they appeared rather to be worldly-minded people, going to church for recreation and in conformity to custom. Here, at times, I would involuntarily doze. I was ashamed, but some of my neighbours, who were in no better case, lightened the shame. I could not go on long like this, and soon gave up attending the service.

    My connection with the family I used to visit every Sunday was abruptly broken. In fact it may be said that I was warned to visit it no more. It happened thus.[M12] My hostess was a good and simple woman, but somewhat narrow-minded. We always discussed religious subjects. I was then re-reading[326] Arnold's *Light of Asia*. Once we began to compare the life of Jesus with that of Buddha. 'Look at Gautama's compassion!' said I. 'It was not confined to mankind, it was extended to all living beings. Does not one's heart overflow with love to think of the lamb joyously perched on his shoulders? One fails to notice this love for all living beings in the *life*[M13] of Jesus.' The comparison pained the good lady. I could understand her feelings. I cut the matter short,

[M10] where universal love could take a person

[M11] imbued with devotion. The congregation at eleven did not appear to be

[M12] It could be said that the family I visited every Sunday told me to absent myself.

[M13] history

---

[324] Of Oswald Askew, the family to which Balasundaram's indenture was transferred.

[325] 'Wesleyan' to add.

[326] The original has 'reading'. 'Re-reading' is factually correct as MKG read it for the first time in London with his theosophist friends.

and we went to the dining-room. Her son, a cherub aged scarcely five, was also with us. I am happiest when in the midst of children, and this youngster and I had long been friends. I *spoke derisively of*[M14] the piece of meat on his plate and *in high praise of*[M15] the apple on mine. The innocent boy was carried away and joined in my praise of the fruit.

M14 poked fun at

M15 praised

But the mother? *She was dismayed.*[M16]

I was warned.[M17] I checked myself and changed the subject. The following week I visited the family as usual,[327] but not without trepidation. I did not see that I should stop going there, I did not think it proper either. But the good lady made my way easy.

M16 The poor lady was hurt.

M17 I became vigilant.

'Mr. Gandhi,' she said, 'please don't take it ill if I feel obliged to tell you that *my boy is none the better for your company.*[M18] Everyday he hesitates to eat meat and asks for fruit, reminding me of your argument. *This is too much.*[M19] If he gives up meat, he is bound to get weak, if not ill. How could I bear it? Your discussions should henceforth be only with us elders. They are sure to react badly on children.'[328]

M18 your company is beginning to have a bad effect on my boy

M19 I cannot afford this.

'Mrs.——,' I replied, 'I am sorry. I can understand your feelings as a *parent,*[M20] for I too have children. We can very easily end this unpleasant state of things. What I eat and omit to eat is bound to have a greater effect on the child than what I say. The best way, therefore, is for me to stop these[329] visits. That certainly need not affect our friendship.'

M20 mother

'I thank you,' she said with evident relief.

---

[327] 'having resolved to be cautious' to add.

[328] MKG wrote, 'Vegetarianism and Children' for *The Vegetarian* of 5 May 1894. See *CWMG*, vol. 1, pp. 126–27.

[329] 'Sunday' to add.

XXIII

AS A HOUSEHOLDER

To set up a household was no new experience for me. But the establishment in Natal was different from the ones that I had had in Bombay and London.[M1] This time part of the expense was solely for the sake of prestige. I thought it necessary to have a household in keeping with my position as an Indian barrister in Natal and as a representative.[330] So I had a nice little house in a prominent locality.[331] It was also suitably furnished. Food was simple, but as I used to invite English friends and Indian co-workers, the housekeeping bills were always fairly high.

A good servant is essential in every household. But[M2] I have never known how to keep anyone as a servant.

I had a friend[332] as companion and help,[333] and a cook who had become a member of the family. I also had[334] office clerks[335] boarding and lodging with me.

[M1] I had set up households in Bombay and in England, but setting up a household in Natal was different.

[M2] The servant has always been a problem with me as

---

[330] 'of the Indian community' to add.

[331] Burnett Britton describes the house, which was called Beach Grove Villa: 'a semi-detached, ginger-brown house, with a dull red corrugated roof and fancy wood-worked balcony and verandah, facing on the lane, between Mrs. Favill's tea room and Pope's carriage works on Smith Street, which ran down to the water's edge and which the corporation thoughtfully had retained with a wall and then paved for Harry Escombe. Across the lane from Gandhi's thin iron gate was the Attorney General's manse, Bay View. In the back was a yard of gray soil with a combination of swing and chinning bar.' Britton, *Gandhi Arrives in South Africa*, p. 130.

[332] Sheikh Mehtab.

[333] 'and help' added in the English translation.

[334] 'help from one of the' to add.

[335] Vincent Lawrence and his wife.

M3 also gave me

I think I had a fair amount of success in this experiment, but it *was not without its modicum of*M3 the bitter experiences of life.

The companion was very clever and, I thought, faithful to me. But in this I was deceived. He became jealous of an office clerk who was staying with me, and wove such a tangled web that I suspected the clerk. *This clerical friend had a temper of his own.*M4 Immediately he saw that he had been the object of my suspicion,[336] he left both the house and the office. I was pained. I felt that perhaps I had been unjust to him, and my conscience always stung me.

M4 This clerk was independent-minded.

In the meanwhile, the cook needed a few days' leave, or for some other cause was away.[337] It was necessary to procure another during his absence. Of this new man I learnt later that he *was a perfect scamp.*M5 But for me he proved a godsend. Within two or three days of his arrival, he discovered *certain irregularities that were*M6 going on under my roof without my knowledge, and he made up his mind to warn me. I had the reputation of[338] being a credulous but straight man. The discovery[339] was to him, therefore, all the more shocking. Every day at one o'clock I used to go home from office for lunch. At about twelve o'clock one day the cook came panting to the office, and said, 'Please come home at once. *There is a surprise for you.*'M7

M5 could bring down a flying bird

M6 the rottenness that was

M7 If you wish to see something.

'Now, what is this?' I asked. 'You must tell me what it is. How can I leave the office at this hour to go and see it?'

---

[336] 'Immediately he saw that he had been the object of my suspicion,' added in the English translation.

[337] 'I had kept him to look after the needs of the friend.' To add.

[338] 'for' in the first edition.

[339] 'of the dirt' to add.

'You will regret it, if you don't come. That is all I can say.'

I felt an appeal in his persistence. I went home accompanied by a clerk and the cook who walked ahead of us. He took me straight to the upper floor, pointed at my companion's room, and said, 'Open this door and see for yourself.'

I saw it all. I knocked at the door. No reply! I knocked heavily so as to make the very walls shake. The door was opened. I saw a prostitute inside. *I asked her to leave the house, never to return.*[M8]

To the companion I said, 'From this moment I cease to have anything to do with you. I have been thoroughly deceived and have made a fool of myself. *That is how you have requited my trust in you?*'[M9]

Instead of coming to his senses,[M10] he threatened to expose me. 'I have nothing to conceal,' said I. 'Expose whatever I may have done. But you must leave me this moment.'

This made him worse. There was no help for it.[340] So I said to the clerk standing downstairs: 'Please go and inform the Police Superintendent, with my compliments, that a person living with me has *misbehaved himself.*[M11] I do not want to keep him in my house, but he refuses to leave. I shall be much obliged if police help can be sent me.'

This showed him that I was in earnest.[341] His guilt unnerved him. He apologized to me, entreated me not to inform the police, and agreed to leave the house immediately, which he did.

The incident *came as a timely warning in my life.*[M12] Only now could I see clearly how *thoroughly I had been beguiled by this evil genius.*[M13] In harbouring him I had

[M8] I told her, 'Please, sister, you must leave at once. Never step into this house ever again.'

[M9] My trust did not deserve this reward.

[M10] My companion was enraged

[M11] deceived me

[M12] purged my life of much impurity

[M13] this companion was for me a form of attachment and evil influence

---

[340] 'There was no help for it.' Added in the English translation.

[341] To add at the beginning of this paragraph: 'The wrong are cowardly.'

chosen a bad means for a good end. I had expected to 'gather figs of thistles'.[342] I had known that the companion was a bad character, and yet I believed in his faithfulness to me. In the attempt to reform him I was near ruining myself. I had disregarded the warnings of kind friends. Infatuation had completely blinded me.

But for the new cook I should never have discovered the truth and, being under the influence of the companion, I should probably have been unable to lead the life of detachment that I then began.[M14] I should always have been wasting time on him. He had the power to keep me in the dark and to mislead me.

But God came to the rescue as before.[M15] My intentions were pure, and so I was saved in spite of my mistakes, and this early experience thoroughly forewarned me for the future.

The cook had been almost a messenger sent from Heaven. He did not know cooking, and as a cook he could not have remained at my place. But no one else could have opened my eyes. This was not the first time, as I subsequently learnt, that the woman had been brought into my house. She had come often before,[343] but no one had the courage of this cook. For everyone knew how blindly I trusted the companion. *The cook had, as it were, been sent to me just to do this service, for he begged leave of me that very moment.*[M16]

'I cannot stay in your house,' he said. 'You are so easily misled. This is no place for me.'

I let him go.[M17]

I now discovered that the man who had poisoned my ears against the clerk was no other than this companion. I tried very hard to make amends to the clerk for the injustice I had done him. It has, however,

[M14] If the aforesaid accident had not opened my eyes, if I had not been cognizant of the truth, it is likely that I should not have become fit for the sacrifices I have been able to make. My service would have forever remained incomplete, for my companion would inevitably have impeded my progress.

[M15] But how can one protected by Ram come to harm?

[M16] Having done this service the cook sought leave of me that day and at that very moment.

[M17] I did not insist otherwise.

---

[342] In the original a Gujarati idiomatic phrase; literally, 'expected mogra flowers from a creeper of bitters'.

[343] 'She had come often before,' added in the English translation.

been my eternal regret that I could never satisfy him fully. *Howsoever you may repair it, a rift is a rift.*[M18]

HOMEWARD

By now I had been three years in South Africa. I had got to know the people and they had got to know me. In 1896 I asked permission to go home for six months, for I saw that I was in for a long stay *there*.[M1] I had established a fairly good practice, and could see that people felt the need of my presence.[344] *So I made up my mind to go home, fetch my wife and children, and then return and settle out there.*[M2] I also saw that, if I went home, I might be able to do there some public work by educating public opinion and creating more interest in *the Indians of South Africa*.[M3] The £3 tax was an open sore. There could be no peace until it was abolished.

But who was to take charge of the Congress work and Education Society *in my absence?*[M4] I could think of two men—Adamji Miyakhan and Parsi Rustomji. There were many workers now available from the commercial class. But the foremost among those who could fulfil the duties of the secretary by regular work, and who also commanded the regard of the *Indian community*,[M5] were these two. The secretary certainly needed a working knowledge of English. I recommended the late Adamji Miyakhan's name to the Congress, and it approved of his appointment as secretary. Experience showed that the choice was[345] a very happy one. Adamji Miyakhan satisfied all with his perseverance, liberality, amiability and courtesy, and proved to everyone that the secretary's

[M18] A broken utensil, however well mended, will always be broken, it will never be whole again.

[M1] in South Africa

[M2] Therefore, I decided to live in South Africa with my family and for that reason I considered it necessary to go home.

[M3] this question

[M4] if I went to my home country

[M5] Indians born in South Africa

---

[344] 'in public work. I too felt the same.' To add.

[345] 'had been' in the first edition.

work did not require a man with a barrister's degree or high English education.

About the middle of 1896[346] I sailed for home in the s.s. *Pongola*[347] which was bound for Calcutta.

There were very few[348] passengers on board. Among them were two English officers, with whom I came in close contact. With one of them I used to play chess for an hour daily. The ship's doctor gave me a *Tamil Self-teacher*[349] which I began to study. My experience in Natal had shown me that I should acquire a knowledge of Urdu to get into closer contact with the Mussalmans, and of Tamil to get into closer touch with the Madras Indians.

At the request of the English friend, who read Urdu with me,[350] I found out a good Urdu munshi from

---

[346] MKG sailed on 5 June 1896. On 4 June Tamil and Gujarati Indians gave him a send-off at the Indian Congress Hall, with Dada Abdullah presiding and Vincent Lawrence acting as the Tamil interpreter. MKG was presented with a gold medal and an address in Gujarati, Hindi and Urdu eulogizing his services.

[347] *The Natal Advertiser* of 5 June 1896 gave the name of the ship as *S.S Clan Macleod*. The full report under the title 'Mr. Gandhi's Departure' reads: 'Mr. Gandhi sailed for India this morning by Clan Macleod. He was accompanied from his house in Beach Grove to the point by a crowd of about 500 Indians and several leading Indian merchants in Durban, who cheered him loudly after he had gone on board.' Sabarmati Nidhi 1005 (henceforth SN).

[348] In the Gujarati first edition, reproduced in *Akshar Deha*, the word is 'many'. *Navajivan* of 24 October 1926 has 'very few'.

[349] George Uglow Pope, *A Tamil Hand-Book: Or Full Introduction to the Common Dialect of that Language on the plan of Ollendrof and Arnold*, Madras, 1859 (second edition). Dr. G.U. Pope (1820–1908) did missionary work in south India (1839–81), took holy orders in Madras (1845), was university lecturer in Tamil and Telugu at Oxford (1884–96), chaplain of Balliol College, author of *First Lesson in Tamil, A Handbook of the Ordinary Dialect of the Tamil Language*, and *A Textbook of Indian History*, and translated the *Kural* and the *Tiruvachagam*. For his obituary by MKG, see *CWMG*, vol. 8, pp. 136–37.

[350] 'who read Urdu with me' added in the English translation.

amongst the deck passengers, and we made excellent progress in our studies. The officer had a better memory than I. He would never forget a word after once he had seen it; I often found it difficult to decipher Urdu letters. I brought more perseverance to bear, but could never overtake the officer.

With Tamil I made fair progress. There was no help available, but the *Tamil Self-teacher was a well-written book, and*[M6] I did not feel in need of much outside help.   [M6] book was so written that

I had hoped to continue these studies even after reaching India, but it was impossible. Most of my reading[351] since 1893 has been done in jail. I did make some progress in Tamil and Urdu, in jails—Tamil in South African jails, and Urdu in Yeravda Jail. But I never learnt to speak Tamil, and the little I could do by way of reading is now rusting away for want of practice.

I still feel what a handicap this ignorance of Tamil or Telugu[352] has been. The affection that the *Dravidians*[M7] in   [M7] 'Madrasi' Indians
South Africa showered on me has remained a cherished memory.[353] Whenever I see a Tamil or Telugu friend, I cannot but recall the faith, perseverance and selfless sacrifice of many of his compatriots in South Africa. And they were mostly illiterate, the men no less than the women. The fight in South Africa was for such, and it was fought by illiterate soldiers; it was for the poor, and the poor took their full share in it. Ignorance of their language, however, was never a handicap to me in stealing the hearts of these simple and good countrymen. They spoke broken Hindustani or broken English, and we found no difficulty in getting on with our work. But I wanted to requite their affection by learning Tamil and Telugu. In Tamil, as I have said, I

---

[351] 'and study' to add.

[352] 'of Tamil or Telugu' added in the English translation.

[353] 'with me a cherished memory' in the first edition.

M8 speakers of the Dravidian languages

M9 The Dravid 'Madrasis' of South Africa speak a little bit of Hindi.

made some little progress, but in Telugu, which I tried to learn in India, I did not get beyond the alphabet. I fear now I can never learn these languages, and am therefore hoping that the *Dravidians*M8 will learn Hindustani. *The non-English-speaking among them in South Africa do speak Hindi or Hindustani, however indifferently.*M9 It is only the English-speaking ones who will not learn it, as though a knowledge of English were an obstacle to learning our own languages.

But I have digressed. Let me finish the narrative of my voyage. I have to introduce to my readers[354] the Captain of the *s.s. Pongola*. We had become friends. The good Captain was a Plymouth Brother. Our talks were more about spiritual subjects than nautical. He drew a line between morality and faith. The teaching of the Bible was to him child's play. Its beauty lay in its simplicity. Let all, men, women and children, he would say,[355] have faith in Jesus and his sacrifice, and their sins were sure to be redeemed. This friend revived my memory of the Plymouth Brother of Pretoria. The religion that imposed any moral restrictions was to him no good. My vegetarian food had been *the occasion of the whole of this discussion.*M10 Why should I not eat meat, or for that matter beef? Had not God created all the lower animals for the enjoyment of mankind as, for instance, He had created the vegetable kingdom? These questions inevitably drew us into religious discussion.

M10 at the root of this friendship and religious discussion

We could not convince each other.[356] I was confirmed in my opinion that religion and morality were *synonymous.*M11 The Captain had no doubt about the correctness of his opposite[357] conviction.

M11 manifestations of the same thing

---

[354] 'to my readers' added in the English translation.

[355] 'he would say' added in the English translation.

[356] 'one another' in the first edition.

[357] 'opposite' added in the English translation.

At the end of twenty-four days the pleasant voyage came to a close, and admiring the beauty of the Hooghly, I landed at Calcutta.[358] The same day I took the train for Bombay.

XXV

IN INDIA

On my way to Bombay the train stopped at Allahabad[359] for forty-five minutes. I decided to utilize the interval for a *drive*[M1] through the town. I also had to purchase   [M1] walk some medicine at a chemist's shop. The chemist was half asleep, and took an unconscionable time in dispensing the medicine, with the result that when I reached the station, the train had just started. The Station Master had kindly detained the train one minute for my sake, but not seeing me coming,[360] had carefully ordered my luggage to be taken out of the train.

I took a room at Kellner's,[361] and decided to start work there and then. I had heard a good deal about *The Pioneer*[362] published from Allahabad, and I had understood it to be an opponent of Indian aspirations.

---

[358] MKG reached the shores of Calcutta on 4 July 1896, making this a voyage of twenty-nine days.

[359] 'Prayag' in the original.

[360] 'when he did not see me coming, he' in the first edition.

[361] John Murray in his *A Hand Book for Travellers in India, Burma and Ceylon* (1901), p. 465, describes the Kellner's rooms thus: 'attached to the railway station, afford one comfortable sleeping accommodation, and are perhaps the best place to stop at, Chhota-hazri is provided in the rooms, but other meals have to be taken in the Railway Refreshment Room.'

[362] Started by Sir George Allen in 1865, was the first newspaper in north India owned and edited by the British.

I have an impression that Mr. Chesney Jr.[363] was the editor at that time. I wanted to secure the help of every party, so I wrote a note to Mr. Chesney, telling him how I had missed the train, and asking for an appointment so as to[364] enable me to leave the next day. He immediately gave me one, at[365] which I was very happy especially when I found that he gave me a patient hearing. He promised to notice in his paper anything that I might write, but added *that he could not promise to endorse all the Indian demands, inasmuch as he was bound to understand and give due weight to the viewpoint of the Colonials as well.*[M2]

'It is enough,' I said, 'that you should study the question and discuss it in your paper. I ask and desire nothing but *the barest justice that is due to us.*'[M3]

The rest of the day was spent in having a look round admiring[366] the magnificent confluence of the three rivers, the *Triveni*, and planning the work before me.

This unexpected interview *with the editor of The Pioneer laid the foundation of the series of incidents which ultimately led to my being lynched in Natal.*[M4]

I went straight to Rajkot[367] without halting at Bombay and began to make preparations for writing a pamphlet on the situation in South Africa.[368] The writing and publication of the pamphlet took about a month. It had a green cover and[369] came to be known afterwards as the Green Pamphlet.[370] In it I drew a

M2 'I cannot assure you that I shall accept all your demands. We must understand and represent the Colonial perspective as well.'

M3 pure justice

M4 sowed the seeds of the attack on me in Natal

---

[363] Sir George Maclagan Chesney (Jr.).

[364] 'which would' in the first edition.

[365] 'for' in the first edition.

[366] 'and admiring' in the first edition.

[367] He reached Rajkot on 7 July 1896.

[368] 'on the situation in South Africa' added in the English translation.

[369] 'and hence' in the first edition.

[370] The drafting of the pamphlet was completed at Rajkot on 14 August 1896. The pamphlet was titled 'The Grievances of the

purposely subdued picture of the condition of Indians in South Africa. The language I used was more moderate than that of the two pamphlets[371] which I have referred to before, as I knew that *things heard of from a distance appear bigger than they are.*[M5]

[M5] little suffering seen from afar seems large

Ten thousand copies[372] were printed and sent[373] to all the papers and leaders of every party in India. *The Pioneer* was the first to notice it editorially. A summary of the article was cabled by Reuter[374] to England, and a summary of that summary was cabled to Natal by Reuter's London office.[375] This cable was not longer than three lines in print. It was a miniature, but exaggerated,[376] edition of the picture I had drawn of the treatment accorded to the Indians in Natal, and it was not in my words. We shall see later on the effect this had in Natal. In the meanwhile every paper of note commented at length on the question.

To get these pamphlets ready for posting was no small matter. It would have been expensive too, if I had employed paid help[377] for preparing wrappers, etc.[378] But I hit upon a much simpler plan. I gathered together all the children in my locality and asked them to volunteer two or three hours' labour of a morning, when they

---

British Indians in South Africa: An Appeal to Indian Public'. For the full text, see *CWMG*, vol. 2, pp. 2–50.

[371] 'written in Natal' to add.

[372] The first print run printed at Rajkot was of 6000 copies, the second print run done from Madras was of 4000 copies.

[373] 'and they were sent' in the first edition.

[374] 'by Reuter' added in the English translation.

[375] 'London office' added in the English translation.

[376] 'but exaggerated' added in the English translation.

[377] 'and an expensive one too, if I should employ paid help' in the first edition.

[378] 'for preparing wrappers, etc.' added in the English translation.

had no school.[379] This they willingly agreed to do. I promised to bless them and give them, as a reward, used postage stamps which I had collected. *They got through the work in no time.*[M6] That was my first experiment of having little children as volunteers. Two of those little friends are my co-workers today.

Plague broke out[380] in Bombay about this time, and there was panic all around. There was fear of an outbreak in Rajkot. As I felt that I could be of some help in the sanitation department, I offered my services to the State.[381] They were accepted, and I was put on the committee[382] which was appointed to look into the question. I laid especial emphasis on the cleanliness of latrines, and the committee decided to inspect these in every street. The poor people had no objection to their latrines being inspected, and what is more, they carried out the improvements suggested to them. But when we went to inspect the houses of *the upper ten,*[M7] some of them even refused us admission,[383] not to talk of listening to our suggestions. It was our common experience that the latrines of the rich were more unclean. They were dark and stinking and reeking with filth and worms.[384] The improvements we[385] suggested were quite simple, e.g., to have buckets for excrement instead of allowing it to drop on the ground; to see that urine also was collected in buckets, instead of allowing it to soak into the ground, and to demolish the partitions between the outer walls and the latrines, so as to give the latrines more light and

[M7] officials and statesmen

---

[379] 'when they had no school' added in the English translation.

[380] 'for the first time' to add.

[381] 'State' English word in the original.

[382] 'committee' English word in the original.

[383] 'to have a look at their latrines' to add.

[384] 'It was like going into hell daily, even while alive.' To add.

[385] 'we had' in the first edition.

air and enable[386] the scavenger to clean them properly. The upper classes raised numerous objections to this last improvement, and in most cases it was not carried out.

The committee had to inspect the untouchables' quarters also. Only one member of the committee was ready to accompany me there. To the rest it was something preposterous[387] to visit those quarters, still more so to inspect their latrines. But for me those quarters were an agreeable surprise. That was the first visit in my life to such a locality. The men and women there were surprised to see us. I asked them to let us inspect their latrines.

'Latrines for us!' they exclaimed in astonishment. *'We go and perform our functions out in the open.*[M8] Latrines are for you big people.'

M8 The wilderness is our latrine.

'Well, then, you won't mind if we inspect your houses?' I asked.

'You are perfectly welcome, sir. You may see every nook and corner of our houses. Ours are no houses, they are holes.'[388]

I went in and was delighted to see that the insides were as clean as the outsides. The entrances were well swept, the floors were beautifully smeared with cow-dung, and the few pots and pans were clean and shining. There was no fear of an outbreak in those quarters.[389]

In the upper class quarters[390] we came across a latrine which I cannot help describing in some detail. Every room had its gutter, which was used both for water and

---

[386] 'to enable' in the first edition.

[387] 'To the rest it was something preposterous' added in the English translation. In the original Gujarati, it is: 'To visit those quarters and to inspect those latrines.'

[388] 'they are holes' added in the English translation.

[389] 'There was no fear of an outbreak in those quarters.' Added in the English translation.

[390] 'In the upper class quarters' added in the English translation.

urine, which meant that the whole house would stink. But one of the houses had a storeyed bed-room with a gutter which was being used both as a urinal and a latrine. The gutter had a pipe descending to the ground floor. It was not possible to stand the foul smell in this room. How the occupants could sleep there I leave the readers to imagine.

The committee also visited the Vaishnava[391] *Haveli*. The priest in charge of the *Haveli* was very friendly with my family. So he agreed to let us inspect everything and suggest whatever improvements we liked. There was a part of the *Haveli* premises that he himself had never seen. It was the place where refuse and leaves used as dinner-plates used to be thrown over the wall. It was the haunt of crows and kites. The latrines were of course dirty. I was not long enough in Rajkot to see how many of our suggestions the priest carried out.

M9 at the *Haveli*

It pained me to see so much uncleanliness *about a place of worship*.[M9] One would expect a careful observance of the rules of sanitation and hygiene in a place which is regarded as holy. The authors of the *smritis*, as I knew even then, have laid the greatest emphasis on cleanliness both inward and outward.

XXVI

M1 Loyalty and Nursing

TWO PASSIONS[M1]

Hardly ever have I known anybody to cherish such loyalty as I did to the British Constitution.[392] I can see now that my[393] love of truth was at the root of this

---

[391] 'Vaishnava' added in the English translation.

[392] 'to the British Constitution' added in the English translation.

[393] 'intrinsic' to add.

loyalty. It has never been possible for me to simulate loyalty or, for that matter, any other virtue. *The National Anthem*[M2] used to be sung at every meeting that I attended in Natal.[394] I then felt that I must also join in the singing. Not that I was unaware of the defects in[395] British rule, but I thought that it was on the whole acceptable. In those days I believed that[396] British rule[397] was on the whole beneficial to the ruled.

> [M2] 'God Save the King'

The colour prejudice that I saw in South Africa was, I thought, quite contrary to British traditions, and I believed that it was only temporary and local. I therefore vied with Englishmen in loyalty to the throne. With careful perseverance I learnt the tune of the *National Anthem*[M3] and[398] joined in the singing whenever it was sung.[399] Whenever there was an occasion for the expression of loyalty without fuss or ostentation, I readily took part in it.

> [M3] British national anthem, 'God Save the King'

Never in my life did I exploit this loyalty, never did I seek to gain a selfish end by its means. *It was for me more in the nature of an obligation, and I rendered it without expecting a reward.*[M4]

> [M4] I discharged my loyalty thinking of it as a debt.

Preparations were going on for the celebration of Queen Victoria's[400] Diamond Jubilee when I reached India. I was invited to join the committee appointed for the purpose in Rajkot. I accepted the offer, but[401]

---

[394] The period that is referred to here was the period of Queen Victoria's reign. The anthem would have been 'God Save the Queen'. At the time of writing the *Autobiography* George V was the monarch.

[395] 'the' in the first edition.

[396] 'the' in the first edition.

[397] 'and administrators' to add.

[398] 'always' in the first edition.

[399] 'at the meetings' to add.

[400] 'Victoria's' added in the English translation.

[401] 'I' in the first edition.

had a suspicion that the celebrations would be largely a matter of show. I discovered much humbug about them and was considerably pained. I began to ask myself whether I should remain on the committee or not, but ultimately decided to rest content with doing[402] my part of the business.

One of the proposals was to plant trees. *I saw that many did it merely for show and for pleasing the officials.*[M5] I tried to plead with them that tree-planting was not compulsory, but merely a suggestion. It should be done seriously or not at all. I have an impression that they laughed at my ideas. I remember that I was in earnest when I planted the tree allotted to me and *that I carefully watered and tended it.*[M6]

I likewise taught *the National Anthem*[M7] to the children of my family. I recollect having taught it to students of the local Training College, but I forget whether it was on the occasion of the Jubilee or of King Edward VII's coronation as Emperor of India.[403] Later on the *text*[M8] began to jar on me. As my conception of ahimsa went on maturing, I became more vigilant about my thought and speech. The lines in the Anthem:

> Scatter her enemies,
> And make them fall;
> Confound their politics,
> Frustrate their knavish tricks.

particularly jarred upon my sentiment of ahimsa.[404] I shared my feelings with Dr. Booth[405] who agreed that it ill became a believer in ahimsa to sing those lines. How could we assume that the so-called 'enemies' were

[M5] I perceived some pretence in it. It seemed that tree planting was to be done only to please the Sahibs.

[M6] it grew.

[M7] 'God Save the King'

[M8] singing of the anthem

---

[402] 'having done' in the first edition.

[403] 'as Emperor of India' added in the English translation. At the time of the coronation on 9 August 1902, MKG was in India, albeit in Bombay.

[404] 'upon my sentiment of ahimsa' added in English translation.

[405] Dr. Robert Booth, minister of St Aidan's Church, Durban.

'knavish'? And because they were enemies, were they bound to be in the wrong? From God we could only ask for justice. Dr. Booth entirely endorsed my sentiments, and[406] composed a new anthem for his congregation. But of Dr. Booth more later.

Like loyalty an aptitude for nursing was also deeply rooted in my nature. I was fond of nursing people, whether *friends*[M9] or strangers.

M9 relatives

Whilst busy in Rajkot with the pamphlet on South Africa, I had an occasion to pay a flying[407] visit to Bombay. It was my intention to[408] educate public opinion in cities on this question by organizing meetings,[409] and Bombay was the first city I chose. First of all I met Justice Ranade,[410] who listened to me with attention, and advised me to meet Sir Pherozeshah Mehta.[411] Justice Badruddin Tyabji, whom I met next, also gave the same advice. 'Justice Ranade and I can guide you but little,' he said. 'You know our position. We cannot take an active part in public affairs, but our sympathies are with you. The man who can effectively guide you is Sir Pherozeshah Mehta.'[412]

I certainly wanted to see Sir Pherozeshah Mehta,[413] but the fact that these senior men advised me to act according to his advice gave me a better idea of the immense influence that Sir Phirozeshah had on the

---

[406] 'he' in the first edition.

[407] 'flying' added in the English translation. MKG did not ever travel by air.

[408] 'further' to add.

[409] 'there' in the first edition.

[410] Mahadev Govind Ranade (1842–1901), social reformer and author, judge of the Bombay High Court, one of the founders of the Indian National Congress.

[411] 'Mehta' added in the English translation.

[412] 'Mehta' added in the English translation.

[413] 'Mehta' added in the English translation.

public. In due course I met him. I was prepared to
be awed by his presence. I had heard of the popular
titles that he had earned, and[414] knew that I was to see
the 'Lion of Bombay', the 'Uncrowned King of *the
Presidency*'.[M10] But the king did not overpower me. He
met me, as a loving father would meet his grown-up
son. Our meeting took place at his chamber.[415] He was
surrounded by a circle of friends and followers. Amongst
them were Mr. D.E. Wacha[416] and Mr. Cama,[417] to
whom I was introduced. I had already heard of Mr.
Wacha. He was regarded as the right-hand man of Sir
Pherozeshah, and Sjt. Virchand Gandhi had described
him to me as a great statistician. Mr. Wacha said,
'Gandhi, we must meet again.'

These introductions could scarcely have taken two
minutes. Sir Pherozeshah carefully listened to me. I
told him that I had seen Justices Ranade and Tyabji.
'Gandhi,' said he, 'I see that I must help you. I must
call a public meeting here.' With this he turned to Mr.
Munshi, the secretary,[418] and told him to fix up the
date of the meeting. The date was settled, and he bade
me good-bye, asking me to see him again on the day
previous to the meeting. The interview removed my
fears, and I went home delighted.

During this stay in Bombay I called on my brother-
in-law,[419] who was staying there and lying ill. He was not

---

[414] 'I' in the first edition.

[415] 'chamber', English word in the original.

[416] Mr. (later Sir) Dinshaw Edulji Wacha (1844–1936), one of the
founders of the Indian National Congress and its president in
1901, member, Bombay Legislative Council, the Imperial
Legislative Council and the Council of States, knighted 1917.

[417] Probably Rustom Cama, a leading lawyer, married to Madam
Bhikhaji Cama.

[418] 'the secretary,' added in the English translation.

[419] Vrindavandas, husband of Raliyatbehn.

a man of means, and my sister (his wife)[420] was not equal to nursing him. The illness was serious, and I offered to take him to Rajkot. He agreed, and so I returned home with my sister and her husband. The illness was much more *prolonged*[M11] than I had expected. I put my brother-in-law in my room and remained with him night and day. I was obliged to keep awake part of the night and had to get through some of my South African work whilst I was nursing him. Ultimately, however, *the patient*[M12] died, but it was a great consolation to me that I had had an opportunity to nurse him during his last days.

M11 severe

M12 brother-in-law

My *aptitude*[M13] for nursing gradually developed into a passion, so much so that it often led me to neglect my work, and on occasions I engaged not only my wife but the whole household in such service.

M13 hobby

Such service can have no meaning unless one takes pleasure in it.[M14] When it is done[421] for show or for fear of public opinion, it stunts the man and crushes his spirit. Service which is rendered without joy helps neither the servant nor the served. But all other pleasures and possessions[422] pale into nothingness before service which is rendered in a spirit of joy.

M14 I describe this inclination as a hobby because I have seen that such qualities are sustained only when they become a source of joy.

XXVII

THE BOMBAY MEETING

On the very day after my brother-in-law's death I had to go to Bombay for the public meeting.[423] There had

---

[420] '(his wife)' added in the English translation.

[421] 'under strain' to add.

[422] 'etc.' to add.

[423] The meeting was held on 26 September 1896, MKG reached Bombay on the 25th, his brother-in-law died on 23rd September.

hardly been time for me to think out my speech. I was feeling exhausted after days and nights of anxious vigil, and my voice had become husky. However, I went to Bombay trusting entirely to God. I had never dreamt of writing out my speech.

In accordance with Sir Pherozeshah's instructions I reported myself at his office at 5 p.m. on the eve of the meeting.

'Is your speech ready, Gandhi?' he asked.

'No sir,' said I, trembling with fear, 'I think of speaking extempore.'

'That will not do in Bombay. Reporting here is bad, and if we would benefit by this meeting, you should write out your speech, and it should be printed before daybreak tomorrow. I hope you can manage this?'

I felt rather nervous, but I said I would try.

'Then, tell me, what time Mr. Munshi should come to you for the *manuscript*?'[M1]

'Eleven o'clock tonight,' said I.[424]

On going to the meeting the next day, I saw the wisdom of Sir Pherozeshah's advice. The meeting was held in the hall of Sir Cowasji Jehangir Institute.[425] I had heard that when Sir Pherozeshah Mehta addressed meetings the hall was always packed, chiefly by the students intent on hearing him, leaving not *an inch of room*.[M2] This was the first meeting of the kind in my experience. I saw that my voice could reach only a few.[426] I was trembling as I began to read my speech.[427]

[M1] speech

[M2] even standing room

---

[424] 'Sir Pherozeshah instructed Mr. Munshi to collect the speech at that hour and have it printed that very night and bade me good-bye.' To add.

[425] The meeting was held at Framji Cowasji Institute and not at Sir Cowasji Jehangir Institute. The original Gujarati has Framji Cowasji Institute; also *CWMG*, vol. 2, p. 50, n. 1, has Framji Cowasji Institute.

[426] 'no one' in the first edition.

[427] For the text of the speech. See *CWMG*, vol. 2, pp. 50–60.

Sir Pherozeshah cheered me up continually by asking me to speak louder and still louder. I have a feeling that, far from encouraging me, it made my voice sink lower and lower.

My old friend Sjt. Keshavrao Deshpande came to my rescue. I handed my speech to him. His was just the proper voice. But the audience refused to listen. The hall rang with the cries of 'Wacha', 'Wacha'. So Mr. Wacha *stood up and read the speech, with wonderful results.*[M3] The audience became perfectly quiet, and listened to the speech to the end, punctuating it with applause and cries of 'shame'[428] where necessary. This gladdened my heart.

[M3] stood up, took the papers from Deshpande and fulfilled my task

Sir Pherozeshah liked the speech. *I was supremely happy.*[M4]

[M4] For me it was akin to having bathed in the Ganga.

The meeting won me the active sympathy of Sjt. Deshpande and a Parsi friend, whose name I hesitate to mention, as he is a high-placed Government official today.[429] Both expressed their resolve to accompany me to South Africa.[430] *Mr. C.M. Cursetji, who was then Small Causes Court Judge, however, moved the Parsi friend from his resolve as he had plotted his marriage.*[M5] He had to choose between marriage and going to South Africa, and he chose the former. But Parsi Rustomji made amends for the broken resolve, and a number of Parsi sisters are now making amends for the lady who helped in the breach by dedicating themselves to khadi work. I have therefore gladly forgiven that couple. Sjt. Deshpande had no temptations of marriage, but he too could not come. Today he is himself doing enough reparation for the broken pledge. On my way back to South Africa I met one of the Tyabjis at Zanzibar. He also promised

[M5] Judge Cursetji, however, moved the Parsi friend from his resolve. The reason was a Parsi sister.

---

[428] 'shame' English word in the original.

[429] The Parsi lawyer was F.S. Talyarkhan. See MKG's letter to him, *CWMG*, vol. 2, pp. 67–69.

[430] 'Both expressed their resolve to accompany me to South Africa.' Added in the English translation.

M6 why would he come to South Africa?

to come and help me, but[431] *never came.*[M6] Mr. Abbas Tyabji is atoning for that offence. Thus none of my three attempts to induce barristers to go to South Africa bore any fruit.

In this connection I remember Mr. Pestonji Padshah. I had been on friendly terms with him ever since my stay in England. I first met him in a vegetarian restaurant in London. I knew of his brother Mr. Barjorji Padshah[432] by his reputation as a 'crank'. I had never met him, but friends said that he was eccentric. Out of pity for the horses, he would not ride in tram-cars, he refused to take degrees in spite of a prodigious memory, he had developed an independent spirit,[433] and he was a vegetarian, though a Parsi. Pestonji had not quite this reputation, but he was famous for his erudition even in London. The common factor between us, however, was vegetarianism, and not scholarship in which it was beyond my power to approach him.

I found him out again in Bombay. He was Prothonotary[434] in the High Court.[435] When I met him he was engaged on his contribution to a Higher Gujarati Dictionary. There was not a friend I had not approached for help in my South African work. Pestonji Padshah, however, not only refused to aid me, but even advised me not to return to South Africa.

'It is impossible to help you,' he said. 'But I tell you I do not like even *your* going to South Africa. Is there lack of work in our own country? Look, now,

---

[431] 'he never came.' In the first edition.

[432] Barjorji Jamaspji Padshah (1864–91), studied at universities of Bombay and Cambridge, professor and vice-principal of Dayaram Jethamal College, Sindh, close associate of Jamsetji Tata.

[433] 'that he would yield to nobody' to add.

[434] 'Prothonotary' English word in the original.

[435] 'in the High Court' added in the English translation.

there is not a little to do for our language. I have to find
out scientific words. But this is only one branch of the
work. Think of the poverty of the land. Our people
in South Africa are no doubt in difficulty, but I do not
want a man like you to be sacrificed for that work. Let
us win self-government here, and we shall automatically
help our country-men there. I know I cannot prevail
upon you, but I will not encourage anyone of your type
to throw in his lot with you.'

I did not like this advice, but it increased my regard
for Mr. Pestonji Padshah. I was struck with his love for
the country and for the *mother tongue*.[M7] The incident M7 language
brought us closer to each other. I could understand
his point of view. But far from giving up my work in
South Africa, *I became firmer in my resolve*.[M8] A patriot M8 I felt that even from his point
cannot afford to ignore any branch of service to the of view I should cling to it
motherland.[436] And for me the text of the Gita was clear
and emphatic:

> Finally, this is better, that one do
> His own task as he may, even though he fail,
> Than take tasks not his own, though they seem good.
> To die performing duty is no ill;
> But who seeks other roads shall wander still.[437]

XXVIII

POONA AND MADRAS[M1]   M1 In Poona

Sir Pherozeshah had made my way easy. So from
Bombay I went to Poona.[438] Here there were two

---

[436] 'to the motherland' added in the English translation.

[437] Discourse III, verse 35. Sir Edwin Arnold's translation.

[438] MKG reached Poona on 12 October 1896. For other recollections
of the visit, see *CWMG*, vol. 20, pp. 369–71 and vol. 29, pp. 44–46.

parties. I wanted the help of people of every shade of opinion. First I met Lokamanya Tilak.[439] He said:

'You are quite right in seeking the help of all parties. There can be no difference of opinion on the South African question. But you must have *a non-party*[M2] man for your President. Meet Professor Bhandarkar.[440] He has been taking no part of late in any public movement. But this question might possibly draw him out. See him and let me know what he says. I want to help you to the fullest extent.[441] Of course you will meet me whenever you like. I am at your disposal.'

This was my first meeting with the Lokamanya. It revealed to me the secret of his unique popularity.

Next I met Gokhale.[442] I found him on the Fergusson College[443] grounds. *He gave me an affectionate welcome, and his manner immediately won my heart.*[M3] With him too this was my first meeting, and yet it seemed as though we *were renewing an old friendship.*[M4] Sir Pherozeshah had seemed to me like the Himalaya, the Lokamanya like the ocean. But Gokhale was the Ganges. One could have a refreshing bath in the holy river. The Himalaya was unscalable, and *one could not easily launch forth on*[M5] the sea but the Ganges invited one to its bosom. It was a joy to be on it with a boat and an

M2 an impartial

M3 He embraced me affectionately and made me one of his own.

M4 had met before

M5 there is the fear of being drowned in

---

[439] 'Tilak' added in the English translation. Bal Gangadhar Tilak (1856–1920), the first one to articulate 'Swaraj', at various points associated with the Indian National Congress and the Indian Home Rule League, sentenced to six years imprisonment to Mandalay Prison for sedition, author of *Gita Rahasya*.

[440] Ramkrishna Gopal Bhandarkar (1837–1925), scholar, orientalist, taught at Elphinstone College, Bombay, and Deccan College, Poona, served as vice-chancellor of Bombay University.

[441] 'You must also meet Professor Gokhale.' To add.

[442] Gopal Krishna Gokhale (1866–1915), founder of the Servants of India Society, mentor to both MKG and Muhammad Ali Jinnah.

[443] Established in 1885 by the Deccan Education Society, named after Sir James Fergusson, Governor of Bombay.

oar. Gokhale closely examined me, as a schoolmaster would examine a candidate seeking admission to a school. He told me whom to approach and how to approach them. He asked to have a look at my speech. He showed me over the college, assured me that he was always at my disposal, asked me to let him know the result of the interview with Dr. Bhandarkar, and sent me away exultantly happy.[444] In the sphere of politics the place that Gokhale occupied in my heart during his lifetime and occupies even now was[445] and is absolutely unique.

Dr. Bhandarkar received me with the warmth of a father. It was noon when I called on him. The very fact that I was busy seeing people at that hour appealed greatly to this indefatigable savant, and my insistence of *a non-party man for the* [M6] president of the meeting had his ready approval, which was expressed in the spontaneous exclamation, 'That's it,' 'That's it.'[446]

[M6] an impartial

After he had heard me out he said: 'Anyone will tell you that I do not take part in politics.[447] But I cannot refuse you. Your case is so strong and your industry is so admirable that I cannot decline to take part in your meeting. You did well in consulting Tilak and Gokhale. Please tell them that I shall be glad to preside over the meeting to be held under the joint auspices of the two *Sabhas*.[M7] You need not have the time of the meeting from me. Any time that suits them will suit me.' With this he bade me good-bye with congratulations and blessings.

[M7] parties

Without any ado this erudite and selfless band of workers in Poona held a meeting in an unostentatious

---

[444] 'exultantly happy' added in the English translation.

[445] 'has been' in the first edition.

[446] 'That's it.' English phrase in the original.

[447] 'these days' to add.

little place, and sent me away rejoicing and more confident of my mission.

I next proceeded to Madras.[448] It was wild with enthusiasm. The Balasundaram incident made a profound impression on the meeting. My speech[449] was printed and was, for me, fairly long. But the audience listened to every word with attention. At the close of the meeting there was a regular run on the 'Green Pamphlet'. I brought out[450] a second and revised edition of 10,000 copies. *They sold like hot cakes,*[M8] but I saw that it was not necessary to print such a large number. In my enthusiasm I had overcalculated the demand. It was the English-speaking public to which my speech had been addressed, and in Madras that class alone could not take the whole ten thousand.

The greatest help here came to me from the late Sjt. G. Parameshvaran Pillay,[451] the editor of *The Madras Standard*. He had made a careful study of the question, and he often invited me to his office and gave me guidance. Sjt. G. Subramaniam[452] of *The Hindu*[453] and Dr. Subramaniam[454] also were very sympathetic. But

[M8] A large portion of it was sold

---

[448] MKG reached Madras on 14 October 1896 and left it on 27 October. He stayed at Buckingham Hotel on Mount Road, where his bill was some Rs 74.

[449] See, *CWMG*, vol. 2, pp. 94–121. The meeting was held on 26 October at Pachaippa's Hall.

[450] 'in Madras' to add.

[451] Barrister G.P. Pillay (1864–1903), admitted to the Middle Temple, 1898, called to the Bar in 1902. The *Madras Standard* began publication a few years before *The Hindu*.

[452] Ganapathy Dikshitiar Subramania Iyer (1855–1916), founder, proprietor, editor of *The Hindu* from 1878–98 and founded and edited the Tamil newspaper *Swadesamitran* in 1881.

[453] Founded in September 1878, began as a weekly, became a tri-weekly (1883) and then a daily in 1889.

[454] Sir S. Subramania Iyer (1842–1924), one of the founders of the Indian National Congress, hon. president, Home Rule League,

Sjt. G. Parameshvaran Pillay placed the columns of *The Madras Standard* entirely at my disposal, and I freely availed myself of the offer. The meeting in Pachaiappa Hall, so far as I can recollect, was with Dr. Subramaniam in the chair.

The affection showered on me by most of the friends I met and their enthusiasm for the cause were so great that, in spite of my having to communicate with them in English, I felt myself entirely at home. What barrier is there that love cannot break?

XXIX

'RETURN SOON'

From Madras I proceeded to Calcutta[455] where I found myself hemmed in by difficulties. I knew no one there. So I took a room in the Great Eastern Hotel.[456] Here I became acquainted with Mr. Ellerthorpe,[457] a representative of *The Daily Telegraph*. He invited me to the Bengal Club,[458] where he was staying. He did not then realize that an Indian could not be taken to the drawing-room of the club. Having discovered the restriction, he took me to his room. He expressed his sorrow regarding this prejudice of the local Englishmen

---

vice-president, Theosophical Society (1907–11), judge, Madras High Court (1895–1907), knighted 1900, conferred Doctor of Law, honoris causa (1908).

[455] MKG left Madras on 27 October, reaching Calcutta on 31 October 1896, via Nagpur.

[456] Founded in 1841 as Auckland Hotel, situated on Old Church Street, regarded as Asia's first luxury hotel.

[457] John Ellerthorpe. See Gopalkrishna Gandhi, *A Frank Friendship* (Kolkata: Seagull, 2007), p. 6

[458] Founded on 1 February 1827, it is the oldest surviving club of its kind; Indian members have been admitted since 1959.

and apologized to me for not having been able to take me to the drawing-room.

I had of course to see Surendranath Banerji,[459] the 'Idol of Bengal'. When I met him, he was surrounded by a number of *friends*.[M1] He said:

M1 other visitors

> 'I am afraid people will not take interest in your work. As you know, our difficulties here are by no means few. But you must try as best you can. You will have to enlist the sympathy of Maharajas. Mind, you meet the representatives of the British Indian Association.[460] You should meet Raja Sir Pyarimohan Mukarji[461] and Maharaja Tagore.[462] Both are liberal-minded and take a fair share in public work.'

M2 I could not even wet my beak there

I met these gentlemen, but *without success*.[M2] Both gave me a cold reception and[463] said it was no easy thing to call a public meeting in Calcutta, and if anything could be done, it would practically all depend on Surendranath Banerji.

I saw that my task was becoming more and more difficult. I called at the office of the *Amrita Bazar Patrika*.[464] The gentleman whom I met there took me

---

[459] Surendranath Banerjee (1848–1925) was for a brief period in the Indian Civil Service, twice president, Indian National Congress (1895, 1902).

[460] Founded in 1851 at Calcutta, with Raja Radhakanta Deb as president and Devendranath Tagore as secretary.

[461] Pyari Mohun Mukherjee (1840–1923), C.S.I., M.A., B.L. See Gandhi, *A Frank Friendship*, p. 6.

[462] Jatindramohan Tagore (1831–1908).

[463] 'gave me a cold reception and' added in the English translation.

[464] First published on 20 February 1868 as a Bengali weekly, published bilingually from the following year; as an English weekly from March 1878; as an English daily from 1889. Ceased publication in 1996. See Gandhi, *A Frank Friendship*, p. 7, n. 22.

to be a *wandering Jew*.[M3] *The Bangabasi*[465] went even one better. The editor kept me waiting for an hour. He had evidently many interviewers, but he would not so much as look at me, even *when he had disposed of the rest*.[M4] On my venturing to broach my subject after the long wait, he said: 'Don't you see our hands are full? There is no end to the number of visitors like you. You had better go. I am not disposed to listen to you.' For a moment I felt offended, but I quickly understood the editor's position. I had heard of the fame of *The Bangabasi*. I could see that there was a regular stream of visitors there. And they were all people acquainted with him. His paper had no lack of topics to discuss, and South Africa was hardly known at that time.

However serious a grievance may be in the eyes of the man who suffers from it, he will be but one of the numerous people invading the editor's office, each with a grievance of his own. How is the editor to meet them all? Moreover, the aggrieved party imagines that the editor is a power in the land. Only he knows that his power can hardly travel beyond the threshold of his office. But I was not discouraged. I kept on seeing editors of other papers. As usual I met *the Anglo-Indian editors also*.[M5] *The Statesman*[466] and *The Englishman*[467] *realized*[M6] the importance of the[468] question. I gave them long interviews, and they published them in full.[469]

Mr. Saunders,[470] editor of *The Englishman*, claimed me as his own. He placed his office and paper at my

[M3] wanderer

[M4] as they left one after another

[M5] Englishmen as well

[M6] were aware of

---

[465] First published on 10 December 1881 with Jnanendralal Roy as editor. See ibid, n. 23.

[466] Started as *The Indian Statesman* in 1875 by Robert Knight.

[467] Founded in 1821, merged with *The Statesman* in 1934.

[468] 'South African' to add.

[469] See *CWMG*, vol. 2, pp. 124–27, 131–35.

[470] John O'Brien Saunders (1852–1905), given C.I.E. for his conduct of the newspaper at the Delhi Durbar in 1903.

disposal. He even allowed me the liberty of making whatever changes I liked in the leading article he had written on the situation, the proof of which he sent me in advance.[471] It is no exaggeration to say that a friendship grew up between us. He promised to render me all the help he *could, carried out the promise to the letter, and*[M7] kept on his correspondence with me until the time when he was seriously ill.

Throughout my life I have had the privilege of many such friendships, which have sprung up quite unexpectedly. What Mr. Saunders liked in me was my freedom from exaggeration and my devotion to truth. He subjected me to a searching cross-examination before he began to sympathize with my cause,[472] and he saw that I had spared neither will nor pains to place before him an impartial statement of the case even of the white man in South Africa and also to appreciate it.

My experience has shown me that we win justice quickest by rendering justice to the other party.

The unexpected help of Mr. Saunders had begun to encourage me to think that I might succeed after all in holding a public meeting in Calcutta, when I received the following cable from Durban:[473] 'Parliament opens January. Return soon.'

So I addressed a letter to the Press,[474] in which I explained why I had to leave Calcutta so abruptly, and set off for Bombay. Before starting I wired to the Bombay agent of Dada Abdulla & Co. to arrange for my passage by the first possible boat to South Africa. Dada Abdulla had just then purchased the steamship *Courland*

[M7] could. He asked me to write to him even after I had returned to South Africa and promised to do his best. He

---

[471] 'the proof of which he sent me in advance' added in the English translation.

[472] 'before he began to sympathize with my cause,' added in the English translation.

[473] It was received on 12 November 1896.

[474] See *CWMG*, vol. 2, pp. 127–30.

and insisted[475] on my travelling on that boat, offering to take me and my family free of charge. I gratefully accepted the offer, and in the beginning of December[476] set[477] sail a second time for South Africa, now with my wife and two sons[478] and the only son[479] of my *widowed sister*.[M8]

[M8] late brother-in-law

Another steamship *Naderi* also sailed for Durban at the same time.[480] The agents of the Company were Dada Abdulla & Co. The total number of[481] passengers these boats carried must have been about eight hundred, half of whom were bound for the Transvaal.

---

[475] 'he insisted' in the first edition.

[476] *S.S Courland* set sail on 30 November 1896.

[477] 'I set' in the first edition.

[478] Harilal and Manilal.

[479] Gokuldas (1887–1908), son of Raliyatbehn (1863–1960).

[480] *S.S Naderi* set sail on 28 November 1896.

[481] 'Indian' to add.

PART III

I

RUMBLINGS OF THE STORM

This was my first voyage with my *wife and children.*[M1]
I have often observed in the course of this narrative[1]
that, on account of child marriages amongst middle-
class Hindus, the husband will be literate whilst the wife
remains practically unlettered. A wide gulf thus separates
them, and the husband has to become his wife's teacher.
So I had to think out the details of the dress to be
adopted by my wife and children, the food they were
to eat, and the manners which would be suited to their
new surroundings. Some of the recollections of those
days are amusing to look back upon.

A Hindu wife regards implicit obedience to her
husband as the highest religion. A Hindu husband
regards himself as lord and master of his wife *who must
ever dance attendance upon him.*[M2]

I believed, at the time of which I am writing,
that in order to look civilized, our dress and manners
had as far as possible to approximate to the European
standard. Because, I thought, only thus could we have
some influence, and without influence it would not be
possible to serve the community.

I therefore determined the style of dress for my wife
and children. How could I like them to be known as

[M1] family

[M2] and hence she must dance to
his commands

---

[1] 'in the course of this narrative' added in the English translation.

311

Kathiawad Banias? The Parsis used then to be regarded as the most civilized people amongst Indians,[2] and so, when the complete European style seemed to be unsuited, we adopted the Parsi style. Accordingly my wife wore the Parsi sari, and the boys the Parsi coat and trousers. Of course no one could be without shoes and stockings. It was long before my wife and children could get used to them. The shoes cramped their feet and the stockings stank with perspiration. The toes often got sore. I always had my answers ready to[3] all these objections. But I have an impression that[4] it was not so much the answers as the force of authority that carried conviction. They agreed to the changes in dress as there was no alternative. In the same spirit and with even more reluctance they adopted the use of knives and forks. When my infatuation for these signs of civilization[5] wore away, they gave up[6] the knives and forks. After having become long accustomed to the new style, it was perhaps no less irksome for them to return to the original mode. But I can see today that we feel all the freer and lighter for having cast off the *tinsel*[M3] of 'civilization'.

On board the same steamer with us were some relatives and acquaintances. These and other deck passengers I frequently met, because, the boat belonging to my client friends,[7] I was free to move about anywhere and everywhere I liked.

Since the steamer was making straight for Natal, without calling at intermediate ports, our voyage was

[M3] worn-out skin

---

[2] 'amongst Indians' added in the English translation.

[3] 'for' in the first edition.

[4] 'But I have an impression that' added in the English translation.

[5] 'for these signs of civilization' added in the English translation.

[6] 'shoes and stockings and' to add.

[7] 'which seemed like home to me,' to add.

of only eighteen days. But as though to warn us of the coming real storm on land, a terrible gale overtook us, whilst we were only four days from Natal. December is a summer month of monsoon in the Southern hemisphere, and gales,[8] great and small, are therefore[9] quite common in the Southern sea at that season. The gale in which we were caught was so violent and prolonged that the passengers became alarmed. It was a solemn scene. All became one in face of the common danger. They forgot their differences and began to think of the one and only God—Mussalmans, Hindus, Christians[10] and all. Some took various vows. The captain[11] also joined the passengers in their prayers. He assured them[12] that, though the storm was not without danger, he had had experience of many worse ones, and explained to them that a well-built ship *could stand almost any weather.*[M4] But they were inconsolable. Every minute were heard sounds and crashes which foreboded breaches and leaks. The ship rocked and rolled to such an extent that it seemed as though she would capsize at any moment. It was out of the question for anyone to remain on deck. 'His will be done' was the only cry on every lip. So far as I can recollect, we must have been in this plight for about twenty-four hours. At last the sky cleared, the sun[13] made his appearance, and the captain said that the storm had blown over. People's faces beamed with gladness, and with the disappearance of danger disappeared also the name of God from their lips. Eating and drinking, singing and merry-making

[M4] does not sink all of a sudden

---

[8] 'so gales,' in the first edition.

[9] 'therefore' added in the 1940 edition.

[10] 'Christians' added in the English translation.

[11] Captain Alexander Milne.

[12] 'them all' in the first edition.

[13] 'god' to add.

again became the order of the day. The fear of death was gone, and the momentary mood of earnest prayer gave place to *maya*.[14] There were of course the usual *namaz*[15] and the prayers,[16] yet they had none of the solemnity of that dread hour.

But the storm had made me one with the passengers. *I had little fear of the storm,*[M5] for I had had experience of similar ones. I am a good sailor and do not get sea-sick. So I could fearlessly move amongst the passengers, bringing them comfort and good cheer, and conveying to them hourly reports of the captain. The friendship I thus formed stood me, as we shall see, in very good stead.

The ship cast anchor in the port of Durban on the 18th or 19th of December. The *Naderi* also reached the same day.[17]

But the real storm was still to come.

[M5] I can say that I had no fear of the storm or at any rate the least fear

II

THE STORM

We have seen that the two ships cast anchor in the port of Durban[18] on or about the 18th of December. No passengers are allowed to land at any of the South African ports before being subjected to a thorough medical examination. If the ship has any passenger suffering

---

[14] MD's footnote: 'The famous word in Hindu philosophy which is nearly untranslatable, but has been frequently translated in English as, "delusion", "illusion".'

[15] MD's footnote: 'The prayer prescribed by the Koran.'

[16] 'bhajan' in the original.

[17] *S.S Naderi* and *S.S Courland* cast anchor on 18 December 1896, at 2 p.m. and 5.30 p.m. respectively.

[18] 'in the port of Durban' added in the English translation.

from a contagious disease, she has to undergo a period of quarantine.[19] As there had been plague in Bombay when we set sail, we feared that[20] we might have to go through a brief quarantine. Before the examination every ship has to fly a yellow flag, which is lowered only when the doctor has certified her to be healthy. Relatives and friends of passengers are allowed to come on board only after the yellow flag has been lowered.

Accordingly our ship was flying the yellow flag, when the doctor[21] came and examined us. He ordered a five days' quarantine because, in his opinion, plague germs took twenty-three days at the most to develop. Our ship was therefore ordered to be put in quarantine until the twenty-third day of our sailing from Bombay. But this quarantine order had more than health reasons behind it.

The white residents of Durban had been agitating for our repatriation, and the agitation was one of the reasons for the order. Dada Abdulla and Co.[22] kept us regularly informed about the daily happenings in the town.[23] The whites were holding monster meetings

---

[19] 'quarantine' English word in the original, it is preceded by the Gujarati word 'sutak', literally, segregation.

[20] 'lest' in the first edition.

[21] The officer of health, Durban, was Dr. Robert Thomas Sutherland. He refused to take orders from Harry Escombe and the demonstration committee to extend the period of quarantine and was subsequently discharged with three months' pay. Dr. Daniel Birtwell was appointed by Harry Escombe as the port's Acting Health Officer.

[22] 'and Co.' added in the English translation.

[23] The Reuters cable appeared in the Natal newspapers on 16 September 1896; on the same day a European Protection League was formed in Maritzburg to defend and preserve the rights of the European colonists. In Durban, the Colonial Protection Union was formed to prevent further influx of Asians. On 30 December Harry Sparks, a butcher by trade, called a public meeting to protest against landing of passengers from the *Courland*

every day. They were addressing all kinds of threats and at times offering even inducements to Dada Abdulla and Co.[24] They were ready to indemnify the Company if both the ships should be sent back.[25] But Dada Abdulla and Co.[26] were not the people to be afraid of threats. Sheth Abdul Karim Haji Adam was then the managing partner of the firm. He was determined to moor the ships at the wharf and disembark the passengers at any cost. He was daily sending me detailed letters. Fortunately the late Sjt. Mansukhlal Naazar[27] was then in Durban having gone there to meet me. He was capable and fearless and guided the Indian community.

---

and the *Naderi*, attended by nearly 2000 persons; a demonstration committee comprising representatives of various tradesmen was formed that continued to challenge the Government of Natal. On 13 January 1897, the day on which both the ships were to commence disembarkation of passengers, a crowd of over 3300 men gathered to oppose the landing of 600-odd Indians, and took possession of the wharf. The *Naderi* had 356 passengers, including infants in arms, of which 100 to 120 were old Natal residents returning after a home visit and forty women waiting to join either their fathers or husbands; the *Courland*'s passengers or cargo did not contain either a printing press or skilled artisans of any kind.

[24] 'and Co.' added in the English translation.

[25] On 11 January 1897 a delegation of demonstration committee, comprising Arthur Saville (produce merchant), James Fletcher (poultry farmer) and James Scott Wylie (attorney), went aboard the *Courland* and the *Naderi* with an offer to indemnify the ships if the passengers were returned to the port of embarkation. The captain of the *Courland*, Alexander Milne, presented a claim of £10,000 to £7500, while the captain of the *Naderi*, Francis John Raffin, made a claim of £2500; both were found to be 'exorbitant' and rejected by the demonstration committee.

[26] 'and Co.' added in the English translation.

[27] Mansukhlal Hiralal Naazar (1862–1906), first emigrated to England from Bombay and to Durban in 1896, a close associate of MKG, served as one of the secretaries of the Natal Indian Congress during MKG's visit to India in 1901. First editor of *Indian Opinion* from June 1903 till his death on 20 January 1906.

Their advocate Mr. Laughton[28] was an equally fearless man. He condemned the conduct of the white residents and advised the community, not merely as their paid advocate, but also as their true friend.

Thus Durban had become the scene of an unequal[29] duel. On one side there was a handful of poor Indians and a few of their English friends, and on the other were ranged the white men, strong in arms, in numbers, in education and in wealth. They had also the backing of the State, for the Natal Government openly helped them. Mr. Harry Escombe, who was the most influential of the members of the Cabinet, openly took part in their meetings.

The real object of the quarantine was thus to coerce the passengers into returning to India by somehow intimidating them or the Agent Company.[30] For now threats began to be addressed to us also: 'If you do not go back, you will surely be pushed into the sea. But if you consent to return, you may even get your passage money back.'[31] I constantly moved amongst my fellow-passengers cheering them up. I also sent messages of comfort to the passengers of the *s.s. Naderi*. All of them kept calm and courageous.

---

[28] Frederick Augustus Laughton, the solicitor for Dada Abdullah & Co., formerly a partner of A.W. Baker.

[29] 'unequal' added in the English translation.

[30] 'Threats were held out to the Agent.' To add.

[31] The captain of the *Courland* received a letter signed by Harry Sparks: 'As your passengers are ignorant of the state of feeling, and have come here in ignorance, and we have it from the Attorney-General that if your people are willing to return to India, the Colony will pay the expense. We shall, therefore, be glad to receive an answer from you before the ship comes alongside the wharf, whether the passengers elect to return to India at the Colony's expense, or endeavour to force landing against thousands of men who are ready and waiting to oppose their landing.' *CWMG*, vol. 2, p. 158.

We arranged all sorts of games on the ship for the entertainment of the passengers. On Christmas Day the captain invited the saloon passengers to dinner. The principal among these were my family and I.[32] *In the speeches after dinner*[M1] I spoke on Western civilization. I knew that this was not an occasion for a serious speech. But mine could not be otherwise. I took part in the merriment, but my heart was in the combat that was going on in Durban. For I was the real target. There were two charges against me:

1. that whilst in India I had indulged in unmerited condemnation of the Natal whites;
2. that with a view to swamping Natal with Indians I had specially brought the two shiploads[33] of passengers to settle there.

I was conscious of my responsibility. I knew that Dada Abdulla and Co.[34] had incurred *grave risks*[M2] on my account, the lives of the passengers were in danger, and by bringing my family with me I had *put them likewise in jeopardy.*[M3]

But I was absolutely innocent. I had induced no one to go to Natal. *I did not know the passengers when they embarked.*[M4] And with the exception of a couple of relatives,[35] I did not know the name and address of even one of the hundreds of passengers on board. Neither had I said, whilst in India, a word about the whites in Natal that I had not already said in Natal itself. And I had ample evidence in support of all that I had said.

[M1] A dinner is always followed by speeches.

[M2] heavy losses

[M3] plunged them into suffering

[M4] I did not even know the passengers of the *Naderi.*

---

[32] 'I and my family' in the first edition.

[33] In the original, names of the ships are given, i.e., *Courland* and *Naderi.*

[34] 'and Co.' added in the English translation.

[35] 'on board the *Courland*' to add.

I therefore deplored the civilization of which the
Natal whites were the fruit, and which they represented
and championed. This civilization[36] had all along been on
my mind, and I therefore offered my views concerning it
in my speech before that little meeting.[37] The captain and
other friends gave me a patient hearing, and[38] received
my speech in the spirit in which it was made. I do not
know that it in any way affected the course of their lives,
but afterwards I had long talks with the captain and other
officers regarding the civilization of the West.[39] *I had in
my speech described Western civilization as being, unlike the
Eastern, predominantly based on force.*[M5] The questioners
pinned me to my faith, and one of them—the captain so
far as I recollect—said to me:

    'Supposing the whites carry out their threats, how
will you stand by your principle of non-violence?' To
which I replied: 'I hope God will give me the courage
and the sense to forgive them and to refrain from
bringing them to law. I have no anger against them.[40] I
am only sorry for their ignorance and their narrowness.
I know that they sincerely believe that what they are[41]
doing today is right and proper. I have no reason
therefore to be angry with them.'

    The questioner smiled, possibly distrustfully.

    Thus the days dragged on their weary length.[42] When
the quarantine would terminate was still uncertain. The
Quarantine Officer said that the matter had passed out

[M5] I described the Western civilization as predominantly violent; the Eastern as non-violent.

---

[36] 'civilization' added in the English translation.

[37] 'which they tolerated' to add.

[38] 'gave me a patient hearing, and' added in the English translation.

[39] 'civilization of the West.' Added in the English translation.

[40] 'even today' to add.

[41] 'saying and' to add.

[42] 'weary way' in the first edition.

of his hands and that, as soon as he had orders from the Government, he would permit us to land.

At last ultimatums were served on the passengers and me. We were asked to submit, if we would escape with our lives. In our reply the passengers and I both maintained our right to land at Port Natal, and intimated our determination to enter Natal at any risk.

At the end of twenty three days the ships were permitted to enter the harbour, and orders permitting the passengers to land were passed.

III

THE TEST[43]

So the ships were brought into the dock and the passengers began to go ashore. But Mr. Escombe had sent word to the captain that, *as the whites were highly enraged against me and my life was in danger, my family and I*[44] *should be advised to land at dusk, when the Port Superintendent Mr. Tatum*[45] *would escort us home.*[M1] The captain communicated the message to me, and I agreed to act accordingly. But scarcely half an hour after this, Mr. Laughton came to the captain. He said: 'I would like to take Mr. Gandhi with me,[46] should he have no objection. As the legal adviser of the Agent Company I tell you that you are not bound to carry out the message you have received *from Mr. Escombe.*'[M2] After this he came to me and said somewhat to this effect: 'If you

M1 'Please disembark Gandhi and his family at dusk. The whites are highly enraged against him and his life is in danger. The Port Superintendent Tatum would escort him in the evening.'

M2 regarding Mr. Gandhi

---

[43] MKG has described the events narrated in this chapter in *Satyagraha in South Africa* as well. See *CWMG*, vol. 29, pp. 50–56.

[44] 'I and my family' in the first edition.

[45] G.E. Tautam.

[46] 'at my risk' to add.

are not afraid,[47] I suggest that Mrs. Gandhi and the children should drive to Mr. Rustomji's house, whilst you and I follow them on foot.[48] I do not at all like the idea of your entering the city *like a thief in the night.*[M3] I do not think there is any fear of anyone hurting you. Everything is quiet now. The whites have all dispersed. But in any case I am convinced that you ought not to enter the city stealthily.'[49] I readily agreed. My wife and children drove[50] safely to Mr. Rustomji's place. With the captain's permission I went ashore with Mr. Laughton. Mr. Rustomji's house was about two miles from the dock.

As soon as we landed, some youngsters recognized me and shouted 'Gandhi, Gandhi'. About half a dozen men rushed to the spot and joined in the shouting. Mr. Laughton feared that the crowd might swell and hailed[51] a rickshaw.[52] I had never liked the idea of being in a rickshaw. This was to be my first experience. But the youngsters would not let me get into it. They frightened the rickshaw boy out of his life, and he took to his heels. As we went ahead, the crowd continued to swell, *until it became impossible to proceed further.*[M4] They first caught hold of Mr. Laughton and separated us. Then they pelted me with stones, brickbats and rotten eggs. Someone snatched away my turban, whilst others began to batter

[M3] in a clandestine way after dark

[M4] and it was quite a crowd

---

[47] 'for your life' to add.

[48] 'through the main road' to add.

[49] The Governor of Natal in a dispatch to the Secretary of State for the Colonies wrote that MKG had come ashore at an inappropriate moment and that MKG now accepts that the advice was 'bad'. MKG wrote to the Secretary of State for the Colonies: 'As I have always considered, and still consider, the advice upon which I acted was excellent.' *CWMG*, vol. 2, p. 236.

[50] 'in a carriage' to add.

[51] 'he hailed' in the first edition.

[52] 'rickshaw' in the original, refers to a hand–drawn carriage.

and kick me. I fainted and caught hold of the front railings of a house and stood there to get my breath.[53] But it was impossible.[54] They came upon me boxing and battering. The wife of the Police Superintendent,[55] who knew me, happened to be passing by. *The brave lady came up, opened her parasol though there was no sun then, and stood between the crowd and me.*[M5] This checked the fury of the mob, as it was difficult for them to deliver blows on me without harming Mrs. Alexander.

Meanwhile an Indian youth who witnessed the incident had run to the police station. The Police Superintendent Mr. Alexander sent a posse of men to ring me round and escort me safely to my destination. They arrived in time. The police station lay on our way. As we reached there, the Superintendent asked me to take refuge in the station, but I gratefully[56] declined the offer. 'They are sure to quiet down when they realize their mistake,' I said. 'I have trust in their sense of fairness.' Escorted by the police, I arrived without further harm at Mr. Rustomji's place.[57] I had bruises all over, but no abrasions except in one place. Dr. Dadi Barjor, the ship's doctor, who was on the spot, rendered the best possible help.

There was quiet inside, but outside the whites surrounded the house. Night was coming on, and the yelling crowd was shouting, 'We must have Gandhi.' The quick sighted Police Superintendent was already

[M5] The moment she saw me, she came and stood beside me and opened her parasol though there was no sun then.

---

[53] According to Burnett Britton, the attack took place on West Street. MKG caught hold of the railing of a house between Ship Hotel and Parker, Wood & Company. Britton, *Gandhi Arrives in South Africa*, p. 644.

[54] 'to stand there' to add.

[55] Mrs. Jane Alexander; the Police Superintendent was Richard C. Alexander.

[56] 'gratefully' added in the English translation.

[57] The house was on Field Street.

there trying to keep the crowds under control, not by threats, but by humouring them. But he was not entirely free from anxiety. He sent me a message to this effect: 'If you would save your friend's house and property and also your family, you should escape from the house in disguise, as I suggest.'

Thus on one and the same day I was faced with two contradictory positions. When danger to life had been no more than imaginary, Mr. Laughton advised me to launch forth openly. I accepted the advice. When the danger was quite real, another friend gave me the[58] contrary advice, and I accepted that too. Who can say whether I did so because I saw that my life was in jeopardy, or because I did not want to put my friend's life and property or the lives of my wife and children in danger?[59] Who can say for certain that I was right both when *I faced the crowd in the first instance bravely, as it was said, and when I escaped from it in disguise?*[M6]

It is idle to adjudicate upon the right and wrong of incidents that have already happened. It is useful to understand them and, if possible, to learn a lesson from them for the future. It is difficult to say for certain how a particular man would act in a particular set of circumstances. We can also see that judging a man from his outward act is *no more than a doubtful inference, inasmuch as it is not based on sufficient data.*[M7]

Be that as it may, the preparations for escape made me forget my injuries. As suggested by the Superintendent, I put on an Indian constable's uniform[60] and wore on my head a Madrasi scarf, wrapped round a plate to serve

[M6] I landed from the steamer bravely and when subsequently, faced with real danger, I escaped in disguise?

[M7] mere speculation as the examination is incomplete

---

[58] 'the' added in the 1940 edition.

[59] 'Or for all three reasons?' To add.

[60] This was the uniform of one Richard, the Town Clerks' Indian messenger. Britton, *Gandhi Arrives in South Africa*, p. 646.

as a helmet. Two detectives[61] accompanied me, one of them disguised as an Indian merchant and with his face painted to resemble that of an Indian. I forget the disguise of the other. We reached a neighbouring shop by a by-lane and, making our way through the gunny bags piled in the godown, escaped by the gate of the shop and threaded our way through the crowd to a carriage that had been kept for me at the end of the street. In this we drove off to the same police station where Mr. Alexander had offered me refuge a short time before,[62] and I thanked him and the detective officers.[63]

Whilst I had been thus effecting my escape, Mr. Alexander had kept the crowd amused by singing the tune:

---

[61] These were Sergeant Ball and Detective Sergeant McBeath.

[62] In the four days that MKG spent at the Central Police Station he was accommodated in a spare bedroom of the officer's quarters. He visited the magistrate at the courthouse, met Harry Escombe at the Minister's Room at Star Building and visited Kastur, pregnant with their third son at Dada Abdullah's house.

[63] The Indian community expressed their gratitude to the couple by making a gift of a gold watch each, with a suitable inscription, and a chain and locket to Mrs. Alexander for 'saving the life of one whom we delight to love'. They also sent £10 for distribution among the police force.

In response, Richard Alexander wrote to MKG, 'I am very sorry indeed that I had not sufficient force at my back, to do that duty without inflicting upon you, and yours, a further degradation, by compelling you to escape the mob, in the disguise of one so very far beneath you, and for having to use so much deceit, to procure your safety, which I trust you and your people, will forgive, and that you like our own Prophet, when placed under a similar trial, will forgive your accusers, for they knew not what they did.' See SN 1938.

Jane Alexander wrote: 'My only thought at the time was your safety, and I feel I really ought not to accept anything, as my actions in this matter could in no way atone for the gross injustice done by my countrymen, and I feel that to return your generous gift would be but adding another insult to the many you have had to endure since your return.' See SN 1939.

'Hang old Gandhi
On the sour apple tree.'[64]

When he was informed of my safe arrival at the police station, he thus broke the news to the crowd: 'Well, your victim has made good his escape through a neighbouring shop. You had better go home now.'[65] Some of them were angry, others laughed, some refused to believe the story.

'Well then,' said the Superintendent, 'if you do not believe me,[66] you may appoint one or two representatives, whom I am ready to take inside the house. If they succeed in finding out Gandhi, I will gladly deliver him to you. But if they fail, you must disperse. I am sure that you have no intention of destroying Mr. Rustomji's house or of harming Mr. Gandhi's wife and children.'

The crowd sent their representatives[67] to search the house. They soon returned with disappointing news, and the crowd broke up at last, most of them admiring the Superintendent's tactful handling of the situation, and a few fretting and fuming.

The late Mr. Chamberlain, who was then Secretary of State for the Colonies,[68] cabled asking the Natal Government to prosecute my assailants.[69] Mr. Escombe

---

[64] The original song dates back to the American civil war, where in the refrain is to hang Old Jeff Davis on the sour apple tree. In Gujarati 'sour apple tree' is rendered as 'tamarind tree'.

[65] 'You had better go home now.' Added in the English translation.

[66] 'if you do not believe me,' added in the English translation.

[67] The representatives were George Spradbrow, Mr. Trimble and Inspector of Nuisance W.C. Daugherty. Britton, *Gandhi Arrives in South Africa*, p. 648.

[68] 'who was then the Secretary of State for the Colonies,' added in the English translation.

[69] There was apparently no cable but a letter dated 5 February 1897, wherein Chamberlain stated: 'I trust that proceedings have been

sent for me, expressed his regret for the injuries I had sustained, and said: 'Believe me, I cannot feel happy over the least little injury done to your person. You had a right to accept Mr. Laughton's advice and to face the worst, but I am sure that, if you had considered my suggestion favourably, these sad occurrences would not have happened. If you can identify the assailants, I am prepared to arrest and prosecute them. Mr. Chamberlain also desires me to do so.'

To which I gave the following reply:

'I do not want to prosecute anyone. It is possible that I may be able to identify one or two of *them, but what is the use of*[M8] getting them punished? Besides, I do not hold the assailants to blame. They were given to understand that I had made exaggerated statements in India about the whites in Natal and calumniated them. If they believed these reports, it is no wonder that they were enraged. The leaders, and, if you will permit me to say so, you are to blame. You could have guided the people properly, but you also believed Reuter and assumed that I must have indulged in exaggeration. I do not want to bring anyone to book. I am sure that, when the truth becomes known, they will be sorry for their conduct.'

'Would you mind giving me this in writing?' said Mr. Escombe. 'Because I shall have to cable to Mr. Chamberlain to that effect. I do not want you to make any statement in haste. You may, if you like, consult Mr. Laughton and your other friends, before you come to a final decision. I may confess, however, that, if you waive the right of bringing your assailants to book, you

[M8] the assailants, but what do I gain by

---

taken against the perpetrators of this assault for their breach of peace.' Britton, *Gandhi Arrives in South Africa*, Notes, p. xxxvii, note 50.

will considerably help me in restoring quiet, besides enhancing your own reputation.'

'Thank you,' said I. 'I need not consult anyone. I had made my decision in the matter before I came to you. It is my conviction that I should not prosecute the assailants, and I am prepared this moment to reduce my decision to writing.'[M9]

With this I gave him the necessary statement.[70]

[M9] 'My views on the matter are formed. It is certain that I do not wish to bring prosecution on anyone, and I will give that to you in writing just now.'

IV

THE CALM AFTER THE STORM[71]

I had not yet left the police station, when, after two days, I was taken to see Mr. Escombe. Two constables were sent to protect me, though no such precaution was then needed.

On the day of landing, as soon as the yellow flag was lowered, a representative of *The Natal Advertiser* had come to interview me.[72] He had asked me a number of questions, and in reply I had been able to refute every one of the charges that had been levelled against me. Thanks to Sir Pherozeshah Mehta,[73] I had delivered only written speeches in India, and I had copies of them all, as well as of my other writings. I had given the interviewer all this literature and showed him that in India I had said nothing which I had not already said in South Africa in stronger language. I had also shown him that I had no hand in bringing the passengers of the *Courland* and *Naderi* to South Africa. Many of them were old residents, and most of them, far from wanting

---

[70] See *CWMG*, vol. 2, pp. 126–27.

[71] 'After the Storm' added in the English translation.

[72] For the text of the interview, see *CWMG*, vol. 2, pp. 118–26.

[73] 'Mehta' added in the English translation.

M1 there was recession in Natal. The Transvaal had better prospects for earning

M2 clarification

M3 whites

M4 Thus the end result was to my benefit. And benefit to me was benefit to the cause.

M5 The whites realized that the Indians had the capacity to fight with determination, and this increased their fear.

to stay in Natal, meant to go to the Transvaal. In those days *the Transvaal offered better prospects than Natal to those coming in search of wealth,*M1 and most Indians, therefore, preferred to go there.

This *interview*M2 and my refusal to prosecute the assailants produced such a profound impression that the *Europeans of Durban*M3 were ashamed of their conduct. The Press declared me to be innocent and condemned the mob. *Thus the lynching ultimately proved to be a blessing for me, that is, for the cause.*M4 It enhanced the prestige of the Indian community in South Africa and made my work easier.

In three or four days I went to my house, and it was not long before I settled down again. The incident added also to my professional practice.

But if it enhanced the prestige of the community, it also fanned the flame of prejudice against it. *As soon as it was proved that the Indian could put up a manly fight, he came to be regarded as a danger.*M5 Two bills were introduced in the Natal Legislative Assembly, one of them calculated to affect the Indian trader adversely, and the other to impose a stringent restriction on Indian immigration.[74] Fortunately the fight for the franchise had resulted in a decision to the effect that no enactment might be passed against the Indians as such, that is to say, that the law should make no distinctions of colour or race. The language of the bills above mentioned made them applicable to all, but their object undoubtedly was to impose further restrictions on the Indian residents of Natal.[75]

---

[74] The four bills introduced in March 1897 related to the Quarantine, Trade Licences, Immigration and Uncovenanted Indians Protection bills. For the text of these bills, see *CWMG*, vol. 2, pp. 272–80.

[75] Indians were not specifically mentioned in three of the four measures, only the Uncovenanted Indian Protection Bill referred to Indians by name.

The bills considerably increased my public work[76] and made the community more alive than ever to their sense of duty. They were translated into Indian languages and fully explained, so as to bring home to the community their subtle implications. *We appealed to the Colonial Secretary, but he refused to interfere and the bills became law.*[M6]

Public work now began to absorb most of my time. Sjt. Mansukhlal Naazar, who, as I have said, was already in Durban, came to stay with me, and as he gave[77] his time to public work, he lightened my burden to some extent.

Sheth Adamji Miyakhan had, in my absence, discharged his duty[78] with great credit. He had increased the membership and added about £1,000 to the coffers of the Natal Indian Congress. The awakening caused by the bills and the demonstration against the passengers I turned to good account by making an appeal for membership and funds, which now amounted to £5,000. My desire was to secure for the Congress a permanent fund, so that[79] it might procure property of its own and then carry on its work out of the rent of the property.[80] This was my first experience of managing a public institution. I placed my proposal before my co-workers, and they welcomed it. The property that was purchased was leased out, and the rent was enough to meet the current expenses of the Congress. The property was vested in a strong body of trustees and is

[M6] The dispute eventually reached England. But the laws were not annulled.

---

[76] Petitions were sent to the Natal Legislative Assembly (*CWMG*, vol. 2, pp. 231–35), the Natal Colonial Secretary (ibid., pp. 235–36), the Natal Legislative Council (ibid., pp. 236–37), and the Secretary of State for the Colonies (ibid., pp. 260–80). Letters were sent to Dadabhai Naoroji and others (ibid., pp. 284–88).

[77] 'more of' to add.

[78] 'as a secretary' to add.

[79] 'with which' in the first edition.

[80] 'The Congress could then be fearless about its future.' To add.

still there today, but it has become the source of much internecine quarrelling with the result that the rent of the property now accumulates in the court.

This sad situation developed after my departure from South Africa, but my idea of having permanent funds for public institutions underwent a change *long before this difference arose.*[M7] And now after considerable experience *with the many public institutions which I have managed,*[M8] it has become my firm conviction that *it is not good to run public institutions*[M9] on permanent funds. A permanent fund carries in itself the seed of the moral fall of the institution. A public institution means an institution conducted with the approval,[81] and from the funds, of the public. When such an institution ceases to have public support, it forfeits its right to exist. Institutions maintained on permanent funds are often found to ignore public opinion, and are frequently responsible for acts contrary to it. In our country we experience this at every step. Some of the so-called religious trusts have ceased to render any accounts. The trustees have become the owners and are responsible to none. I have no doubt that the ideal is for public institutions to live, like nature, from day to day. The institution that *fails to win public support*[M10] has no right to exist as such. The subscriptions that an institution annually receives are a test of its popularity and the honesty of its management; and I am of opinion that every institution should submit to that test. But let no one misunderstand me. My remarks do not apply to the bodies which cannot, by their very nature, be conducted without permanent buildings. What I mean to say is that[82] the current expenditure should be found from subscriptions voluntarily received from year to year.

These views were confirmed during the days of the satyagraha in South Africa. That magnificent campaign

[M7] in South Africa

[M8] of the establishment and management of many public institutions

[M9] no public institution should run

[M10] the public is not willing to support

---

[81] 'approval of' in the first edition.

[82] 'What I mean to say is that' added in the English translation.

extending over six years was carried on without permanent funds, though lakhs of rupees were necessary for it. I can recollect times when I did not know what would happen the next day if no subscriptions came in. But I shall not anticipate[83] future events. The reader will find the opinion expressed above amply borne out in the coming narrative.

V

EDUCATION OF CHILDREN

When I landed at Durban in January 1897, I had three children with me, my sister's son ten years old, and my own sons nine and five years of age. Where was I to educate them?

I could have sent them to the schools for European children, but only as a matter of favour and exception. No other Indian children were allowed to attend them. For these there were schools established by Christian missions, but I was not prepared to send my children there, as I did not like the education imparted in those schools.[84] For one thing,[85] the medium of instruction would be only English, or perhaps incorrect Tamil or Hindi; this too could only have been arranged with difficulty.[86] I could not possibly put up with this and other disadvantages. In the meantime[87] I was making my own attempt to teach them. But that was at best

---

[83] 'the future events' in the first edition.

[84] 'How was education through Gujarati possible therein?' To add.

[85] 'For one thing,' added in the English translation.

[86] 'which too could be arranged not without difficulty' in the first edition.

[87] 'In the meantime' added in the English translation.

irregular, and I could not get hold of a suitable Gujarati teacher.

I was at my wit's end. I advertised for an English teacher who should[88] teach the children under my direction. Some regular instruction was to be given them by this teacher, and for the rest they should be satisfied with what little I could give them irregularly. So I engaged an English *governess*[M1] on £7 a month. *This went on for some time, but not to my satisfaction. The boys acquired some knowledge of Gujarati through my conversation and intercourse with them, which was strictly in the mother-tongue.*[M2] I was loath to send them back to India, for I believed even then that young children should not be separated from their parents. The education that children naturally imbibe in a well-ordered household is impossible to obtain in hostels. *I therefore kept my children with me.*[M3] I did send my nephew and elder son to be educated at residential schools in India for a few months, but I soon had to recall them. Later, the eldest son, long after he had come of age, *broke away from me,*[M4] and went to India to join a High School in Ahmedabad.[89] I have an impression that the nephew was satisfied with what I could give him. Unfortunately he died in the prime of youth after a brief illness.[90] The other three of my sons have never been at a public school, though they did get some regular schooling in an improvised[91] school which I started *for the children of satyagrahi parents in South Africa.*[M5]

These experiments were all inadequate. I could not devote to the children all the time I had wanted to give

[M1] woman

[M2] We pulled along somehow. My dealings with the boys were only through Gujarati, and they learnt some Gujarati through this.

[M3] Therefore for the most part they stayed with me.

[M4] on his own will left South Africa

[M5] in the context of the satyagraha

---

[88] 'would' in the first edition.

[89] Harilal left Johannesburg on 17 May 1911 and joined New English High School in Ahmedabad.

[90] Gokuldas passed away in 1908.

[91] 'improvised' added in the English translation.

them. My inability to give them enough attention[92] and other unavoidable causes prevented me from providing them with the *literary education*[M6] I had desired, and all my sons have had complaints[93] to make against me in this matter. Whenever they come across an M.A. or a B.A., or even a matriculate, they seem to feel[94] the handicap of a want of school education.

M6 knowledge of letters

Nevertheless I am of opinion that, if I had insisted on their being educated somehow at public schools, they would have been deprived of the training that can be had only at the school of experience, or from constant contact with the parents.[95] I should never have been free, as I am today, from anxiety on their score, and the artificial education that they could have had in England or South Africa, torn from me, would never have taught them the simplicity and the spirit of service that they show in their lives today, while their artificial ways of living might have been a serious handicap in my public work. Therefore, though I have not been able to give them a *literary education*[M7] either to their or[96] to my satisfaction, I am not quite sure, as I look back on my past years, that I have not done my duty by them to the best of my capacity. Nor do I *regret not having sent them to public schools*.[M8] [97] I have always felt that the *undesirable traits*[M9] I see today in my eldest son are an echo[98] of my own undisciplined and unformulated early life. I regard that time as a period of *half-baked knowledge*[M10] and

M7 knowledge of letters

M8 have any regret

M9 painful results

M10 unconsciousness

---

92 'My inability to give them enough attention' added in the English translation.

93 'to a lesser or greater extent' to add.

94 'labour under' in the first edition.

95 'and the object-lesson in self-reliance they received' to add.

96 'either to their or' added in the English translation.

97 'On the contrary,' to add.

98 'echo rather of' in the first edition.

indulgence. *It coincided with the most impressionable years of my eldest son, and naturally he has refused to regard it as my time of indulgence and inexperience. He has on the contrary believed that that was the brightest period of my life, and the changes, effected later, have been due to delusion miscalled enlightenment. And well he might. Why should he not think that my earlier years represented a period of awakening, and the later years of radical change, years of delusion and egotism?*[M11] Often have I been confronted with various posers from friends: What harm had there been, if *I had given my boys an academical education?*[M12] What right had I thus to clip their wings? Why should I have come in the way of their taking degrees and choosing their own careers?

I do not think that there is much point in these questions. I have come in contact with numerous students. *I have tried myself or through others to impose my educational 'fads' on other children too*[M13] and have[99] seen the results thereof. There are within my knowledge a number of young men[100] today contemporaneous with my sons. I[101] do not think that[102] *man to man*[M14] they are any better than my sons, or that my sons have much to learn from them.

But the ultimate result of my experiments is in the womb of the future. My object in discussing this subject here is that a student of the history of civilization may have some measure of the difference between disciplined[103] home education and school education, and also of the effect produced on children through changes introduced by parents in their lives. The purpose of this

[M11] At a time which I consider to be my period of stupefaction and indulgence, he was at an age where he would have clear recollections. How is he to believe that it was my period of unconsciousness? Why should he not believe that it was my period of wisdom and the subsequent changes were undesirable and born of delusion? Why should he not believe that at that time I was on the royal road, recognized by the world as such, and for that reason secure, and the subsequent changes are the signs of refined egotism and ignorance?

[M12] my boys had acquired degrees of barrister and suchlike

[M13] I have carried out, or helped others carry out, different experiments on some other children,

[M14] in terms of humanity

---

[99] 'and I have' in the first edition.

[100] 'There are a number of young men today whom I know' in the first edition.

[101] 'And I' in the first edition.

[102] 'that' added in the 1940 edition.

[103] 'disciplined' added in the English translation.

chapter is also to show the lengths to which a votary of truth is driven by his experiments with truth, as also to show the votary of liberty how many are the sacrifices demanded by that stern goddess. *Had I been without*[104] *a sense of self-respect and satisfied myself*[105] *with having for my children the education that other children could not get,*[M15] I should have deprived them of the object-lesson in liberty and self-respect that I gave them at the cost of the literary training. And where a choice has to be made between liberty and learning, who will not say that the former has to be preferred a thousand times to the latter?

The youths whom I called out in 1920 from those citadels of slavery—their schools and colleges—and whom I advised that it was far better to remain unlettered and break stones for the sake of liberty than to go in for a literary education in the chains of slaves will probably be able now to trace my advice to its source.

[M15] Despite raising the boys under my care, had I given up self-respect and not cherished the idea of restraining my desire to give my own what was not available to other Indian children

VI

SPIRIT OF SERVICE

My profession progressed satisfactorily, but that was far from satisfying me.[106] The question of further simplifying my life and of doing some *concrete act of service*[M1] to my fellowmen[107] had been constantly agitating me, when a *leper*[M2] came to my door. I had not the heart[108] to dismiss him with a meal. So I offered him shelter, dressed his wounds, and began to look after him. But I could not

[M1] bodily service

[M2] person disabled and suffering from leprosy

---

[104] 'blind to' in the first edition.

[105] 'allowed myself to be' in the first edition.

[106] 'but that far from satisfied me' in the first edition.

[107] 'to my fellowmen' added in the English translation.

[108] 'not got the heart' in the first edition.

M3 I lacked the wherewithal and
courage

M4 nursing

M5 to take on this responsibility

go on like that indefinitely. *I could not afford, I*[109] *lacked the will*M3 to keep him always with me. So I sent him to the Government Hospital for indentured labourers.

But I was still ill at ease. I longed for some *humanitarian*M4 work of a permanent nature. Dr. Booth was the head of the St. Aidan's Mission. He was a kind-hearted man and treated his patients free. Thanks to Parsi Rustomji's charities, it was possible to open a small charitable[110] hospital under Dr. Booth's charge. I felt strongly inclined to serve as a nurse[111] in this hospital. The work of dispensing medicines took from one to two hours daily, and[112] I made up my mind to find that time from my office-work, *so as to be able to fill the place of a compounder in the dispensary attached to the hospital.*M5 Most of my professional work was chamber work, conveyancing and arbitration. I of course used to have a few cases in the magistrate's court, but most of them were of a non-controversial character, and Mr. Khan,[113] who had followed me to South Africa and was then living with me, undertook to take them if I was absent. So I found time to serve in the small hospital. This meant two hours every morning, including the time taken in going to and from the hospital. This work brought me some peace. It consisted in ascertaining the patient's complaints,

---

[109] 'and I' in the first edition.

[110] 'charitable' added in the English translation.

[111] 'nurse' English word in the original.

[112] 'a paid or voluntary worker was required for it' to add.

[113] Rahimkhan Karimkhan, only son of Karimkhan, private secretary to the Aga Khan, admitted to Lincoln's Inn on 21 April 1894, decided to leave the Society, but petitioned again for readmission in October 1897, passed his examination in Easter Term of 1898, called to the Bar on 22 June 1898 (Source: *Black Book*, vol. 38, hon'ble society of Lincoln's Inn). Went to South Africa in 1899, introduced Hermann Kallenbach to MKG.

laying the facts before the doctor and dispensing the prescriptions. It brought me in close touch with suffering Indians, most of them indentured Tamil, Telugu or North India men.

The experience stood me in good stead, when during the Boer War I offered my services for nursing the sick and wounded soldiers.

The question of the rearing of children had been ever before me. I had two sons[114] born in South Africa, and my service in the hospital was useful[115] in solving the question of their upbringing. My independent spirit was[116] a constant source of trial.[117] My wife and I had decided to have the best medical aid at the time of her delivery,[118] but if the doctor and the nurse were to leave us in the lurch at the right moment, what was I to do? Then the nurse had to be an Indian. *And the difficulty of getting a trained Indian nurse in South Africa can be easily imagined from the similar difficulty in India.*[M6] So I studied the things necessary for safe labour. I read Dr. Tribhuvandas' book, *Ma-ne Shikhaman*[119]—Advice to a Mother—and I nursed both my[120] children according to the instructions given in the book, tempered here and there by such experience as I had gained elsewhere. The services of a nurse were utilized[121]—not for more than

[M6] It is difficult to get a trained Indian nurse in India, what to speak of South Africa?

---

[114] Ramdas (1898–1969) and Devadas (1900–57).

[115] 'useful to me' in the first edition.

[116] 'and remains' to add.

[117] 'trial to me' in the first edition.

[118] 'for which we had arranged for a doctor and a nurse,' to add.

[119] Tribhuvandas Motichand Shah, *Ma-ne Shilkhaman*, probably based on Pye Henry Chavasse's (1810–1879) *Advice to a Mother on the Management of Her Children and on the Treatment on the Moment of Some of Their More Pressing Illnesses and Accidents.*

[120] 'younger' to add.

[121] 'availed of' in the first edition.

M7 in the initial period I bathed and cleaned the infants

two months each time—chiefly for helping my wife, *and not for taking care of the babies, which I did myself.*M7

The birth of the last child put me to the severest test. The travail came on suddenly. The doctor was not immediately available, and some time was lost in fetching the midwife. Even if she had been on the spot, she could not have helped delivery. I had to see through the safe delivery of the baby. My careful study of the subject in Dr. Tribhuvandas' work was of inestimable help. I was not nervous.

I am convinced that for the proper upbringing of children the parents ought to have a general knowledge of the care and nursing of babies. At every step I have seen the advantages of my careful study of the subject. My children would not have enjoyed the general health that they do today, had I not studied the subject and turned my knowledge to account. We labour under a sort of superstition that the child has nothing to learn during the first five years of its life. On the contrary the fact is that the child never learns in after life what it does in its first five years. The education of the child begins with conception.[122] The physical and mental states of the parents at the moment of conception *are reproduced*

M8 have an effect on

*in*M8 the baby. Then during the period of pregnancy it continues to be affected by the mother's moods, desires and temperament, as also by her[123] ways of life. After birth the child imitates the parents, and[124] for a considerable number of years entirely depends on them for its growth.

The couple who realize these things will never have sexual union for the fulfilment of their lust, but

M9 progeny.

only when[125] they desire *issue.*M9 *I think it is the height*

---

[122] 'I can say this based on my experience.' To add.

[123] 'diet and' to add.

[124] 'being helpless' to add.

[125] 'but will unite only when' in the first edition.

of ignorance to believe that the sexual act is an independent function necessary like sleeping or eating.[M10] The world depends for its existence on the act of generation, and as the world is the play-ground of God and a reflection of His glory, the act of generation should be controlled for the ordered growth of the world. He who realizes this will control his lust *at any cost*,[M11] equip[126] himself with the knowledge necessary for the physical, mental and spiritual well-being of his progeny,[127] and give the benefit of that knowledge to posterity.

[M10] I think it is deep, dark ignorance to believe that sexual gratification is an autonomous act.

[M11] with great effort

VII

BRAHMACHARYA–I

We now reach the stage in this story when I began seriously to think of taking the brahmacharya vow. I had been wedded to a monogamous ideal[M1] ever since my marriage, faithfulness to my wife being part of the love of truth. But it was in South Africa that I came to realize the importance of observing *brahmacharya* even with respect to my wife. I cannot definitely say what circumstance or what book it was, that set my thoughts in that direction, but I have a recollection that the predominant factor was the influence of Raychandbhai, of whom I have already written.[128] I can still recall a conversation that I had with him. On one occasion I spoke to him in high praise of Mrs. Gladstone's devotion to her husband.[129] I had read somewhere that Mrs. Gladstone insisted on preparing tea

[M1] It is time now to consider *brahmacharya*. Monogamy as an ideal had a place in my heart

---

126 'will equip' in the first edition.

127 'born out of the sexual act' to add.

128 'of whom I have already written' added in the English translation.

129 William Ewart Gladstone (1809–98), British Liberal politician, served as prime minister of Britain on four separate occasions. Mrs. Catherine Gladstone (1812–1900).

M2 I read this out

M3 prepared tea for him

M4 affection

M5 like a magnet

M6 Husband and wife have a sense of oneness, hence love between them is not surprising.

for Mr. Gladstone even in the House of Commons, and that this had become a rule in the life of this illustrious[130] couple, whose actions were governed by regularity. I *spoke of this*[M2] to the poet, and incidentally eulogized conjugal love. 'Which of the two do you prize more,' asked Raychandbhai, 'the love of Mrs. Gladstone for her husband as his wife, or her devoted service irrespective of her relation to Mr. Gladstone? Supposing she had been his sister, or his devoted servant, and *ministered*[131] *to him*[M3] with the same *attention,*[M4] what would you have said? Do we not have instances of such devoted sisters or servants? Supposing you had found the same loving devotion in a male servant,[132] would you have been pleased in the same way as in Mrs. Gladstone's case?[133] Just examine the view-point suggested by me.'

Raychandbhai was himself married. I have an impression that at the moment his words sounded harsh, but they gripped me *irresistibly.*[M5] The devotion of a[134] servant was, I felt, a thousand times more praiseworthy than that of a wife to her husband. *There was nothing surprising in the wife's devotion to her husband, as there was an indissoluble bond between them. The devotion was perfectly natural.*[M6] But it required a special effort to cultivate equal devotion between master and servant. The poet's point of view began gradually to grow upon me.

What then, I asked myself,[135] should be my relation with my wife? Did my faithfulness consist in making my wife the instrument of my lust? So long as I was the slave

---

[130] 'illustrious' added in the English translation.

[131] 'and had ministered' in the first edition.

[132] 'servant' added in the English translation. 'instead of a female' to add.

[133] 'as in Mrs. Gladstone's case' added in the English translation.

[134] 'male' to add.

[135] 'I asked myself' added in the English translation.

of lust, my faithfulness was worth nothing.[136] To be fair
to my wife, I must say that she was never the *temptress*.[M7]   ᴹ⁷ aggressor
It was therefore the easiest thing for me to take the vow
of *brahmacharya*, if only I willed it. It was my weak will
or lustful attachment that was the obstacle.

Even after my conscience had been roused in the
matter,[137] I failed twice. I failed because the motive
that actuated the effort was none the highest. My main
object was to escape having more children. Whilst in
England I had read something about *contraceptives*.[M8] I   ᴹ⁸ external remedies
have already referred to Dr. Allinson's birth-control
propaganda in the chapter on Vegetarianism.[138] If it had
some temporary effect on me, Mr. Hills'[139] opposition
to those methods and his advocacy of internal efforts as
opposed to outward means, in a word, of self-control,
had a far greater effect, which in due time came to be
abiding. Seeing, therefore, that I did not desire more
children I began to strive after self-control. There was
endless difficulty in the task. We began to sleep in

---

[136] 'worth nothing' translates the word 'Prakrut', the word in
this context refers to the low value of the language Prakrut in
comparison to Sanskrit.

[137] 'in the matter' added in the English translation.

[138] MKG does not refer to Dr. Thomas Allinson's propaganda
on birth control in the chapter on vegetarianism, but to Dr.
Allinson's writings on 'health and hygiene'. The book being
referred to here is *A Book for Married Women*, which advocated
'artificial' birth control.

[139] Arnold F. Hills (1872–1927), wealthy industrialist, chairman of
the Thames Iron Works, president of the London Vegetarian
Society. The opposition that is referred to here was a public
debate between Allinson and Hills on 13 February 1891 on 'The
Meaning of Sexual Morality', which MKG attended. A week
later, Hills moved a proposal before the executive committee of
the London Vegetarian Society to have Allinson expelled. MKG,
though sympathetic to Hills' views on sexual morality, wished to
uphold the freedom of opinion and had prepared a speech on the
subject, which, given his nervousness, was read by someone else.
Hills carried the motion.

separate beds. I decided to retire to bed only after the day's work had left me completely exhausted. All these efforts did not seem to bear much fruit, but when I look back upon the past, I feel that the final resolution was the cumulative effect of those unsuccessful[140] strivings.

The final resolution could only be made as late as 1906. Satyagraha had not then been started. I had not the least notion of its coming. I was practising in Johannesburg at the time of the Zulu 'Rebellion'[141] in Natal, which came soon after the Boer War.[142] I felt that I must offer my services to the Natal Government on that occasion.[143] The offer was accepted, as we shall see in another chapter. But the work set me furiously thinking in the direction of self-control and according to my wont I discussed my thoughts with my co-workers. It became my conviction that procreation and the consequent care of children were inconsistent with public service. I had to break up my household at Johannesburg[144] to be able to serve during the 'Rebellion'. Within one month of offering my services, I had to give up the house I had so carefully furnished. I took my wife and children to Phoenix and led the Indian ambulance corps attached to the Natal forces. During the difficult marches that had then to be performed, the idea flashed upon me that if I wanted to devote myself to the service of the community in this manner, I must relinquish the desire for children

---

[140] 'unsuccessful' added in the English translation.

[141] The Zulu Rebellion or the Bambatha Rebellion of mid-1906; the immediate contributing factor was the imposition of 'poll tax'.

[142] The Boer War (11 October 1899–31 May 1902), fought between the Transvaal Republic and Orange Free State on one side and the United Kingdom, assisted by imperial forces, on the other; resulted in the victory of the United Kingdom and annexation of both the republics.

[143] 'as well' to add.

[144] This house was at 11, Albemarle Street.

and wealth and live[145] the life of a *vanaprastha*—of one retired from household cares.[146]

The 'Rebellion' did not occupy me for more than six weeks, but this brief period proved to be a very important epoch in my life. The importance of vows grew upon me more clearly than ever before. I realized that a vow, *far from closing the door to real freedom, opened it*.[M9] Up to this time I had not met with success because the will had been lacking, because I had had no faith in myself, no faith in the grace of God, and therefore, my mind had been tossed on the boisterous sea of doubt.[147] I realized that in refusing to take a vow man was drawn into temptation, and that to be bound by a vow was like a passage from libertinism to a real[148] monogamous marriage. 'I believe in effort, I do not want to bind myself with vows,' is the mentality of weakness and betrays a subtle desire for *the thing to be avoided. Or where can be the difficulty in making a final decision?*[M10] I vow to flee from the serpent which I know will bite me, I do not simply make an effort to flee from him. I know that mere effort may mean certain death.

Mere effort means ignorance of the certain fact that the serpent is bound to kill me. The fact, therefore, that I could rest content with an effort *only*,[M11] means that I have not yet clearly realized the *necessity of definite action*.[M12] 'But supposing my views are changed in the future, how can I bind myself by a vow?'[149] Such a doubt often deters us.[150] But that

[M9] was not bondage but a door to freedom

[M10] pleasures. What can impede complete renunciation of a thing that is undesirable?

[M11] to renounce

[M12] appropriateness of giving up that thing

---

[145] 'and must live' in the first edition.

[146] The explanatory part, 'of one retired from household cares', added in the English translation.

[147] 'and enslaved by all manner of passions' to add.

[148] 'real' added in the English translation.

[149] 'how can I bind myself by a vow' added in the English translation.

[150] 'from taking a vow' to add.

doubt also betrays a lack of clear perception that a particular thing must be renounced. That is why Nishkulanand[151] has sung:

Renunciation without aversion is not lasting.

Where therefore the desire is gone, a vow of renunciation is the natural and[152] inevitable fruit.

VIII

BRAHMACHARYA–II

After full discussion and mature deliberation I took the vow in 1906.[153] I had not shared my thoughts with my wife until then, but only consulted her at the time of taking the vow. She had no objection. But I had great difficulty[154] in making the final resolve. I had not the necessary strength. How was I to control my passions? The elimination of carnal relationship with one's wife seemed then a strange thing. *But I launched forth with faith in the sustaining power of God.*[M1]

As I look back upon the twenty years of the vow, I am filled with pleasure and wonderment. *The more or less successful practice of self-control had been going on since 1901.*[M2] But the freedom and joy that came to me after taking the vow had never been experienced before 1906. Before the vow I had been open to

[M1] And yet I could clearly see that it was my duty. My intentions were pure. I launched forth thinking that God would give me strength.

[M2] The desire for self-control had been intense since 1901 and I did practise it as well.

---

[151] Nishkulanand Swami (1766–1848), an ascetic poet of the Swaminarayan sect. He composed the *Bhaktachintamani*, his poems have been collected as *Nishkulanand Kavya*, and he was an accomplished carpenter.

[152] 'natural and' added in the English translation.

[153] On 20 July 1906.

[154] 'I was hard put to it' in the first edition.

being overcome by temptation at any moment. *Now the vow was a sure shield against temptation.*[M3] The great potentiality of *brahmacharya* daily became more and more patent to me. The vow was taken when I was in Phoenix. As soon as I was free from ambulance work, I went to Phoenix, whence I had to return to Johannesburg. In about a month of my returning there, the foundation of satyagraha was laid. As though unknown to me, the *brahmacharya* vow had been preparing me for it. Satyagraha had not been a preconceived plan. It came on spontaneously, without my having willed it.[155] But I could see that all my previous steps had *led up to that goal.*[M4] I had cut down my heavy household expenses at Johannesburg and gone to Phoenix to take, as it were, the *brahmacharya* vow.

[M3] Now passions became incapable of riding over me.

[M4] been a preparation for it

The knowledge that a perfect observance of *brahmacharya* means realization of Brahman, I did not owe to a study of the Shastras. It slowly grew upon me with experience. The shastric texts on the subject I read only later in life. Every day of the vow has taken me nearer the knowledge that in *brahmacharya* lies the protection of the body, the mind and the soul. For *brahmacharya* was now no process of hard penance, *it was a matter of consolation and joy.*[M5] Every day revealed a fresh beauty in it.

[M5] but a source of joy

But if it was a matter of ever-increasing joy, let no one believe that it was an easy thing for me. Even when[156] I am past fifty-six years, I realize how hard a thing it is. Every day I realize more and more that it is like walking on the sword's edge, and I see every moment the necessity for eternal vigilance.

Control of the palate is the first essential in the observance of the vow. I found that complete control

---

[155] On 11 September 1906.

[156] 'while' in the first edition.

of the palate made the observance very easy, and so I now pursued my dietetic experiments not merely from the vegetarian's but also from the *brahmachari's* point of view. As the result of these experiments I saw that the *brahmachari's* food should be limited, simple, spiceless, and, if possible, uncooked.

Six years of experiment have showed me that the *brahmachari's* ideal food is fresh fruit and nuts. The immunity from passion that I enjoyed when I lived on this food was unknown to me after I changed that diet. *Brahmacharya needed no effort on my part in South Africa*[M6] when I lived on fruits and nuts alone. It has been a matter of very great effort ever since I began to take milk. How I had to go back to milk from a fruit diet will be considered in its proper place. It is enough to observe here that I have not the least doubt that milk diet makes the *brahmacharya* vow difficult to observe. Let no one deduce from this that all *brahmacharis* must give up milk. The effect on *brahmacharya* of different kinds of food can be determined only after numerous experiments. I have yet to find a fruit-substitute for milk which is an equally good muscle-builder and easily digestible. The doctors, *vaidyas* and *hakims* have alike failed to *enlighten me*.[M7] Therefore, though I know milk to be partly a stimulant, I cannot, for the time being, advise anyone to give it up.

As an external aid to *brahmacharya*, fasting is as necessary as selection and restriction in diet. So overpowering are the senses that they can be kept under control only when they are completely hedged in on all sides, from above and from beneath. It is common knowledge that they are powerless without food, and so fasting[157] undertaken with a view to control of the senses is, I have no doubt, very helpful. With some, fasting is of no avail, because assuming that mechanical

[M6] *Brahmacharya* was natural and effortless

[M7] point out such fruit or grains

---

[157] 'wilfully' to add.

fasting alone will make them immune, they keep their bodies without food, but feast their minds upon all sorts of delicacies, thinking all the while what[158] they will eat and what they will drink after the fast terminates. Such fasting[159] helps them in controlling neither palate nor lust. Fasting is useful, when mind co-operates with starving body, that is to say, when it cultivates a distaste for the objects that are denied to the body. Mind is at the root of all sensuality. Fasting, therefore, has a limited use, for a fasting man may continue to be swayed by passion. But it may be said that[160] extinction of the sexual passion is as a rule impossible without fasting, which may be said to be indispensable for the observance of *brahmacharya*. Many aspirants after *brahmacharya* fail, because *in the use of their other senses*[M8] they want to carry on like[161] those who are not *brahmacharis*. Their effort is, therefore, identical with the effort to experience the bracing cold of winter in the scorching summer months. There should be a clear line between the life of *a brahmachari and of one who is not.*[M9] The resemblance that there is between the two is only apparent. The distinction ought to be clear as daylight. Both use their eyesight, but whereas the *brahmachari* uses it to see the glories of God, the other uses it to see the[162] frivolity around him. Both use their ears, but whereas the one hears nothing but praises of God, the other feasts his ears upon ribaldry. Both often keep late hours, but whereas the one *devotes them to prayer,*[M10] the other fritters them away in wild and wasteful mirth. Both *feed the inner man, but the one only to keep the temple of God in good repair,*[M11]

[M8] in matters of food, drink and seeing etc.

[M9] the one practising self-control and the one leading a licentious life, between the life of one who submits to passions and one who renounces them

[M10] prays to Rama enthroned in his heart

[M11] eat. But one eats only to pay rent to sustain the temple of God in the form of the body

---

[158] 'as to what' in the first edition.

[159] 'they complain' to add.

[160] 'it may be said that' added in the English translation.

[161] 'as' in the first edition.

[162] 'drama of' to add.

while[163] the other gorges himself and makes the sacred vessel a stinking gutter. Thus both live as the poles apart, and the distance between them will grow and not diminish with the passage of time.

Brahmacharya means control of[164] the senses in thought, word and deed. Every day I have been realizing more and more the necessity for restraints of the kind I have detailed above.[165] There is no limit to the possibilities of renunciation even as there is none to those of *brahmacharya*. Such *brahmacharya* is impossible of attainment by limited effort. For *many*[M12] it must remain only as an ideal. An aspirant after *brahmacharya* will always be conscious of his shortcomings, will seek out the passions lingering in the innermost recesses of his heart and will incessantly strive to get rid of them. So long as thought is not under complete control of the will, *brahmacharya* in its fullness is absent. Involuntary thought is an affection of the mind, and curbing of thought, therefore, means curbing of the mind which is even more difficult to curb than the wind. Nevertheless *the existence of God within makes even control of the mind possible.*[M13] Let no one think that it is impossible because it is difficult. It is the highest goal, and it is no wonder that the highest effort should be necessary to attain it. But it was after coming to India that I realized that such *brahmacharya* was impossible to attain by mere human effort. Until then I had been labouring under the delusion that fruit diet alone would enable me to eradicate all passions, and *I had flattered myself with the belief*[M14] that I had nothing more to do.

But I must not anticipate the chapter of my struggle. Meanwhile let me make it clear that those who desire

M12 the millions

M13 if the *atman* exists, even this is attainable

M14 in my pride I had believed

---

163 'and' in the first edition.

164 'all' to add.

165 'I see it even today.' To add.

to observe *brahmacharya*[M15] with a view to realizing God need not despair, provided *their faith in God is equal to their confidence in their own effort.*[M16]

[M15] such *brahmacharya* as I have described

[M16] they have faith in God along with confidence in their endeavour

विषया विनिवर्तन्ते निराहारस्य देहिनः ।
रसवर्ज रसोऽप्यस्य परं दृष्ट्वा निवर्तते ।।

'The sense-objects turn away from an abstemious soul, leaving the relish behind. The relish also disappears with the realization of the Highest.'[166] Therefore His name and His grace are the last resources of the aspirant after *moksha*. This truth came to me only after my return to India.

IX

SIMPLE LIFE[M1]

[M1] Simplicity

I had started on a life of ease and comfort, but the experiment[167] was short-lived. Although I had furnished the house with care, yet *it failed to have any hold on me.*[M2] So no sooner had I *launched forth on that life,*[M3] than I began to cut down expenses. The washerman's bill was heavy, and as he was besides by no means[168] noted for his punctuality, even two or three dozen shirts and collars[169]

[M2] I failed to cultivate any attraction for it

[M3] established a household

---

[166] The translation of the Sanskrit verse added in the English translation. Sir Edwin Arnold's translation of the verse reads:

'Things that solicit sense
Hold off from the self-governed; nay, it comes,
The appetites of him who lives beyond
Depart—aroused no more.'
Bhagvad Gita, Verse 59, Discourse II.

[167] 'the experiment' added in the English translation.

[168] 'as also he was by no means' in the first edition.

[169] 'collars' in the original.

proved insufficient for me. Collars had to be changed daily and shirts, if not daily, at least every alternate day. This meant a double expense, which appeared to me unnecessary. So I equipped myself with a washing outfit to save it. I bought a book on washing, studied the art and taught it also to my wife. This no doubt added to my work, but its novelty made it a pleasure.

I shall never forget the first collar that I washed myself. I had used more starch than necessary, the iron had not been made hot enough, and for fear of burning the collar I had not pressed it sufficiently. The result was that, though the collar was fairly stiff, the superfluous starch continually dropped off it. I went to court with the collar on, thus inviting the ridicule of brother barristers, but even in those days I could be impervious to ridicule.

'Well,' said I, 'this is my first experiment at washing my own collars and hence the loose starch. But it does not trouble me, and then there is the advantage of providing you with so much fun.'

'But surely there is no lack of laundries here?' asked a friend.

'The laundry bill is very heavy,' said I. 'The charge for washing a collar is almost as much as its price, and even then there is the eternal dependence on the washerman. I prefer by far to wash my things myself.'

But I could not make my friends appreciate the beauty of self-help. In course of time I became an expert washerman so far as my own work went, and my washing was by no means inferior to laundry washing. My collars were no less stiff or shiny than others.

When Gokhale came to South Africa,[170] he had[171] with him a scarf which was a gift from Mahadeo

---

[170] Gopal Krishna Gokhale reached Cape Town on 22 October 1912. MKG gave him a send-off at Zanzibar on 29 November 1912.

[171] 'Gokhale had' in the original.

Govind Ranade. He treasured the memento with the utmost care and used it only on special occasions. One such occasion was the banquet given in his honour by the Johannesburg Indians.[172] The scarf was creased and needed ironing. It was not possible to send it to the laundry and get it back in time. I offered to try my art.

'I can trust to your capacity as a lawyer, but *not as a washerman*,'[M4] said Gokhale. 'What if you should soil it? Do you know what it means to me?'

With this he narrated, with much joy, the story of the gift. I still insisted, guaranteed good work, got his permission to iron it, and won his certificate. After that I did not mind if the rest of the world refused me its certificate.

In the same way, as I freed myself from slavery to the washerman, I *threw off*[M5] dependence on the barber. All people who go to England learn there at least the art of shaving, but none, to my knowledge, learn to cut their own hair. I had to learn that too.[173] I once went to an English hair-cutter in Pretoria. He contemptuously refused to cut my hair. I certainly felt hurt, but immediately[174] purchased a pair of clippers and cut my hair before the mirror. I succeeded more or less in cutting the front hair, but *I spoiled the back*.[M6] The friends in the court shook with laughter.

'What's wrong with your hair, Gandhi?[175] Rats have been at it?'

M4 I would not allow you to use your skill as a washerman on this scarf

M5 I got an opportunity to rid myself of the

M6 found it extremely difficult to cut the hair at the back. They were not even in any case

---

172 This banquet, hosted by the British Indian Association at Freemason Hall, was held on 31 October 1912. To add here: 'It was to be his most important speech in South Africa. He, therefore, wished to wear that scarf.'

173 'I had to learn that too.' Added in the English translation.

174 'went to the market and' to add.

175 'What's wrong with your hair, Gandhi?' added in the English translation.

'No. The white barber would not condescend to touch my black hair,' said I, 'so I preferred to cut it myself, no matter how badly.'

The reply did not surprise the friends.

The barber was not at fault in having refused to cut my hair. There was every chance of his losing his custom, if he should serve black men. We do not allow our barbers to serve our untouchable brethren. I got the reward of this in South Africa, not once, but many times, and the conviction that it was the punishment for our own sins saved me from becoming angry.

The extreme forms in which my passion for self-help and simplicity ultimately expressed itself will be described in their proper place. The seed had been long sown. It only needed watering to take root, to flower and to fructify, and the watering came in due course.

X

THE BOER WAR

^{M1} shall

I *must*^{M1} skip many other experiences of the period between 1897 and 1899 and come straight to the Boer War.

When the war was declared, my personal sympathies were all with the Boers, but I believed then that I had yet no right, in such cases, to *enforce*^{M2} my individual convictions. I have minutely dealt with the inner struggle regarding this in my history of the Satyagraha in South Africa,[176] and I must not repeat the argument here. I invite the curious to *turn to those pages*.^{M3} Suffice it to say that my loyalty to the British rule drove me to participation with the British in that war. I felt that,

^{M2} act according to

^{M3} read that account

---

[176] See *CWMG*, vol. 29, *Satyagraha in South Africa*, Chapter IX, pp. 59–68.

if I demanded rights as a British citizen, it was also my duty, as such, to participate in the defence of the British Empire. I held then that India could achieve her complete emancipation only[177] within and through[178] the British Empire. So I collected together as many comrades as possible, and with very great difficulty got their services accepted as an ambulance corps.

The average Englishman believed that the Indian was a coward, incapable of taking risks or looking beyond his immediate self-interest. Many English friends, therefore, threw cold water on my plan. But Dr. Booth supported it whole-heartedly. He trained us in ambulance work. We secured medical certificates of fitness for service. Mr. Laughton and the late Mr. Escombe *enthusiastically*[M4] supported the plan, and we applied at last for service at the front.[179] The Government thankfully acknowledged our application, but said that our services were not then needed.[180]

[M4] also

I would not rest satisfied, however, with this refusal. *Through the introduction of Dr. Booth,*[M5] I called on the Bishop of Natal.[181] There were many Christian Indians in our corps. The Bishop was delighted with my proposal and promised to help us in getting our services accepted.

[M5] With the help of Dr. Booth and accompanied by him

---

[177] 'only' added in the English translation.

[178] 'and through' added in the English translation.

[179] 'Letter to Colonial Secretary', 19 October 1899. See *CWMG*, vol. 3, pp. 134–35.

[180] In his reply of 23 October 1899, C. Bird, the principal undersecretary informed MKG: 'The Government is deeply impressed with the offer of Her Majesty's loyal Indian subjects in Durban who have offered their services . . . and should the occasion arise, the Government will be glad to avail itself of these services.' SN: 3303.

[181] Arthur Hamilton Baynes (1854–1942), a Church of England priest and Bishop of Natal from 1893 to 1901. For MKG's letter to Bishop Baynes, see *CWMG*, vol. 3, pp. 151–52.

Time too was working with us. The Boer had shown more pluck, determination and bravery than had been expected; and our services were ultimately needed.[182]

Our corps was 1,100-strong, with nearly 40 leaders. About three hundred were free Indians and the rest indentured.[183] Dr. Booth was also with us. The corps acquitted itself well. Though our work was to be outside the firing line, and though we had the protection of the Red Cross, we *were asked*[M6] at a critical moment to serve within the firing line. The reservation had not been of our seeking. The authorities did not want us to be within the range of fire. The situation, however, was changed after the repulse at Spion Kop,[184] and General Buller[185] sent the message that, though we were not bound to take the risk, Government would be thankful if we would do so and fetch the wounded from the field. *We had no hesitation,*[M7] and so the action at Spion Kop found us working within the firing line. During these days we had to march from twenty to twenty-five miles a day,[186] bearing the wounded on stretchers. Amongst the wounded we had the honour of carrying soldiers like General Woodgate.[187]

M6 also had the opportunity

M7 We were only too eager for this risk

---

[182] 'The Government needed many recruits.' To add. 'Recruits' translates the word *rangroot*, which is a corruption of the word recruit in many Indian languages.

[183] The largest numbers of indentured labourers came from Messrs Marshall Campbell Shire & Co., Reynolds Bros., and Wilson and the Collieries companies.

[184] The Battle of Spion Kop was fought on 23–24 January 1900, some thirty-eight miles south-west from Ladysmith.

[185] General Sir Redvers Henry Buller (1839–1908).

[186] 'and on one occasion we had to do so' to add.

[187] Major General Sir Edward Robert Prevost Woodgate (1845–1900).

The corps was disbanded after six weeks' service. After the reverses at Spion Kop and Vaalkranz,[188] the British Commander-in-Chief abandoned the attempt to relieve Ladysmith and other places by summary procedure, and decided to proceed slowly, awaiting reinforcements from England and India.

Our humble work was at the moment much applauded, and the Indians' prestige was enhanced. The newspapers published laudatory rhymes with the refrain, 'We are sons of Empire after all.'

General Buller mentioned with appreciation the work of the corps in his despatch, and the leaders were awarded the War Medal.

The Indian community became better organized. I got into closer touch with the indentured Indians. There came a greater awakening amongst them, and the feeling that Hindus, Mussalmans, Christians, Tamilians, Gujaratis and Sindhis were all Indians and children of the same motherland took deep root amongst them. Everyone believed that the Indians' grievances were now sure to be redressed. At the moment the white man's attitude seemed to be distinctly changed. The relations formed with the whites during the war were of the sweetest. We had come in contact with thousands of tommies.[189] They were friendly with us and thankful[190] for being there to serve them.

I cannot forbear from recording a sweet reminiscence of how human nature shows itself at its best in moments of trial. We were marching towards Chievely[191]

---

[188] The Battle of Vaal Krantz was fought from 5 to 7 February 1900.

[189] 'tommies' English word in the original.

[190] 'and were thankful to us' in the first edition.

[191] Chieveley.

Camp where Lieutenant Roberts,[192] the son of Lord Roberts,[193] had received a mortal wound. Our corps had the honour of carrying the body from the field. It was a sultry day—the day of our march. Everyone was thirsting for water. There was a tiny brook on the way where we could slake our thirst. But who was to drink first? We had proposed to come in after the tommies had finished. But they would not begin first and urged us to do so, and for a while a pleasant competition went on for giving precedence to one another.

XI

SANITARY REFORM AND FAMINE RELIEF

M1 The desolate state of any aspect of the social body has pinched me.

It has always been impossible for me to reconcile myself to any one member of the body politic remaining out of use.[M1] I have always been loath to hide or connive at the weak points of the community or to press for its rights without having purged it of its blemishes. Therefore, ever since my settlement in Natal, I had been endeavouring to clear the community of a charge that had been levelled against it, not without a certain amount of truth. The charge had often been made that the Indian was slovenly in his habits and did not keep his house and surroundings clean. The principal men of the community had, therefore, already begun to put their houses in order, but house-to-house inspection was undertaken only when plague was reported to be imminent in Durban. This was done after consulting, and gaining the approval

---

[192] Frederick Hugh Sherston Roberts V.C. (1872–99), mortally wounded on 15 December 1899 at the Battle of Colenso.

[193] Frederick Roberts, 1st Earl Roberts (1832–1914), also served as the commander-in-chief of the imperial forces during the Boer War.

of, the *city fathers*,[M2] who had desired our co-operation.   ^{M2} municipal officers
Our co-operation made work easier for them and at
the same time lessened our hard-ships. For whenever
there is an outbreak of epidemics,[194] the executive, as a
general rule, get impatient, take excessive measures and
behave to such as may have incurred their displeasure
with a heavy hand. The community saved itself from
this oppression by voluntarily taking sanitary measures.

But I had some bitter experiences. I saw that I could
not so easily count on the help of the community in
getting it to do its own duty, as I could in claiming for
rights.[195] At some places I met with insults, at others
with polite indifferences. It was too much for people to
bestir themselves to keep their surroundings clean. To
expect them to find money for the work was out of the
question. These experiences taught me, better than ever
before, that without infinite patience it was impossible
to get the people to do any work. It is the reformer
who is anxious for the reform, and not society, from
which he should expect nothing better than opposition,
abhorrence and even *mortal persecution*.[M3] Why may not   ^{M3} threat to his life
society regard as retrogression what the reformer *holds
dear as life itself?*[M4]   ^{M4} considers reform? If not
                                                                    retrogression, why would
Nevertheless the result of this agitation was that the   society not remain indifferent
Indian community learnt to recognize more or less the   to it?
necessity for keeping their houses and environments
clean. I gained the esteem of the authorities. They saw
that, though I had made it my business to ventilate
grievances and press for rights, I was no less keen and
insistent upon self-purification.

There was one thing, however, which still remained
to be done, namely, the awakening in the Indian settler
of a sense of duty to the motherland. India was poor, the
Indian settler went to South Africa in search of wealth,

---

[194] 'of plague, etc.' to add.

[195] 'from the local Government' to add.

and he was bound to contribute part of his earnings for the benefit of his countrymen in the hour of their adversity. This the settler did during the terrible famines in 1897 and 1899. They contributed handsomely for famine relief, and more so in 1899 than in 1897.[196] We had appealed to Englishmen also for funds, and they had responded well. Even the indentured Indians gave their share to the contribution, and the system inaugurated at the time of these famines has been continued ever since, and we know that Indians in South Africa never fail to send handsome contributions to India in times of national calamity.

Thus service of the Indians in South Africa *ever revealed to me new implications of truth at every stage.*[M5] Truth is like a vast tree, which yields more and more fruit, the more you nurture it.[197] The deeper the search in the mine of truth[198] the richer the discovery of the gems buried there, *in the shape of openings for an ever greater variety of service.*[M6]

[M5] taught me a number of things one after another

[M6] the opportunities for service

XII

RETURN TO INDIA

On my relief from war-duty I felt that my work was no longer in South Africa but in India. *Not that there was nothing to be done in South Africa,*[M1] but I was afraid that my main business might become merely money-making.

Friends at home were also pressing me to return, and I felt that I should be of more service in India. And

[M1] I could have certainly done some service sitting in South Africa

---

[196] Total collection amounted to £1535.1.9 of which £1194 was subscribed by the Indians.

[197] 'There is no limit to this.' To add.

[198] 'in the mine of truth' added in the English translation.

for the work in South Africa, there were, of course, Messrs Khan and Mansukhlal Naazar. So I requested my co-workers to relieve me. After very great difficulty my request was conditionally accepted, the condition being that I should be ready to go back to South Africa if, within a year, the community should need me. I thought it was a difficult condition but the love that bound me to the community made me accept it.

> The Lord has bound me
> With the cotton-thread of love,
> I am His bondslave,[199]

sang Mirabai. And for me, too, the cotton-thread of love that bound me to the community was too strong to break. The voice of the people is the voice of God, and here the voice of friends was too real to be rejected. I accepted the condition and got their permission to go.

At this time I was intimately connected only with Natal. The Natal Indians bathed me with the nectar of love. Farewell meetings were arranged at every place, and costly gifts were presented to me.[200]

Gifts had been bestowed on me before when I returned to India in 1896, but *this time the farewell was overwhelming*.[M2] The gifts of course included things in gold and silver, but there were articles of costly diamond as well.

[M2] the gifts and the scenes at the meeting this time overwhelmed me

What right had I to accept all these gifts? Accepting them, how could I persuade myself that I was serving the community without remuneration? All the gifts, excepting a few from my clients, were purely for my service to the community, and I could make no

---

[199] The original has 'I am pierced by a dagger of love.'

[200] At 3.30 on the afternoon of 12 October 1901, Parsi Rustomji gave a party to about 100 guests at his residence. On 15 October a public farewell was given at the Natal Indian Congress Hall.

difference between my clients and co-workers; for the clients also helped me in my public work.

One of the gifts was a gold necklace worth fifty guineas, meant for my wife. But even that gift was given because of my public work, and so it could not be separated from the rest.

The evening I was presented with the bulk of these things I *had a sleepless night.*[M3] I walked up and down my room deeply agitated, but could find no solution. It was difficult for me to forgo gifts worth hundreds, it was more difficult to keep them.

And even if I could *keep*[M4] them, what about my children? What about my wife? They were being trained to a life of service and to an understanding that service was its own reward.

I had no costly ornaments in the house. We had been fast simplifying our life. How then could we afford to have gold watches? How could we afford to wear gold chains and diamond rings? Even then I was exhorting people to conquer the infatuation for jewellery. What was I now to do with the jewellery that had come upon me?

I decided that I could not keep these things. I drafted a letter,[201] creating a trust of them in favour of the community and appointing Parsi Rustomji and others trustees. In the morning I held a consultation with my wife and children and finally got rid of the heavy incubus.

I knew that I should have some difficulty in persuading my wife, and I was sure that I should have none so far as the children were concerned. So I decided to constitute them my attorneys.

The children readily agreed to my proposal. 'We do not need these costly presents, we must return them

M3 spent a sleepless night like a man whose sense had taken his leave

M4 remain unaffected by them

---

[201] See *CWMG*, vol. 3, pp. 246–47.

to the community, and should we ever need them, we could easily purchase them,' they said.

I was delighted. 'Then you will plead with Mother, won't you?' I asked them.

'Certainly,' said they. 'That is our business. She does not need to wear the ornaments. She would want to keep them for us, and if we don't want them, why should she not agree to part with them?' But it was easier said than done. 'You may not need them,' said my wife. 'Your children may not need them. Cajoled they will dance to your tune. I can understand your not permitting me to wear them. But what about my daughters-in-law? They will be sure to need them. And who knows what will happen tomorrow? *I would be the last person to part with*[M5] gifts so lovingly given.'

M5 One cannot return

And thus the torrent of argument went on, reinforced, in the end, by tears. But the children were adamant. And I was unmoved.

I mildly put in: 'The children have yet to get married. We do not want to see them married young. When they are grown up, they can take care of themselves. And surely we shall not have, for our sons, brides who are fond of ornaments. And if after all, we need to provide them with ornaments, I am there. You will ask me then.'

'Ask you? I know you by this time. You deprived me of my ornaments, you would not leave me in peace with them. Fancy you offering to get ornaments for the daughters-in-law! You who are trying to make *sadhus*[202] of my boys from today! No, the ornaments will not be returned. And pray what right have you to my necklace?'

'But,' I rejoined, 'is the necklace given you for your service or for my service?'

---

[202] In the original, *vairagi*.

'I agree. But service rendered by you is as good as rendered by me. I have toiled and moiled for you day and night. Is that no service? You forced all and sundry on me, making me weep bitter tears, and I slaved for them!'

These were pointed thrusts, and some of them went home. But I was determined to return the ornaments. I somehow succeeded in extorting a consent from her. The gifts received in 1896 and 1901 were all returned. A trust-deed was prepared, and they were deposited with a bank, to be used for the service of the community, according to my wishes or to those of the trustees.[203]

Often, when I was in need of funds for public purposes, and felt that I must draw upon the trust, I have been able to raise the requisite amount, leaving the trust money intact. The fund is still there, being operated upon in times of need, and it has regularly accumulated.

I have never since regretted the step, and as the years have gone by, *my wife*[M6] has also seen its wisdom. It has saved us from many temptations.

I am definitely of opinion that a public worker should accept no *costly*[M7] gifts.

M6 Kasturba

M7 personal

---

[203] The following articles were deposited within the African Banking Corporation.

- Gold medal presented in 1896
- Gold coin presented by Tamil Indians in 1896
- Gold chain presented by the Johannesburg Committee in 1899
- Gold chain, sovereign purse and seven gold coins presented by Parsi Rustomji
- Gold watch presented by Mr. Joosub of Messrs Dada Abdulla & Co.
- Diamond ring presented by the community
- Gold necklace presented by Gujarati Hindus
- Diamond ring presented by Abdul Cadir

CWMG, vol. 3, p. 247.

XIII

IN INDIA AGAIN[204]

So I sailed for home.[205] Mauritius was one of the ports of call,[206] and as the boat made a long halt there,[207] I went ashore and acquainted myself fairly well with the local conditions.[208] For one night I was the guest of Sir Charles Bruce,[209] the Governor of the Colony.

After reaching India I spent some time in going about the country.[210] It was the year 1901 when the Congress met at Calcutta under the presidentship of Mr.

---

[204] 'Again' added in the English translation.

[205] There are discrepancies in the various sources regarding the date of travel. According to C.B. Dalal, *Gandhiji Ni Dinvari*, vol. 1, p. 41, he travelled on 19 October, *CWMG*, vol. 3, p. 576, gives the date as 18 October, while Pyarelal, *Mahatma Gandhi: The Discovery of Satyagraha on the Threshold*, vol. II, p. 378, gives the date as 20 October 1901. MKG accompanied by Kasturba and their four sons sailed on *S.S Nowshera*.

[206] Reached Port Louis on 30 October 1901.

[207] According to C.B. Dalal, MKG sailed for India on 19 November, while Pyarelal gives the date as 1 December 1901, which was impossible.

[208] On 4 November MKG visited the Supreme Court accompanied by the attorney general. On 13 November he was given a public reception in Port Louis by the Indian community. Another reception was organized for him on 16 November at St Pierre. MKG visited local spots including Tamarin, Rose Hill, Gentilly, Moka and the waterfalls.

[209] Sir Charles Bruce (1836–1920), also a Sanskrit scholar who worked on the Sanskrit dictionary published by the Imperial Academy of Saint Petersburg.

[210] MKG reached Bombay on 28 November 1901, went to Rajkot on 14 December via Porbandar, preferring to make a sea voyage, and reached Bombay again on 19 December, and wrote a public letter on the condition of South African Indians.

(later Sir) Dinshaw Wacha. And I of course attended it. It was my first experience of the Congress.

From Bombay I travelled[211] in the same train as Sir Pherozeshah Mehta, as I had to speak to him about conditions in South Africa. I knew the kingly style in which he lived. He had engaged a special saloon for himself, and I had orders to take my opportunity of speaking to him by travelling in his saloon for one stage. I, therefore, went to the saloon and reported myself at the appointed station. With him were *Mr. Wacha, and Mr. (now Sir) Chimanlal Setalvad.*[M1] They were discussing politics. As soon as Sir Pherozeshah saw me, he said, 'Gandhi, it seems nothing can be done for you. Of course we will pass the resolution you want. But what rights have we in our own country? I believe that, so long as we have no power in our own land, you cannot fare better in the Colonies.'

I was taken aback. Mr. Setalvad[212] seemed to concur in the view; Mr.[213] Wacha cast a *pathetic*[M2] look at me.

I tried to plead with Sir Pherozeshah, but it was out of the question for one like me to prevail upon the uncrowned king of Bombay. I contented myself with the fact that I should be allowed to move my resolution.

'You will of course show me the resolution,' said Mr. Wacha, to cheer me up. I thanked him and *left them at the next stop.*[M3]

So we reached Calcutta.[214] The President was taken to his camp with great *eclat* by the Reception Committee. I asked a volunteer where I was to go.

[M1] Dinshawji and Chimanlal Setalvad of that time

[M2] pitying

[M3] as soon as the train stopped at the next station, I hurried out and ran into my compartment

[211] On 20 December.

[212] Sir Chimanlal Harilal Setalvad (1864–1947), lawyer, served as a member of the Hunter Commission following the Jallianwala Bagh massacre, knighted in 1919.

[213] Sir Chimanlal and Sir Dinshaw in the original; both were knighted after the incident in narration.

[214] On 23 December 1901.

He took me to the Ripon College,[215] where a number of delegates were being put up. Fortune favoured me. Lokamanya was put up in the same block as I. I have a recollection that he came a day later.

And as was natural, Lokamanya would never be without his durbar. Were I a painter, I could paint him as I saw him seated on his bed—so vivid is the whole scene in my memory. Of the numberless people that called on him, I can recollect today only one, namely the late Babu Motilal Ghose, editor of the *Amrita Bazar Patrika*.[216] Their loud laughter and their talks about the wrong-doings of the ruling race cannot be forgotten.

But I propose to examine in some detail the appointments in this camp. The volunteers were clashing against one another. You asked one of them to do something. He delegated it to another, and he in his turn to a third, and so on; and as for the delegates, they were *neither here nor there*.[M4]

I made friends with a few volunteers. I told them some things about South Africa, and they felt somewhat ashamed. I tried to bring home to them the secret of service. They seemed to understand, but service is no mushroom growth. It presupposes the will first, and then experience. There was no lack of will on the part of those good, simple-hearted young men, but their experience[217] was nil. The Congress would meet three days every year and then go to sleep. What training

[M4] not among the three, or the thirteen or even counted among the fifty-six

---

[215] Founded in 1884 by Surendranath Banerji and named after Lord Ripon, Viceroy of India (1880–84), located on 24, Harrison Road. According to Gopalkrishna Gandhi, *A Frank Friendship*, p. 18, MKG stayed at the India Club from 24 to 29 December. India Club was established in 1882 by the Raja of Cooch Behar and was located at 6, Bankshall Street.

[216] One of the oldest newspapers in India, commenced publication in February 1868. It was started by brothers Sisir Ghosh and Motilal Ghosh.

[217] 'and training' to add.

could one have out of a three days' show once a year? And the delegates were of a piece with the volunteers. They had no better or longer training. They would do nothing themselves. 'Volunteer, do this,' 'Volunteer, do that,' were their constant orders.

Even here I was face to face with untouchability in a fair measure.[M5] The Tamilian kitchen was far away from the rest. To the Tamil delegates even the sight of others, whilst they were dining, meant pollution.[218] So a special kitchen had to be made for them in the College compound, walled in by wicker-work. It was full of smoke which choked you. It was a kitchen, dining-room, washroom, all in one—a close safe with no outlet. To me this looked like a travesty of *Varnadharma*.[219] If, I said to myself, there was such untouchability between the delegates of the Congress, one could well imagine the extent to which it existed amongst their constituents. I heaved a sigh at the thought.[220]

There was no limit to insanitation. Pools of water were everywhere. There were only a few latrines, and the recollection of their stink still oppresses me. I pointed it out to the volunteers. They said point-blank: 'That is not our work, it is the scavenger's work.' I asked for a broom. The man stared at me in wonder. I procured one and cleaned the latrine. But that was for myself. The rush was so great, and the latrines were so few, that they needed frequent cleaning, but that was more than I could do. So I had to content myself with simply ministering to myself. And the others did not seem to mind the stench and the dirt.

[M5] I had a fairly good experience of what Akha Bhagat calls 'superfluous limb'. Many practised untouchability.

---

[218] *Drishti dosha* in the original. *Navajivan* of 27 February 1927 carries a footnote, which in translation would read: 'Among the Madrasi Brahmins, mere sight of persons of other castes would pollute them while they eat. Hence they have the practice of keeping the doors of their homes closed while eating.'

[219] MD's footnote: 'Duties of the four fundamental divisions of Hindu Society.'

[220] 'of this number derived from multiplication' to add.

But that was not all. Some of the delegates did not scruple to use the verandahs outside their rooms for calls of nature at night. In the morning I pointed out the spots to the volunteers. No one was ready to undertake the cleaning, and I found no one to share the honour with me of doing it. Conditions have since considerably improved, but even today thoughtless delegates are not wanting who disfigure the Congress camp by *committing nuisance*[M6] wherever they choose, and all the volunteers are not always ready to clean up after them.

[M6] defecating

I saw that, if the Congress session were to be prolonged, conditions would be quite favourable for the outbreak of an epidemic.

XIV

CLERK AND BEARER[221]

There were yet two days for the Congress session to begin. I had made up my mind to offer my services to the Congress office in order to gain some experience. So as soon as I had finished the daily ablutions on arrival at Calcutta, I proceeded to the Congress office.

Babu Bhupendranath Basu[222] and Sjt. Ghosal[223] were the secretaries. I went to Bhupenbabu and offered my

---

[221] *Bera* in the original. *Navajivan* of 6 March 1927 carries a footnote, which in translation would read: 'Bera appears to be a corruption of the English word bearer. "Bera" means the one who provides personal service. In Calcutta, all household servants are called "Bera".'

[222] Bhupendranath Basu (1859–1924), lawyer, member, Executive Council of the Bengal government (1904–10), president, Indian National Congress (1914), vice-chancellor, Calcutta University. *A Frank Friendship*, p. 18.

[223] Janki Nath Ghosal (1840–1913), husband of Rabindranath Tagore's sister Swarnakumari Devi, close associate of A.O. Hume, father of Sarladevi Chowdharani, who figured later in MKG's life. *A Frank Friendship*, p. 19.

services. He looked at me, and said: 'I have no work, but possibly Ghosalbabu[224] might have something to give you. Please go to him.'

So I went to him. He scanned me and said with a smile: 'I can give you only clerical work. Will you do it?'

'Certainly,' said I. 'I am here to do anything that is not beyond my capacity.'

'That is the right spirit, young man,' he said. Addressing the volunteers who surrounded him, he added, 'Do you hear what this young man says?'

Then turning to me he proceeded: 'Well then, here is a heap of letters for disposal. Take that chair and begin. As you see, hundreds of people come to see me. What am I to do? Am I to meet them, or am I to answer these busybodies inundating me with letters? I have no clerks to whom I can entrust this work. Most of these letters have nothing in them, but you will please look them through. Acknowledge those that are worth it, and refer to me those that need a considered reply.'

I was delighted at the confidence reposed in me.

Sjt. Ghosal did not know me when he gave me the work. Only later did he enquire about my credentials.

I found my work very easy—the disposal of that heap of correspondence. I had done with it in no time, and Sjt. Ghosal was very glad. He was talkative. He would talk away for hours together. When he learnt something from me about my history, he felt rather sorry to have given me clerical work. But I reassured him: 'Please don't worry. What am I before you? *You have grown gray in the service of*[M1] the Congress,[225] and are as an elder to me. I am but an inexperienced youth. You have put me under a debt of obligation by entrusting me with

M1 You are an old servant of

---

[224] Mr. Ghosal in the original.

[225] Ghosal attended every session of the Congress from 1885 to 1911.

this work. For I want to do Congress work, and you have given me the rare opportunity of understanding the details.'

'To tell you the truth,' said Sjt. Ghosal, 'that is the proper spirit. But young men of today do not realize it. Of course I have known the Congress since its birth. In fact I may claim a certain share with Mr. Hume[226] in bringing the Congress into being.'

And thus we became good friends. He insisted on my having[227] lunch with him.

Sjt. Ghosal[228] used to get his shirt buttoned by his bearer. I volunteered to do the bearer's duty, and I loved to do it, as my regard for elders was always great. When he came to know this, he did not mind my doing little acts of personal service for him. In fact he was delighted. Asking me to button his shirt, he would say,[229] 'You see, now, the Congress secretary has no time even to button his shirt. He has always some work to do.' Sjt. Ghosal's naiveté amused me, but did not create any dislike in me for service of that nature. The benefit I received from this service is incalculable.

In a few days I came to know the working of the Congress. I met most of the leaders. I observed the movements of stalwarts like Gokhale and Surendranath. I also noticed the huge waste of time there. I observed too, with sorrow even then, the prominent place that the English language occupied in our affairs. There was little regard for economy of energy.[230] More than one

---

[226] Allan Octavian Hume (1829–1912), civil servant, ornithologist, botanist and one of the founders of the Indian National Congress.

[227] 'on my having my lunch' in the first edition.

[228] 'even' to add.

[229] 'evidently pleased,' to add.

[230] 'There was little regard for economy of energy.' Added in the English translation.

did the work of one, and many an important thing was no one's business at all.

Critical as my mind was in observing these things, there was enough charity in me, and so I always thought that it might, after all, be impossible to do better in the circumstances, and *that saved me from undervaluing any work.*[M2]

[M2] I did not feel prejudiced against anyone

XV

IN THE CONGRESS

In the Congress at last. The immense pavilion and the volunteers in stately array, as also the elders seated on the dais, *overwhelmed*[M1] me. I *wondered*[M2] where I should be in that vast assemblage.

[M1] unnerved

[M2] was oppressed by the thought

The presidential address was a book by itself. To read it from cover to cover was out of the question. Only a few passages were therefore read.

After this came the election of the Subjects Committee. Gokhale took me to the Committee meetings.

Sir Pherozeshah had of course agreed to admit my resolution, but I was wondering who would put it before the Subjects Committee, and when. For there were lengthy speeches to every resolution, all in English to boot, and every resolution had some well-known leader to back it. Mine was but a feeble pipe amongst those veteran drums, and as the night was closing in, my heart beat fast. The resolutions coming at the fag-end were, so far as I can recollect, rushed through at *lightning speed.*[M3] Everyone was hurrying to go. It was 11 o'clock. I had not the courage to speak. I had already met Gokhale, who had looked at my resolution. So I drew near his chair and whispered to him: 'Please do something for me.' He said: 'Your resolution is not out

[M3] the speed of today's aeroplanes

of my mind. You see the way they are rushing through the resolutions. But I will not allow yours to be passed over.'

'So we have done?' said Sir Pherozeshah Mehta.

'No, no, there is still the resolution on South Africa. Mr. Gandhi has been waiting long,' cried out Gokhale.

'Have you seen the resolution?' asked Sir Pherozeshah.

'Of course.'

'Do you like it?'

'It is quite good.'

'Well then, let us have it, Gandhi.'

I read it trembling.

Gokhale supported it.

'Unanimously passed,' cried out everyone.

'You will have five minutes to speak to it Gandhi,' said Mr. Wacha.

The *procedure*M4 was far from pleasing to me. No one had troubled to understand the resolution, everyone was in a hurry to go and, because Gokhale had seen the resolution, it was not thought necessary for the rest to see it or understand it!

    M4 scene

The morning found me worrying about my speech. What was I to say in five minutes? I had prepared myself fairly well but the words would not come to me. I had decided not to read my speech but to speak extempore.[231] But the facility for speaking that I had acquired in South Africa seemed to have left me for the moment.

As soon as it was time for my resolution, Mr. Wacha called out my name. I stood up. My head was reeling. I read the resolution somehow. Someone had printed and distributed amongst the delegates copies of a poem he had written in praise of foreign emigration. I read the poem and referred to the *grievances of the settlers*M5 in

    M5 suffering

---

[231] 'but to speak extempore' added in the English translation.

South Africa. Just at this moment Mr. Wacha[232] rang the bell. I was sure I had not yet spoken for five minutes. I did not know that the bell was rung in order to warn me to finish in two minutes more. I had heard others speak for half an hour or three quarters of an hour, and yet no bell was rung for them. I felt hurt and sat down as soon as[233] the bell was rung.[234] But my childlike intellect thought then that the poem contained an answer to Sir Pherozeshah. There was no question about the passing of the resolution. In those days there was hardly any difference between visitors and delegates.[235] Everyone raised his hand and all resolutions passed unanimously. My resolution also fared in this wise and so lost all its importance for me. And yet the very fact that it was passed by the Congress was enough to delight my heart. The knowledge that the *imprimatur* of the Congress meant that of the whole country was enough to delight anyone.

XVI

LORD CURZON'S DURBAR

The Congress was over, but as I had to meet the Chamber of Commerce[236] and various people in connection with work in South Africa, I stayed in Calcutta for a month. Rather than stay this time in a hotel, I arranged to get

---

[232] 'Sir Dinshaw' in the original.

[233] 'no sooner than' in the first edition.

[234] For the text of the resolution and MKG's speech. See *CWMG*, vol. 3, pp. 252–55.

[235] 'There was no opposing a resolution.' To add.

[236] 'Chamber of Commerce' in English in the original. The Bengal Chamber of Commerce and Industry was established in 1853.

the required introduction for a room in the India Club. *Among its members were some prominent Indians,*[M1] and I looked forward to getting into touch with them and interesting them in the work in South Africa. Gokhale frequently went to this Club to play billiards, and when he knew that I was to stay in Calcutta for some time, he invited me to stay with him. I thankfully accepted the invitation, but did not[237] think it proper to go there by myself. He waited for a day or two and then took me personally. He discovered my reserve and said: 'Gandhi, you have to stay in the country, and this sort of reserve will not do. You must get into touch with as many people as possible. I want *you to do Congress work.*'[M2]

I shall record here an incident in the India Club, before I proceed to talk of my stay with Gokhale. Lord Curzon[238] held his durbar about this time. Some Rajas and Maharajas who had been invited to the durbar were *members of*[M3] the Club. In the Club I always found them wearing fine Bengali dhotis and shirts and scarves. On the durbar day they put on trousers[239] befitting *khansamas*[240] and shining boots. I was pained and inquired of one of them the reason for the change.

'We alone know our[241] *unfortunate condition.*[M4] We alone know the insults we have to put up with, in order that we may possess our wealth and titles,' he replied.

'But what about these *khansama* turbans and these shining boots?' I asked.

'Do you see any difference between *khansamas* and us?' he replied, and added, 'they are our *khansamas,*

[M1] Prominent Indian leaders often stayed at this club

[M2] take from you Congress-related work

[M3] at

[M4] anguish

---

[237] 'I did not' in the first edition.

[238] George Nathaniel Curzon (1859–1925), Viceroy of India (1899–1905), in 1905 presided over the partition of Bengal.

[239] 'a long shirt, turban' to add.

[240] MD's footnote: 'i.e. waiters'.

[241] 'our own' in the first edition.

we are Lord Curzon's *khansamas*. If I were to absent myself from the levee,[242] I should have to suffer the consequences. If I were to attend it in my usual dress, it should be an offence. And do you think I am going to get any opportunity there of talking to Lord Curzon? Not a bit of it!'

I was moved to pity for this plain-spoken friend.

This reminds me of another durbar.

At the time when Lord Hardinge[243] laid the foundation-stone of Hindu University,[244] there was a durbar. There were Rajas and Maharajas of course, but Pandit Malaviyaji[245] specially invited me also to attend it, and I did so.[246]

I was distressed to see the Maharajas bedecked like women—silk pyjamas and silk *achkans*, pearl necklaces round their necks, bracelets on their wrists, pearl and diamond tassels on their turbans and, besides all this, swords with golden hilts hanging from their waist-bands.

M5 was told by someone

I *discovered*[MS] that these were insignia not of their royalty, but of their slavery. I had thought that they must be wearing these badges of impotence of their own free will, but I was told that it was obligatory for these Rajas to wear all their costly jewels at such functions. I also gathered that some of them had a positive dislike

---

242 'levee' English word in the original.

243 Charles Hardinge (1858–1944), Viceroy of India (1910–16).

244 The foundation stone of the Banaras Hindu University was laid on 4 February 1916.

245 Pandit Madan Mohan Malaviya (1861–1946), founder of the Banaras Hindu University (1916), president of the Indian National Congress (1908, 1918), president of the Special Session of the Hindu Mahasabha, Gaya (1922), and Kashi (1923). In the original he is described as 'Bharat Bhushan'.

246 MKG spoke at the ceremony on 6 February 1916. For the text of his speech, see *CWMG*, vol. 13, pp. 210–16.

for wearing these jewels, and that they never wore them except on occasions like the durbar.

I do not know how far my information was correct. But whether they wear them on other occasions or not, it is distressing enough to have to attend viceregal durbars[247] in jewels that only some women wear.

How heavy is the toll of sins and wrongs that wealth, power and prestige exact from man!

XVII

A MONTH WITH GOKHALE–I

From the very first day of my stay with him Gokhale made me feel completely at home.[248] He treated me as though I were his younger brother, he acquainted himself with all my requirements and arranged to see that I got all I needed. Fortunately my wants were few, and as I had cultivated the habit of self-help, I needed very little personal attendance. He was deeply impressed with my habit of fending for myself, *my personal cleanliness,*[M1] perseverance and regularity, and would often overwhelm me with praise.

[M1] by the cleanliness of my attire of that period

He seemed to keep nothing private from me. He would introduce me to all the important people that called on him. Of these the one who stands foremost in my memory is Dr. (now Sir) P.C. Ray.[249] He lived practically next door and was a very frequent visitor.

---

247 'or any other occasion' to add.

248 MKG shifted to Gokhale's residence at 91, Upper Circular Road, on 29 December 1901.

249 Sir Prafulla Chandra Ray (1861–1944), first chemist outside of Europe to be honoured with the Chemical Landmark Plaque by the Royal Society of Chemistry. He was educated at Edinburgh University, taught at Presidency College, Calcutta (1889–1916),

This is how he introduced Dr. Ray: 'This is Prof. Ray who, having a monthly salary of Rs. 800, keeps just Rs. 40 for himself and devotes the balance to public purposes. He is not, and does not want to get married.'

I see little difference between Dr. Ray as he is today and[250] as he used to be then. His dress used to be nearly as simple as it is, with this difference of course that whereas it is khadi now,[251] it[252] used to be Indian mill-cloth in those days. I felt I could never hear too much of the talks between Gokhale and Dr. Ray, as they all pertained to public good or were of educative value. At times they were painful too, containing, as they did, strictures on public men. As a result, some of those whom I had regarded as stalwart fighters began to look quite puny.

To see Gokhale at work was as much a joy as an education. He never wasted a minute. His private relations and friendships were all for public good. All his talks had reference only to the good of the country and were absolutely free from any trace of[253] untruth or insincerity. India's poverty and subjection were matters of constant and intense[254] concern to him. Various people sought to interest him in different things. But he gave every one of them the same reply: 'You do the thing yourself. Let me do my own work. What I want is freedom for my country. After that is won, we can

---

was the first Palit Professor of Chemistry at Calcutta University, wrote *A History of Hindu Chemistry* (1902), and founded India's first pharmaceutical company, Bengal Chemicals and Pharmaceuticals (1901).

[250] 'Prof. Ray' to add.

[251] 'there was no khadi in those days,' to add.

[252] 'probably' to add.

[253] 'impurity,' to add.

[254] 'exclusive' in the first edition.

think of other things. Today that one thing is enough to engage all my time and energy.'

His reverence for Ranade could be seen every moment. Ranade's authority was final in every matter, and he would cite it at every step. The anniversary of Ranade's death[255] (or birth, I forget which) occurred during my stay with Gokhale, who observed it regularly. There were with him then, besides myself, his friends Prof. Kathavate[256] and a Sub-Judge. He invited us to take part in the celebrations and in his speech he gave us his reminiscences of Ranade. He compared incidentally Ranade, Telang[257] and Mandlik.[258] He eulogized Telang's *charming style*[M2] and Mandlik's greatness as a reformer. Citing an instance of Mandlik's solicitude for his clients, he told us an anecdote as to how once, having missed his usual train, he engaged a special train so as to be able to attend the court[259] in the interest of his client. But Ranade, he said, towered above them all, as a versatile genius. He was not only a great judge, he was an equally great historian, an economist and a reformer. Although he was a judge, he fearlessly attended the Congress, and everyone had such confidence in his sagacity that they unquestioningly accepted his decisions. Gokhale's joy knew no bounds, as he described these qualities

[M2] language

---

[255] 16 January 1902, the first death anniversary of M.G. Ranade.

[256] Professor Abaji Vishnu Kathavate, a scholar of Sanskrit.

[257] Justice Kashinath Trimbak Telang (1850–93), judge of the Bombay High Court, one of the founders of the Indian National Congress and the Bombay Presidency Association. His translation of the Gita appeared in Max Muller's *Sacred Books of the East*, and he translated *Mudrarakshasa* of Vishakadatta into English.

[258] R.N. Mandalik, member, executive committee, Satyagraha Sabha, Bombay.

[259] 'so as to be able to attend the court' added in the English translation.

of head and heart which were all combined in[260] his master.

Gokhale used to have a horse-carriage in those days. I did not know the circumstances that had made a horse-carriage a necessity for him, and so I remonstrated with him: 'Can't you make use of the tram-car in going about from place to place? Is it derogatory to a leader's dignity?'

Slightly pained, he said, 'So you also have failed to understand me! I do not use my Council allowances for my own personal comforts. I envy your liberty to go about in tram-cars, but I am sorry I cannot do likewise. *When you are the victim of as wide a publicity as I am*,[M3] it will be difficult, if not impossible, for you to go about in a tram-car. There is no reason to suppose that everything that the leaders do is with a view to personal comfort. I love your simple habits. I live as simply as I can, but some expense is almost inevitable for a man like myself.'[261]

He thus satisfactorily disposed of one of my complaints, but there was another which he could not dispose of to my satisfaction.

'But you do not even go out for walks,' said I. 'Is it surprising that you should be always ailing? Should public work leave no time for physical exercise?'

'When do you ever find me free to go out for a walk?' he replied.

I had such a great regard for Gokhale that I never strove with him. Though this reply was far from satisfying me, I remained silent. I believed then and I believe even now, that, no matter what amount of work one has, one

[M3] When you will be known to as many people as I am,

---

[260] 'head and heart which were all combined in' added in the English translation.

[261] On 30 January 1902 MKG wrote to Gokhale, 'I feel that I had no right to question your taste on Monday evening. I was too presumptuous. Had I known that I would cause you thereby the pain I did cause, I should certainly never have taken the liberty. I trust you will forgive me the folly.' *CWMG*, vol. 3, pp. 266–67.

should always find some time for exercise, just as one does for one's meals. It is my humble opinion that, far from taking away from one's capacity for work, it adds to it.

XVIII

A MONTH WITH GOKHALE–II

Whilst living under Gokhale's roof I was far from being a stay-at-home.

I had told my Christian friends in South Africa that in India I would meet the Christian Indians and acquaint myself with their condition. I had heard of Babu Kalicharan Banerji[262] and held him in high regard. He took a prominent part in the Congress, and I had none of the misgivings about him that I had about the average Christian Indian, who stood aloof from the Congress and isolated himself from Hindus and Mussalmans. I told Gokhale that I was thinking of meeting him. He said: 'What is the good of your seeing him? He is a very good man, but I am afraid he will not satisfy you. I know him very well. However, you can certainly meet him if you like.'

I sought an appointment, which he readily gave me. When I went, I found that his wife was on her death-bed. His house was simple. In the Congress I had seen him in a coat and trousers, but I *was glad to find*[M1]   [M1] found him now wearing a Bengal dhoti and shirt. I liked his simple mode of dress, though I myself then wore a Parsi coat and trousers. Without much ado I presented my difficulties to him. He asked: 'Do you believe in the doctrine of original sin?'

'I do,' said I.

---

[262] Kalicharan Banerji (1847–1907), prominent Christian personality of Calcutta and an active Congressman. *A Frank Friendship*, p. 22. 'Babu' added in the English translation.

'Well then, Hinduism offers no absolution therefrom, Christianity does,' and added: 'The wages of sin is death, and the Bible says that the only way of deliverance is surrender unto Jesus.' I put forward *Bhakti-marga* (the path of devotion) of the Bhagavad Gita, but to no avail. I thanked him for his goodness. He failed to satisfy me, but I benefited by the interview.

During these days I walked up and down the streets of Calcutta. I went to most places on foot. I met Justice Mitter[263] and Sir Gurudas Banerji,[264] whose help I wanted in my work in South Africa. And about this time I met Raja Sir Pyarimohan Mukarji.[265]

Kalicharan Banerji had spoken to me about the Kali temple, which I was eager to see, especially as I had read about it in the books. So I went there one day. Justice Mitter's house was in the same locality, and I therefore went to the temple on the same day that I visited him. On the way I saw a stream of sheep going to be sacrificed to Kali. Rows of beggars lined the lane leading to the temple. There were religious mendicants too, and even in those days I was sternly opposed to giving alms to sturdy beggars. A crowd of them pursued me. One of such men was found seated on a verandah. He stopped me, and accosted me: 'Whither are you going, my boy?'[266] I replied to him.

He asked my companion and me to sit down, which we did.

I asked him: 'Do you regard this sacrifice as religion?'

'Who would regard killing of animals as religion?'

'Then, why don't you preach against it?'

---

[263] Justice Dwarkanath Mitter, judge, High Court of Calcutta.

[264] Sir Gurudas Banerji (1844–1918), judge, High Court of Calcutta, first Indian to be the vice-chancellor of Calcutta University.

[265] Raja Sir Pyarimohan Mukherjee, member, Imperial Legislative Council.

[266] In the original this sentence is in Hindustani.

'That's not my business. Our business is to worship God.'

'But could you not find any other place in which to worship God?'

'All places are equally good for us. The people are like a flock of sheep, following where leaders lead them. It is no business of us *sadhus*.'

We did not prolong the discussion but passed on to the temple. *We were greeted by rivers of blood*.[M2] I could not bear to stand there. I was *exasperated*[M3] and restless. I have never forgotten that sight.

[M2] There was a river of blood facing us.

[M3] oppressed

That very evening I had an invitation to dinner at a party of Bengali friends. There I spoke to a friend about this cruel form of worship. He said: 'The sheep[267] don't feel anything. The noise and the drum-beating there deaden all sensation of pain.'

I could not swallow this. I told him that, if the sheep had speech, they would tell a different tale. I felt that the cruel custom ought to be stopped. I thought of the story of Buddha,[268] but I also saw that the task was beyond my capacity.

I hold today the same opinion as I held then. To my mind the life of a lamb is no less precious than that of a human being. I should be unwilling to take the life of a lamb for the sake of the human body. I hold that, the more helpless a creature, the more entitled it is to protection by man from the cruelty of man. But he who has not qualified himself for such service is unable to afford to it any protection. I must go through[269] more self-purification and sacrifice, before I can hope to save these lambs from this unholy sacrifice. Today I think I

---

[267] ', we believe,' to add.

[268] The story of Buddha and King Bimbisara: Buddha's teaching of mercy stopped the practice of offering sacrifice during fire worship.

[269] 'a great deal' to add.

must die pining for this self-purification and sacrifice. It is my constant prayer that there may be born on earth some great spirit, man or woman, fired with divine pity, who will deliver us from this heinous sin, save the lives of the innocent creatures, and purify the temple. How is it that Bengal with all its knowledge, intelligence, sacrifice, and *emotion*[M4] tolerates this slaughter?

[M4] idealism

XIX

A MONTH WITH GOKHALE–III

The terrible sacrifice offered to Kali in the name of religion enhanced my desire to know Bengali life. I had read and heard a good deal about the Brahmo Samaj.[270] I knew something about the life of Pratap Chandra Mazmudar.[271] I had attended some of the meetings addressed by him. I secured his *Life of Keshav Chandra Sen*, read it with great interest, and understood the distinction between Sadharan Brahmo Samaj and Adi Brahmo Samaj.[272] I met Pandit Shivanath Shastri[273] and in company with Prof. Kathavate[274] went to see

---

[270] Founded in 1828 by Raja Ram Mohan Roy and Keshav Chandra Sen, among others.

[271] Pratap Chandra Mazumdar (1840–1905).

[272] In 1866 due to differences between Devendranath Tagore and Keshav Chandra Sen, Tagore founded the Adi (the original) Brahmo Samaj to distinguish it from the reformist Keshav Chandra Sen. At the time of this schism there were fifty-four samajs, fifty in Bengal, two in the North-West Frontier Province and one each in the Punjab and Madras. In 1878 there was another schism in the group led by Sen, which led to the establishment of the Sadharan Brahmo Samaj on 15 May 1878 by Anand Mohan Bose, Shibchandra Deb and Umesh Chandra Dutta.

[273] Shivanath Shastri (1847–1919), leader of the Sadharan Brahmo Samaj, educationist, poet and novelist. His collections of poems include *Pushpamala* and *Pushpanjali*, his novels include *Yugantar* and *Nayantara*.

[274] 'I went' in the first edition.

Maharshi Devendranath Tagore,[275] but as no interviews
with him were allowed then, we could not see him. We
were, however, invited to a celebration of the Brahmo
Samaj held at his place, and there we had the privilege
of listening to fine Bengali music. Ever since I have
been a lover of Bengali music.

Having seen *enough*[M1] of the Brahmo Samaj,[276] it   ^M1 as much
was impossible to be satisfied without seeing Swami
Vivekanand.[277] So with great enthusiasm I went to Belur
Math, mostly, or maybe all the way, on foot. I loved
the sequestered site of the Math. I was disappointed
and sorry to be told that the Swami was at his Calcutta
house,[278] lying ill, and could not be seen.

I then ascertained the place of residence of Sister
Nivedita,[279] and met her in a Chowringhee mansion.
I was taken aback by the splendour that surrounded
her, and even in our conversation, there was not much
meeting ground. I spoke to Gokhale about this, and he
said he did not wonder that there could be no point of
contact between me and a volatile[280] person like her.

---

[275] Devendranath Tagore (1817–1905), father of Rabindranath
Tagore, adopted Brahomism in 1843.

[276] 'as I possibly could' to add.

[277] Swami Vivekananda (1863–1902), disciple of Swami
Ramakrishna, eminent exponent of Vedantic philosophy,
founder of Belur Math, a monastery along the Hooghly.

[278] Gopalkrishna Gandhi suggests that the Swami was at the house
of his prominent disciple Balaram Bose at Bagbazar. *A Frank
Friendship*, p. 22.

[279] Sister Nivedita (born Margaret Noble, 1867–1911), Irishwoman,
met Swami Vivekananda in London in 1895, became his disciple
and took the name of Nivedita.

[280] MD's footnote: 'Regarding the use of the word "volatile", see note
"In Justice to Her Memory." *Young India*, 30th June, 1927.' *Modern
Review* of July 1927 took objection to this adjective 'volatile' and the
description of 'splendour'. It wrote: 'The mention of "the splendour
that surrounded her" without any other details conveys a wrong
idea of Sister Nivedita's mode of living. The fact is, at the time
when Mr. Gandhi saw her, she was the guest of Mrs. Ole Bull and

M2 giving a sermon

I met her again at Mr. Pestonji Padshah's place. I happened to come in just as she was *talking*[M2] to his old mother, and so I became an interpreter between the two. In spite of my failure to find any agreement with her, I could not but notice and admire her overflowing love for Hinduism. I came to know of her books later.

I used to divide my day between seeing the leading people in Calcutta regarding the work in South Africa, and visiting and studying the religious and public institutions of the city. I once addressed a meeting, presided over by Dr. Mullick, on the work of the Indian Ambulance Corps in the Boer War.[281] My acquaintance with *The Englishman* stood me in good stead on this occasion too. Mr. Saunders was ill then but rendered[282] me as much help as in 1896. Gokhale liked this speech of mine, and he was very glad to hear Dr. Ray praising it.

Miss Josephine MacLeod at the American Consulate, and, as such, was not responsible for "splendour." . . . We do not know whether Mr. Gokhale spoke to Mr. Gandhi in English and actually used the word "volatile" to describe her . . . But whoever may be responsible for the use of the word "volatile" has wronged her memory.' MKG 'gladly' published this in *Young India* and wrote a note on it. He said: 'Such references should be regarded merely as the impression left upon my mind at the time to which they may relate.' Regarding the adjective 'volatile' he said, 'As to the use of the word "volatile", though the translation is not mine, I cannot disassociate myself from its use, because as a rule I revise these translations, and I remember having discussed the adjective with Mahadev Desai. We both had doubts about the use of the adjective being correct. The choice lay between volatile, violent and fantastical. The last two were considered to be too strong. Mahadev had chosen volatile and I passed it.' *CWMG*, vol. 34, pp. 80–81.

[281] The meeting was held on 27 January 1902, at Albert Hall, on 15, College Square. According to Gopalkrishna Gandhi, the meeting was chaired by Gokhale. *A Frank Friendship*, p. 30. For the text of the speech, see *CWMG*, vol. 3, pp. 260–66. MKG had earlier addressed a meeting at the same venue on 19 January 1902 on the condition of Indians in South Africa, with Narendranath Sen in Chair and Gokhale in attendance. *A Frank Friendship*, p. 26.

[282] 'he rendered' in the first edition.

Thus my stay under the roof of Gokhale made my work in *Calcutta*[M3] very easy, brought me into touch with the foremost Bengali families, and was the beginning of my intimate contact with Bengal.

[M3] Bengal

I must needs skip over many a reminiscence of this memorable month. *Let me simply mention my flying visit to Burma,*[283] *and the foongis*[284] *there.*[M4] I was pained by their lethargy. I saw the golden pagoda. I did not like the innumerable little candles burning in the temple, and the rats running about the sanctum brought to my mind thoughts of Swami Dayanand's experience at Morvi.[285] The freedom and energy of the Burmese women charmed just as[286] the indolence of the men pained me. I also saw, during my brief sojourn, that just as Bombay was not India, Rangoon was not Burma, and that just as we in India have become commission agents[287] of English merchants, even so in Burma have we combined with the English merchants in making the Burmese people our commission agents.

[M4] During that month I also swam across to Brahmadesh. I visited the *foongis* there.

On my return from Burma I took leave of Gokhale. The separation was a wrench, but my work in Bengal, or rather Calcutta, was finished, and I had no occasion to stay any longer.[288]

---

[283] MKG left Calcutta on 28 January 1902 by *S.S. Goa*, reaching Rangoon on 31st. He left Rangoon on 17 February 1902, reaching Calcutta on the 20th. The letters from Rangoon bear the address line as 7, Moghul Street.

[284] MD's footnote: 'Monks.'

[285] This refers to an experience that Swami Dayanand had at the age of fourteen, when he kept a vigil at the Shiva temple on the night of Shivaratri. He was shocked to find mice frolicking over the Shivalinga. 'at Morvi' added in the English translation.

[286] 'charmed me and the indolence' in the first edition.

[287] 'commission agents' English term in the original.

[288] 'and I had no occasion to stay any longer' added in the English translation.

Before settling down I had thought of making a[289] tour through India travelling third class, and of acquainting myself with the hardships of third-class[290] passengers. I spoke to Gokhale about this. To begin with he ridiculed the idea, but when I explained to him what I hoped to see, he cheerfully approved. I planned to go first to Benares[291] to pay my respects to Mrs. Besant,[292] who was then ill.

M5 brass

It was necessary to equip myself anew for the third-class tour. Gokhale himself gave me a *metal*[M5] tiffin-box and got it filled[293] with sweetballs[294] and *puris*. I purchased a canvas bag worth twelve annas and a long coat[295] made of *Chhaya*[296] wool. The bag was to contain this coat, a dhoti, a towel and a shirt. I had a blanket as well to cover myself with and a water jug. Thus equipped I set forth on my travels. Gokhale and Dr. Ray came to the station to see me off. I had asked them both not to trouble to come, but they insisted. 'I should not have come if you had gone first class, but now I had to,'[297] said Gokhale.

No one stopped Gokhale from going on to the platform. He was in his silk turban, jacket and dhoti. Dr. Ray was in his Bengali dress. He was stopped by

---

[289] 'short' to add.

[290] 'the third-class' in the first edition.

[291] 'Kashiji' in the original.

[292] The original has 'Vidushi [literally, learned] Anne Besant'.

[293] 'replenished' in the first edition.

[294] 'magas ladu' in the original, made from gram flour, a long-lasting sweet.

[295] 'got a long coat' in the first edition.

[296] MD's footnote: 'A place in Porbandar state noted for its coarse woollen fabrics.'

[297] 'but now I must come' in the first edition.

the ticket collector, but on Gokhale's telling him that he was his friend, he was admitted.

Thus with their good wishes I started on my journey.[298]

XX

IN BENARES[299]

The journey was from Calcutta to Rajkot, and I planned to halt at Benares, Agra, Jaipur and Palanpur *en route*.[300] I had not the time to see any more places than these. In each city I stayed one day and put up in dharmsalas or with *pandas*[301] like the ordinary[302] pilgrims, excepting at Palanpur.[303] So far as I can remember, I did not spend more than Rs. 31 (including the train fare) on this journey.

In travelling third class I mostly preferred the ordinary to the mail trains, as I knew that the latter were more crowded and the fares in them higher.[304]

The third-class compartments are practically as dirty, and the closet arrangements as bad, today as they were then.[M1] There may be a little improvement now, but the difference

[M1] The third-class compartments were practically as dirty, and the closet arrangements as bad, then as they are today.

---

[298] On 21 February 1902.

[299] 'Kashi' in the original. Throughout this chapter Kashi has been rendered as Benares, from Varanasi.

[300] MKG was in Benares on 22nd, in Agra on 23rd, in Jaipur on 24th and 25th in Palanpur, reaching Rajkot on 26 February 1902.

[301] MD's footnote: 'Priests'.

[302] 'ordinary' added in the English translation.

[303] In Palanpur MKG was the guest of Mr. Patwari, the executive officer of the state.

[304] 'the latter were crowded, and there was of course the objection of the fare being higher for third class by mail' in the first edition.

between the facilities provided for the first and the third classes *is*[M2] out of all proportion to the difference between the fares for the two classes. Third-class passengers are treated like sheep and their comforts are sheep's comforts. In Europe I travelled third—and only once first just to see what it was like—but there I noticed no such difference between the first and the third classes. In South Africa third-class passengers are mostly Negroes, yet the third-class comforts are better there than here. In parts of South Africa third-class compartments are provided with sleeping accommodation and cushioned seats. The accommodation is also regulated, so as to prevent overcrowding, whereas here I have *found the regulation limit usually exceeded.*[M3]

M3 never found the regulation limit observed

The indifference of the railway authorities to the comforts of the third-class passengers,[305] combined with the dirty and inconsiderate habits of the passengers themselves, makes third-class travelling a trial for a passenger of cleanly ways. These unpleasant habits commonly include throwing of rubbish on the floor of the compartment, smoking at all hours and in all places, betel and tobacco chewing, *converting of the whole carriage into a spittoon,*[M4] shouting and yelling, and using foul language, regardless of the convenience or comfort of fellow-passengers.[306] I have noticed little difference between my experience of the third-class travelling in 1902 and that of my unbroken third-class tours from 1915 to 1919.

M4 spitting at the place where one is seated, throwing left-overs on the floor,

I can think of only one remedy for this awful state of things[307]—that educated men should make a point of travelling third class and reforming the habits of the people, as also of never letting the railway authorities

---

[305] 'to the comforts of the third-class passengers' added in the English translation.

[306] 'This can be experienced everywhere.' To add.

[307] ', and it is this' added in the first edition.

rest in peace, sending[308] in complaints wherever necessary, never resorting to bribes or any unlawful means[309] for obtaining their own comforts, and never putting up with infringements of rules on the part of anyone concerned. This, I am sure, would bring about considerable improvement.

My serious illness in 1918-19[310] has unfortunately compelled me practically to give up third-class travelling,[311] and it has been a matter of[312] constant pain and shame to me, especially because the disability came at a time when the agitation for the removal of the hardships of third-class passengers was making fair headway. The hardships of poor railway and steamship passengers, accentuated by their bad habits, the undue facilities allowed by Government to foreign trade, and such other things, make an important group of subjects,[313] worthy to be taken up by one or two enterprising and persevering *workers*[M5] who could devote their full time to it.

[M5] gentlemen

But I shall leave the third-class passengers at that,[314] and come to my experience in Benares. I arrived[315] there in the morning. I had decided to put up with a *panda*. Numerous Brahmins surrounded me as soon as I got out of the train, and I selected one who struck me to be comparatively cleaner and better than the rest.

---

[308] 'by sending' in the first edition.

[309] 'or any unlawful means' added in the English translation.

[310] 'in 1918–19' added in the English translation.

[311] 'since 1920' to add.

[312] 'for' in the first edition.

[313] 'subject by itself' in the first edition.

[314] MKG wrote to Gokhale from Rajkot on 4 March, narrating at length his experience of the journey. See *CWMG*, vol. 3, pp. 272–73.

[315] 'reached' in the first edition.

M6 ritualistic

M7 ritual worship

It proved to be a good choice. There was a cow in the courtyard of his house and an upper storey where I was given a lodging.[316] I did not want to have any food without ablution in the Ganges in the *proper orthodox*[M6] manner. The *panda* made preparations for it. I had told him beforehand that on no account could I give him more than a rupee and four annas as *dakshina*,[317] and that he should therefore keep this in mind while making the preparations.

The *panda* readily assented. 'Be the pilgrim rich or poor,' said he, 'the *service*[M7] is the same in every case. But the amount of *dakshina* we receive depends upon the will and the ability of the pilgrim.'[318] I did not find that the *panda* at all abridged the usual formalities in my case. The *puja*[319] was over at 12 o'clock, and I went to the Kashi Vishvanath temple for *darshan*. I was deeply pained by what I saw there. When practising as a barrister in Bombay in 1891, I had occasion to attend a lecture on 'Pilgrimage to Kashi' in the Prarthana Samaj hall. I was therefore prepared for some measure of disappointment. But the[320] actual disappointment was greater than I had bargained for.

The approach was through a narrow and slippery lane. Quiet there was none. The swarming flies and the noise made by the shopkeepers and pilgrims were perfectly insufferable.

Where one expected an atmosphere of meditation and communion, it was conspicuous by its absence. One had to seek that atmosphere in oneself. I did observe

---

[316] 'my lodging' in the first edition.

[317] MD's footnote: 'Gift.'

[318] 'Pilgrim' translates the original word *yajman*, the institutor of sacrifice.

[319] MD's footnote: 'Worship.'

[320] 'my' in the first edition.

Seven-year-old M.K. Gandhi, Porbandar.

With elder brother Laxmidas (L), Rajkot, 1886.

With friend Sheikh Mehtab, Rajkot, circa 1886.

As a barrister: wearing the London Vegetarian
Society badge, Johannesburg, 1906.

With his wife, Kasturba.

With C.F. Andrews (L) and W.W. Pearson, 1914.

With the Indian Ambulance Corps during the Boer War (1899–1902).

With the Indian Stretcher Bearers Corps during the Zulu Rebellion, 1906.

Gandhi and Kasturba with fellow settlers at the Phoenix Settlement, Natal, 1906.

With Hermann Kallenbach (on Gandhi's left) at Tolstoy Farm, 1910.

સત્યાગ્રહના મિત્ર અને ટોલ્સ્ટોય ફાર્મના માલીક મો. એચ. કેલનબેક

Gandhi with his secretary, Mrs. Sonja Schlesin, and Mr. H.S.L. Polak in front of his office in Johannesburg, 1905.

A portrait of Hermann Kallenbach, 'The Owner of Tolstoy Farm', published in *Indian Opinion* on 5 August 1911 in recognition of his contribution to the Satyagraha Movement.

Gopal Krishna Gokhale with Gandhi, Kallenbach and other members of the Reception Committee, Durban, 1912.

A page from the handwritten constitution of the Natal Indian Congress.

A page from Mahadev Desai's manuscript of his translation of *An Autobiography*: Chapter XXII, 'Comparative Study of Religions', Part II.

A copy of the menu for the farewell dinner hosted at Johannesburg.

Indian Opinion, 14 January 1905.

Mahadev Desai's translation of *An Autobiography* commenced with the 3 December 1925 issue of *Young India*.

A page with testimonies collected from the peasants during the Champaran Satyagraha, 1917.

The 29 December 1925 edition of the Gujarati newspaper *Navajivan*.

A note in one of the volumes of the first edition of *An Autobiography*, from Mahadev Desai's personal collection of books.

The first Satyagraha Ashram at Kochrab, 1915.

People marching on the street during the Non-cooperation Movement, 1919.

With Mahadev Desai at Sevagram,
January 1942.

devout sisters, who were absorbed in meditation, entirely unconscious of the environment. But for this the authorities of the temple could scarcely claim any credit. The authorities should be responsible for creating and maintaining about the temple a pure, sweet and serene atmosphere, *physical as well as moral.*[M8] Instead of this I found a bazar where cunning shopkeepers were selling sweets and toys of the latest fashion.

[M8] outer as well as inner

When I reached the temple, I was greeted at the entrance by a stinking mass of rotten flowers. The floor was paved with fine marble, which was however broken by some devotee innocent of aesthetic taste[321] who had set it with rupees serving as[322] an excellent receptacle for dirt.

I went near the *Jnana-vapi* (well of knowledge). I searched[323] here for God but failed to find Him. *I was not therefore in particularly good mood.*[M9] The surroundings of the *Jnana-vapi* too I found to be dirty. I had no mind to give any *dakshina.* So I offered a pie. The panda in charge got angry and threw away the pie. He swore at me and said: 'This insult will take you straight to hell.'

[M9] I seethed within.

This did not perturb me. 'Maharaj,' said I, 'whatever fate has in store for me, it does not behove one of your class to indulge in such[324] language. You may take this pie if you like, or you will lose that too.'

'Go away,' he replied, 'I don't care for your pie.'[325] And then followed a further volley of abuse.

I took up the pie and went my way, flattering myself that the Brahmin had lost a pie and I had saved one. But the Maharaj was hardly the man to let the pie

---

[321] 'innocent of aesthetic taste' added in the English translation.

[322] 'which served as' in the first edition.

[323] 'had searched' in the first edition.

[324] 'foul' to add.

[325] This sentence is in Hindustani in the original.

go. He called me back and said, 'All right, leave the pie here, I would rather not be as you are. If I refuse your pie, it will be bad for you.'[326]

I silently gave him the pie and, with a sigh, went away.

Since then I have twice been to Kashi Vishvanath, but that has been after I *had already been afflicted with the title of*[M10] Mahatma and experiences such as I have detailed above had become impossible. People eager to have my *darshan* would not permit me to have a *darshan* of the temple. The woes of mahatmas are known to mahatmas *alone*.[M11] Otherwise the dirt and the noise were the same as before.

If anyone doubts the infinite mercy of God, let him have a look at these sacred places. How much hypocrisy and irreligion does the Prince of Yogis suffer to be perpetrated in His holy name? He proclaimed long ago:

ये यथा मां प्रपद्यन्ते तांस्तथैव भजाम्यहम्[327]

'Whatever a man sows, that shall he reap.' The law of karma is inexorable and impossible of evasion. There is thus hardly any need for God to interfere. He laid down the law and, *as it were, retired*.[M12]

After this visit to the temple, I *waited upon*[M13] Mrs. Besant. I knew that she had just recovered from an illness. I sent in my name. She came at once. As I wished only to pay my respects to her, I said, 'I am aware that you are in delicate health. I only wanted to pay my respects. I am thankful that you have been good enough to receive me in spite of your indifferent health. I will not detain you any longer.'

So saying, I took leave of her.

[M10] became

[M11] like myself

[M12] washed off his hands

[M13] sought *darshan* of

---

[326] In Hindustani in the original.

[327] Bhagvad Gita, IV, 11. 'Whoso worship me, Them I exalt.' In Edwin Arnold's translation.

XXI

SETTLED IN BOMBAY[328]

Gokhale was very anxious that I should settle down in Bombay, practise at the bar and help him in public work. Public work in those days meant Congress work, and the chief work of the institution which he had *assisted to found*[M1] was carrying on the Congress administration.[329]

I liked Gokhale's advice but I was not overconfident of success as a barrister.[M2] The unpleasant memories of past failure were yet with me, and I still hated as poison the use of flattery for getting briefs.[330]

I therefore decided to start work first at Rajkot. Kevalram Mavji Dave, my old well-wisher, who had induced me to go to England, was there, and he started me straightaway with three briefs. Two of them were appeals before the Judicial Assistant to the Political Agent[331] in Kathiawad and one was an original case in Jamnagar. This last was rather important. *On my saying that I could not trust myself to do it justice,*[M3] Kevalram Dave exclaimed: *'Winning or losing is no concern of yours.*[M4] You

M1 created

M2 That was also my wish. But I lacked self-confidence that I would get professional work.

M3 I hesitated to take the risk of this case.

M4 'In case of a loss, it will be our loss, isn't it?

---

[328] The original has a question mark: 'Settled in Bombay?'

[329] V.S. Srinivas Sastri, while providing editorial comments for the revised edition of the *Autobiography*, raised certain factual questions pertaining to this line. He appended a note, which reads: 'What is the institution meant here? The Servants of India Society had not been founded. The Fergusson College didn't dabble in politics. Neither this college nor Congress owed its foundation even in part to Gokhale.' This note was placed for MKG's consideration. The note is cancelled with two broad strokes made in blue ink. MKG's three-word remark are in blue ink and circled. The original Gujarati reads: *Mool barabar chhe.* (The original is correct.) No changes were made in revised edition.

[330] 'for getting briefs' added in the English translation.

[331] 'to the Political Agent' added in the English translation.

will simply try your best, and I am of course there to assist you.'

The counsel on the other side was the late Sjt. Samarth. I was fairly well prepared. Not that I knew much of Indian law, but Kevalram Dave had instructed me very thoroughly. I had heard friends say, before I went out to South Africa, that Sir Pherozeshah Mehta had the law of evidence at his finger-tips and that that was the secret of his success. I had borne this in mind, and during the voyage had carefully studied the Indian Evidence Act with commentaries thereon. There was of course also the advantage of my legal experience in South Africa.

I won the case and gained some confidence.[332] I had no fear about the appeals, which were successful. All this inspired a hope in me that after all I might not fail even in Bombay.

But before I set forth the circumstances in which I decided to go to Bombay, I shall narrate my experience of the inconsiderateness and ignorance of English officials. The Judicial Assistant's court was peripatetic. He was constantly touring, and *vakils* and their clients had to follow him wherever he moved his camp. The *vakils* would charge more whenever they had to go out of head-quarters, and so the clients had naturally to incur double the expenses. *The inconvenience*[M5] was no concern of the judge.

[M5] This

The appeal of which I am talking was to be heard at Veraval where plague was raging. I have a recollection that there were as many as fifty cases daily in the place with a population of 5,500. It was practically deserted, and I put up in a deserted dharmsala at some distance from the town. But where were the clients to stay? If they were poor, they had simply to trust themselves to God's mercy.

---

[332] 'confidence in myself.' In the first edition.

A friend who also had cases before the court had wired[M6]   [M6] Some *vakil* friends had wired
that I should put in an application for the camp to be   me
moved to some other station because of the plague at
Veraval. On my submitting the application, the sahib
asked me: 'Are you afraid?'

I answered: 'It is not a question of my being
afraid, I think I can shift for myself, but what about
the clients?'

'The plague has come to stay in India,' replied the
sahib. 'Why fear it? The climate of Veraval is lovely.
(The sahib lived far away from the town in a palatial
tent pitched on the seashore.) Surely people must learn
to live thus in the open.'

It was no use arguing against this philosophy. The
sahib told his *shirastedar*: 'Make a note of what Mr.
Gandhi says, and let me know if it is very inconvenient
for the *vakils* or the clients.'

The sahib of course had honestly done what he
thought was the right thing. But how could the man
have an idea of the hardships of poor India? How was
he to understand the needs, habits, idiosyncrasies and
customs of the people? How was one, accustomed to
measure things in gold sovereigns, all at once to make
calculations in tiny bits of copper? As the elephant is
powerless to think in the terms of the ant, in spite of the
best intentions in the world, even so is the Englishman[333]
powerless to think in the terms of, or legislate for, the[334]
Indian.[335]

But to resume the thread of the story. In spite of my
successes, I had been thinking of staying on in Rajkot
for some time longer when one day Kevalram Dave

---

[333] 'whose habits were those of an elephant' to add.

[334] 'ant-like' to add.

[335] 'even so is the Englishman with the needs of an elephant
powerless to think in terms of, or legislate for, the Indian, with
the needs of an ant' in the first edition.

came to me and said: 'Gandhi, we will not *suffer you to vegetate here*.[M7] You must settle in Bombay.'

'*But who will find work for me there?*'[M8] I asked. 'Will you find the expenses?'

'Yes, yes, I will,' said he. 'We shall bring you down here sometimes as a big barrister from Bombay[336] and drafting work we shall send you there. It lies with us *vakils* to make or mar a barrister.[337] You have proved your worth in Jamnagar and Veraval, and I have therefore not the least anxiety about you. You are destined to do public work, and we will not allow you to be buried in Kathiawad. So tell me, then, when you will go to Bombay.'

'I am expecting a remittance from Natal. As soon as I get it I will go,' I replied.

The money came in about two weeks, and I went to Bombay. I took chambers in Payne, Gilbert and Sayani's[338] offices, and it looked as though I had settled down.

XXII

FAITH ON ITS TRIAL

Though I had hired chambers in the Fort[339] and a house in Girgaum,[340] God would not let me settle down. Scarcely had I moved into my new house when my

---

[336] 'from Bombay' added in the English translation.

[337] 'to magnify or belittle a barrister' in the first edition.

[338] Henry Alfred Handley Payne, Reginald Gilbert, Rahimtulla Mahomed Sayani. The chambers were at Agakhan's Building, 2nd floor, opposite High Court, Fort, Bombay.

[339] 'in the Fort' added in the English translation.

[340] MKG rented a part of a house on Girgaum Backroad belonging to one Keshavji Tulsidas.

second son Manilal, who had already been through an acute attack of smallpox some years back, had[341] a severe attack of typhoid, combined with pneumonia and signs of delirium at night.

The doctor was called in. He said medicine would have little effect, but[342] eggs and chicken broth might be given with profit.

Manilal was only ten years old. To consult his wishes was out of the question. Being his guardian I had to decide. The doctor was a very *good*[M1] Parsi. I told   [M1] kind
him that we were all vegetarians and that I could not possibly give either of the two things to my son. Would he therefore recommend something else?

'Your son's life is in danger,' said the good doctor. 'We could give him milk diluted with water, but that will not give him enough nourishment. As you know, I am called in by many Hindu families, and they do not object to anything I prescribe. I think you will be well advised not to be so hard on your son.'

'What you say is quite right,' said I. 'As a doctor you could not do otherwise. But my responsibility is very great. If the boy had been grown up, I should certainly have tried to ascertain his wishes and respected them. But here I have to think and decide for *him*.[M2]   [M2] the child
To my mind it is only on such occasions that a man's faith is truly tested. Rightly or wrongly it is part of my religious conviction that man may not eat meat, eggs,[343] and the like. There should be a limit even to the means of keeping ourselves alive. Even for life itself we may not do certain things. Religion, as I understand it, does not permit me to use meat *or eggs*[M3] for me or mine even   [M3] and the like
on occasions like this, and I must therefore take the risk

---

[341] 'started' in the first edition.

[342] 'but that' in the first edition.

[343] 'eggs,' added in the English translation.

that you say is likely. But I beg of you one thing. As I cannot avail myself of your treatment, I propose to try some hydropathic remedies which I happen to know. But I shall not know how to examine the boy's pulse, chest, lungs, etc. If you will kindly look in from time to time to examine him and keep me informed of his condition, I shall be grateful to you.'

The good doctor appreciated my difficulty and agreed to my request. Though Manilal could not have made his choice, I told him what had passed between the doctor and myself and asked him his opinion.

'Do try your hydropathic treatment,' he said. 'I will not have eggs or chicken broth.'

This made me glad, though I realized that, if I had given him either of these, he would have taken it.

I knew Kuhne's treatment[344] and had tried it too. I knew as well that fasting also could be tried with profit. So I began to give Manilal hip-baths according to Kuhne, never keeping him in the tub for more than three minutes, and kept him on orange juice mixed with water for three days.

But the temperature persisted, going up to 104°. At night he would be delirious. I began to get anxious. What would people say of me?[345] What would my elder brother think of me? Could we not call in another doctor? Why not have an Ayurvedic physician? What right had the parents to inflict their *fads*[M4] on their children?

I was haunted by thoughts like these. Then a contrary current would start. *God would surely be pleased to see that I was giving*[M5] the same treatment to my son as I would give myself. I had faith in hydropathy, and little

M4 unlettered intellect

M5 It would be enough for God that I gave

---

[344] Louis Kuhne (1835–1901), German naturopath and vegetarian, devised methods of cold water hydropathy to detoxify the body, author of *The New Science of Healing* (1899).

[345] 'if I were to lose the child' to add.

faith[346] in allopathy. The doctors could not *guarantee recovery*.[M6] At best they could experiment. The thread of life was in the hands of God. *Why not trust it to Him and in His name go on with what I thought was the right treatment?*[M7]

My mind was torn between these conflicting thoughts. It was night. I was in Manilal's bed lying by his side. I decided to give him a wet sheet pack. I got up, wetted a sheet,[347] wrung the water out of it and wrapped it about Manilal, keeping only his head out and then covered him with two blankets. To the head I applied a wet towel. The whole body was burning like hot iron, and quite parched. There was absolutely no perspiration.

I was sorely tired. I left Manilal in the[348] charge of his mother, and went out for a walk on Chaupati to refresh myself. It was about ten o'clock. Very few pedestrians were out. Plunged in deep thoughts, I scarcely looked at them. 'My honour is in Thy keeping, oh Lord, in this hour of trial,' I repeated to myself. Ramanama was on my lips. After a short time I returned, my heart beating within my breast.

No sooner had I entered the room than Manilal said, 'You have returned, Bapu?'

'Yes, darling.'[349]

'Do please pull me out. I am burning.'

'Are you perspiring, my boy?'

'I am simply soaked. Do please take me out.'

I felt his forehead. It was covered with beads of perspiration. The temperature was going down. I thanked God.

[M6] make a gift of life

[M7] In His name and with faith in Him, do not give up your path.

---

[346] 'faith' added in the 1940 edition.

[347] 'in cold water' to add.

[348] 'the' added in the 1940 edition.

[349] 'Bhai' in the original.

^{M8} Won't you perspire a little
more?

'Manilal, your fever is sure to go now. *A little more perspiration and then I will take you out.*'^{M8}

'Pray, no. Do deliver me from this furnace. Wrap me some other time if you like.'

I[350] just managed to keep him under the pack for a few minutes more by diverting him. The perspiration streamed down his forehead. I undid the pack and dried his body. Father and son fell asleep in the same bed.

^{M9} a great deal

And each slept *like a log.*^{M9} Next morning Manilal had much less fever. He went on thus for forty days on diluted milk and fruit juices. I had no fear now. It was an obstinate type of fever, but it had been got under control.

Today Manilal is the healthiest of my boys. Who can say whether his recovery was due to God's grace, or to hydropathy, or to careful dietary and nursing? Let everyone decide according to his own faith. For my part I was sure that God had saved my honour, and that belief remains unaltered to this day.

XXIII

TO SOUTH AFRICA AGAIN

Manilal was[351] restored to health, but I saw that the Girgaum house was not habitable. It was damp and ill-lighted. So in consultation with Shri Revashankar Jagjivan I decided to hire some well-ventilated bungalow in a suburb of Bombay. I wandered about in Bandra and Santa Cruz. The slaughter-house in Bandra prevented our choice falling there. Ghatkopar and places near it were too far from the sea. At last we hit upon a fine bungalow in Santa Cruz, which we hired as being the best from the point of view of sanitation.

---

[350] 'So reassured' to add at the beginning.

[351] 'was thus' in the first edition.

I took a first-class season ticket from Santa Cruz to Churchgate, and remember having frequently felt a certain pride in being the only first-class passenger in my compartment. Often I walked to Bandra in order to take the fast train from there direct to Churchgate.

I prospered in my profession better than I had expected. My South African clients often entrusted me with some work, and it *was*[M1] enough to enable me to pay my way.

[M1] seemed

I had not yet succeeded in securing any work in the High Court, but I attended the 'moot'[352] that used to be held in those days, though I never ventured to take part in it. I recall Jamiatram Nanabhai taking a prominent part. Like other fresh barristers I made a point of attending the hearing of cases in the High Court, more, I am afraid, for enjoying[353] the soporific breeze coming straight from the sea than for adding to my knowledge. I observed that I was not the only one to *enjoy this pleasure.*[M2] It seemed to be the fashion[354] and therefore nothing to be ashamed of.

[M2] doze off

However I began to make use of the High Court library and make fresh acquaintances and[355] felt that before long I should secure work in the High Court.

Thus whilst on the one hand I began to feel somewhat at ease about my profession, on the other hand Gokhale, whose eyes were always on me, had been busy making his own plans on my behalf. He peeped in

---

[352] 'moot' in the original. The original has *charcha* ('debate') within brackets. The word 'moot' has Scandinavian origins, meaning a meeting. The present usage is derived from the practice instituted by the Inns of Court in the sixteenth century where 'pupils' would present legal arguments on a given set of factual circumstances or legal points before senior lawyers or judges.

[353] 'a little snooze and' to add.

[354] 'fashion' English word in the original.

[355] 'and I' in the first edition.

at my chambers twice or thrice every week, often in company with friends whom he wanted me to know, and he kept me acquainted with his mode of work.

But it may be said that God has never allowed any of my own plans to stand. He has disposed them in His own way.

Just when I seemed to be settling down as I had intended, I received an unexpected cable from South Africa: 'Chamberlain expected here. Please return immediately.'[356] I remembered my promise and cabled to say that I should be ready to start the moment they put me in funds. They promptly responded, I gave up the chambers and started for South Africa.

I had an idea that the work there would keep me engaged for at least a year, so I kept the bungalow and *left my wife and*[M3] children there.

^{M3} thought it desirable to leave the

I believed then that enterprising youths who could not find an opening in the country should emigrate to other lands. I therefore took with me four or five such youths, one of whom was Maganlal Gandhi.[357]

The Gandhis were and are a big family. *I wanted to find out all those who wished to leave the trodden path and venture abroad.*[M4] My father used to accommodate a number of them in some State service. I wanted them

^{M4} I wanted those among them who desired to be independent to be encouraged to do so.

---

[356] The first message was received before 3 November 1902. 'Yes, I received a cablegram from Natal asking me if I could go to London and thence to the Transvaal. I replied "No" unless it was absolutely necessary . . . I have not heard in reply to the cable from me.' *CWMG*, vol. 3, p. 314. By 8 November a reply had been received with remittance of funds. On 14 November MKG conveyed his decision to Gokhale: 'When I was just feeling that I had settled down in Bombay, I received a message from Natal asking me to go there . . . I propose to leave by the first steamer available. That would be probably the 20th instant.' *CWMG*, vol. 3, p. 316.

[357] Maganlal Gandhi (1883–1928), son of Khushalchand Gandhi; the other person was Anandlal Amrutlal Gandhi, a solicitor. The two of them initially opened a shop at Tongat.

to be free from this spell. I neither could nor would secure other service for them;[358] I wanted them to be self-reliant.

But as my ideals advanced,[359] I tried to persuade these youths also to conform their ideals to mine, and I had the greatest success in guiding Maganlal Gandhi. But about this later.

The separation from wife and[360] children, the breaking up of a *settled establishment*,[M5] and the going from the certain to the uncertain—all this was for a moment painful, but I had inured myself to an uncertain life. I think it is wrong to expect certainties in this world, where all else but God that is Truth is an uncertainty. All that appears and happens about and around us is uncertain, transient. But there is a Supreme Being hidden therein as a certainty, *and one would be blessed if one could catch a glimpse of that Certainty and hitch one's waggon to it. The quest for that Truth is the summum bonum of life.*[M6]

I reached Durban not a day too soon.[361] There was work waiting for me. The date for the deputation to wait on Mr. Chamberlain had been fixed.[362] I had to draft the memorial to be submitted to him and accompany the deputation.[363]

[M5] carefully built nest

[M6] if one could have a glimpse of it, if one could have faith in it, only then would life be meaningful. The quest for this is the highest vocation.

---

[358] 'Not that I could secure other service for them, I would not even if I could.' In the first edition.

[359] '(so I presume)' to add.

[360] 'wife and' added in the English translation.

[361] MKG sailed from Bombay on 25 November 1902, reaching Durban on Christmas day.

[362] The date fixed was 26 December 1902, Friday—a day of prayer for many members of the delegation. MKG wrote to the mayor of Durban, expressing this difficulty and seeking a time for Saturday. The delegation waited upon Mr. Joseph Chamberlain, the Secretary of State for Colonies on Saturday 27 December.

[363] For the memorial, see *CWMG*, vol. 3, pp. 317–22.

PART IV

I

'LOVE'S LABOUR'S LOST'?

Mr. Chamberlain had come to *get a gift of*[M1] 35 million pounds from South Africa,[1] and to win the hearts of Englishmen and[2] Boers. So he gave a cold shoulder to the Indian deputation.

'You know,' he said, 'that the Imperial Government has *little*[M2] control over self-governing Colonies. Your grievances seem to be genuine. I shall do what I can, but you must try your best to placate the Europeans, if you wish to live in their midst.'

The reply cast a chill over the members of the deputation. I was also disappointed. It was an eye-opener for us all, and I saw that we should start with our work *de novo*.[3] I explained the situation to my colleagues.

As a matter of fact there was nothing wrong about Mr. Chamberlain's reply.[M3] It was well that he did not mince

[M1] take

[M2] only nominal

[M3] Was Mr. Chamberlain's response wrong?

---

[1] The main purpose of the visit was to obtain from South Africa a substantial contribution towards the ruinous cost of the war, which would have been levied as war indemnity. Given the policy of assimilation, the British did not wish to impose war indemnity. The British Imperial Government obtained a loan of £35,000,000 at 3 per cent rate of interest from British Transvaalers as an equitable return for the benefits they had obtained from the war.

[2] ', if possible,' to add.

[3] In the original a colloquial expression, *ekda ghuntva*, literally, to write and rewrite numerical 1.

matters. He had brought home to us in a rather gentle way the rule of might being right or[4] the law of the sword.

But sword we had none. We scarcely had the nerve and the muscle even to receive sword-cuts.

Mr. Chamberlain had given only a short time to the subcontinent.[M4] If Srinagar to Cape Comorin is 1,900 miles, Durban to Cape Town is not less than 1,100 miles, and Mr. Chamberlain had to cover the long distance at hurricane speed.

From Natal he hastened to the Transvaal. I had to prepare the case for the Indians there as well and submit it to him. But how was I to get to Pretoria? Our people there were not in a position to procure the necessary legal facilities for my getting to them in time. The war had reduced the Transvaal to a howling wilderness. There were neither provisions nor clothing available. Empty or closed shops were there, waiting to be replenished or opened, but that was a matter of time. Even refugees could not be allowed to return until the shops were ready with provisions. Every Transvaaler had therefore to obtain a permit. The European had no difficulty in getting one, but the Indian found it very hard.

During the war many officers and soldiers had come to South Africa from India and Ceylon, and it was considered to be the duty of the British authorities to provide for such of them as decided to settle there. They had in any event to appoint new officers, and these experienced men came in quite handy. The quick ingenuity of some of them created a new department. It showed their resourcefulness. There was a special department for the Negroes. Why then should there not be one for the Asiatics? The argument seemed to be quite plausible. When I reached the Transvaal, this new

[M4] Mr. Chamberlain was to stay for only a few weeks. South Africa is not a small province. It is a country, a continent. Africa consists of many sub-continents.

---

[4] 'the rule of might being right or' added in the English translation.

department had already been opened and was[5] gradually spreading its *tentacles*.[M5] The officers who issued permits to the returning refugees might issue them to all, but how could they do so in respect of the Asiatics without the intervention of the new department? And if the permits were to be issued on the recommendation of the new department, some of the responsibility and burden of the permit officers could thus be lessened. This was how they had argued. The fact, however, was that the new department wanted some apology for work, and the men wanted money. If there had been no work, the department would have been found unnecessary and would have been discontinued. So they found this work for themselves.

The Indians had to apply to this department. A reply would be vouchsafed many days after. And as there were large numbers wishing to return to the Transvaal, there grew up an army of intermediaries or[6] touts who, with the officers, looted the poor Indians to the tune of thousands. I was told that no permit could be had without influence and that in some cases one had to pay up to hundred pounds in spite of the influence which one might bring to bear. Thus there seemed to be no way open to me. I went to my old friend, the Police Superintendent of Durban, and said to him: 'Please introduce me to the Permit Officer and help me to obtain a permit. You know that I have been a resident of the Transvaal.' He immediately put on his hat, came out and secured me a permit. There was hardly an hour left before my train was to start. I had kept my luggage ready. I thanked Superintendent Alexander and started for Pretoria.[7]

[M5] net

---

[5] 'it was' in the first edition.

[6] 'an army of intermediaries or' added in the English translation.

[7] MKG probably left on 31 December 1902.

I now had a fair idea of the difficulties ahead. On reaching Pretoria I drafted the memorial.[8] In Durban I do not recollect the Indians having been asked to submit in advance the names of their representatives, but here there was the new department and it[9] asked to do so. The Pretoria Indians had already come to know that the officers wanted to exclude me.[10]

But another chapter is necessary for this painful though amusing incident.

II

AUTOCRATS[11] FROM ASIA

The officers at the head of the new department were at a loss to know how I had entered the Transvaal.[12] They inquired of the Indians[13] who used to go to them, but these could say nothing definite. The officers only ventured a guess that I might have succeeded in entering without a permit on the strength of my old connections. If that was the case, I was liable to be arrested!

---

[8] For the text of the memorial, see *CWMG*, vol. 3, pp. 325–29.

[9] 'so they were' in the first edition.

[10] On 6 January 1903 Sheth Tyeb Haji Khan Muhammad under his signature sent two representations drafted by MKG, one to the colonial secretary, Transvaal, and the other to the private secretary to the governor, urging them to permit 'Mr. Advocate M.K. Gandhi' on whose advice the Indians were being guided.

[11] 'Autocrats' translates 'nawabshahi', the rule/manners of the nawab.

[12] E.J. Burgess, earlier supervisor of Indian Immigrants, was now supervisor of Asiatics and Captain Hamilton Fowles was the chief secretary of permits and registrar of Asiatics.

[13] According to Pyarelal, one Sardar Ladha Singh was appointed as a secret agent to shadow MKG. See Pyarelal, *Mahatma Gandhi: The Birth of Satyagraha* (Ahmedabad: Navajivan, 1986), p. 10.

It is a general practice, on the termination of a big war, to invest the Government of the day with special powers.[14] This was the case in South Africa. The Government had passed a Peace Preservation Ordinance,[15] which[16] provided that anyone entering the Transvaal without a permit should be liable to arrest and imprisonment. The question of arresting me under this provision was mooted, but no one could summon up courage enough to ask me to produce my permit.[17]

The officers had of course sent telegrams to Durban, and when they found that I had entered with a permit, they were disappointed. But they were not the men to be defeated by such disappointment. Though I had succeeded in entering the Transvaal, they could still successfully prevent me from waiting on Mr. Chamberlain.

So the community was asked to submit the names of the representatives who were to form the Deputation. Colour prejudice was of course in evidence everywhere in South Africa, *but I was not prepared to find here the dirty and underhand dealing among officials that I was familiar with in India.*[M1] In South Africa the public departments were maintained for the good of the people and were responsible to public opinion. Hence officials in charge had a certain courtesy of manner and humility about them, and *coloured*[M2] people also got the benefit of it more or less. With the coming of the officers from Asia, came also its autocracy, *and the habits that the autocrats had imbibed there.*[M3] In South Africa there was a kind of responsible government or democracy, whereas the

[M1] but here I smelled the decay of dirt and corruption like in India

[M2] black- and yellow-skinned

[M3] its intrigues and other rottenness

---

[14] 'for a short time' to add.

[15] Peace Preservation Ordinance No. 38 of 1902.

[16] 'one clause of' to add before 'which'.

[17] There was no provision to interrogate a person on mere suspicion under the Ordinance.

commodity imported from Asia was autocracy pure and simple; *for the Asiatics had no responsible government, there being a foreign power governing them.*[M4] In South Africa the Europeans were settled emigrants. They had become South African citizens and had control over the departmental officers. But the autocrats from Asia now appeared on the scene, and the Indians in consequence found themselves between the devil and the deep sea.[18]

I had a fair taste of this autocracy. I was first summoned to see the chief of the department, an officer from Ceylon.[19] Lest I should appear to exaggerate when I say that I was 'summoned' to see the chief, I shall[20] make myself clear. No written order was sent to me. Indian leaders often had to visit the Asiatic officers. Among these was the late Sheth Tyeb Haji Khan Muhammad. The chief of the office asked him who I was and why I had come there.

'He is our adviser,' said Tyeb Sheth, 'and he has come here at our request.'

'Then what are we here for? Have we not been appointed to protect you? What can Gandhi know of the conditions here?' asked the *autocrat.*[M5]

Tyeb Sheth answered the charge as best he could: 'Of course you are there. But Gandhi is our man. He knows our language and understands us. You are after all officials.'

The Sahib ordered Tyeb Sheth to fetch me before him. I went to the Sahib in company with Tyeb Sheth and others. No seats were offered, we were all kept standing.

[M4] for in Asia people had no power, there was only power over people

[M5] Sahib.

---

[18] 'between devil and the deep sea': In the original, there is the idiomatic expression *sudi vacche sopari*, literally, 'like a betel nut in a nutcracker'.

[19] Assistant colonial secretary, W.H. Moor, formerly of the Ceylon Civil Service.

[20] 'would' in the first edition.

'What brings you here?' said the Sahib addressing me.

'I have come here at the request of my fellow-countrymen to help them with my advice,' I replied.

'But don't you know that you have no right to come here? The permit you hold was given you by mistake. You cannot be regarded as a domiciled Indian. You must go back. You shall not wait on Mr. Chamberlain. It is for the protection of the Indians here that the Asiatic Department has been especially created. Well, you may go.' With this he bade me good-bye, giving me no opportunity for a reply.

But he detained my companions. He gave them a sound scolding and advised them to send me away.

They returned *chagrined*.^M6 We were now confronted with an unexpected situation.

M6 embittered

III

POCKETED THE INSULT^M1

M1 Swallowed the Bitter Draught

I smarted under the insult, but as I had pocketed many such in the past, I had become inured to them. I therefore decided to forget this latest one and take what course a dispassionate view of the case might suggest.

We had a letter from the Chief of the Asiatic Department to the effect that, as I had seen Mr. Chamberlain in Durban, it had been found necessary to omit my name from the Deputation which was to wait on him.

The letter was more than my co-workers could bear. They proposed to drop the idea of the Deputation altogether. I pointed out to them the awkward situation of the community.

'If you do not represent your case before Mr. Chamberlain,' said I, 'it will be presumed that you have

M2 hardships

no *case*[M2] at all. After all, the representation has to be made in writing, and we have got it ready. It does not matter in the least whether I read it or someone else reads it. Mr. Chamberlain is not going to argue the matter with us. I am afraid, we must swallow the insult.'

I had scarcely finished speaking when Tyeb Sheth cried out, 'Does not an insult to you amount to an insult to the community? How can we forget that you are our representative?'

'Too true,' said I. 'But even the community will have to pocket insults like these. Have we any alternative?'

'Come what may, why should we swallow a fresh insult? Nothing worse can possibly happen to us. Have we many rights to lose?' asked Tyeb Sheth.

M3 I liked this

It was a[M3] spirited reply, but of what avail was it?[21] I was fully conscious of the limitations of the community. I pacified my friends and advised them to have, in my place,[22] Mr. George Godfrey, an Indian barrister.

So Mr. Godfrey led the Deputation.[23] Mr. Chamberlain referred in his reply to my exclusion. 'Rather than hear the same representative over and over again, is it not better to have someone new?' he said, and tried to heal the wound.

But all this, far from ending the matter, only added to the work of the community and also to mine. We had to start afresh.

'It is at your instance that the community helped in the war, and you see the result now,' were the words with which some people taunted me. But the taunt had

---

[21] 'I liked the spirited reply, but I also knew that the spirit was of no avail.' In the first edition.

[22] 'the late' to add.

[23] The deputation waited upon Mr. Chamberlain on 7 January 1903.

no effect. 'I do not regret my advice,' said I. 'I maintain that we did well in taking part in the war. In doing so we simply did our duty. We may not look forward to any reward[24] for our labours, but it is my firm conviction that all good action is bound to bear fruit in the end. Let us forget the past and think of the task before us.' With which the rest agreed.

I added: 'To tell you the truth, the work for which you had called me is practically finished. But I believe I ought not to leave the Transvaal, so far as it is possible, even if you permit me to return home.[25] Instead of carrying on my work from Natal, as before, I must now do so from here. I must no longer think of returning to India within a year, but must get enrolled in the Transvaal Supreme Court. I have confidence enough to deal with this new department. If we do not do this, the community will be hounded out of the country, besides being thoroughly robbed. Every day it will have fresh insults heaped upon it. The facts that Mr. Chamberlain refused to see me and that the official insulted me, are nothing before the humiliation of the whole community. *It will become impossible to put up with the veritable dog's life that we shall be expected to lead.'*[M4]

[M4] We cannot tolerate that we would live like dogs here.

So I set the ball rolling,[26] discussed things with Indians in Pretoria and Johannesburg, and ultimately decided to set up office in Johannesburg.

It was indeed doubtful whether I would be enrolled in the Transvaal Supreme Court. But the Law Society

---

[24] 'reaping the reward' in the first edition.

[25] MKG was uncertain about his plans at least till 6 February 1903. He wrote to Chhaganlal Gandhi, 'There is a great uncertainty about me. Despite my best efforts, I am not in a position to give you more satisfactory news . . . It is no bed of roses here. I cannot offer more definite news.' *CWMG*, vol. 3, p. 336.

[26] 'set the ball rolling,' added in the English translation.

did not oppose my application, and the Court allowed it.[27] It was difficult for an Indian to secure rooms for office in a suitable locality. But I had come in fairly close contact with Mr. Ritch,[28] who was then one of the merchants there. Through the good offices of a house agent known to him, I succeeded in securing suitable rooms for my office in *the legal quarters*[M5] of the city, and I started on my professional work.[29]

M5 a good locality

---

[27] MKG enrolled as an attorney and not as an advocate. Under the Administration of Justice Proclamation, a legal practitioner had to make this choice; advocates had 'right to audience' in all courts, while attorneys had a limited right to audience. The attorneys were like solicitors. MKG filed the petition to be admitted to the Supreme Court of Transvaal on 31 March 1903, which was granted on 14 April 1903. He was administered the oath as an attorney by Mr. Justice Wessels. See DiSalvo, *M.K. Gandhi, Attorney at Law*, p. 162. The Law Society did scrutinize MKG's application but under the provisions could not bring itself to oppose it. Their minutes bear this out: 're-Admission: M.K. Gandhi. It was reported that this gentleman, who is an Indian, has been admitted as an Attorney of the Supreme Court of this Colony, but as his qualifications were sufficient and as there was nothing in the Administration of Justice Proclamation against admission of such persons, the Council did not think anything could be done in the matter'. Ibid., p. 163.

[28] Lewis Walter Ritch, articled clerk under MKG, in 1902 manager of a commercial firm, later passed his Bar examinations in London, Hon. Secretary of the South African British Committee set up in 1906, was solicitor in MKG's office from 1911.

[29] Lewis Ritch and estate agent C.H. Kew found Court Chambers on 15, Rissik Street, adjacent to the High Court and the magistrate's court located in Government Square. Eric Itzkin, in *Gandhi's Johannesburg: Birthplace of Satyagraha*, has shown that till 1904 MKG occupied Nos. 25 and 26 Court Chambers, in 1908 he occupied 21 to 24 Court Chambers (p. 13). MKG lived in rented rooms behind the chambers at the southern end of Rissik Street. Joseph Doke describes the interiors of the chambers: 'The office, at the corner of Rissik and Anderson streets, I found to be like any other offices . . . The first room was given up to a lady-typist; the second, into which I was ushered, was the Sanctum Sanctorum. It was meagerly furnished and dusty. A few pictures were scattered along the walls. They were chiefly photographs

IV

QUICKENED SPIRIT OF SACRIFICE

Before I narrate[30] the struggle for the *Indian settlers*'[M1] rights in the Transvaal and their dealings[31] with the Asiatic Department, I must turn to some other aspects of my life.

Up to now there had been in me a mixed desire. The spirit of self-sacrifice was tempered by the desire to lay by something for the future.[M2]

About the time I took up chambers in Bombay, an American insurance agent had come there—a man with a pleasing countenance and a sweet tongue. As though we were old friends he discussed my future welfare.[32] 'All men of your status in America have their lives insured. Should you not also insure yourself against the future? Life is uncertain. We in America regard it as a religious obligation to get insured. Can I not tempt you to take out a small policy?'[33]

Up to this time I had *given the cold shoulder to all*[M3] the agents I had met in South Africa and India, for I had thought that life assurance implied fear and want of faith in God. But now I succumbed to the temptation of the American agent. As he proceeded with his argument, I had before my mind's eye a

[M1] community's

[M2] Hitherto there was in me a desire to accumulate wealth, service to others was mixed with self-interest.

[M3] not given into any of

---

of no great merit. The Indian Stretcher Bearers Corps was in evidence—photographs of Mrs. Besant, Sir William Wilson Hunter, and Justice Ranade—several separate Indian portraits— and a beautiful picture of Jesus Christ. Some indifferent chairs, and shelves filled with law books completed the inventory.' Doke, *Gandhi: A Patriot in South Africa*, p. 10.

[30] 'Before I proceed with my narrative of' in the first edition.

[31] 'and of the dealings' in the first edition.

[32] 'discussed with me matters for' in the first edition.

[33] 'policy' English word in the original.

picture of my wife and children. 'Man, you have
sold almost all the ornaments of your wife,' I said
to myself. 'If something were to happen to you, the
burden of supporting her and the children would fall
on your poor brother, who has so nobly filled the
place of father. How would that become you?' With
these and similar arguments I persuaded myself to take
out a policy for Rs. 10,000.

But when my mode of life changed in South
Africa, my outlook changed too.[34] All the steps I took
at this time of trial were taken *in the name of God and
for His service*.[M4] I did not know how long I should
have to stay in South Africa. I had a fear that I might
never be able to get back to India; so I decided to
keep my wife and[35] children with me and earn enough
to support them.[36] This plan[37] made me deplore the
life policy and feel ashamed of having been caught in
the net of insurance agent. If, I said to myself, my
brother is really in the position of my father, surely he
would not consider it too much of a burden to support
my widow, if it came to that. And what reason had
I to assume that death would claim me earlier than
the others? After all the real protector was neither I
nor my brother, but the Almighty. In getting my life
insured I had robbed my wife and children of their
self-reliance. Why should they not be expected to take
care of themselves? What happened to the families of
the numberless poor in the world? Why should I not
count myself as one of them?

[M4] with God as witness

---

[34] 'But the changed mode of my life in South Africa altered my
outlook.' In the first edition.

[35] 'wife and' added in the English translation.

[36] '. . . India and so I had decided that I should have . . . with me and
no longer impose separation upon them, and that I should earn
enough to support them.' In the first edition.

[37] 'This train of reasoning' in the first edition.

A multitude of such[38] thoughts passed through my mind, but I did not immediately act upon them. I recollect having paid at least one insurance premium in South Africa.

Outward circumstances too supported this train of thought. During my first sojourn in South Africa it was[39] Christian influence that had kept alive in me the religious sense. Now it was theosophical influence that added strength to it. Mr. Ritch was a theosophist and put me in touch with the Society at Johannesburg. I never became a member, as I had my differences, but I came in close contact with almost every theosophist.[40] I had religious discussions with them every day. There used to be readings from theosophical books and sometimes I had occasion to address their meetings.[41] The chief thing about theosophy is to cultivate and promote the idea of brotherhood. We had considerable discussion over this, and I criticized the members where their conduct did not appear to me to square with their ideal. The criticism was not without its wholesome effect on me. It led to introspection.[42]

---

[38] 'such' added in the 1940 edition.

[39] 'had been' in the first edition.

[40] The group of theosophists included Miss Bissicks (who ran the Alexandra Tea Room), Lewis Ritch, Herbert Kitchin, an engineer who settled at the Phoenix, Lewis Playford, the chief magistrate of Johannesburg, and William Wyberg, the commissioner of mines. Itzkin, *Gandhi's Johannesburg*, p. 21.

[41] MKG lectured on Hinduism to the Johannesburg Lodge of the Theosophical Society on 18 August 1903; the meeting took place at the Masonic Hall on 95, Jeppe Street (ibid.). In March 1905 MKG gave four lectures on religion at the invitation of the Theosophical Society. The lectures were held at the Masonic Temple, then located at 80, Plein Street. *The Star* of 10 March 1905 reported on the speech (ibid., p. 25).

[42] 'self-introspection' in the first edition.

V

RESULT OF INTROSPECTION

When, in 1893, I came in close contact with Christian
friends, I was a mere novice. They tried hard[43] to bring
home to me, and make me accept, the message of *Jesus*,[M1]
and I was a humble and respectful listener with an open
mind. At that time I naturally studied Hinduism to the
best of my ability and endeavoured to understand other
religions.

In 1903 the position was somewhat changed.
Theosophist friends certainly intended to draw me
into their society, but that was with a view to getting
something from me as a Hindu. Theosophical literature
is replete with Hindu influence, and so these friends
expected that I should be helpful[44] to them. I explained
that my Samskrit study was not much to speak of, that
I had not read the[45] Hindu scriptures in the original,
and that even my acquaintance with the translations[46]
was of the slightest. But being believers[47] in *samskara*
(tendencies caused by[48] previous births) and *punarjanma*
(rebirth), they assumed that I should be able to render
at least some help. And so I felt like a Triton among
the minnows.[49] I started reading Swami Vivekananda's
Rajayoga[50] with some of these friends and M.N.

M1 the Bible

---

[43] 'were trying hard' in the first edition.

[44] 'very helpful' in the first edition.

[45] 'ancient' to add.

[46] 'them through translations' in the first edition.

[47] 'being believers as they were' in the first edition.

[48] 'impressions of' in the first edition.

[49] 'Triton among the minnows' is a line from Shakespeare's *Coriolanus*,
Act III, scene 1. It translates the original idiomatic expression 'in a
land bereft of trees, a castor-bean plant is the prime minister'.

[50] Interpretation of Patanjali's *Yoga Sutra*, first published in 1896.

Dvivedi's[51] *Rajayoga* with others. I had to read Patanjali's *Yoga Sutras* with one friend and the *Bhagavad Gita* with quite a number. We formed a sort of Seekers' Club where we had regular readings. I already had faith in the *Gita*, which had a fascination for me. Now I realized the necessity of diving deeper into it. I had[52] one or two translations, by means of which I tried to understand the original Samskrit. I decided also to get by heart one or two verses every day. For this purpose I employed the time of my morning ablutions. The operation took me thirty-five minutes,[53] fifteen minutes for the tooth brush and twenty for the bath. The first I used to do standing in western fashion. So on the wall opposite I stuck slips of paper on which were written the *Gita* verses and referred to them now and then to help my memory.[54] This time was found sufficient for memorizing the daily portion and recalling the verses already learnt. I remember having thus committed to memory thirteen chapters. But the memorizing of the *Gita* had to give way to other work[55] and the creation and nurture of satyagraha,[56] which absorbed all my thinking time, as the latter may be said to be doing even now.

What effect this reading of the *Gita* had on my friends[57] only they can say, but to me the *Gita* became an infallible guide of conduct. *It became my dictionary of daily reference.*[M2] Just as I turned to the English dictionary

[M2] That book became for me a spiritual reference.

---

[51] Manibhai Nabhubhai Dwivedi (1858–98), philosopher, poet, for some time professor of philosophy at Samaldas College, Bhavnagar. His *Rajyoga* was published in 1885.

[52] 'had with me' in the first edition.

[53] 'The operation took me thirty-five minutes' added in the English translation.

[54] 'I repeated them during the bath.' To add.

[55] 'the increase of other work' in the first edition.

[56] 'birth and nursing of satyagraha' in the first edition.

[57] 'Gita had on the friends with whom I read it,' in the first edition.

M3 I turned to Gitaji for
difficulties in mode of conduct
and other such conundrums

for the meanings of[58] English words that I did not understand, *I turned to this dictionary of conduct for a ready solution of all my troubles and trials.*[M3] Words like *aparigraha* (non-possession) and *samabhava* (equability) gripped me. How to cultivate and preserve that equability was the question. How was one to treat alike[59] insulting, insolent and corrupt officials, co-workers of yesterday raising meaningless opposition, and men who had always been good to one? How was one to divest oneself of all possessions? Was not the body itself possession enough? Were not wife and children possessions? Was I to destroy all the cupboards of books I had? Was I to give up all[60] I had and follow Him? Straight came the answer: I could not follow Him unless I gave up all I had. My study of English law came to my help. Snell's discussion of the maxims of Equity came to my memory. I understood more clearly in the light of the *Gita* teaching the implication of the word 'trustee'.[61] My regard for jurisprudence increased, I discovered in it religion. I understood the *Gita* teaching of non-possession to mean that those who desired salvation should act like the trustee who, though having control over great possessions, regards not an iota of them as his own. It became clear to me as daylight that non-possession and equability presupposed a change of heart, a change of attitude. I then wrote to Revashankerbhai to allow the insurance policy to lapse and get whatever could be recovered or else to regard the premiums already paid as lost, for I had become convinced that God, who created my wife and children as well as

---

[58] 'the meanings of' added in the 1940 edition.

[59] 'What was the meaning of making no distinction between' in the first edition.

[60] 'Was I to burn my boats, give up all' in the first edition.

[61] 'trustee' English word in the original. The Gujarati language does not have a word for trustee.

myself, would take care of them. To my brother, who had been as father to me, I wrote explaining that I had given[62] him all that I had saved up to that moment, but that henceforth he should expect nothing from me, for future savings,[63] if any, would be utilized for the benefit of the community.[64]

I could not easily make my brother understand this. In stern language he explained to me my duty towards him. I should not, he said, aspire to be wiser than our father. I must support the family as he did. I pointed out to him that I was doing exactly what our father had done. The meaning of[65] 'family' had but to be slightly widened and the wisdom of my step would become clear.

My brother gave me up and practically stopped all communication.[66] I was deeply distressed, but it would have been a greater distress to give up what I considered to be my duty, and I preferred the lesser. But that did not affect my devotion to him,[67] which remained as pure and great as ever. His great[68] love for me was at the root of his misery. He did not so much want my money as that I should be well-behaved towards the family. Near the end of his life, however, he appreciated my view-point. When almost on his death-bed, he realized that my step had been right and wrote me a most pathetic letter. He apologized to me, if indeed a father may apologize to his son. He commended his sons to my care, to be brought up as I thought fit, and expressed his impatience to meet

---

[62] 'always offered' in the first edition.

[63] 'all future savings' in the first edition.

[64] See *CWMG*, vol. 6, pp. 430–35.

[65] 'It only needed that the meaning of' in the first edition.

[66] 'communication with me' in the first edition.

[67] 'my brother' in the first edition.

[68] 'excessive' in the first edition.

me. He cabled[69] that he would like to come to South
Africa and I cabled in reply that he could. But that was
not to be. Nor could his desire as regards his sons be
fulfilled. He died *before he could start for South Africa.*[M4]
His sons had been brought up in the old atmosphere and
could not change their course of life. I could not draw
them to me. It was not their fault. 'Who can say thus
far, no further, to the tide of his own nature?' Who can
erase the impressions[70] with which he is born? It is idle to
expect one's children and wards necessarily to follow the
same course of evolution as oneself.

M4 in India

This instance to some extent serves to show what a
terrible responsibility it is to be a parent.

VI

A SACRIFICE TO VEGETARIANISM

As the ideals of sacrifice and simplicity *were becoming
more and more realized,*[M1] and the religious consciousness
was becoming more and more quickened in my daily
life, the passion for vegetarianism as a mission went
on increasing. I have known only one way of carrying
on missionary[71] work, viz., by personal example and
discussion with searchers for knowledge.

M1 grew

There was in Johannesburg a vegetarian restaurant
conducted by a German[72] who believed in Kuhne's
hydropathic treatment. I visited[73] the restaurant myself

---

[69] 'cabled to me' in the first edition.

[70] 'indelible impressions' in the first edition.

[71] 'missionary' translates 'prachar', literally, propaganda.

[72] This restaurant was run by Adolf Ziegler. Pyarelal, *The Birth of Satyagraha*, vol. III, p. 358.

[73] 'began visiting' in the first edition.

and helped it by taking English friends there. But I saw that it could not last as[74] it was always in financial difficulties. I assisted it as much as I thought it deserved, and spent some money on it, but it had ultimately to be closed down.

Most theosophists are vegetarians more or less, and an enterprising lady belonging to that society now came upon the scene with a vegetarian restaurant on a grand scale.[75] She was fond of art, extravagant and ignorant[76] of accounts. Her circle of friends was fairly large. She had started in a small way, but later decided to extend the venture by taking large rooms, and asked me for help. I knew nothing of her finances when she thus approached me, but I took it that her estimate must be fairly accurate. And I was in a position to accommodate her. My clients used to keep large sums as deposits with me. Having received the consent of one of these clients,[77] I lent about a thousand pounds from the amount to his credit. This client was most large-hearted and trusting. He had originally come to South Africa as an indentured labourer. He said: 'Give away the money, if you like. I know nothing in these matters. I only know you.'[78] His name was Badri. He afterwards took a prominent

---

[74] 'could not last for any length of time as' in the first edition.

[75] Miss Ada Bissicks. The restaurant, located on the first floor of Livingstone Building, 18 Rissik Street, was named The Alexandra Tea Room. Eric Itzkin, *Gandhi's Johannesburg*, p. 11. H.S.L. Polak met MKG in this tea room. For MKG's letter to Miss Bissicks, see *CWMG*, vol. 5, p. 33.

[76] 'knew little' in the first edition.

[77] This was Budree Ahir, originally from Bihar, arrived as an indentured labourer in 1881; after completion of his indenture amassed considerable property in the Transvaal, was part of the deputation that saw Mr. Chamberlain; a satyagrahi, arrested on 25 September 1913 and again on 30 September 1913; sentenced to three months of hard labour.

[78] These lines are in Hindustani in the original.

part in satyagraha, and suffered imprisonment as well. So I advanced the loan assuming that this consent was enough.

In two or three months' time I came to know that the amount would not be recovered. I could ill afford to sustain such a loss. There were many other purposes to which I could have applied this amount. The loan was never repaid. But how could trusting Badri be allowed to suffer? He had known me only. I made good the loss.

A client friend to whom I spoke about this transaction sweetly chid me for my folly.

'Bhai,'—I had fortunately not yet become 'Mahatma', nor even 'Bapu' (father), friends[79] used to call me by the loving name of 'Bhai' (brother)—said he, 'this was not for you to do. *We depend upon you in so many things*.[M2] You are not going to get back this amount. I know you will never allow Badri to come to grief, for you will pay him out of your pocket, but if you go on helping your reform schemes by operating on your clients' money, the poor fellows will be ruined, and you will soon become a beggar.[80] *But you are our trustee and must know that, if you become a beggar, all our public work will come to a stop*.[M3]'

[M2] We are guided by our confidence in you.

[M3] As a result your public work would suffer.

The friend, I am thankful to say, is still alive. I have not yet come across a purer man than he, in South Africa or anywhere else. I have known him to apologize to people and to cleanse himself, when, having happened to suspect them, he had found his suspicion to be unfounded.

I saw that he had rightly warned me. For though I made good Badri's loss, I should not have been able to meet[81] any similar loss and should have been driven to incur debt—a thing I have never done in my life and always abhorred. I realized that even a man's reforming

---

[79] 'client friends' in the original.

[80] 'and sit at home' to add.

[81] 'able to find another thousand pounds for any similar loss' in the first edition.

zeal ought not to make him exceed his limits. I also saw that in thus lending trust-money I had disobeyed the cardinal teaching of the *Gita*, viz., the duty of a man of equipoise to act without desire for the fruit. The error became for me a beaconlight of warning.

The sacrifice offered on the altar of vegetarianism was neither intentional nor expected. It was a virtue of necessity.

VII

EXPERIMENTS IN EARTH AND WATER TREATMENT

With the growing simplicity of my life, my dislike for medicines steadily increased. While practising in Durban, I suffered for some time from debility and rheumatic inflammation. Dr. P.J. Mehta,[82] who had come to *see me*,[M1] gave me treatment, and I got well. After that, up to the time when I returned to India, I do not remember having suffered from an ailment to speak of.

[M1] take me back

But I used to be troubled with constipation and frequent headaches, while at Johannesburg. I kept myself fit with occasional laxatives and a well-regulated diet. But I could hardly call myself healthy, and always wondered when I should get free from the incubus of these laxative medicines.

About this time I read of the formation of a 'No Breakfast Association'[83] in Manchester. The argument of the promoters was that Englishmen ate too often and too much, that their doctors' bills were heavy because they ate until midnight, and that they should at least

---

[82] Dr. P.J. Mehta visited MKG in 1898.

[83] This association probably owes its origins to Dr. Edward Hooker Dewey (1837–1904) who in 1900 published *The No-Breakfast Plan and the Fasting Cure* (London: L.N. Fowler and Co., 1900).

give up breakfast, if they wanted to improve this state of affairs. Though all these things could not be said of me, I felt that the argument did partly apply in my case. I used to have three square meals daily in addition to afternoon tea. I was never a spare eater and enjoyed as many delicacies as could be had with a vegetarian and spiceless diet. I scarcely ever got up before six or seven. I therefore argued that, if I also dropped the morning breakfast, I might become free from headaches. So I tried the experiment. For a few days it was rather hard, but the headache entirely disappeared. This led me to conclude that I was eating more than I needed.

But the change was far from relieving me of constipation. I tried Kuhne's hip-baths, which gave some relief but did not completely cure me. In the meantime the German who had a vegetarian restaurant, or some other friend, I forget who, placed in my hands Just's *Return to Nature*.[84] In this book I read about earth treatment. The author also advocated fresh fruit and nuts as the natural diet of man. I did not at once take to the exclusive fruit diet, but immediately began experiments in earth treatment, and with wonderful results. The treatment consisted in applying to the abdomen a bandage of clean earth moistened with cold water and spread like a poultice on fine[85] linen. This I applied at bed-time, removing it during the night or in the morning, whenever I happened to wake up. *It proved a radical cure.*[M2] Since then I have tried the treatment on myself and my *friends and never had reason to regret it.*[M3] In India I have not been able to try this treatment with equal confidence. For one thing,[86] I have never had time to settle down in one place to conduct the experiments.

[M2] It cured me of my constipation.

[M3] associates, and I can scarcely remember it failing on someone

---

[84] Adolf Just (1859–1936), *Return to Nature: Paradise Regained*, translated into English in 1903.

[85] ', wet' to add.

[86] 'For one thing,' added in the English translation.

But my faith in the earth and water treatment remains practically the same as before. Even today I give myself the earth treatment to a certain extent and recommend it to my co-workers, whenever occasion arises.

Though I have had two serious illnesses in my life, I believe that man has little need to drug himself. 999 cases out of a thousand can be brought round by means of a well-regulated diet, water and earth treatment and similar household remedies. He who runs to the doctor, *vaidya* or *hakim for every little ailment,*[M4] and swallows all kinds of vegetable and mineral drugs, not only curtails his life, but, by becoming the slave of his body instead of remaining its master, loses self-control, and ceases to be a man.

Let no one discount these observations because they are being written in a sick-bed.[87] I know the reasons for my illnesses.[88] I am fully conscious that I alone am responsible for them, and it is because of that consciousness that I have not lost patience. In fact I have thanked God for them as lessons and successfully resisted the temptation of taking numerous drugs. I know my obstinacy often tries my doctors, but they kindly bear with me and do not give me up.

However, I must not digress.[M5] Before proceeding further, I should give the reader a word of warning. Those who purchase Just's book on the strength of this chapter should not take everything in it to be gospel truth.[89] A writer almost always presents one aspect of a case, whereas every case can be seen from no less than

[M4] at every moment

[M5] I should not prolong the description of my present condition. Hence, we turn towards the period of 1904–05.

---

[87] This chapter appeared in *Navajivan* on 26 June 1927, when MKG was suffering from high blood pressure.

[88] In Gujarati, *Mari jindagi na karano hu janu chu.* MD's translation brings clarity, but a literal translation would be 'I know the reasons of my life.'

[89] 'gospel truth' translates *veda vakya,* literally, 'a statement from the Veda'.

seven points of view, all of which are probably correct by themselves, but not correct at the same time and in the same circumstances. And then many books are written with a view to gaining customers and earning name and fame. Let those, therefore, who read such books as these do so with discernment, and take advice of some experienced man before trying any of the experiments set forth, or let them read the books with patience and digest them thoroughly before acting upon them.

VIII

A WARNING

I am afraid I must continue the digression until the next chapter. Along with my experiments in earth treatment, those in dietetics were also being carried on, and it may not be out of place here to make a few observations as regards the latter, though I shall have occasion to refer to them again later.

I may not, now or hereafter, enter into a detailed account of the experiments in dietetics,[90] for I did so in a series of Gujarati articles which appeared years ago in *Indian Opinion*, and which were afterwards published in the form of a book popularly known in English as *A Guide to Health*.[91] Among my little books this has been

---

[90] 'and my views on the subject' to add.

[91] 'General Knowledge about Health', a series of thirty-four articles spread over *CWMG*, vols 11 and 12. These were later translated into Hindi and based on the Hindi version was *A Guide to Health*, an English adaption by A. Rama Iyer, published by S. Ganesan, Madras, in July 1921. In August–December 1942, during his imprisonment at the Aga Khan Palace, Poona, MKG wrote in Gujarati what became in Dr. Sushila Nayar's translation *A Key to Health*, published by Navajivan in 1948. This book, according

the most widely read alike in the East and in the West, a thing that I have not yet been able to understand. It was written for the benefit of the readers of *Indian Opinion*. But I know that the booklet has profoundly influenced the lives of many, both in the East and in the West, who have never seen *Indian Opinion*.[92] For they have been corresponding with me on the subject. It has therefore appeared necessary to say something here about the booklet, for though I see no reason to alter the views set forth in it, yet I have made certain radical changes in my actual practice, of which all readers of the book do not know, and of which, I think, they should be informed.

The booklet was written, like all my other writings, with a spiritual end, which has always inspired every one of my actions, and therefore it is a matter for deep distress[93] to me that I am unable today to practise some of the theories propounded in the book.

It is my firm conviction that man need take no milk at all, beyond the mother's milk that he takes as a baby. His diet should consist of nothing but sunbaked fruits and nuts. He can secure enough nourishment both for the *tissues and the nerves*[M1] from fruits like grapes and nuts like almonds. Restraint of the sexual and other passions becomes easy for a man who lives on such food. My co-workers and I have seen by experience that there is much truth in the Indian proverb that as a man eats, so shall he become.[94] These views have been set out elaborately in the book.

[M1] body and the mind

---

to MKG, though not based on *Indian Opinion* articles, did not fundamentally differ from them.

[92] 'both in the East and in the West, who have never seen *Indian Opinion*' added in the English translation.

[93] 'and shame' to add.

[94] In the original there are two proverbs, the other translates as 'a man burps as he eats.'

But unfortunately in India I have found myself obliged to deny some of my theories in practice. Whilst I was engaged on the recruiting campaign in Kheda, an error in diet laid me low, and I was at death's door.[95] I tried in vain to rebuild a shattered constitution without milk. I sought the help of the doctors, *vaidyas* and[96] scientists whom I knew, to recommend a substitute for milk. Some suggested *mung* water, some *mowhra* oil, some almond-milk. I wore out my body in experimenting on these, but nothing could help me to leave the sick-bed. The *vaidyas* read verses to me from Charaka[97] to show that religious scruples about diet have no place in therapeutics. So they could not be expected to help me to continue to live without milk. And how could those who recommended beef-tea and brandy[98] without hesitation help me to persevere with a milkless diet?

I might not take cow's or buffalo's milk, as I was bound by a vow. The vow of course meant the giving up of all milks, but as I had mother cow's and mother buffalo's only in mind when I took the vow, and as I wanted to live, I somehow beguiled myself into emphasizing the letter of the vow and decided to take goat's milk.[99] I was fully conscious, when I started

---

[95] This was in August 1918; in a letter of 12 August he wrote, 'Nor did I exercise self-restraint in deciding what to eat; I ate *ghens*. If I had taken vegetable soup only, the painful result would certainly not have followed. Today I am too weak to get up or walk.' *CWMG*, vol. 15, p. 18.

[96] 'chemical' to add.

[97] The *Charaka Samhita*, a foundational text of Ayurveda, consists of eight books and 120 chapters. Its date of composition is uncertain, dated between the fourth century BC and second century AD.

[98] 'beef-tea' and 'brandy', English words in the original.

[99] This was a suggestion made by Kasturba. MKG wrote in a letter; 'Only four days ago, she was making herself miserable about milk, and, on the impulse of the moment, asked me why, if I might not

taking mother goat's milk, that the spirit of my vow was destroyed.

But the idea of leading a campaign against the Rowlatt Act[100] had possessed me. And with it grew the desire to live. Consequently one of the greatest experiments in my life came to a stop.

I know it is argued that the soul has nothing to do with what one eats or drinks, as the soul neither eats nor drinks; that it is not what you put inside from without, but what you express outwardly from within, that matters. There is, no doubt, some force in this. But rather than examine this reasoning, I shall content myself with merely declaring my firm conviction that, for the seeker who would live in fear of God and who would see Him face to face, *restraint in diet both as to quantity and quality is as essential as restraint in thought and speech.*[M2]

In a matter, however, where my theory has failed me, *I should not only give the information, but issue a grave warning against adopting it.*[M3] I would therefore urge those who, on the strength of the theory propounded by me, may have given up milk, not to persist in the experiment, unless they find it beneficial in every way, or unless they are advised by experienced physicians. Up to now my experience here has shown me that for those with a weak digestion and for those who are confined to bed there is no light and nourishing diet equal to that of milk.

I should be greatly obliged if *anyone*[M4] with experience in this line, who happens to read this chapter,

[M2] the choice with regard to diet—both its acceptance and rejection—is as essential as the choice—both its acceptance and rejection—of thought and speech

[M3] I should not only not advise them to follow it but actively dissuade them from doing so

[M4] any vaidya, doctor, *hakim* or anybody else

---

take cow's milk, I would not take goat's milk. This went home.' *CWMG*, vol. 15, pp. 70–71.

[100] The Anarchical and Revolutionary Crimes Act, 1919—based on Justice S.A.T. Rowlatt Committee's (1918) recommendation and passed by the Imperial Legislative Council—extended indefinitely measures of preventive detention, incarceration without trial and judicial review enacted under the Defence of India Act, 1915.

would tell me, if he has known from experience, and not from reading, of a vegetable substitute for milk, which is equally nourishing and digestible.

IX

A TUSSLE WITH POWER

To turn now to the Asiatic Department.

Johannesburg was the stronghold of the Asiatic officers. I had been observing that, far from protecting the Indians, Chinese and others, these officers were grinding them down.[101] Every day I had complaints like this: 'The rightful ones are not admitted, whilst those who have no right are smuggled in on payment of £100. If you will not remedy this state of things, who will?' I shared the feeling. If I did not succeed in stamping out this evil, I should be living in the Transvaal in vain.

So I began to collect evidence, and as soon as I had gathered a fair amount, I approached the Police Commissioner. He appeared to be a[102] just man. Far from *giving me the cold shoulder*,[M1] he listened to me patiently and asked me to show him all the evidence in my possession. He examined the witnesses himself and was satisfied, but he knew as well as I that it was difficult in South Africa to get a white jury to convict a white offender against coloured men. 'But,' said he, 'let us try at any rate. It is not proper either, to let such criminals go scot-free for fear of the jury[103] acquitting

M1 dismissing the matter altogether

---

[101] In the original there is a play between *rakshan* (protection) and *bhakshan* (devouring). 'Instead of being protected they were being devoured.'

[102] 'kind and' to add.

[103] 'jury' English word in the original. In the earlier instance jury translates the word *panch*.

them. I must get them arrested. I assure you I shall leave no stone unturned.'

I did not need the assurance. I suspected quite a number of officers, but as I had no unchallengeable evidence against them all, warrants of arrest were issued against the two[104] about whose guilt I had not the slightest doubt.

My movements could never be kept secret. Many knew that I was going to the Police Commissioner practically daily. The two officers against whom warrants had been issued had spies more or less efficient. They used to patrol my office and report my movements to the officers. I must admit, however, that *these officers were so bad that they could not have had many spies.*[M2] Had the Indians and the Chinese not helped me, they would never have been arrested.

M2 the tyranny of the officers was so much that they could not find too many to spy for them

One of these absconded. The Police Commissioner obtained an extradition warrant against him and got him arrested and brought to the Transvaal. They were tried, and although there was strong evidence against them, and in spite of the fact that the jury had evidence of one of them having absconded, both were declared to be not guilty and acquitted.[105]

I was sorely disappointed. The Police Commissioner also was very sorry. I got disgusted with the legal profession. The very intellect became an abomination to me inasmuch as it could be *prostituted*[M3] for screening crime.[106]

M3 used

However, the guilt of both these officers was so patent that in spite of their acquittal the Government could not harbour them. Both were cashiered, and the

---

[104] The two officials were Cecil Price Jackson, supervisor of Asiatics in the Asiatic Permit Department, and Charles Walton, a clerk in the same department.

[105] The case was tried in the court of Judge H.H. Jordan.

[106] Mr. Stellard appeared for the defence.

Asiatic Department became comparatively clean, and the Indian community was somewhat re-assured.

The event enhanced my prestige and brought me more business. The bulk, though not all, of the hundreds of pounds that the community was monthly squandering in peculation, was saved. All could not be saved, for the dishonest still plied their trade. But it was now possible for the honest man to preserve his honesty.

I must say that, though these officers were so bad, I had nothing against them personally. They were aware of this themselves, and when in their straits they approached me, I helped them too. They had a chance of getting employed by the Johannesburg Municipality in case I did not oppose the proposal. A friend of theirs saw me in this connection and I agreed *not to thwart*[M4] them, and they succeeded.

M4 to help

M5 White classes

This attitude of mine put the *officials*[M5] with whom I came in contact perfectly at ease, and though I had often to fight with their department and use strong language, they remained quite friendly with me. I was not then quite conscious that such behaviour was part of my nature. I learnt later that it was an essential part of satyagraha, and an attribute of ahimsa.

Man and his deed are two distinct things. Whereas a good deed should call forth approbation and a wicked deed disapprobation, the doer of the deed, whether good or wicked, always deserves respect or pity as the case may be. *'Hate the sin and not the sinner' is a precept which,*[107] [M6] though easy enough to understand, is rarely practised, and that is why the poison of hatred spreads in the world.

M6 This matter

This ahimsa is the basis of the search for truth. I am realizing every day that the search is vain unless it is founded on ahimsa as the basis. It is quite proper to resist

---

[107] This phrase was introduced by MD in the English translation. Its source is St. Augustine's Letter 211 (c. 424 AD) that contains the phrase *cum dilectione hominum et odio vitiorum*, which translates roughly to 'With love for mankind and hatred of sins'.

and attack a system, but to resist and attack its author is tantamount to resisting and attacking oneself. For we are all tarred with the same brush, and are children of one and the same Creator,[108] and as such the divine powers within us are infinite. To slight a single human being is to slight those divine powers, and thus to harm not only that being but with him the whole world.

X

A SACRED RECOLLECTION AND *PENANCE*[M1]

[M1] Atonement

A variety of incidents in my life have conspired to bring me in close contact with people of many creeds and many communities, and my experience with all of them warrants the statement that I have known no distinction between relatives and strangers, countrymen and foreigners, white and coloured, Hindus and Indians of other faiths, whether[109] Mussalmans, Parsis, Christians or Jews. I may say that my heart has been incapable of making any such distinctions. I cannot claim this as a special virtue, as it is in my very nature, rather than a result of any effort on my part, whereas in the case of ahimsa (non-violence), *brahmacharya* (celibacy), *aparigraha* (non-possession) and other cardinal virtues, I am fully conscious of a continuous striving for their cultivation.

When I was practising in Durban, my office clerks often stayed with me, and there were among them Hindus and Christians, or to describe them by their provinces, Gujaratis and Tamilians. I do not recollect having ever regarded them as anything but my kith and

---

[108] 'Creator' translates 'Brahma'.

[109] 'Indians of other faiths, whether' added in the English translation.

kin. I treated them as members of my family, and had unpleasantness with my wife if ever she stood in the way of my treating them as such. One of the clerks was a Christian,[110] born of *Panchama*[111] parents.

The house was built after the Western model and the rooms rightly had no outlets for dirty water. Each room had therefore chamber-pots. Rather than have these cleaned by a servant or a sweeper, my wife or I attended to them. The clerks who made themselves completely at home would naturally clean their own pots, but the *Christian clerk*[M2] was a newcomer, and it was our duty to *attend to his bedroom*.[M3] My wife managed the pots of the others, but *to clean those used by one who had been a Panchama*[M4] seemed to her to be the limit, and we fell out. She could not bear the pots being cleaned by me, neither did she like doing it herself. Even today I can recall the picture of her chiding me, her eyes red with anger, and pearl drops streaming down her cheeks, as she descended the ladder, pot in hand. *But I was a cruelly kind husband.*[M5] I[112] regarded myself as her teacher, and so harassed her out of my blind love for her.

I was far from being satisfied by her merely carrying the pot. I would have her do it cheerfully. So I said, raising my voice: 'I will not stand this *nonsense*[M6] in my house.'

The words pierced her like an arrow.

[M2] but the clerk born in a *Panchama* family

[M3] to remove his chamber-pot

[M4] this

[M5] But I was a loving as also a cruel husband.

[M6] quarrel

---

[110] Vincent Lawrence.

[111] *Panchama* means the fifth. The earliest references to the fifth caste or panchama castes 'are, in the Madras Census Report, 1871, summed up as being "that great division of the people, spoken of by themselves as the fifth caste"'. In the Madras Presidency 'the Panchamas were, in the Department of Public Instruction, called "Paraiyas and kindred classes" till 1893. From Edgar Thurston, *Castes and Tribes of Southern India* (Madras: Government Press, 1909). The communities classified as panchama were outside the pale of caste and hence considered 'untouchable'.

[112] 'also' to add.

She shouted back: 'Keep your house to yourself and let me go.' *I forgot myself, and the spring of compassion dried up in me.*[M7] I caught her by the hand, dragged the helpless woman to the gate, which was just opposite the ladder, and proceeded to open it with the intention of pushing her out.[113] *The tears were running down her cheeks in torrents,*[M8] and she cried: '*Have you no sense of shame? Must you so far forget yourself?*[M9] Where am I to go? I have no parents or relatives here to harbour me. Being your wife, you think I must put up with your cuffs and kicks? *For Heaven's sake behave yourself,*[M10] and shut the gate. *Let us not be found making scenes like this!*'[M11]

I put on a brave face, but was really ashamed and shut the gate. If my wife could not leave me, neither could I leave her. We have had numerous bickerings, but the end has always been peace between us. The wife, with her matchless powers of endurance, has always been the victor.

Today I am in a position to narrate the incident with some detachment, as it belongs to a period out of which I have fortunately emerged. I am no longer a blind, infatuated husband, I am no more my wife's teacher. *Kasturba*[114] *can, if she will, be as unpleasant to me today, as I used to be to her before.*[M12] We are tried friends, the one no longer regarding the other as the object of lust. She has been a faithful nurse throughout my illnesses, serving without any thought of reward.

The incident in question occurred in 1898, when I had no conception of[115] *brahmacharya*. It was a time when I thought that the wife was the object of her husband's lust, born to do her husband's behest, rather than a helpmate, a comrade and a partner in the husband's joys and sorrows.

[M7] I had forgotten God. Not a drop of compassion remained in me.

[M8] The Ganga and the Jamuna flowed from her eyes

[M9] You have no shame, but I do. Have some sense of decency at least.

[M10] Feel some shame

[M11] If someone were to see us, neither of us would look good.

[M12] Kasturbai can, if she wishes, scold me today.

---

[113] 'with the intention of pushing her out' added in the English translation.

[114] 'Mrs. Gandhi' in the first edition.

[115] 'the practice of' to add.

M13 From the year 1900 onwards

It was in the year 1900 that[M13] these ideas underwent a radical transformation, and in 1906 they took concrete shape. But of this I propose to speak in its proper place. Suffice it to say that with the gradual disappearance in me of the carnal appetite, my domestic life became and is becoming more and more peaceful, sweet and happy.

Let no one conclude from this narrative of a sacred recollection that we are by any means an ideal couple,[116] or that there is a complete identity of ideals between us. Kasturba[117] herself does not perhaps know whether she has any ideals independently of me. It is likely that many of my doings have not her approval even today. We never discuss them, I see no good in discussing them. For she was educated neither by her parents nor by me at the time when I ought to have done it. But she *is*

M14 has

blessed with[M14] one great quality to a very considerable degree, a quality which most Hindu wives possess in some measure. And it is this: willingly or unwillingly, consciously or unconsciously, she has *considered herself*

M15 sought fulfilment in her life

blessed[M15] in following in my footsteps, and has never stood in the way of my endeavour to lead a life of restraint. Though, therefore, there is a wide difference between us intellectually, I have always had the feeling that ours is a life of contentment, happiness and[118] progress.

XI

INTIMATE EUROPEAN CONTACTS

This chapter has brought me to a stage where it becomes necessary for me to explain to the reader how this story[119] is written from week to week.

---

[116] 'or that there is no blemish in my wife,' to add.

[117] 'Mrs. Gandhi' in the first edition, and Kasturbai in Gujarati.

[118] 'spiritual' to add.

[119] 'of Experiments with Truth' to add.

When I began writing it, I had no definite plan before me. I have no[120] diary or documents on which to base the story of my experiments. I write just as the *Spirit*[M1] moves me at the time of writing. *I do not claim to know definitely that all conscious thought and action on my part is directed by the Spirit.*[M2] But on an examination of the greatest steps that I have taken in my life, as also of those that may be regarded as the least, I think it will not be improper to say that all of them were *directed by the Spirit.*[M3]

I have not seen Him, neither have I known Him. I have made the world's faith in God my own, and as my faith is ineffaceable, I regard that faith as amounting to experience. However, as it may be said that to describe faith as experience is to tamper with truth, it may perhaps be more correct to say that I have no word for *characterizing my belief in God.*[M4]

It is perhaps now somewhat easy to understand why[121] I believe that I am writing this story *as the Spirit prompts me.*[M5] When I began the last chapter I gave it the heading I have given to this, but as I was writing it, I realized that before I narrated my experiences with Europeans, I must write something *by way of a preface.*[M6] This I did and altered the heading.

Now again, as I start on this chapter, I find myself confronted with a fresh problem. What things to mention and what to omit regarding the English friends of whom I am about to write is a serious problem. If things that are relevant are omitted, truth will be dimmed. And it is difficult to decide straightaway what is relevant, when I am not even sure about the relevancy of writing this story.

I understand more clearly today what I read long ago about the inadequacy[122] of all autobiography as

[M1] the dweller within

[M2] I do not know with any certainty whether all my actions may be considered as those of the dweller within.

[M3] inspired by the dweller within

[M4] describing my faith in God in pure form

[M5] in submission to the prompting of the invisible dweller within

[M6] about that sacred recollection

---

[120] 'books,' to add.

[121] 'It is perhaps now somewhat easy to understand why' added in the English translation.

[122] 'and difficulty' to add.

history. I know that I do not set down in this *story*[M7] all that I remember. Who can say how much I must give and how much omit in the interests of truth? And what would be the value in a court of law of the inadequate *ex parte* evidence being tendered by me of certain events in my life?[123] If some busybody were to cross-examine me on the chapters already written, he could probably shed much more light on them, and if it were a hostile[124] critic's cross-examination, he might even flatter himself for having shown up 'the hollowness of many of my pretensions'.

I, therefore, wonder for a moment whether it might not be proper to stop writing these chapters. But so long as there is no prohibition from the *voice*[M8] within, I must continue the writing. I must follow the sage maxim that nothing once begun should be abandoned unless it is proved to be morally wrong.

M8 dweller

I am not writing the autobiography to please critics. Writing it is itself one of the experiments with truth. One of its objects is certainly to provide some comfort and food for reflection[125] for my co-workers. Indeed I started writing it in compliance with their wishes. It might not have been written, if Jairamdas and Swami Anand[126] had not persisted in their suggestion. If, therefore, I am wrong in writing the autobiography, they must share the blame.

But to take up the subject indicated in the heading. Just as I had Indians living with me as members of my family, *so had I*[M9] English friends living with me in Durban.[127] Not that all who lived with me liked

M9 I began to have

---

[123] 'being tendered by me of certain events in my life' added in the English translation.

[124] 'hostile' added in the English translation.

[125] 'and food for reflection' added in the English translation.

[126] In the original the order is Swami Anand and Jairamdas.

[127] 'in Durban' added in the English translation.

it. But I persisted in having them. Nor was I wise in every case. I had some bitter experiences, but these included both Indians and Europeans. And I do not regret the experiences. In spite of them, and in spite of the inconvenience and worry that I have often caused to friends, I have not altered my conduct and friends have kindly borne with me. Whenever my contacts with strangers have been painful to friends, I have not hesitated to blame them. I hold that believers who have to see the same God in others that they see in themselves, must be able to live amongst all with sufficient detachment. And the ability to live thus can be cultivated, not by fighting shy of unsought opportunities for such contacts, but by hailing them in a spirit of service and withal keeping oneself unaffected by them.

Though, therefore, my house was full when the Boer War broke out, I received two Englishmen who had come from Johannesburg. Both were theosophists, one of them being Mr. Kitchin,[128] of whom we shall have occasion to know more later. These[129] friends often cost my wife bitter tears. Unfortunately she has had many such trials on my account. This was the first time that I had English friends to live with me as intimately as members of my family. I had stayed in English houses during my days in England, but there I conformed to their ways of living, and it was more or less like living in a boarding house. Here it was quite the contrary. The English friends became members of the family. They adopted the Indian style in many matters. Though the appointments in the house were in the Western fashion, the *internal life*[M10] was mostly Indian. I do remember   [M10] mode of life and food
having had some difficulty in keeping them as members of the family, but I can certainly say that they had no difficulty in making themselves perfectly at home under

---

[128] Herbert Kitchin.

[129] 'Living with' to add before 'These'.

my roof. In Johannesburg these contacts developed further than in Durban.

XII

EUROPEAN CONTACTS (*CONTD.*)[130]

In Johannesburg I had at one time as many as four[131] Indian *clerks, who were perhaps more like my sons than clerks.*[M1] But even these were not enough for my work. It was impossible to do without typewriting,[132] which, among us, if at all, only I knew. I taught it to two of the clerks, but they never came up to the mark because of their poor English. And then one of these I wanted to train as an accountant. I could not get out anyone from Natal, for *nobody*[M2] could enter the Transvaal without a permit, and for my own personal convenience I was not prepared to ask a favour of the Permit Officer.

I was at my wit's end. Arrears were fast mounting up, so much so that it seemed impossible for me, however much I might try, to cope with professional and public work. I was quite willing to engage a European clerk, but I was not sure to get a white man or woman to serve a coloured man like myself.[133] However I decided to try. I approached a typewriter's agent whom I knew, and asked him to get me a *stenographer. There were girls available, and he*[M3] promised to try to secure the services of one. He came across a Scotch girl called Miss Dick, who had just come fresh from Scotland. She had no

[M1] clerks. I cannot say whether they should be called clerks or sons.

[M2] no Indian

[M3] typewriting person, man or woman, who would not object to working under a 'black' man. In South Africa stenographers and typists are mostly women. This agent

---

[130] '(Contd.)' added in the English translation.

[131] See Chapter XV for the names of the three clerks who have been identified.

[132] 'type', 'typewriting' and 'shorthand', all English words in the original.

[133] 'like myself' added in the English translation.

objection to earning an honest livelihood, wherever available, and she was in need. So the agent sent her on to me. She immediately prepossessed me.

'Don't you mind serving under an Indian?' I asked her.

'Not at all,' was her firm reply.

'What salary do you expect?'

'Would £17/10 be too much?'

'Not too much if you will give me the work I want from you. When can you join?'

'This moment, if you wish.'

I was very pleased and straightaway started dictating letters to her.

Before very long she became more a daughter or a sister to me than a mere stenotypist.[134] I had scarcely any reason to find fault with her work. She was *often*[M4] ᴹ⁴ at one time even
entrusted with the management of funds amounting to thousands of pounds, and she was in charge of account books. She won my complete confidence, but what was perhaps more, she confided to me her innermost thoughts and feelings. She sought my advice in the final choice of her husband, and I had the privilege to give her away in marriage. As soon as Miss Dick became Mrs. Macdonald, she had to leave me, but even after her marriage she did not fail to respond, whenever under pressure I made a call upon her.

But a permanent stenotypist was now needed in her place, and I was fortunate in getting another girl. She was Miss Schlesin,[135] introduced to me by Mr. Kallenbach,[136]

---

[134] 'I never had to speak to her in a raised voice.' To add.

[135] Sonja Schlesin (1888–1956); for her biography, see George Paxton, *Sonja Schlesin: Gandhi's South African Secretary* (Scotland: Pax Books, 2006).

[136] Hermann Kallenbach (1871–1945), introduced to MKG by barrister Rahim Karim Khan. For the correspondence between Kallenbach and MKG, see *CWMG*, vol. 96. For Kallenbach's

whom the reader will know in due course. She is at present a teacher in one of the High Schools in the Transvaal.[137] She was about seventeen when she came to me. Some of her idiosyncrasies were at times too much for Mr. Kallenbach and me. She had come less to work as a stenotypist than to gain experience. Colour

---

biographies, see Isa Sarid and Christian Bartolf, *Hermann Kallenbach: Mahatma Gandhi's Friend in South Africa* (Berlin: Gandhi Information Centre, 1997) and Shimon Lev, *Soul Mates: The Story of Mahatma Gandhi and Hermann Kallenbach* (New Delhi: Orient Blackswan, 2012). Kallenbach and Sonja's uncle Victor Rosenburg came from the same Lithuanian town of Neustadt, hence were acquainted. This acquaintance led to Kallenbach recommending Sonja to MKG.

[137] In *Navajivan* of 7 August 1927 and *Young India* of 11 August 1927 this sentence read: 'She is at present at the head of a girls' school in the Transvaal.' The correction was made at the instance of Sonja Schlesin. On 2 June 1928 she wrote, 'Dear Mr. Gandhi, Time for just a line by this mail to ask you *on no account* to publish the allusions to myself in your wretched autobiography in a book-form until I send you a revised copy which I shall do by next mail. You say that I am at the head of a girls' school. I have never had anything to do with a girls' school and it would take many more years of experience than I possess to attain to the principalship at a high school, even if I desired such a position, which I don't.' She wrote further, 'The whole thing is simply a fabrication of your own fancy. Your brain is so tired that you have just the haziest recollection of things, you jumble up facts and you unconsciously invent. I therefore seriously think you should cease writing until you are in a normal state again . . . In fact so far as your allusions to myself are concerned, at any rate, the autobiography should indeed be entitled not "The Story of My Experiments with Truth" but *Illustrations of My Experiments with Untruth.*"' SN 15040. Emphasis in the original.

In a letter to Manilal and Sushila Gandhi, MKG remarked, 'I follow what you say about Miss Schlesin. But, then, isn't she half crazy? She has written a sort of wild letter even to me.' *CWMG,* vol. 37, p. 66.

MKG issued a correction in *Young India* of 28 June 1928: 'Miss Schlesin of whom mention has been made in the Autobiography chapters tells me that she is not, as I have stated, principal of a girls' school but that she is a teacher at a High School. The error has given her pain for which I am sorry. I may at once say that she is in no way responsible for the error.' *CWMG,* vol. 36, p. 468.

prejudice was foreign to her temperament. *She seemed to mind neither age nor experience.*[M5] She would not hesitate even to the point of insulting a man and telling him to his face what she thought of him. Her impetuosity often landed me in difficulties, but her open and guileless temperament removed them as soon as they were created. I have often signed without revision letters typed by her, as I considered her English to be better than mine, and had the fullest confidence in her loyalty.

Her sacrifice was great. For a considerable period she did not draw more than £6, and refused ever to receive more than £10 a month. When I urged her to take more, she would give me a scolding and say, 'I am not here to draw a salary from you. I am here because I like to work with you and I like your ideals.'

She had once an occasion to take £40 from me, but she insisted on having it as a loan, and repaid the full amount last year.[138] Her courage was equal to her sacrifice. She is one of the few women I have been privileged to come across, with a character as clear as crystal and courage that would shame a warrior. She is a grown-up[139] woman now. *I do not know her mind quite as well as when she was with me,*[M6] but my contact with this young lady will ever be for me a sacred recollection. I would therefore be false to truth if I kept back what I know about her.

She knew neither night nor day in toiling for the cause. She ventured out on errands in the darkness of the

[M5] She feared no one.

[M6] I am not fully acquainted with her mind at present

---

[138] Sonja Schlesin in her letter stated that she had demanded as a matter of right and obtained a loan of £150. 'Thus you speak of my educational loan which I had begged you to treat as a personal matter. I have the copy of a letter strongly reproving you for disclosing the matter of loan even to Rustomjee. *Please omit all reference to this* when the autobiography appears in a book-form. You do not even know the amount of loan—it was £150 and not £40, and I have all your acknowledgements for £110 sent to you, £40 were sent to Rustomjee.' SN 15040. Emphasis in the original.

[139] 'unmarried' to add.

M7 When all of us were in prison, when hardly any responsible man was outside,

M8 lakhs

M9 he was fond of giving marks to each one's character

night all by herself, and angrily scouted any suggestion of an escort. Thousands of stalwart[140] Indians looked up to her for guidance. *When during the satyagraha days almost every one of the leaders was in jail,*[M7] she led the movement single-handed. She had the management of *thousands,*[M8] a tremendous amount of correspondence and *Indian Opinion* in her hands, but she never wearied.

I could go on without end writing thus[141] about Miss Schlesin, but I shall conclude this chapter with citing Gokhale's estimate of her. Gokhale knew every one of my co-workers. He was pleased with many of them, *and would often give his opinion of them.*[M9] He gave the first place to Miss Schlesin amongst all the Indian and European co-workers. 'I have rarely met with the sacrifice, the purity and the fearlessness[142] I have seen in Miss Schlesin,' said he. 'Amongst your co-workers, she takes the first place in my estimation.'

XIII

'INDIAN OPINION'[143]

Before I proceed with the other intimate European contacts, I must note two or three items of importance.

---

[140] In the original 'bearded'.

[141] 'I could go on thus indefinitely writing' in the first edition.

[142] 'and the ability' to add.

[143] For the history of *Indian Opinion* and its print culture, see Surendra Bhana and James D. Hunt (eds), *Gandhi's Editor: Letters of M.H. Nazar (1902–1903)* (New Delhi: Promila and Co., 1898) and Isabel Hofmeyr, *Gandhi's Printing Press: Experiments in Slow Reading* (Harvard University Press, 2013); for satyagraha poems published in *Indian Opinion*, see *The Fire that Blazed in the Ocean: Gandhi and the Poems of Satyagraha in South Africa, 1909–1911*, introduced and translated by Surendra Bhana and Neelima Shukla-Bhatt (New Delhi: Promila and Co., 2011).

One of the contacts, however, should be mentioned at once. The appointment of Miss Dick was not enough for my purpose. I needed more assistance. I have in the earlier chapters referred to Mr. Ritch. I knew him well. He was manager in a commercial firm. He approved my suggestion of leaving the firm and getting articled under me, and he considerably lightened my burden.

About this time Sjt. Madanjit[144] approached me with a proposal to start *Indian Opinion* and sought my advice.[145] He had already been conducting a press, and I approved of his proposal. The journal was launched in 1904[146] and Sjt. Mansukhlal Naazar[147] became the first editor. But I had to bear the brunt of the work, having for most of the time to be practically in charge of the journal.[148] Not that Sjt. Mansukhlal could not carry it on. He had been doing a fair amount of journalism whilst in India, but he would never venture to write on intricate South African problems so long as I was there. He had the greatest confidence in my discernment, and therefore threw on me the responsibility of attending to the editorial columns. The journal has been until this day a weekly. In the beginning, it used to be issued

---

[144] Madanjit Vyavaharik, a former Bombay schoolteacher, established the International Printing Press with MKG's help and guidance.

[145] 'and help' to add.

[146] The first issue of *Indian Opinion* was published on 4 June 1903; MKG took over the management of the weekly in October 1904 when Madanjit Vyavaharik returned to India; the press was shifted to Phoenix in December 1904.

[147] Mansukhlal Hiralal Nazaar (1862–1906), born in Surat, studied at Elphinstone College, Bombay, had unfinished education in medicine from Grant Medical College, Bombay; first immigrated to England and then to South Africa in 1896, worked in the Indian Ambulance Corps and also served as a joint secretary of the Natal Indian Congress with Rahim Karim Khan.

[148] 'It has always been my lot to run papers from a distance.' To add.

in Gujarati, Hindi, Tamil and English. I saw, however, that the Tamil and Hindi sections were a make-believe. They did not serve the *purpose for which they were intended*,[M1] so I discontinued them as I even felt that there would be a certain amount of deception involved in their continuance.[149]

I had no notion that I should have to invest any money in this journal, but I soon discovered that it could not go on without my financial help. The Indians and the Europeans both knew that, though I was not avowedly[150] the editor of *Indian Opinion*, I was virtually responsible for its *conduct*.[M2] It would not have mattered if the journal had never been started, but to stop it after it had once been launched would have been both a loss and a disgrace.[151] So I kept on pouring out my money, until ultimately I was practically sinking all my savings in it. I remember a time when I had to remit £75 each month.

But after all these years I feel that the journal has served the community well. It was never intended to be a commercial concern. So long as it was under my control, the changes in the journal were indicative of changes in my life. *Indian Opinion* in those days, like *Young India* and *Navajivan* today, was a mirror of part of my life. Week after week I poured out my soul in its columns, and expounded the principles and practice of satyagraha as I understood it. During ten years, that is, until 1914, excepting the intervals of my *enforced rest*[M3] in prison, there was hardly an issue of *Indian Opinion* without an article from me. I cannot recall a word in those articles set down without thought or deliberation, or a word of conscious exaggeration, or anything merely to please. Indeed the journal became for me a training

M1 community

M2 writings

M3 terms

---

[149] 'and thus obtained some relief' to add.

[150] 'nominally' in the first edition.

[151] 'to the community' to add.

in self-restraint, and for friends a medium through which to keep in touch with my thoughts. The critic found very little to which he could object. In fact the tone of *Indian Opinion* compelled the critic to put a curb on his own pen. Satyagraha would probably have been impossible without *Indian Opinion*. The readers looked[152] forward to it for a trust-worthy account of the satyagraha campaign as also of the real condition of Indians in South Africa. For me it became a means for the study of human nature in all its casts and shades, as I always aimed at establishing an intimate and clean bond between the editor and the readers, I was inundated with letters containing the outpourings of my correspondents' hearts. They were friendly, critical or bitter, according to the temper of the writer. It was a fine education for me to study, digest and answer all this correspondence. It was as though the community thought audibly through this correspondence with me. It made me thoroughly understand the responsibility of a journalist, and the hold I secured in this way over the community made the future campaign workable, dignified and irresistible.

In the very first month of *Indian Opinion*, I realized that the sole aim of journalism should be service. The newspaper Press is a great power, but just as an unchained torrent of water submerges whole countrysides and devastates crops, even so an uncontrolled pen serves but to destroy. If the control is from without, it proves more poisonous than want of control. It can be profitable only when exercised from within. If this line of reasoning is correct, how many of the journals in the world would stand the test? But who would stop those that are useless? And who should be the judge? The useful and the useless must, like good and evil generally,[153] go on together, and man must make his choice.

---

[152] 'upon it as their own and looked' to add.

[153] 'like good and evil generally' added in the English translation.

XIV

[M1] Scavengers' Quarters   COOLIE LOCATIONS[154] OR *GHETTOES*?[M1]

Some of the classes which render us the greatest social
service, but[155] which we Hindus have chosen to regard
as 'untouchables', are relegated to remote quarters of a
town or a village, called in Gujarati *dhedvado*, and the
name has acquired a bad odour. Even so in Christian
Europe the Jews were once 'untouchables', and the
quarters[156] that were assigned to them had the offensive
name of 'ghettoes'.[157] In a similar way today we have
become the untouchables of South Africa. It remains
to be seen how far the sacrifice of Andrews[158] and the
magic wand of Shastri[159] succeed in rehabilitating us.

---

[154] 'Coolie Locations' in English in the original.

[155] 'which render us the greatest social service, but' not in the original
Navajivan of 21 August 1927. This was added in the English
translation. Curiously, the Gujarati equivalent of this portion was
incorporated into the first Gujarati edition as also in the *Akshar
Deha*. It is the first instance in the *Autobiography* wherein a portion
added in the English translation was incorporated in the Gujarati.

[156] 'quarters' translates *dhedvado*. Thus the original reads, 'and the
dhedvado assigned to them had the offensive name of "ghettoes".'

[157] 'ghetto' English word in the original.

[158] Charles Freer Andrews, 'Deenbandhu' (1871–1940), came to
India as a member of the Cambridge Brotherhood, left the order
in 1913, lifelong friend of Tagore and MKG. 'CFA' and his
colleague, Willie Pearson, (1881–1923) went to South Africa at the
instance of Gokhale to study the South African Indian question.
For biographical studies of CFA, see Banarasidas Chaturvedi
and Marjorie Sykes, *Charles Freer Andrews: A Narrative* (London:
George, Allen and Unwin, 1949), Hugh Tinker, *The Ordeal of
Love: C.F. Andrews and India* (New Delhi: Oxford University
Press, 1980), and Daniel O'Conner, *A Clear Star: C.F. Andrews
and India 1904–1914* (New Delhi: Chronicle Books, 2005).

[159] Rt. Hon'ble Srinivas Sastri was appointed the agent-general of
Government of India to South Africa in 1927.

The ancient[160] Jews[161] regarded themselves as the chosen people of God to the exclusion of all others, with the result that their descendants[162] were visited with a strange and even unjust retribution. Almost in a similar way the Hindus have considered themselves *Aryas* or civilized, and a section of their own kith and kin as *Anaryas* or untouchables, with the result[163] that a strange, if unjust, nemesis is being visited not only upon the Hindus in South Africa,[164] but the Mussalmans and Parsis as well, inasmuch as they belong to the same country and have the same colour as their Hindu brethren.

The reader will have now realized to some extent the meaning of the word 'locations'[165] with which I have headed this chapter. In South Africa we have acquired the odious name of 'coolies'. The word 'coolie' in India means only a porter or hired workman,[166] but in South Africa it has contemptuous connotation. It means what a pariah or an untouchable means to us, and the quarters assigned to the 'coolie' are known as 'coolie locations'. Johannesburg had one such location,[167] but

---

[160] 'ancient' added in the English translation.

[161] 'like the Hindus' to add.

[162] 'with the result that their descendants' added in the English translation.

[163] 'of this sin' to add.

[164] 'and other Colonies' to add.

[165] 'Coolie Locations' in the original.

[166] 'carrier' in the first edition.

[167] The Indian Location, New Town, bounded by Carr Street (north), Malherbe Street (west), Goch Street (east) and Pim Street (south). New Town's 'Coolie Location' was established in 1887 as Johannesburg's first Indian settlement. When it was evacuated in 1904 its population comprised 1642 Indians, 1420 Africans and 146 'Cape Coloured'. Itzkin, *Gandhi's Johannesburg*, p. 50.

unlike other places with locations where[168] the Indians had tenancy rights, in the Johannesburg location the Indians had acquired their plots on a lease of 99 years. People were densely packed in the location, the area of which never increased with the increase in population. Beyond arranging to clean the latrines in the location in a haphazard way, the Municipality did nothing to provide any sanitary facilities, much less good roads or lights. It was hardly likely that it would safeguard its sanitation, when it was indifferent to the welfare of the residents. *These were too ignorant of the rules of municipal sanitation and hygiene to do without the help or supervision of the Municipality. If those who went there had all been Robinson Crusoes, theirs would have been a different story. But we do not know of a single emigrant colony of Robinson Crusoes in the world.*[M2] Usually people migrate abroad in search of wealth and trade, but the bulk of the Indians who went to South Africa were ignorant, pauper agriculturists, who needed all the care and protection that could be given them. The traders and *educated*[M3] Indians who followed them were very few.

The criminal negligence of the Municipality and the ignorance of the Indian settlers thus conspired to render the location thoroughly insanitary. The Municipality, far from doing anything to improve the condition of the location, used the insanitation caused by their own neglect as a pretext[169] for destroying the location, and for that purpose obtained from the local legislature authority to dispossess the settlers.[170]

[M2] The Indians who lived there were not well-educated, ideal Indians knowledgeable about the rules of municipal sanitation and hygiene, and, therefore, could not do without the help or the supervision of the municipality. If those Indians who went there had been the kind who could make merry in the forest and transform dust into wealth, theirs would have been a different history. We do not know anywhere large numbers of people of this type prospecting in foreign lands.

[M3] free

---

[168] 'but unlike the other places where there were locations and where' in the first edition.

[169] 'lever' in the first edition.

[170] This was being done under the 'Unsanitary Area Commissioner's Report'. See *CWMG*, vol. 3, p. 414. The move to confine Asiatics within specified locations was based on Government Notice No. 356 of 1903, the so-called 'Bazar Notice'. This

This was the condition of things when I settled in Johannesburg.

The settlers, having proprietary rights in their land, were naturally entitled to compensation. A special tribunal was appointed to try the land acquisition cases. If the tenant was not prepared to accept the offer of the Municipality, he had a right to appeal to the tribunal, and if the latter's award exceeded the Municipality's offer, the Municipality had to bear the costs.

Most of the tenants engaged me as their legal adviser. I had no desire to make money out of these cases, so I told the tenants that I should be satisfied with whatever costs the tribunal awarded, in case they won, and a fee of £10 on every lease, irrespective of the result of the case. I also told them that I proposed to set apart half of the money paid by them for the building of a hospital or similar institution for the poor. This naturally pleased them all.

Out of about 70 cases only one was lost. So the fees amounted to a fairly big figure. But *Indian Opinion* was there with its persistent claim and devoured, so far as I can recollect, a sum of £1,600. I had worked hard for these cases. The clients always surrounded me. Most of them were originally indentured labourers from Bihar and its neighbourhood and from[171] South India. For the redress of their peculiar grievances they had formed an association of their own,[172] separate from that of the

---

notice drawing on the provisions of Law No. 3 of 1885 resolved 'that the Government takes immediate steps to have Bazars in every town set apart in which alone Asiatics may reside and trade; the Colonial Secretary shall be charged with the duty of defining such Asiatic Bazars in consultation with the Resident Magistrate, or where such exists in Town Council or Health Board'. See *CWMG*, vol. 3, pp. 352–53. Accordingly, provisions were made for fifty-four such locations across the Transvaal.

[171] 'the Tamil and Telugu regions of' to add.

[172] Transvaal Indian Association.

free Indian merchants and traders. Some of them were open-hearted, liberal men and had[173] high character. Their leaders were Sjt. Jairamsing,[174] the president, and Sjt. Badri, who was as good as the president. Both of them are now no more. They were exceedingly helpful to me. Sjt. Badri came in very close contact with me and took a prominent part in satyagraha. Through these and other friends I came in intimate contact with numerous Indian settlers from North and South India. I became more their brother than a mere legal adviser, and shared in *all their private and public sorrows and hardships.*[M4]

M4 three kinds of sorrows

It may be of some interest to know how the Indians used to name me.[175] Abdulla Sheth refused to address me as Gandhi. *None, fortunately, ever insulted me by calling or regarding me as 'saheb'.*[M5] Abdulla Sheth hit upon a fine appellation—'bhai', i.e., brother. Others followed[176] him and continued to address me as 'bhai' until the moment I left South Africa. There was a sweet[177] flavour about the name[178] when it was used by the ex-indentured Indians.

M5 Who would either call me or regard me a 'Sahib'?

---

[173] 'of' in the first edition.

[174] Jairamsingh arrived in Natal as an indentured labourer, moved to Johannesburg after completing his indenture, was president of the Transvaal Indian Association. His son Bhawani Dayal and daughter-in-law Jagrani were for some time residents of Phoenix, both were active in the Satyagraha Movement, Bhawani Dayal was the editor of the Hindi section of *Indian Opinion* from 28 June 1914, and president of Natal Indian Congress, 1938.

[175] 'It may be of some interest to know how the Indians used to name me.' Added in the English translation.

[176] 'copied' in the first edition.

[177] 'sweeter' in the first edition.

[178] 'especially' to add.

XV

THE BLACK[179] PLAGUE–I

The Indians were not removed from the location as soon as the Municipality secured its ownership. It was necessary to find the residents suitable new quarters before dislodging[180] them, but as the Municipality could not easily do this, the Indians were suffered to stay in the same 'dirty' location, with this difference that their condition became worse than before.[181] Having ceased to be proprietors they became tenants of the Municipality, with the result that their surroundings became more insanitary than ever. When they were proprietors, they had to maintain some sort of cleanliness, if only for fear of the law. The Municipality had no such fear! The number of tenants increased, and with them the squalor and the disorder.

While the Indians were fretting over this state of things, there was a sudden outbreak of the black plague,[182] also called pneumonic plague, more terrible and fatal than the bubonic.

---

[179] The illness acquired the name Black Death in the Middle Ages because the patients were covered with black boils that oozed blood and pus. In the original, the word 'black' is not used.

[180] 'dispossessing' in the first edition.

[181] 'with this difference that their condition became worse than before' added in the English translation.

[182] MKG had repeatedly warned Dr. C. Porter, medical officer of health, Johannesburg, about the squalor and insanitary conditions of the Indian Location. On 11 February 1904 MKG wrote to Dr. Porter: 'From what I hear, I believe the Mortality in the location has increased considerably and it seems to me that, if the present state of things is continued, the outbreak of some epidemic disease is merely a question of time.' *CWMG*, vol. 4, p. 129. At MKG's instance Dr. Porter visited the location on Saturday, 13 February 1904 and suggested that neither overcrowding nor

Fortunately it was not the location but one of the[183] gold mines in the vicinity of Johannesburg that was responsible for the outbreak. The workers in this mine were for the most part Negroes, for whose cleanliness their white employers were solely responsible. There were a few Indians also working in connection with the mine, twenty-three of whom suddenly caught the infection, and returned one evening to their quarters in the location with an acute attack of the plague. Sjt. Madanjit, who was then canvassing[184] subscribers for *Indian Opinion* and realizing subscriptions, happened to be in the location at this moment.[185] He was a remarkably fearless man. His heart wept to see these victims of the scourge, and he sent a pencil-note to me to the following effect: 'There has been a sudden outbreak of the black plague. You must come immediately and take prompt measures, otherwise we must be prepared for dire consequences. Please come immediately.'

Sjt. Madanjit bravely broke open the lock of a vacant house, and put all the patients there.[186] I cycled to the location, and wrote to the Town Clerk to inform him of the circumstances in which we had taken possession of the house.[187]

---

insanitation could be helped. MKG contended and warned: 'I feel convinced that every minute wasted over the matter merely hastens a calamity for Johannesburg and that through absolutely no fault of the British Indians.' *CWMG*, vol. 4, p. 130.

[183] 'many' to add.

[184] 'going about canvassing' in the first edition.

[185] This was on the evening of 18 March 1904.

[186] The Emergency Hospital, as it came to be called, was in a house marked as 'Stand 36'. Itzkin, *Gandhi's Johannesburg*, p. 51.

[187] MKG also informed Dr. Porter the same evening and requested for an appropriate place to set up a temporary hospital, urged the Town Council to do its duty and assured him that the Indian

Dr. William Godfrey,[188] who was practising in Johannesburg, ran to the rescue as soon as he got the news, and became both nurse and doctor to the patients. But twenty-three patients were more than three of us could cope with.

It is my faith, based on experience, that if one's heart is pure, calamity brings in its train men and measures to fight it. I had at that time four Indians in my office—Sjts. Kalyandas, Maneklal, Gunvantrai Desai[189] and another whose name I cannot recollect. Kalyandas had been entrusted to me by his father. In South Africa I have rarely come across anyone more obliging and willing to render implicit obedience than Kalyandas. Fortunately he was unmarried then, and I did not hesitate to impose on him duties involving risks, however great. Maneklal I had secured in Johannesburg. He too, so far as I can remember, was unmarried. So I decided to sacrifice all four—call them clerks, co-workers or sons. There was no need at all to consult Kalyandas. The others expressed their readiness as soon as they were asked. 'Where you are, we will also be,' was their short and sweet reply.

Mr. Ritch had a large family. He was ready to take the plunge, but I prevented him. I had not the heart to expose him to the risk. So he attended to the work outside the danger zone.[190]

---

community would provide both the men and money required to assist in the effort.

[188] Dr. William Godfrey, son of Subhan Godfrey, acquired a medical degree in Calcutta and later studied at Glasgow.

[189] The original does not have the name of Gunvantrai Desai. It states 'and two others'.

[190] On 9 March 1905 at a farewell meeting for England-bound Ritch MKG recalled, 'He insisted upon tending the Indian plague-patients, regardless of the possible consequence to himself.' CWMG, vol. 4, p. 370.

It was a terrible night—that night of vigil and nursing. I had nursed a number of patients before, but never any attacked by the black plague. Dr. Godfrey's pluck proved infectious. There was not much nursing required. To give them their doses of medicine, to attend to their wants, to keep them and their beds clean and tidy, and to cheer them up was all that we had to do.

The indefatigable zeal and fearlessness with which the[191] youths worked rejoiced me beyond measure. One could understand the bravery of Dr. Godfrey and of an experienced man like Sjt. Madanjit. But the spirit[192] of these callow youths!

So far as I can recollect, we pulled all the patients through that night.[193] But the whole incident, apart from its pathos, is of such absorbing interest and, *for*[M1] me, of such religious value, that I must devote to it at least two more chapters.

[M1] according to

XVI

THE BLACK PLAGUE–II

The Town Clerk expressed his gratitude to me for having taken charge of the vacant house and the patients. He frankly confessed that the Town Council had no immediate means to cope with such an emergency, but promised that they would render all the help in their power. Once awakened to a sense of their duty, the Municipality made no delay in taking prompt measures.

---

[191] 'four' to add.

[192] 'oh for the spirit' in the first edition.

[193] 'The night passed somehow.' To add at the beginning of this paragraph.

The next day they placed a vacant godown at my disposal, and suggested that the patients be removed there, but the Municipality did not undertake to clean the premises. The building was unkempt and unclean. We cleaned it up ourselves, raised a few beds and other necessaries through the offices of charitable Indians, and improvised a temporary hospital. The Municipality lent the services of a nurse,[194] who came with brandy[195] and other *hospital equipment.*[M1] Dr. Godfrey still remained in charge.

[M1] items necessary for the patients

The nurse was a kindly lady and would fain have attended to the patients, but we rarely allowed her to touch them, lest she should catch the contagion.

We had instructions to give the patients frequent doses of brandy. The nurse even asked us to take it for precaution, just as she was doing herself. But none of us would touch it. I had no faith in its beneficial effect even for the patients. With the permission of Dr. Godfrey, I put three patients, who were prepared to do without brandy, under the earth treatment, applying wet earth bandages to their heads and chests. Two of these were saved. The other twenty died in the godown.[196]

---

[194] This nurse was Emily Blake (1877–1904), daughter of James and Sarah of Richmond, having worked in Western Fever Hospital, London, came to South Africa in 1901. According to the Rand Plague Report of 1905, she was the only nurse to have succumbed to plague while serving patients. She died on 31 March 1904. See Tim Capon, 'Plague, Gandhi and the Parliamentary Clerk's Daughter', www.theheritageportal.co.za. Published on 9 November 2005, accessed on 3 April 2016.

[195] 'nurse' and 'brandy' English words in the original.

[196] The first case of plague death was on 19 March and the last on 9 July. On 16 July 1904 the epidemic was announced to be over. There were 113 identified cases of which sixty-seven (sixty-five fatal) were of pneumonic plague, thirty-eight (nine fatal) of bubonic plague, six (all fatal) of mixed variety and two (both fatal) of septicemia.

Meanwhile the Municipality was busy taking other measures. There was a lazaretto[197] for contagious diseases about seven miles from Johannesburg. The two[198] surviving patients were removed to tents near the lazaretto, and arrangements were made for sending any fresh cases there. We were thus relieved of our work.

In the course of a few days we learnt that the good nurse had had an attack and immediately succumbed. It is impossible to say how the two patients were saved and how we remained immune, but the experience enhanced my faith in earth treatment, as also my scepticism of[199] the efficacy of brandy, even as a medicine. I know that neither this faith nor this scepticism[200] is based upon any solid grounds, but I still retain[201] the impression which I then received, and have therefore thought it necessary to mention[202] it here.

On the outbreak of the plague, I had addressed a strong letter to the Press,[203] holding the Municipality guilty of negligence after the location came into its possession and responsible for the outbreak of the plague itself. This letter secured me Mr. Henry Polak,[204]

---

[197] 'lazaretto' English word in the original. It also provides an explanation, which translates as 'a hospice for patients of contagious diseases'.

[198] 'three' in the original.

[199] 'diffidence in' in the first edition.

[200] 'diffidence' in the first edition.

[201] 'I cannot efface' in the first edition.

[202] 'take note of' in the first edition.

[203] Letter of 5 April 1904. See *CWMG*, vol. 4, pp. 159–60.

[204] Henry Solomon Leon Polak came to South Africa in 1903 and was assistant editor of the *Transvaal Critic* when he met MKG at Ada Bissick's vegetarian restaurant. MKG stood witness to Henry Polak and Millie Graham Downs's marriage in 1905 and the couple lived with the Gandhis in their home at Albermarle Street and later in a four-roomed house in Bellevue East. Polak

and was partly responsible for the friendship of the late Rev. Joseph Doke.[205]

I have said in an earlier chapter that I used to have my meals at a vegetarian restaurant. Here I met Mr. Albert West.[206] We used to meet in this restaurant every evening and go out walking after dinner. Mr. West was a partner in a small printing concern. He read my letter in the Press about the outbreak of the plague and, not finding me in the restaurant, felt uneasy.

My co-workers and I had reduced our diet since the outbreak, as I had long made it a rule to go on a light diet during[207] epidemics. In these days I had therefore given up my evening dinner. Lunch also I would finish before the other guests arrived.[208] I knew the proprietor of the restaurant very well, and I had informed him that, as I was engaged in nursing the plague patients, I wanted to avoid the contact of *friends*[M2] as much as possible.

M2 others

---

at the instance of MKG qualified himself as an attorney and helped in his work, visited India and England to propagate the case of South African Indians and wrote *The Indians of South Africa: Helots within the Empire and how They are Treated* (Madras: G.A. Natesan & Co., 1909). He succeeded Herbert Kitchin as the editor of *Indian Opinion* and was imprisoned during the satyagraha in South Africa. He also wrote, along with H.N. Brailsford and Lord Pethick-Lawrence, a biographical work, *Mahatma Gandhi* (London: Odham Press, 1949).

[205] Rev. Joseph Doke (1861–1913), Baptist missionary, married to Agnes Biggs with whom he had four children: Willey, Clement, Comber and Olive. MKG recuperated at the Doke household after an assault by Mir Alam and others on 10 February 1908. Doke also wrote two romances, *The Secret City: The Romance of Karoo* (1913) and *The Queen of the Secret City* (1916).

[206] Albert West along with his wife, mother and sister Ada (Devi) West joined the Phoenix Settlement and was arrested during the Satyagraha Movement.

[207] 'plague' to add.

[208] 'so as to keep them as far away from danger as possible' to add.

Not finding me in the restaurant for a day or two, Mr. West knocked at my door early one morning[209] just as I was getting ready to go out for a walk. As I opened the door Mr. West said: 'I did not find you in the restaurant and was really afraid lest something should[210] have happened to you. So I decided to come and see you in the morning in order to make sure of finding you at home. Well, here I am at your disposal. I am ready to help in nursing the patients. You know that I have no one depending on me.'

I expressed my gratitude, and without taking even a second to think, replied: 'I will not have you as a nurse. If there are no more cases we shall be free in a day or two. There is one thing however.'

'Yes, what is it?'

'Could you take charge of the *Indian Opinion* press at Durban? Mr. Madanjit is likely to be engaged here and someone is needed at Durban. If you could go, I should feel quite relieved on that score.'

'You know that I have a press. Most probably I shall be able to go, but may I give my final reply in the evening? We shall talk it over during our evening walk.'[211]

I was delighted. We had the talk. He agreed to go. Salary was no consideration to him, as money was not his motive. But a salary of £10 per month and a part of the profits, if any, was fixed up. The very next day Mr. West left for Durban by the evening mail, entrusting me with the recovery of his dues. From that day until the time I left the shores of South Africa, he remained a partner of my joys and sorrows.

Mr. West belonged to a peasant family in Louth (Lincolnshire). He had had an ordinary school education,

---

[209] 'one early morning' in the first edition.

[210] 'might' in the first edition.

[211] 'if you can come out.' To add.

but had learnt a good deal in the school of experience and by dint of self-help. I have always known him to be a pure, sober, god fearing, humane Englishman.

We shall know more of him and his family in the chapters to follow.

XVII

LOCATION IN FLAMES

Though my co-workers and I were relieved of the charge of the patients, there remained many things arising out of the black plague still to be dealt with.

I have referred to the negligence of the Municipality regarding the location. But it was wide awake so far as the health of its white citizens was concerned. It had spent large amounts for the preservation of their health and now it poured forth money like water in order to stamp out the plague. In spite of the many *sins of omission and commission against*[M1] the Indians that I had laid at the door of the Municipality, I could not help commending its solicitude for the white citizens, and I rendered it as much help as I could in its laudable efforts. I have an impression that, if I had withheld my co-operation, the task would have been more difficult for the Municipality, and that it would not have hesitated to use armed force and *do its worst.*[M2]

But all that was averted. The Municipal authorities were pleased at the Indians' behaviour, and much of the future work regarding plague measures[212] was simplified. I used all the influence I could command with the Indians to make them submit to the requirements of the Municipality. It was far from easy for the Indians to go

[M1] faults regarding

[M2] enforce its will

---

[212] 'regarding plague measures' added in the English translation.

all that length, but I do not remember anyone having resisted my advice.

The location was put under a strong guard, passage in and out being made impossible without permission. My co-workers and I had free permits of entry and exit. The decision was to make the whole location population vacate, and live under canvas for three weeks in an open plain about thirteen miles from Johannesburg, and then to set fire to the location. To settle down under canvas with provisions and other necessaries was bound to take some time, and a guard became necessary during the interval.[213]

The people were in a terrible fright, but my constant presence was a consolation to them. Many of the poor people used to hoard their scanty savings underground. This had to be unearthed. They had no bank, they knew none. I became their banker.[214] *Streams of money poured into my office.*[M3] I could not possibly charge my fees for my labours in such a crisis. I coped with the work somehow. I knew my bank manager very well.[215] I told him that I should have to deposit these moneys with him.[216] The banks were by no means anxious to accept large amounts of copper and silver. There was also the fear of bank clerks refusing to touch money coming from a plague-affected area. But the manager accommodated me in every way. It was decided to disinfect all the money before sending it to the bank. So far as I can remember, nearly sixty thousand pounds were thus deposited. I advised such of the people as had enough money to place it as fixed deposit, and

[M3] There was heaps of money at my place.

---

[213] All inhabitants of the Indian location were removed to the tent camp on 30 March 1904.

[214] 'bank' in the original.

[215] 'My bank manager I knew very well.' In the first edition.

[216] 'have to deposit with him these moneys' in the first edition.

they accepted the advice. The result was some of them became accustomed to invest their money in banks.

The location residents were removed by special train to Klipspruit Farm[217] near Johannesburg, where they were supplied with provisions by the Municipality at public expense. This city under canvas looked like a military camp. The people who were unaccustomed to this camp life were distressed and astonished over the arrangements, but they did not have to put up with any particular inconvenience. I used to cycle out to them daily. Within twenty-four hours of their stay they forgot all their misery and began to live merrily. Whenever I went there I found them enjoying themselves with song and mirth. Three weeks' stay in the open air evidently improved their health.

So far as I recollect, the location was put to the flames on the very next day after its evacuation. The Municipality showed not the slightest inclination to save anything from the conflagration. About this very time, and for the same reason, the Municipality burnt down all its timber in the market, and sustained a loss of some ten thousand pounds. The reason for this drastic step was the discovery of some dead rats in the market.

The Municipality had to incur heavy expenditure, but it successfully arrested the further progress of the plague, and the city once more breathed freely.

XVIII

THE MAGIC SPELL OF A BOOK

The black plague enhanced my influence with the poor Indians, and increased my business and my responsibility.

---

[217] According to Eric Itzkin the origins of Soweto go back to the evacuation camp at Klipspruit. *Gandhi's Johannesburg*, p. 50.

Some of the new contacts with Europeans became so close that they added considerably to my moral obligations.

I made the acquaintance of Mr. Polak in the vegetarian restaurant, just as I had made that of Mr. West. One evening a young man dining at a table a little way off sent me his card expressing a desire to see me. I invited him to come to my table, which he did.

'I am sub-editor of *The Critic*,'[218] he said. 'When I read your letter to the Press about the plague, I felt a strong desire to see you. I am glad to have this opportunity.'

Mr. Polak's candour drew me to him. The same evening we got to know each other. We[219] seemed to hold closely similar views on the essential things of life. He liked simple life. He had a wonderful faculty of translating into practice anything that appealed to his intellect. Some of the changes that he had made in his life were as prompt as they were radical.

Indian Opinion was getting more and more expensive every day. The very first report from Mr. West was alarming. He wrote: 'I do not expect the concern to yield the profit that you had thought probable. I am afraid there may be even a loss. The books are not in order. There are heavy arrears to be recovered, but one cannot make head or tail of them. Considerable overhauling will have to be done. But all this need not alarm you. I shall try to put things right as best I can. I remain on, whether there is profit or not.'

Mr. West might have left when he discovered that there was no profit, and I could not have blamed him. In fact, he had a right to arraign me for having described the concern as profitable without proper proof. But he never so much as uttered one word of complaint. I have,

---

[218] *The Transvaal Critic*, established by Herbert Hess.

[219] 'and we' in the first edition.

however, an impression that this discovery[220] led Mr. West to regard me as credulous. I had simply accepted Sjt. Madanjit's estimate without caring to examine it, and told Mr. West to expect a profit.

I now realize that a public worker should not make statements of which he has not made sure.[221] Above all, a votary of truth must exercise the greatest caution. To allow a man to believe a thing which one has not fully verified is to compromise truth. I am pained to have to confess that, in spite of this knowledge, I have not quite conquered my credulous habit, for which my ambition to do more work than I can manage is responsible. This ambition has often been a source of worry more to my co-workers than to myself.

On receipt of Mr. West's letter I left for Natal.[222] I had taken Mr. Polak into my fullest confidence. He came to see me off at the station,[223] and left with me a book to read during the journey, which he said I was sure[224] to like. It was Ruskin's *Unto This Last*.[225]

The book was impossible to lay aside, once I had begun it. It gripped me. Johannesburg to Durban was a twenty-four hours' journey. The train reached there in the evening. I could not get any sleep that night. I determined to change my life in accordance with the ideals of the book.

---

[220] 'must have' to add.

[221] 'not made himself sure' in the first edition.

[222] Between 8 and 25 June 1904 MKG made two visits to Durban; this incident is from that period.

[223] 'station' in the original. This was the Old Park Station in Eloff Street.

[224] 'I should be sure' in the first edition.

[225] John Ruskin, *Unto This Last*, first published in December 1860 in the monthly journal *Cornhill Magazine* in four essays. The title comes from the 'Parable of the Workers in the Vineyard': 'I will give unto this last, even as unto thee.'

This was the first book of Ruskin I had ever read. During the days of my education I had read practically nothing outside text-books, and after I launched into active life I had very little time for reading.[226] I cannot therefore claim much book knowledge. However, I believe I have not lost much because of this enforced[227] restraint. On the contrary, the limited reading may be said to have enabled me thoroughly to digest what I did read. Of these books, the one that brought about an instantaneous and *practical*[M1] transformation in my life was *Unto This Last*. I translated it later into Gujarati, entitling it *Sarvodaya*[228] (the welfare of all).[229]

I believe that I discovered some of my deepest convictions reflected in this great book[230] of Ruskin, and that is why it so captured me and made me transform my life. A poet is one who can call forth the good latent in *the human breast*.[M2] Poets do not influence all alike, for *everyone is not evolved in an equal measure*.[M3]

The teachings of *Unto This Last*[231] I understood to be:

1. That the good of the individual is contained in the good of all.
2. That a lawyer's work has the same value as the barber's inasmuch as all have the same right of earning their livelihood from their work.

M1 constructive

M2 us

M3 not all have good ideals in equal measure

---

[226] 'little time left me for reading' in the first edition.

[227] 'or unattempted' to add.

[228] This is a paraphrase and not a complete translation. It was published in *Indian Opinion* in instalments during May–July 1908. See *CWMG*, vol. 8.

[229] '(the welfare all)', as explanation of the term *Sarvodaya*, added in the English translation.

[230] 'great book' translates *granth ratna*, literally, 'gem of a book'.

[231] Hereafter the title *Sarvodaya* is used in Gujarati.

3. That a life of labour, i.e., the life of the tiller of the soil and the handicraftsman[232] is the life worth living.

The first of these I knew. The second I had dimly realized. The third had never occurred to me. *Unto This Last* made it as clear as daylight for me that the second and the third were contained in the first. I arose with the dawn, ready to reduce these principles to practice.

XIX

THE PHOENIX SETTLEMENT

I talked over the whole thing[M1] with Mr. West, described to him the effect *Unto This Last* had produced on my mind, and proposed that *Indian Opinion* should be removed to a farm, on which everyone should labour, drawing the same living wage, and attending to the press work in spare time. Mr. West approved of the proposal, and £3 was laid down as the monthly allowance per head, irrespective of *colour or nationality*.[M2]

But it was a question whether all the ten or more workers in the press would agree to go and settle *on an out-of-the-way farm, and be satisfied with bare maintenance*.[M3] We therefore proposed that those who could not fit in with the scheme should continue to draw their salaries and gradually try to reach the ideal of becoming members of the Settlement.

I talked to the workers in the terms of this proposal. It did not appeal to Sjt. Madanjit, who considered my proposal to be foolish and held that it would ruin a venture on which he had *staked his all*;[M4] that the

[M1] In the morning I first talked over the matter

[M2] whether they were white or black

[M3] in the wilderness, and whether all would agree to withdraw an equal amount sufficient for food and clothing was the other question

[M4] poured his soul

---

[232] 'and the handicraftsman' added in the English translation.

workers would bolt, *Indian Opinion* would come to a stop, and the press would have to be closed down.

Among the men working in the press was Chhaganlal Gandhi,[233] *one of my cousins.*[M5] I had put the proposal to him at the same time as to West. He had a wife and children, but he had from childhood chosen to be trained and to work under me. He had full faith in me. So without any argument he agreed to the scheme and has been with me ever since. The machinist[234] Govindaswami also fell in with the proposal. The rest did not join the scheme, but agreed to go wherever I removed the press.[235]

I do not think I took more than two days to fix up these matters with the men. Thereafter I at once advertised for a piece of land situated near a railway station in the vicinity of Durban. An offer came in respect of Phoenix. Mr. West and I went to inspect the estate. Within a week we purchased twenty acres of land. It had a nice little spring and a few orange and mango trees. Adjoining it was a piece of 80 acres which had many more fruit trees and a dilapidated cottage.[236] We purchased this too, the total cost being a thousand pounds.

[M5] a nephew of mine

---

[233] Chhaganlal Khushalchand Gandhi, son of MKG's cousin, went to South Africa in 1902 and became a founder member and joint manager of the Phoenix and editor of the Gujarati *Indian Opinion* in 1908. MKG sent him to England to study law in 1911, which he could not complete. He was among the sixteen pioneering satyagrahis who left Phoenix on 15 September 1913 and crossed the Transvaal border, and was sentenced to three months with hard labour. After return to India he joined the Satyagraha Ashram and worked as its manager for a time.

[234] 'machineer' in the original.

[235] Uma Dhupelia-Mesthrie lists twelve such persons, who were day workers. Anandlal Gandhi, Virji Damodardas Mehta, Mr. Mannering, Mr. Orchard, Hemchand, Kababhai, Ramnath, Behary, Muthu, Rajcoomar, Harilal Thakkar and Brian Gabriel. *Gandhi's Prisoner? The Life of Gandhi's Son Manilal* (New Delhi: Permanent Black, 2004), p. 69.

[236] 'After some days,' to add.

The late[237] Mr. Rustomji always *supported*[M6] me in such enterprises. He liked the project. He placed at my disposal second-hand corrugated iron sheets of a big godown[238] and other building material, with which we started work. Some Indian carpenters and masons, who had worked with me in the Boer War, helped me in erecting a shed for the press. This structure, which was 75 feet long and 50 feet broad, was ready in less than a month. Mr. West and others, at great personal risk, stayed with the carpenters and masons. The place, uninhabited and thickly overgrown with grass, was infested with snakes and obviously dangerous to live in.[239] At first all lived under canvas.[240] We carted most of our things to Phoenix in about a week. It was fourteen[241] miles from Durban, and two and a half miles from Phoenix station.[242]

[M6] partnered

---

[237] 'The late' added. The original has Sheth Parsi Rustomji.

[238] 'godown' English word in the original.

[239] Isabel Hofmeyr has described Phoenix as part of an experiment in segregated self-sufficiency. 'While some accounts portray Phoenix as a remote and isolated outpost, it formed part of a crowded ideological hinterland where African American inspired Zulu nationalists, Protestant evangelists, Arya Samajists, and Bombay Muslims intersected. The International Printing Press comprised but one element in this mosaic of projects in which ideas of self-help, improvement, and uplift from both black Atlantic and Indian Ocean encountered each other.' *Gandhi's Printing Press*, p. 55. The other neighbouring institute was at Ohlange, established in June 1901 by John Langalibalele Dube; it also comprised a printing press from which his newspaper *Ilanga Lase Natal: Ipe pa la Bantu* (Sun of Natal: The Black People's Paper) was published. Hofmeyr concludes, 'The hinterland around Phoenix constituted a brave new world of evangelical experiment comprising proselytizing Trappists, mid-Western Protestants, Zulu internationalists, Bombay Muslim holy men and Punjabi Aryasamajists.' P. 59.

[240] 'When the main building was ready,' to add.

[241] 'thirteen' in the original.

[242] The Phoenix Settlement was established on 26 June 1904. For the announcement of the scheme, see *CWMG*, vol. 4, pp. 319–21.

Only one issue of *Indian Opinion* had to be printed outside, in the Mercury Press.

I now endeavoured to draw to[243] Phoenix those relations and friends who had come with me from India to try their fortune, and who were engaged in business of various kinds. They had come in search of wealth, and it was therefore difficult to persuade them; but some agreed. Of these I can single out here only Maganlal Gandhi's[244] name. The others went back to business.[245] Maganlal Gandhi left his business for good to cast in his lot with me, and by ability, sacrifice and[246] devotion stands foremost among my original co-workers in my ethical experiments. As a self-taught handicraftsman his place among them is unique.

Thus the Phoenix Settlement was started in 1904,[247] and there, in spite of numerous odds, *Indian Opinion* continues to be published.[248] But the initial difficulties,

---

[243] 'my way of thinking and' to add.

[244] Maganlal Khushalchand Gandhi (1883–1928), nephew of MKG, described as 'the soul of the Ashram'. He went to South Africa in December 1902 and lived as a trader in Tongat. He and his wife, Santok, joined the Phoenix Settlement and became central to the life of the community and the International Printing Press. He led the 'Phoenix Party' of about forty-five boys to India in 1914 and lived at various places, including Shantiniketan. He was the manager of the Satyagraha Ashram and led the technical experiments in weaving and spinning. At his untimely death in 1928 MKG expressed his grief: 'I am more widowed the she.' A bunch of his letters have recently been edited for publication: Tridip Suhrud and Uma Gohil (eds), *Tongat Thi Patro* (1903–1904) (Ahmedabad: Navajivan, forthcoming).

[245] 'having stayed at Phoenix for longer or shorter duration' to add.

[246] 'matchless' to add.

[247] For aims of the Phoenix Settlement, see *CWMG*, vol. 11, pp. 321–22.

[248] 'published at the Settlement' in the first edition. The last issue of *Indian Opinion* was published on 4 August 1961.

the changes made,[249] the hopes and the disappointments
demand a separate chapter.

XX

THE FIRST NIGHT

It was no easy thing to issue the first number of
Indian Opinion from Phoenix. Had I not taken two
precautions, the first issue would have had to be
dropped or delayed. The idea of having an engine[250]
to work the press had not appealed to me. I had
thought that hand-power would be more in keeping
with an atmosphere where agricultural work was
also to be done by hand. But as the idea had[251] not
appeared feasible, we had installed an oil-engine.[252] I
had, however, suggested to West to have something
handy to fall back upon in case the engine failed.
He had therefore arranged a wheel which could be
worked by hand. The size of the paper, *that of a daily,
was considered unsuitable for an out-of-the-way place like
Phoenix. It was reduced to foolscap size,*[M1] so that, in case
of emergency, copies might be struck off with the
help of a treadle.

In the initial stages, we all had to keep late hours
before the day of publication. Everyone, young and old,
had to help in folding the sheets. We usually finished
our work between ten o'clock and mid-night. But the
first night was unforgettable. The pages were locked,
but the engine refused to work. We had got out an

[M1] was that of a daily. This
place did not have the facility
to repair a large machine
immediately. That also would
have stopped the publication.
The size therefore was changed
to that of an ordinary weekly.

---

[249] 'the changes made' added in the English translation.

[250] 'engine' English word in the original.

[251] 'But as it had' in the first edition.

[252] 'oil-engine' in the original.

engineer from Durban[253] to put up the engine and set it going. He and West tried their hardest, but in vain.[254] Everyone was anxious. West, in despair, at last came to me, with tears in his eyes, and said, 'The engine will not work, I am afraid we cannot issue the paper in time.'

'If that is the case, we cannot help it. No use shedding tears.[255] Let us do whatever else is[256] humanly possible.[257] What about the handwheel?' I said, comforting him.

'Where have we the men to work?' he replied. 'We are not enough to cope with the job. It requires relays of four men each, and *our own men*[M2] are all tired.'

Building work had not yet been finished, so the carpenters were still with us. They were sleeping on the press floor. I said pointing to them, 'But can't we make use of these carpenters? And we may have a whole night of work. I think this device is still open to us.'

'I dare not wake up the carpenters.[258] And our men are really too tired,' said West.

'Well, that's for me to negotiate,' said I.

'Then it is possible that we may get through the work,' West replied.

I woke up the carpenters and requested their co-operation. They needed no *pressure*.[M3] They said, 'If we cannot be called upon in an emergency, *what use are we?*[M4] You rest yourselves and we will work the wheel. For us it is easy work.' Our own men were of course ready.

West was greatly delighted and started singing a hymn as we set to work. I partnered the carpenters, all the rest joined turn by turn, and thus we went on until

[M2] we

[M3] pleading

[M4] how are we to be considered human

---

[253] 'from Durban' added in the English translation.

[254] 'but to no avail' in the first edition.

[255] 'But it is no use shedding tears over it.' In the first edition.

[256] 'it is' in the first edition.

[257] 'possible to do' in the first edition.

[258] 'and seek their help' to add.

7 a.m. There was still a good deal to do. I therefore suggested to West that the engineer might now be asked to get up and try again to start the engine, so that if we succeeded we might finish in time.

West woke him up and he immediately went into the engine room. And lo and behold![259] The engine worked almost as soon as he touched it. The whole press rang with peals of joy. 'How can this be? How is it that all our labours last night were of no avail, and this morning it has been set going as though there were nothing wrong with it?' I enquired.

'It is difficult to say,' said West or the engineer, I forget which.[260] 'Machines also sometimes seem to behave as though they required rest like us.'

For me the failure of the engine had come as a test for us all, and its working in the nick of time as the fruit of our honest and earnest labours.

The copies were despatched[261] in time, and everyone was happy.

This initial insistence ensured the regularity of the paper, and created an atmosphere of self-reliance in Phoenix. There came a time when we deliberately gave up the use of the engine and worked with hand-power only. Those were, to my mind, the days of the highest moral uplift for Phoenix.

XXI

POLAK TAKES THE PLUNGE

It has always been my regret that, although I started the Settlement at Phoenix, I could stay there only for

---

[259] 'And lo and behold!' added in the English translation.

[260] 'I forgot which' added in the English translation.

[261] 'to the station' to add.

brief periods.[262] My original idea had been gradually to
retire from practice, go and live at the Settlement, earn
my livelihood by manual work[263] there, and find the
joy of service in the fulfilment of Phoenix. But it was
not to be. I have found by experience that *man makes*

M1 we desire something and
what happens is something else
altogether.

his plans to be often upset by God,[M1] but at the same
time[264] where the ultimate goal is the search of truth,
no matter how a man's plans are frustrated, the issue
is never injurious and often better than anticipated.
The unexpected turn that Phoenix took and the
unexpected happenings were certainly not injurious,
though it is difficult to say that they were better than
our original expectations.

In order to enable every one of us to make a living
by manual labour, we parcelled out the land round the
press in pieces of three acres each. One of these fell to
my lot. On all these plots we, much against our wish,[265]
built houses with corrugated iron. Our desire had been
to have mud huts thatched with straw or small brick
houses such as would become ordinary peasants, but it
could not be. They would have been more expensive
and would have meant more time, and everyone was
eager to settle down as soon as possible.

The editor was still Mansukhlal Naazar. He had
not accepted the new scheme and was directing the
paper from Durban where there was a branch office
for *Indian Opinion*. Though we had paid compositors,
the idea was for every member of the Settlement to
learn type-setting, the easiest, if the most tedious, of the
processes in a printing-press. Those, therefore, who did
not already know the work learnt it. I remained a dunce

---

[262] 'intervals' in the first edition.

[263] 'by manual work' added in the English translation.

[264] 'but I have also found that' in the first edition.

[265] 'inspite of ourselves' in the first edition.

to the last. Maganlal Gandhi surpassed us all.[266] Though he had never before worked in a press, he became an expert compositor and not only achieved great speed but, to my agreeable surprise, quickly mastered all the other branches of press work. I have always thought that he was not conscious of his own capacity.

We had hardly settled down, the buildings were hardly ready, when I had to leave the newly *constructed nest*[M2] and go to Johannesburg. I was not in a position to allow the work there to remain without attention for any length of time.

M2 created family

On return to Johannesburg,[267] I informed Polak of the important changes I had made. His joy knew no bounds when he learnt that the loan of his book had been so fruitful. 'Is it not possible,' he asked,[268] 'for me to take part in the new venture?' 'Certainly,' said I, 'You may if you like join the Settlement.' 'I am quite ready,' he replied, 'if you will admit me.'

His determination captured me. He gave a month's notice[269] to his chief to be relieved from *The Critic*, and reached Phoenix in due course. By his sociability he won the hearts of all and soon became a member of the family. *Simplicity was so much a part of his nature that, far from feeling the life at Phoenix in any way strange or hard, he took to it like a duck takes to water.*[M3] But I could not keep him there long. Mr. Ritch had decided to finish his legal studies in England,[270] and it was impossible for me to bear the burden of the office single-handed, so

M3 Simplicity was in his bones, far from feeling the life at Phoenix in any way strange or hard, it seemed natural and to his liking.

---

266 The last line of this paragraph, 'I have always thought that he was not conscious of his own capacity,' appears here in the original.

267 'On return from Johannesburg' in the original, which is an apparent mistake, corrected in the translation.

268 'with enthusiasm' to add.

269 'notice' English word in the original.

270 A farewell was organized for him on 9 March 1905.

I suggested to Polak that he should join the office and qualify as an attorney. I had thought that ultimately both of us would retire and settle at Phoenix, but that never came to pass. Polak's was such a trustful nature that, when he reposed his confidence in a friend, he would try to agree with him instead of arguing with him. He wrote to me from Phoenix that though he loved the life there, was perfectly happy, and had hopes of developing the Settlement, still he was ready to leave and join the office to qualify as an attorney, if I thought that thereby we should more quickly realize our ideals. I heartily welcomed the letter. Polak left Phoenix, came to Johannesburg and signed his articles with me.

About the same time a Scotch theosophist, whom I had been coaching for a local legal examination, also joined as an articled clerk, on my inviting him to follow Polak's example. His name was Mr. MacIntyre.[271]

Thus, with the laudable object of quickly realizing the ideals at Phoenix, I seemed to be going deeper and deeper into a contrary current, and had God not willed otherwise, I should have found myself entrapped in this net spread in the name of simple life.

It will be after a few more chapters that I shall describe[272] how I and my ideals were saved in a way no one had imagined or expected.

---

[271] William J. MacIntyre. He was to play an important role in the first test case of a non-European riding the newly inaugurated electric tramcars in Johannesburg. He and a wealthy Indian merchant, Ebrahim Saleji Coovadia, boarded a tramcar and since Coovadia was not a servant of MacIntyre's, he was refused a ride. See DiSalvo, *M.K. Gandhi, Attorney at Law*, pp. 181–85, for the details of this test case.

[272] 'it will take a few more chapters before I describe' in the first edition.

XXII

WHOM GOD PROTECTS[273]

I had now given up all hope of returning to India[274] in the near future. I had promised my wife that I would return home within a year. The year was gone without any prospect of my return, so[275] I decided to send for her and[276] the children.

On the boat bringing them to South Africa, Ramdas, my third son, broke his arm while playing with the ship's captain.[M1] The captain looked after him[277] well and had him[278] attended to by the ship's doctor. Ramdas landed[279] with his hand in a sling. The doctor had advised that, as soon as we reached home,[280] the wound should be dressed by a qualified doctor. But this was the time when I was full of faith in my experiments in earth treatment. I had even succeeded in persuading some of my clients who had faith in my quackery to try the earth and water treatment.

What then was I to do for Ramdas?[M2] He was just eight years old. I asked him *if he would mind my dressing his wound.*[M3] With a smile he said *he did not mind at all.*[M4]

[M1] The children came. My third son, Ramdas, was among them. He had become quite friendly with the steamer's captain while on board, and broke his arm while playing with the captain.

[M2] What else could I do for Ramdas?

[M3] 'Would you be afraid if I were to dress your wound?'

[M4] he allowed me to conduct the experiment

---

[273] In the original, *Jene Ram Rakhe*. This is from a poem by medieval Gujarati saint-poet Dhiro Bhagat (1753–1825). The poem also forms part of the *Ashram Bhajanavali*, a book of hymns that formed part of the daily Ashram prayers.

[274] 'and settling there' to add.

[275] 'and so' in the first edition.

[276] 'her and' added in the English translation. They reached South Africa in the last quarter of 1904.

[277] 'had looked after him' in the first edition.

[278] 'had had him' in the first edition.

[279] 'therefore landed' in the first edition. 'in Johannesburg' to add.

[280] 'as soon as we reached home' added in the English translation.

It was not possible for him at that age to decide what was the best thing for him, but he knew very well the distinction between quackery and proper medical treatment. And he knew my habit of *home treatment*[M5] and had faith enough to trust himself to me. In fear and trembling I undid the bandage, washed the wound, applied a clean earth poultice and tied the arm up again. This sort of dressing went on daily for about a month until the wound was completely healed. There was no hitch, and the wound took no more time to heal than the ship's doctor had said it would[281] under the usual treatment.

This and other[282] experiments enhanced my faith in such household remedies, and I now proceeded with them with more self-confidence. I widened the sphere of their application, trying the earth and water and fasting treatment[283] in cases of wounds, fevers, dyspepsia, jaundice and other complaints, with success on most occasions. But nowadays I have not the confidence I had in South Africa and experience has even shown that these experiments involve obvious risks.

The reference here, therefore, to these experiments is not meant to demonstrate their success. I cannot claim complete success for any experiment. Even medical men can make no such claim for[284] their experiments.[285] My object is only to show that he who would go in for novel experiments must begin with himself. That leads to a quicker discovery of truth, and God always protects the honest[286] experimenter.

---

[281] 'would do' in the first edition.

[282] 'and other' added in the English translation.

[283] 'on women and men, young and old' to add.

[284] 'about' in the first edition.

[285] 'for their experiments' added in the English translation.

[286] 'honest' added in the English translation.

The risks involved in experiments in cultivating intimate contacts with Europeans were as grave as those in the nature-cure experiments. Only those risks were of a different kind. But in cultivating those contacts I never so much as thought of the risks.

I invited Polak to come and stay with me,[287] and we began to live like blood-brothers. The lady who was soon to be[288] Mrs. Polak and he had been engaged for some years, but the marriage had been postponed for a propitious time. I have an impression that Polak wanted to put some money by before he settled down to a married life. He knew Ruskin much better than I, but his Western surroundings were a bar against his translating Ruskin's teaching immediately into practice. But I pleaded with him: 'When there is a heart union, as in your case, it is hardly right to postpone marriage merely for financial considerations. If poverty is a bar,

---

[287] The house was at 11, Albermarle Street on the eastern limit of the city. The majority of Indians lived in western Johannesburg. The rental was arranged by Charles Kew, the agent who had secured for MKG his chambers in Rissik Street. Polak's wife, Millie Graham Polak, describes the house: 'The house was situated in a fairly good middle-class neighbourhood, on the outskirts of town. It was a double-storied, detached, eight-roomed building of the modern villa type, surrounded by a garden, and having in the front, open spaces of the Kopies. The upstairs verandah was roomy enough to sleep on, if one wished to do so, and, indeed, in warm weather, it was often so used.' In *Mr. Gandhi: The Man* (London: George Allen and Unwin, 1931), p. 18. This arrangement was not done without any opposition though. In October 1947 Charles Kew wrote to MKG, recalling how the residents had tried to keep him out of the whites-only suburb. Displaying 'considerable indignation they tried before you took possession to offset the tenancy but the owner of the house supported me, and in a few weeks the agitation died down' Itzkin, *Gandhi's Johannesburg*, p. 61. On 5 June 1905 MKG wrote to the owner M.H. Thurston to seek reduction in the rent and to have the chimney in the dining room repaired. See *CWMG*, vol. 4, p. 462.

[288] 'The lady who was soon to be' added in the 1940 edition.

poor men can never marry. And then you are now staying with me. There is no question of household expenses. I think you should get married as soon as possible.' As I have said in a previous chapter, I had never to argue a thing twice with Polak. He appreciated the force of my argument, and immediately opened correspondence on the subject with[289] Mrs. Polak, who was then in England. She gladly accepted the proposal and in a few months reached Johannesburg.[290] Any expense over the wedding was out of the question, not even a special dress was thought necessary. They needed no religious rites to seal the bond. Mrs. Polak was a Christian by birth and Polak a Jew. Their common religion was the religion of ethics.

I may mention in passing an amusing incident in connection with this wedding. The Registrar of European marriages in the Transvaal could not register marriages between black or coloured people. In the wedding in question, I acted as the best man. Not that we could not have got a European friend for the purpose, but Polak would not brook the suggestion. So we three went to the Registrar of marriages. How could he be sure that the parties to a marriage in which I acted as the best man would be whites? He proposed to postpone registration pending inquiries. The next day was a Sunday.[291] The day following was New Year's Day, a public holiday.[292] To postpone the date of a solemnly arranged wedding on such a flimsy pretext was more than one could put up with. I knew the Chief Magistrate, who was head of the Registration

---

[289] 'future' to add.

[290] She reached Johannesburg on 30 December 1905.

[291] 'Christmas Day' in the original, an apparent error.

[292] 'The day following was New Year's Day, a public holiday.' Added in the English translation.

Department. So I appeared before him with the couple. He laughed and gave me a note to the Registrar and the marriage was duly registered.

Up to now the Europeans living with us had been more or less known to me before. But now an English lady who was an utter stranger to us entered the family. I do not remember our ever having had a difference with the newly-married couple, but even if Mrs. Polak and my wife[293] had had some unpleasant experiences, they would have been no more than what happen in the best-regulated homogeneous families. And let it be remembered that mine would be considered an essentially heterogeneous family, where people of all kinds and temperaments were freely admitted.[294] When we come to think of it, the distinction between heterogeneous and homogeneous is discovered to be merely imaginary. We are all one family.

I had better celebrate West's wedding also in this chapter. At this stage of my life, my ideas about *brahmacharya* had not fully matured, and so *I was interesting myself in getting*[M6] all my bachelor friends married. When, in due course, West made a pilgrimage to Louth to see his parents, I advised him to return married if possible. Phoenix was the common home, and as we were all supposed to have become farmers, we were not afraid of marriage *and its usual consequences.*[M7] West returned with Mrs. West,[295] a beautiful young lady from Leicester. She came of a family of shoemakers working in a Leicester

[M6] I made it my business to get

[M7] or procreation

---

[293] 'who hitherto did not have much experience of such kind' to add.

[294] 'And let it be remembered that mine would be considered an essentially heterogeneous family, where people of all kinds and temperaments were freely admitted.' Added in the English translation.

[295] Ada West, née Pywell. They had two children, Hilda and Harry. Albert West's sister was also called Ada, known to Phoenix community as 'Devi Behn'.

factory. Mrs. West had herself some experience of work in this factory. I have called her beautiful, because it was her moral beauty that at once attracted me. True beauty after all consists in purity of heart. With Mr. West had come his mother-in-law too. The old lady is still alive. She put us all to shame by her industry and her buoyant, cheerful nature.

In the same way as I persuaded these European friends to marry, I encouraged the Indian friends to send for their families from home. Phoenix thus developed into a little village, half a dozen[296] families having come and settled and begun to increase there.[297]

XXIII

A PEEP INTO THE HOUSEHOLD[M1]

It has already been seen that, though household expenses were heavy, the tendency towards simplicity began in Durban. But the Johannesburg house came in for much severer overhauling in the light of *Ruskin's teaching*.[M2]

I introduced as much simplicity as was possible in a barrister's house. It was impossible to do without a certain amount of furniture. *The change was more internal than external*.[M3] The liking for doing personally all the physical labour increased. I therefore began to bring my children also under that discipline.

Instead of buying baker's bread, we began to prepare unleavened wholemeal bread at home according to Kuhne's recipe. Common mill flour was no good for this, and the use of handground flour, it was thought,

---

[296] 'Indian' to add.

[297] These included Maganlal and Santok Gandhi, Chhaganlal and Kashi Gandhi, Sam Govindasaami Raju's family, Anandlal Gandhi and his family and Purshottamdas Desai and Ani.

would ensure more simplicity, health and economy. So I purchased a hand-mill for £7. The iron[298] wheel was too heavy to be tackled by one man, but easy for two. Polak and I and the children usually worked it. My wife also occasionally lent a hand, though the grinding hour was her usual time for commencing kitchen work. Mrs. Polak now joined us on her arrival. The grinding proved a very beneficial exercise for the children. Neither this nor any other work was ever imposed on them, but it was a pastime to them to come and lend a hand, and they were at liberty to break off whenever tired. But the children, including those whom I shall have occasion to introduce later, *as a rule never failed me*.[M4] Not that I had no laggards at all, but most did their work cheerfully enough. I can recall few youngsters in those days fighting shy of work or pleading fatigue.

M4 have always done for me tremendous work

We had engaged a servant to look after the house. He lived with us as a member of the family, and the children used to help him in his work. The municipal sweeper removed the night-soil, but we personally attended to the cleaning of the closet instead of asking or expecting the servant to do it. This proved a good training for the children. The result was that none of my sons developed any aversion for scavenger's work, and they naturally got a good grounding in general sanitation. There was hardly any illness in the home at Johannesburg, but whenever there was any, the nursing was willingly done by the children. I will not say that I was indifferent to their *literary education*,[M5] but I certainly did not hesitate to sacrifice it. My sons have therefore some reason for a grievance against me.[299] Indeed they have occasionally given expression to it, and I must plead guilty to a certain extent. The desire to give them *a literary education*[M6] was there. I even endeavoured to

M5 education of letters

M6 an education of letters

---

[298] 'iron' added in the English translation.

[299] 'because of the deficiency in this regard' to add.

give it to them myself, but every now and then there was some hitch or other. As I had made no other arrangement for their private tuition, I used to get them to walk with me daily to the office and back home—a distance of about 5 miles in all. This gave them and me a fair amount of exercise. I tried to instruct them by conversation during these walks, if there was no one else *claiming my attention.*[M7] All my children, excepting the eldest, Harilal, who had stayed away in India, were brought up in Johannesburg in this manner. Had I been able to devote at least an hour to their *literary education*[M8] with strict regularity, I should have given them, in my opinion, an ideal education. But it has been their, as also my, regret that I *failed to ensure them enough literary training.*[M9] The eldest son has often given vent to his distress privately before me and publicly in the Press;[300] the other sons[301] have generously forgiven the failure as unavoidable. *I am not heart-broken over it*[M10] and the regret, if any, is that I did not prove an ideal father. But I hold that I sacrificed their *literary training*[M11] to what

[M7] walking with me. In the office they would talk with the clients and clerks, read whatever was put in their hands, run errands or do shopping for the house.

[M8] education of letters

[M9] did not insist on its adherence

[M10] I do not regret this lack

[M11] education of letters

---

[300] The reference is to Harilal Gandhi's 'semi-public' letter of 31 March 1915. He wrote, 'In 1906, at the age of nineteen, I implored and beseeched you, I made innumerable arguments and pleaded that I should be allowed to chart the course of my life. I wanted to study, to gain knowledge; I had no other desire. I demanded that I should be sent to England. I wept and wandered aimlessly for a year but you paid no heed. You told me that character building should precede everything else.' Chandubhai Bhagubhai Dalal, *Harilal Gandhi: A Life*, translated from the original Gujarati by Tridip Suhrud (Delhi: Orient Blackswan, 2007), p. 131. The full text of the letter is in Appendix 1, pp. 127–45.

[301] Uma Dhupelia-Mesthrie writes of Manilal, 'As Manilal approached his seventeenth year, he began a dialogue with his father about his education. He was full of questions: What class must I tell people I am in? People ask me—what are you going to do with your life? What is the purpose of all the activity at Phoenix? Should not one be learning a skill to earn a living? Gandhi had answers to all the boy's queries. "You are in Bapu's class," he was told.' *Gandhi's Prisoner?*, p. 75.

I genuinely, though maybe wrongly, believed to be service to the community. I am quite clear that I have not been negligent in doing whatever was needful for building up their character. I believe it is the bounden duty of every parent to provide for this properly. Whenever, in spite of my endeavour, my sons have been found wanting, it is my certain conviction that they have reflected, not want of care on my part, but[302] the defects of both their parents.

Children inherit the qualities of the parents, no less than their physical features. Environment does play an important part, but the original capital on which a child starts in life is inherited from its ancestors. I have also seen children successfully surmounting the effects of an evil inheritance. That is due to purity being[303] an inherent attribute of the soul.[304]

Polak and I had often very heated discussions about the desirability or otherwise of[305] giving the children an English education. It has always been my conviction that Indian parents who train their children to think and talk in English from their infancy betray their children and their country. They deprive them of the spiritual and social heritage of the nation, and render them to that extent unfit for the service of the country.[306] Having these convictions, I made a point of always talking to my children in Gujarati. Polak never liked this. He thought I was spoiling their future. He contended, with all the vigour and love at his command, that, if children were to learn a universal language like English from their infancy, they would

---

[302] 'not want of care on my part, but' added in the English translation.

[303] 'purity being' added in the English translation.

[304] 'It is its uniqueness.' To add.

[305] 'the desirability or otherwise of' added in the English translation.

[306] 'and the world' to add.

easily gain considerable advantage[307] over others in the race of life. He failed to convince me. I do not now remember whether I convinced him of the correctness of my attitude, or whether he gave me up as too obstinate. This happened about twenty years ago, and my convictions have only deepened with experience. Though my sons have suffered for want of full literary education, the knowledge of the mother-tongue that they naturally acquired has been all to their and the country's good, inasmuch as they do not appear the foreigners they would otherwise have appeared. They naturally became bi-lingual, speaking and writing English with fair ease, because of daily contact with a large circle of English friends, and because of their stay in a country where English was the chief language spoken.

XXIV

THE ZULU 'REBELLION'

[M1] It has been my lot never to settle down to a steady life after setting up a home.

Even after I thought I had settled down in Johannesburg, there was to be no settled life for me.[M1] Just when I felt that I should be breathing in peace, an unexpected event happened. The papers brought the news of the outbreak of the Zulu 'rebellion' in Natal.[308] I bore no grudge

---

[307] 'advance' in the first edition.

[308] 'In mid-1906, the Natal colonialist in the face of rising Zulu resentment against the imposition of a "Poll Tax" unleashed one of the most brutal and bloody armed campaign to suppression the challenge to British colonial rule. The protest and subsequent armed rebellion against the tax has become popularly known as the Bambatha Rebellion after Chief Bambatha kaMancinza, head of the Zondi, a Zulu clan . . . Chief Bambatha, with the support of other chiefs in the area, refused to accept a new tax that was being implemented by the colonial administration.

against the Zulus, they had harmed no Indian. I had doubts about the[309] 'rebellion' itself. But I then believed that the British Empire *existed for the welfare of the world. A genuine sense of loyalty prevented me from even wishing ill to the Empire. The rightness or otherwise of the 'rebellion'*[M2] was therefore not likely to affect my decision. Natal had a volunteer Defence Force, and it was open to it to recruit more men.[310] I read that this force had already been mobilized to quell the 'rebellion'.

I considered myself a citizen of Natal, being intimately connected with it. So I wrote to the Governor, expressing my readiness, if necessary, to form

[M2] was beneficial to the world. My loyalty was heartfelt. I did not desire the withering of the Empire. The consideration of morality and immorality of the use of force

---

Together with a small group of supporters, he launched a series of attacks against the colonial forces, using the Nkandla Forest as a base. The campaign . . . culminated in a battle . . . at Mome Gorge, where Bambatha and his followers were finally defeated.

'In 1887 Zululand was annexed by the colony of Natal and the Zulu were gradually stripped of most of their arable land. There was widespread poverty, made worse by a series of natural disasters. In 1903 an epidemic of East Coast fever decimated the cattle, there were swarms of locusts and enormous damage was caused by a severe hailstorm in 1905. All these factors led to a serious economic depression. Africans had to pay a Hut Tax and a Dog Tax, and were subjected to a system of forced labour called *isibalo*, which caused widespread hardship and resentment. White farmers occupied more and more land, establishing farms and sugar plantations. After the South African War there was a shortage of agricultural labour. Rather than work for the white farmers, the black workforce was increasingly attracted to the gold mines of the Witwatersrand, where they could earn better wages. In 1905, in an attempt to increase the supply of labour and force more black men into becoming agricultural labourers, the Natal government under Charles Smythe, imposed a Poll Tax of £1 on all men over the age of eighteen. To pay the tax, African men would have to work for cash.

'The Bambatha Rebellion claimed the lives of 4000 Zulu. More than 7000 people were imprisoned and 4000 were flogged. [This] was the last armed resistance against white rule before the formation of the Union of South Africa in 1910.' Source: http://www.sahistory.org.za.

[309] 'correctness of the term' to add.

[310] 'in times of crisis' to add.

an Indian Ambulance Corps. He replied immediately accepting the offer.[311]

I had not expected such prompt acceptance.[312] Fortunately I had made all the necessary arrangements even before writing the letter. If my offer was accepted, I had decided to break up the Johannesburg home. Polak was to have a smaller house, and my wife was to go and settle at Phoenix. I had her full consent to[313] this decision. I do not remember her having ever stood in my way in matters like this. As soon, therefore, as I got the reply from the Governor, I gave the landlord the usual month's notice of vacating the house, sent some of the things to Phoenix and left some with Polak.

I went to Durban and appealed for men. A big contingent was not necessary. We were a party of twenty-four, of whom, besides me, four were Gujaratis. The rest were ex-indentured men from South India, excepting one who was a free Pathan.[314]

---

[311] 'He sent immediately an affirmative reply.' In the first edition. In a meeting held on 24 April 1906 the Natal Indian Congress resolved to offer to raise an ambulance corps, which was communicated to the colonial secretary on 25 April; see *CWMG*, vol. 5, p. 292. The offer was accepted on 30 May 1906, see ibid., p. 348.

[312] 'acceptance of my offer' in the first edition.

[313] 'her full co-operation in' in the first edition.

[314] The *Indian Opinion* of 16 June 1916 gave the following list: M.K. Gandhi (Sgt. Major), U.M. Shetlat (Sgt.), H.I. Joshi (Sgt.), S.B. Medh (Sgt.), Khan Mahomed, Mahomed, Sheikh Dada Mian, Pooti Naiken, Appalsamy, Kunjee, Sheikh Madar, Mahomed, Alwar, Muthusamy Copoosamy, Ajadhyasing, Kistana, Ali, Bhailal, Jamaluddin. See *Indian Opinion*, vol. IV, no. 24, p. 398. *CWMG*, vol. 5, p. 368, adds the name of Prabhu Hari (Corporal). The photograph of the Indian Ambulance Corps on the page facing p. 368 has twenty men and not twenty-four as mentioned in the *Autobiography*. Of these, thirteen were ex-indentured, two were engine drivers, one goldsmith, three agents and bookkeepers and one a barrister.

In order to give me a status and to facilitate work, as also in accordance with the existing convention, the Chief Medical Officer appointed me to the temporary rank of Sergeant Major and three men selected by me to the rank of sergeants and one to that of corporal.[315] We also received our uniforms from the Government. Our Corps was on active service for nearly six weeks. On reaching the scene of the 'rebellion', I saw that there was nothing there to justify the name of 'rebellion'. There was no resistance that one could see. The reason why the disturbance had been magnified into a rebellion was that a Zulu chief had advised non-payment of a new tax imposed on his people, and had assagaied a sergeant who had gone to collect the tax. At any rate my heart was with the Zulus, and I was delighted, on reaching headquarters, to hear that our main work was to be the nursing of the wounded Zulus. The Medical Officer in charge welcomed us. He said the white people were not willing nurses for the wounded Zulus, that their wounds were festering, and that he was at his wit's end. He hailed our arrival as a godsend for those innocent people, and he equipped us with bandages, disinfectants, etc., and took us to the improvised hospital. The Zulus[M3] were delighted to see us. The M3 patients white soldiers used to peep through the railings that separated us from them and tried to dissuade us from attending to the wounds. And as we would not heed them, they became enraged and poured unspeakable abuse[316] on the Zulus.

Gradually I came into closer touch with these soldiers, and they ceased to interfere. Among the commanding

---

[315] 'Sergeant Major', 'sergeant' and 'corporal' English words in the original.

[316] 'unspeakable abuse' translates *kan na kida khare*, literally, abuse such that 'worms would fall from the ears'.

officers were Col. Sparks[317] and Col. Wylie,[318] who had
bitterly opposed me in 1896. They were surprised at
my attitude and specially called and thanked me. They
introduced me to General Mackenzie. Let not the
reader think that these were professional soldiers. Col.
Wylie was a well-known Durban[319] lawyer. Col. Sparks
was well known as the owner of a butcher's shop in
Durban. General Mackenzie was a noted Natal farmer.
All these gentlemen[320] were volunteers, and as such had
received military training and experience.

The wounded in our charge were not wounded
in battle. A section of them had been taken prisoners
as suspects. The General had sentenced them to be
flogged. The flogging had caused severe sores. These,
being unattended to, were festering. The others were
Zulu friendlies. Although these had badges given them
to distinguish them from the 'enemy', they had been
shot at by the soldiers by mistake.

Besides this work, I had to compound and dispense
prescriptions for the white soldiers. This was easy
enough for me as I had received a year's training in Dr.
Booth's little hospital. This work brought me in close
contact with many Europeans.

We were attached to a swift-moving column. It
had orders to march wherever danger was reported. It
was for the most part mounted infantry. As soon as our
camp was moved, we had to follow on foot with our

---

[317] Harry Sparks was among the main organizers of the demonstration
against the landing of the passengers of *S.S. Courland* and
S.S. Naderi in 1896 that had led to the assault on MKG. Apart
from being the biggest butcher in the Colony he was also a
captain in the Natal Mounted Rifles in the Volunteer Force.

[318] James Scott Wylie, attorney of Wylie and Binns, member of the
protest committee.

[319] 'Durban' added in the English translation.

[320] 'gentlemen' added in the English translation.

stretchers on our shoulders. Twice or thrice we had to march forty miles a day. But wherever we went, I am thankful that we had God's good work to do, having to carry to the camp on our stretchers those Zulu friendlies who had been inadvertently wounded, and to attend upon them as nurses.[321]

XXV

HEART SEARCHINGS

The Zulu 'rebellion' was full of new experiences and gave me much food for thought. The Boer War had not brought home to me the horrors of war with anything like the vividness that the 'rebellion' did. This was no war but a man-hunt, not only in my opinion, but also in that of many Englishmen with whom I had occasion to talk. To hear every morning reports of the soldiers' rifles exploding like crackers in innocent hamlets, and to live in the midst of them was a trial. But I swallowed the bitter draught, especially as the work of my Corps consisted only in nursing the wounded Zulus. I could see that but for us the Zulus would have been uncared for. This work, therefore, eased my conscience.

But there was much else to set one thinking.[322] It was a sparsely populated part of the country. Few and far between in hills and dales were the scattered Kraals of the simple and so-called 'uncivilized' Zulus. Marching, with or without the wounded,[323] through these solemn solitudes, I often fell into deep thought.

---

[321] For MKG's report from the 'front', see *CWMG*, vol. 5, pp. 368–78.

[322] 'But there was much else to set one thinking.' Added in the English translation.

[323] 'miles after miles' to add.

I pondered over *brahmacharya* and its implications, and my convictions took deep root. I discussed it with my co-workers. I had not realized then how indispensable it was for self-realization, but clearly saw that *one aspiring to serve humanity with his whole soul could not do without it.*[M1] It was borne in upon me that I should have more and more occasions for service of the kind I was rendering, and that I should find myself unequal to my task if I were engaged in the pleasures of family[324] life and in the propagation and rearing of children.

In a word, I could not live both after the flesh and the spirit.[M2] On the present occasion, for instance, I should not have been able to throw myself into *the fray,*[M3] had my wife been expecting a baby. *Without the observance of brahmacharya service of the family would be inconsistent with service of the community. With brahmacharya they would be perfectly consistent.*[M4]

So thinking, I became somewhat impatient to take a final vow. The prospect of the vow brought a certain kind of exultation. Imagination also found free play and opened out limitless vistas of service.

Whilst I was thus in the midst of strenuous physical and mental work, a *report*[M5] came to the effect that the *work of suppressing the 'rebellion' was nearly over,*[M6] and that we should soon be discharged. A day or two after this our discharge came and in a few days we got back to our homes.[325]

After a short while I got a letter from the Governor specially thanking the Ambulance Corps for its services.

On my arrival at Phoenix I eagerly broached the subject of *brahmacharya* with Chhaganlal, Maganlal, West and others. They liked the idea and accepted the necessity of taking the vow, but they also represented

[M1] it was an imperative for service

[M2] I could not ride two horses.

[M3] this service

[M4] The absence of *brahmacharya* would result in the enlargement of the family, which would run contrary to one's endeavour for uplift of society. The observance of *brahmacharya* in marriage would enable one to render service to the family in a form consistent with the service to society.

[M5] rumour

[M6] rebellion had been quelled

---

[324] 'family' added in the English translation.

[325] The Ambulance Corps returned to Durban on 20 July 1906.

the difficulties of the task. Some of them set themselves bravely to observe it, and some, I know, succeeded also.

I too took the plunge[326]—the vow to observe *brahmacharya* for life.[327] I must confess that I had not then fully realized the magnitude and immensity of the task I undertook. The difficulties are even today staring me in the face. The importance of the vow is being more and more borne in upon me. Life without *brahmacharya* appears to me to be insipid and animal-like. The brute by nature knows no self-restraint. *Man is man because he is capable of, and only in so far as he exercises, self-restraint.*[M7] What formerly appeared to me to be extravagant praise of *brahmacharya* in our religious books seems now, with increasing clearness every day, to be absolutely proper and founded on experience.

[M7] The humanity of man lies in voluntary self-restraint.

I saw that *brahmacharya*, which is so full of wonderful potency, is by no means an easy affair, and certainly not a mere matter of the body. It begins with bodily restraint, but does not end there.[328] The perfection of it precludes even an impure thought. A true *brahmachari* will not even dream of satisfying the fleshly appetite, and *until he is in that condition, he has a great deal of ground to cover.*[M8]

[M8] so long as the desire persists in dreams, consider that *brahmacharya* imperfect

For me the observance of even bodily *brahmacharya* has been full of difficulties. Today I may say that I feel myself fairly[329] safe, but I have yet to achieve complete mastery over thought, which is so essential. Not that the will or effort is lacking, but it is yet a problem to me wherefrom undesirable thoughts spring their insidious

---

[326] 'the plunge' added in the English translation.

[327] This was in July 1906. C.B. Dalal gives the date as 20 July 1906, the day he returned to Durban.

[328] 'but does not end there' added in the English translation.

[329] 'fairly' added in the English translation.

M9 Great men

M10 which guide our path. They are not perfect.

invasions. I have no doubt that there is a key[330] to lock out undesirable thoughts, but[331] everyone has to find it out for himself. *Saints and seers*[M9] have left their experiences for us, *but they have given us no infallible and universal prescription.*[M10] For perfection or freedom from error[332] comes only from grace, and so seekers after God have left us *mantras*, such as Ramanama, hallowed by their own austerities and charged with their purity. Without an unreserved surrender to His grace, complete mastery over thought is impossible. This is the teaching of every great book of religion, and I am realizing the truth of it every moment of my striving after that *perfect*[M11] *brahmacharya*.

M11 most subtle

But part of the history of that striving and struggle will be told in chapters to follow. *I shall conclude this chapter with an indication of how I set about the task.*[M12] In the first flush of enthusiasm, I found the observance quite easy. The very first change I made in my mode of life was to stop sharing the same bed with my wife or seeking privacy with her.

M12 In concluding this chapter I would only say that

Thus *brahmacharya*, which I had been observing willy-nilly since 1900, was sealed with a vow in the middle of 1906.

XXVI

THE BIRTH OF SATYAGRAHA

Events were so shaping themselves in Johannesburg as to make this self-purification on my part a preliminary as it were to satyagraha. I can now see that all the

---

[330] 'no doubt that man possesses the key' in the first edition.

[331] 'for the present I have come to the conclusion that' to add.

[332] 'or freedom from error' added in the English translation.

principal events of my life, culminating in the vow of
brahmacharya, were secretly preparing me for it. *The*
principle called satyagraha[333] *came into being before that name*
was invented.[M1] Indeed when it was born, I myself could
not say what it was. In Gujarati also we used the English

[M1] Before the word 'satyagraha'
was invented, the thing itself
had come into being.

---

[333] The advent of satyagraha was in a historic mass meeting of more
than 3000 persons (including a delegation of persons of Chinese
origin), which took place to oppose the Transvaal Asiatic Law
Amendment Ordinance. The Ordinance was published in the
Transvaal Government Gazette Extraordinary of 22 August
1906. MKG described the impact of the Ordinance on him: 'I
went up a hill near the house in company of a friend and began
to translate the draft Ordinance into Gujarati for *Indian Opinion*.
I shuddered as I read the sections of the Ordinance one after
another. I saw nothing in it except hatred of Indians . . . I clearly
saw that this was a question of life and death for them. I further
saw that even in case of memorials and representations proving
fruitless, the community must not sit with folded hands. Better
to die than submit to such a law.' *Satyagraha in South Africa*,
CWMG, vol. 29, p. 83. The Ordinance required every Asiatic
of eight years of age or above to register before the Registrar
of Asiatics; further they were required as identification to give
finger and thumb impressions and produce such registration
permits whenever asked for. Failure to register was a punishable
offence, and the sentence included deportation.

The meeting of the Asiatics was called by the Transvaal British
Indian Association under the chairmanship of Abdul Gani. The
meeting took place at the Empire Theatre on 11 September
1906. During the course of this meeting, one of the speakers,
Sheth Haji Habib, proposed to administer an oath in the name
of God and with God as witness. MKG explained the nature of
an oath made in the name of God and with Him as witness and
ordinary resolution, however deliberately made. The meeting
resolved to oppose the Ordinance, if it became law, in the name
of God. The origins of satyagraha are in this event.

The Resolution 4 adopted by the assembly reads: 'British Indians
here assembled solemnly and regretfully resolve that, rather than
submit to the galling, tyrannous, and un-British requirements
laid down in the above Draft Ordinance, every British Indian
in the Transvaal shall submit himself to imprisonment and shall
continue so to do until it shall please His Most Gracious Majesty
the King–Emperor to grant relief.' *CWMG*, vol. 5, p. 423.

The Empire Theatre was destroyed in an accidental fire the
day the satyagraha pledge was taken.

phrase 'passive resistance' to describe it. When in a meeting of Europeans[334] I found that the term 'passive resistance' was too narrowly construed, that it was supposed to be a weapon of the weak, that it could be characterized by hatred, and that it could finally manifest itself as violence, I had to demur to all these statements and explain the real nature of the Indian movement. It was clear that a new word must be coined by the Indians to designate their struggle.

But I could not for the life of me find out a new[335] name, and therefore offered a nominal prize through *Indian Opinion* to the reader who made the best suggestion on the subject. As a result Maganlal Gandhi coined the word 'Sadagraha' (*sat*—truth, *agraha*—firmness) and won the prize.[336] But in order to make it clearer I changed the word to 'Satyagraha' which has since become current in Gujarati as a designation for the struggle.

The history of this struggle is for all practical purposes a history of the remainder of my life in South Africa and especially of my experiments with truth in that subcontinent.[337] I wrote the major portion of this history in Yeravda jail and finished it after I was released. It was published in *Navajivan* and subsequently issued in book form.[338] Sjt. Valji Govindji Desai has been translating it

---

[334] This meeting took place on 7 July 1909 at Germiston. MKG was invited to speak on 'The Ethics of Passive Resistance' by the Germiston Literary and Debating Society. The meeting, attended by leading citizens of Germiston, took place at the council chamber and the president of the society, Linton Jones, presided. See *CWMG*, vol. 9, pp. 243–44.

[335] ', unencumbered' to add.

[336] For the offer of the prize, see *CWMG*, vol. 7, p. 435, and for the announcement of the result, see *CWMG*, vol. 8, pp. 22–23.

[337] 'in that sub-continent' added in the English translation.

[338] 'with the title *History of Satyagraha in South Africa*' to add.

into English for *Current Thought*, but I am now arranging to have the English translation published in book form[339] at an early date, so that those who will may be able to familiarize themselves with my most important experiments in South Africa. I would recommend a perusal of my history of satyagraha in South Africa to such[340] readers as have not seen it already. I will not repeat what I have put down there, but in the next few chapters will deal only with a few personal incidents of my life in South Africa which have not been covered by that history. And when I have done with these, I will at once proceed to give the reader some idea of my experiments in India. Therefore, anyone who wishes to consider these experiments in their strict chronological order will now do well to keep the history of satyagraha in South Africa before him.

XXVII

MORE EXPERIMENTS IN DIETETICS

I was anxious to observe *brahmacharya* in thought, word and deed, and equally[341] anxious to devote the maximum of time to the satyagraha struggle and fit myself for it by cultivating[342] purity. I was therefore led to make further changes and to impose greater restraints upon myself in the matter of food. The motive for the previous changes had been largely *hygienic*,[M1] but the new experiments were made from a religious standpoint.

[M1] from the point of view of health

---

[339] It was published by S. Ganesan of Madras in 1928.

[340] 'Gujarati' to add.

[341] 'and I was equally' in the first edition.

[342] 'utmost possible' to add.

Fasting and restriction in diet now played a more important part in my life. Passion in man is generally co-existent with a hankering after the pleasures of the palate. And so it was with me. I have encountered many difficulties in trying to control passion as well as taste, and I cannot claim even now to have brought them under complete subjection. I have considered myself to be a heavy eater. What friends have thought to be my restraint has never appeared to me in that light. If I had failed to develop restraint to the extent that I have, I should have descended lower than the beasts and met my doom long ago. However, as I had adequately realized my shortcomings, I made great efforts to get rid of them, and thanks to this endeavour I have all these years pulled on with my body and *put in with it my share of work*.[M2]

M2 have been able to take some work from it

Being conscious of my weakness and unexpectedly coming in contact with congenial company, I began to take an exclusive fruit diet or to fast on the *Ekadashi* day, and also to observe *Janmashtami* and similar holidays.[343]

I began with a fruit diet,[344] but from the standpoint of restraint I did not find much to choose between a fruit diet and a diet of food grains. I observed that the same indulgence of taste was possible with the former as with the latter, and even more, when one got accustomed to it. I therefore came to attach greater importance to fasting or having only one meal a day on holidays. And if there was some occasion for penance or the like, I gladly utilized it too for the purpose of fasting.[345]

But I also saw that, the body now being drained more effectively, the food yielded greater relish and the

---

[343] 'holiday' translates the original term *tithi*, which is indicative of lunar movements—each movement of twelve degrees indicating a *tithi*—here, a day of observance.

[344] 'I began with a fruit diet' added in the English translation.

[345] 'by having only one meal' to add.

appetite grew keener. It dawned upon me that fasting could be made as powerful a weapon of indulgence as of restraint. Many similar later experiences of mine as well as of others can be adduced as evidence of this startling[346] fact. I wanted to improve and train my body, but as my chief object now was to achieve restraint and a conquest of the palate, I selected first one food and then another, and at the same time restricted the amount. But the relish was after me, as it were. As I gave up one thing and took up another, this latter afforded me a fresher and greater relish than its predecessor.[347]

In making these experiments I had several companions, the chief of whom was Hermann Kallenbach. I have already written about this friend in the history of satyagraha in South Africa, and will not go over[348] the same ground here. Mr. Kallenbach was always with me whether in fasting or in dietetic changes. I lived with him at his own place when the satyagraha struggle was at its height.[349] We discussed our changes in food and derived more pleasure from the new diet than from the old. Talk of this nature sounded quite pleasant in those days, and did not strike me as

---

[346] 'startling' added in the English translation.

[347] 'than its predecessor' added in the English translation.

[348] 'will not therefore go over' in the first edition.

[349] Kallenbach's house in Pine Road, designed by Kallenbach and Reynolds, was called The Kraal. Building plans were approved on 28 June 1907. On the back of a photograph of the house Kallenbach wrote in German, 'The Kraal, our first house, where Gandhi lived with me for several years. In this house the Rev. J. Doke came many times while writing the book about Gandhi, "An Indian Patriot." 18 September 1928. H.K.' See Itzkin, *Gandhi's Johannesburg*, p. 70. MKG began to live in this house with Kallenbach in March 1908. During his visit to India in 1937 Kallenbach recalled in a conversation with Mahadev Desai, 'Though we worked in our own offices, we lived in the same rooms—almost in the same bed—and whilst he cooked for us I did the cleaning.' *Harijan*, vol. 5, no. 16.

M3 functions for the body and through the body to come face-to-face with the soul

at all improper. Experience has taught me, however, that it was wrong to have dwelt upon the relish of food. One should eat not in order to please the palate, but just to keep the body going. When each organ of sense *subserves the body and through the body the soul*,M3 its special relish disappears, and then alone does it begin to function in the way nature intended it to do.

Any number of experiments is too small and no sacrifice is too great for attaining this symphony with nature. But unfortunately the current is nowadays flowing strongly in the opposite direction. We are not ashamed to[350] sacrifice a multitude of other lives in decorating the perishable body and trying to prolong its existence for a few fleeting moments[351] with the result that we kill ourselves, both body and soul. In trying to

M4 many

cure one old disease, we give rise to *a hundred*M4 new ones; in trying to enjoy the pleasures of sense,[352] we lose in the end even our capacity for enjoyment. All this is passing before our very eyes, but there are none so blind as those who will not see. *Having thus set forth their object and the train of ideas which led up to them, I now propose to describe the dietetic experiments at some length.*M5

M5 In order that the experiments in dietetics that I propose to discuss at length are understood, it was necessary to set forth their object and the train of thought that was followed.

M1 Wife's Determination

XXVIII

*KASTURBAI'S COURAGE*M1

Thrice in her life my wife narrowly escaped death through serious illness.[353] The cures were due to

---

[350] 'are not ashamed to' added in the English translation.

[351] 'for a few fleeting moments' added in the English translation.

[352] 'in trying to enjoy the pleasures of sense' added in the English translation.

[353] The three illnesses referred to here were in November 1908, January 1909 and February–March 1914.

household remedies. At the time of her first attack satyagraha was going on or was about to commence.[354] She had frequent haemorrhage. A medical friend advised a surgical operation, to which she agreed after some hesitation. She was extremely emaciated, and the doctor had to perform the operation without chloroform.[355] It was successful, but she had to suffer much pain. *She, however, went through it with wonderful bravery.*[M2] The doctor[356] and his wife who nursed her were all attention. This was in Durban.[357] The doctor gave me leave to go to Johannesburg, and told me not to have any anxiety about the patient.[358]

[M2] I was wonderstruck by her forbearance.

In a few days, however, I received a letter to the effect that Kasturbai was worse, too weak to sit up in bed, and had once become unconscious. The doctor knew that he might not, without my consent, give her wines or meat.[359] So he telephoned to me at Johannesburg for permission to give her beef tea.[360] I replied saying I could not grant the permission, but that, if she was in a condition to express her wish in the matter she might be consulted, and she was free to do as she liked. 'But,' said the doctor, 'I refuse to consult the patient's wishes in the matter. You must come yourself. If you do not leave me free to prescribe whatever diet I like, I will not hold myself responsible for your wife's life.'

---

[354] 'or was about to commence' added in the English translation. MKG was in Volkrust prison at this time.

[355] 'chloroform', English word in the original.

[356] The operation was performed by Dr. Nanji, a Parsi doctor, on 10 January 1909. His wife was a trained nurse.

[357] 'After two or three days' to add before next sentence.

[358] 'about the patient' added in the English translation.

[359] 'either in medicine or as food' to add.

[360] 'beef tea' in English in the original.

I took the train for Durban the same day, and met the doctor who quietly broke this news to me: 'I had already given Mrs. Gandhi beef tea when I telephoned to you.'

'Now, doctor, I call this a fraud,' said I.

'No question of fraud in prescribing medicine or diet for a patient. In fact we doctors consider it a virtue to deceive patients or their relatives, if thereby we can save our patients,' said the doctor with determination.

I was deeply pained, but kept cool. The doctor was a good man and a personal friend. He and his wife had laid me under a debt of gratitude, but I was not prepared to put up with his *medical morals*.[M3]

M3 conduct

'Doctor, tell me what you propose to do now. I would never allow my wife to be given meat or beef, even if the denial[361] meant her death, unless of course she desired to take it.'

'You are welcome to your philosophy. I tell you that, so long as you keep your wife under my treatment, *I must have the option to give her anything I wish*.[M4] If you don't like this, I must regretfully ask you to remove her. I can't see her die under my roof.'

M4 I will give her the necessary meat or anything else that is required

'Do you mean to say that I must remove her at once?'

'Whenever did I ask you to remove her? I only want to be left entirely free. If you do so, my wife and I will do all that is possible for her, and you may go back without the least anxiety on her score. But if you will not understand this simple thing, you will compel me to ask you to remove your wife from my place.'

I think one of my sons[362] was with me.[363] He entirely agreed with me, and said his mother should not

---

[361] 'denial' added in the 1940 edition, 'it' in the first edition.

[362] Probably Manilal Gandhi. See MKG's letter to him, *CWMG*, vol. 9, pp. 417–18. 'I would have preferred Ba's passing away without the soup, but would not have allowed it to be given to her without her consent.'

[363] 'I consulted him.' To add.

be given beef tea.[364] I next spoke to Kasturbai herself. *She was really too weak to be consulted in this matter. But I thought it my painful duty to do so.*[M5] I told her what had passed between the doctor and myself. She gave a resolute reply: 'I will not take beef tea. It is a rare thing in this world to be born as a human being, and I would far rather die in your *arms*[M6] than pollute my body with such abominations.'[365]

I pleaded with her. I told her that she was not bound to follow me. I cited to her the instances of Hindu friends and acquaintances who had no scruples about taking meat or wine as medicine. But she was adamant. 'No,' said she, 'pray remove me at once.'

I was delighted. Not without some agitation I decided to take her away. I informed the doctor of her resolve. He exclaimed in a rage: 'What a callous man you are! You should have been ashamed to broach the matter to her in her present condition. I tell you your wife is not in a fit state to be removed. She cannot stand the least little hustling. I shouldn't be surprised if she were to die on the way. But if you must persist, you are free to do so. If you will not give her beef tea, I will not take the risk of keeping her under my roof even for a single day.'

So we decided to leave the place at once.[366] It was drizzling and the station was some distance. We had to take the train from Durban for Phoenix, whence our Settlement was reached by a road of two miles and a half. I was undoubtedly taking a very great risk, but I trusted in God, and proceeded with my task. I sent a messenger to Phoenix in advance, *with a message to West*

[M5] She was very weak. To ask her anything was painful.

[M6] lap

---

[364] *mansa*, meat, in the original. In Gujarati meat is often used to indicate all types of non-vegetarian food.

[365] 'with such abominations' added in the English translation.

[366] 'So we decided to leave the place at once.' Added in the English translation.

M7 We had a 'hammock' at
Phoenix. Hammock means a
bed made of rope mesh or
canvas, supported by bamboos
on all ends, a patient can rest
easily in it. West was asked to
meet us at the Phoenix station.

to receive us at the station with a hammock, a bottle of hot milk and one of hot water, and six men to carry Kasturbai in the hammock.M7 I got a rickshaw to enable me to take her by the next available train, put her into it in that dangerous condition, and marched away.

Kasturbai needed no cheering up. On the contrary she comforted me, saying: 'Nothing will happen to me. Don't worry.'

She was mere skin and bone, having had no nourishment for days. The station platform was very large, and as the rickshaw could not be taken inside, one had to walk some distance before one could reach the train. So I carried her in my arms and put her into the compartment. From Phoenix we carried her in the hammock, and there she slowly picked up strength under hydropathic treatment.

In two or three days of our arrival at Phoenix a Swami came to our place. He had heard of *the resolute way in which we had rejected the doctor's advice*,M8 and he had, out of sympathy, come to plead with us. My second and third sons[367] Manilal and Ramdas were, so far as I can recollect, present when the Swami came. He held forth on the religious harmlessness of taking meat, citing authorities from Manu. I did not like his carrying on this disputation in the presence of my wife, but I suffered him to do so out of courtesy. I knew the verses from the *Manusmriti*, I did not need them for my conviction. I knew also that there was a school which regarded these verses as interpolations: but even if they were not, I held my views on vegetarianism independently of religious texts, and Kasturbai's faith was unshakable. *To her the scriptural texts were a sealed book, but the traditional religion of her forefathers was enough for her.*M9 The children swore by their father's creed and so they made light of the Swami's discourse. But Kasturbai put an end to the

M8 our obstinacy

M9 What was she, poor woman, to know of the authority of the scriptural texts? To her the traditions of her forefathers was religion.

---

[367] 'My second and third sons' added in the English translation.

dialogue *at once. 'Swamiji,' she said, 'whatever*[M10] *you may say, I do not want to recover by means of beef tea. Pray don't worry me anymore.*[M11] You may discuss the thing with *my husband and children*[M12] if you like. But my mind is made up.'[368]

XXIX

DOMESTIC SATYAGRAHA

My first experience of jail life was in 1908.[369] I saw that some of the regulations that the prisoners had to

---

[368] 'my mind has been made up.' In the first edition.

[369] On 27 December 1907 H.F. Papenfus, acting commissioner of police, Transvaal, called MKG for a meeting and informed him that the order of his arrest along with twenty-two others had been received. MKG assured Papenfus that he along with the other defendants would voluntarily appear before the court the next day, 28 December. In the case of *Rex vs. Mohandas K. Gandhi*, P.J. Schuurman appeared for the prosecution in magistrate H.H. Jordan's court. MKG represented himself. He was given a notice to leave the Transvaal within forty-eight hours or face arrest under the Asiatic Registration Act. MKG was arrested on 10 January 1908 for defying the court's orders. During the trial MKG requested the court to give him the maximum penalty, £500 fine and six months' hard labour. MKG was taken to the Fort Prison Complex on Hospital Hill and lodged in section 4 of the 'Native Prison'. Their ward could accommodate fifty-one prisoners, but the number increased to 151, and tents had to be pitched in the prison yard. See DiSalvo, *M.K. Gandhi, Attorney at Law*, pp. 202–13, for the details of the trial.

In what was to become a lifelong pattern, something that MKG looked forward to and often meticulously planned, he used the jail time to read. He records, 'I borrowed some of Carlyle's work and the Bible. From a Chinese interpreter who used to visit the place I borrowed a copy of the Koran in English, Huxley's lectures, biographies of Burns, Johnson and Scott, and Bacon's essays on civil and moral counsel. I also had some books of my own, those included an edition of the Gita with a commentary by Manilal Nabhubhai, some Tamil books, an observe were such as should be voluntarily observed by a *brahmachari*, that is, one desiring to practise self-restraint.[370] Such, for instance, was the regulation requiring the last meal to be finished before sunset.[371] Neither the Indian nor the African prisoners were allowed tea or coffee. They could add salt to the cooked food if they wished, but they might not have anything for the mere satisfaction of the palate. When I asked the jail medical officer to give us curry powder, and to let us add salt to the food whilst it was cooking, he said: 'You are not here for satisfying your palate. From the point of view of health, curry powder is not necessary, and it makes no difference whether you add salt during or after cooking.'

Ultimately these restrictions were modified, though not without much difficulty,[372] *but both were wholesome*

Urdu book presented by Maulvi Sahib, the writings of Tolstoy, Ruskin and Socrates.' *CWMG*, vol. 8, p. 159.

Following an agreement with General Jan Christian Smuts (1870–1950), then the colonial secretary, MKG was released on 30 January 1908; but his release papers were given to him on 31 January. MKG wrote a series of essays in *Indian Opinion* on his 'Gaol Experience'. See *CWMG*, vol. 8.

[370] *Navajivan* of 4 December 1928 has the following two footnotes:

(a) 'My jail experiences have also been published in a book form. They were originally written in Gujarati and have been published in English as well. So far as I know both are available. M K Gandhi'

(b) 'These books are not available in Navajivan office, it is likely that they are available with Bombay book sellers. Manager, Navajivan.'

The English translation in the 8 December 1928 *Young India* did not carry these, and are absent from subsequent English editions.

[371] 'by 5 o'clock' to add.

[372] On 21 January 1908 MKG petitioned the director of prisons about diet. The prisoners were served 'mealie meal', which was found 'totally unsuitable'. MKG wrote, 'The Petitioners,

rules of self-restraint.[M1] Inhibitions imposed from without rarely succeed, but when they are self-imposed, they have a decidedly salutary effect. So, immediately after release from jail, I imposed on myself the two rules. As far as was then possible, I stopped taking tea, and finished my last meal before sunset. Both these now require no effort in the observance.

There came, however, an occasion which compelled me to give up salt altogether, and this restriction I continued for an unbroken period of ten years. I had read in some books on vegetarianism that salt was not a necessary article of diet for man, that on the contrary saltless diet was better for the health. I had deduced that a *brahmachari* benefited by a saltless diet. I had[373] read and realized[374] that the weak-bodied should avoid pulses.[375] I was very fond of *them.*[M2]

Now it happened that Kasturbai, who had a brief respite after her operation, had again begun getting haemorrhage, and the malady seemed to be obstinate. Hydropathic treatment by itself did not answer. She had not much faith in my remedies, though she *did not resist them. She certainly did not ask for outside help.*[M3] So when all my[376] remedies had failed, I entreated her to give up salt and pulses. She would not agree, however much I pleaded with her, supporting myself with authorities. At last she challenged me, saying that even I could not

[M1] but solely from the point of view of self-restraint, both were desirable

[M2] both these things.

[M3] was not averse to them either. There was no insistence upon getting other medical treatment.

---

therefore, humbly pray that the diet according to European scale with the exception of mealie meal may be prescribed for them, or such other diet as may be considered suitable to keep body and soul together and may be consistent with their national habits, or habits formed by prolonged residence in South Africa.' *CWMG*, vol. 8, p. 39.

[373] 'also' to add.

[374] 'from experience' to add.

[375] 'But I had not been able to give them up immediately.' To add.

[376] 'other' to add.

M4 vaidya

give up these articles if I was advised to do so. I was pained and equally delighted—delighted in that I got an opportunity to shower my love on her. I said to her: 'You are mistaken. If I was ailing and the *doctor*[M4] advised me to give up these or any other articles, I should unhesitatingly do so. But there! Without any medical advice,[377] I give up salt and pulses for one year, whether you do so or not.'

She was rudely shocked and exclaimed in deep sorrow: 'Pray forgive me. Knowing you, I should not have provoked you. I promise to abstain from these things, but for heaven's sake take back your vow. This is too hard on me.'[M5]

M5 She was filled with deep remorse. She exclaimed: 'Pray forgive me. Despite knowing you, I said this somehow. I will not eat pulses and salt henceforth. But, please take back your words. This punishment is harsh for me.'

'It is very good for you to forgo these articles. I have not the slightest doubt that you will be all the better without them. As for me, I cannot retract a vow seriously[378] taken. And it is sure to benefit me, for all restraint, whatever prompts it, is wholesome for men. You will therefore leave me alone. It will be a test for me, and a moral support to you in carrying out your resolve.'

So she gave me up. 'You are too obstinate. You will listen to none,' she said, and sought relief in tears.

I would like to count this incident as an instance of satyagraha and it is one of the sweetest recollections of my life.

After that Kasturbai began to pick up quickly—whether as a result of the saltless and pulseless diet or of the other consequent changes in her food, whether as a result of my strict vigilance in exacting observance of the other rules of life, or as an effect of the mental exhilaration produced by the incident, and if so to what extent, I cannot say. But she rallied quickly, haemorrhage

---

377 'Without any medical advice' added in the English translation.

378 'seriously' added in the English translation.

completely stopped, and I added somewhat to my reputation as a quack.[379]

As for me, I was all the better for the new denials. I never craved for the things I had left, the year sped away, and I found the senses to be more subdued than ever. The experiment stimulated the inclination for self-restraint, and I continued the abstention from the articles until long after I returned to India. Only once I happened to take both the articles whilst I was in London in 1914. But of that occasion, and as to how I resumed both,[380] I shall speak in a later chapter.

I have tried the experiment of a saltless and pulseless diet on many of my co-workers, and with good results in South Africa. Medically there may be two opinions as to the value of this diet, but morally I have no doubt that *all self-denial is good for the soul*.[M6] The diet of a man of self-restraint must be different from that of a man of pleasure, just as their ways of life must be different. Aspirants after *brahmacharya* often defeat their own end by adopting courses suited to a life of pleasure.

[M6] from the view of self-restraint, the exclusion of both these articles is beneficial

XXX

TOWARDS SELF-RESTRAINT

I have described in the last chapter how Kasturbai's illness was instrumental in bringing about some changes in my diet. At a later stage more changes were introduced *for the sake of supporting brahmacharya*.[M1]

[M1] from the perspective of *brahmacharya*

---

[379] This incident is from February 1911. In July MKG wrote, 'I am still on saltless diet. I personally feel better for it and as for Ba, it appears her very life has been saved. So far as I can see, she is a new woman altogether.' *CWMG*, vol. 11, p. 130. MKG also wrote at length on saltless diet in his essay 'General Knowledge About Health'. *CWMG*, vol. 11, pp. 507–08.

[380] 'after my return to India' to add.

The first of these was the giving up of milk. It was from Raychandbhai that I first learnt that milk stimulated animal passion. Books on vegetarianism strengthened the idea, but so long as I had not taken the *brahmacharya* vow I could not make up my mind to forgo milk. I had long realized that milk was not necessary for supporting the body, but it was not easy to give it up. While the necessity for avoiding milk in the interest of self-restraint was growing upon me, I happened to come across some literature from Calcutta, describing the tortures to which cows and buffaloes were subjected by their keepers. This had a wonderful effect on me. I discussed it with Mr. Kallenbach.

Though I have introduced Mr. Kallenbach to the readers of the history of satyagraha in South Africa, and referred to him in a previous chapter, I think it necessary to say something more about him here. We met quite by accident. He was a friend of Mr. Khan's,[381] and as the latter had discovered deep down in him a vein of otherworldliness he introduced him to me.

When I came to know him I was startled at his love of luxury and extravagance. But in our very first meeting, he asked searching questions concerning matters of religion. We incidentally talked of Gautama Buddha's renunciation. Our acquaintance soon ripened into very close friendship, so much so that we thought alike, and he was convinced that he must carry out in his life the changes I was making in mine.

At that time he was single, and was expending Rs. 1,200 monthly on himself, over and above house rent. Now he reduced himself to such simplicity that his expenses came to Rs. 120 per month. After the breaking up of my household and my first release from

---

[381] Rahimkhan Karimkhan, Bar-at-law. See n. 113 in Chapter VI, Part III.

jail, we began to live together.[382] It was a fairly hard life that we led.

It was during this time that we had the discussion about milk. Mr. Kallenbach said, 'We constantly talk about the harmful effects of milk. Why then do not we give it up? It is certainly not necessary.' I was agreeably surprised at the suggestion, which I warmly welcomed, and both of us pledged ourselves to abjure milk there and then. This was at Tolstoy Farm[383] in the year 1912.

But this denial was not enough to satisfy me. Soon after this I decided to live on a pure[384] fruit diet, and that too composed of the cheapest fruit possible. Our ambition was to live the life of the poorest people.

The fruit diet turned out to be very convenient also. Cooking was practically done away with. Raw groundnuts, bananas, dates, lemons, and olive oil composed our usual diet.

I must here utter a warning for the aspirants of *brahmacharya*. Though I have made out an intimate connection between diet[385] and *brahmacharya*, it is certain that mind is the principal thing. *A mind consciously unclean cannot be cleansed by fasting.*[M2] Modifications in diet have no effect on it. The concupiscence of the mind cannot be rooted out except by intense self-examination,

[M2] An unclean mind is not purified by fasting.

---

[382] MKG addressed Kallenbach as 'Lower House', while Kallenbach called MKG 'Upper House'. Both shared lodgings first at Kallenbach's home in Johannesburg, 'The Kraal', on Pine Road for nearly one and a half years and then 'tent' in Mountain View on Linksfield Ridge near Johannesburg for nearly seven months. The two later founded Tolstoy Farm. Under MKG's influence, Kallenbach had given up meat and experimented with celibacy. He reported to his brother in 1908 that 'for the last 18 months I have given up my sex life'. Guha, *Gandhi Before India*, p. 287.

[383] Kallenbach bought about 1100 acres at Lawley near Johannesburg and pledged it for the satyagrahis on 30 May 1910.

[384] 'purely' in the first edition.

[385] ', fasting' to add.

^{M3} meditation on

surrender to^{M3} God and, lastly, grace. But there is an intimate connection between the mind and the body, and the carnal mind always lusts for delicacies and luxuries.[386] To obviate this tendency dietetic restrictions and fasting would appear to be necessary. The carnal mind, instead of controlling the senses, becomes their slave, and therefore the body always needs clean non-stimulating foods and periodical fasting.

Those who make light of dietetic restrictions and fasting are as much in error as those who stake their all on them. My experience teaches me that, for those whose minds are working towards self-restraint, dietetic restrictions and fasting are very helpful. In fact without their help concupiscence cannot be completely rooted out of the mind.

XXXI

FASTING

^{M1} In this too Mr. Kallenbach

^{M2} mortification of the body

Just about the time when I gave up milk and cereals, and started on the experiment of a fruit diet, I commenced fasting[387] as a means of self-restraint. *In this Mr. Kallenbach also*^{M1} joined me. I had been used to fasting now and again, but for purely health reasons. That fasting was necessary for *self-restraint*^{M2} I learnt from a friend.

Having been born in a Vaishnava family and of a mother who was given to keeping all sorts of hard

---

[386] 'Such foods and luxuries in turn affect the mind.' To add.

[387] 'fasting' translates the word *upvas*, literally, 'to dwell closer to God'. There are five recorded instances of fasting in South Africa and twenty-nine such instances in India. A fast includes a one-meal-a-day diet as well. After April 1919 MKG fasted on every 13 and 16 April, and after 28 November 1921, on each Monday.

vows, I had observed, while in India, the *Ekadashi* and other fasts, but in doing so I had merely copied my mother and sought to please my parents.

At that time I did not understand, nor did I believe in, the *efficacy of fasting*.[388] M3 But seeing that the friend I have mentioned was observing it with benefit,[389] and with the hope of supporting the *brahmacharya* vow, I followed his example and began keeping the *Ekadashi* fast. *As a rule Hindus*M4 allow themselves milk and fruit on a fasting day, but such fast I had been keeping daily. So now I began complete fasting, allowing myself only water.

When I started on this experiment, the Hindu month of *Shravan* and the Islamic month of *Ramzan* happened to coincide. The Gandhis used to observe not only the Vaishnava but also the Shaivite vows, and visited the Shaivite as also the Vaishnava temples.[390] Some of the members of the family used to observe *pradosha*[391] in the whole of the month of *Shravan*. I decided to do likewise.

These important experiments were undertaken while we were at Tolstoy Farm,[392] where Mr. Kallenbach and I were staying with a few satyagrahi families, including young people and children. For these last we had a school. Among them were four or five Mussalmans. I always helped and encouraged them in keeping all their religious observances. I took care to see that they offered their daily *namaz*. There

M3 beneficial effects of such vows

M4 Generally people

---

[388] In the original '*vrata*', vow or an observance, often used as a synonym for fasting.

[389] 'with benefit' added in the English translation.

[390] 'visited the Vaishnava as also the Shaivite temples' in the first edition.

[391] MD's footnote: 'Fasting until evening.'

[392] 'Tolstoy Ashram' in the original.

were Christian and Parsi youngsters[393] too, whom I considered it my duty to encourage to follow their respective religious observances.

During this month, therefore, I persuaded the Mussalman youngsters to observe the *Ramzan* fast. I had of course decided to observe *pradosha* myself, but I now asked the Hindu, Parsi and Christian youngsters[394] to join *me*.[M5] I explained to them that it was always a good thing to join[395] with others in any matter of self-denial. Many of the Farm inmates welcomed my proposal. The Hindu and the Parsi youngsters[396] did not copy the Mussalman ones in every detail; it was not necessary. The Mussalman youngsters had to wait for their breakfast until sunset, whereas the others did not do so, and were thus able to prepare delicacies for the Mussalman friends and serve them. Nor had the Hindu and other youngsters to keep the Mussalmans company when they had their last meal before sunrise next morning, and of course all except the Mussalmans allowed themselves water.[397]

The result of these experiments was that all were convinced of the value of fasting, and *a splendid esprit de corps grew up among them.*[M6]

We were all vegetarians on Tolstoy Farm, thanks, I must gratefully confess, to the readiness of all to respect my feelings. The Mussalman youngsters[398] must have missed their meat during *Ramzan*, but none of them ever let me know that they did so. They delighted in and relished the vegetarian diet, and the Hindu youngsters often prepared vegetarian delicacies for them, in keeping with the simplicity of the Farm.

[M5] the Muslim youngsters

[M6] generosity and the feeling of love among them increased

---

[393] 'youngsters' added in the English translation.

[394] 'youngsters' added in the English translation.

[395] 'participate' in the first edition.

[396] 'youngsters' added in the English translation.

[397] 'during the day' to add.

[398] 'youngsters' added in the English translation.

I have purposely digressed in the midst of this chapter on fasting, as I could not have given these pleasant reminiscences anywhere else, and I have indirectly described a characteristic of mine, namely that I have always loved to have my co-workers with me in anything that has appealed to me as being good. They were quite new to fasting, but thanks to the *pradosha* and *Ramzan* fasts, it was easy for me to interest them in fasting as a means of self-restraint.[399]

Thus an atmosphere of self-restraint naturally sprang up on the Farm. All the Farm inmates now began to join us in keeping partial and complete fasts,[400] which, I am sure, was entirely to the good. I cannot definitely say how far this self-denial touched their hearts and helped them in their striving to conquer the flesh. For my part, however, I am convinced that I greatly benefited by it both *physically and morally*.[M7] But I know that it does not necessarily follow that fasting and similar disciplines would have the same effect for all.

M7 from the perspective of health as well as control over desires

Fasting can help to curb animal passion, only if it is undertaken with a view to self-restraint. Some of my friends have actually found their animal passion and palate stimulated as an after-effect of fasts. *That is to say, fasting is futile unless it is accompanied by an incessant longing for self-restraint.*[401] [M8] The famous[402] verse from the second chapter of the Bhagvad Gita is worth noting in this connection:

M8 That is, fasting can have beneficial effect only if accompanied by an incessant desire for self-restraint and control over the palate. It is a folly to believe that a bodily fast done without a purpose and involvement of the mind would result in the control of passions.

> 'For a man who is fasting his senses
> Outwardly, the sense-objects disappear,
> Leaving the yearning behind; but when

---

[399] 'as a means of self-restraint' added in the English translation.

[400] 'on other occasions' to add.

[401] 'It is a mistake to think that mere physical fasting can by itself effect self-restraint.' This sentence deleted in the 1940 edition.

[402] 'famous' added in the English translation.

> He has seen the Highest,
> Even the yearning disappears.'[403]

Fasting and similar discipline is, therefore, one of the means to the end of self-restraint, but it is not all, and if physical fasting is not accompanied by mental fasting, it is bound to end in hypocrisy and disaster.[404]

XXXII

AS SCHOOLMASTER

The reader will, I hope, bear in mind the fact that I am, in these chapters, describing things not mentioned, or only cursorily mentioned in the history of satyagraha in South Africa. If he does so, he will easily see[405] the connection between the recent chapters.

As the Farm grew[406] it was found necessary to make some provision for the education of its boys and girls. There were, among these, Hindu, Mussalman, Parsi and Christian boys and some Hindu girls. It was not possible, and I did not think it necessary, to engage special teachers for them. It was not possible, for qualified Indian teachers were scarce, and even when available, none would be ready to go to a place 21 miles distant from Johannesburg[407] on a small salary. Also we were certainly not overflowing with money. And I did not think it necessary to import teachers from outside the Farm. I did not believe in the existing

---

[403] Verse 59, Discourse II. Sir Edwin Arnold's translation.

[404] 'consequent disaster' in the first edition.

[405] 'easily be able to see' in the first edition.

[406] 'As the Farm grew' added in the English translation.

[407] 'Durban' in the original. Corrected in the English translation.

system of education, and I had a mind to find out by experience and experiment the true system. Only this much I knew—that, under ideal conditions, true education could be imparted only by the parents, and that then there should be the minimum of outside help, that Tolstoy Farm was a family, in which I occupied the place of the father, and that I should so far as possible shoulder the responsibility for the training of the young.

The conception no doubt was not without its flaws. All the young people had not been with me since their *childhood*,[M1] they had been brought up in different conditions and environments, and they did not belong to the same religion. How could I do full justice to the *young people*,[M2] thus circumstanced, even if I assumed the place of paterfamilias?

But I had always given the first place to the *culture*[M3] of the heart or the building of character, and as I felt confident that moral training could be given to all alike, no matter how different their ages and their upbringing, I decided to live amongst them all the twenty-four hours of the day as their father. I regarded character building as the proper foundation for their education and, if the foundation was firmly laid, I was sure that[408] the children could learn all the other things themselves or with the assistance of friends.

But as I fully appreciated the necessity of[409] a literary training in addition, I started some classes with the help of Mr. Kallenbach and Sjt. Pragji Desai.[410] Nor did I

M1 birth

M2 boys and girls

M3 cultivation

---

[408] 'when they got the opportunity' to add.

[409] 'some measure' to add.

[410] Pragji Khandubhai Desai, arrived in South Africa in 1906 at the age of twenty-two, for some time the editor of the Gujarati section of *Indian Opinion*, arrested twice in 1910 (March, July) and sentenced to three months' hard labour, jailed six times

underrate the building up of the body. This they got in the course of their daily routine. For there were no servants on the Farm, and all the work, from cooking down to scavenging,[411] was done by the inmates. There were many fruit trees to be looked after, and enough gardening to be done as well. Mr. Kallenbach was fond of *gardening*[M4] and had gained some experience of this work in one of the governmental model *gardens*.[M5] It was obligatory on all, young and old, who were not engaged in the kitchen, to give some time to gardening. The children had the lion's share of this work, which included digging pits, felling timber and lifting loads. This gave them ample exercise. They took delight in the work, and so they did not generally need any other exercise or games. Of course some of them, and sometimes all of them, malingered and shirked. Sometimes I connived at their pranks, but often[412] I was strict with them. I dare say they did not like the strictness, but I do not recollect their having resisted it. Whenever I was strict, I would, by argument, convince them that it was not right to play *with*[M6] one's work. The conviction would, however, be shortlived, the next moment they would again leave their work and go to play. All the same we got along, and at any rate they built up fine physiques. There was scarcely any illness on the Farm, though it must be said that good air and water and regular hours of food were not a little responsible for this.

A word about vocational training. It was my intention to teach every one of the youngsters some useful manual vocation.

[M4] farming

[M5] farms

[M6] while doing

---

during various phases of the Satyagraha Movement, pioneer settler on Tolstoy Farm in 1910 and later lived at the Phoenix Settlement.

[411] In the original the order is 'from scavenging to cooking'.

[412] 'and often' in the first edition.

For this purpose Mr. Kallenbach went to a Trappist monastery[413] and returned having learnt shoe-making.[414] I learnt it from him and taught the art to such as were ready to take it up. Mr. Kallenbach had some experience of carpentry, and there was another inmate who knew it; so we had a small class in carpentry. Cooking almost all the youngsters knew.

All this was new to them.[415] They had never even dreamt that they would have to learn these things some day. For generally the only training that Indian children received in South Africa was in *the three R's*.[416] [M7]

M7 elementary literacy

On Tolstoy Farm we made it a rule that the youngsters should not be asked to do what[417] the teachers did not do, and therefore, when they were asked to do any work, there was always a teacher co-operating and actually working with them. Hence whatever the youngsters learnt, they learnt cheerfully. Literary training and character building must be dealt with in the following chapters.

---

[413] This Trappist monastery is on marianhill, on the outskirts of Pinetown near Durban. It was founded in 1882 by Abbot Francis Pfanner.

[414] While MKG was his prisoner General Jan Christian Smuts sent him two books on religion (*CWMG*, vol. 9, pp. 238–39); MKG had in response sent him a 'stout pair of leather sandals' made at Tolstoy Farm. J.C. Smuts, *Jan Christian Smuts: By His Son* (London: Cassell and Company, 1952), p. 107.

[415] 'for them' in the first edition.

[416] The 'three R's' refer to 'reading, writing, arithmetic', so called because of the strong R phoneme at the beginning of each word. This first gained currency in the 1830s, and since then has been used to describe other trifecta (e.g., reduce, reuse, recycle).

[417] 'we' to add.

XXXIII

LITERARY TRAINING[418]

It was seen in the last chapter how we provided for the physical training on Tolstoy Farm, and incidentally for the vocational. Though this was hardly done in a way to satisfy me, it may be claimed to have been more or less successful.

Literary training, however, was a more difficult matter. I had neither the resources nor the literary equipment necessary; and I had[419] not the time I would have wished to devote to the subject. The physical work that I was doing used to leave me thoroughly exhausted at the end of the day, and I used to have the classes just when I was most in need of some rest. Instead, therefore, of my being fresh for the class, I could with the greatest difficulty keep myself awake. The mornings had to be devoted to work on the farm and domestic duties, so the school hours had to be kept[420] after the midday meal. There was no other time suitable for the school.

M1 hours

M2 mother-tongue

We gave three *periods*[M1] at the most to literary training. Hindi, Tamil, Gujarati and Urdu were all taught, and tuition was given through the *vernaculars*[M2] of the boys. English was taught as well. It was also necessary to acquaint the Gujarati Hindu children with a little Samskrit,[421] and to teach all the children elementary history, geography and arithmetic.

I had undertaken to teach Tamil and Urdu. The little Tamil I knew was acquired during voyages and

[418] 'Literary Training' translates *akshar kelavani*, literally, 'training of letters'.

[419] 'necessary resources, nor the literary equipment besides which I had' in the first edition.

[420] 'soon' to add.

[421] 'and all with a little Hindi' to add.

in jail. I had not got beyond Pope's[422] excellent Tamil handbook. My knowledge of the Urdu script was all that I had acquired on a single voyage, and my knowledge of the language was confined to the familiar Persian and Arabic words that I had learnt from contact with Mussalman friends. Of Samskrit I knew no more than I had learnt at the high school, even my Gujarati was no better than that which one acquires at the school.

Such was the capital with which I had to carry on. *In poverty of literary equipment my colleagues went one better than I.*[M3] But my love for the languages of my country, my confidence in my capacity as a teacher as also the ignorance of my pupils, and more than that, their generosity, stood me in good stead.

The Tamil boys were all born in South Africa, and therefore knew very little Tamil, and did not know the script at all. So I had to teach them the script and the rudiments of grammar. That was easy enough. My pupils knew that they could any day beat me in Tamil conversation, and when Tamilians, not knowing English, came to see me, they became my interpreters. I got along merrily, because I never attempted to disguise my ignorance from my pupils. In all respects I showed myself to them exactly as I really was. Therefore in spite of my colossal ignorance of the language I never lost their love and respect. It was comparatively easier to teach the Mussalman boys Urdu. They knew the script. I had simply to stimulate in them an interest in reading and to improve their handwriting.

These youngsters were for the most part unlettered and unschooled. But I found in the course of my work that I had very little to teach them, beyond weaning them from their laziness,[423] and supervising their studies. As I was content with this, I could pull on with boys of

M3 My helpers knew even less than I.

---

[422] George Uglow Pope, see n. 349 in Chapter XXIV, Part II.

[423] 'making them read by themselves' to add.

different ages and learning different subjects in one and the same class-room.

Of textbooks, about which we hear so much, I never felt the want. I do not even remember having made much use of the books that were available. I did not find it at all necessary to load the boys with quantities of books. I have always felt that the true textbook for the pupil is his teacher. I remember very little that my teachers taught me from books, but I have even now a clear recollection of the things they taught me *independently of books.*[M4]

M4 orally

Children take in much more and with less labour through their ears than through their eyes. I do not remember having read any book from cover to cover with my boys. But I gave them, in my own language, all that I had digested from my reading of various books, and I dare say they are still carrying a recollection of it in their minds. It was laborious for them to remember what they learnt from books, but what I imparted to them by word of mouth, they could repeat[424] with the greatest ease. Reading was a task for them, but listening to me was a pleasure, *when I did not bore them by failure*[425] *to make my subject interesting.*[M5] And from the questions that my talks prompted them to put,[426] I had a measure of their power of understanding.

M5 when I myself, through fatigue or some other reason, was not dull or uninteresting

XXXIV

TRAINING OF THE SPIRIT[427]

M1 students

The spiritual training of the *boys*[M1] was a much more difficult matter than their physical and mental training.

---

[424] 'immediately' to add.

[425] 'failing' in the first edition.

[426] 'make' in the first edition.

[427] 'Spirit' translates *aatmik*, literally, of the *atman*.

I relied little on religious books for the training of the spirit. Of course I believed that every student should be acquainted with the elements of his own religion and have a general knowledge of his own scriptures, and therefore I provided for such knowledge as best I could. But that, to my mind, was part of the intellectual training. Long before I undertook the education of the youngsters of the Tolstoy Farm I had realized that the training of the spirit was a thing by itself. To develop the spirit is to build character and to *enable one to work towards a knowledge of God and self-realization. And I held that this was an essential part of the training of the young,*[M2] and that all training without culture of the spirit was of no use, and might be even harmful.

[M2] acquire knowledge of God and of the Self. And children need a great deal of help in acquiring this knowledge.

I am familiar with the superstition that self-realization is possible only in the fourth stage of life, i.e., *sannyasa* (renunciation).[428] But it is a matter of common *knowledge*[M3] that those who defer preparation for this invaluable experience until the last stage of life attain not self-realization but old age amounting to a second and pitiable childhood, living as a burden on this earth. I have a full recollection that I held these views even whilst I was teaching, i.e., in 1911–12, though I might[429] not then have expressed them in identical language.

[M3] experience

How then was this spiritual training to be given? I made the children memorize and[430] recite hymns, and read to them from books on moral training. But that was far from satisfying me. As I came into closer contact with them I saw that it was not through books that one could impart training of the spirit. Just as physical training was to be imparted through physical exercise,

---

[428] 'i.e., *sannyasa* (renunciation)' added in the English translation.

[429] 'though possibly I should' in the first edition.

[430] 'memorize and' added in the English translation.

and intellectual through intellectual exercise, even so the training of the spirit was possible only through the exercise of the spirit. And the exercise of the spirit entirely depended on the life and character of the teacher. The teacher had always to be *mindful of his p's and q's*,[M4] whether he was in the midst of his boys or not.

It is possible for a teacher situated miles away[431] to affect the spirit of the pupils[432] by his way of living. It would be idle for me, if I were a liar, to teach boys[433] to tell the truth. A cowardly teacher would never succeed in making his boys valiant, *and a stranger to self-restraint could never teach his pupils the value of self-restraint.*[M5] I saw, therefore, that I must be an eternal[434] object-lesson to the boys and girls living with me. They thus became my teachers, and I learnt I must be good and live straight, if only for their sakes. I may say that the increasing discipline and restraint I imposed on myself at Tolstoy Farm was mostly due to those wards of mine.

One of them was wild, unruly, given to lying, and quarrelsome. On one occasion he broke out most violently. I was *exasperated*.[M6] I never punished my *boys*,[M7] but this time I was very angry.[435] I tried to reason with him. But he was adamant and even tried to over-reach me. At last I picked up a ruler lying at hand and delivered a blow on his arm. I trembled as I struck him. I dare say he noticed it. This was an entirely novel experience for them all. The boy cried out and begged

[M4] watchful

[M5] how is a debauched teacher to impart self-restraint?

[M6] alarmed

[M7] pupils

---

[431] 'miles away' translates 'Lanka'; in Gujarati, Lanka indicates both the Lanka of Ravana in the Ramayana, as also any island.

[432] 'his pupils' in the first edition.

[433] 'my boys' in the first edition.

[434] 'eternal' added in the English translation.

[435] 'I went up to him.' To add.

to be forgiven. He cried not because the beating was painful to him; he could, if he had been so minded, have paid me back in the same coin, being a stoutly-built youth of seventeen; but he realized my pain in being driven to this violent resource. Never again after this incident did he disobey me. But I still repent *that violence.*^{M8} I am afraid I exhibited before him that day not the spirit, but the brute, in me.

M8 beating him with a ruler

I have always been opposed to corporal punishment. I remember only one occasion on which I physically punished one of my sons. I have therefore never until this day been able to decide whether I was right or wrong in using the ruler. *Probably it was improper,*^{M9} for it was prompted by anger and a desire to punish. Had it been an expression only of my distress, I should have considered it justified. But the motive in this case was mixed.

M9 I have doubts regarding the propriety of this punishment

This incident set me thinking and[436] taught me a better method of correcting students. I do not know whether[437] that method would have availed on the occasion in question. The youngster soon forgot the incident, and I do not think he ever showed great improvement. But the incident made me *understand better*^{M10} the duty of a teacher towards his pupils.

M10 think further about

Cases of[438] misconduct on the part of the boys often occurred after this, but I never resorted to corporal punishment. Thus in my endeavour to impart spiritual training to the boys and girls under me, I came to understand better and better the *power*^{M11} of the spirit.

M11 quality

---

[436] 'set me thinking and' added in the English translation.

[437] 'how' in the first edition.

[438] 'similar' to add.

XXXV

TARES AMONG THE WHEAT[439]

It was at Tolstoy Farm that Mr. Kallenbach drew my attention to a problem that had never before struck me. As I have already said,[440] some of the boys at the Farm[441] were bad and unruly. There were loafers, too, amongst them. *With these my three boys came in daily contact, as also did other children of the same type as my own sons. This troubled Mr. Kallenbach, but his attention was centred on the impropriety of keeping my boys with these unruly youngsters.*[M1]

M1 Among them were three of my sons. There were other children too, similarly raised. But Mr. Kallenbach's attention was on how those loafers and my sons could live together.

One day he spoke out: 'Your way of mixing your own boys with the bad ones does not appeal to me. It can have only one result. They will become demoralized through this bad company.'

I do not remember whether the question puzzled me at the moment, but I recollect what I said to him:

'How can I distinguish between my boys and the loafers? I am equally responsible for both.[442] The youngsters have come because I invited them. If I were to dismiss them with some money, they would immediately run off to Johannesburg and fall back into their old ways. To tell you the truth,[443] it is quite likely that they and their guardians believe that, by having come here, they have laid me under an obligation. That they have to put up with a good deal of inconvenience here, you and I know very well. But my duty is clear. I must have them here, and therefore

---

[439] 'Mixture of Good and Bad' in the original.

[440] 'As I have already said,' added in the English translation.

[441] 'Ashram' in the original.

[442] 'for the present' to add.

[443] 'To tell you the truth' added in the English translation.

my boys also must needs live with them. And surely, you do not want me to teach my boys to feel from today that they are superior to other boys. To put that sense of superiority into their heads would be to lead them astray. This association with other boys will be a good discipline for them. They will, of their own accord, learn to discriminate between good and evil. Why should we not believe that, if there is really anything good in them, it is bound to react on their companions? However that may be, I cannot help keeping them here, and if that means some risk, we must run it.'

Mr. Kallenbach shook his head.

The result, I think, cannot be said to have been bad. I do not consider my sons were any the worse for the experiment. On the contrary[444] I can see that they gained something. If there was the slightest trace of superiority in them, it was destroyed and they learnt to mix with all kinds of children. They were tested and disciplined.

This and similar experiments have shown me that, if good children are taught together with bad ones and thrown into their company, they will lose nothing, provided the experiment is conducted under the watchful care of their parents and guardians.[445]

Children[446] *wrapped up in cottonwool are not always proof against all temptation or contamination.*[M2] It is true, however, that when boys and girls of all kinds of upbringing are kept and taught together, the parents and the teachers are put to the severest test. They have constantly to be on the alert.

[M2] There is no rule that our children locked up in iron safes remain pure and are contaminated when brought out.

---

[444] 'In fact' in the first edition.

[445] 'and guardians' added in the English translation.

[446] 'It does not necessarily follow that children' in the first edition.

XXXVI

FASTING AS PENANCE

Day by day it became increasingly clear to me how very difficult it was to bring up and educate boys and girls in the right way. If I was to be their real[447] teacher and guardian, I must touch their hearts. I must share their joys and sorrows, I must help them to solve the problems that faced them, and I must take along the right channel the surging aspirations of their youth.

On the release of some of the satyagrahis from jail, Tolstoy Farm was almost denuded of its inmates. The few that remained mostly belonged to Phoenix. So I removed them there.[448] Here I had to pass through a fiery ordeal.

In those days I had to move between Johannesburg and Phoenix. Once when I was in Johannesburg I received tidings of the moral fall of two of the inmates of the Ashram.[449] *News of an apparent failure or reverse in the satyagraha struggle would not have shocked me, but this news came upon me like a thunderbolt.*[M1] The same day I took the train for Phoenix. Mr. Kallenbach insisted on accompanying me. He had noticed the state I was in. He would not brook the thought of my going alone, *for he happened to be the bearer of the tidings which had so upset me.*[M2]

During the journey my duty seemed clear to me.[450] I felt that the guardian or teacher was responsible, to

[M1] After putting the remaining Ashramites of the Tolstoy Ashram at Phoenix, I went to Johannesburg. I had been in Johannesburg a few days when I received the news of the terrible fall of two persons. News of an apparent failure in the great satyagraha struggle never shocked me, but this incident came upon me like a thunderbolt. I was wounded.

[M2] as it was he who had told me about the fall

---

[447] 'real' added in the English translation.

[448] The Tolstoy Farm was closed on 9 January 1913.

[449] The two persons involved in the incident were Manilal Gandhi and Jaykuvar (Jeki) Doctor, daughter of P.J. Mehta, married to Manilal Doctor. For a compassionate account of the incident, see Dhupelia-Mesthrie, *Gandhi's Prisoner?*, pp. 106–10.

[450] 'seemed to become clear to me' in the first edition. 'or one could say that it seemed to me to have become clear' to add.

some extent at least, for the lapse of his ward or pupil. So my responsibility regarding the incident in question became clear to me as daylight. My wife had already warned me in the matter, but being of a trusting nature, I had ignored her caution.[451] I felt that the only way the guilty parties could be made to realize my distress and the depth of their own fall would be for me to do some penance. So I imposed upon myself a fast for seven days and a vow to have only one meal a day for a period of four months and a half.[452] Mr. Kallenbach tried to dissuade me, but in vain. He *fully*[M3] conceded   [M3] finally
the propriety of the penance, and insisted on joining me. I could not resist his transparent affection.

I felt greatly relieved, for the decision meant a heavy load off my mind. The anger against the guilty parties subsided and gave place to the purest pity for them. Thus considerably eased, I reached Phoenix. I made further investigation and acquainted myself with some more details I needed to know.

My penance pained everybody, but it cleared the atmosphere. Everyone came to realize what a terrible thing it was to be sinful, and the bond that bound me to the boys and girls became stronger and truer.

A circumstance arising out of this incident compelled me, a little while after, to go into a fast for fourteen days, the results of which[453] exceeded even my expectations.[454]

---

[451] 'cautioning' in the first edition.

[452] The fast commenced on 12 July 1913 and was completed on 11 November 1913. MKG's one-meal-a-day fast did not end here. From 12 November 1913 to 1 May 1914 he did a one-meal-a-day fast for removal of the £3 tax on Asiatics and from 2 May 1914 to 15 May 1914 he observed complete fast due to a moral lapse at Phoenix and continued the one-meal-a-day fast until 26 June 1914.

[453] 'I believe' to add.

[454] On 22 April 1914, several days before undertaking this fast, MKG described his condition: 'Never perhaps have I spent such

It is not my purpose to make out from these incidents that it is the duty of a teacher to resort to fasting whenever there is a delinquency on the part of his pupils. *I hold, however, that some occasions do call for this drastic remedy. But it presupposes clearness of vision and spiritual fitness.*[M4] Where there is no true love between the teacher and the pupil, where the pupil's delinquency has not touched the very being of the teacher and where the pupil has no respect for the teacher, fasting is *out of place*[M5] and may even be harmful. Though there is thus room for doubting the propriety of fasts in such cases, there is no question about the teacher's responsibility[455] for the errors of his pupil.

The first penance did not prove difficult for any of us.[M6] I had to suspend or stop none of my normal activities. It may be recalled that[456] during the whole of this period of penance[457] I was a strict fruitarian. The latter part of the *second*[M7] fast went fairly hard with me. I had not then completely understood the wonderful efficacy of Ramanama, and my capacity for suffering was to that extent less. Besides, I did not know the technique of fasting, especially the necessity of drinking plenty of water, however nauseating or distasteful it might be.[458] Then the fact that the first had been an easy affair had made me rather careless as to the *second*.[M8] Thus during the first I took Kuhne baths every day, but during the *second*[M9] I gave them

[M4] I hold, however, that under certain circumstances such fasts as penance have a definite place. But it requires discernment and fitness.

[M5] bereft of meaning

[M6] The seven-day fast and subsequent one-meal-a-day fast did not prove difficult for any one of us.

[M7] fourteen-day

[M8] fourteen-day fast

[M9] fourteen-day fast

---

days of agony as I am doing now. I talk and smile, I walk and eat and work, all mechanically these days. I can do no writing whatever. The heart seems to have gone dry. The agony that I am going through is unspeakable.' *CWMG*, vol. 12, p. 410.

[455] 'to a lesser or greater degree' to add.

[456] 'It may be recalled that' added in the English translation.

[457] 'of penance' added in the English translation.

[458] 'however distasteful or nauseating it might be' added in the English translation.

up after two or three days, and drank very little water, as it was distasteful and produced nausea. The throat became parched and weak and during the last days I could speak only in a very low voice. In spite of this, however, my work was carried on through dictation where writing was necessary. I regularly listened to readings from the Ramayana *and other sacred books.*[M10]   [M10] etc.
I had also sufficient strength to discuss and advise in all urgent matters.

XXXVII

TO MEET GOKHALE

I must skip many of the recollections of South Africa.

At the conclusion of the satyagraha struggle in 1914,[459] I received Gokhale's instructions to return home via London.[460] So in July Kasturbai, Kallenbach and I sailed for England.[461]

During satyagraha I had begun travelling third class. I therefore took third-class passages for this voyage. But there was a good deal of difference between *third-class accommodation on the boat on this route and that provided on Indian coastal boats or railway trains.*[M1] There is hardly   [M1] this third-class and our third-class.
sufficient sitting, much less sleeping, accommodation in the Indian service, and little cleanliness. During the

---

[459] The satyagraha could be considered to have concluded with the passage of the Indians' Relief Act of 26 June 1914.

[460] On 27 February 1914 MKG wrote to Gokhale, 'My present ambition you know. It is to be by your side as your nurse and attendant.' *CWMG*, vol. 12, p. 361. On 6 May MKG wrote to Gokhale that he and Kasturba wished to return to India via London. On 5 June MKG informed Gokhale that he would be accompanied by Kasturba and Kallenbach.

[461] They sailed from Cape Town on 18 July 1914 on board *S.S Kinfaus Castle*.

voyage to London, on the other hand, there was enough room and cleanliness,[462] and the steamship company had provided special facilities for us. The company had provided reserved closet accommodation for us, and as we were fruitarians, the steward had orders to supply us with fruits and nuts. As a rule third-class passengers get little fruit *or nuts*.[M2] These facilities made our eighteen days on the boat quite comfortable.[463]

Some of the incidents during the voyage are well worth recording. Mr. Kallenbach was very fond of binoculars, and had one or two costly pairs. We had daily discussions over *one of these*.[M3] I tried to impress on him that this possession was not in keeping with the ideal of simplicity that we aspired to reach. Our discussions *came to a head*[M4] one day, as we were standing near the porthole of our cabin.

'Rather than allow these to be a bone of contention between us, why not throw them into the sea and be done with them?'[M5] said I.

'Certainly throw the *wretched*[M6] things away,' said Mr. Kallenbach.

'I mean it,' said I.

'So do I,' quickly came the reply.

And forthwith I flung them into the sea. They were worth some £7, but their value lay less in their price than in Mr. Kallenbach's infatuation for them. However,[464] having got rid of them, he never regretted it.

This is but one out of the many[465] incidents that happened between Mr. Kallenbach and me.

M2 and no nuts at all

M3 this

M4 led to a pungent argument

M5 'Rather than quarrel, will it not be good if we were to throw the binoculars into the sea and not talk about it at all?'

M6 inauspicious

---

[462] 'equal cleanliness' in the first edition.

[463] On board MKG explained the Gita and read the Ramayana to Kasturba and gave Gujarati lessons to Kallenbach.

[464] 'But' in the first edition.

[465] 'similar' to add.

Every day we had to learn something new in this way, for both of us were trying to tread the path of truth. In the march towards truth, anger, selfishness, hatred, etc., naturally give way, for otherwise truth would be impossible to attain. A man who is swayed by passions may have good enough intentions, may be truthful in word, but he will never find the[466] truth. A successful[467] search for[468] truth means complete deliverance from the dual throng such as of love and hate, happiness and misery.[469]

Not much time had elapsed since my fast when we started on our voyage. I had not regained my normal strength. I used to stroll on deck to get a little exercise, so as to revive my appetite and digest what I ate. But even this exercise was beyond me, causing pain in the calves, so much so that on reaching London I found that I was worse rather than better. There I came to know Dr. Jivraj Mehta.[470] I gave him the history of my fast and subsequent pain, and he said, 'If you do not take complete rest for a few days, there is a fear of your legs going out of use.'[471]

It was then that I learned that a man emerging from a long fast should not be in a hurry to regain lost

---

[466] 'unsullied' to add.

[467] 'successful' added in the English translation.

[468] 'pure' to add.

[469] 'happiness and misery' added in the English translation.

[470] Jivraj Narayan Mehta (1887–1978), studied medicine in Bombay and London (1909–15) and obtained FRCS, participated in the movement for national independence and was twice incarcerated (1938, 1942) and held various public offices in post-Independence India, including those of the first chief minister of Gujarat (1960–63) and high commissioner to UK (1963–66).

[471] Several months of prolonged fasting with one meal a day, consisting of a diet of fruits and nuts, had caused a deficiency of vitamin B.

strength, and should also put a curb on his appetite. More caution and perhaps more restraint are necessary in breaking a fast than in keeping it.

In Madeira[472] we heard that the Great War might break out at any moment. As we entered the English Channel, we received the news of its actual outbreak. We were stopped for some time. It was a difficult business to tow the boat through the submarine mines which had been laid throughout the Channel, and it took about two days to reach Southampton.

War was declared on the 4th of August. We reached London on the 6th.

XXXVIII

MY PART IN THE WAR

On arrival in England I learned that Gokhale had been stranded in Paris[473] where he had gone for reasons of health, and as communication between Paris and London had been cut off, there was no knowing when he would return. I did not want to go home without having seen him, but no one could say definitely when he would arrive.

What then was I to do in the meanwhile?[474] What was my duty as regards the War? Sorabji Adajania,[475] my

---

[472] A Portuguese archipelago situated in the north Atlantic Sea. The only port of call on this journey.

[473] Gokhale had gone to Vichy in France to take healing waters.

[474] The party first took rooms with Deepchand Zaveri, a Gujarati diamond merchant, at 60, Talbot Road, Bayswater, and in early October moved to the hostel of M.M. Gandevia at 16, Trebovir Road, West Kensington.

[475] Sorabji Shapurji (Adajania) (1883–1918), born in Adajan, near Surat; a cousin of Parsi Rustomji, worked as a bookkeeper and

comrade in jail and a satyagrahi, was then reading for the bar in London. As one of[476] the best satyagrahis he had been sent to England to qualify himself as a barrister, so that he might take my place on return to South Africa. Dr. Pranjivandas Mehta was paying[477] his expenses.[478] With him, and through him, I had conferences with Dr. Jivraj Mehta and others who were prosecuting their studies in England. In consultation with them, a meeting of the Indian residents in Great Britain and Ireland was called.[479] I placed my views before them.

I felt that Indians residing in England ought to do their bit in the War. English students had volunteered to serve in the army, and Indians might do no less. A

---

manager in a store in Natal. Joined the satyagraha in 1908 and served several sentences with hard labour. In 1911 he attended the Indian National Congress, chosen by MKG for a scholarship offered by P.J. Mehta to study in England and qualify for the Bar. He died on 13 July 1918. In his obituary MKG wrote, 'He was a prince among passive resisters.' *CWMG*, vol. 14, p. 507.

[476] 'one of' added in the English translation. In a farewell meeting organized on 16 June 1911 to mark Sorabji's departure for India to participate in the Indian National Congress MKG said, 'As a satyagrahi Mr. Sorabji has displayed many fine qualities. He has rightly been described as the greatest of satyagrahis.' *CWMG*, vol. 11, p. 107.

[477] 'finding' in the first edition.

[478] P.J. Mehta had offered this scholarship with a view that one of MKG's sons would benefit from it. One of Harilal Gandhi's grievances was that his father first chose Chhaganlal Gandhi and later Sorabji for this scholarship. Chhaganlal could not complete the envisaged course of study.

[479] On 8 August 1914 a reception was held for MKG, Kasturba and Kallenbach at Hotel Cecil by Indian and British friends. Among those present were Sarojini Naidu, Satchidanand Sinha, Lala Lajpat Rai, M.A. Jinnah and Albert Cartwright, with Bhupendranath Basu presiding. In this reception MKG asked the question as to what was his duty and that of other Indians given the 'tremendous crisis that has overwhelmed the Empire'. *CWMG*, vol. 12, p. 523.

number of objections were taken to this line of argument. There was, it was contended, a world of difference[480] between the Indians and the English. We were slaves and they were masters. How could a slave co-operate[481] with the master in the hour of the latter's need? Was it not the duty of the slave, seeking to be free, to make the master's need his opportunity? This argument failed to appeal to me then. I knew the difference of status between an Indian and an Englishman, but I did not believe that we had been quite reduced to slavery. I felt then that it was more the fault of individual British officials than of the British system, and that we could convert them by love. If we would improve our status through the help and co-operation of the British, it was our duty to win their help by standing by them in their hour of need. Though the system was faulty, it did not seem to me to be intolerable, as it does today. But if, having lost my faith in the system, I *refuse to co-operate with*[M1] the British Government today, how could those friends then do so, having lost their faith not only in the system but in the officials as well?

M1 would refuse to help

The opposing friends felt that that was the hour for making a bold declaration of Indian demands and for improving the status of Indians.[482]

I thought that England's need should not be turned into our opportunity, and that it was more *becoming*[M2] and far-sighted not to press our demands while the War lasted. I therefore adhered to my advice and invited those who would to enlist as volunteers.[483] There was a

M2 civil

---

[480] 'a world of difference' translates 'the difference between an elephant and a horse' in the original.

[481] 'voluntarily' to add.

[482] 'Indians' status' in the first edition.

[483] On 13 August 1914 the following circular was prepared with signatures of MKG, Kasturbai, Sarojini Naidu and fifty others: 'We, the undersigned have, after mature deliberation, decided

good response, practically all the provinces and all the religions being represented among the volunteers.

I wrote a letter to Lord Crewe,[484] acquainting him with these facts, and expressing our readiness to be trained for ambulance work, if that should be considered a condition precedent to the acceptance of our offer.[485]

Lord Crewe accepted the offer after some hesitation,[M3] and thanked us for having tendered our services to the Empire at that critical hour.   M3 deliberations

The volunteers began their preliminary training in first aid to the wounded under the well-known Dr. Cantlie.[486] It was a short course of six weeks, but it covered the whole course of first aid.

We were a class of about 80. In six weeks we were examined, and all except one passed. For these the Government now provided military drill and other training. Colonel Baker[487] was placed in charge of this work.[488]

London[M4] in these days was a sight worth seeing.   M4 England
There was no panic, but all were busy helping to the best of their ability. Able-bodied adults began training

---

for the sake of the Motherland and the Empire to place our services unconditionally, during this crisis, at the disposal of the authorities. We advisedly used the word "unconditionally" as we believe that, at a moment like this, no service that can be assigned to us can be considered to be beneath our dignity or inconsistent with our self-respect.' *CWMG*, vol. 12, p. 527.

[484] Robert Crewe-Milnes, 1st Marquess of Crew (1858–1945), Secretary of State for India (1910–11, 1911–15).

[485] For the letter to Lord Crewe, see *CWMG*, vol. 12, pp. 527–28.

[486] Sir (Dr.) James Cantlie (1851–1926), pioneered first aid, wrote the Red Cross *First Aid Manual*, helped set up the *Journal of Tropical Medicine* and the London School of Tropical Medicine.

[487] Lt. Col. Richard J. Baker, formerly of the Indian Medical Service. The unit was officially recognized at a ceremony on 1 October 1914, attended by the Aga Khan.

[488] 'and was appointed Corps Commandant' to add.

as combatants, but what were the old, the infirm and the women to do? There was enough work for them, if they wanted. So they employed themselves in cutting and making clothes and dressings for the wounded.

The Lyceum,[489] a ladies' club, undertook to make as many clothes for the soldiers as they could. Shrimati Sarojini Naidu[490] was a member of this club, and threw herself whole-heartedly into the work. This was my first acquaintance with her. She placed before me a heap of clothes which had been cut to pattern, and asked me to get *them all*[M5] sewn up and return them to her. I welcomed her demand and with the assistance of friends got as many clothes made as I could manage during my training for first-aid.

[M5] as many of them as possible

XXXIX

A SPIRITUAL DILEMMA

As soon as the news reached South Africa that I along with other Indians had offered my services in the War, I received two cables. One of these was from Mr. Polak who questioned *the consistency of my action with my profession of ahimsa.*[491] [M1]

[M1] 'Is your action not inconsistent with your profession of ahimsa?'

---

[489] The Lyceum Club, founded in 1904 by writer and suffragist Constance Smedly (1876–1941) at 138, Piccadilly, for ladies interested in literature, journalism, art, science and medicine.

[490] Sarojini Naidu (1879–1949), poet and nationalist, president of the Indian National Congress (1925), Governor, Uttar Pradesh (1947–49).

[491] In a letter to Maganlal Gandhi of 18 September 1914, MKG explained his attitude towards war and his duty: 'When thousands have come forward to lay down their lives only because they thought it their duty to do so, how could I sit still? A rifle this hand will never fire. And so there only remained nursing the wounded and I took it up. This is how I communed to myself.' *CWMG*, vol. 12, p. 531. MKG invoked the Gita in a letter to

I had to a certain extent anticipated this objection, for I had discussed the question in my *Hind Swaraj* or *Indian Home Rule*,[492] and used to discuss it day in and day out with friends in South Africa. All of us recognized the immorality of war. If I was not prepared to prosecute my assailant, *much less should I be willing to*[M2]   M2 how could I participate in a war, especially when I knew nothing of the justice or otherwise of the cause of the combatants. Friends of course knew that I had previously served in the Boer War, but they assumed that my views had since undergone a change.

As a matter of fact the very same line of argument that persuaded me to take part in the Boer War had weighed with me on this occasion. It was quite clear to me that participation in war could never be consistent with ahimsa. But it is not always given to one to be equally clear about one's duty. A votary of truth is often obliged to grope in the dark.

Ahimsa is a comprehensive principle. We are helpless mortals caught in the conflagration of *himsa*. The saying that life lives on life *has a deep meaning in it.*[M3]   M3 is not false

---

Pragji Desai: 'The *Gita* says that he who eats without performing *Yajna* is a thief. In the present situation here sacrifice meant, and means, self-sacrifice. I saw, therefore, that I too must perform *Yajna*. I myself could not shoot, but could nurse the wounded.' *CWMG*, vol. 12, pp. 554–55.

[492] *Hind Swaraj*, written on board the steamer *Kildonan Castle*, between 13 and 22 November 1909, was first published under the title *Hind Swarajya* in the Gujarati columns of *Indian Opinion* in two instalments: 11 December (twelve chapters) and 18 December (eight chapters) 1909. In January 1910, published as a book under the same title and proscribed in India by the Government of Bombay on 24 March 1910; translated in English by MKG, with a foreword dated 20 March 1910 under the title 'Indian Home Rule' and published by the International Printing Press, Phoenix. See *CWMG*, vol. X, pp. 6–64. For a bilingual critical edition, see *M.K. Gandhi's Hind Swaraj: A Critical Edition*, annotated, translated and edited by Suresh Sharma and Tridip Suhrud (New Delhi: Orient Blackswan, 2010).

Man cannot for a moment live without consciously or unconsciously committing outward *himsa*. The very fact of his living[493]—eating, drinking and moving about—[494] necessarily involves some *himsa*, destruction of life, be it ever so minute. A votary of ahimsa therefore remains true to his faith if the spring of all his actions is compassion, if he shuns to the best of his ability the destruction of the tiniest creature, tries to save it, and thus incessantly strives to be free from the deadly coil of *himsa*. He will be constantly growing in self-restraint and compassion, but he can never become entirely free from outward *himsa*.[495]

Then again, because underlying ahimsa is the unity of all life, the *error*[M4] of one cannot but affect all, and hence man cannot be wholly *free from*[M5] himsa. So long as he continues to be a social being, he cannot but participate in the *himsa that the very existence of society involves*.[M6] When two nations are fighting, the duty of a votary of ahimsa is to stop the war. He who is not equal to that duty, he who has no power of resisting war, he who is not qualified to resist war, may take part in war, and yet whole-heartedly try to free himself, his nation and the world from war.

I had hoped to improve my status *and*[M7] that of my people through the British Empire. Whilst in England I was enjoying the protection of the British Fleet, and taking shelter as I did under its armed might, I was directly participating in its potential violence. Therefore, if I desired to retain my connection with the Empire and to live under its banner, one of three courses was open to me: I could declare open resistance to the War and, in accordance with the law

M4 sin

M5 untouched by

M6 committed by society

M7 that is,

---

[493] 'The very fact of his living' added in the English translation.

[494] 'all action' to add.

[495] 'so long as he lives in the body' to add.

of satyagraha, boycott the Empire until it changed its military policy; or I could seek imprisonment by civil disobedience of such of its laws as were fit to be disobeyed; or I could participate in the War on the side of the Empire and thereby acquire the capacity and fitness for resisting the violence of war. I lacked this capacity and fitness, so I thought there was nothing for it but to serve[496] in the War.

I make no distinction, from the point of view of ahimsa, between combatants and non-combatants. He who volunteers to serve a band of dacoits, by working as their carrier, or their watchman while they are about their business, or their nurse when they are wounded, is as much guilty of dacoity as the dacoits themselves. In the same way those who confine themselves to attending to the wounded in battle cannot be absolved from the guilt of war.

I had argued the whole thing out to myself in this manner, before I received Polak's cable, and soon after its receipt, I discussed these views with several friends and concluded that it was my duty to offer to serve in the War. Even today I see no flaw in that line of argument, nor am I sorry for my action, holding, as I then did, *views favourable to the British connection.*[M8]

[M8] certain views regarding the British Empire

I know that even then I could not carry conviction with all my friends about the correctness of my position. The question is subtle. It admits of differences of opinion, and therefore I have submitted my argument as clearly as possible to those who believe in ahimsa and who are making serious efforts to practise it in every walk of life. A devotee of Truth may not do anything in deference to convention. He must *always hold himself open to correction,*[M9] and whenever he discovers himself to be wrong he must confess it at all costs and atone for it.

[M9] not obstinately hold on to his opinion

---

[496] 'but for me to serve' in the first edition.

XL

MINIATURE SATYAGRAHA

Though I thus took part in the War as a matter of duty, it chanced that[497] I was not only unable directly to participate in it, but actually compelled to offer what may be called miniature satyagraha[498] even at that critical juncture.

I have already said that an officer[499] was appointed in charge of our training, as soon as our names were approved and enlisted. We were all under the impression that this Commanding Officer was to be our chief only so far as technical matters were concerned, and that in all other matters I was the head of our Corps, which was directly responsible to me in matters of internal discipline; that is to say, the Commanding Officer had to deal with the Corps through me. *But from the first the Officer left us under no such delusion.*[M1]

Mr. Sorabji Adajania was a shrewd man. He warned me. 'Beware[500] of this man,' he said. 'He seems inclined to lord it over us.[501] We will have none of his orders. We are prepared to look upon him as our instructor. But the youngsters he has appointed to instruct us also feel as though they had come as our masters.'[502]

[M1] Just as the ways of a son can be seen even while he is in the cradle, we discerned a different look in the eyes of the officer on the first day.

---

[497] 'as chance would have it' in the first edition.

[498] 'what may be called miniature satyagraha' added in the English translation.

[499] Col. Richard J. Baker.

[500] 'Bhai' to add before 'Beware'.

[501] 'lord it over us' translates 'Jahangiri', literally, 'rule like Emperor Jahangir'.

[502] Sorabji's first impression of Col. Baker and the work was favourable. On 7 October 1914 he wrote to Chhaganlal Gandhi, 'Col. Baker is a kind man. We do not have much hard work. At present it is a play.' SN 6059, translated from the Gujarati by TS.

These youngsters were Oxford students who had come to instruct us and whom the Commanding Officer had appointed to be our section leaders.

I also had not failed to notice *the high-handedness of the Commanding Officer*,[M2] but I asked Sorabji not to be anxious and tried to pacify him. But he was not the man to be easily convinced.

M2 what Sorabji had told me

'You are too trusting. These people will deceive you with *wretched*[M3] words, and when at last you see through them, you will ask us to resort to satyagraha, and *so come to grief, and bring us all to grief along with you*,'[M4] said he with a smile.

M3 honeyed

M4 and so bring us all to grief

'What else but grief can you hope to come to after[503] having cast in your lot with me?' said I. 'A satyagrahi is born to be deceived. Let the Commanding Officer deceive us. Have I not told you times without number that ultimately a deceiver only deceives himself?'

Sorabji gave a loud laugh. 'Well, then,' said he, 'continue to be deceived. You will some day meet your death in satyagraha and drag poor mortals like me behind you.'

These words put me in mind of what the late Miss Emily Hobhouse[504] wrote to me with regard to non-co-operation: 'I should not be surprised if one of these days you have to go to the gallows for the sake of truth. May God show you the right path and protect you.'

The talk with Sorabji took place just after the appointment of the Commanding Officer. In a very few

---

On 24 October he reported the dispute to Chhaganlal, 'Because of our dispute with the Commanding Officer, both the drill and camping have stopped.' SN 6058, translated from the original Gujarati by TS.

[503] 'by' in the first edition.

[504] Emily Hobhouse (1860–1926) brought to light the depraved condition of concentration camps built in South Africa to incarcerate Boer women and children during the Second Boer War.

days our relations with him reached the breaking point. I had hardly regained my strength after the fourteen days' fast, when I began to take part in the drill, often walking to the appointed place about two miles from home. This gave me pleurisy[505] and laid me low. In this condition I had to go week-end camping. Whilst the others stayed there, I returned home. It was here that an occasion arose for satyagraha.

The Commanding Officer began to exercise his authority somewhat freely. He gave us clearly to understand that he was our head in all matters, military and non-military,[506] giving us at the same time a taste of his authority. Sorabji hurried to me. He was not at all prepared to put up with this high-handedness.[507] He said: 'We must have all orders through you. We are still in the training camp and all sorts of absurd orders are being issued. Invidious distinctions are made between ourselves and those youths who have been appointed to instruct us.[508] We must have it out with the Commanding Officer, otherwise *we shall not be able to go on any longer.*[M5] The Indian students and others who have joined our Corps are not going to abide by any absurd orders. In a cause which has been taken up for the sake of self-respect, it is unthinkable to put up with loss of it.'

I approached the Commanding Officer[509] and drew his attention to the complaints I had received. He wrote asking me to set out the complaints in writing,

[M5] our work is certain to break down

---

[505] In the Gujarati the term used is *pasali no varam*, meaning pain in the ribcage, which is a possible symptom of pleurisy.

[506] 'military and non-military' added in the English translation.

[507] 'high-handedness' translates 'Jahangiri'.

[508] 'who have been appointed to instruct us' added in the English translation.

[509] MKG wrote to Col. Baker on 13 October 1914. See *CWMG*, vol. 12, pp. 536–37.

at the same time asking me 'to impress upon those who complain that the proper direction in which to make complaints is to me through their section commanders, now appointed, who will inform me through the instructors'.[510]

To this I replied saying that I claimed no authority, that in the military sense I was no more than any other private, but that I had believed that as *Chairman of the Volunteer Corps*,[M6] I should be *allowed unofficially to act*[M7] as their representative. I also set out the grievances and requests that had been brought to my notice, namely, that grievous dissatisfaction had been caused by the appointment of section leaders without reference to the feeling of the members of the Corps; that they be recalled, and the Corps be invited to elect section leaders, subject to the Commander's approval.

This did not appeal to the Commanding Officer, who said it was repugnant to all military discipline that the section leaders should be elected by the Corps, and that the recall of appointments already made would be subversive of all discipline.[511]

So we held a meeting and decided upon withdrawal.[512] I brought home to the members the serious consequences of satyagraha. But a very large majority voted for the resolution,[513] which was to the

[M6] leader of our group of volunteers

[M7] accepted

---

[510] This is reproduced from Col. Baker's letter to MKG of 13 October 1914. SN 6069A. The original in Gujarati reads: 'Complaints cannot be made through you, complaints should be made directly to me through section officers.'

[511] Col. Baker in a letter of 14 October 1914 wrote to MKG, 'It is an idea repugnant to military discipline that these promotions should be made by election by the members of the Corps.' SN 6069.

[512] 'and decided upon withdrawal' added in the English translation.

[513] Fifty-three members attended, the resolution was carried by a vote of 49-2. The meeting took place on 13 October 1914.

effect that, unless the appointments of Corporals already made were recalled and the members of the Corps given an opportunity of electing their own Corporals, the members would be obliged to abstain from further drilling and week-end camping.[514]

I then addressed a letter[515] to the Commanding Officer telling him what a severe disappointment his letter rejecting my suggestion had been. I assured him that I was not fond of any exercise of authority and that I was most anxious to serve.[516] I also drew his attention to a precedent.[517] I pointed out that, although I occupied no official rank in the South African Indian Ambulance Corps[518] at the time of the Boer War, there was never a hitch between Colonel Gallwey and the Corps, and the Colonel never took a step without reference to me with a view to ascertain the wishes of the Corps. I also enclosed a copy of the resolution we had passed the previous evening.[519]

This had no good[520] effect on the officer, who felt that the meeting and the resolution were a grave breach of discipline.[521]

---

[514] For the full text of the resolution, see *CWMG,* vol. 12, p. 538.

[515] Letter of 14 October 1914, see *CWMG,* vol. 12, pp. 538–39.

[516] 'and carry the work to fruition' to add.

[517] 'I also drew his attention to a precedent.' Added in the English translation.

[518] 'in the South African Indian Ambulance Corps' added in the English translation.

[519] 'the previous evening' added in the English translation.

[520] 'good' added in the English translation.

[521] Col. Baker wrote to MKG at 4.15 p.m. on 16 October, 'I would strongly advise you not to venture to drill this afternoon—the more so as any attempt on your part to address the Corps is unnecessary—as I myself will convey the decision arrived at to those who attend—to say nothing of the fact that it would be a grave breach of discipline on your part.' SN 6069B.

Hereupon I addressed a letter to the Secretary of State for India,[522] acquainting him with all the facts and enclosing a copy of the resolution. He replied[523] explaining that conditions in South Africa were different, and drawing my attention to the fact that under the rules[524] the section commanders were appointed by the Commanding Officer, but assuring me that in future, when appointing section commanders, the Commanding Officer would consider my recommendations.

A good deal of correspondence passed between us after this, but I do not want to prolong the bitter tale. Suffice it to say that my experience was of a piece with the experiences we daily have in India. What with threats and what with adroitness the Commanding Officer succeeded in creating a division in our Corps. Some of those who had voted for the resolution yielded to the Commander's threats or persuasions and went back on their promise.

About this time an unexpectedly large contingent of wounded soldiers arrived at the Netley Hospital, and the services of our Corps were requisitioned.[525] Those whom the Commanding Officer could persuade went

---

[522] See Letter to Charles Roberts, dated 16 October 1914, *CWMG*, vol. 12, pp. 540–41.

[523] Roberts wrote three letters to MKG, on 16, 18 and 22 October 1914, all bear SN 6069B, the letter referred to here is of 22 October.

[524] Roberts sent MKG an 'Extract From the Army Field Service Regulation, chapter XI, No. 97 (4)', which stated, 'Voluntary medical units will be required to adhere to the service regulations governing the constitution, personnel and equipment of war of corresponding units of the army. They will, when accepted, come under orders of the military authorities, and be incorporated with the medical units of the army in such a manner and for such purposes as the Commander-in-Chief may determine.'

[525] On 14 October Col. Baker requested MKG, 'I would be glad if you can exert your influence to have as full a muster of the Corps tomorrow as possible.' SN 6069B.

to Netley. The others refused to go.[526] I was on my back, but was in communication with the members of the Corps. *Mr. Roberts, the Under-Secretary of State, honoured me with many calls during those days.*[527] *He insisted on my persuading the others to serve.*[M8] He suggested that they should form a separate Corps and that at the Netley Hospital they could be responsible only to the Commanding Officer there, so that there would be no question of loss of self-respect, Government would be placated, and at the same time helpful service would be rendered to the large number of wounded received at the hospital. This suggestion appealed both to my companions and to me, with the result that those who had stayed away also went to Netley.[528]

Only I remained away, lying on my back *and making the best of a bad job.*[M9]

[M8] I had come to be well acquainted with Mr. Roberts. He came to see me and insisted on me sending the others as well.

[M9] , grinding my teeth

XLI

GOKHALE'S CHARITY

I have already referred to the attack of pleurisy I had in England. *Gokhale returned to London soon after.*[M1] Kallenbach and I used regularly to go to him.[529] Our talks were mostly about the War, and as Kallenbach had

[M1] At the time of this illness Gokhale had already returned to England.

---

[526] 'The India Office was not pleased with this.' To add.

[527] Roberts visited MKG on 17 October 1914 at 10.15 a.m. at his lodgings at 16, Trebovir Road, West Kensington.

[528] On 30 October twelve members reported to Netley, on 31st, a further eight and on 1 November two more volunteers reported to duty. SN 6069A.

[529] Gokhale returned to London on 16 August 1914 and stayed till 24 October, when he returned to India. He was in England in connection with his work on the Royal Commission on Public Service. He stayed in a cottage in suburban Twickenham as a guest of Sir Ratanji Tata (1871–1918). MKG and Kallenbach

the geography of Germany at *his fingertips*,[M2] and had
travelled much in Europe, he used to show him on the
map the various places in connection with the War.

[M2] at the tip of his tongue

When I got pleurisy[530] this also became a topic of
daily discussion. My dietetic experiments were going
on even then. My diet consisted, among other things,
of groundnuts, ripe and unripe bananas, lemon, olive
oil, tomatoes and grapes. I completely eschewed milk,
cereals, pulses and other things.

Dr. Jivraj Mehta treated me. He pressed me hard
to resume milk and cereals, but I was obdurate. *The
matter reached Gokhale's ears.*[M3] He had not much regard
for my reasoning in favour of a fruitarian diet, and he
wanted me to take whatever the doctor prescribed for
my health.

[M3] The complaint was taken to Gokhale.

It was no easy thing for me not to yield to Gokhale's
pressure. When he would not take a refusal, I begged
him to give me twenty-four hours for thinking over
the question. As Kallenbach and I returned home that
evening, we discussed where my duty lay. He had
been with me in my experiment. He liked it, but I saw
that he was agreeable to my giving it up if my health
demanded it. So I had to *decide for myself according to the
dictates of the inner voice.*[M4]

[M4] search the inner voice

I spent the whole night thinking over the matter.
To give up the experiment would mean renouncing
all my ideas in that direction, and yet I found no flaw
in them. The question was how far I should yield to
Gokhale's loving pressure, and how far I might modify
my experiment in the so-called[531] interests of health. I
finally decided to adhere to the experiment in so far as
the motive behind was chiefly religious, and to yield

---

used to meet him at the National Liberal Club in the Whitehall
Place and Northumberland Avenue.

[530] 'the disease' in the original; pleurisy is not mentioned.

[531] 'so-called' added in the English translation.

^{M5} in all other matters

^{M6} cruel practice perpetrated on cows and buffaloes in Calcutta

to the doctor's advice *where the motive was mixed.*^{M5} Religious considerations had been predominant in the giving up of milk. I had before me a picture of the *wicked processes the govals in Calcutta adopted to extract the last drop of milk from their cows and buffaloes.*^{M6} I also had the feeling that, just as meat was not man's food, even so animal's milk could not be man's food. So I got up in the morning with the determination to adhere to my resolve to abstain from milk. This greatly relieved me. I dreaded to approach Gokhale, but I trusted him to respect my decision.

In the evening Kallenbach and I called on Gokhale at the National Liberal Club. The first question he asked me was: 'Well, have you decided to accept the doctor's advice?'

I gently but firmly[532] replied: 'I am willing to yield on all points except one about which I beg you not to press me. I will not take milk, milk-products or meat. If not to take these things should mean my death, I feel *I had better face it.*'^{M7}

^{M7} therein lies my duty

'Is this your final decision?' asked Gokhale.

'I am afraid I cannot decide otherwise,' said I. 'I know that my decision will pain you, but I beg your forgiveness.'

With a certain amount of pain but with deep affection, Gokhale said: 'I do not approve of your decision. I do not see any religion in it. But I won't press you anymore.' With these words he turned to Dr. Jivraj Mehta and said: 'Please don't worry him anymore. Prescribe anything you like within the limit he has set for himself.'

The doctor expressed dissent, but was helpless. He advised me to take *mung* soup, with a dash of asafoetida in it. To this I agreed. I took it for a day or two, but it increased my pain. As I did not find it suitable, I went

---

[532] 'but firmly' added in the English translation.

back to fruits and nuts.[533] The doctor of course went on with his external treatment. The latter somewhat relieved my pain, but my restrictions were to him a sore handicap.

Meanwhile Gokhale left for home, as he could not stand the October[534] fogs of London.

XLII

TREATMENT OF PLEURISY[M1]

[M1] What Was Done for the Disease?

The persistence of the pleurisy[535] caused some anxiety, but I knew that the cure lay not in taking medicine internally but in dietetic changes assisted by external remedies.

I called in Dr. Allinson of vegetarian fame, who treated diseases by dietetic modifications and whom I had met in 1890. *He thoroughly overhauled me.*[M2] I explained to him how I had pledged myself not to take milk. He cheered me up and said: 'You need not take milk. In fact I want you to do without any fat for some days.' He then advised me to live on *plain brown*[M3] bread, raw vegetables such as beet, radish, onion and other tubers and greens, and also fresh fruit, mainly oranges. The vegetables were not to be cooked but merely grated fine,[536] if I could not masticate them.[537]

[M2] I showed him my body.

[M3] dry

I adopted this for about three days, but raw vegetables did not quite suit me. My body was not in a condition

---

[533] 'and nuts' added in the English translation.

[534] 'October–November' in the original.

[535] 'chest pain' in the original.

[536] 'or ground' to add.

[537] 'if I could not masticate them' added in the English translation.

to enable me to do full justice to the experiment.[538] I was nervous about taking raw vegetables.

Dr. Allinson also advised me to keep all the windows of my room open for the whole twenty-four hours, bathe in tepid water, have an oil massage on the affected parts and a walk in the open for fifteen to thirty minutes. I liked all these suggestions.

My room had French windows which, if kept wide open, would let in the rain. The fanlight could not be opened. I therefore got the glass broken, so as to let in fresh air, and I partially opened the windows in a manner not to let in rain.

All these measures somewhat improved my health, but did not completely cure me.

Lady Cecilia Roberts[539] occasionally called on me. *We became friends.*[M4] She wanted very much to persuade me to take milk. But as I was unyielding, she hunted about for a substitute for milk. Some friend suggested to her malted milk, assuring her quite unknowingly that it was absolutely free from milk, and that it was a chemical preparation with all the properties of milk. Lady Cecilia, I knew, had a great regard for my religious scruples, and so I implicitly trusted her. I dissolved the powder in water and took it only to find that it tasted just like milk.[540] I read the label on the bottle, to find, only too late,[541] that it was a preparation of milk. So I gave it up.[542]

[M4] We were well acquainted.

---

[538] 'nor had I the necessary faith' to add.

[539] Lady Cecilia Maude Roberts (1868–1947), wife of Charles Roberts and daughter of the Earl and Countess of Carlisle.

[540] 'It was akin to asking about the antecedents of the household after having accepted its water.' To add.

[541] 'only too late' added in the English translation.

[542] 'after having taken it once' to add.

I informed Lady Cecilia about the discovery, asking her not to worry over it. She came post-haste to me to say how sorry she was. Her friend had not read the label at all. I begged her not to be anxious and expressed my regret that I could not avail myself of the thing she had procured with so much trouble. I also assured her that I did not at all feel upset or guilty over having taken milk under a misapprehension.

I must skip over many other sweet reminiscences of my contact with Lady Cecilia. I could think of many friends who have been a source of great comfort to me in the midst of trials and disappointments. One who has faith reads in them the merciful providence of God, who thus sweetens sorrow itself.

Dr. Allinson, when he next called, relaxed his restrictions and permitted me to have groundnut butter or olive oil for the sake of fat, and to take the vegetables cooked, if I chose, with rice. These changes were quite welcome, but they were far from giving me a complete cure. Very careful nursing was still necessary, and I was obliged to keep mostly in bed.

Dr. Mehta occasionally looked in to examine me and held out a standing offer to cure me if only I would listen to his advice. Whilst things were going on in this way, Mr. Roberts one day came to see me and urged me very strongly to go home.

'You cannot possibly go to Netley in this condition. There is still severer cold ahead of us. I would strongly advise you to get back to India, for it is only there that you can be completely cured. If, after your recovery, you should find the War still going on, you will have many opportunities there of rendering help. As it is, I do not regard what you have already done as by any means a mean contribution.'

I accepted his advice and began to make preparations for returning to India.

XLIII

M1 Departure

HOMEWARD[M1]

Mr. Kallenbach had accompanied me to England with a view to going to India. We were staying together and of course wanted to sail by the same boat.[543] Germans, however, were under such strict surveillance that we had our doubts about Mr. Kallenbach getting a passport.[544] I did my best to get it,[545] and Mr. Roberts, who was in favour of his getting his passport, sent a cable to the Viceroy in this behalf. But straight came Lord Hardinge's[546] reply: 'Regret Government of India not prepared to take any such risk.' All of us understood the force of the reply.[547]

It was a great wrench for me to part from Mr. Kallenbach, but I could see that his pang was greater. Could he have come to India, he would have been leading today the simple *happy*[M2] life of a farmer and weaver. Now he is in South Africa, leading his old life and doing brisk business as an architect.

M2 beautiful

---

[543] 'and of course wanted to sail by the same boat' added in the English translation.

[544] 'pass' in the original.

[545] MKG wrote two letters to the undersecretary for Colonies. In one he also mentioned Kallenbach's desire to join the Indian Volunteers Corps. See *CWMG*, vol. 12, pp. 526, 528–29.

[546] Charles Hardinge, 1st Baron Hardinge of Penhurts (1856–1944), Viceroy of India (1910–16); his viceroyalty was marked by the visit of King George V and the Delhi Durbar of 1911 and the shifting of the capital of British-administered India from Calcutta to Delhi in 1912.

[547] Kallenbach registered with the London police as an alien enemy on 10 September 1914; on 17 June 1915 he was assigned to a detention camp. He remained at the detention camps at Stanford, Knockaloe and Douglass Small Camp till his release in January 1917.

We *wanted*[M3] a third-class passage, but as there was   [M3] tried to secure
none available on P. and O. boats,[548] we had to go
second.[549]

We took with us the dried fruit we had carried from
South Africa, as most of it would not be procurable on
the boat, where fresh fruit was easily available.

Dr. Jivraj Mehta had bandaged my ribs with
'Mede's Plaster'[550] and had asked me not to remove it
till we reached the Red Sea.[551] For two days I put up
with the discomfort, but finally it became too much for
me. It was with considerable difficulty that I managed
to undo the plaster and regain the liberty of having a
proper wash and bath.

My diet consisted mostly of nuts and fruits.[552]
I found that I was improving every day and felt
very much better by the time we entered the Suez
Canal. I was weak, but felt entirely out of danger,
and I gradually went on increasing my exercise. The
improvement I attributed largely to the pure air of the
temperate zone.

Whether it was due to past experience or to any
other reason, I do not know, but the kind of distance
I noticed between the English and Indian passengers
on the boat was something I had not observed even

---

[548] Peninsular and Oriental Steam Navigation Company, dating
back to 1822.

[549] MKG and Kasturba sailed from London on *S.S. Arabia* on
19 December 1914.

[550] A rigid corset cast from plaster of Paris, fixed around the torso,
fortified with a layer of belladonna plant; originally a costume
worn by the Medes, an ancient tribe of Persia.

[551] 'till we reached the Red Sea' added in the English translation.

[552] On 23 December MKG reported on his diet: 'We live on the
food we have brought from England. Mixing two parts banana
flour and one part wheat flour, we have made biscuits and *rotis*.
We eat these and dry fruit, soaked in water. Ripe fruit we obtain
from the ship.' *CWMG*, vol. 12, p. 566.

on my voyage from South Africa.[553] I did talk to a few Englishmen, but the talk was mostly formal.[554] There were hardly any cordial conversations such as had certainly taken place on the South African boats.[555] The reason for this was, I think, to be found in the conscious or unconscious feeling at the back of the Englishman's mind that he belonged to the ruling race, and the feeling at the back of the Indian's mind that he belonged to the subject race.

I was eager to reach home and get free from this atmosphere.

On arriving at Aden we already began to feel somewhat at home. We knew the Adenwallas very well, having met Mr. Kekobad Kavasji Dinshaw[556] in Durban and come in close contact with him and his wife. A few days more and we reached Bombay.[557] *It was such a joy to get back to the homeland after an exile of ten years.*[M4]

M4 I returned after ten years to a country that I had hoped to return to in 1905, which gave me great joy.

Gokhale had inspired a reception for me in Bombay,[558] where he had come in spite of his delicate health. *I had approached India in the ardent hope of merging*

---

[553] 'There was distance there too, but this appeared to be of a different type.' To add.

[554] 'mostly formal' translates *Sahib, saalam*, literally, 'Salutations, Sir'.

[555] 'and in South Africa' to add.

[556] Kekobad Cowasji Dinshaw (Adenwala), manager and partner of Cowasji Dinshaw firm in Aden.

[557] MKG and Kasturba reached Bombay on 9 January 1915.

[558] A public reception was accorded to him and Kasturba on 12 January 1915 at Mount Petit, with over 600 guests present and with Sir Pherozeshah Mehta presiding. On the previous day a reception was given to them in Ghatkopar, Bombay, with Rao Bahadur Vasanji Khimji presiding. On 13 January a meeting to welcome him was held by the Bombay National Union, with Lokmanya G.B. Tilak present. On 14 January the Gurjar Sabha gave him a reception with M.A. Jinnah presiding.

myself in him, and thereby feeling free.[M5] But fate had willed it otherwise.

[M5] I had reached Bombay in the ardent hope of meeting him, merging with his life and of freeing myself of all burden.

XLIV

SOME REMINISCENCES OF THE BAR

Before coming to a narrative of the course my life took in India, it *seems*[M1] necessary to recall a few of the South African[559] experiences which I have[560] deliberately left out.

[M1] has become

Some lawyer friends have asked me to give my reminiscences of the bar. The number of these is so large that, if I were to describe them all, they would occupy a volume by themselves and take me out of my scope. But it may not perhaps be improper to recall some of those which bear upon the practice of truth.

So far as I can recollect, I have already said that I never resorted to untruth in my profession, and that a large part of my legal practice was in the interest of public work, for which I charged nothing beyond out-of-pocket expenses, and these too I sometimes met myself. I had thought that in saying this I had said all that was necessary as regards my legal practice. But friends want me to do more. They seem to think that, if I described[561] however slightly some of the occasions when I refused to swerve from the truth, the *legal profession might profit by it.*[M2]

[M2] lawyers might learn something from it

As[562] a student I had heard that the lawyer's profession was a liar's profession. But this did not influence me, as

---

[559] 'South African' added in the English translation.

[560] 'had' in the first edition.

[561] 'were to describe' in the first edition.

[562] 'Even' to add before 'As'.

I had no intention of earning either position or money by lying.

My principle was put to the test many a time in South Africa. Often I knew[563] that my opponents had tutored their witnesses, and if I only encouraged my client or his witnesses to lie, we could[564] win the case. But I always resisted the temptation. I remember only one occasion when, after having won a case, I suspected that my client had deceived me. In my heart of hearts I always wished that I should win only if my client's case was right. In fixing my fees I do not recall ever having made them conditional on my winning the case. Whether my client won or lost, I expected nothing more nor less than *my fees*.[M3]

M3 what I had earned for my work

I warned every new client at the outset that he should not expect me to take up a false case or to coach the witnesses, with the result that I *built up*[M4] such a reputation that no false cases used to come to me. Indeed some of my clients would keep their clean cases for me, and take the doubtful ones elsewhere.

M4 acquired

There was one case which proved a severe trial. It was brought to me by one of my best clients. It was a case of highly complicated accounts and had been a prolonged one. It had been heard in parts before several courts. Ultimately the bookkeeping portion of it was entrusted by the court to the arbitration of some qualified accountants.[565] The award was entirely in favour of my client, but the arbitrators had inadvertently committed an error in calculation which, however small, was serious, inasmuch as an entry which ought to have been on the debit side was made on the credit side. The opponents had *opposed the award on other grounds*.[M5] I was

M5 appealed for the arbitrator's award to be set aside

---

563 'would know' in the first edition.

564 'would' in the first edition.

565 'appointed by it' to add.

junior counsel for my client. When the senior counsel became aware of the error, he was of opinion that our client was not bound to admit it. He was clearly of opinion that no counsel was bound to admit anything that went against his client's interest. I said we ought to admit the error.

But the senior counsel contended: 'In that case there is every likelihood of the court cancelling the whole award, and no sane counsel would imperil his client's case to that extent. At any rate I would be the last man to take any such risk. If the case were to be sent up for a fresh hearing, one could never tell what expenses our client might have to incur, and what the ultimate result might be!'

The client was present when this conversation took place.

I said: 'I feel that both our client and we ought to run the risk. Where is the certainty of the court[566] upholding a wrong award simply because we do not admit the error? And supposing the *admission*[M6] were to bring the client to grief, what harm is there?'

'But why should we make the admission at all?' said the senior counsel.

'Where is the surety of the court not detecting the error or our opponent not discovering it?' said I.

'Well then, will you argue the case? I am not prepared to argue it on your terms,' replied the senior counsel with decision.

I humbly answered: 'If you will not argue, then I am prepared to do so, if our client so desires. I shall have nothing to do with the case if the error is not admitted.'

With this I looked at my client. He was a little embarrassed. I had been in the case from the very first. The client fully trusted me, and knew me through and through. He said: 'Well, then, you will argue the case

[M6] verification of the error

---

[566] 'upon discovery of the error' to add.

and admit the error. Let us lose,[567] if that is to be our lot.
God defends the right.'

I was delighted. I had expected nothing less from
him. The senior counsel again warned me, pitied me for
my obduracy, but congratulated me all the same.

What happened in the court we shall see in the next
chapter.

XLV

SHARP PRACTICE?

I had no doubt about the soundness of my advice, but
I doubted very much my fitness for doing full justice to
the case. I felt it would be a most hazardous undertaking
to argue such a difficult case before the Supreme Court,
and I appeared before the Bench in fear and trembling.

As soon as I referred to the error in the accounts,
one of the judges said:

'Is not this sharp practice, Mr. Gandhi?'[568]

I boiled within to hear this charge. It was intolerable
to be accused of sharp practice when there was not the
slightest warrant for it.

'With a judge prejudiced from the start like this,
there is little chance of success in this difficult case,' I said
to myself. But I composed my thoughts and answered:

'I am surprised that Your Lordship should suspect
sharp practice without hearing me out.'
'No question of a charge,' said the judge. 'It is a
mere suggestion.'

---

[567] 'We will lose' in the first edition.

[568] 'Mr. Gandhi' added in the English translation.

'The suggestion here seems to me to amount to a charge. I would ask Your Lordship to hear me out and then arraign me if there is any occasion for it.'

'I am sorry to have interrupted you,' replied the judge. 'Pray do go on with your explanation of the discrepancy.'

I had enough material in support of my explanation. Thanks to the judge having raised this question, I was able to rivet the Court's attention on my argument from the very start. I felt much encouraged and took the opportunity of entering into a detailed explanation. The Court gave me a patient hearing, and I was able to convince the judges that the discrepancy was due entirely to inadvertence. They therefore did not feel disposed to cancel the whole award, which had involved considerable labour.

The opposing counsel seemed to feel secure in the belief that not much argument would be needed after the error had been admitted. *But the judges continued to interrupt him, as they were convinced that the error was a slip*[M1] which could be easily rectified. The counsel laboured hard to attack the award, but the judge who had originally started with the suspicion had now come round definitely to my side.

'Supposing Mr. Gandhi had not admitted the error, what would you have done?' he asked.

'It was impossible for us to secure the services of a more competent and honest expert accountant than the one appointed by us.'

'The Court must presume that you know your case best. If you cannot point out anything beyond the slip which any expert accountant is liable to commit, the Court will be loath to compel the parties to go in for fresh litigation and fresh expenses because of a patent mistake. We may not order a fresh hearing when such an error can be easily corrected,' continued the judge.

[M1] But the judges were not inclined to set aside the award of the arbitrators on account of such an evident slip

And so the counsel's objection was overruled. The Court either confirmed the award, with the error rectified, or ordered the arbitrator to rectify the error, I forget which.

I was delighted.[569] So were client and senior counsel; and I was confirmed in my conviction that it was not impossible to practise law without compromising truth.

Let the reader, however, remember that even truthfulness in the practice of the profession cannot cure it of the fundamental defect that vitiates it.

XLVI

CLIENTS TURNED CO-WORKERS

The distinction between the legal practice in Natal and that in the Transvaal was that in Natal *there was a joint bar; a barrister, whilst he was admitted to the rank of advocate, could also practise as an attorney; whereas in the Transvaal, as in Bombay, the spheres of attorneys and advocates were distinct.*[M1] A barrister had the right of election whether he would practise as an advocate or as an attorney. So whilst in Natal I was admitted as an advocate, in the Transvaal I sought admission as an attorney. For as an advocate I could not have come in direct contact with the Indians and the white attorneys in South Africa would not have briefed me.

But even in the Transvaal it was open to attorneys to appear before magistrates. On one occasion, whilst I was conducting a case before a magistrate in Johannesburg, I discovered that my client had deceived me.[570] I saw him completely break down in the witness[571] box. So

[M1] despite the difference between an advocate and an attorney, both could appear before all courts without any distinction. While in the Transvaal, they were distinct like in Bombay. There an advocate may deal with his client only through an attorney.

---

[569] 'beyond measure' to add.

[570] 'His case was false.' To add.

[571] 'witness' added in the English translation.

without any argument I asked the magistrate to dismiss the case. The opposing counsel was astonished, and the magistrate was pleased. I rebuked my client for bringing a false case to me.[572] He knew that I never accepted false cases, and when I brought the thing home to him, he admitted his mistake, and I have an impression that he was not angry with me for having asked the magistrate to decide against him. At any rate my conduct in this case did not affect my practice for the worse, indeed it made my work easier. I also saw that my devotion to truth enhanced my reputation amongst the members of the profession, and in spite of the *handicap of colour*[M2]   [M2] strange circumstances
I was able in some cases to win even their affection.

During my professional work it was also my habit never to conceal[573] my ignorance from my clients or my colleagues. Wherever I *felt myself at sea*,[M3] I would   [M3] did not know
advise my client to consult some other counsel, or if he preferred to stick to me, I would ask him to let me seek the assistance of senior counsel. This frankness earned me the unbounded affection and trust of my clients. They were always willing to pay the fee whenever consultation with senior counsel was necessary. This affection and trust served me in good stead in my public work.

I have indicated in the foregoing chapters that my[574] object in practising in South Africa was service of the community. Even for this purpose, winning the confidence of the people was an indispensable condition. The large-hearted Indians magnified into service professional work done for money, and when I advised them to suffer the hardships of imprisonment for the sake of their rights, many of them cheerfully[575]

---

[572] 'for bringing a false case to me' added in the English translation.

[573] 'disguise' in the first edition.

[574] 'sole' to add.

[575] 'cheerfully' added in the English translation.

accepted the advice, not so much because they had reasoned out the correctness of the course, as because of their confidence in, and affection for, me.

As I write this, many a sweet reminiscence comes to my mind. Hundreds of clients became friends and real co-workers in public service, and their association sweetened a life that was otherwise full of difficulties and dangers.[576]

XLVII

HOW A CLIENT WAS SAVED[577]

The reader, by now, will be quite familiar with Parsi Rustomji's name.[578] He was one who became at once my client and co-worker, or perhaps it would be truer to say that he first became co-worker and then client. I won his confidence to such an extent that he sought and followed my advice also in private domestic matters. Even when he was ill, he would seek my aid, and though there was much difference between our ways of living, he did not hesitate to accept my quack[579] treatment.

This friend once got into a very bad scrape. Though he kept me informed of most of his[580] affairs,

---

[576] 'and dangers' added in the English translation.

[577] 'from Imprisonment' to add.

[578] In a letter of 15 July 1928 to Manilal and Sushila Gandhi, MKG explained as to why he mentioned Parsi Rustomji's name. 'I was prompted by love in writing what I did about the Rustomji case in the "Autobiography". I have omitted other names but given this one; my aim in giving certain names is that they should be remembered as long as the "Autobiography" is recognized as an important work.' *CWMG*, vol. 37, p. 66.

[579] 'quack' added in the English translation.

[580] 'business' to add.

he had studiously kept back one thing. He was a large importer of goods from Bombay and Calcutta, and[581] not infrequently[582] he resorted to smuggling. But as he was on the best terms with customs officials, no one was inclined to suspect him. In charging duty, they used to take his invoices on trust. Some might even have connived at the smuggling.

But to use the telling simile of the Gujarati[583] poet Akho, theft like quicksilver won't be suppressed, and Parsi Rustomji's *proved no exception. The good friend*[M1] ran post-haste to me, the tears rolling down his cheeks as he said:[584] 'Bhai, I have deceived you. My *guilt*[M2] has been discovered today. I have smuggled and I am doomed.[585] I must go to jail and be ruined. You alone may be able to save me from this predicament. I have kept back nothing else from you, but I thought I ought not to bother you with such tricks of the trade, and so I never told you about this smuggling. But now, how much I repent it!'

I calmed him and said: 'To save or not to save you is in His hands. As to me you know my way. I can but try to save you by means of confession.'

The good *Parsi felt deeply mortified.*[M3]

'But is not my confession before you enough?' he asked.

'You have wronged not me but Government. How will the confession made before me avail you?' I replied gently.

'Of course I will do just as you advise, but will you not consult with my old counsel Mr. —? He is a friend too,' said Parsi Rustomji.

[M1] theft was caught. He

[M2] sin

[M3] Parsi's face withered

---

[581] 'and it turned out that' in the first edition.

[582] 'not infrequently' added in the English translation.

[583] 'Gujarati' added in the English translation.

[584] 'in Parsi tongue' to add.

[585] 'and I am doomed' added in the English translation.

Inquiry revealed that the smuggling had been going on for a long time, but the actual offence detected involved a trifling sum. We went to his counsel. He perused the papers, and said: 'The case will be tried by a jury, and a Natal jury will be the last to acquit an Indian. But I will not give up hope.'

I did not know this counsel intimately. Parsi Rustomji intercepted: 'I thank you, but I should like to be guided by Mr. Gandhi's advice in this case. He knows me intimately. Of course you will advise him whenever necessary.'

Having thus shelved the counsel's question,[586] we went to Parsi Rustomji's shop.

And now explaining my view I said to him: 'I don't think this case should be taken to court at all. It rests with the Customs Officer to prosecute you or to let you go, and he in turn will have to be guided by the Attorney General. I am prepared to meet both.[587] I propose that you should offer to pay the penalty they fix, and the odds are that they will be agreeable. But if they are not, you must be prepared to go to jail. I am of opinion that the shame lies not so much in going to jail as in committing the offence. The deed of shame has already been done. Imprisonment you should regard as a penance. The real penance lies in resolving never to smuggle again.'

I cannot say that Parsi Rustomji took all this quite well. He was a brave man, but his courage failed him for the moment. His name and fame were at stake, and where would he be if the edifice he had reared with such care and labour should go to pieces? 'Well, I have told you,' he said, 'that *I am entirely in your hands.*[M4] You may do just as you like.'

M4 my head is in your lap

---

586 'shelved the counsel's question' translates the expression 'bhinu sankeli', literally, 'having folded up still wet clothes'.

587 'But I shall have to admit to the smuggling that they are unaware of.' To add.

I brought to bear on this case all my powers of persuasion. I met the Customs Officer and fearlessly apprised him of the whole affair. I also promised to place all the books at his disposal and told him how penitent Parsi Rustomji was feeling.

The Customs Officer said: 'I like the old Parsi. I am sorry he has made a fool of himself. You know where my duty lies. I must be guided by the Attorney General and so I would advise you to use all your persuasion with him.'

'I shall be *thankful*,'[M5] said I, 'if you do not insist on dragging him into court.'

[M5] satisfied

Having got him to promise this, I entered into correspondence with the Attorney General and also met him.[588] I am glad to say that he appreciated my *complete frankness*[M6] and was convinced that I had kept back nothing.

[M6] love of truth

I now forget whether it was in connection with this or with some other case that *my persistence and frankness extorted from him the remark*:[M7] 'I see you will never take a no for an answer.'

[M7] he gave me the testimonial

The case against Parsi Rustomji was compromised.[M8] He was to pay a penalty equal to twice the amount he had confessed to having smuggled. Rustomji reduced to writing the facts of the whole case, got the paper framed and hung it up in his office to serve as a perpetual reminder to his heirs and fellow-merchants.

[M8] Parsi Rustomji was not prosecuted.

These friends of Rustomji warned me *not to be taken in by this transitory contrition*.[M9] When I told Rustomji about this warning he said: 'What would be my fate if I deceived you?'

[M9] that this was not true contrition. It was the detachment of the one in a crematorium. I do not know how far they were right.

---

[588] 'whom I also met' in the first edition.

PART V

I

THE FIRST EXPERIENCE

Before I reached home, the party which had started from Phoenix had already arrived. According to our original plan I was to have preceded them, *but my preoccupation in England with the War had upset all our calculations, and when I saw that I had to be detained in England indefinitely,*[M1] I was faced with the question of finding a place for accommodating the Phoenix party. I wanted them all to stay together in India, if possible, and to live the life they had led at Phoenix. I did not know of any[1] Ashram to which I could recommend them to go, and therefore cabled to them to meet Mr. Andrews and do as he advised.

So they were first put in the Gurukul, Kangri, where the late Swami Shraddhanandji[2] treated them as his own children. After this they were put in the

[M1] but I stayed back in London on account of the war.

---

[1] 'head of an' to add.

[2] Swami Shraddhananda (1856–1926), also known as Mahatma Munshiram, Arya Samaj missionary, participated in the shuddhi movement and was active in nationalist politics during the agitation against the Rowlatt Act, established Gurukul Kangri near Haridwar in 1902, assassinated in 1926.

Shantiniketan Ashram,[3] where the Poet[4] and his people showered similar love upon them. The experiences they gathered at both these places too stood[5] them and me in good stead.

The Poet, Shraddhanandji and Principal Sushil Rudra,[6] as I used to say to Andrews, composed his trinity. When in South Africa[7] he was never tired of *speaking of them, and of my many sweet memories of South Africa, Mr. Andrews's talks, day in and day out, of this great trinity, are amongst the sweetest and most vivid.*[M2]

[M2] praising these three. Of the many memories of our loving companionship in South Africa, what is vivid before my eyes is how the names of these three great men were always in his heart and on his lips.

---

[3] The Shantiniketan school was founded by Rabindranath Tagore (1861–1941) in 1901. He located the school in rural southern Bengal, about 140 km north-west of Calcutta. There his father Maharshi Devendranath (1817–1905) had endowed an ashram for Brahmo householders in the 1860s and named it 'Shantiniketan'. Devendranath's endowment provided for an annual village fair, a hall of prayer and a school. Rabindranath was concerned over the growing cultural divide between city and village in modern India. He hoped to redeem this at Shantiniketan where boys from the city would live and study in a school surrounded by villages. Shantiniketan was home for a year to Gandhi's Phoenix Farm boys when they left South Africa and came to India in 1914. Tagore wrote to thank Gandhi 'for allowing your boys to become our boys as well, and thus form a living link in the *sādhanā* of both of our lives'. February 1915 (not dated), *Visva-Bharati Quarterly*, 35, Nos. 1–4 (Gandhi Number), May 1969–April 1970, p. 237.

[4] 'the Poet' refers to Rabindranath Tagore.

[5] 'served' in the first edition.

[6] Sushil Kumar Rudra (1861–1925), eldest son of Rev. Pyari Mohan Rudra, a missionary of the Church Mission Society, joined St. Stephen's College in 1883 and became its fourth and first Indian principal in 1912. A friend of C.F. Andrews who dedicated two of his books to Rudra: *North India* (1908) and *Sadhu Sundar Das* (1936); the non-cooperation plan was 'hatched under his roof' as MKG wrote in his obituary. See *CWMG*, vol. 27, p. 351. Sushil Rudra is buried at the English chapel in Solan.

[7] C.F. Andrews sailed for South Africa from Calcutta on 30 November 1913, reaching Durban on 2 January 1914. He gave a public lecture on Tagore at the Town Hall in Cape Town on 12 February and sailed from there for England on 21 February 1914.

Mr. Andrews naturally[8] put *the Phoenix party*[M3] in touch also with Sushil Rudra. Principal Rudra had no Ashram, but he had a home which he placed completely at the disposal of *the Phoenix*[M4] family. Within a day of their arrival, his *people*[M5] made them feel so thoroughly at home that they did not seem to miss Phoenix at all.

[M3] my children

[M4] my

[M5] sons and daughter

It was only when I landed in Bombay that I learnt that *the Phoenix party*[M6] was at Shantiniketan. I was therefore impatient to meet them as soon as I could after my meeting with Gokhale.

[M6] this family

The receptions in Bombay[9] *gave me an occasion for offering what might be called a little satyagraha.*[M7]

At the party given in my honour at Mr. Jehangir Petit's place, I did not dare to speak in Gujarati. In those palatial surroundings of dazzling splendour I, who had lived my best life[10] among indentured labourers, felt myself a complete rustic. With my Kathiawadi cloak, turban and dhoti, I looked somewhat more civilized than I do today, but the pomp and splendour of Mr. Petit's mansion made me feel absolutely out of my element. However, I acquitted myself tolerably well, having taken shelter under Sir Pherozeshah's protecting wing.

[M7] In Bombay, while accepting the honours I had to offer a little satyagraha.

Then there was the Gujarati function. The Gujaratis would not let me go without a reception,[11] which was organized by the late Uttamlal Trivedi.[12] I had acquainted myself with the programme beforehand.

---

[8] 'therefore' in the first edition.

[9] See n. 557 of Chapter XLIII, Part IV, for details of the receptions.

[10] 'my best life' added in the English translation.

[11] 'The Gujaratis would not let me go without a reception,' added in the English translation.

[12] Uttamlal Keshavlal Trivedi (1872–1923), versatile literary critic, trained in law, and practised it first at Rajkot and later in Bombay. Translated Lokmanya Tilak's *Gita Rahasya* into Gujarati.

Mr. Jinnah was present, being a Gujarati, I forget whether as president or as the principal speaker.[13] He made a short and sweet little speech in English. As far as I remember most of the other speeches were also in English. When my turn came, I expressed my thanks in Gujarati explaining[14] my partiality for Gujarati and Hindustani, and entering my humble protest against the use of English in a Gujarati gathering. This I did, not without some hesitation, for I was afraid lest it should be considered discourteous for an inexperienced man, returned home after a long exile, to enter his protest against established practices. But no one seemed to misunderstand my insistence on replying in Gujarati. In fact I was glad to note that everyone seemed reconciled to my protest.

The meeting thus emboldened me to think that I should not find it difficult to place my[15] new-fangled notions before my countrymen.

After a brief stay in Bombay, full of these preliminary experiences, I went to Poona whither[16] Gokhale had summoned me.

---

[13] Muhammad Ali Jinnah (1876–1948), revered as Quaid-i-Azam, called to the Bar from Lincoln's Inn; his early public life was in the Indian National Congress and the All India Home Rule League, and he played a prominent part in the Lucknow Pact (1915). He joined the All India Muslim League in 1913; his break from the Congress came in 1920. After a brief interlude from public life he became a member of the Central Legislative Assembly (1934), made a demand for a separate, sovereign nation state of Pakistan through the Lahore Resolution of the Muslim League in 1940. With the creation of Pakistan he became its first governor general. Married Ruttie Petit. Jinnah, as the chairman of the Gurjar Sabha, presided over the reception for MKG held on 14 January 1915.

[14] 'in few words' to add.

[15] 'other' to add.

[16] 'where' in the first edition.

II

WITH GOKHALE IN POONA

The moment I reached Bombay Gokhale sent me word
that the Governor[17] was desirous of seeing me, and that
it might be proper for me to respond before I left for
Poona. Accordingly I *called on His Excellency*.[18] [M1] After
the usual inquiries, he said:

[M1] went to meet him

> 'I ask *one thing*[M2] of you. I would like you to come
> and see me whenever you propose to take any steps
> concerning Government.'

[M2] a promise

I replied:

> 'I can very easily give the promise, inasmuch as it is my
> rule, as a satyagrahi, to understand the viewpoint of the
> party I propose to deal with, and to try to agree with
> him as far as may be possible. I strictly observed the rule
> in South Africa and I mean to do the same here.'

Lord Willingdon thanked me and said:

> 'You may come to me whenever you like, and you
> will see that my Government do not wilfully do
> anything wrong.'

---

[17] Lord Willingdon, Freeman Thomas, 1st Marquess of Willingdon
(1866–1941), Governor of Bombay (1913–17), Governor of
Madras (1919–24), governor general of Canada (1926–31),
Viceroy of India (1931–36).

[18] MKG visited the Bombay branch of the Servants of India Society
on 14 January 1915 and met Lord Willingdon, the Governor
of Bombay, on the same day. Gokhale reached Bombay on 15
January (and thus he did not attend the reception at Mount Petit
as stated in Chapter XLIII of Part IV) and MKG having met
him left for Rajkot the same evening. MKG reached Poona on
8 February 1915, remaining there till 13 February. His diary of
1915 bears this out. See *CWMG*, vol. 13, pp. 156–59.

To which I replied: 'It is that faith which sustains me.'

After this I went to Poona. It is impossible for me to set down all the reminiscences of this precious[19] time. Gokhale and the members of the Servants of India Society[20] overwhelmed me with affection. So far as I recollect, Gokhale had summoned all of them to meet me. I had a frank talk with them all on every sort of subject.

Gokhale was very keen that I should join the Society and so was I. But the members felt that, as there was a great difference between my ideals and methods of work and theirs, it might not be proper for me to join the Society.[21] Gokhale believed that, in spite of my insistence on my own principles, I was equally ready and able to *tolerate theirs*.[M3]

[M3] abide by the ideals of others and work in harmony with them

'But,' he said, 'the members of the Society have not yet understood your readiness for compromise. They are tenacious of their principles, and quite independent. I am hoping that they will accept you, but if they don't you will not for a moment think that they are lacking in respect or love for you. They are hesitating to take any risk lest their high regard for you should be jeopardized. But whether you are formally admitted as a member or not, I am going to look upon you as one.'

I informed Gokhale of my intentions. Whether I was admitted as a member or not, I wanted to have an

---

[19] 'precious' added in the English translation.

[20] In the original 'the Society'. The Servants of India Society was founded by Gokhale in 1905 with the object of serving the people of India without any discrimination. It started an English daily, *The Hitavada*, in 1911; after Gokhale's death in 1915, Rt. Hon'ble Srinivas Sastri became its president (1915–45).

[21] *The Mahratta* of 14 February 1915 reported a conversation with MKG: 'Asked about his future plans he replied that he had not yet settled anything and that it was not certain that he would join the Servants of India Society.' *CWMG*, vol. 13, p. 20.

Ashram where I could settle down with my Phoenix family, preferably somewhere in Gujarat, as, being a Gujarati, I thought I was best fitted to serve the country through serving Gujarat. Gokhale liked the idea. He said: 'You should certainly do so. Whatever may be the result of your talks with the members, you must look to me for the expenses of the Ashram, which I will regard as my own.'

My heart overflowed with joy. It was a pleasure to feel free from the responsibility of raising funds, and to realize that I should not be obliged to set about the work all on my own, but that I should be able to count on a sure guide whenever I was in difficulty. This took a great load off my mind.

So the late Dr. Dev[22] was summoned and told to open an account for me in the Society's books and to give me whatever I might require for the Ashram and for public expenses.

I now prepared to go to Shantiniketan. On the eve of my departure Gokhale arranged a party of selected friends, taking good care to order refreshments of my liking, i.e., fruits and nuts. The party was held just a few paces from his room, and yet he was hardly in a condition to walk across and attend it. *But his affection for me got the better of him and he insisted on coming.*[M4] He came, but fainted[23] and had to be carried away. Such fainting was not a new thing with him and so when he came to, he sent word that we must go on with the party.

This party was of course no more than a conversazione in the open space opposite the Society's guesthouse, during which friends[24] had heart-to-heart

[M4] But how would his love let him be?

---

[22] Dr. H.S. Deva, secretary of the Servants of India Society.

[23] In his diary MKG noted. 'Mr. Gokhale fainted.' *CWMG*, vol. 13, p. 159.

[24] 'sat on carpets and' to add.

chats over light refreshments of groundnuts, dates and fresh fruits of the season.[25]

But the fainting fit was to be no common event in my life.

III

WAS IT A THREAT?

From Poona[26] I went to Rajkot and Porbandar, where I had to meet my brother's widow and other relatives.[27]

During the satyagraha in South Africa I had altered my style of dress so as to make it more in keeping with that of the indentured labourers, and in England also I had adhered to the same style for indoor use.[28] For landing in Bombay I had a Kathiawadi suit of clothes consisting of a shirt, a dhoti, a cloak and a white scarf, all made of Indian mill-cloth. But as I was to travel third from Bombay, I regarded the scarf and the cloak as too much of an encumbrance, so I shed them, and invested in an eight-to-ten-annas Kashmiri cap. One dressed in that fashion was sure to pass muster as a poor man.

On account of the plague prevailing at that time third-class passengers were being medically inspected at Viramgam or Wadhwan—I forget which. I had slight fever. The inspector on finding that I had a temperature asked me to report myself to the Medical Officer at Rajkot and noted down my name.

---

[25] 'and fresh fruits of the season' added. In the original 'groundnuts, dates etc.'

[26] 'Bombay' in the original, which is factually correct.

[27] MKG reached Rajkot on 17 January and left it on 1 February 1915.

[28] 'I intended to wear, on return to India, Kathiawadi attire, which I had kept with me in South Africa.' To add.

Someone had perhaps sent *the information*[M1] that I was
passing through Wadhwan, for the tailor Motilal,[29] a noted
public worker of the place, met me at the station. He
told me about the Viramgam customs, and the hardships
railway passengers had to suffer on account of it. I had
little inclination to talk because of my fever, and tried to
finish with a brief reply which took the form of a question:

'Are you prepared to go to jail?'

I had taken Motilal to be one of those impetuous youths
who do not think before speaking. But not so Motilal.
He replied with firm deliberation:

> 'We will certainly go to jail, provided you lead us.
> As Kathiawadis, we have the first right on you. Of
> course we do not mean to detain you now, but you
> must promise to halt here on your return. You will
> be delighted to see the work and the spirit of our
> youths, and *you may trust us to respond as soon as you
> summon us.*'[M2]

Motilal captivated me. His comrade eulogizing him,
said:

> 'Our friend is but a tailor. But he is such a master of
> his profession that he easily earns Rs. 15 a month—
> which is just what he needs—working an hour a
> day, and gives the rest of his time to public work.
> He leads *us all, putting our education to shame.*'[M3]

Later I came in close contact with Motilal, and I saw
that there was no exaggeration in the eulogy. He made
a point of spending some days in the then newly started
Ashram every month to teach the children tailoring

M1 a cable letter

M2 you can summon us to join
your army and we shall enlist

M3 the educated and puts us to
shame

---

[29] Motilal Parshottam Parmar (1888–1918), a committed Swadeshi
worker, died while serving plague patients.

and to do some of the tailoring of the Ashram himself. He would talk to me every day of Viramgam, and the hardships of the passengers, which had become absolutely unbearable for him. He was cut off in the prime of youth by a sudden illness, and public life at Wadhwan suffered without him.

On reaching Rajkot, I reported myself to the Medical Officer the next morning. I was not unknown there. The doctor felt ashamed and was angry with the inspector. This was unnecessary, for the inspector had only done his duty. He did not know me, and even if he had known me, he should not have done otherwise. The[30] Medical Officer would not let me go to him again and insisted on sending an inspector to me instead.

Inspection of third-class passengers for sanitary reasons is essential on such occasions. If *big men*[M4] choose to travel third, whatever their position in life,[31] they must voluntarily submit themselves to all the regulations that the poor are subject to, and the officials ought to be impartial. My experience is that the officials, instead of looking upon third-class passengers as fellowmen, regard them *as so many sheep.*[M5] They talk to them contemptuously, and brook no reply or argument. The third-class passenger has to obey the official as though he were his servant, and the latter may with impunity belabour and blackmail him, and book him his ticket only after putting him to the greatest possible inconvenience, including often missing the train. All this I have *seen with my own eyes.*[M6] No reform is possible unless some of the educated and the rich voluntarily accept the status of the poor, travel third, refuse to enjoy the amenities denied to the poor and, instead of taking avoidable hardships, discourtesies and injustice[32] as a matter of course, fight for their removal.

[M4] men considered big

[M5] akin to animals

[M6] experienced

---

[30] 'Since I was known' to add before 'The'.

[31] 'whatever their position in life,' added in the English translation.

[32] 'and abuse' to add.

Wherever I went in Kathiawad I heard complaints about the Viramgam customs hardships. I therefore decided immediately to make use of Lord Willingdon's offer. I collected and read all the literature available on the subject, convinced myself that the complaints were well-founded, and opened correspondence with the Bombay Government. I called on the Private Secretary to Lord Willingdon and waited on His Excellency also. The latter expressed his sympathy but shifted the blame on Delhi. 'If it had been in our hands, we should have removed the *cordon*[M7] long ago. You should approach the Government of India,' said the Secretary.

[M7] custom

I communicated with the Government of India, but got no reply beyond an acknowledgement. It was only when I had an occasion to meet Lord Chelmsford[33] later[34] that redress could be had. When I placed the facts before him, he expressed his astonishment. He had known nothing of the matter. He gave me a patient hearing, telephoned that very moment for papers about Viramgam and promised to remove the cordon if the authorities had no explanation or defence to offer. Within a few days of this interview I read in the papers that the Viramgam customs cordon had been removed.[35]

---

[33] Frederic John Napier Thesiger, 1st Viscount Chelmsford (1868–1933), British statesman, called to the Bar from the Inner Temple in 1893, served as Governor of Queensland (1905–1909), Governor of New South Wales (1909-1913), also served as First Lord of Admiralty and Agent-General of New South Wales, Viceroy of India (1916–21), saw the implementation of the Montague–Chelmsford Reform with Secretary of State for India Edwin Samuel Montague, also imposed the repressive Rowlatt Act.

[34] 'that is after about two years' correspondence' to add.

[35] The Viramgam Custom was removed on 10 November 1917; MKG announced its removal to the Gujarat Political Conference on 4 November and Resolution 5 of the conference expressed its thanks to the Viceroy for this action.

M8 victory as fundamental to

M9 A people who seek freedom
must possess the means to
their ultimate defence.

I regarded this *event as the advent of*[M8] satyagraha in India. For during my interview with the Bombay Government the Secretary had expressed his disapproval of a reference to satyagraha in a speech which I had delivered in Bagasra (in Kathiawad).[36]

'Is not this a threat?' he had asked. 'And do you think a powerful Government will yield to threats?'

'This was no threat,' I had replied. 'It was educating the people. It is my duty to place before the people all the legitimate remedies for grievances. *A nation that wants to come into its own ought to know all the ways and means to freedom.*[M9] Usually they include violence as the last remedy. Satyagraha, on the other hand, is an absolutely non-violent weapon. I regard it as my duty to explain its practice and its limitations. I have no doubt that the British Government is a powerful Government but, I have no doubt also that satyagraha is a sovereign remedy.'

The clever Secretary sceptically[37] nodded his head and said: 'We shall see.'

IV

SHANTINIKETAN

From Rajkot I proceeded to Shantiniketan.[38] The teachers and students overwhelmed me with affection.

---

[36] The Bombay Secret Abstracts, 1916, do not contain any reference to 'satyagraha'. See *CWMG*, vol. 3, p. 151. The phrase 'and of which he had a report' deleted in the 1940 edition.

[37] 'sceptically' added in the English translation.

[38] MKG left Rajkot on 1 February, reaching Poona via Ahmedabad and Bombay on the 8th, remained there till the 13th and left for Shantiniketan on the 15th from Bombay, reaching there on 17 February 1915.

The reception was a beautiful combination of simplicity, art and love. It was here I met Kakasaheb Kalelkar[39] for the first time.

I did not know then why Kalelkar was called 'Kakasaheb'. But I learnt later on that Sjt. Keshavrao Deshpande,[40] who was a contemporary and *a close friend of mine*[M1] in England, and who had conducted a school in the Baroda State called 'Ganganath Vidyalaya', had given the teachers family names with a view to investing the Vidyalaya with a family atmosphere. Sjt. Kalelkar who was a teacher there came to be called 'Kaka' (literally, paternal uncle). Phadke[41] was called 'Mama' (literally, maternal uncle), and Harihar Sharma received the name 'Anna' (literally, brother). Others also got similar names. Anandanand (Swami) as Kaka's friend and Patwardhan (Appa) as Mama's friend later joined the family, and all in course of time became my co-workers one after another. Sjt. Deshpande himself used to be called 'Saheb'. When the Vidyalaya had to be dissolved, the family also broke up, but they never gave up their spiritual relationship or their assumed names.

[M1] and with whom I was well acquainted

Kakasaheb went out to gain experience of different institutions, and at the time I went to Shantiniketan, he happened to be there. Chintaman Shastri, belonging to the same fraternity, was there also. Both helped in teaching Samskrit.

The Phoenix family had been assigned separate quarters at Shantiniketan. Maganlal Gandhi was at their head, and he had made it his business to see that all

---

[39] Dattatreya Balkrishna Kalelkar (1885–1981), educationist, writer, constructive worker, member, Rajya Sabha (1952–64), president, Backward Classes Commission (1953).

[40] Bar-at-law, a close friend of Sri Aurobindo during their Cambridge days, for some time editor of the English section of *Indu Prakash*.

[41] Vitthal Laxman Phadke, dedicated his life to sanitation work.

the rules of the Phoenix Ashram should be scrupulously observed. I saw that, by dint of his love, knowledge and perseverance, he had made his fragrance felt in the whole of Shantiniketan.

Andrews was there, and also Pearson.[42] Amongst the Bengali teachers with whom we came in fairly close contact were Jagadanandbabu,[43] Nepalbabu,[44] Santoshbabu,[45] Kshitimohanbabu,[46] Nagenbabu,[47] Sharadbabu[48] and Kalibabu.[49]

As is my wont, I quickly mixed with the teachers and students, and engaged them in a discussion on self-help. I put it to the teachers that, if they and the boys dispensed with the services of paid cooks and cooked their food themselves, it would enable the teachers to control the kitchen from the point of view of the boys' physical and moral health, and it would afford to the students an object-lesson in self-help. One or two of them were inclined to shake their heads. Some of them strongly approved of the proposal. The boys

[42] William Winstanley Pearson (1881–1923), close friend of C.F. Andrews, worked as a missionary in Bengal, accompanied Andrews to South Africa.

[43] Jagadananda Ray (1869–1933), taught science and mathematics to Rabindranath Tagore's children and later a teacher at Shantiniketan.

[44] Nepalchandra Ray (1867–1944), educationist and writer.

[45] Santosh Chandra Majumdar (1886–1926) of Sriniketan or Santosh Kumar Mitra (1893–1979) of Sishu Vibhaga and Gardening departments of Shantiniketan.

[46] Kshitimohan Sen (1880–1960), Sanskritist and educationist.

[47] Nagendranath Aich (1878–1956), teacher of art and Bengali.

[48] Possibly Sarat Kumar Ray (1878–1935), teacher of English and mathematics.

[49] Kalidas Basu (1888–1933), teacher of Bengali and mathematics or Kalimohan Ghosh (1884–1940) of Sriniketan (footnotes 43 to 49, Dr. Uma Dasgupta to Gopalkrishna Gandhi; taken from *Gandhi and Bengal: A Frank Friendship*, pp. 54–55).

welcomed it, if only because of their instinctive taste for novelty. So we launched the experiment. When I invited the Poet to express his opinion, he said that he did not mind it provided the teachers were favourable. To the boys he said, 'The experiment contains the key to swaraj.'[50]

Pearson began to wear away his body in making the experiment a success. *He threw himself into it with zest.*[M2] A batch was formed to cut vegetables, another to clean the grain, and so on. Nagenbabu and others undertook to see to the sanitary cleaning of the kitchen and its surroundings. It was a delight to me to see them working spade in hand.

[M2] He liked this very much.

But it was too much to expect the hundred and twenty-five boys with their teachers to take to this work of physical labour *like ducks to water.*[M3] There used to be daily discussions. Some began early to show fatigue. But Pearson was not the man to be tired. One would always find him with his smiling face doing something or other in or about the kitchen. He had taken upon himself the cleaning of the bigger utensils. A party of students played on their sitar before this cleaning party in order to beguile the tedium of the operation. All alike took the thing up with zest and Shantiniketan became a busy hive.

[M3] all at once

Changes like these when once begun always develop. Not only was the Phoenix party's kitchen self-conducted,[51] but the food cooked in it was of the simplest. Condiments were eschewed. Rice, dal, vegetables and even wheat flour were all cooked at one

---

[50] This was during MKG's second visit to Shantiniketan from 6 to 11 March 1915. He and Tagore met on 6 March. Tagore was away from Shantiniketan during MKG's first visit there from 17–20 February.

[51] 'The Phoenix party's kitchen was not only a self-conducted one' in the first edition.

and the same time in a steam cooker. And Shantiniketan boys started a similar kitchen with a view to introducing reform in the Bengali kitchen. One or two teachers and some students ran this kitchen.[52]

The experiment was, however, dropped after some time. I am of opinion that the[53] famous institution lost nothing by having conducted the experiment for a brief interval, and some of the experiences gained could not but be of help to the teachers.

I had intended to stay at Shantiniketan for some time, but fate *willed otherwise*.[M4] I had hardly been there a week when I received from Poona a telegram announcing Gokhale's death.[54] Shantiniketan was immersed in grief. All the members came over to me to express their condolences. A special meeting was called in the Ashram[55] temple to mourn the national loss.[56] It was a solemn function. The same day I left for Poona with my wife and Maganlal. All the rest stayed at Shantiniketan.

Andrews accompanied me up to Burdwan. 'Do you think,' he asked me, 'that a time will come for satyagraha in India? And if so, have you any idea when it will come?'

'It is difficult to say,' said I. 'For one year I am to do nothing. For Gokhale took from me a promise that

[M4] dragged me away forcefully

---

[52] 'From such experiments it was possible to initiate the self-help experiment in the general kitchen.' To add.

[53] 'world' to add.

[54] Gokhale died at 10.25 p.m. on 19 February, MKG received the telegram on the 20th; he had spent three days at Shantiniketan.

[55] 'Ashram' added in the English translation.

[56] 'to mourn the national loss' added in the English translation. For MKG's speech at the condolence meet, see *CWMG*, vol. 3, pp. 26–28. MKG and the Phoenix party commenced a 'half-fast', i.e. one meal a day. MKG also took a vow not to use any footwear for one year as a sign of mourning.

I should travel *in India*[M5] for gaining experience,[57] and[58] express no opinion on public questions until I have finished the period of probation.[59] Even after the year is over, *I will be in no hurry to speak and pronounce opinions.*[M6] And so I do not suppose there will be any occasion for satyagraha for five years or so.'

    I may note in this connection that Gokhale used to laugh at some of my ideas in *Hind Swaraj* or *Indian Home Rule* and say: 'After you have stayed a year in India, your views will correct themselves.'

[M5] for one year

[M6] I will speak on a question only when it is important for me to do so.

V

WOES OF THIRD-CLASS PASSENGERS

At Burdwan we came face to face with the hardships that a third-class passenger has to go through even in securing his ticket.[M1] 'Third-class tickets are not booked so early,' we were told. I went to the Station Master, *though that too was a difficult business.*[M2] Someone kindly directed me to where he was, and I represented to him our difficulty. He also made the same reply. As soon as the booking window opened, I went to purchase the tickets. But it was no easy thing to get them. Might was right, and passengers, who were forward and indifferent to others, coming one after another, continued to push me out. *I was therefore about the last of the first crowd to get a ticket.*[M3]

    The train arrived, and *getting into it was another trial.*[M4] There was a free exchange of abuse and pushes between passengers already in the train and those trying

[M1] At Burdwan we had to secure third-class tickets. We faced hardships in doing so.

[M2] but who would let me approach him?

[M3] At last I got the tickets.

[M4] here too the strong ones forced themselves in

---

[57] 'for gaining experience' added in the English translation.

[58] 'to form or' to add.

[59] 'until I have finished the period of probation' added in the English translation. The original further adds, 'I intend to keep this promise word for word.'

to get in.[60] We ran up and down the platform, but were everywhere met with the same reply: 'No room here.' I went to the guard. He said, 'You must try to get in where you can or take the next train.'

'But I have urgent business,' I respectfully replied. He had no time to listen to me. I was disconcerted. I told Maganlal to get in wherever possible, and I got into an inter-class compartment with my wife. The guard saw us getting in. At Asansol station he came to charge us excess fares. I said to him:

> 'It was your duty to find us room. We could not get any, and so we are sitting here. If you can accommodate us in a third-class compartment, we shall be only too glad to go there.'
> 'You may not argue with me,' said the guard. 'I cannot accommodate you. You must pay the excess fare, or get out.'

I wanted to reach Poona somehow. I was not therefore prepared to fight the guard, so I paid the excess fare he demanded, i.e., up to Poona. But I resented the injustice.

In the morning we reached Mogalsarai. Maganlal had managed to get a seat in the third class, to which I now shifted. I acquainted the ticket examiner[61] with all the facts, and asked him to give me a certificate to the effect that I had shifted to a third-class compartment at Mogalsarai. This he declined to do. I applied[62] to the railway authorities for redress and got a reply to this effect: 'It is not our practice to refund excess fares without the production of a certificate, but we make an

---

[60] 'It was not for me to join the fray.' To add.

[61] 'ticket collector' in the original.

[62] For MKG's letter to the chief manager, East Indian Railways, see *CWMG*, vol. 13, pp. 28–29.

exception in your case. It is not possible, however, to refund the excess fare from Burdwan to Mogalsarai.'[63]

Since this I have had experiences of third-class travelling which, if I wrote them all down, would easily fill a volume. But I can only touch on them casually in these chapters. It has been and always will be my profound regret that physical incapacity should have compelled me to give up third-class travelling.

The woes of third-class passengers are undoubtedly due to the high-handedness of railway authorities. But the rudeness, dirty habits, selfishness and ignorance of[64] the passengers themselves are no less to blame. The pity is that they often do not realize that they are behaving ill, dirtily or selfishly. They believe that everything they do is in the natural way. *All this may be traced to the indifference towards them of us 'educated' people.*[M5]

We reached Kalyan dead tired.[65] Maganlal and I got some water from the station water-pipe and had our bath. As I was proceeding to arrange for my wife's bath, Sjt. Kaul of the Servants of India Society recognizing us came up. He too was going to Poona. He offered to take my wife to the second-class bath-room. I hesitated to accept the courteous offer. I knew that my wife had no right to avail herself of the second-class bath-room, but I ultimately connived at the impropriety. This, I know, does not become a votary of truth. Not that my wife was eager to use the bath-room, *but a husband's partiality for his wife got the better of his partiality for truth.*

[M5] We the civilized have not cared for it.

---

[63] The acting divisional traffic manager replied on 27 March, 'As the difference in fares was correctly realized according to rules, and there is no record at Mugalsarai of your having travelled from that point to Jubbulpur 3rd Class, under ordinary circumstances refunds are not granted, but I am prepared to accept your statement and will send by Postal Money Order the difference in fares between Mugalsarai and Jubbulpur.' *CWMG*, vol. 13, p. 29.

[64] 'some of' to add.

[65] 'We made preparations for bathing.' To add.

M6 But the husband's
attachment in the form of the
golden lid hid the truth.

The face of truth is hidden behind the golden veil of maya, says the Upanishad.[66] M6

VI

*WOOING*M1

M1 My Effort

On arrival in Poona,[67] we found ourselves, after the performance of the *shraddha* ceremonies, discussing the future of the Society, and the question as to whether I should join it or not. *This question of membership proved a very delicate matter for me to handle.*M2 Whilst Gokhale was there I did not have to seek admission as a member. I had simply to obey his wish, a position I loved to be in. Launching on the stormy sea of Indian public[68] life, I was in need of a sure pilot. I had had one in Gokhale and had felt secure in his keeping. Now that he was gone, I was thrown on my own resources, and[69] I felt that it was my duty to seek admission. That, I thought, would please Gokhale's spirit. So, without hesitation and with firmness, I began the *wooing*.M3

M2 I had a large burden to bear.

M3 effort

Most of the members of the Society were in Poona at this juncture. I set about pleading with them and tried to dispel their fears about me. But I saw that they were divided. One section favoured my admission,

---

[66] The reference is to Verse 15 of the *Ishopanishad* that characterized truth as being hidden by a golden orb. 'The door of the True is covered with a golden disk. Open that, O Pushan, that we may see the nature of the True.' Friedrich Max Müller (trans.), *The Upanishads*, vol. 1 (Oxford: Clarendon Press, 1879), p. 313.

[67] MKG reached Poona on 22 February and stayed there till 3 March 1915.

[68] 'public' added in the English translation.

[69] 'Now that he was gone, I was thrown on my own resources, and' added in the English translation.

the other was strongly against it. *I knew that neither yielded to the other in its affection for me,*[M4] but possibly their loyalty to the Society was greater, at any rate not less than their love for me. All our discussions were therefore free from bitterness, and strictly confined to matters of principle. The section that was opposed to me held that they and I were as the poles asunder in various vital matters, and they[70] felt my membership was likely to imperil the very objects for which the Society was founded.[71] This naturally was more than they could bear.

We dispersed after prolonged discussions, the final decision being postponed to *a later date.*[M5]

I was considerably agitated as I returned home. Was it right for me to be admitted by a majority vote? Would it be consonant with my loyalty to Gokhale?[72] I saw clearly that, when there was such a sharp division amongst the members of the Society over admitting me, by far the best course for me was to withdraw my application for admission and save those opposed to me from a delicate situation. Therein I thought lay my loyalty to the Society and Gokhale. The decision came to me in a flash, and immediately I wrote to Mr. Shastri asking him not to have the adjourned meeting at all.[73] Those who had opposed my application fully appreciated the decision. *It saved them from an awkward position*[M6] and bound us in closer bonds of friendship.

[M4] I could see the love of both for me

[M5] another meeting

[M6] They were saved from a moral dilemma

---

[70] 'moreover' to add.

[71] 'by Gokhale' to add.

[72] 'If the votes were cast against me, would I not be instrumental in placing the Society in an embarrassing situation?' To add.

[73] The letter mentioned herein is not available. However, a letter of 13 January 1916 seems to suggest that Srinivas Sastri wrote to MKG to inform him of the views of the members. MKG in response wrote, 'The members are coming to a just decision in not having me as a member.' *CWMG,* vol. 13, p. 200.

The withdrawal of my application made me truly a member of the Society.

Experience now tells me that it was well that I did not formally become a member, and that the opposition of those who had been against me was justified. Experience has shown too that our views on matters of principle were widely divergent. But the recognition of the differences has meant no estrangement or *bitterness*[M7] between us. We have remained as brothers,[74] and the Society's Poona home has always been for me a place of pilgrimage.

It is true that I did not officially become a member of the Society, but I have ever been a member in spirit. Spiritual relationship is far more precious than physical. Physical relationship divorced from spiritual is body without soul.[75]

M7 sourness

VII

KUMBHA MELA[76]

I next went to Rangoon[77] to meet Dr. Mehta,[78] and on my way I halted at Calcutta. I was the guest of the late Babu Bhupendranath Basu.[79] Bengali hospitality reached

74 'and friends' to add.

75 'divorced from the spiritual is like body without soul' in the first edition.

76 'Mela' added in the English translation.

77 MKG reached Shantiniketan on 6 March and then Calcutta on 12 March; he left for Rangoon on 14 March and returned to Calcutta on 26 March 1915.

78 'I next went to Rangoon, where I wanted to meet Dr. Mehta' in the first edition.

79 Bhupendra Nath Bose (1859–1924), president, Indian National Congress (1914), vice-chancellor, University of Calcutta (1923–24). His residence was 14, Balram Ghosh Street.

its climax here. In those days I was a strict fruitarian,[80] so all the fruits and nuts available in Calcutta were ordered for me. The ladies of the house kept awake all night skinning various nuts. Every possible care was taken in dressing fresh fruit in the Indian style.[81] Numerous delicacies were prepared for my companions, amongst whom was my son Ramdas.[82] Much as I could appreciate this affectionate hospitality, I could not bear the thought of a whole household being occupied in entertaining two or three guests. But as yet I saw no escape from such embarrassing attentions.

On the boat going to Rangoon I was a deck passenger.[83] If excess of attention embarrassed us in Sjt. Basu's house, grossest inattention, even to the elementary comforts of deck passengers, was our lot on the boat. *What was an apology for a bath-room was unbearably dirty,*[M1] the latrines were stinking sinks. To use the latrine one had to wade through urine and excreta or jump over them.

[M1] The place for bathing was so dirty that one could hardly stand there

This was more than *flesh and blood*[M2] could bear. I approached the Chief Officer without avail. *If anything was lacking to complete the picture of stink and filth, the passengers furnished it by their thoughtless habits.*[M3] They spat where they sat, dirtied the surroundings with the leavings of their food, tobacco and betel leaves. There was no end to the noise, and everyone tried to monopolize as much room as possible.[84] Their luggage took up more room than they. We had thus two days of the severest trial.

[M2] I

[M3] The passengers through their filth made the deck worse.

---

80 'and my son Ramdas was with me,' to add.

81 'in the Indian style' added in the English translation.

82 'amongst whom was my son Ramdas' added in the English translation.

83 MKG, Kasturba, Ramdas and four others left by *S.S. Lanka.*

84 'No one considered the comfort of anyone else.' To add.

On reaching Rangoon I wrote to the Agent of the Steamship Company, acquainting him with all the facts.[85] Thanks to this letter and to Dr. Mehta's efforts in the matter, the return journey though on deck was less unbearable.[86]

In Rangoon my fruitarian diet was again a source of additional trouble to the host. But since Dr. Mehta's home was as good as my own, I could control somewhat the lavishness of the menu. However, as I had not set any limit to the number of[87] articles I might eat,[88] the palate and the eyes refused to put an effective check on the supply of varieties ordered. There were no regular hours for meals. Personally I preferred having the last meal before nightfall. Nevertheless as a rule it could not be had before eight or nine.

This year—1915—was the year of the Kumbha fair, which is held at Hardvar once every 12 years.[89] I was by no means eager to attend the fair, but I was anxious to meet Mahatma Munshiramji who was in his Gurukul. Gokhale's Society had sent a big volunteer corps for service at the Kumbha. Pandit Hridayanath Kunzru[90]

---

[85] MKG wrote to the agent of the British India Steam Navigation Company on 19 March 1915. 'I have been in the habit of travelling as a deck passenger now for sometime. I was surprised to find that the arrangements for the deck passengers on *S.S. Lanka* were the worst I have yet seen.' *CWMG*, vol. 13, p. 41.

[86] Bulloch and Brothers, the agents of the BISN Company, replied on 20 March expressing regret at the inconvenience and assured that 'We are taking up the matter with the Commander of "Lanka" in regard to your complaint about the state of the latrines and as requested your letter will be forwarded to Managing Agents, Calcutta.' SN 6168.

[87] 'number of' added in the 1940 edition.

[88] 'I might eat' added in the English translation.

[89] 'which is held at Hardvar once every 12 years' added in the English translation.

[90] Dr. Hridaynath Kunzru (1887–1978), president of the Servants of India Society (1937–78), member, Central Legislative Assembly (1927–30), member, Rajya Sabha (1952–62).

was at the head, and the late Dr. Dev was the medical officer. I was invited to send the Phoenix party to assist them, and so Maganlal Gandhi had already preceded me. On my return from Rangoon, I joined the band.

The journey from Calcutta to Hardvar[91] was particularly trying. Sometimes the compartments had no lights. From Saharanpur we were huddled into carriages for goods or cattle. These had no roofs, and what with the blazing midday sun overhead and the scorching iron floor beneath, we were all but roasted. The pangs of thirst, caused by even such a journey as this, could not persuade orthodox Hindus to take water, if it was 'Mussalmani'. They waited until they could get the 'Hindu' water. These very Hindus, let it be noted, do not so much as hesitate or inquire when during illness the doctor administers them wine or prescribes beef tea or a Mussalman or Christian compounder gives them water.

Our stay in Shantiniketan had taught us that the scavenger's work would be our special function in India. Now for the volunteers in Hardvar tents had been pitched in a dharmsala, and Dr. Dev had dug some pits to be used as latrines. He had had to depend on paid scavengers for looking after these. Here was work for the Phoenix party.[92] We[M4] offered to cover up the excreta with earth and to see to their disposal, and Dr. Dev gladly accepted our offer. The offer was naturally made by me, but it was Maganlal Gandhi who had to[93] execute it. My business was mostly to keep sitting in the tent giving *darshan* and holding religious and other discussions with numerous pilgrims who called on me.[94] This left me not a minute which I could call my own. I

[M4] The Phoenix party

---

[91] MKG reached Haridwar on 5 April 1915.

[92] 'Here was work for the Phoenix party.' Added in the English translation.

[93] 'bear the burden and' to add.

[94] 'Giving *darshan* perturbed me.' To add.

was followed even to the bathing ghat by these *darshan-seekers*, nor did they leave me alone whilst I was having my meals.[95] Thus it was in Hardvar that I realized what a deep impression my humble services in South Africa had made throughout the whole of India.

But this was no enviable position to be in.[96] I felt as though I was *between the devil and the deep sea.*[M5] Where no one recognized me, I had to put up with the hardships *that fall to the lot of the millions in this land, e.g., in railway travelling. Where I was surrounded by people who had heard of me I was the victim of their craze for darshan.*[M6] Which of the two conditions was more pitiable, I have often been at a loss to determine. This at least I know that the *darshan-walas'* blind love has often made me angry, and more often sore at heart. Whereas travelling, though often trying, has been uplifting and has hardly ever roused me to anger.

I was in those days strong enough to roam about a lot, and was fortunately not so known as not to be able to go in the streets without creating much fuss. During these roamings I came to observe more of the pilgrims' absent-mindedness, hypocrisy and slovenliness, than of their piety. The swarm of sadhus, who had descended there, seemed to have been born but to *enjoy the good things of life.*[M7]

Here I saw a cow with five feet! I was astonished, but knowing men soon disillusioned me. The poor five-footed cow was a sacrifice to the greed of the wicked. I learnt that the fifth foot was nothing else but a foot cut off from a live calf and grafted upon the shoulder of the cow! The result of this double cruelty was exploited to fleece the ignorant of their money. There was no Hindu but would be attracted by a five-footed cow,

M5 being squeezed between two stones of a quern

M6 as a third-class passenger. When I alighted, the love of *darshan*-seekers troubled me.

M7 eat *malpua* and *kheer*

---

[95] 'I could not sit by myself even for a moment anywhere in the tent.' To add.

[96] 'But this was no enviable position to be in.' Added in the English translation.

and no Hindu but would lavish his charity on such a miraculous cow.

The day of the *fair*[M8] was now upon us. *It proved a red-letter day for me.*[M9] I had not gone to Hardvar with the sentiments of a pilgrim. I have never *thought*[M10] of frequenting places of pilgrimage in search of piety. But the seventeen lakhs of men that were reported to be there could not all be hypocrites or mere sight-seers. I had no doubt that countless people amongst them had gone there to earn merit and for self-purification. It is difficult, if not impossible, to say to what extent this kind of faith uplifts the soul.

I therefore passed the whole night immersed in deep thought. There were those pious souls in the midst of the hypocrisy that surrounded them. They would be free of guilt *before their Maker.*[M11] If the visit to Hardvar was in itself a sin, I must publicly protest against it, and leave Hardvar on the day of Kumbha. *If the pilgrimage to Hardvar and to the Kumbha fair was not sinful, I must impose some act of self-denial on myself in atonement for the iniquity prevailing there and purify myself. This was quite natural for me. My life is based on disciplinary resolutions.*[M12] I thought of the unnecessary trouble I had caused to my hosts at Calcutta and Rangoon, who had so lavishly entertained me.[97] I therefore decided to limit the articles of my daily[98] diet and to have my final meal before sunset. I was convinced that, if I did not impose these restrictions on myself, I should put my future hosts to considerable inconvenience and should engage them in serving me rather than engage myself in service. So I pledged myself never whilst in India[99] to take more than five articles in twenty-four hours, and never to eat after

[M8] Kumbh

[M9] It was a blessed day for me.

[M10] been enamoured

[M11] in the kingdom of God

[M12] If there was no sin in coming here and staying on the day of Kumbh, I must take a difficult vow and atone for the sin prevalent here and seek self-purification. My life is based on vows, hence I decided to take some difficult vows.

---

[97] 'who had so lavishly entertained me' added in the English translation.

[98] 'daily' added in the 1940 edition.

[99] 'whilst in India' added in the English translation.

dark.[100] I gave the fullest thought to the difficulties I might have to face. But I wanted to leave no loophole. I rehearsed to myself what would happen during an illness, if I counted medicine among the five articles, and made no exception in favour of special articles of diet. I finally decided that there should be no exception on any account whatsoever.

I have been under these vows for now thirteen years. They have subjected me to a severe test, but I am able to testify that[101] they have also served as my shield.

^{M13} prolonged

I am of opinion that they have *added a few years to*[M13] my life and saved me from many an illness.

VIII

LAKSHMAN JHULA

It was a positive relief to reach the Gurukul and meet

^{M1} who resembled a mountain

Mahatma Munshiramji *with his giant frame*.[M1] I at once felt the wonderful contrast between the peace of the Gurukul and the din and noise of Hardvar.

The Mahatma overwhelmed me with affection. The *brahmacharis* were all attention. It was here that I was first introduced to Acharya Ramadevji,[102] and I could immediately see what a force and a power he must be. We[103] had different viewpoints in several matters, nevertheless our acquaintance soon ripened into friendship.

---

[100] MKG wrote in his diary for 9 April 1915: 'Water not included in five articles. Cardamom etc. included. Groundnut and its oil to count as one article.' *CWMG*, vol. 13, p. 164.

[101] 'I am able to testify that' added in the English translation.

[102] Acharya Ramdev (1881–1939), Arya Samajist, educationist, principal of the Gurukul, author of *Bharat Varsha ka Itihas*.

[103] 'saw that we' to add.

I had long discussions with Acharya Ramadevji and other *professors*[M2] about the necessity of introducing industrial training into the Gurukul. When the time came for going away it was a wrench to leave the place. I had heard much in praise of the Lakshman Jhula (a hanging bridge over the Ganges) some distance from Hrishikesh,[104] and many friends pressed me not to leave Hardvar without having gone as far as *the bridge*.[M3] I wanted to do this pilgrimage on foot and so I did it in two stages.

M2 teachers

M3 Hrishikesh

Many sannyasis called on me at Hrishikesh. One of them[105] was particularly attracted towards me. The Phoenix party was there and their presence drew from the Swami many questions.

We had discussions about religion and he realized that I *felt deeply about matters of religion*.[M4] He saw me bare-headed and shirtless as I had returned from my bath in the Ganges. He was pained to miss the *shikha* (tuft of hair)[106] on my head and the sacred thread about my *neck*[M5] and said:

M4 had a strong religious inclination

M5 body

> 'It pains me to see you, a believing Hindu, going without a sacred thread and the *shikha*. These are the two external symbols of Hinduism and every Hindu ought to wear them.'

Now there is a history as to how I came to dispense with both.[107] When I was an urchin of[108] ten, I envied

---

[104] '(a hanging bridge over the Ganges) some distance from Hrishikesh' added in the English as an explanation.

[105] Mangalnathji, vide the entry under 7 April, 'Diary for 1915', *CWMG*, vol. 13, p. 164.

[106] '(tuft of hair)' added in the English as an explanation.

[107] 'Now there is a history as to how I came to dispense with both.' Added in the English translation.

[108] 'an urchin of' added in the English translation.

M6 Brahmins in Porbandar

the *Brahmin lads*^M6 sporting bunches of keys tied to their sacred threads, and I wished I could do likewise. The practice of wearing the sacred thread was not then common among the Vaishya families in Kathiawad. But a movement had just been started for making it obligatory for the first three varnas.[109] As a result several members of the Gandhi clan adopted the sacred thread. The Brahmin who was teaching two or three of us boys *Ram Raksha*[110] invested us with the thread, and although I had no occasion to possess a bunch of keys, I got one and began to sport it. Later, when the thread gave way, I do not remember whether *I missed it very much.*^M7 But I know that I did not go in for a fresh one.

M7 my infatuation had gone or not

As I grew up several well-meaning[111] attempts were made both in India and South Africa to reinvest me with the sacred thread, but with little success. If the Shudras may not wear it, I argued, what right have the other varnas to do so? And I saw no adequate reason for adopting what was to me an *unnecessary custom.*^M8 I had no objection to the thread as such, but the reasons for wearing it were lacking.

M8 external practice not customary in our family

As a Vaishnava I had naturally[112] worn round my neck the *kanthi*, and the *shikha* was considered obligatory by elders.[113] On the eve of my going to England, however, I got rid of the *shikha*, lest when I was bare-headed it should expose me to ridicule and make me look, as I then thought, a barbarian in the eyes of the Englishmen. In fact this cowardly feeling carried me so

---

[109] 'to wear the sacred thread' to add.

[110] See n. 184 in Chapter X, Part I.

[111] 'well-meaning' added in the English translation.

[112] 'naturally' added in the English translation.

[113] 'for us, the two brothers' to add.

far that[114] in South Africa I got my *cousin*[M9] Chhaganlal
Gandhi who was religiously wearing the *shikha*, to do
away with it. I feared that it might come in the way of
his public work and so, even at the risk of paining him,
I made him get rid of it.[115]

      M9 nephew

I therefore made a clean breast of the whole matter
to the Swami and said:

> 'I will not wear the sacred thread, for I see no
> necessity for it, when countless Hindus can go
> without it and yet remain Hindus. Moreover,
> *the sacred thread should be a symbol of spiritual
> regeneration*,[M10] presupposing a deliberate attempt
> on the part of the wearer at a higher and purer
> life. *I doubt whether in the present state of Hinduism
> and of India, Hindus can vindicate the right to wear a
> symbol charged with such a meaning.*[M11] That right
> can come only after Hinduism has purged itself
> of untouchability, has removed all distinctions of
> superiority and inferiority, and shed a host of other
> evils and *shames that have become rampant in it. My
> mind therefore rebels against the idea*[M12] of wearing the
> sacred thread. But I am sure your suggestion about
> the *shikha* is worth considering. I once used to have
> it, and I discarded it from a false[116] sense of shame.[117]
> And so I feel that I should start growing it again. I
> shall discuss the matter with my comrades.'

M10 to adopt the sacred thread
is to be born again

M11 Today Hinduism and India
are in a fallen state. Do we have
the right to wear the sacred
thread?

M12 got rid of the irreligion and
fraud that have made home in
it. I therefore cannot swallow
your argument

The Swami did not appreciate my position with regard
to the sacred thread. The very reasons that seemed to
me to point to not wearing it appeared to him to favour
its wearing. Even today my position remains about

---

[114] 'this cowardly feeling carried me so far that' added in the English
translation.

[115] 'Thus I was ashamed of the *shikha*.' To add.

[116] 'false' added in the English translation.

[117] 'and fear' to add.

the same as it was at Hrishikesh. So long as there are different religions, every one of them may need some outward distinctive symbol. But when the symbol is made into a fetish and an instrument of proving the superiority of one's religion over others', it is fit only to be discarded. The sacred thread does not appear to me today to be a means of uplifting Hinduism. I am therefore indifferent to it.

As for the shikha, cowardice having been the reason for discarding it,[M13] after consultation with friends I decided to re-grow it.

But to return to Lakshman Jhula. I was charmed with the natural scenery about Hrishikesh and the Lakshman Jhula, and bowed my head in reverence to our ancestors for their sense of the beautiful in Nature, and for their foresight in investing beautiful manifestations of Nature with a religious significance.

But the way in which men were using these beauty spots was far from giving me peace.[M14] As at Hardvar, so at Hrishikesh, people dirtied the roads and the fair banks of the Ganges. They did not even hesitate to desecrate the sacred water of the Ganges. It filled me with agony to see people performing natural functions on the thoroughfares and river banks, when they could easily have gone a little farther away from public haunts.

Lakshman Jhula was, I saw, nothing but an iron suspension bridge over the Ganges.[M15] I was told that originally there had been a fine[118] rope-bridge.[119] But a philanthropic Marwadi got it into his head to destroy the rope-bridge and erect an iron one at a heavy cost and then entrusted the keys to the Government! *I am at a loss to say anything about the rope-bridge*[M16] as I have never seen it, but the iron bridge is entirely out of place in such surroundings and mars their beauty. The making over of the keys of

M13 Discarding the *shikha* was a matter of shame for me, and

M14 But human creations did not give peace to the mind.

M15 At Lakshman Jhula I saw an iron suspension bridge.

M16 Of the rope-bridge I have no idea

---

[118] 'fine' added in the English translation.

[119] 'albeit very strong' to add.

this pilgrims' bridge to Government was too much even for my loyalty of those days.

The Svargashram which one reaches after crossing the bridge was a wretched place, being nothing but a number of shabby-looking sheds of galvanized iron sheets. These, I was told, were made for *sadhakas* (aspirants).[120] There were hardly any living there at the moment. *Those who were in the main building gave one an unfavourable impression.*[M17]

But the Hardvar experiences proved for me to be of inestimable value. They helped me *in no small way*[M18] to decide where I was to live and what I was to do.

[M17] Nor did those who were in the main building produce a favourable impression on me.

[M18] a great deal

IX

FOUNDING OF THE ASHRAM

The pilgrimage to the Kumbha fair was my second visit to Hardvar.

The Satyagraha Ashram was founded on the 25th of May, 1915.[121] Shraddhanandji wanted me to settle in Hardvar. Some of my Calcutta friends recommended Vaidyanathadham.[122] Others strongly urged me to choose Rajkot. But when I happened to pass through Ahmedabad, many friends pressed me to settle down

---

[120] '(aspirants)' added in the English as an explanation.

[121] On 11 May 1915 MKG saw the bungalow at Kochrab, which belonged to Barrister Jivanlal Desai. On the same day he prepared an estimate of expenditure and other requirements for the Ashram and gave them to Sheth Mangaldas Girdharlal. The list contains the names of the first forty inhabitants of the Ashram. See *CWMG*, vol. 13, pp. 84–87. On 20 May MKG performed the *Vastu Puja* at Kochrab.

[122] Vaidyanath Dham, one of the twelve Jyotirlingas of Shiva, located in the earlier Santhal Pargana, in the present-day state of Jharkhand.

there, and they volunteered to find the expenses of the Ashram, as well as a house for us to live in.

^{M1} My eyes had come to rest on Ahmedabad.

I had a predilection for Ahmedabad.^{M1} Being a Gujarati I thought I should be able to render the greatest service to the country through the Gujarati language. And then, as Ahmedabad was an ancient centre of handloom weaving, it was likely to be the most favourable field for the *revival of the cottage industry of hand-spinning.*^{M2} There was also the hope that, the city being the capital of Gujarat, monetary help from its wealthy citizens would be more available here than elsewhere.

^{M2} work related to the spinning-wheel

The question of untouchability was naturally[123] among the subjects discussed with the Ahmedabad friends. I made it clear to them that I should take the first opportunity of admitting an untouchable candidate to the Ashram if he was otherwise worthy.

'Where is the untouchable who will satisfy your condition?' said a Vaishnava friend self-complacently.

^{M3} settle down

I finally decided to *found the Ashram*^{M3} at Ahmedabad.

So far as accommodation was concerned, *Sjt. Jivanlal Desai, a barrister in Ahmedabad, was the principal man to help me. He offered to let, and we decided to hire, his Kochrab bungalow.*^{M4} The first thing we had to settle was the name of the Ashram. I consulted friends. Amongst the names suggested were 'Sevashram' (the abode of service).[124] 'Tapovan' (the abode of austerities),[125] etc. I liked the name 'Sevashram' but for the absence of emphasis on the method of service. *'Tapovan' seemed to be a pretentious title, because though tapas was dear to us we could not presume to be tapasvins (men of austerity). Our creed was devotion to truth, and our business was the search for and insistence on truth.*^{M5} I wanted to acquaint India with

^{M4} it was decided to hire the Kochrab Bungalow of Sjt. Jivanlal Desai, a barrister of Ahmedabad, who was the principal man in persuading me to settle in Ahmedabad.

^{M5} *Tapovan* could not be chosen as a name because though *tapas* was dear to us, the name seemed pretentious. We wished to worship truth, seek truth and insist upon it.

---

[123] 'naturally' added in the English translation.

[124] '(the abode of service)' added as translation in the English.

[125] '(the abode of austerities)' added as translation in the English.

the method I had tried in South Africa, and I desired to test in India[126] the extent to which its application might be possible. So my companions and I selected the name 'Satyagraha Ashram', as conveying both our goal and our method of service.

For the conduct of the Ashram a code of rules and observances was necessary. A draft[127] was therefore prepared, and friends were invited to express their opinions on it. Amongst the many opinions that were received, that of Sir Gurudas Banerji[128] is still in my memory. He liked the rules, but suggested that humility should be added as one of the observances,[129] as he believed that the younger generation sadly lacked humility. Though I noticed this fault, I feared humility would cease to be humility the moment it became a matter of vow. The true connotation of humility is self-effacement. Self-effacement is *moksha* (salvation),[130] and whilst it cannot, by itself, be an observance, there may be other observances necessary for its attainment. If the acts of an aspirant after *moksha* or a servant have no humility or selflessness about them, there is no longing for *moksha* or service. Service without humility is selfishness and egotism.

---

[126] 'in India' added in the English translation.

[127] For the draft rules of the Ashram, see *CWMG*, vol. 13, pp. 91–98. The third revised draft was adopted on 7 November 1915. The revised draft had two significant inclusions: a vow against untouchability and a paragraph on Varnashrama Dharma, which clearly states, 'The Ashram does not follow the *varnashrama* dharma.' Ibid., p. 94.

[128] Sir Gurudas Banerji (1844–1918), judge of Calcutta High Court, first Indian to be appointed vice-chancellor of the University of Calcutta (1890–92), chairman, Banga Jatiya Vidya Parishad (Society for the Promotion of National Education in Bengal).

[129] The first draft had six observances: truth, non-violence, celibacy, control of palate, non-stealing, non-possession and two subsidiary observances, swadeshi and fearlessness.

[130] '(salvation)' added as translation in the English.

There were at this time about thirteen Tamilians in our party. Five Tamil youngsters had accompanied me from South Africa, and the rest came from different parts of the country. We were in all about twenty-five men and women.[131]

This is how the Ashram was started. All had their meals in a common kitchen and strove to live as one family.

X

ON THE ANVIL

The Ashram had been in existence only a few months when we were put to a test such as I had scarcely expected. I received a letter from Amritlal Thakkar[132] to this effect: 'A humble and honest untouchable family is desirous of joining your Ashram. Will you accept them?'

I was perturbed. I had never expected that an untouchable family with an introduction from no less a man than Thakkar Bapa would so soon be seeking admission to the Ashram. I shared the letter with my companions. They welcomed it.

I wrote to Amritlal Thakkar expressing our willingness to accept the family, provided all the members were ready to abide by the rules of the Ashram.

---

[131] In his note to Mangaldas Girdharlal, MKG had given the number as forty, with their names. In the draft rules the number is thirty-five.

[132] Amritlal Thakkar (1869–1951), known as Thakkar Bapa, worked as a civil engineer in East Africa, joined the Servants of India Society in 1914 and dedicated his life to the service of 'untouchable' and tribal communities, founded Bhil Seva Mandal (1922) and became general secretary of the Harijan Sevak Sangh (1932).

The family consisted of Dudabhai, his wife Danibehn and their daughter Lakshmi[133] *then a mere toddling babe.*[M1] Dudabhai had been a teacher in Bombay. They all agreed to abide by the rules and were accepted.[134]

[M1] who still crawled and was fed at the breast

---

[133] Danibehn and Dudabhai handed over their daughter Lakshmi to MKG on 5 October 1920. MKG said later, 'Lakshmi, lives in my house moving like Lakshmi indeed.' *CWMG*, vol. 19, p. 154.

[134] Dudabhai Dafda sent a letter on 6 September 1915 expressing his intent to join the Ashram and abide by its rules. He visited the Ashram on 11 September and joined it with his family on Sunday, 26 September 1915. The letter written in Gujarati is given below in English translation.

Bombay
Date 6.9.15

Pujya Deshbhakta Sriyut Mohandas Karamchand Gandhi at Ahmedabad

Respected Sir

The applicant Dudabhai Malji requests with Namaskar and in humility that—since I am desirous of joining the Satyagraha Ashram recently opened by you, I take the liberty, with respect, of giving a brief account of my life.

I was born in an *antyaja* (scavenger) Hindu caste in a small village called Devrajya of Amreli in Kathiawad. In my infancy my parents died in the terrible famine of 1956 (i.e. 1900 AD). I was then aged about four. My other relatives did not care for me and hence I had to spend many days in great hardship. The Patel Talati of the village in order to save me admitted me in an orphanage in Amreli opened by Namdar Maharaja Gaikwad Sarkar. When I joined the orphanage food, clothing and all other needs were provided for by the Namdar Maharaja. Moreover, all of us were given education and vocational training of various kinds. I lived there, passed Gujarati class six and joined weaving class. I have passed elementary, middle and highest grade examinations. I am an expert on traditional loom. I have average knowledge of shuttle loom.

At the age of eighteen I was asked to leave the orphanage and was appointed in the same institution as a teacher. At that time my salary was Rs. 7. After I had worked for two months the State got me married to a girl named Danibai, who was also an inhabitant of the orphanage. Danibai has studied up to Gujarati class four and has average knowledge of embroidery and

But their admission created a flutter amongst the friends who had been helping the Ashram.[135] The very

---

tailoring. We could not meet our expenses in our salary of Rs. 7 and it became necessary for me to come to Bombay. I came to Bombay. I stayed with a teacher from my community named Sampat Nanji Marwadi and acquainted him with my condition. Hence, he took me to the Superintendent of the Municipal Gujarati Schools. He acquainted himself with my story and admitted me as a teacher at a salary of Rs. 15. He assessed my work and gave me an increase of Rs. 4. After that I called my wife Danibai to Bombay from Amreli. She too found work as a teacher in the Depressed Class Mission School. Her salary is Rs. 12. Both of us work as teachers and our combined monthly salary is Rs. 31 and from that, with the grace of god, we are able to meet our expenses quite well. We have a daughter of fifteen months. My Danibai is aged approximately eighteen years and I am about twenty-one years of age. We are, as enumerated above, three of us in the family. Sometime ago I received the rules of Sevashram opened by you from Rajman Rajeshri Amrutlal V. Thakker, LCE of the Servants of Indian Society. It gave me great joy to read the rules. I met Ra. Ra. Thakker Saheb two–four times and sought clarifications on them and now I have full comprehension of them. Moreover, I have also explained the full import of these rules to my wife, Danibai. Therefore, she has also given an assurance to observe all rules. I have ascertained that she will abide by the rules.

Based on this I make a humble submission that I, my wife and our daughter, all three of us be admitted as novices in your Ashram. I am hopeful of obtaining this grace. I conclude this letter with the hope and faith in god that my aspiration shall be fulfilled. If you wish to try me out for some days before admitting me to the Ashram at Ahmedabad, I will be quite happy to do so as well.

Bombay   Hopeful of your grace
                                    Dust of thy feet
                                    Dudabhai Malji Dafda

Babula Talav
Post no. 8.

SN: 6229. Translated from the original Gujarati by TS.

[135] There was quite a 'flutter' at the Ashram as well. On 11 September, the day of Dudabhai's visit, Santok Maganlal Gandhi, a satyagrahi in South Africa, fasted in protest. MKG

first difficulty was found with regard to the use of the well, which was partly controlled by the owner of the bungalow. The man in charge of the water-lift objected that drops of water from our bucket would pollute him. So he took to swearing at us and molesting Dudabhai. I told everyone to put up with the abuse and continue drawing water at any cost.[136] When he saw that we did not return his abuse, the man became ashamed and ceased to bother us.

All monetary help, however, was stopped. The friend who had asked that question about an untouchable being able to follow the rules of the Ashram had never expected that any such would be forthcoming.

With the stopping of monetary help came rumours of proposed social boycott. We were prepared for all this. I had told my companions that, if we were boycotted and denied the usual facilities, we would not leave Ahmedabad. We would rather go and stay in the untouchables' quarter and live on whatever[137] we could get by manual labour.

Matters came to such a pass that Maganlal Gandhi one day gave me this notice: 'We are out of funds and there is nothing for the next month.'

I quietly replied: 'Then we shall go to the untouchables' quarter.'

---

wrote in his diary, 'There was quite a scene. Santok refused to eat, and I, too, therefore.' *CWMG*, vol. 13, p. 177. Kasturba also expressed her deep unhappiness at the admission. MKG wrote to Srinivas Sastri on 23 September. 'There was quite a flutter at the Ashram. There is a flutter even in Ahmedabad. I have told Mrs. Gandhi she could leave me and we should part as good friends.' *CWMG*, vol. 13, pp. 127–28. Maganlal and Santok Gandhi left the Ashram on Friday, 24 September, but returned on 3 October 1915.

[136] 'all costs' in the first edition.

[137] 'help we could get or what' to add.

This was not the first time I had been faced with such a trial. On all such occasions God[138] has sent help at the last moment. One morning, shortly after Maganlal had given me warning of our monetary plight, one of the children came and said that a Sheth[139] who was waiting in a car outside wanted[140] to see me. I went out to him. 'I want to give the Ashram some help. Will you accept it?' he asked.

'Most certainly,' said I. 'And I confess I am at the present moment at the end of my resources.'

'I shall come tomorrow at this time,' he said. 'Will you be here?'

'Yes,' said I, and he left.

Next day, exactly at the appointed hour, the car drew up near our quarters, and the horn was blown. The children came with the news. The Sheth did not come in. I went out to see him. He placed in my hands currency notes of the value of Rs. 13,000, and drove away.

I had never expected this help, and what a novel way of rendering it! The gentleman had never before visited the Ashram. So far as I can remember, I had met him only once. No visit, no enquiries, simply rendering

---

[138] In the original 'Shamla', that is, 'the dark god' or Krishna. The reference is to the help sent by Krishna to the poet Narsinha Mehta to meet the customary expenses for his daughter Kuvarbai, as also to God in the form of Shamalshah Sheth, honouring a promissory note made out by Narsinha Mehta.

[139] Ambalal Sarabhai (1890–1967), leading industrialist, played an important role in India's freedom struggle. President of Ahmedabad Mill Owners' Association in 1918–19. MKG had a meal at his and Sarladevi Sarabhai's house on 3 February 1915, his first visit to Ahmedabad after his return to India. A close associate of MKG, he and several members of the Sarabhai family had a deep and abiding relationship with MKG and the institutions that he founded.

[140] 'a Sheth was waiting in a car outside and that he wanted' in the first edition.

help and going away! This was a unique experience for me. The help deferred the exodus to the untouchables' quarter. We now felt quite safe for a year.

Just as there was a storm outside, so was there a storm in the Ashram itself. Though in South Africa untouchable friends used to come to my place and live and feed with me, my wife and other women did not seem quite to relish the admission into the Ashram of the untouchable friends. My[141] eyes and[142] ears easily detected their indifference, if not their dislike, towards Danibehn. The monetary difficulty had caused me no anxiety, but this internal storm was more than I could bear. Danibehn was an ordinary woman. Dudabhai was a man with slight education but of good understanding. I liked his patience. Sometimes he did flare up, but on the whole I was well impressed with his forbearance. I pleaded with him to swallow minor insults. He not only agreed, but prevailed upon his wife to do likewise.

The admission of this family proved a valuable lesson to the Ashram. In the very beginning we proclaimed to the world that the Ashram would not countenance untouchability. *Those who wanted to help the Ashram were thus put on their guard,*[M2] and the work of the Ashram in this direction was considerably simplified. The fact that it is mostly the real orthodox Hindus who have met the daily growing expenses of the Ashram is perhaps a clear indication that untouchability is shaken to its foundation. There are indeed many other proofs of this, but the fact that *good*[M3] Hindus do not scruple to help an Ashram where we go to the length of dining with the untouchables is no small proof.

I am sorry that I should have to skip over quite a number of things pertaining to this subject, how we tackled delicate questions arising out of the main

[M2] The Ashram's limits were clearly drawn

[M3] those who consider themselves *Sanatani*

---

[141] 'sharp' to add.

[142] 'attentive' to add.

M4 cheerfully faced

question, how we *had to overcome*^M4 some unexpected difficulties, and various other matters which are quite relevant to a description of experiments with Truth. The chapters that follow will also suffer from the same drawback. I shall have to omit important details, because most of the characters in the drama are still alive, and it is not proper without permission to use their names in connection with events with which they are concerned. It is hardly practicable to obtain their consent or to get them every now and then to revise the chapters concerning themselves. Besides, such procedure is outside the limit of this autobiography. I therefore fear that the rest of the story, valuable as it is in my opinion to seekers after Truth, will be told with inevitable omissions. Nevertheless, it is my desire and hope, God willing, to bring this narrative down to the days of Non-co-operation.

XI

ABOLITION OF INDENTURED EMIGRATION^M1

M1 Indenture System

We shall, for a moment, take leave of the Ashram, which in the very beginning had to weather internal and external storms, and briefly advert to *a matter that*

M2 the system of indenture

engaged my attention.^M2

Indentured labourers were those who had emigrated from India to labour under an indenture for five years

M3 In 1914

or less.[143] *Under the Smuts-Gandhi Settlement of 1914,*^M3 the £3 tax in respect of the indentured emigrants to Natal had been abolished. *But the general emigration from*

M4 But the system had not yet been abolished.

India still needed treatment.^M4

In March 1916 Pandit Madan Mohan Malaviyaji moved a resolution in the Imperial Legislative

---

[143] 'for five or less years' in the first edition.

Council for the abolition of the indenture system. In accepting the motion Lord Hardinge announced that he had 'obtained from *His Majesty's Government*[M5] the promise of the abolition in due course' of the system. *I felt, however, that India could not be satisfied with so very vague an assurance, but ought to agitate for immediate abolition.*[M6] India had tolerated the system through her sheer negligence, and I believed *the time had come when people could successfully agitate for this redress.*[M7] I met some of the leaders, wrote in the Press[144] and saw that public opinion was solidly in favour of immediate abolition. Might this be a fit subject for satyagraha? I had no doubt that it was, but I did not know the *modus operandi*.

In the meantime the Viceroy had *made no secret of*[M8] the meaning of 'the eventual abolition', which, as he said, was abolition 'within such reasonable time as will allow of alternative arrangements being introduced'.

So in February 1917,[145] Pandit Malaviyaji asked for leave to introduce a bill for the immediate abolition of the system. Lord Chelmsford refused permission. It was time for me to tour the country for an all-India agitation.

Before I started the agitation I thought it proper to wait upon the Viceroy. So I applied for an interview. He immediately granted it. Mr. Maffey, now Sir John Maffey,[146] was his private secretary. I came in close contact with him. I had a satisfactory talk with Lord Chelmsford who, without being definite, promised to be helpful.

I began my tour from Bombay. Mr. Jehangir Petit[147] undertook to convene the meeting under the

[M5] The Emperor

[M6] I clearly felt that a decision should be taken for the immediate abolition of the system.

[M7] that people had been sufficiently awakened for the system to be abolished

[M8] taken an opportunity to explain

---

[144] See *CWMG*, vol. 13, pp. 247–50.

[145] 'Bharat Bhushan' to add, which was an honorific used for him.

[146] Sir John Maffey, 1st Baron Rugby (1877–1969), member of the Indian Civil Service (1899–1924), private secretary to the Viceroy (1916–20), chief commissioner of NWFP (1921–24).

[147] Jehangir Bomanji Petit (1879–1946), nationalist, mill owner, philanthropist, secretary, South Africa India Fund, joint-

auspices of the Imperial Citizenship Association.[148] The Executive Committee of the Association met first for framing the resolutions to be moved at the meeting. Dr. Stanley Reed,[149] Sjt. (now Sir) Lallubhai Samaldas,[150] Sjt. Natarajan[151] and Mr. Petit were present at the Committee meeting. The discussion centred round the fixing of the period within which the Government was to be asked to abolish the system. There were three proposals, viz., for abolition 'as soon as possible', abolition 'by the 31st July',[152] and 'immediate abolition'. I was for a definite date as we could then decide what to do if the Government failed to accede to our request within the time limit. Sjt. Lallubhai was for 'immediate' abolition. He said 'immediate' indicated a shorter period than the 31st July. I explained that the people would not understand the word 'immediate'. If we wanted to get them to do something, they must have a more definite word. Everyone would interpret 'immediate' in his own way—Government one way, the people another way. There was no question of misunderstanding 'the 31st of July', and if nothing was done by that date, we could proceed further. Dr. Reed saw the force of the argument, and ultimately Sjt. Lallubhai also agreed. We

---

secretary, South African Indian Passive Resistance Fund, chairman, Bombay Mill Owners' Association.

[148] The Imperial Indian Citizenship Association was founded in 1915. MKG addressed a public meeting on the issue at the Excelsior Theatre.

[149] Sir Herbert Stanley Reed (1872–1969), editor, *The Times of India* (1907–24), later a Conservative member of parliament in the British Parliament.

[150] Sir Lallubhai Samaldas, businessman, a liberal politician of Bombay, pioneered the cooperative movement in western India.

[151] Kamakshi Natarajan, editor, *Indian Social Reformer*, hon. secretary, Imperial Indian Citizenship Association.

[152] Apparently a slip for '31st May'. See *CWMG*, vol. 13, p. 342.

adopted the 31st July as the latest date by which the abolition should be announced, a resolution to that effect was passed at the public meeting, and meetings throughout India resolved accordingly.

Mrs. Jaiji Petit put all her energies into the organization of a ladies' deputation to the Viceroy. Amongst the ladies from Bombay who formed the deputation, I remember the names of Lady Tata[153] and the late Dilshad Begum. The deputation had a great effect. The Viceroy gave an encouraging reply.

I visited Karachi,[154] Calcutta[155] and various other places.[156] There were fine meetings everywhere, and there was unbounded enthusiasm. I had not expected anything like it when the agitation was launched.

In those days I used to travel alone, and had therefore wonderful experiences. The *C.I.D. men*[M9] [M9] detectives were always after me.[157] But as I had nothing to conceal, they did not molest me, nor did I cause them any trouble. Fortunately I had not then received the stamp of Mahatmaship, though the shout of that name was quite common where people knew me.

On one occasion the detectives disturbed me at several stations, asked for my ticket and took down the number. I, of course, readily replied to all the questions they asked. My fellow-passengers had taken me to be a 'sadhu'[158] or a 'fakir'. When they saw that I was

---

[153] Lady Meherbai Dorabji Tata (1879–1931).

[154] MKG addressed a meeting under the aegis of the Citizens' Association at Khalikdina Hall on 2 March 1917.

[155] On 6 March he addressed a meeting in Calcutta at the Town Hall.

[156] The two other recorded meetings were on 4 February at Ahmedabad and 26 February at Surat.

[157] 'I could have no cause of quarrel with them.' To add.

[158] 'an ordinary sadhu' in the original.

being molested at every station, they were exasperated and swore at the detectives. 'Why are you worrying the poor sadhu for nothing?'[159] they protested. 'Don't you show these scoundrels your ticket,'[160] they said, addressing me.

I said to them gently: 'It is no trouble to show them my ticket. They are doing their duty.'[161] The passengers were not satisfied, they evinced more and more sympathy, and strongly objected to this sort of ill-treatment of innocent men.

But the detectives were nothing. The real hardship was the *third-class travelling*.[M10] My bitterest experience was from Lahore to Delhi. I was going to Calcutta from Karachi via Lahore where I had to change trains.[162] It was impossible to find a place in the train. It was full and those who could get in did so by sheer force, often sneaking through windows if the doors were locked. I had to reach Calcutta on the date fixed for the meeting, and if I missed this train I could not arrive in time. I had almost given up hope of getting in. No one was willing to accept me, when a porter discovering my plight came to me and said, 'Give me twelve annas and I'll get you a seat.' 'Yes,' said I, 'you shall have twelve annas if you do procure me a seat.' The young man went from carriage to carriage entreating passengers but no one heeded him. As the train was about to start, some passengers said, 'There is no room here, but you can shove him in here if you like. He will have to stand.'[163] 'Well?' asked the young porter. I readily agreed, and he shoved me in bodily

[M10] crowd in our trains

---

[159] In Hindustani in the original.

[160] In Hindustani in the original.

[161] 'and I do not mind it' to add.

[162] This was on 3 March 1917.

[163] In Hindustani in the original.

through the window. Thus I got in and the porter earned his twelve annas.

The night was a trial. The other passengers were sitting somehow. I stood two hours, holding the chain of the upper bunk. Meanwhile some of the passengers kept worrying me incessantly. 'Why will you not sit down?'[164] they asked. I tried to reason with them saying there was no room but they could not tolerate my standing, though they were lying full length on the upper bunks. They did not tire of worrying me neither did I tire of gently replying to them. This at last mollified them. Some of them asked me my name and, when I gave it they felt ashamed. They apologized and made room for me. *Patience was thus rewarded.*[M11] I was dead tired, and my head was reeling. God sent help just when it was most needed.

[M11] I remembered the saying: 'Sweet are the fruits of patience.'

In that way I somehow reached Delhi and thence[165] Calcutta. The Maharaja of Cassimbazaar, the president of the Calcutta meeting, was my host.[166] Just as in Karachi, here also there was unbounded enthusiasm.

The meeting was attended by several Englishmen. Before the 31st July the Government announced that indentured emigration from India was stopped.[167]

It was in 1894 that I drafted the first petition protesting against the system, and I had then hoped that this 'semi-slavery', as Sir W.W. Hunter used to call the system,[168] would some day be brought to an end.

---

[164] In Hindustani in the original.

[165] 'Delhi and thence' added in the English translation.

[166] MKG stayed at Cassim Bazar House, 302, Upper Circular Road.

[167] The decision of the governor general in Council to prohibit labour emigration from India under the Defence of India Act was gazetted on 12 March 1917.

[168] 'as Sir W.W. Hunter used to call the system' added in the English translation.

There were many who aided in the agitation which was started in 1894, but I cannot help *saying that potential satyagraha hastened the end.*[M12]

[M12] but say that behind this was pure satyagraha

For further details of that agitation and of those who took part in it, I refer the reader to my *Satyagraha in South Africa.*

XII

THE STAIN OF INDIGO

Champaran is the land of King Janaka. Just as it abounds in mango groves, so used it to be full of indigo plantations until the year 1917.[169] The Champaran tenant was bound by law to plant three out of every twenty parts of his land with indigo for his landlord. This system was known as the *tinkathia*[170] system, as three *kathas* out of twenty (which make one acre) had to be planted with indigo.

---

[169] Indigo cultivation in Champaran began in 1830 and reached a peak in terms of area under cultivation in 1899–1900 when 38,849 hectares of land was under indigo cultivation. The same was 8662 and 10,683 for the years 1916–17 and 1917–18. See Jacques Pouchepadass, *Champaran and Gandhi: Planters, Peasants and Gandhian Politics*, translated from the French by James Walker (New Delhi: Oxford University Press, 1999), pp. 236–37, Table A.

In 1917 the district of Champaran contained 2846 villages, of which three-fourths were held by three landholders, who had obtained their rights under Permanent Settlement in 1793. These were the Bettiah Estate, the Ramnagar Estate and the Madhuban Estate, of which the Bettiah Estate had 1719 villages. Of the total number of villages held by the estate only 283 were under their direct management, while the rest were under lease to European planters and Indian peasants. See B.B. Mishra, *Select Documents on Mahatma Gandhi's Movement in Champaran, 1917–18* (Government of Bihar: 1963), p. 6.

[170] The system came into being in 1868. The planters had two options regarding the method of indigo cultivation: either have it cultivated by a tenant on a certain portion of their holding

I must confess that I did not then know even the name, much less the geographical position, of Champaran, and I had hardly any notion of indigo plantations. I had seen packets of indigo, but little dreamed that it was grown and manufactured in Champaran at great hardship to thousands of agriculturists.

Rajkumar Shukla[171] was one of the agriculturists who had been under this harrow, and he was filled with a passion to wash away the stain of indigo for the thousands who were suffering as he had suffered.

This man caught hold of me at Lucknow, where I had gone for the Congress of 1916.[172] 'Vakil Babu will tell you everything about our distress,'[173] he said, and urged me to go to Champaran. 'Vakil Babu' was none other than Babu Brajkishore Prasad,[174] who became my esteemed co-worker in Champaran, and who is the soul of public work in Bihar. Rajkumar Shukla brought him to my tent. He was dressed in a black alpaca *achkan* and trousers. Brajkishore Babu failed then to make an impression on me. I took it that he must be some vakil exploiting the simple agriculturists. Having heard

---

(*asamivar* system) or cultivate it himself (*zirat* system). *Tinkathia* was part of the *asamivar* system.

[171] Rajkumar Shukla was from Satwaria village and resident of village Muli Barharwa in police station Shikarpur of Champaran and was described as 'a well-to-do middle class peasant and money-lender who also managed the farm of a land holder from Allahabad'. Mishra, p. 22.

[172] The 31st annual session of the Indian National Congress held at Lucknow from 26–30 December 1916 was presided by Ambica Charan Majumdar, remembered for the Lucknow Pact of 1916 between the Congress and the Muslim League, and the reunion of the Congress, which had split in 1907.

[173] In Hindustani in the original.

[174] Babu Braj Kishore Prasad, B.A., B.L., of Srinagar village, a leading vakil of Darbhanga, a member of the Bengal Legislative Council (1910), and Bihar and Orissa Legislative Council (1912–16); raised the issue of Champaran in the Council as early as 1913.

from him something of Champaran, I replied as was my wont: 'I can give no opinion without seeing the conditions with my own eyes. You will please move the resolution in the Congress, but leave me free for the present.' Rajkumar Shukla of course wanted some help from the Congress. Babu Brajkishore Prasad moved the resolution, expressing sympathy for the people of Champaran, and it was unanimously passed.[175]

Rajkumar Shukla was glad, but far from satisfied. He wanted me personally to visit Champaran and witness the miseries of the ryots there. I told him that I would include Champaran in the tour which I had contemplated and give it a day or two. 'One day will be enough,' said he, 'and you will see things with your own eyes.'[176]

From Lucknow I went to Cawnpore.[177] Rajkumar Shukla followed me there. 'Champaran is very near here. Please give a day,'[178] he insisted. 'Pray excuse me this time. But I promise that I will come,' said I, further committing myself.

I returned to the Ashram. The ubiquitous Rajkumar was there too. 'Pray fix the day now,' he said. 'Well,' said I, 'I have to be in Calcutta on such and such a date,[179] come and meet me then, and take me from

---

[175] According to the Bihar Special Branch Intelligence Report, Rajkumar Shukla also spoke at the Lucknow Congress on Resolution X: 'Planters and Labourers in Bihar'. See Mishra, *Select Documents*, pp. 54–55.

[176] In Hindustani in the original.

[177] There is no available record of MKG's visit to Kanpur. He left Lucknow on 31 December 1916, reaching Ahmedabad on 2 January 1917.

[178] In Hindustani in the original.

[179] MKG was to be in Calcutta on 7, 8 and 9 April 1917 for the AICC meeting. The Bihar Special Branch Report of 4 March states, 'It is also rumoured that Mr. Gandhi who has once agitated Indians

there.' I did not know where I was to go, what to do, what things to see.

Before I reached Bhupen Babu's[180] place in Calcutta, Rajkumar Shukla had gone and established himself there. Thus this ignorant, unsophisticated but resolute agriculturist captured me.

So early in 1917, we left Calcutta for Champaran, *looking just like fellow-rustics.*[M1] I did not even know the train. He took me to it, and we travelled together, reaching Patna in the morning.[181]

[M1] we were a pair, both looked like peasants.

This was my first visit to Patna. I had no friend or acquaintance with whom I could think of putting up. I had an idea that Rajkumar Shukla, simple agriculturist as he was, must have some influence in Patna. I had come to know him a little more on the journey, and on reaching Patna I had no illusions left concerning him. He was perfectly innocent of everything. The *vakils* that he had taken to be his friends were really nothing of the sort. Poor Rajkumar was more or less as a menial to them. Between such agriculturist clients and their *vakils* there is a gulf as wide as the Ganges in flood.

Rajkumar Shukla took me to Rajendra Babu's place in Patna.[182] Rajendra Babu had gone to Puri or some other place, I now forget which. There were one or two servants at the bungalow who paid us no attention.[183] I had with me something to eat. I wanted

---

in South Africa is coming here to deliver lectures.' Mishra, *Select Documents*, p. 51.

[180] Bhupendra Nath Bose.

[181] MKG and Rajkumar Shukla reached Patna on 10 April 1917.

[182] 'in Patna' added in the English translation.

[183] 'who paid us no attention' added in the English translation. On 10 April MKG wrote to Maganlal Gandhi, 'The man who had brought me here does not know anything. He has dumped me in some obscure place. The master of the house is away and the servants take us both to be beggars. They don't even permit us

dates which my companion procured for me from the bazaar.

There was strict untouchability in Bihar. I might not draw water at the well whilst the servants were using it, lest drops of water from my bucket might pollute them, the servants not knowing to what caste I belonged. Rajkumar directed me to the indoor latrine, the servant promptly directed me to the outdoor one. All this was far from surprising or irritating to me, for I was inured to such things. The servants were doing the duty, which they thought Rajendra Babu would wish them to do.[184]

These entertaining experiences enhanced my regard for Rajkumar Shukla, if they also enabled me to know him better. *I saw now that Rajkumar Shukla could not guide me, and that I must take the reins in my own hands.*[M2]

M2 From Patna I took the reins in my own hands.

XIII

M1 Simple

THE *GENTLE*[M1] BIHARI

I knew Maulana Mazharul Haq[185] in London when he was studying for the bar, and when I met him at

---

the use of their latrine, not to speak of inviting us to meals . . . I have swallowed a good many insults and the queer situation here does not trouble me. If things go on this way I am not likely to see Champaran.' *CWMG*, vol. 13, pp. 360–61.

[184] 'The servants were doing their duty, and as they thought, doing what Rajendra Babu would wish them to do.' In the first edition.

[185] Maulana Mazharul Haq (1866–1930), Bar-at-law, enrolled in the Middle Temple on 8 November 1888, called to the Bar on 10 June 1891, one of the founders of the Muslim League, vice-chairman, Bihar Congress Committee, participated in the Khilafat Non-Cooperation Movement, established the Sadaquat Ashram at Patna, and started an English journal, *The Motherland*.

the Bombay Congress in 1915—the year in which he was President of the Muslim League—he had renewed the acquaintance, and extended me an invitation to stay with him whenever I happened to go to Patna. I bethought myself of this invitation and sent him a note indicating the purpose of my visit. He immediately came in his car, and pressed me to accept his hospitality. I thanked him and requested him to guide me to my destination by the first available train, the railway guide being useless to an utter stranger like[186] me. He had a talk with Rajkumar Shukla and suggested that I should first go to Muzaffarpur. There was a train for that place the same evening, and he sent me off by it.

Principal Kripalani[187] was then in Muzaffarpur. I had known of him ever since my visit to Hyderabad.[188] Dr. Choithram[189] had told me of his great sacrifice, of his simple life, and of the Ashram that Dr. Choithram was running out of funds provided by Prof. Kripalani. He used to be a professor in the Government College, Muzaffarpur, and had just resigned the post when I went there. I had sent a telegram informing him of my arrival,[190] and he met me at the station with a crowd of students, though the train reached there at midnight. He had no rooms of his own, and was staying with

---

[186] 'an utter stranger like' added in the English translation.

[187] Jivatram Bhagvandas Kripalani (1888–1982), professor of English and history at Muzaffarpur College, joined the Non-Cooperation Movement, general secretary (1934–45) and president (1946), Indian National Congress, member of the Constituent Assembly and member of Parliament (1952–71).

[188] Hyderabad (Sindh). MKG and Acharya Kripalani first met at Shantiniketan on 17 December 1915. MKG visited Hyderabad (Sindh) and surrounding areas in February–March 1916.

[189] Dr. Choithram Gidwani (1889–1952), medical practitioner, president, Sindh Provincial Congress Committee, participated in the civil disobedience and quit India movements.

[190] 'informing him of my arrival' added in the English translation.

M2 and took me there

Professor Malkani[191] *who therefore virtually became my host.*[M2] It was an extraordinary thing in those days for a Government professor to harbour a man like me.

Professor Kripalani spoke to me about the desperate condition of Bihar, particularly of the Tirhut division[192] and gave me an idea of the difficulty of my task. He had established very close contact with the Biharis, and had already spoken to them about the mission that took me to Bihar.

In the morning a small group of *vakils* called on me. I still remember Ramnavmi Prasad[193] among them, as his earnestness specially appealed to me.

'It is not possible,' he said, 'for you to do the kind of work you have come for, if you stay here (meaning Prof. Malkani's quarters).[194] You must come and stay with one of us. Gaya Babu[195] is a well-known *vakil* here. I have come on his behalf to invite you to stay with him. I confess we are all afraid of Government, but we shall render what help we can. Most of the things Rajkumar Shukla has told you are true. It is a pity our leaders are not here today. I have, however, wired to them both, Babu Brajkishore Prasad and Babu Rajendra

---

[191] Narayandas Ratanmal Malkani (1890–1974), taught economics at Muzaffarpur College, joined Gujarat Vidyapith (1920–27), participated in the civil disobedience and quit India movements, served as deputy high commissioner of India at Karachi and was nominated member of the Rajya Sabha (1952–62).

[192] Tirhut had 87,000 acres of land under indigo cultivation at the end of the nineteenth Century. Mishra, p. 5.

[193] Ramnavmi Prasad, born in 1981 at village Fahatha, obtained Bachelor of Arts and Bachelor of Law degrees from Calcutta University, practised at the district court, Muzaffarpur, joined the Non-Cooperation Movement.

[194] '(meaning Prof. Malkani's quarters)' added in the English translation.

[195] Gaya Prasad Singh, B.A., B.L., of Kanhauliganj village was elected in 1922 to the Bihar Legislative Assembly.

Prasad.[196] I expect them to arrive shortly, and they are sure to be able to give you all the information you want and to help you considerably. Pray come over to Gaya Babu's place.'

This was a request that I could not resist, though I hesitated for fear of embarrassing Gaya Babu. But he put me at ease, and so I went over to stay with him. He and his people showered all their affection on me.

Brajkishorebabu now arrived from Darbhanga and Rajendra Babu from Puri. Brajkishorebabu was not the Babu Brajkishore Prasad I had met in Lucknow. He impressed me this time with his humility, simplicity, goodness and extraordinary faith, so characteristic of the Biharis, and my heart was joyous over it. The Bihar *vakils'* regard for him was an agreeable surprise to me.

Soon I felt myself becoming bound to this circle of friends in lifelong friendship. Brajkishorebabu acquainted me with the facts of the case. He used to *be in the habit of taking up*[M3] the cases of the poor tenants. There were two such cases pending when I went there. *When he won any such case,*[M4] he consoled himself that he was doing something for these poor people.[197] Not that he did not charge fees from these simple peasants.[198] *Lawyers labour under the belief that,*[M5] if they do not charge fees, they will have no wherewithal to run their households, and will not be able to render effective help to the poor people. The figures of the fees they charged

M3 take up

M4 By taking such cases

M5 The argument being that

---

[196] Babu Rajendra Prasad (1884–1963), studied history and law at Calcutta University, a nationalist leader of the Indian National Congress, chairman of the Constituent Assembly of India (1946–49), the first President of independent India (1950–62).

[197] 'He sometimes failed in them as well.' To add.

[198] 'Though self-sacrificing, Braj Kishore Babu or Rajendra Babu did not hesitate to charge their fees.' To add.

and the[199] standard of a barrister's fees in Bengal and Bihar staggered me.

'We gave Rs. 10,000 to so and so for his opinion,' I was told. Nothing less than *four figures*[M6] in any case.

The friends listened to my kindly reproach and did not misunderstand me.

'Having studied these cases,' said I, 'I have come to the conclusion that we should stop going to law-courts. Taking such cases to the courts does little good. Where the ryots are so crushed and fear-stricken, law-courts are useless. The real *relief*[M7] for them is to be free from fear. We cannot sit still until we have driven *tinkathia* out of Bihar. I had thought that I should be able to leave here in two days, but I now realize that the work might take even two years. I am prepared to give that time, if necessary. I am now feeling my ground, but I want your help.'

I found Brajkishore Babu exceptionally cool-headed. 'We shall render all the help we can,' he said quietly, 'but pray tell us what kind of help you will need.'

And thus we sat talking until midnight.

'I shall have little use for your legal *knowledge*,'[M8] I said to them. 'I want clerical assistance and help in interpretation. It may[200] be necessary to face imprisonment, but much as I would love you to run that risk, you would go only so far as you feel yourselves capable of going. Even turning yourselves into clerks and giving up your profession for an indefinite period is no small thing. I find it difficult to understand the local dialect of Hindi, and I shall not be able to read papers written in Kaithi[201] or Urdu. I shall want you to translate them for me. We cannot afford to pay for this

M6 thousands

M7 remedy

M8 acumen

---

[199] 'unbelievable' to add.

[200] 'even' to add.

[201] Kathi script, also called 'Kayathi' or 'Kayasthi', dates back to 1600s. It derives its name from the Kayastha community, whose members were employed as administrators in princely north India. It was recognized as official script in British courts in Bihar.

work. It should all be done for love and out of a spirit of service.'

Brajkishorebabu understood this immediately, and he now cross-examined me and his companions by turns. He tried to ascertain the implications of all that I had said—how long their service would be required, how many of them would be needed, whether they might serve by turns and so on. Then he asked the *vakils* the capacity of their sacrifice.

Ultimately they gave me this assurance. 'Such and such a number of us will do whatever you may ask. Some of us will be with you for so much time as you may require. The idea of accommodating oneself to imprisonment is a novel thing for us. We will try to *assimilate*[M9] it.'

[M9] acquire fitness for

XIV

FACE TO FACE WITH AHIMSA[202]

My object was to inquire into the condition of the Champaran agriculturists and understand their grievances against the indigo planters. For this purpose it was necessary that I should meet thousands of the ryots. But I deemed it essential, before starting on my inquiry, to know the planters' side of the case and see the Commissioner of the Division.[203] I sought and was granted appointments with both.

The Secretary of the Planters' Association[204] told me plainly that I was an outsider and that I had no business

---

[202] 'Face to face with the Goddess of Ahimsa' in the original.

[203] MKG wrote to Leonard Frederick Morshead, 'Having heard a great deal about the condition of the Indians working in connection with Indigo plantation, I have arrived here to ascertain, so far as possible, for myself the true position.' *CWMG*, vol. 13, p. 362.

[204] Herbert Cox of the Paddumukair factory.

to come between the planters and their tenants, but if I had any representation to make, I might submit it in writing. I politely told him that I did not regard myself as an outsider, and that I had every right to inquire into the condition of the tenants if they desired me to do so.

The Commissioner, on whom I called, proceeded to bully me, and advised me forthwith to leave Tirhut.[205]

I acquainted my co-workers with all this, and told them that there was a likelihood of Government stopping me from proceeding further, and that I might have to go to jail earlier than I had expected,[206] and that,

---

[205] The commissioner, L.F. Morshead, in his note on the interview wrote, 'Mr. Gandhi said that he had had many communications asking him to enquire into conditions in the indigo plantations, and found that there was an insistent public demand that he should enquire . . . It was pointed out to him that the raiyats were not backward in representing their grievances, and that our administrative resources in the shape of courts, the Settlement Officials, the Manager of the Bettiah Estate, the District Magistrate, Subdivision Officer in their executive capacity were all being employed to ascertain and rectify the causes of complaint . . . Mr. Gandhi was asked whether he could produce any credentials to show the insistent public demand of which he spoke.' Mishra, *Select Documents*, pp. 58–59. During this interview Mr. Weston, the magistrate of Muzaffarpur, was also present. The same day MKG sent the commissioner two credentials. One was signed by Braj Kishore Prasad, Ramnavmi Prasad, Gaya Prasad Singh and Ramdayalu Sinha. The other was from Arikshan Sinha who was a delegate at the Lucknow Congress. Ibid., pp. 59–61.

[206] The administration was forewarned and prepared. On 11 April, E.C. Ryland, deputy inspector general of police, crime and railways, wrote to H. Macpherson, chief secretary, Government of Bihar and Orissa, 'As Mr. Gandhi's speeches are not always free from objection it has been decided by the Punjab Government that he should not lecture in the Punjab without first obtaining permission from Government. In view of the rumours that Mr. Gandhi intends visiting Champaran . . . the Local Government will no doubt consider whether similar orders should not be published here.' Mishra, *Select Documents*, p. 57. C. Marshman, the superintendent of police, Champaran, was informed that MKG's visit was 'most undesirable and likely

if I was to be arrested, it would be best that the arrest should take place in Motihari or if possible in Bettiah. It was advisable, therefore, that I should go to those places as early as possible.

Champaran is a district of the Tirhut division and Motihari is its headquarters. Rajkumar Shukla's place was in the vicinity of Bettiah, and the tenants belonging to the *kothis* in its neighbourhood were the poorest in the district. Rajkumar Shukla wanted me to see them and I was equally anxious to do so.

So I started with my co-workers for Motihari the same day. Babu Gorakh Prasad[207] harboured us in his home, which became a caravanserai. It could hardly contain us all. The very same day we heard that about five miles from Motihari a tenant[208] had been ill-treated. It was decided that, in company with Babu Dharanidhar Prasad,[209] I should go and see him the next morning, and we accordingly set off for the place on elephant's back. An elephant, by the way, is about as common in Champaran as a bullock-cart in Gujarat. We had scarcely

---

to cause trouble' and he had not been in the past allowed to speak; but because 'He is not on any list of agitators' the district magistrate was requested to call him and issue a warning that if his visit were to result in trouble, action would be taken against him. The superintendent was told, 'If Gandhi does anything after this warning . . . he can be proceeded against most suitably by an eviction order under rule 3, Defence of India (consolidation) Rules, but as I said before in dealing with men like Gandhi one has to be careful.' Ibid., pp. 56–57.

[207] Babu Gorakh Prasad (1869–1962), pleader, joined the Non-Cooperation Movement (1919–21), Civil Disobedience Movement (1930), individual Satyagraha (1941) and Quit India movement (1942).

[208] This was the case of tenant Lomraj and Mr. Kemp, the manager of the Jagiraha factory, near Jassauli village.

[209] Babu Dharanidhar Prasad (d. 1948), pleader, joined the Non-Cooperation Movement, president, Bihar Provincial Conference (1923).

gone half way when a messenger[210] from the Police
Superintendent overtook us and said that the latter had
sent his compliments. I saw what he meant. Having left
Dharanidhar Babu to proceed to the original destination,
I got into the hired carriage which the messenger had
brought. He then served on me a notice[211] to leave
Champaran, and drove me to my place. On his asking
me to acknowledge the service of the notice, I wrote
to the effect that I did not propose to comply with it
and leave Champaran till my inquiry was finished.
Thereupon I received a summons to take my trial the
next day for disobeying the order to leave Champaran.[212]

I kept awake that whole night writing letters[213] and
giving necessary instructions to Babu Brajkishore Prasad.[214]

---

[210] The messenger was Sub-Inspector Ajodhya Prasad Tiwari.
Mishra, *Select Documents*, p. 63.

[211] The notice was served under Section 144, Criminal Procedure
Code. The notice read:

To: Mr. M.K. Gandhi (at present in Motihari)
Whereas your presence in any part of the district will endanger
the public peace and may lead to serious disturbances . . . I do
hereby order you to abstain from remaining in this district which
you are required to leave by the next available train. Given under
my hand and the seal of the Court, this 16th day of April, 1917.

W. B. Heycock
District Magistrate, Champaran

See ibid., p. 62, n. 4.

[212] MKG responded to the notice, 'Out of sense of public
responsibility, I feel it my duty to say that I am unable to leave
this district, but if it so pleases the authorities, I shall submit to
the order, *viz*, suffering the penalty of disobedience.' *CWMG*,
vol. 13, p. 367. MKG was issued summons on 17 April, under
Section 188, Indian Penal Code.

[213] On 16 April MKG wrote two letters to Maganlal Gandhi and
one to Mr. Maffey, private secretary to the Viceroy, and on the
17th he wrote to Esther Fearing, H.S.L. Polak and Kripalani.
See *CWMG*, vol. 13, pp. 365–73.

[214] MKG wrote, 'The royts should be instructed definitely not
to use violence whether regarding their own grievances or

The news of the notice and[215] the summons spread *like wild-fire,*[M1] and I was told that Motihari that day witnessed unprecedented scenes. Gorakhbabu's house and the court house overflowed with men. Fortunately I had finished all my work during the night and so was able to cope with the crowds. My companions proved the greatest help. They occupied themselves with regulating the crowds, for the latter followed me *wherever I went.*[M2]

M1 in a moment

M2 to the court

A sort of friendliness sprang up between the officials— Collector, Magistrate, Police Superintendent—and myself. I might have legally resisted the notices served on me. Instead I accepted them all, and my conduct towards the officials was correct. They thus saw that I did not want to offend them personally, but that I wanted to offer civil resistance to their orders. In this way they were put at ease, and instead of harassing me they gladly availed themselves of my and my co-workers' co-operation in regulating the crowds. *But it was an ocular demonstration to them of the fact that their authority was shaken.*[M3] The people had for the moment lost all fear of punishment and yielded obedience to the power of love which their new friend exercised.

M3 But they also understood that from that day their authority had vanished.

It should be remembered that no one knew me in Champaran. The peasants were all ignorant. Champaran, being far up north of the Ganges, and right at the foot of the Himalayas in close proximity to Nepal, was cut off from the rest of India. The Congress was practically unknown in those parts.[216] Even those who had heard the name of the Congress shrank from joining it or even mentioning it. And now the Congress and its members had entered this land, though not in the name of the Congress, *yet in a far more real sense.*[M4]

M4 and yet the power of the Congress became evident

---

regarding imprisonment of those who may come to assist them.'
See *CWMG*, vol. 13, pp. 369–70.

[215] 'the notice and' added in the English translation.

[216] 'There were no Congress members to be found.' To add.

In consultation with my co-workers I had decided that nothing should be done in the name of the Congress. What we wanted was work and not name, substance and not shadow.[217] For the name of the Congress was the *bete noire* of the Government and their controllers—the planters. To them the Congress was a byword for lawyers' wrangles, evasion of law through legal loopholes, a byword for bomb and anarchical crime and for diplomacy and hypocrisy. We had to disillusion them both. Therefore we had decided not to mention the name of the Congress and not to acquaint the peasants with the organization called the Congress. It was enough, we thought, if they understood and followed the spirit of the Congress instead of its letter.

No emissaries had therefore been sent there, openly or secretly, on behalf of the Congress to prepare the ground for our arrival.[218] Rajkumar Shukla was incapable of reaching the thousands of peasants. No political work had yet been done amongst them. The world outside Champaran was not known to them. And yet they received me as though we had been age-long friends. It is no exaggeration, but the literal truth, to say that in this meeting with the peasants[219] I was face to face with God, Ahimsa and Truth.

When I come to examine my *title*[M5] to this realization, I find nothing but my love for the people.

[M5] fitness

---

[217] 'substance and not shadow' translates a colloquial expression that literally translates as, 'We wanted food and not the sounds of cooking.'

[218] The government of course did not think so. S.N. Sinha, personal assistant to the commissioner noted on 23 April 1917, 'Everything was pre-arranged. Rs. 10,000 or more was collected in Motihari and the interior of Champaran.' See Mishra, *Select Documents*, p. 84.

[219] 'in this meeting with the peasants' added in the English translation.

And this in turn is nothing but an expression of my unshakable faith in ahimsa.

That day in Champaran was an unforgettable event in my *life and a red-letter day for the peasants and for me.*[M6]

According to the law, I was to be on my trial, but truly speaking Government was to be on its trial. The Commissioner only succeeded in trapping Government in the net which he had spread for me.

[M6] life. It was a day of festivity for the peasants and me.

XV

CASE WITHDRAWN

The trial began. The Government pleader, the Magistrate and other officials were on tenterhooks. They were at a loss to know what to do. The Government pleader was pressing the Magistrate to postpone the case. But I interfered and requested the Magistrate not to postpone the case, as I wanted to plead guilty to having disobeyed the order to leave Champaran and read a brief statement as follows:[220]

> With the permission of the Court I would like to make a brief statement showing why I have taken the very serious step of seemingly disobeying the order passed under Section 144 of Cr.P.C. In my humble opinion it is a question of difference of opinion between the Local Administration and myself. I have entered the country with motives of rendering humanitarian and national service. I have done so in response to a pressing invitation to come and help the ryots, who urge they are not being fairly treated by the indigo planters. I could not

---

[220] *Navajivan* of 22 July 1928 did not carry the statement, which was introduced in the English translation published in *Young India* of 26 July 1928 and later incorporated in the Gujarati.

render any help without studying the problem. I have, therefore, come to study it with the assistance, if possible, of the Administration and the planters. I have no other motive, and I cannot believe that my coming can in any way disturb public peace and cause loss of life. I claim to have considerable experience in such matters. The Administration, however, have thought differently. I fully appreciate their difficulty, and I admit too that they can only proceed upon information they received. As a law-abiding citizen my first instinct would be, as it was, to obey the order served upon me. But I could not do so without doing violence to my sense of duty to those for whom I have come. I feel that I could just now serve them only by remaining in their midst. I could not, therefore, voluntarily retire. Amid this conflict of duties I could only throw the responsibility of removing me from them on the Administration. I am fully conscious of the fact that a person, holding, in the public life of India, a position such as I do, has to be most careful in setting an example.[221] It is my firm belief that in the complex constitution under which we are living, the only safe and honourable course for a self-respecting man is, in the circumstances such as face me, to do what I have decided to do, that is, to submit without protest to the penalty of disobedience. I venture to make this statement not in any way in extenuation of the penalty to be awarded against me, but to show that I have disregarded the order served upon me not for want of respect for lawful authority, but in obedience to the higher law of our being, the voice of conscience.

There was now no occasion to postpone the hearing, but as both the Magistrate and the Government pleader

---

[221] 'setting examples', both in Mishra, *Select Documents*, p. 70, and *CWMG*, vol. 13, p. 375.

had *been taken by surprise*,[M1] the Magistrate postponed judgment. Meanwhile I had wired full details to the Viceroy,[222] to Patna friends, as also to[223] Pandit Madan Mohan Malaviya and others.

Before I could appear before the Court to receive the sentence,[224] the Magistrate sent a written message that the Lieutenant Governor had ordered the case against me to be withdrawn, and the Collector wrote to me saying that I was at liberty to conduct the proposed inquiry, and that I might count on whatever help I needed from the officials. None of us was prepared for this prompt and happy issue.[225]

[M1] not anticipated this result

---

[222] See *CWMG*, vol. 13, pp. 368–69.

[223] 'Bharat Bhushan' to add.

[224] On 18 April 1917, district magistrate Heycock wrote to the commissioner, Tirhut division, 'Mr. Gandhi has pleaded guilty under section 188, I.P.C. He of course still refuses to leave the district unless he is compelled. This can only be done under the Defence of India Act.' Mishra, *Select Documents*, p. 70. MKG agreed to stay on in Motihari 'quietly' till Saturday, 21 April, and 'wait upon' the district magistrate at 7 a.m. that day.

[225] Sir Edward Gait, Lt. Governor of Bihar, sent a telegram to district magistrate, Motihari, seeking a full report on 18 April 1917, which was complied with on the same day. The Government of India sought a similar report from the Lt. Governor on the same day. On 19 April, the Government of Bihar issued telegraphic orders to withdraw the proceedings and take no further action; on the same day the district magistrate was instructed by telegram to give MKG 'facilities for obtaining information regarding facts of agrarian situation'. Mishra, *Select Documents*, p. 74.

On 20 April, the chief secretary wrote to the commissioner and severely indicted his actions, terming them a 'great mistake'. The letter clearly stated, 'In the circumstances His Honour in the Council has no alternative but to direct the abandonment of the proceedings taken against Mr. Gandhi. He fully recognises the fact that Mr. Gandhi will thus appear to have gained a victory over the local officials: and, if he is disposed to cause trouble, will be in a better position to do so, but this is unavoidable. The order issued under section 144, Criminal Procedure Code, was *ultra vires* and action cannot be taken under the Defence of India

I called on the Collector Mr. Heycock. He seemed to be a good man, anxious to do justice. He told me that I might ask for whatever papers I desired to see, and that I was at liberty to see him whenever I liked.

The country thus had its first direct object-lesson in[226] Civil Disobedience. The affair was freely discussed both locally and in the Press, and[227] my inquiry got unexpected publicity.

It was necessary for my inquiry that the Government should remain neutral. But the inquiry did not need support from Press reporters or leading articles in the Press. *Indeed the situation in Champaran was so delicate and difficult that*[M2] over-energetic criticism or highly coloured reports might easily damage the cause which I was seeking to espouse. So I wrote to the editors of the principal papers requesting them not to trouble to send any reporters, as I should send them whatever might be necessary for publication and keep them informed.[228]

I knew that the Government attitude countenancing my presence had displeased the Champaran planters and I knew that even the officials, though they could say nothing openly, could hardly have liked it.[M3] Incorrect or misleading reports, therefore, were likely to incense them all the more, and their ire, instead of descending on me, would be sure to descend on the poor fear-stricken ryots and seriously hinder my search for the truth about the case.

In spite of these precautions[229] the planters engineered against me a poisonous agitation. All sorts of falsehoods appeared in the Press about my co-workers

M2 Not just that, but

M3 I knew that the planters were very angry; I also knew that the officials could not be pleased with this.

Rules unless and until Mr. Gandhi does something to justify such action.' Mishra, *Select Documents*, p. 71.

[226] 'Satyagraha or' to add.

[227] 'Champaran and' to add.

[228] See *CWMG*, vol. 13, pp. 377–78.

[229] 'In spite of these precautions' added in the English translation.

and myself. But my extreme cautiousness and my insistence on truth, even to the minutest detail, *turned the edge of their sword.*[M4]

[M4] made their arrows futile

The planters left no stone unturned in maligning Brajkishorebabu, but the more they maligned him, the more he rose in the estimation of the people.

In such delicate situations as this I did not *think it proper to*[M5] invite any leaders from other provinces. Pandit Malaviyaji had sent me an assurance that, whenever I wanted him, I had only to send him word, but I did not trouble him. I thus prevented the struggle from assuming a political aspect. But I sent to the leaders and the principal papers occasional reports, not for publication, but merely for their information.[230] I had seen[231] that, even where the end might be political, but where the cause was non-political, one damaged it by giving it a political aspect and helped it by keeping it within its non-political limit. The Champaran struggle was a proof of the fact that disinterested service of the people in any sphere ultimately helps the country politically.

[M5] encourage in the least the reporters to come nor did I

XVI

METHODS OF WORK

To give a full account of the Champaran inquiry would be to narrate the history, for the period[232] of the Champaran ryot, which is out of the question in these chapters. The Champaran inquiry was a bold experiment with Truth and Ahimsa, and I am giving week by week

---

[230] 'not for publication, but merely for their information' added in the English translation.

[231] 'from long experience' to add.

[232] 'for the period' added in the English translation.

only what occurs to me as worth giving from that point of view. For more details the reader must turn to Sjt. Rajendra Prasad's history of the Champaran Satyagraha in Hindi, *of which, I am told, an English edition*[233] *is now in the press.*[M1]

M1 and the translation brought out by the 'Yugadharma' Press.

But to return to the subject matter of this chapter. The inquiry could not be conducted in Gorakhbabu's house, without practically asking poor[234] Gorakhbabu to vacate it. And the people of Motihari had not yet shed their fear to the extent of renting a house to us. However, Brajkishorebabu tactfully secured one with considerable open space about it, and we now removed there.

It was not quite possible to carry on the work without money. It had not been the practice hitherto to appeal to the public for money for work of this kind. Brajkishorebabu and his friends were mainly *vakils* who either contributed funds themselves, or found it from friends whenever there was an occasion. How could they ask the people to pay when they and their kind could well afford to do so? That seemed to be the argument. I had made up my mind not to accept anything from the Champaran ryots. It would be bound to be misinterpreted. I was equally determined not to appeal to the country at large for funds to conduct this inquiry. For that was likely to give it an all-India and political aspect. Friends from Bombay offered[235] Rs. 15,000, but I declined the offer with thanks. I decided to get as much as was possible, with Brajkishorebabu's help, from well-to-do Biharis living outside Champaran

---

[233] *Satyagraha in Champaran* (Madras: S. Ganesan, 1928). The original in Hindi was written during long vacations in the High Court in September and October of 1918 and 1919, and was published in 1922.

[234] 'poor' added in the English translation.

[235] 'telegraphically' to add.

and, if more was needed, to approach my friend Dr. P.J. Mehta of Rangoon.[236] Dr. Mehta readily agreed to send me whatever might be needed. We were thus free from all anxiety on this score. We were not likely to require large funds, as we were bent on exercising the greatest economy in consonance with the poverty of Champaran.[237] Indeed it was found in the end that we did not need any large amount. I have an impression that we expended in all not more than three thousand rupees, and, as far as I remember, we saved *a few hundred*[M2] rupees from what we had collected.

[M2] five hundred to a thousand

The curious ways of living of my companions in the early days were a constant theme of raillery at their expense. Each of the *vakils* had a servant and a cook, and therefore a separate kitchen, and they often had their dinner as late as midnight. Though they paid their own expenses, their *irregularity*[M3] worried me, but as we had become close friends there was no possibility of a misunderstanding between us, and they received my ridicule in good part. Ultimately it was agreed that the servants should be dispensed with, that all the kitchens should be amalgamated and that regular hours should be observed. As all were not vegetarians, and as two kitchens would have been expensive, a common vegetarian kitchen was decided upon. It was also felt necessary to insist on simple meals.

[M3] mode of life

These arrangements considerably reduced the expenses and saved us a lot of time and energy, and both these were badly needed. Crowds of peasants came to make their statements, and they were followed by an army of companions who filled the compound and garden to overflowing. The efforts of my companions to save me from *darshan*-seekers were often of no avail,

---

[236] 'of Rangoon' added in the English translation.

[237] 'in consonance with the poverty of Champaran' added in the English translation.

and I had to be exhibited for *darshan* at particular hours. At least five to seven volunteers were required to take down statements, and even then some people had to go away in the evening without being able to make their statements. All these statements were not essential, many of them being repetitions,[238] but the people could not be satisfied otherwise, *and I appreciated their feeling in the matter.*[M4]

M4 and it helped me understand their feelings

Those who took down the statements had to observe certain rules. Each peasant had to be closely cross-examined, and whoever failed to *satisfy the test*[M5] was rejected. This entailed a lot of extra time but most of the statements were thus rendered incontrovertible.

M5 hold

An officer from the C.I.D. would always be present when these statements were recorded.[239] We might have prevented him but we had decided from the very beginning not only not to mind the presence of C.I.D. officers, but to treat them with courtesy and to give them all the information that it was possible to give them.[240] This was far from doing us any harm. *On the contrary the very fact that the statements were taken down in the presence of the C.I.D. officers made the peasants more fearless.*[M6] Whilst on the one hand excessive fear of the C.I.D. was driven out of the peasants' minds, on the other, their presence exercised a natural restraint on exaggeration. *It was the business of C.I.D. friends to entrap people and so the peasants had necessarily to be cautious.*[M7]

M6 This had a beneficial effect; people became more fearless.

M7 The fear that if they were to lie, the officials would entrap them, made them cautious in their statements.

---

[238] 'many of them being repetitions' added in the English translation.

[239] On 28 April the chief secretary, in a letter to the commissioner of Tirhut division wrote, 'His Honour in Council would be glad to know who your confidential informant is and this may be communicated to me secretly. The name will be kept off the record.' Mishra, *Select Documents*, p. 89.

[240] 'All statements were to be recorded in their presence and in their hearing.' To add.

As I did not want to irritate the planters, but to win them over by gentleness, I made a point of writing to and meeting such of them against whom allegations of a serious nature were made. I met the Planters' Association[241] as well, placed the ryots' grievances before them and acquainted myself with their point of view. Some of the planters hated me. Some were indifferent and[242] a few treated me with courtesy.

XVII

COMPANIONS

Brajkishorebabu and Rajendrababu were a matchless pair. Their devotion made[243] it impossible for me to take a single step without their help. Their disciples, or their companions—Shambhubabu,[244] Anugrahababu,[245] Dharanibabu, Ramnavmibabu and other *vakils*—were

---

[241] Herbert Cox was the honorary secretary of the Bihar Planters' Association. The directors of the Association on 5 May 1917 passed a resolution, 'That the Directors of the Bihar Planters' Association place on record its emphatic protest against the manner and methods of enquiry conducted by Mr. Gandhi and his assistants in Champaran district, inasmuch as they are calculated to stir up feelings of animosity between landlords and tenants, planters and tenants.' Mishra, *Select Documents*, p. 119.

[242] 'whilst' in the first edition.

[243] 'me an invalid and made' to add.

[244] Shambhu Saran (1892–1931), M.A., B.L., a lawyer in the Patna High Court, a prominent worker of the Congress in Bihar.

[245] Anugraha Narayan Sinha (1889–1957), M.A., B.L., lawyer in the Patna High Court, member, Central Legislative Assembly (1934–37), finance minister, Government of Bihar (1937–39), finance, agriculture and labour minister, Government of Bihar (1946–57).

always with us. Vindhyababu and Janakdharibabu[246] also came and helped us now and then. *All these were Biharis.*[M1] Their principal work was to take down the ryots' statements.

Professor Kripalani could not but cast in his lot with us. Though a Sindhi he was more Bihari than a born Bihari. I have seen only a few workers capable of merging themselves in the province of their adoption. Kripalani is one of those few. He made it impossible for anyone to feel that he belonged to a different province. He was my gatekeeper in chief. For the time being he made it the end and aim of his life to save me from *darshan*-seekers. He warded off people, calling to his aid now his unfailing humour, now his non-violent threats. At nightfall he would take up his occupation of a teacher and regale his companions with his historical studies and observations,[247] and quicken any timid visitor into bravery.

Maulana Mazharul Haq had registered his name on the standing list of helpers whom I might count upon whenever necessary,[248] and he made a point of looking in once or twice a month. *The pomp and splendour in which he then lived was in sharp contrast to his simple life of today.*[M2] The way in which he associated with us made us feel that he was one of us, though his fashionable habit gave a stranger a different impression.

M2 The difference between the pomp and splendour of those days and his simple life today are as separated as heavens from earth.

As I gained more experience of Bihar, I became convinced that work of a permanent nature was impossible without proper[249] village education. The ryots' ignorance was pathetic. They either allowed their children to roam about, or made them toil on indigo

---

[246] Babu Jankidhar Prasad, B.A., B.L., of Manpura village, vakil in Muzaffarpur.

[247] 'with his historical studies and observations' added in the English translation.

[248] 'whom I might count upon whenever necessary' added in the English translation.

[249] 'proper' added in the English translation.

plantations from morning to night for a couple of coppers a day. In those days a male labourer's wage did not exceed ten pice, a female's did not exceed six, and a child's three. He who succeeded in earning four annas a day was considered most fortunate.

In consultation with my companions I decided to open primary schools in six villages.[250] One of our conditions with the villagers was that they should provide the teachers with board and lodging while we would see to the other expenses. The village folk had hardly any cash in their hands, but they could well afford to provide foodstuffs. Indeed they had already expressed their readiness to contribute grain and other raw materials.

From where to get the teachers was a great problem. It was difficult to find local teachers who would work for a bare allowance or without remuneration. My idea was never to entrust children to commonplace teachers. *Their literary qualification was not so essential as their moral fibre.*[M3]

So I issued a public appeal for voluntary teachers. It received ready response. Sjt. Gangadharrao Deshpande[251] sent Babasaheb Soman[252] and Pundalik,[253]

[M3] A teacher may be lacking in knowledge of letters but requires the force of character.

---

[250] The reports filed by Bachu Narain Lal, deputy superintendent of police on special duty, provide the names of five schools with the teachers working there. The schools were at Bhitwara (thirty-nine enrolled students, twenty-five regular attendees) started in November 1917, Madhubani (eighty-five students) started in January 1918, Bhitwara (eighty-one students) started in February 1918, girls' school at Barharwa (twenty-five students) started in November 1917 and boys' school at Barharwa (150 students) started in November 1917. See Mishra, *Select Documents*, pp. 532–47.

[251] Gangadharrao Deshpande, a political worker from Belgaum, popularly known as 'Lion of Karnataka', associated with the All India Spinners' Association and All India Village Industries Association.

[252] Baba Saheb Soman (d. 1946), from Belgaum.

[253] Pundalik Katgade of Belgaum.

Shrimati Avantikabai Gokhale[254] came from Bombay and Mrs. Anandibai Vaishampayan[255] from Poona.[256] I sent to the Ashram for Chhotalal,[257] Surendranath[258] and my son Devdas. About this time Mahadev Desai[259] and Narahari Parikh[260] with their wives cast in their lot with me. Kasturbai was also summoned for the work. This was a fairly strong contingent.[261] Shrimati Avantikabai

---

[254] Avantikabai Gokhale, the police reports describe her as 'wife of Baban Gopal Gokhale, knows English, Mahrathi, Guzerati and a little of Hindi, fair complexion, stout build; middle size; age about 35 years'. Mishra, *Select Documents*, p. 542. She was in charge of the girls' school at Barharwa.

[255] Anandibai, the police reports describe her as 'daughter of Ramchander Devkar, reads in the 2nd class of the Kurvey Mahila Ashram, knows Hindi and Mahrathi, medium complexion; medium built, pox-pitted face; aged about 19 years'. Ibid., p. 536. Was a student when she joined the movement.

[256] In the original, 'from South'. In Gujarati the term *dakshini* denotes a person or an object from Maharashtra, not including Bombay.

[257] Chhotalal worked as a weaving master, a member of the Satyagraha Ashram. The police records describe him as, 'Bania, Jaipore, entrance passed. Allahabad University, Knows Hindi and weaving, fair complexion, medium build, short stature, age about 20'. Mishra, *Select Documents*, p. 544.

[258] Surendranath, taught Bhasha, arithmetic and drill, member of the Satyagraha Ashram. The police records describe him as 'from district Gorakhpur, middle vernacular passed, knows Urdu and a little of English, medium complexion and medium build, short stature, curly hair, age about 20 years'. Ibid., p. 544.

[259] Mahadev Haribhai Desai (1892–1942), one of MKG's closest associates, worked as his secretary, writer, translator and journalist of great eminence. Translated *Autobiography* into English and rendered works of Tagore and Jawaharlal Nehru in Gujarati. His 'Diary of Mahadev Desai' is the most authentic record of each day that he spent with MKG from 1917 to 1942.

[260] Narahari Dwarkadas Parikh (1891–1957), lawyer, member of the Satyagraha Ashram, worked as a registrar of the Gujarat Vidyapith.

[261] 'of male and female teachers' to add.

and Shrimati Anandibai were educated enough, but Shrimati Durga Desai and Shrimati Manibehn Parikh had nothing more than a bare knowledge of Gujarati, and Kasturbai not even that. How were these ladies to instruct the children in Hindi?

I explained to them that they were expected to teach the children not grammar *and the three R's so much as*[M4] cleanliness and good manners. I further explained that even as regards letters[262] there was not so great a difference between Gujarati, Hindi and Marathi as they imagined, and in the primary classes, at any rate, the teaching of the rudiments of the alphabet and numerals was not a difficult matter. The result was that the classes taken by these ladies were found to be most successful. The experience inspired them with confidence and interest in their work. Avantikabai's became a model school. She threw herself heart and soul into her work. She brought her exceptional gifts to bear on it. Through these ladies we could, to some extent,[263] reach the village women.

But I did not want to stop at providing for primary education. The villages were insanitary, the lanes full of filth, the well surrounded by mud and stink and the courtyards unbearably untidy. The elder people badly needed education in cleanliness. They were all suffering from various skin diseases. So it was decided to do as much sanitary work as possible and to penetrate every department of their lives.

Doctors were needed for this work. I requested *the Servants of India Society*[M5] to lend us the services of the late Dr. Dev.[264] We had been great friends, and he readily offered his services for six months. The teachers—men and women—had all to work under him.

[M4] but

[M5] Gokhale's Society

---

[262] 'even as regards letters' added in the English translation.

[263] 'to some extent' added in the English translation.

[264] See *CWMG*, vol. 13, p. 453.

All of them had express instructions not to concern themselves with grievances against planters or with politics. People who had any complaints to make were to be referred to me. No one was to venture out of his beat. The *friends*[M6] carried out these instructions with wonderful fidelity. I do not remember a single occasion of indiscipline.

M6 Champaran associates

XVIII

PENETRATING THE VILLAGES

As far as was possible we placed each school in charge of one man and one woman. These volunteers had to look after medical relief and sanitation. The womenfolk had to be approached through women.

Medical relief was a very simple affair. Castor oil, quinine and sulphur ointment were the only drugs provided to the volunteers.[265] If the patient showed a furred tongue or complained of constipation, castor oil was administered, in case of fever quinine was given after an opening dose of castor oil, and the sulphur ointment was applied in case of boils and itch after thoroughly washing the affected parts. No patient was permitted to take home any medicine. Wherever there was some complication[266] *Dr. Dev was consulted.*[M1] Dr. Dev used to visit each centre on certain fixed days in the week.

M1 the case was reserved for Dr. Dev.

Quite a number of people availed themselves of this simple relief. This plan of work will not seem *strange*[M2] when it is remembered that the prevailing ailments were few and amenable to simple treatment, by no means requiring expert help. As for the people the arrangement answered excellently.

M2 amusing

---

[265] 'at each of the schools' to add.

[266] 'or when the ailment could not be understood' to add.

Sanitation was a difficult affair. The people were not prepared to do anything themselves. Even the field labourers were not ready to do their own scavenging. But Dr. Dev was not a man easily to lose heart. He and the volunteers concentrated their energies on making a village ideally clean. They[267] swept the roads and the courtyards, cleaned out the wells, filled up the pools nearby, and lovingly persuaded the villagers to raise volunteers from amongst themselves. In some villages they shamed people into taking up the work, and in others the people were so enthusiastic that they[268] even prepared roads to enable my car to go from place to place. These sweet experiences were not unmixed with bitter ones of people's apathy. I remember some villagers frankly expressing[269] their *dislike for this work.*[M3]

[M3] annoyance at the suggestion of improvements.

It may not be out of place here to narrate an experience that I have described before now at many meetings.[270] Bhitiharva was a small village in which was one of our schools.[271] I happened to visit a smaller village in its vicinity and found some of the women dressed very dirtily. *So I told my wife to ask them why they did not wash their clothes.*[M4] She spoke to them. One of the women took her into her hut and said: 'Look now, there is no box or cupboard here containing other clothes. The sari I am wearing is the only one I have. How am I to wash it? Tell Mahatmaji to get me another sari, and I shall then promise to bathe and put on clean clothes every day.'

[M4] I suggested to Kasturbai to persuade these women to wash and change their clothes.

This cottage was not an exception, but a type to be found in many Indian villages. In countless cottages

---

[267] 'concentrated their energies on making a village ideally clean. They' added in the English translation.

[268] 'were so enthusiastic that they' added in the English translation.

[269] 'having frankly expressed' in the first edition.

[270] 'of women' to add.

[271] 'in which was one of our schools' added in the English translation.

M5 bags and boxes and change of clothes. Countless people live with only the clothes on their body and possession.

in India people live without any furniture, *and without a change of clothes, merely with a rag to cover their shame.*M5

One more experience I will note. In Champaran there is no lack of bamboo and grass. The school hut they had put up at Bhitiharva was made of these materials. Someone—possibly some of the neighbouring planters' men—set fire to it one night. It was not thought advisable to build another hut of bamboo and grass. The school was in charge of Sjt. Soman and Kasturbai. Sjt. Soman decided to build a pukka house, and thanks to his infectious labour, many co-operated with him, and a brick-house was soon made ready. There was no fear now of this building being burnt down.

Thus the volunteers with their schools, sanitation work and medical relief gained the confidence and respect of the village folk, and were able to bring good influence to bear upon them.

M6 suitable

M7 six

But I must confess with regret that my hope of putting this constructive work on a permanent footing was not fulfilled. The volunteers had come for temporary periods, I could not secure any more from outside, and permanent *honorary*M6 workers from Bihar were not available. As soon as my work in Champaran was finished, work outside, which had been preparing in the meantime, drew me away. The *few*M7 months' work in Champaran, however, took such deep root that its influence in one form or another is to be observed there even today.

XIX

M1 The Brighter Side

*WHEN A GOVERNOR IS GOOD*M1

Whilst on the one hand social service work of the kind I have described in the foregoing chapters was being carried out, on the other the work of recording statements of the ryots' grievances was progressing apace. Thousands of such statements were taken,[272] and they could not but have their effect. The ever-growing number of ryots coming to make their statements increased the planters' wrath, and they *moved heaven and earth*[M2] to counteract my inquiry.

One day I received a letter from the Bihar Government to the following effect: 'Your inquiry has been sufficiently prolonged; should you not now bring it to an end and leave Bihar?' The letter was couched in polite language, but its meaning was obvious.[273]

I wrote in reply that the inquiry was bound to be prolonged, and unless and until it resulted in bringing relief to the people, I had no intention of leaving Bihar. I pointed out that it was open to Government to terminate my inquiry by accepting the ryots' grievances as genuine and redressing them, or by recognizing that *the ryots had made out a prima facie case for an official inquiry which should be immediately instituted.* [M3]

Sir Edward Gait,[274] the Lieutenant Governor, asked me to see him, expressed his willingness to

M2 increased their efforts

M3 the grievances appoint an official inquiry committee

---

[272] Lt. Governor Sir Edward Gait, in his letter dated 17 June 1917 to F.G. Sly, chairman-designate of the Champaran Agrarian Inquiry Committee, stated, 'Mr. Gandhi claims, with the aid of his assistants, to have examined 7,000 *raiyats*.' Mishra, *Select Documents*, p. 221.

[273] Walter Maude, member of the Executive Council, had a long talk with MKG. In his note on the meeting Maude wrote, 'I explained fully to him what we consider to be the chief danger of the situation, namely, the recording of evidence in sort of court fashion by a number of assistants and at length . . . I suggested that he must have got a very considerable amount of evidence together by now and might be in a position to make a report, he consented at once to send up a preliminary report.' Mishra, *Select Documents*, p. 123. On 13 May 1917 MKG sent 'preliminary conclusions'. See ibid., pp. 126–31, and *CWMG*, vol. 13, pp. 385–90.

[274] Sir Edward Albert Gait (1863–1950), joined the Indian Civil Service in 1884, served as secretary, Government of Bengal

appoint an inquiry and invited me to be a member of the Committee.[275] I ascertained the names of the other members, and after consultation with my co-workers agreed to serve on the Committee, on condition that I should be free to confer with my co-workers during

---

(1905–07), chief secretary, Government of Bengal (1907–08), census commissioner, Government of India (1909–11), and Lt. Governor of Bihar and Orissa (1915–20).

[275] The views of the government rapidly changed, possibly as a result of the preliminary conclusions sent by MKG and his acceptance by people as new 'Mulk-Malik' or 'Guruji'. W.H. Lewis, sub-divisional officer, wrote in his report, 'The impression that Mr. Gandhi has been sent by the king or some other high authority to hold this inquiry has been created here and he is regarded as a new Hakim or Mulk-Malik.' See, D.G. Tendulkar, *Gandhi in Champaran* (New Delhi: Publications Division, 1957). A petition received by the Planters' Association described him as 'Gurujee'. 'A week ago his name was unknown here. To-day he is the *Gurujee* of the whole district who hang upon his words, and hundreds visit him daily merely to touch his feet.' Mishra, *Select Documents*, p. 111, n. 2. On 4 May the chief secretary wrote to the commissioner, 'The Lieutenant Governor in Council takes the view that no useful purpose would be served by appointment of an official or joint commission of enquiry, as there is nothing from the Government point of view to enquire into.' Ibid., p. 112. In a minute the Lt. Governor on 25 May wrote that he had asked MKG for a meeting on 2 June at Ranchi; in his minute he also included a note by Sir E.V. Levinge on the possible terms of reference, should a commission of inquiry be constituted. On 27 May, the chief secretary wrote to the Home Department, Government of India, that 'Local Government adheres to view that committee at present is inexpedient'. Ibid., p. 171. On 2 June, Home Department, Government of India, wrote to the chief secretary, Government of Bihar, 'The Government of India are of the opinion after giving fullest consideration to the views of the Lieutenant Governor in Council, that a committee of enquiry should be appointed and start investigation as early as possible.' Ibid., pp. 190–91. Sir Edward Gait and MKG had meetings on 4, 5 and 6 June, wherein they agreed on the terms of reference and composition of the committee. On 10 June 1917, the government constituted a Committee of Enquiry with F.G. Sly, commissioner of the Central Provinces as its president, *vide*, Government Resolution 1890-C. Ibid., p. 213.

the progress of the inquiry, that Government should recognize that, by being a member of the Committee, I did not cease to be the ryots' advocate, and that in case the result of the inquiry failed to give me satisfaction, I should be free to guide and advise the ryots as to what line of action they should take.

Sir Edward Gait accepted the condition as just and proper and announced the inquiry. The late Sir Frank Sly[276] was appointed Chairman of the Committee. The Committee found in favour of the ryots, and recommended that the planters should refund a portion of the exactions made by them which the Committee had found to be unlawful, and that the *tinkathia* system should be abolished by law.[277]

Sir Edward Gait had a large share in getting the Committee to make a unanimous report and in getting the Agrarian Bill passed in accordance with the Committee's recommendations. Had he not adopted a firm attitude, and had he not brought all his tact to bear on the subject, the report would not have been unanimous, and the Agrarian Act would not have been passed. The planters wielded extraordinary power. *They*[M4] offered strenuous opposition to the Bill in spite of the report, but Sir Edward Gait remained firm up to the last and fully carried out the recommendations of the Committee.

^M4 Some of them

The *tinkathia* system, which had been in existence for about a century, was thus abolished, and with it the planters' raj came to an end. The ryots, who had all along remained crushed, now somewhat came to *their*

[276] Sir Frank George Sly joined the Indian Civil Service, served in the Central Provinces as commissioner of settlement, inspector-general of agriculture, commissioner of Berar, chief commissioner and Governor of the Central Provinces (1920–25).

[277] For the report of the Champaran Agrarian Enquiry Committee see Appendix XI, pp. 578–600, and for the Champaran Agrarian Bill, 1917, see Appendix XIII, pp. 601–04, *CWMG*, vol. 13.

[M5] realize their own power

own,[M5] and the superstition that the stain of indigo could never be washed out was exploded.

It was my desire to continue the constructive work[278] for some years, to establish more schools and to penetrate the villages more effectively. The ground had been prepared, but it did not please God, as often before, to allow my plans to be fulfilled. Fate decided otherwise and drove me to take up work elsewhere.

XX

IN TOUCH WITH LABOUR

Whilst I was yet winding up my work on the Committee, I received a letter from Sjts. Mohanlal Pandya[279] and Shankarlal Parikh[280] telling me of the failure of crops in the Kheda district, and asking me to guide the peasants, who were unable to pay the assessment. I had not the inclination, the ability or the courage to advise without an inquiry on the spot.

At the same time there came a letter from Shrimati Anasuyabai[281] about the condition of labour in Ahmedabad. Wages were low, the labourers had long been agitating for an increment, and I had a desire to guide them if I could. But I had not the *confidence*[M1] to direct even this comparatively small affair from that long distance. So I seized the first opportunity to go

[M1] ability

---

[278] 'in Champaran' to add.

[279] Mohanlal Kameshwar Pandya of Kathlal village. See Chapter XXIV for his role in the Kheda Satyagraha.

[280] Shankarlal Dwarkadas Parikh, of Kathlal village.

[281] Anasuya Sarabhai (1885–1972), sister of Ambalal Sarabhai, studied at the London School of Economics, actively participated in the Ahmedabad mill strike and founded the Majdoor Mahajan Sangh, affectionately called 'Motiben'.

to Ahmedabad.[282] I had hoped that I should be able to finish both these matters quickly and get back to Champaran to supervise the constructive work that had been inaugurated there.[283]

But things did not move as swiftly as I had wished, and I was unable to return to Champaran,[284] with the result that the schools closed down one by one. My co-workers and I had built many castles in the air, but they all vanished for the time being.

One of these was cow-protection work in Champaran, besides rural sanitation and education. I had seen, in the course of my travels, that cow-protection and Hindi propaganda had become the exclusive concern of the Marwadis. A Marwadi friend had sheltered me in his dharmsala whilst at Bettiah. Other Marwadis of the place had interested me in their goshala (dairy).[285] My ideas about cow-protection had been definitely formed then, and my conception of the work was the same as it is today. Cow-protection, in my opinion, included cattle-breeding, improvement of the stock, *humane treatment of bullocks*,[M2] formation of model dairies, etc. The Marwadi friends had promised

[M2] belabouring the bullocks within certain limits

---

[282] MKG wrote to Ambalal Sarabhai from Motihari on 21 December 1917, 'I do not wish to interfere with your business affairs at all . . . I think you should satisfy the weavers for the sake of Shrimati Anasuyabehn at any rate . . . why should not the mill-owners feel happy paying a little more to the workers? . . . In a single letter I have meddled in your business and your family affairs.' *CWMG*, vol. 14, p. 115. MKG discussed the question of the millhands on 4 and 5 December 1917 at Ahmedabad and again on 4, 5, 6 and 8 January 1918 at Ahmedabad. By 6 February MKG was back again in Gujarat addressing himself to the questions in Kheda and Ahmedabad. MKG was in the Patna and Champaran area from 20–25 May 1918.

[283] 'that had been inaugurated there' added in the English translation.

[284] 'for some time' to add.

[285] '(dairy)' added in the English translation.

full co-operation in this work, but as I could not fix myself up in Champaran, the scheme could not be carried out.

The goshala in Bettiah is still there,[286] but it has not become a model dairy, the Champaran bullock is still made to work beyond his capacity, and the so-called Hindu still cruelly belabours the poor animal and disgraces his religion.

That this work should have remained unrealized has been, to me, a continual regret, and whenever I go to Champaran and hear the gentle reproaches of the Marwadi and Bihari friends, I recall with a heavy sigh all those plans which I had to drop so abruptly.

The educational work in one way or another is going on in many places. But the cow-protection work had not taken firm root, and has not, therefore, progressed in the direction intended.

Whilst the Kheda peasants' question was still being discussed, I had already taken up the question of the mill-hands in Ahmedabad.[287]

I was in a most delicate situation. *The mill-hands' case was strong.*[M3] Shrimati Anasuyabai had to battle

[M3] To me the mill-hands' case appeared to be strong.

---

[286] MKG laid the foundation stone of the goshala on 7 October 1917.

[287] The question was regarding the payment of bonus. Since August 1916, Ahmedabad textile mills had begun to pay a 'plague bonus', an increase in wages necessitated by plague and the need of the mills to have workers despite plague. Some mills paid plague bonus as high as 70 to 80 per cent of workers' wages and continued to pay it even after the cessation of plague. The workers demanded a wage hike and hike in dearness allowance instead of a plague bonus. The dispute was about the quantum of this hike. For a chronicle of the Ahmedabad Mill Strike, see Mahadev Desai, *A Righteous Struggle*, translated from the Gujarati by Somnath P. Dave and edited by Bharatan Kumarappa (Ahmedabad: Navajivan, 1951). Erik Erikson's *Gandhi's Truth: On the Origins of Militant Non-Violence* (New York: W.W. Norton & Co.: 1970, 1993), remains an unparalleled inquiry into MKG's mind as also a deep study of the Ahmedabad mill strike.

against her own brother, Sjt. Ambalal Sarabhai, *who led the fray on behalf of the mill-owners.*[M4] My relations with them were friendly, and that made fighting with them the more difficult. I held consultations with them, and requested them to refer the dispute to arbitration, *but they refused to recognize the principle of arbitration.*[M5]

[M4] who played a principal role in this heartless battle between mill-hands and mill-owners

[M5] but the mill-owners refused to recognize the propriety of an intervention by arbitrators between them and the mill-hands

I had therefore to advise the labourers to go on strike. Before I did so, I came in very close contact with them and their leaders, and explained to them the conditions of a successful strike:

1. never to resort to violence,
2. never to molest *blacklegs,*[M6]
3. never to depend upon alms, and
4. to remain firm, no matter how long the strike continued, and to earn bread, *during the strike,*[M7] by any other honest labour.

[M6] those who wish to resume work

[M7] if their resources were exhausted

The leaders of the strike understood and accepted the conditions, and the labourers pledged themselves at a general meeting not to resume work until either their terms were accepted or the mill-owners agreed to refer the dispute to arbitration.

It was during this strike that I came to know intimately Sjt. Vallabhbhai Patel[288] and Shankarlal Banker. Shrimati Anasuyabai I knew well before this.

---

[288] Vallabhbhai Jhaverbhai Patel (1875–1950), later revered as Sardar Patel, leader of the Indian National Congress, called to the Bar from the Middle Temple, joined public life through his work in the Ahmedabad Municipality and the Gujarati Sabha. A close associate of MKG, participated in the Kheda Satyagraha, led the Nagpur Satyagraha (1923) and Bardoli Satyagraha (1928); he was imprisoned along with MKG in Yeravada Prison (1932–34). As independent India's first deputy prime minister and home minister, he played a pioneering role in the political and administrative integration of princely India into the new republic. Married to Jhaverba, with whom he had a daughter, Manibehn, and a son, Dahyabhai.

We had daily meetings of the strikers under the shade of a tree on the bank of the Sabarmati. They attended the meeting in their *thousands*[M8] and I reminded them in my speeches of their pledge and of the duty to maintain peace and self-respect. They daily paraded the streets of the city in peaceful[289] procession,[290] carrying their banner bearing the inscription *'Ek Tek'* (keep the pledge).

M8 hundreds

The strike went on for twenty-one days. During the continuance of the strike I consulted the mill-owners from time to time and entreated them to do justice to the labourers. 'We have our pledge too,' they used to say. 'Our relations with the labourers are those of parents and children . . . How can we brook the interference of a third party? Where is the room for arbitration?'

XXI

A PEEP INTO THE ASHRAM

Before I proceed to describe the progress of the labour dispute it is essential to have a peep into the Ashram. All the while I was in Champaran the Ashram was never out of my mind, and occasionally I *paid*[291] *it flying visits.*[M1]

M1 visited it as well

At that time the Ashram was in Kochrab, a small village near Ahmedabad. Plague broke out in this village, and I saw evident danger to the safety of the Ashram children. It was impossible to keep ourselves immune from the effects of the surrounding insanitation, however scrupulously we might observe the rules of

---

[289] 'peaceful' added in the English translation.

[290] 'and came to the meeting as one' to add.

[291] 'sometimes I used to pay' in the first edition.

cleanliness within the Ashram walls. We were not then equal either to getting the Kochrab people to observe these rules nor to serving the village otherwise.

Our ideal was to have the Ashram at a safe[292] distance both from town and village, and *yet at a manageable distance from either. And we were determined, some day, to settle on ground of our own.*[M2]

The plague, I felt, was sufficient notice to quit Kochrab. Sjt. Punjabhai Hirachand, a merchant in Ahmedabad,[293] had come in close contact with the Ashram, and used to serve us in a number of matters in a pure and selfless spirit. He had a wide experience of things in Ahmedabad, and he volunteered to procure us suitable land.[294] I went about with him north and south of Kochrab in search of land, and then suggested to him to find out a piece of land three or four miles to the north. He hit upon the present site.[295] Its vicinity to the Sabarmati Central Jail was for me a special attraction. As jail-going was understood to be the *normal lot*[M3] of satyagrahis, I liked this position. And I knew that the sites selected for jails have generally clean surroundings.

In about eight days the sale was executed. There was no building on the land and no tree. But its situation on the bank of the river and its solitude were great advantages.

We decided to start by living under canvas, and having a tin shed for a kitchen, till permanent houses were built.

[M2] not so far that reaching there would be difficult. And some day the Ashram had to settle on its own open land to justify the name, Ashram.

[M3] fate

---

[292] 'safe' added in the English translation.

[293] 'a merchant in Ahmedabad' added in the English translation.

[294] 'as soon as possible' to add.

[295] The stamp paper on which the sale deed was to be written was purchased on 11 December 1916. On 11 May 1917 an agreement to sale was done and the deed of conveyance was signed on 31 May 1917, which was registered on 13 June 1917. The Ashram at Sabarmati was established on 17 June 1917.

The Ashram had been slowly growing. We were now over forty souls, men, women and children, having our meals at a common kitchen. The whole conception about the removal was mine, the execution was as usual left to[296] Maganlal.

Our difficulties, before we had permanent living accommodation, were great. The rains were impending, and provisions had to be got from the city four miles away. The ground, which had been a waste, was infested with snakes, and it was no small risk to live with little children under such conditions. The general rule was not to kill the snakes, though I confess none of us had shed the fear of these reptiles, nor have we even now.

The rule of not killing venomous reptiles[297] has been practised for the most part at Phoenix, Tolstoy Farm and Sabarmati. At each of these places we had to settle on waste lands.[298] We have had, however, no loss of life occasioned by snakebite. I see, with the eye of faith, in this circumstance the hand of the God of Mercy. Let no one cavil at this, saying that God can never be partial, and that He has no time to meddle with the humdrum affairs of men. I have no other language to express the fact of the matter, to describe this uniform experience of mine. *Human language can but imperfectly describe God's ways. I am sensible of the fact that they are indescribable and inscrutable.*[M4] But if mortal man will dare to describe them, he has no better medium than his own *inarticulate speech.*[M5] Even if it be a superstition to believe that complete immunity from harm for twenty-five years in spite of a fairly regular practice of non-killing is not a fortuitous accident but a grace of God, I should still hug that superstition.

[M4] Despite using this-worldly language to describe God's actions, I know that His 'work' is indescribable.

[M5] child-like prattle

---

[296] 'Late' to add. Maganlal Gandhi died on 23 April 1928 at Patna.

[297] 'venomous reptiles' translates *hinsak jiva*, literally, 'carnivorous animals'.

[298] 'All of them were fairly well infested with snakes.' To add.

During the strike of the mill-hands in Ahmedabad the foundation of the Ashram weaving-shed was being laid. For the principal activity of the Ashram was then weaving. Spinning had not so far been *possible for* [M6] us.[299]

[M6] discovered by

XXII

THE FAST

For the first two weeks the mill-hands exhibited great courage and self-restraint and *daily held monster meetings*.[M1] On these occasions I used to remind them of their pledge,[300] and they would shout back to me the assurance that they would rather die than break their word.

[M1] attended the daily meetings in large numbers

But at last they began to show signs of flagging.[301] Just as physical weakness in men manifests itself in

---

[299] 'Therefore we decided to first build the weaving shed and its foundation was being laid.' To add.

[300] The Workers' Pledge:

The Workers have resolved:

(1) that they will not resume work until a 35 per cent increase on the July wage is secured;
(2) that they will not, during the period of lock-out, cause any disturbance or resort to violence or indulge in looting, nor damage any property of the employers or abuse anyone but will remain peaceful.

CWMG, vol. 14, p. 215.

[301] There were those in the city who also argued that the millhands should end their hardships by accepting lower increase in wages. One of them was Barrister Jivanlal Desai, whose bungalow in Kochrab was the site of the first Ashram at Ahmedabad. MKG wrote to him, 'Considering it useless to persuade me, why do you not try to persuade the mill-owners? They do not have to humiliate themselves.' *CWMG*, vol. 14, p. 247. MKG also wrote

irascibility, their attitude towards the blacklegs became more and more menacing as the strike seemed to weaken, and I began to fear an outbreak of rowdyism on their part. The attendance at their daily meetings also began to dwindle by degrees, and despondency and despair were writ large on the faces of those who did attend. Finally the information was brought to me that the strikers had begun to totter.[302] I felt deeply troubled and set to thinking furiously[303] as to what my duty was in the circumstances. I had had experience of a *gigantic strike in South Africa, but the situation that confronted me here was different. The mill-hands had taken the pledge at my suggestion. They had repeated it before me day after day, and the very idea that they might now go back upon it was to me inconceivable. Was it pride or was it my love for the labourers*

---

to Mangaldas Parekh, who had not joined the millowners and had kept his mills working by paying workers the same bonus as the 'plague bonus'. 'Why is it taken for granted that I can get the workers to accept anything I want? I claim that the workers are under my control because of the means I have adopted. Shall I now see to it that they break their pledge? . . . But why don't you participate in this? It does not become you merely to watch this great struggle unconcernedly.' *CWMG*, vol. 14, p. 248.

[302] On 12 March 1918 the millowners lifted the lockout and expressed their willingness to take back all those who would accept a 20 per cent increase, as against the 35 per cent demanded by the workers. On the day the lockout was lifted, Ambalal Sarabhai sent MKG a letter, which he destroyed after reading and did not allow MD to make a copy of the reply but permitted only a summary of it from memory. The summary of the reply suggests that Ambalal Sarabhai's letter was about threats being issued to those workers who had decided to accept the 20 per cent raise and resume work. 'I never wished that there should be any pressure on the workers . . . I am even ready, myself, to escort any worker who says he wants to attend the mill.' *CWMG*, vol. 14, p. 250. MKG counselled the workers, 'Workers should remember our pledge that, if they bring pressure to bear on their fellows and use threats to stop them from going to work, we shall not find it possible to help them.' Ibid.

[303] 'furiously' added in the English translation.

and my passionate regard for truth that was at the back of this feeling—who can say?[M2]

One morning[304]—it was at a mill-hands' meeting—while I was still groping and unable to see my way clearly, the light came to me. Unbidden and all by themselves the words came to my lips: 'Unless the strikers rally,' I declared to the meeting, 'and continue the strike till a settlement is reached or till they leave the mills altogether,[305] I will not touch any food.'

The labourers[306] were thunderstruck. Tears began to course down Anasuyabehn's cheeks. The labourers broke out, 'Not you but we shall fast. *It would be monstrous if you were to fast.*[M3] Please forgive us for our lapse,[307] we will now remain faithful to our pledge to the end.'[308]

'There is no need for you to fast,' I replied. 'It would be enough if you could remain true to your pledge. As you know we are without funds, and we do not want to continue our strike by living on public charity. You should therefore try to eke out a bare existence by some kind of labour, so that you may be able to remain unconcerned, no matter how long the

[M2] labourers' strike in South Africa, but this was a new experience. The pledge that was taken at my suggestion, a pledge to which I bore witness every day, how was that pledge to be broken? This idea could be considered as pride, or it could be considered as love for the labourers and for truth.

[M3] But fast you cannot.

---

[304] 15 March 1918. MD describes the circumstances preceding the meeting: 'One day Shri Chhaganlal Gandhi was requesting the workers of the Jugaldas Chawl to attend the morning meeting, when they confronted him with these words, "What is it to Anasuyabehn and Gandhiji? They come and go in their car; they eat sumptuous food, but we are suffering death agonies; attending meetings does not prevent starvation." These rumours reached Gandhiji's ears. Generally Gandhiji does not mind criticism, but these bitter words which described the situation realistically, pierced this heart.' Desai, *A Righteous Struggle*, pp. 25–26.

[305] 'or till they leave the mills altogether' added in the English translation.

[306] 'who were present' to add.

[307] 'for our lapse' added in the English translation.

[308] 'to the end' added in the English translation.

strike may continue. As for my fast, it will be broken only after the strike is settled.'

In the meantime Vallabhbhai was trying to find some employment for the strikers under the Municipality, but there was not much hope of success there. Maganlal Gandhi suggested that, as we needed sand for filling the foundation of our weaving school in the Ashram, a number of them might be employed for that purpose. The labourers welcomed the proposal. Anasuyabehn led the way with a basket on her head and soon an endless stream of labourers carrying baskets of sand on their heads could be seen issuing out of the hollow of the river-bed. It was a sight worth seeing. The labourers felt themselves infused with a new strength, and it became difficult to cope with the task of paying out wages to them.

My fast was not free from a grave defect. For as I have already mentioned in a previous chapter, I enjoyed very close and cordial relations with the mill-owners, and my fast could not but affect their decision. As a satyagrahi I knew that I might not fast against them, but ought to leave them free to be influenced by the mill-hands' strike alone. My fast[M4] was undertaken not on account of lapse of the mill-owners, but on account of that of the labourers in which, as their representative, I felt I had a share. With the mill-owners, I could only plead; to fast against them would amount to coercion.[309]

M4 penance

---

[309] 'coercion' translates the word '*tragu*' in the original. In Gujarat and Rajasthan, *trag* or *tragu* was widely practised almost until the end of the nineteenth century. The word does not find place in the Sanskrit dictionary of Monier Williams, collated in the last quarter of the nineteenth century. George Abraham Grierson wrote, 'One is tempted to connect it with the Sanskrit root *trai* or *tra* "to protect", but the termination *ga* presents difficulties which I cannot get over.' See Henry Yule and A.C. Burnell, *Hobson-Jobson: A Glossary of Colloquial Anglo-Indian Words and Phrases* (first published 1886; reprint edition: London: Curzon Press, 1995, p. 937). The practice of *tragu* entailed fasting unto

Yet in spite of my knowledge that my fast was bound to put pressure upon them, as in fact it did, I felt I could not help it. The duty to undertake *it*[M5] seemed to me to be clear.

I tried to set the mill-owners at ease. 'There is not the slightest necessity for you to withdraw from your position,' I said to them. But they received my words coldly and even flung keen, delicate bits of sarcasm at me, as indeed they had a perfect right to do.[310]

The principal man at the back of the mill-owners' unbending attitude towards the strike was Sheth Ambalal. His resolute will and transparent sincerity were wonderful and captured my heart. It was a pleasure to be pitched against him. The strain produced by my fast upon the opposition, of which he was the head, cut me, therefore, to the quick. And then, Sarladevi, his wife, was attached to me with the affection of a blood-sister, and I could not bear to see her anguish on account of my action.

Anasuyabehn and a number of other friends and labourers shared the fast with me on the first day. But after some difficulty I was able to dissuade them from continuing it further.

[M5] such a tainted fast

---

death, and, in extreme situations, to enforce an agreement or to avenge a perceived wrong, injustice or dishonour, men and women of the Bhat and Charan communities would sacrifice their body parts and their lives.

[310] Erik Erikson has captured something of the anger and predicament of the mill-owners, particularly of Ambalal Sarabhai, given his close relations with MKG and the fact that his sister Anasuya was one of the leaders of the labourers. MKG stayed the first night of the fast at Anasuya Sarabhai's house. 'Ambalal's feelings, as usual, were more complex. He felt more personally touched, and went out to sit by Gandhiji, who had reclined on his mat to preserve his strength. Ambalal felt angry, too. The fast, as he put it, was a "dirty trick". "Look here," he is said to have told Gandhiji, in essence, "You are changing the very premise of this whole affair. This is between owners and the workers—where does *your* life come in?"' *Gandhi's Truth*, p. 353.

The net result of it was that an atmosphere of goodwill was created all round. The hearts of the mill-owners were touched, and they set about discovering some means for a settlement. Anasuyabehn's house became the venue of their discussions. Sjt. Anandshankar Dhruva[311] intervened and was in the end appointed arbitrator, and the strike was called off after I had fasted only for three days.[312] The mill-owners commemorated the event by distributing sweets among the labourers, and thus a settlement was reached after 21 days' strike.

At the meeting held to celebrate the settlement, both the mill-owners and the Commissioner were present. The advice which the latter gave to the mill-hands on this occasion was: 'You should always act as Mr. Gandhi advises you.' Almost immediately after these events I had to engage in a tussle with this very gentleman. But circumstances were changed, and he had changed with the circumstances. He then set about warning the Patidars of Kheda against following my advice!

I must not close this chapter without noting here an incident, as amusing as it was pathetic. It happened in connection with the distribution of sweets.[313] The mill-owners had ordered a very large quantity, and it was a problem how to distribute it among the thousands

---

[311] Anandshankar Bapubhai Dhruva (1859–1942), eminent littérateur, scholar and educationist, appointed vice-chancellor of the Banaras Hindu University in 1920, a position that he held for twenty years.

[312] According to the terms of settlement an increase of 35 per cent was given on the first day—in keeping with the pledge of the workers—20 per cent on the second day as determined by the millowners and 27. 5 per cent from the third day, till such time as the arbitrator's award was made; the remaining 7.5 per cent was to be settled by either the owners or the workers, depending upon the arbitrator's award. The arbitrator's award was given on 10 August 1918, upholding the 35 per cent increase.

[313] 'It happened in connection with the distribution of sweets.' Added in the English translation.

of labourers. It was decided that it would be the fittest thing to distribute it in the open, beneath the very tree under which the pledge had been taken, especially as it would have been extremely inconvenient to assemble them all together in any other place.

I had taken it for granted that the men who had observed strict discipline for full 21 days would without any difficulty be able to remain standing in an orderly manner while the sweets were being distributed, and not make an impatient scramble for them. But when it came to the test, *all the*[M6] methods that were tried for making the distribution failed. Again and again their ranks would break into confusion after distribution had proceeded for a couple of minutes. The leaders of the mill-hands tried their best to restore order, but in vain. The confusion, the crush and the scramble at last became so great that quite an amount of the sweets was spoiled by being trampled underfoot, and the attempt to distribute them in the open had finally to be given up. With difficulty we succeeded in taking away the remaining sweets to Sheth Ambalal's bungalow in Mirzapur.[314] Sweets were distributed comfortably[315] the next day within the compound of that bungalow.

[M6] two or three

The comic side of this incident is obvious, but the pathetic side bears mention. Subsequent inquiry revealed the fact that the beggar population of Ahmedabad, having got scent of the fact that sweets were to be distributed under the *Ek-Tek* tree, had gone there in large numbers, and it was their hungry[316] scramble for the sweets that had created all the confusion and disorder.

The grinding poverty and starvation with which our country is afflicted is such that it drives more and more men every year into the ranks of the beggars, *whose*

---

[314] Shanti Sadan.

[315] 'comfortably' added in the English translation.

[316] 'hungry' added in the English translation.

M7 and in order to secure food they break normal boundaries

M8 rich

desperate struggle for bread renders them insensible to all feelings of decency and self-respect.[M7] And our *philanthropists,*[M8] instead of providing work for them and insisting on their working for bread,[317] give them alms.

XXIII

THE KHEDA SATYAGRAHA

No breathing time was, however, in store for me. Hardly was the Ahmedabad mill-hands' strike over, when I had to plunge into the Kheda Satyagraha struggle.[318]

A condition approaching famine had arisen in the Kheda district owing to a widespread failure of crops, and the Patidars of Kheda were considering the question of getting the revenue assessment for the year suspended.

Sjt. Amritlal Thakkar had already inquired into and reported on the situation and[319] personally discussed the question with the Commissioner, before I gave definite advice to the cultivators. Sjts. Mohanlal Pandya and Shankarlal Parikh had also thrown themselves into the fight, and had set up an agitation in the Bombay Legislative Council through Sjt. Vithalbhai Patel[320] and

---

[317] 'and insisting on their working for bread' added in the English translation.

[318] The last leaflet on the millstrike was issued on 19 March 1918 and on 21 March MKG in a public meeting in Ahmedabad declared the necessity of intervention in the Kheda situation. He reached Nadiad the same evening to commence the campaign. For a history of the Kheda Satyagraha, see David Hardiman, *Peasant Nationalists of Gujarat: Kheda District, 1917–1934* (New Delhi: Oxford University Press, 1982).

[319] 'I' to add.

[320] Vithalbhai Patel (1873–1933), called to the Bar from the Middle Temple, one of the founders of the Swaraj Party, member of the Bombay Legislative Council, member of the Central Legislative

the late Sir Gokuldas Kahandas Parekh.[321] *More than one deputation had waited upon the Governor in that connection.*[M1]

I was at this time President of the Gujarat Sabha.[322] The Sabha sent petitions and telegrams to the Government and even patiently swallowed the insults and threats of the Commissioner.[323] The conduct of the officials on this occasion was so ridiculous and undignified as to be almost incredible now.[324]

The cultivators' demand was as clear as daylight, and so moderate as to *make out a strong case for its acceptance.*[M2] Under the Land Revenue Rules, if the crop was four annas[325] or under, the cultivators could claim full suspension of the revenue assessment for the year. According to the official figures the crop was said to be over four annas. The contention of the cultivators, on the other hand, was that it was less than four annas. *But the Government was in no mood to listen, and regarded*

[M1] Deputations had met the Government.

[M2] require no agitation

Council, elected its president in 1925. He was the elder brother of Sardar Patel.

[321] Sir Gokuldas Kahandas Parekh, a pleader from Bombay, member of the Bombay Legislative Council, knighted in 1921.

[322] Gujarat Sabha, a body established in 1884 to represent the grievances of people to the government. By 23 June 1917 MKG was a member of its executive committee.

[323] On 1 January 1918 the Gujarat Sabha wrote to the Government of Bombay, urging exemption in some cases, and postponement in others, of the assessment of land revenue. The Sabha also advised the farmers of Kheda to suspend payments till a reply had been received. On 10 January 1918 the Sabha delegation met F.G. Pratt, the commissioner of the Northern Division, who agreed to meet only its secretaries and also stated that he might advise the government to declare the Sabha an illegal body.

[324] 'undignified as now to appear almost incredible' in the first edition.

[325] Sixteen annas made a rupee; four annas equalled a quarter of a rupee. This was used to measure agricultural yield; a four-anna crop indicated one-fourth of the average yield per unit. This unit continues to be in use even for the measure of crop insurance.

*the popular demand for arbitration as lese majeste.*M3 At last all petitioning and prayer having failed, after taking counsel with co-workers, I advised the Patidars to resort to satyagraha.[326]

Besides the *volunteers*M4 of Kheda, my principal comrades in this struggle were Sjts. Vallabhbhai Patel, Shankarlal Banker, Shrimati Anasuyabehn, Sjts. Indulal Yagnik,[327] Mahadev Desai and others. Sjt. Vallabhbhai, in joining the struggle, had to suspend a splendid and growing practice at the bar, which for all practical purposes he was never able to resume.

We fixed up our headquarters at the Nadiad Anathashram,[328] no other place being available which would have been large enough to accommodate all of us.

The following pledge was signed by the satyagrahis:

'Knowing that the crops of our villages are less than four annas, we requested the Government to

[326] MKG wrote to the Governor of Bombay, 'But if this last request of mine is ignored and properties are confiscated or sold, or land forfeited, I shall be compelled to advise the peasants openly not to pay up land revenue.' *CWMG*, vol. 14, p. 259. To this the Governor replied on 17 March, 'The Government has been kept fully informed of what has been happening in Kheda district and is satisfied that the Collector and other officers of the Revenue Department while acting strictly according to rules and regulations have the interests of the agriculturalists at heart.' Ibid., p. 260. On 22 March MKG made one final effort at settlement before holding public meetings or launching satyagraha; that having failed, the first mass meeting was held at Nadiad on 22 March 1918.

[327] Indulal Kanaiyalal Yagnik (1892–1972), member of the Home Rule League and the Servants of India Society, founder editor of *Young India*, which was later handed over to MKG, one of the founders of the All India Kisan Sabha, post-Independence led the Maha Gujarat Movement for the creation of the separate state of Gujarat, elected to the 2nd, 3rd, 4th and 5th Lok Sabha (1957–72).

[328] 'let nobody consider any special merit in living at Anathashram' to add. Anathashram is an orphanage, founded in 1908.

suspend the collection of revenue assessment till the ensuing year, but the Government has not acceded to our prayer. Therefore, we, the undersigned, hereby solemnly declare that we shall not, of our own accord, pay to the Government the full or the remaining revenue for the year. We shall let the Government take whatever legal steps it may think fit and gladly suffer the consequences of our non-payment. We shall rather let our lands be forfeited than that by voluntary payment we should allow our case to be considered false or should compromise our self-respect. Should the Government, however, agree to suspend collection of the second instalment of the assessment throughout the district, such amongst us as are in a position to pay will pay up the whole or the balance of the revenue that may be due. The reason why those[329] who are able to pay still withhold payment is that, if they pay up, the poorer ryots may in a panic sell their chattels or incur debts to pay their dues, and thereby bring suffering upon themselves. In these circumstances we feel that, for the sake of the poor, it is the duty even of those who can afford to pay to withhold payment of their assessment.'[330]

I cannot devote many chapters to this struggle. So a number of sweet recollections in this connection will have to be *crowded*[M5] out. Those who want to make a [M5 left] fuller and deeper study of this important fight would do well to read the full and authentic history of the Kheda Satyagraha by Sjt. Shankarlal Parikh[331] of Kathlal, Kheda.

---

[329] 'of us' to add.

[330] For the pledge, see *CWMG*, vol. 14, p. 279. There are some variations between the two texts.

[331] Shankarlal Dwarkadas Parikh, *Kheda Satyagraha* (Ahmedabad: Gujarat Vidya Sabha, first published 1922; second edition 1954).

XXIV

'THE ONION THIEF'

Champaran being in a far away corner of India, and the Press having been kept out of the campaign, it did not attract *visitors*[M1] from outside. *Not so with the Kheda campaign, of which the happenings were reported in the Press from day to day.*[M2]

The Gujaratis were deeply interested in the fight, which was to them[332] a novel experiment. They were ready to pour forth their riches for the success of the cause.[333] It was not easy for them to see that satyagraha could not be conducted simply by means of money. Money is the thing that it least needs. In spite of my remonstrance, the Bombay merchants sent us more money than necessary, so that we had some balance left at the end of the campaign.

At the same time the satyagrahi *volunteers*[M3] had to learn the new lesson of simplicity. I cannot say that they imbibed it fully, but they considerably changed their ways of life.

For the Patidar farmers,[334] too, *the*[M4] fight was quite a new thing. We had, therefore, to go about from village to village explaining the principles of satyagraha.

The main thing was to rid the agriculturists of their fear by making them realize that the officials were not the masters but the servants of the people, inasmuch as they received their salaries from the *taxpayer*.[M5] And then it seemed well nigh impossible to make them realize the duty of combining civility with fearlessness.

[M1] spectators

[M2] The Kheda struggle had become a subject for the Press.

[M3] army

[M4] this kind of

[M5] people's money

---

[332] 'the fight, which was to them a' added in the English translation. The original read, 'this novel experiment'.

[333] 'for the success of the cause' added in the English translation.

[334] 'farmers' added in the English translation.

Once they had shed the fear of the officials, how could
they be stopped from returning their insults? And yet if
they resorted to incivility it would spoil their satyagraha,
like a drop of arsenic in milk. I realized later that they
had less fully learnt the lesson of civility than I had
expected.[335] Experience has taught me that civility is the
most difficult part of satyagraha. Civility does not here
mean the mere outward gentleness of speech cultivated
for the occasion, *but an inborn gentleness and desire to do
the opponent good. These should show themselves in every act
of a satyagrahi.*[M6]

> [M6] Civility means an inward respect for the opponent, pure feelings, a concern for their interests, and conduct to match these.

In the initial stages, though the people exhibited
much courage, the Government did not seem inclined to
take strong action. But as the people's firmness showed
no signs of wavering, the Government began coercion.
The attachment officers sold people's cattle and seized
whatever movables they could lay hands on. Penalty
notices were served, and in some cases standing crops
were attached. This unnerved the *peasants*,[M7] some of
whom paid up their dues, while others desired to place
safe movables in the way of the officials so that they
might attach them to realize the dues. On the other
hand some were prepared to fight to the bitter end.

> [M7] people

While these things were going on, one of Sjt.
Shankarlal Parikh's tenants paid up the assessment
in respect of his land. This created a sensation. Sjt.
Shankarlal Parikh immediately *made amends*[M8] for his
tenant's mistake by giving away for charitable purposes
the land for which the assessment had been paid. He
thus saved his honour and set a good example to others.

> [M8] atoned

With a view to steeling the hearts of those who were
frightened, I advised the people, under the leadership of
Sjt. Mohanlal Pandya, to remove the crop of onion,
from a field which had been in my opinion wrongly
attached. I did not regard this as *civil disobedience*,[M9] but

> [M9] a breach of law

---

[335] 'than I had expected' added in the English translation.

even if it was, I suggested that this attachment of standing crops,[336] though it might be in accordance with law, was morally wrong, and was nothing short of looting, and that therefore it was the people's duty to remove the onion in spite of the order of attachment. *This was a good opportunity for the people to learn a lesson in courting fines or imprisonment, which was the necessary consequence of such disobedience.*[M10] For Sjt. Mohanlal Pandya it was a thing after his heart. He did not like the campaign to end without someone undergoing suffering in the shape of[337] imprisonment for something done consistently with the principles of satyagraha. So he volunteered to remove the onion crop from the field, and in this seven or eight friends joined him.

It was impossible for the Government to leave them free.[M11] The arrest of Sjt. Mohanlal and his companions added to the people's enthusiasm. When the fear of jail disappears, *repression puts heart into the people.*[M12] Crowds of them besieged the court-house on the day of the hearing. Pandya and his companions were convicted and sentenced to a brief term of imprisonment.[338] I *was*[M13] of opinion that the conviction was wrong, because the act of removing the onion crop could not come under the definition of 'theft' in the Penal Code. *But no appeal was filed as the policy was to avoid the law-courts.*[M14]

A procession escorted the 'convicts' to jail, and on that day Sjt. Mohanlal Pandya earned from the people the honoured title of *'dungli chor'* (onion thief) which he enjoys to this day.

[M10] I had clearly shown to the people that this entailed the danger of fine as also imprisonment.

[M11] How could the Government not arrest them?

[M12] punishment by the State, instead of repressing people, gives them valour.

[M13] am

[M14] But no one was inclined to file an appeal.

---

[336] 'for a meagre amount of revenue' to add.

[337] 'suffering in the shape of' added in the English translation.

[338] Mohanlal Pandya and five others from village Navagam were charged on 8 June 1918, in the court of the collector acting as a district magistrate. Two of them were given ten days of imprisonment while the rest were awarded twenty days' imprisonment.

The conclusion of the Kheda Satyagraha I will leave to the next chapter.

XXV

END OF KHEDA SATYAGRAHA

The campaign *came to an unexpected end.*[M1] It was clear that the people were exhausted, and I hesitated to let the unbending be driven to utter ruin. I was casting about for some graceful way of terminating the struggle which would be acceptable to a satyagrahi. Such a one appeared quite unexpectedly. The Mamlatdar of the Nadiad Taluk sent me word that, if well-to-do Patidars paid up, the poorer ones would be granted suspension. I asked for a written undertaking to that effect, which was given. But as a Mamlatdar could be responsible only for his Taluk, I inquired of the Collector, who alone could give an undertaking in respect of the whole district, whether the Mamlatdar's undertaking was true for the whole district.[339] He replied that orders declaring suspension in terms of the Mamlatdar's letter had been already issued. I was not aware of it, but if it was a fact, the people's pledge had been fulfilled. The pledge, it will be remembered,[340] had the same thing for its object, and so we expressed ourselves satisfied with the orders.

However, the end was far from making *me*[M2] feel happy, in-as much as it lacked the *grace*[M3] with which the termination of every satyagraha campaign ought to be accompanied. The Collector carried on as though he had done nothing by way of a settlement. The poor were to be granted suspension, but hardly any got the

[M1] ended in a strange manner

[M2] any of us

[M3] sweetness

---

[339] 'whether the Mamlatdar's undertaking was true for the whole district' added in the English translation.

[340] 'it will be remembered' added in the English translation.

benefit of it. It was the people's right to determine
who was poor, but they could not exercise it. I was
sad that they had not the strength to exercise the right.
Although, therefore, the termination was celebrated as
a triumph of satyagraha, *I could not enthuse over it, as it*
lacked the essentials of a complete triumph.[M4]

The end of a satyagraha campaign can be described
as *worthy*,[M5] only when it leaves the satyagrahis stronger
and more spirited than they are in the beginning.[341]

The campaign was not, however, without its
indirect results which we can see[342] today and the benefit
of which we are reaping. The Kheda Satyagraha marks
the beginning of an awakening among the peasants of
Gujarat, the beginning of their true political education.

Dr. Besant's[343] brilliant Home Rule agitation had
certainly touched the peasants, but it was the Kheda
campaign that compelled the educated public workers to
establish contact with the actual life of the peasants. They
learnt to identify themselves with the latter. They found
their proper sphere of work, their capacity for sacrifice
increased. That Vallabhbhai found himself during this
campaign was by itself no small achievement. We could
realize its measure during the *flood*[M6] relief operations last
year[344] and the Bardoli Satyagraha[345] this year. Public life

[M4] it appeared to me lustreless
from this point of view

[M5] pure

[M6] emergency

---

[341] 'This I did not see.' To add.

[342] 'even' to add.

[343] 'The learned' to add before her name.

[344] Many towns of Gujarat suffered floods in 1927 due to unusually
higher than average rainfall in parts of central and south Gujarat.
Vallabhbhai Patel led the relief efforts and persuaded Viceroy
Lord Irwin to visit Ahmedabad on 9 December 1927 and provide
government assistance for flood relief.

[345] Bardoli, then a taluka in Surat district of Gujarat, had a 222 sq.
miles area with 173 villages. The land revenue assessment of
the area was revised in 1926 and increased by 30 per cent. The
peasants of the area, led by Vallabhbhai Patel, took a pledge
of satyagraha on 12 February 1928, after all efforts to reason

in Gujarat became instinct with a new energy and a new vigour. The Patidar peasant[346] came to an unforgettable consciousness of his strength. The lesson was indelibly imprinted on the public mind that the salvation of the people depends upon themselves, upon their capacity for suffering and sacrifice. Through the Kheda campaign satyagraha took firm root in the soil of Gujarat.

Although, therefore, I found nothing to enthuse over in the termination of the satyagraha, the Kheda peasants were jubilant, because they knew that what they had achieved was commensurate with their effort, and they had found the true and infallible method for a redress of their grievances. This knowledge was enough justification for their jubilation.[347]

Nevertheless the Kheda *peasants*[M7] had not fully understood the inner meaning of satyagraha, and they saw it to their cost, as we shall see in the chapters to follow.

[M7] people

XXVI

PASSION FOR UNITY

The Kheda campaign was launched while the *deadly war*[M1] in Europe was still going on. Now a crisis had arrived, and[348] the Viceroy had invited various leaders to a war conference in Delhi.[349] I had also been urged

[M1] Great War

---

with the government had failed; intense agitation culminated in the government accepting the chief demands of the peasants in August 1928. Vallabhbhai came to be called 'Sardar'—the leader—after this satyagraha.

[346] 'peasant' added in the English translation.

[347] 'against the government' to add.

[348] 'Now a crisis had arrived, and' added in the English translation.

[349] The Viceroy opened the war conference on 25 April 1918.

to attend the conference. I have already referred to the cordial relations between Lord Chelmsford, the Viceroy, and myself.

In response to the invitation I went to Delhi.[350] I had, however, objections to taking part in the conference,[351] the principal one being the exclusion from it of leaders like the Ali Brothers.[352] They were then in jail. I had met them only once or twice, though I had heard much about them. Everyone had spoken highly of their services and their courage. I had not then come in close[353] touch with Hakim Saheb,[354] but[355] Principal Rudra and Dinabandhu Andrews had told me

[350] MKG reached Delhi on 26 April and stayed at Professor Sushil Rudra's house at St Stephen's College.

[351] On 10 April MKG wrote to J.L. Maffey, the PS to the Viceroy, 'What vexes me, however is the case of the Ali Brothers.' *CWMG*, vol. 14, p. 321. On 14 April he wrote a note to Maffey, 'In all humility I ask Lord Chelmsford not only to release the brothers but take them in his counsel, as also Mr. Tilak. They are *not* enemies of the state.' Ibid., p. 338. Having gone to Delhi, MKG wrote to Sir Claude Hill that he would not be able to serve on any committee nor speak on the main resolution. On 27 April MKG had interviews with Maffey and later with the Viceroy on the matter of participating in the conference.

[352] 'Lokmanya and others' to add. Ali brothers refer to Maulana Shaukat Ali (1873–1937) and his brother Maulana Mohammad Ali (1878–1931). Maulana Mohammad Ali, who studied at Aligarh Muslim University and Oxford University, was a poet, scholar, journalist and one of the founders of the All Indian Muslim League as also the Jamia Millia Islamia. The Ali brothers founded and edited an Urdu journal, *Hamdard*, and English journal, *Comrade*. In 1924 MKG undertook a twenty-one-day fast from 17 September to 8 October, during which he stayed at the house of Maulana Mohammad Ali from 17 September to 25 September.

[353] 'close' added in the English translation.

[354] Hakim Ajmal Khan (1868–1927), took great interest in the expansion of the Unani system of medicine, one of the co-founders of Jamia Millia Islamia and its first chancellor (1920–27).

[355] 'the late' to add.

a deal in his praise. I had met Mr. Shuaib Qureshi[356] and *Mr.*[M2] Khwaja[357] at the Muslim League in Calcutta. I had also come in contact with Drs. Ansari[358] and Abdur Rehman.[359] I was seeking the friendship of good Mussalmans, and was eager to understand the Mussalman mind through contact with their purest and most patriotic representatives. I therefore never needed any pressure to go with them, *wherever they took me, in order to get into intimate touch with them.*[M3]

    I had realized early enough in South Africa that there was no genuine friendship between the Hindus and the Mussalmans. I never missed a single opportunity to remove *obstacles in the way of unity.*[M4] It was not in my nature to placate anyone by adulation, or at the cost of self-respect. *But my South African experiences had convinced me*[M5] that it would be on the question of Hindu–Muslim unity that my ahimsa would be put to its severest test, and that the question presented the widest field for my experiments in ahimsa. The conviction is still there. Every moment of my life I realize that[360] God is putting me on my trial.[361]

    Having such strong convictions on the question when I returned from South Africa, I prized the contact with the Brothers. *But before closer touch could be established they were isolated.*[M6] Maulana Mahomed Ali used to

[M2] Barrister

[M3] to their society

[M4] the sourness between them

[M5] I knew from then

[M6] Our affection grew. But soon after our acquaintance the Government buried the Ali Brothers alive.

---

[356] Shuaib Qureshi, editor, *New Era.*

[357] Khwaja Abdul Majid (1885–1962), studied at Cambridge, called to the Bar in 1910, chancellor, Jamia Millia Islamia (1936–62), founded the All India Muslim Majlis to oppose the two-nation theory and the partition.

[358] Dr. Mukhtar Ahmed Ansari (1880–1936), studied medicine in Madras and in England, president, All India Muslim League (1918, 1920), and of the Indian National Congress (1927).

[359] Dr. Abdur Rahman, general secretary, Delhi Satyagraha Sabha.

[360] 'of my life I realize that' added in the English translation.

[361] 'My experiment continues.' To add.

write long letters to me from Betul and Chhindwada whenever his jailers allowed him to do so. I applied for permission to visit the Brothers, but to no purpose.

It was after the imprisonment of the Ali Brothers that I was invited by Muslim friends to attend the session of the Muslim League at Calcutta. Being requested to speak, I addressed them on the duty of the Muslims to secure the Brothers' release. A little while after this I was taken by these friends to the Muslim College at Aligarh. There I invited the young men to be fakirs for the service of the motherland.[362]

Next I opened correspondence with the Government for the release of the Brothers. In that connection I studied the Brothers' views and activities about the Khilafat.[363] I had discussions with Mussalman friends. I felt that, if I would become a true friend of the Muslims, I must render all possible help in securing the release of the Brothers, and a just settlement of the Khilafat question.[364] It was not for me to enter into the absolute merits of the question, provided there was nothing immoral in their demands.[365] In matters of

---

[362] MKG had gone to Aligarh before attending the All India Muslim League at Calcutta. He was at Aligarh on 28 November 1917 (*CWMG*, vol. 14, p. 98) and spoke at the Muslim League meeting on 31 December 1917. His next visit to Aligarh was from 11–13 October 1920.

[363] The Khilafat movement (1919–24) sought to hold the British Empire to maintain the authority of the Ottoman Sultan as the Caliph of Islam. A deputation was sent to England in 1920 but failed to influence the provisions of the Treaty of Sevres. The Lucknow Pact of 1916 led to the Indian National Congress and the All India Muslim League working closely on the non-cooperation and the Khilafat movements. The abolition of the Ottoman Sultanate in 1922 and the Caliphate in 1924 led to the dissolution of the Khilafat Movement, while MKG suspended the Non-Cooperation Movement in 1922.

[364] 'For me the Khilafat question was simple.' To add.

[365] 'I felt I must render help.' To add.

religion *beliefs differ, and each one's is supreme for himself.*[M7] [M7] faith is supreme.
If all had the same belief about all matters of religion,
there would be only one religion in the world. As time
progressed I found that the Muslim demand about the
Khilafat was not only not against any ethical principle,
but that the British Prime Minister[366] had admitted the
justice of the Muslim demand. I felt, therefore, bound
to render what help I could in securing a due fulfilment
of the Prime Minister's pledge. The pledge had been
given in such clear terms that the examination of the
Muslim demand on the merits[367] was needed only to
satisfy my own conscience.

Friends and critics have[368] criticized my attitude
regarding the Khilafat question. *In spite of the criticism*[M8] [M8] I have reflected over it all
I feel that I have no reason to revise it or to regret my and yet
co-operation with the Muslims. I should adopt the same
attitude, should a similar occasion arise.

When, therefore, I went to Delhi, I had fully
intended to submit the Muslim case to the Viceroy. The
Khilafat question had not then assumed the shape it did
subsequently.

But on my reaching Delhi another difficulty in the
way of my attending the conference arose. Dinabandhu
Andrews raised a question about the morality of my
participation in the war conference. He told me of the[369]
controversy in the British Press regarding secret treaties
between England and Italy. How could I participate in
the conference, if England had entered into secret treaties
with another European power?—asked Mr. Andrews. I
knew nothing of the treaties. Dinabandhu Andrews's

---

[366] 'Lloyd George' to add. David Lloyd George (1863–1945),
chancellor of the Exchequer (1908–15), prime minister of the
War-time Coalition Government (1916–22).

[367] 'from a limited point of view' to add.

[368] 'severely' to add.

[369] 'then current' to add.

word was enough for me. I therefore addressed a letter to Lord Chelmsford explaining my hesitation to take part in the conference. He invited me to discuss the question with him. I had a prolonged discussion with him and his Private Secretary Mr. Maffey. As a result I agreed to take part in the conference. This was in effect the Viceroy's argument: 'Surely you do not believe that the Viceroy knows everything done by the British Cabinet. I do not claim, no one claims, that the British Government is infallible. But if you agree that the Empire has been, on the whole, a power for good, if you believe that India has, on the whole, benefited by the British connection, would you not admit that it is the duty of every Indian citizen to help the Empire in the hour of its need? I too have read what the British papers say about the secret treaties. I can assure you that I know nothing beyond what the papers say, and you know the canards that these papers frequently start. Can you, acting on a mere newspaper report, refuse help to the Empire at such a critical juncture? You may raise whatever moral issues you like and challenge us as much as you please after the conclusion of the war, not today.'

The argument was not new. It appealed to me as new because of the manner in which, and the hour at which, it was presented, and I agreed to attend the conference. As regards the Muslim demands I was to address a letter to the Viceroy.

XXVII

RECRUITING CAMPAIGN[370]

So I attended the conference. The Viceroy was very keen on my supporting the resolution about recruiting.

---

[370] The original would translate 'Enlisting Rangroot'; *rangroot*, a widely prevalent corruption of 'recruit'.

I asked for permission to speak in Hindi-Hindustani. The Viceroy acceded to my request, but suggested that I should speak also in English. I had no speech to make. I spoke but one sentence to this effect: 'With a full sense of my responsibility I beg to support the resolution.'[371]

Many congratulated me on my having spoken in Hindustani. That was, they said, the first instance *within living memory*[M1] of anyone having spoken in Hindustani at *such a*[M2] meeting. The congratulations and the discovery that I was the first to speak in Hindustani at a Viceregal meeting hurt my national pride. *I felt like shrinking into myself.*[M3] What a tragedy that the language of the country should be taboo[372] in meetings held in the country, for work relating to the country, and that a speech there in Hindustani by a stray individual like myself should be a matter for congratulation? Incidents like these are reminders of the low state to which we have been reduced.

[M1] in our times

[M2] the Viceroy's

[M3] I was ashamed.

The one sentence that I uttered at the conference had for me considerable significance. It was impossible for me to forget either the conference or the resolution I supported. There was one undertaking that I had to fulfil while yet in Delhi. I had to write a letter to the Viceroy. This was no easy thing for me. I felt it my duty both in the interests of the Government and of the people to explain therein how and why I attended the conference, and to state clearly what the people expected from Government.

In the letter[373] I expressed my regret for the exclusion from the conference of leaders like Lokamanya Tilak and the Ali Brothers, and stated the people's minimum

---

[371] For the speech, see *CWMG*, vol. 14, p. 375.

[372] 'tabooed' in the first edition.

[373] In *Navajivan* of 14 October 1928, a footnote from the editor (that is, MKG) states, 'A translation of the letter is given at the end of the chapter.' For the letter, also see *CWMG*, vol. 14, pp. 377–80.

political demand as also the demands of the Muslims on account of the situation created by the War. I asked for permission to publish the letter, and the Viceroy gladly gave it.

The letter had to be sent to Simla, where the Viceroy had gone immediately after the conference.[374] The letter had for me considerable importance, and sending it by post would have meant delay. I wanted to save time, and yet I was not inclined to send it by any messenger I came across. I wanted some pure man to carry it and hand it personally at the Viceregal Lodge.[375] Dinabandhu Andrews and Principal Rudra suggested the name of the good Rev. Ireland[376] of the Cambridge Mission.[377] He agreed to carry the letter if he might read it and if it appealed to him as good. I had no objection as the letter was by no means private. He read it, liked it and expressed his willingness to carry out the mission. I offered him the second-class fare, but he declined it saying he was accustomed to travelling intermediate. This he did though it was a night journey. His simplicity and his straight and plain-spoken manner captivated me. The letter thus delivered at the hands

---

[374] The practice of governor generals and Viceroys shifting the capital to Simla began in 1823.

[375] 'and hand it personally at the Viceregal Lodge' added in the English translation. The Viceregal Lodge was built atop the Observatory Hill, Simla, during the viceroyalty of Lord Dufferin. He and Lady Dufferin took up residence at the Lodge designed by Henry Irwin on 23 July 1888. After Independence it became Rashtrapati Nivas, which was transferred to the Indian Institute of Advanced Study in October 1964.

[376] Rev W.F. Ireland, educated at Cambridge, joined St Stephen's College in 1916, left the college in 1920 to do 'District work'. F.F. Monk, *St Stephen's College: A History* (1935), p. 247 (Staff List).

[377] Cambridge Mission, an Anglican Christian missionary initiative in India led by graduates of Cambridge University. The Brotherhood established St Stephen's College in Delhi in 1881.

of a pure-minded man had, as I thought, *the desired*[M4] ᴹ⁴ a good
result. It eased my mind and[378] cleared my way.

The other part of my obligation consisted in raising
recruits. Where could I make a beginning except in
Kheda? And whom could I invite to be the first recruits
except my own co-workers? So as soon as I reached
Nadiad, I had a conference with Vallabhbhai and
other friends. Some of them could not *easily take to the
proposal.*[M5] Those who liked the proposal had misgivings ᴹ⁵ immediately swallow it
about its success. There was no love lost between the
Government and the classes to which I wanted to make
my appeal. The bitter experience they had had of the
Government officials was still fresh in their memory.

And yet they were in favour of starting work. As
soon as I set about my task, my eyes were opened. My
optimism *received a rude shock.*[M6] Whereas during the ᴹ⁶ was shaken a bit
revenue campaign the people readily offered their carts
free of charge, and *two*[M7] volunteers came forth when ᴹ⁷ three or four
one was needed, it was difficult now to get a cart even
on hire, to say nothing of volunteers. But we would
not be dismayed. We decided to dispense with the use
of carts and to do our journeys on foot. At this rate we
had to trudge about 20 miles a day. If carts were not
forthcoming, it was idle to expect people to feed us. It
was hardly proper to ask for food. So it was decided that
every volunteer must carry his food in his satchel. No
bedding or sheet was necessary as it was summer.

We had meetings wherever we went. People did
attend, but hardly one or two would offer themselves
as recruits. 'You are a votary of ahimsa, how can you
ask us to take up arms?' 'What good has Government
done for India to deserve our co-operation?' These and
similar questions used to be put to us.

However, our steady work began to tell. Quite a
number of names were registered, and we hoped that

---

[378] 'eased my mind and' added in the English translation.

we should be able to have a regular supply as soon as the first batch was sent. I had already begun to confer with the Commissioner as to where the recruits were to be accommodated.

The Commissioners in every division were holding conferences on the Delhi model. One such was held in Gujarat.[379] My co-workers and I were invited to it. We attended, but I felt there was even less place for me here than at Delhi. In this atmosphere of servile submission I felt ill at ease. I spoke somewhat at length. I *could say*[M8] nothing to please the officials, and had certainly one or two hard things to say.

I used to issue leaflets asking people to enlist as recruits.[380] One of the arguments I had used was distasteful to the Commissioner: 'Among the many misdeeds of the British rule in India, history will look upon the Act depriving a whole nation of arms as the blackest. If we want the Arms Act to be repealed, if we want to learn the use of arms, here is a golden opportunity. If the middle classes render voluntary help to Government in the hour of its trial, distrust will disappear, and the ban on possessing arms will be withdrawn.' The Commissioner referred to this and said that he appreciated my presence in the conference in spite of the differences between us. And I had to justify my standpoint as courteously as I could:

Here is the letter to the Viceroy referred to above:

'As you are aware, after careful consideration, I felt constrained to convey to Your Excellency that

M8 said

---

[379] No record of this is available. Though on 10 June 1918 the Governor of Bombay Lord Willingdon chaired a stormy meeting of the Bombay Provincial War Conference, from which Tilak, Gandhi, Jinnah and others staged a walkout and on 16 June MKG presided over a mass meeting in Bombay to protest against Lord Willingdon's intemperate utterances with regard to the Home Rule League.

[380] 'Appeal for Enlistment', *CWMG*, vol. 14, p. 439–43.

I could not attend the Conference for reasons stated in the letter of the 26th instant (April), but after the interview you were good enough to grant me, I persuaded myself to join it, if for no other cause, then certainly out of my great regard for yourself. One of my reasons for abstention and perhaps the strongest was that Lokamanya Tilak, Mrs. Besant and the Ali Brothers, whom I regard as among the most powerful leaders of public opinion, were not invited to the Conference. I still feel that it was a grave blunder not to have asked them, and I respectfully suggest that that blunder might be possibly repaired if these leaders were invited to assist the Government by giving it the benefit of their advice at the Provincial Conferences, which I understand are to follow. I venture to submit that no Government can afford to disregard the leaders, who represent the large masses of the people as these do, even though they may hold views fundamentally different. At the same time it gives me pleasure to be able to say that the views of all parties were permitted to be freely expressed at the Committees of the Conference. For my part, I purposely refrained from stating my views at the Committee at which I had the honour of serving or at the Conference itself. I felt that I could best serve the objects of the Conference by simply tendering my support to the resolutions submitted to it, and this I have done without any reservation. I hope to translate the spoken word into action as early as the Government can see its way to accept my offer, which I am submitting simultaneously herewith in a separate letter.

I recognize that in the hour of its danger we must give, as we have decided to give, ungrudging and unequivocal support to the Empire of which we aspire in the near future to be partners in the same sense as the Dominions overseas. But it is the simple truth that our response is due to the expectation that our goal will be reached all the more speedily. On that account, even as performance of duty automatically confers a corresponding right, people are entitled to believe that the imminent reforms alluded to in your speech will embody the main general principles of the Congress-League Scheme, and I am sure that it is this faith which has enabled many members of the Conference to tender to the Government their full-hearted co-operation.

If I could make my countrymen retrace their steps, I would make them withdraw all the Congress resolutions, and not whisper "Home Rule" or "Responsible Government" during the pendency of the War. I would make India offer all her able-bodied sons as a sacrifice to the Empire at its critical moment, and I know that India, by this very act, would become the most favoured partner in the Empire, and racial distinctions would become a thing of the past. But practically the whole of educated India has decided to take a less effective course, and it is no longer possible to say that educated India does not exercise any influence on the masses. I have been coming into most intimate touch with the ryots ever since my return from South Africa to India, and I wish to assure you that the desire for Home Rule has widely penetrated them. I was present at the sessions of the last Congress, and I was a party to the resolution that full Responsible Government should be granted to British India within a period to be fixed definitely by a Parliamentary Statute. I admit that it is a bold step to take, but I feel sure that nothing less than a definite vision of Home Rule to be realized in the shortest possible time will satisfy the Indian people. I know that there are many in India who consider no sacrifice as too great in order to achieve the end, and they are wakeful enough to realize that they must be equally prepared to sacrifice themselves for the Empire in which they hope and desire to reach their final status. It follows then that we can but accelerate our journey to the goal by silently and simply devoting ourselves heart and soul to the work of delivering the Empire from the threatening danger. It will be national suicide not to recognize this elementary truth. We must perceive that, if we serve to save the Empire, we have in that very act secured Home Rule.

Whilst, therefore, it is clear to me that we should give to the Empire every available man for its defence, I fear that I cannot say the same thing about financial assistance. My intimate intercourse with the ryots convinces me that India has already donated to the Imperial Exchequer beyond her capacity. I know that in making this statement I am voicing the opinion of the majority of my countrymen.

The Conference means for me, and I believe for many of us, a definite step in the consecration of our lives to the common cause, but ours is a peculiar position. We are today outside the partnership. Ours is a consecration based on hope of better future. I should be untrue to you and to my country if I did not clearly and unequivocally tell you what that hope is. I do not bargain for its fulfilment, but you should know that disappointment of hope means disillusion.

There is one thing I may not omit. You have appealed to us to sink domestic differences. If the appeal involves the toleration of tyranny and wrongdoing on the part of officials, I am powerless to respond. I shall resist organized tyranny to the uttermost. The appeal must be to the officials that they do not ill-treat a single soul, and that they consult and respect popular opinion as never before. In Champaran by resisting an age-long tyranny I have shown the ultimate sovereignty of British justice. In Kheda a population that was cursing the Government now feels that it, and not the Government, is the power when it is prepared to suffer for the truth it represents. It is, therefore, losing its bitterness and is saying to itself that the Government must be a Government for people, for it tolerates orderly and respectful disobedience where injustice is felt. Thus Champaran and Kheda affairs are my direct, definite and special contribution to the War. Ask me to suspend my activities in that direction and you ask me to suspend my life. If I could popularize the use of soul-force, which is but another name for love-force, in place of brute force, I know that I could present you with an India that could defy the whole world to do its worst. In season and out of season, therefore, I shall discipline myself to express in my life this eternal law of suffering, and present it for acceptance to those who care, and if I take part in any other activity, the motive is to show the matchless superiority of that law.

Lastly, I would like you to ask His Majesty's Ministers to give definite assurance about Mohammedan States. I am sure you know that every Mohammedan is deeply interested in them. As a Hindu, I cannot be indifferent to their cause. Their sorrows must be our sorrows. In the most scrupulous regard for the rights of those States and for the Muslim sentiment as to their places of worship, and your just and timely treatment of India's claim to Home Rule lies the safety of the Empire. I write this, because I love the English nation, and I wish to evoke in every Indian the loyalty of Englishmen.'

XXVIII

NEAR DEATH'S DOOR

I very nearly ruined my constitution during the recruiting campaign. In those days my food principally consisted of *groundnut butter and lemons*.[M1] I knew that it was possible to eat too much *butter*[M2] and injure one's health, and yet I allowed myself to do so.[381] This gave me a slight attack of dysentery. I did not take serious notice of this, and

[M1] roasted and pounded groundnut mixed with jaggery, fruits like banana, etc., and juice of two or three lemons.

[M2] nuts

---

[381] 'I knew that the butter could be easily overeaten to the detriment of one's health, and yet I allowed myself to overeat it.' In the first edition.

went that evening to the Ashram, as was my wont every now and then. I scarcely took any medicine in those days. I thought I should get well if I skipped a meal, and indeed I felt fairly free from trouble as I omitted the morning meal next day. I knew, however, that to be entirely free I must prolong my fast and, if I ate anything at all, I should have nothing but fruit juices.

There was some festival that day,[382] and although[383] I had told Kasturbai that I should have nothing for my midday meal, she tempted me and I succumbed. As I was under a vow of taking no milk or milk products, she[384] had specially prepared for me a sweet wheaten porridge with oil added to it instead of ghee. She had reserved too a bowlful of[385] mung for me. *I was fond of these things,*[M3] and I readily took them, hoping that without coming to grief I should eat just enough to please Kasturbai and to satisfy my palate. But the devil had been only waiting for an opportunity. Instead of eating very little I had my fill of the meal. This was sufficient invitation to the angel of death.[386] Within an hour the dysentery appeared in acute form.

The same evening I had to go back to Nadiad. I walked with very great difficulty to the Sabarmati station, a distance of only[387] ten furlongs.[388] Sjt. Vallabhbhai, who joined me at Ahmedabad, saw that I was unwell, but I did not allow him[389] to guess how unbearable the pain was.

[M3] I gave in to taste

---

[382] The date was 11 August 1918.

[383] 'I recollect' to add.

[384] 'told me that she' to add.

[385] 'whole' to add. That is, 'unsplit'.

[386] 'angel of death' translates as 'Yamaraj', 'the god of death.'

[387] 'only' added in the English translation.

[388] 'one and a quarter mile' in the original.

[389] 'or other companions' to add.

We reached Nadiad at about ten o'clock.[390] The Hindu[391] Anathashram where we had our headquarters[392] was only half a mile from the station; but it was as good as ten for me. I somehow managed to reach the quarters, but the griping pain was steadily increasing.[393] Instead of using the usual latrine which was a long way off, I asked for a commode to be placed in the adjoining room. I was ashamed to have to ask for this, but there was no escape. Sjt. Fulchand[394] immediately procured a commode. All the friends surrounded me deeply concerned. They were all love and attention, but they could not relieve my pain. And my obstinacy added to their helplessness. I refused all medical aid. I would take no medicine, but preferred to suffer the penalty for my folly.[M4] So they looked on in helpless dismay. I must have had thirty to forty motions in twenty-four hours. I fasted, not taking even fruit juices in the beginning. The appetite had all gone. I had thought all along that I had an iron frame,[M5] but I found that my body had now become a lump of clay. It had lost all power of resistance. Dr. Kanuga[395] came and pleaded with me to take medicine. I declined. He offered to give me an injection. I declined that too. My ignorance about injections was in those days quite ridiculous. I believed that an injection must be some kind of serum. Later I discovered that the injection that the doctor suggested

[M4] sin

[M5] a body hard as stone

---

[390] 'at about ten o'clock' added in the English translation.

[391] 'Hindu' added in the English translation.

[392] 'where we had our headquarters' added in the English translation.

[393] 'I had to go to the lavatory every fifteen minutes. At last I was defeated. I made public my unbearable pain, and took to bed.' To add.

[394] 'Bapooji' to add. Fulchand Bapooji Shah.

[395] Dr. Balwantrai Narasinhprasad Kanuga. Dr. Kanuga and Dr. G.R. Talwalkar reached Nadiad from Ahmedabad on 22 August 1918.

was a vegetable substance, but the discovery was too late to be of use. The motions still continued, leaving me completely exhausted. The exhaustion brought on a delirious fever. The friends got more nervous, and called in more doctors. But what could they do with a patient who would not listen to them?

Sheth Ambalal with his good wife came down to Nadiad, conferred with my co-workers and removed me with the greatest care to his Mirzapur bungalow in Ahmedabad.[396] It was impossible for anyone to receive more loving and selfless service than I had the privilege of having during this illness. But a sort of low fever persisted, wearing away my body from day to day. I felt that the illness was bound to be prolonged and possibly fatal. Surrounded as I was with all the love and attention that could be showered on me under Sheth Ambalal's roof, I began to get restless and urged him to remove me to the Ashram. He had to yield to my importunity.[397]

Whilst I was thus tossing on the bed of pain in the Ashram, Sjt. Vallabhbhai brought the news that Germany had been completely defeated, and that the Commissioner had sent word that recruiting was no longer necessary. The news that I had no longer to worry myself about recruiting came as a very great relief.

I had now been trying hydropathy which gave some relief, but it was a hard job to build up the body. The many medical advisers overwhelmed me with advice, but I could not persuade myself to take anything. Two or three suggested meat broth as a way out of the milk vow, and cited authorities from Ayurveda in support of their advice. One of them strongly recommended eggs.[398] But for all of them I had but one answer—no.

---

[396] MKG was taken to Shanti Sadan on 23 August 1918.

[397] MKG was removed to the Ashram on 7 September 1918.

[398] 'But I could not accept anyone's advice.' To add.

For me the question of diet was not one to be determined on the authority of the Shastras. It was one interwoven with my course of life *which is guided by principles no longer depending upon outside authority. I had no desire to live at the cost of them.*[M6] How could I relinquish a principle in respect of myself, when I had enforced it relentlessly in respect of my wife, children and friends?

[M6] independent of anything else. I had no greed to live by eating all types of things and by whichever remedy.

This protracted and first long illness in my life thus afforded me a unique opportunity to examine my principles and to test them. One night I gave myself up to despair.[399] I felt that I was at death's door. I sent word to Anasuyabehn. She ran down to the Ashram. Vallabhbhai came up with Dr. Kanuga, who felt my pulse and said: 'Your pulse is quite good. I see absolutely no *danger*.[M7] This is a nervous breakdown due to extreme weakness.' But I was far from being reassured. I passed the night without sleep.

[M7] signs of death

The morning broke without death coming. But I could not get rid of the feeling that the end was near, and so I began to devote all my waking hours to listening to the *Gita* being read to me by the inmates of the Ashram.[400] I was incapable of reading. I was hardly inclined to talk. The slightest talk meant a strain on the brain. All interest in living had ceased, as I have never liked to live for the sake of living. It was such an agony to live on in that helpless state, doing nothing, receiving the service of friends and co-workers, and watching the body slowly wearing away.

Whilst I lay thus ever expectant of death, Dr. Talvalkar came one day with a strange creature. He hailed from Maharashtra. *He was not known to fame,*[M8] but the moment I saw him I found that he was a crank like myself. He had come to try his treatment on me.

[M8] India does not know him

---

[399] 1 October 1918.

[400] 'I had no strength for any work.' To add.

He had almost finished his course of studies in the Grant Medical College without taking the degree.[401] Later I came to know that he was a member of the Brahmo Samaj. Sjt. Kelkar, for that is his name, is a man of an independent and obstinate[402] temperament. He swears by the ice treatment, which he wanted to try on me. We gave him the name of 'Ice Doctor'.[403] He is quite confident that he has discovered certain things which have escaped qualified doctors. It is a pity both for him and me that he has not been able to infect me with his faith in his system. I believe in his system up to a certain point, but I am afraid he has been hasty in arriving at certain conclusions.

But whatever may be the merits of his discoveries, I allowed him to experiment on my body. I did not mind external treatment.[404] The treatment consisted in the application of ice all over the body. Whilst I am unable to endorse his claim about the effect his treatment had on me, it certainly infused in me a new hope and a new energy, and the mind naturally reacted on the body. I began to have appetite, and to have a gentle walk for five to ten minutes. He now suggested a reform in my diet. Said he: 'I assure you that you will have more energy and regain your strength quicker if you take raw eggs. Eggs are as harmless as milk. They certainly cannot come under the category of meat. And do you know that all eggs are not fertilized? There are sterilized[M9] eggs on the market.' I was not, however,   [M9] unfertilized

---

[401] 'without taking the degree' translates the original 'had not received the imprint from Dwarka'.

[402] 'and obstinate' added in the English translation.

[403] See *CWMG*, vol. 15, p. 98. MKG and the ashramites were considering other names for him. 'We are thinking of giving him a third name, Dudabhai (Brother Milk) as these days he has gone milk-crazy.'

[404] 'which was that of ice, which is water' to add.

M10 unfertilized

M11 some interest in the
activities around me

prepared to take even the *sterilized*M10 eggs. But the
improvement was enough to give me *interest in public
activities.*M11

XXIX

THE ROWLATT BILLS AND
MY[405] DILEMMA

M1 staying there for a patient
such as me

Friends and doctors assured me that I should recuperate
quicker by a change to Matheran, so I went there.[406]
But the water at Matheran being very hard, it made
*my stay there*M1 extremely difficult. As a result of the
attack of the dysentery that I had, my anal tract had
become extremely tender, and owing to fissures, I felt
an excruciating pain at the time of evacuation, so that
the very idea of eating filled me with dread. Before
the week was over I had to flee from Matheran.[407]
Shankarlal Banker now constituted himself the guardian
of my health, and pressed me to consult Dr. Dalal.[408]
Dr. Dalal was called accordingly. His capacity for taking
instantaneous decisions captured me.

He said: 'I cannot rebuild your body unless you take
milk. If in addition you would take iron and arsenic
injections, I would guarantee[409] fully to renovate your
constitution.'

M2 milk I will not take

'You can give me the injections,' I replied, 'but
milk is a different question; I have a vow against it.'M2

---

[405] 'Moral' to add.

[406] MKG stayed at Ambalal Sarabhai's house, Bombay View, from
2–12 December 1918.

[407] MKG left Matheran on the 13th, reaching Bombay on 14
December where he stayed till 9 February 1919.

[408] Dr. A.K. Dalal.

[409] 'guarantee' English word in the original.

'What exactly is the nature of your vow?' the doctor inquired.

I told him the whole history and the reasons behind my vow, how,[410] since I had come to know that the cow and the buffalo were subjected to the process of *phooka*, I had conceived a strong disgust for milk. Moreover, I had always held that milk is not the natural diet of man. I had therefore abjured its use altogether. Kasturbai was standing near my bed listening all the time to this conversation.[411]

'But surely you cannot have any objection to goat's milk then,' she interposed.

The doctor too took up the strain. 'If you will take goat's milk, it will be enough for me,' he said.

I succumbed.[412] My intense eagerness to take up the satyagraha fight had created in me a strong desire to live, and so I contented myself with adhering to the letter of my vow only, and sacrificed its spirit. For although I had only the milk of the cow and the she-buffalo in mind when I took the vow, by natural implication it covered the milk of all animals. Nor could it be right for me to use milk at all, so long as I held that milk is not the natural diet of man. Yet knowing all this I agreed to take goat's milk. The will to live proved stronger than the devotion to truth, and for once the votary of truth compromised his sacred ideal by his eagerness to take up the satyagraha fight. The memory of this action even now rankles in my breast and fills me with remorse, and I am constantly thinking how to give up goat's milk. But I cannot yet free myself from that subtlest of temptations, the desire to serve, which still holds me.

---

[410] 'I told him the whole history and reasons behind my vow, how' added in the English translation.

[411] 'listening all the while that this conversation was going on' in the first edition.

[412] The date was 8 January 1919.

M3 from the point of view of
ahimsa

My experiments in dietetics are dear to me *as a part
of my researches in ahimsa.*^M3 They give me recreation and
joy. But my use of goat's milk today troubles me not
from the view-point of dietetic ahimsa so much as from
that of truth, being no less than in breach of pledge. It
seems to me that I understand the ideal of truth better
than that of ahimsa, and my experience tells me that, if
I let go my hold of truth, I shall never be able to solve
the riddle of ahimsa. The ideal of truth requires *that vows
taken should be fulfilled in the spirit as well as in the letter.*^M4

M4 protection of the body
and the soul of the vow and
adherence to it in letter and
spirit

In the present case I killed the spirit—the soul of my
vow—by adhering to its outer form only,[413] and that
is what galls me. But in spite of this clear knowledge
I cannot see my way straight before me.^M5 In other words,
perhaps, I have not the courage *to follow the straight
course.*^M6 Both at bottom mean one and the same thing,
for doubt is invariably the result of want or weakness[414]
of faith. 'Lord, give me faith' is, therefore, my prayer
day and night.[415]

M5 I have not been able to
discern my duty towards my
vows

M6 for their observance

Soon after I began taking goat's milk, Dr. Dalal
performed on me a successful operation for fissures.[416]
As I recuperated, my desire to live revived, especially
because God had kept work in store for me.[417]

I had hardly begun to feel my way towards
recovery, when I happened casually to read in the
papers the Rowlatt Committee's[418] report which had

---

[413] 'by adhering to its outer form only' added in the English translation.

[414] 'or weakness' added in the English translation.

[415] 'is, therefore, my prayer day and night' added in the English
translation.

[416] The operation was performed on 21 January 1919.

[417] 'As I recuperated, my desire to live revived, especially because
God had kept work in store for me.' Added in the English
translation.

[418] The Rowlatt Committee, appointed in 1918 to evaluate
political terrorism in India, especially in Bengal and the Punjab,

just been published.[419] Its recommendations startled me. Shankarlal Banker and Umar Sobani approached me with the suggestion that I should take some *prompt*[M7] action in the matter. In about a month I went to Ahmedabad. I mentioned my apprehensions to Vallabhbhai, who used to come to see me almost daily. 'Something must be done,' said I to him. 'But what can we do in the circumstances?' he asked in reply. I answered, 'If even a handful of men can be found to sign the pledge of resistance, and the proposed measure is passed into law in defiance of it,[420] we ought to offer satyagraha at once. If I was not laid up like this, I should give battle against it all alone, and expect others to follow suit. But in my present helpless condition I feel myself to be altogether unequal to the task.'

    M7 definite

As a result of this talk, it was decided to call a small meeting of such persons as were in touch with me. The recommendations of the Rowlatt Committee seemed to me to be altogether unwarranted by the evidence published in its report, and were, I felt, such that no self-respecting people could submit to them.

The proposed conference was at last held at the Ashram.[421] Hardly a score of persons had been invited to it. So far as I remember, among those who attended were, besides Vallabhbhai, Shrimati Sarojini Naidu,

---

and their links with the German government and the Bolsheviks in Russia. Justice Sidney Rowlatt (president), J.D.V. Hodge (secretary), Justice Basil Scott, Justice C.V. Kumaraswami Sastri, Verney Lovett and P.C. Mitter (members) comprised the committee.

[419] Called Bill No. 1 and Bill No. 2 of 1919, the bills made provision for the ordinary criminal law to be supplemented and gave emergency powers to the government. For a summary of the bills, see *CWMG*, vol. 15, pp. 110–18.

[420] 'in defiance of it' added in the English translation.

[421] The conference was held on 24 February 1919.

Mr. Horniman,[422] the late Mr. Umar Sobani, Sjt. Shankarlal Banker and Shrimati Anasuyabehn. The satyagraha pledge[423] was drafted at this meeting, and as far as I recollect, was signed by all present. I was not editing any journal at that time, but I *used occasionally to ventilate my views through*[M8] the daily Press. I followed the practice on this occasion. Shankarlal Banker took up the agitation in right earnest, and for the first time I got an idea of his wonderful[424] capacity for organization and sustained work.

As all hope of any of the existing institutions adopting a novel weapon like satyagraha seemed to me to be in vain, a separate body called the Satyagraha Sabha[425] was established at my instance. Its principal members were drawn from Bombay where, therefore, its headquarters were fixed. The intending covenanters began to sign the satyagraha pledge in large numbers, bulletins were issued, and popular meetings began to be held everywhere recalling all the familiar features of the Kheda campaign.

I became the president of the Satyagraha Sabha. I soon found that there was not likely to be much chance of agreement between myself and the intelligentsia composing this Sabha. My insistence on the use of Gujarati in the Sabha, as also some of my other methods of work that would appear to be peculiar,[426] caused them no small worry and embarrassment. I must say to

---

[422] Benjamin Guy Horniman (1873–1948), British journalist, editor of the daily *British Chronicle* founded by Sir Pherozeshah Mehta; he broke the story of the massacre at Jallianwala Bagh, was arrested and deported to England for his criticism of the colonial government.

[423] For the satyagraha pledge, see *CWMG*, vol. 15, pp. 101–02.

[424] 'wonderful' added in the English translation.

[425] For the Satyagraha Sabha rules, see *CWMG*, vol. 15, pp. 132–33.

[426] 'that would appear to be peculiar' added in the English translation.

their credit, however, that most of them generously put up with my *idiosyncrasies*.[M9]

But from the very beginning it seemed clear to me that the Sabha was not likely to live long. I could see that already my emphasis on truth and ahimsa had begun to be disliked by some of its members. Nevertheless in its early stages our new activity went on at full blast, and the movement gathered head rapidly.[427]

XXX

THAT WONDERFUL SPECTACLE!

Thus, while on the one hand the agitation against the Rowlatt Committee's report gathered volume and intensity, on the other the Government grew more and more determined to give effect to its recommendations, and the Rowlatt Bill was published. I have attended the proceedings of India's legislative chamber only once in my life, and that was on the occasion of the debate on this Bill. Shastriji[428] delivered an impassioned speech, in which he uttered a solemn note of warning to the Government. The Viceroy seemed to be listening spell-bound, his eyes riveted on Shastriji as the latter poured forth the hot stream of[429] his eloquence. For the moment it seemed to me as if the Viceroy could not but be deeply moved by it, it was so true and so full of feeling.

But you can wake a man only if he is really asleep; no effort that you may make will produce any effect upon him if he is merely pretending sleep.[M1] That was precisely the

[M9] methods

[M1] A sleeping man can be awakened, but how would a man pretending to be asleep listen to the beating of drums in his ears?

---

[427] 'and the movement gathered head rapidly' added in the English translation.

[428] V.S. Srinivas Sastri.

[429] 'the hot stream of' added in the English translation.

M2 The farce of discussing the Bills in the legislature had to be enacted. The Government enacted the farce.

M3 And who would listen to my feeble tune?

Government's position.[430] *It was anxious only to go through the farce of legal formality.*[M2] Its decision had already been made. Shastriji's solemn warning was, therefore, entirely lost upon the Government.

In these circumstances mine could only be a cry in the wilderness.[M3] I earnestly pleaded with the Viceroy, I addressed him private letters as also public letters, in the course of which I clearly told him that the Government's action left me no other course except to resort to satyagraha. But it was all in vain.[431]

The Bill had not yet been gazetted as an Act. I was in a very weak condition, but when I received an invitation from Madras[432] I decided to take the risk of the long journey. I could not at that time sufficiently raise my voice at meetings. The incapacity to address meetings standing still abides. My entire frame would shake, and heavy throbbing[433] would start on an attempt to speak standing for any length of time.[434]

I have ever felt at home in the South.[435] Thanks to my South African work I[436] felt I had some sort of special right over the Tamils and Telugus,[437] and *the good people of the South have never belied my belief.*[M4] The invitation had come over the signature of the late Sjt. Kasturi

M4 hitherto I have not felt that I have erred in my belief

---

[430] 'That was precisely the Government's position.' Added in the English translation.

[431] See *CWMG*, vol. 15, pp. 129–30, 218–20, 225, 274–75, 302–03, 311.

[432] 'but when I received an invitation from Madras' added in the English translation.

[433] 'throbs' in the first edition.

[434] MD read out MKG's speeches in Madras.

[435] 'But I felt that I must accept the invitation from Madras.' To add before this sentence.

[436] 'have' to add.

[437] 'and the people of Southern provinces' to add.

Ranga Iyengar.[438] But the man behind the invitation, as I subsequently learnt on my way to Madras, was Rajagopalachari.[439] This might be said to be my first acquaintance with him; at any rate this was the first time that *we came to know each other personally.*[M5]

[M5] I could recognize him on sight

Rajagopalachari had then only recently left Salem to settle down for legal practice in Madras at the pressing invitation of friends like the late Sjt. Kasturi Ranga Iyengar, and that with a view to taking a more active part in public life. It was with him that we had put up in Madras.[440] This discovery I made only after we had stayed with him for a couple of days. For since the bungalow that we were staying in belonged to Sjt. Kasturi Ranga Iyengar, I was under the impression that we were his guests. Mahadev Desai, however, corrected me. He very soon formed a close acquaintance with Rajagopalachari, who, from his innate shyness, kept himself constantly in the background. But Mahadev put me on my guard. 'You should cultivate this man,' he said to me one day.

And so I did. We daily discussed together plans of the fight, but beyond the holding of public meetings I could not then think of any other programme. I felt myself at a loss to discover how to offer civil disobedience against

---

[438] S. Kasturi Ranga Iyengar (1859–1923), lawyer, nationalist, journalist, purchased *The Hindu* in 1905 and became its editor and managing director till his death in 1923.

[439] Chakravarti Rajagopalachari (1878–1972), joined the Rowlatt Satyagraha and the non-cooperation movements, edited *Young India* during MKG's imprisonment in the early 1920s, member of the Congress Working Committee (1922–42), Governor of Bengal (1947–48), the only Indian Governor General of independent India (1948–50), served as Premier of Madras (1937–39) and as chief minister of Madras (1952–54), awarded the Bharat Ratna (1954), founder of the Swatantra Party (1959), accomplished writer. His daughter Lakshmi married MKG's youngest son, Devadas.

[440] MKG stayed in Madras from 18 March to 23 March 1919.

the Rowlatt Bill if it was finally passed into law. One could disobey it only if the Government gave one the opportunity for it. Failing that, could we civilly disobey other laws? And if so, where was the line to be drawn? These and a host of similar questions formed the theme of these discussions of ours.

Sjt. Kasturi Ranga Iyengar called together a small conference of leaders to thrash out the matter. Among those who took a conspicuous part in it was Sjt. Vijayaraghavachari.[441] He suggested that I should draw up a comprehensive manual of the science of satyagraha, embodying even minute details. I felt the task to be beyond my capacity, and I confessed as much to him.

While these cogitations were still going on, news was received that the Rowlatt Bill had been published as an Act. That night I fell asleep while thinking over the question. Towards the small hours of the morning I woke up somewhat earlier than usual. I was still in that twilight condition between sleep and consciousness when suddenly the idea broke upon me—it was as if in a dream. Early in the morning I related the whole story to Rajagopalachari.

'The idea came to me last night in a dream that we should call upon the country to observe a general *hartal*.[442] Satyagraha is a process of self-purification, and ours is a sacred fight, and it seems to me to be in the fitness of things that it should be commenced with an act of self-purification. Let all the people of India, therefore, suspend their business on that day and observe the day as one of fasting and prayer. The Mussalmans may not fast for more than one day; so

---

[441] C. Vijayaraghavachari (1852–1944), member of the Indian National Congress and its president (1920), member, Madras Legislative Council (1895–1901), Imperial Legislative Council (1913–16).

[442] 'as a response to this Act' to add.

the duration of the fast should be 24 hours. It is very difficult to say whether all the provinces would respond to this appeal of ours[443] or not, but I feel fairly sure of Bombay, Madras, Bihar and Sind. I think we should have every reason to feel satisfied even if all these places observe the *hartal* fittingly.'

Rajagopalachari was at once taken up with my suggestion. Other friends too welcomed it when it was communicated to them later. I drafted a brief appeal.[444] The date of the *hartal* was first fixed on the 30th March 1919, but was subsequently changed to 6th April. The people thus had only a short notice of the *hartal*. As the work had to be started at once, it was hardly possible to give longer notice.[445]

But who knows how it all came about? The whole of India from one end to the other,[446] towns as well as villages, observed a complete *hartal* on that day. It was a most wonderful spectacle.

XXXI

THAT MEMORABLE[447] WEEK!–I

After a short tour in South India I reached Bombay, I think on the 4th April,[448] having received a wire from

---

[443] 'to this appeal of ours' added in the English translation.

[444] See *CWMG*, vol. 15, pp. 145–46. MKG called for the observation as a 'day of humiliation and prayer'. This was drafted and released on 23 March 1919.

[445] 'there was hardly any time to give longer notice' in the first edition.

[446] 'from one end to the other' added in the English translation.

[447] 'Memorable' added in the English translation.

[448] MKG reached Bombay on 3 April 1919.

Sjt. Shankarlal Banker asking me to be present there for the 6th of April celebrations.

But in the meanwhile Delhi had already observed the *hartal* on the 30th March. The word of the late Swami Shraddhanandji and Hakim Ajmal Khan Saheb was law there. The *wire*[M1] about the postponement of the *hartal* till the 6th of April had reached there too late. Delhi had never witnessed a *hartal* like that before. Hindus and Mussalmans seemed united *like one man*.[M2] Swami Shraddhanandji was invited to deliver a speech in the Jumma Masjid which he did. All this was more than the authorities could bear. The police checked the *hartal* procession as it was proceeding towards the railway station and opened fire, *causing a number of casualties*,[M3] and the reign of repression commenced in Delhi. Shraddhanandji urgently summoned me to Delhi. I wired back, saying I would start for Delhi immediately after the 6th of April celebrations were over in Bombay.

The story of happenings in Delhi was repeated with variations in Lahore and Amritsar.[M4] From Amritsar Drs. Satyapal[449] and Kitchlew[450] had sent me a pressing invitation to go there. I was altogether unacquainted with them at that time, but I communicated to them my intention to visit Amritsar after Delhi.

On the morning of the 6th citizens of Bombay flocked in their thousands to the Chaupati for a bath in the sea, after which they moved on in a procession to Thakurdvar.[451] The procession included a fair sprinkling

[M1] news

[M2] at heart

[M3] many were injured, some killed,

[M4] As in Delhi, so in Lahore and Amritsar.

---

[449] Dr. Satyapal, a medical practitioner, whose arrest led to protests which finally resulted in the Jallianwala Bagh massacre.

[450] Dr. Saifuddin Kitchlew (1888–1963), nationalist politician, studied at Cambridge and obtained a doctorate from Munster University, Germany, member of the Punjab Congress Committee and general secretary, AICC, was the first Indian recipient of the Lenin Peace Prize; he was arrested along with Dr. Satyapal.

[451] The procession moved to Madhav Baug and not Thakurdvar. This is indicated in a footnote in the Gujarati edition of the

of women and children, while the Mussalmans joined it in large numbers. From Madhav Baug some of us who were in the procession were taken by the Mussalman friends to a mosque near by,[452] where Mrs. Naidu and myself were persuaded to deliver speeches. Sjt. Vithaldas Jerajani[453] proposed that we should then and there administer the Swadeshi and Hindu–Muslim unity pledges to the people, but I resisted the proposal on the ground that pledges should not be administered or taken in precipitate hurry, and that we should be satisfied with what was already being done by the people. A pledge once taken, I argued, must not be broken afterwards; therefore it was necessary that the implications of the Swadeshi pledge should be clearly understood, and the grave responsibility entailed by the pledge regarding Hindu–Muslim unity fully realized by all concerned. In the end I suggested that those who wanted to take the pledges should again assemble[454] on the following morning for the purpose.

Needless to say[455] the *hartal* in Bombay was a complete success. Full preparation had been made for starting civil disobedience. Two or three things had been discussed in this connection. It was decided that civil disobedience might be offered in respect of *such laws only as*[M5] easily lent themselves to being disobeyed by the masses. The salt tax was extremely unpopular and a powerful movement had been for some time past going on to secure its repeal. I therefore suggested

M5 only one law from among those which

Autobiography—Gandhiji No Akshrdeha, vol. 39, p. 298, as also *CWMG*, vol. 15, p. 188.

452 Sonapuri Mosque, near Peal House.

453 Vithaldas Jerajani, a constructive (*rachnatmak*) worker, started the Shuddha Swadeshi Bhandar in Bombay.

454 'at the Chaupati grounds' to add.

455 'Needless to say' added in the English translation.

that the people might prepare salt from sea-water[456] in their own houses in disregard of the salt laws. My other suggestion was about the sale of proscribed literature. *Two of my books, viz, Hind Swaraj and Sarvodaya (Gujarati adaptation of Ruskin's Unto This Last), which had been already proscribed, came handy for this purpose.*[M6] To print and sell them openly seemed to be the easiest way of offering civil disobedience. A sufficient number of copies of the books was therefore printed, and it was arranged to sell them at the end of the monster meeting that was to be held that evening after the breaking of the fast.

On the evening of the 6th *an army of*[M7] volunteers issued forth accordingly with this prohibited literature to sell it among the people. Both Shrimati Sarojini Devi and I went out in cars. All the copies were soon sold out. The proceeds of the sale were to be utilized for furthering the civil disobedience campaign. Both these books were priced at four annas per copy, but I hardly remember anybody having *purchased them from me at their face value merely.*[M8] Quite a large number of people simply poured out all the cash that was in their pockets to purchase their copy. *Five and ten rupee notes just flew out to cover the price of a single copy,*[M9] while in one case I remember having sold a copy for fifty rupees! It was duly explained to the people that they were liable to be arrested and imprisoned for purchasing the proscribed literature. But for the moment they had shed all fear of jail-going.

It was subsequently learnt[457] that the Government had conveniently taken the view that the books that had been proscribed by it had not in fact been sold, and that what we had sold was not held as coming under the definition of proscribed literature. The reprint was

[M6] Two of these books were mine, viz *Hind Swaraj* and *Sarvodaya*.

[M7] many

[M8] placed four annas either in my or Sarojini Devi's hands

[M9] Some even gave ten or five rupee notes

---

[456] 'from sea-water' added in the English translation.

[457] 'on the 7th' to add.

held by the Government to be a new edition of the books that had been proscribed, and to sell them did not constitute an offence under the law. This news caused general disappointment.

The next morning another meeting was held for the administration of the pledges with regard to Swadeshi and Hindu–Muslim unity. Vithaldas Jerajani for the first time realized that all is not gold that glitters.[458] Only a handful of persons came. I distinctly remember some of the sisters who were present on that occasion. The men who attended were also very few. I had already drafted the pledge and brought it with me. I thoroughly explained its meaning to those present before I administered it to them. The paucity of the attendance neither pained nor surprised me, for I have noticed this characteristic difference in the popular attitude—partiality for exciting work, dislike for quiet constructive effort. The difference has persisted to this day.

But I shall have to devote to this subject a chapter by itself. To return to the story. On the night of the 7th I started for Delhi and Amritsar.[459] On reaching Mathura on the 8th I first heard rumours[460] about my probable arrest. At the next stoppage after Mathura, Acharya Gidwani came to meet me, and gave me definite news that I was to be arrested, and offered his services to me if I should need them. I thanked him for the offer, assuring him that I would not fail to avail myself of it, if and when I felt it necessary.

Before the train had reached Palwal railway station, I was served with a written order[461] to the effect that

---

458 In the original, 'all that is white is not milk'.

459 MKG boarded the train on the afternoon of 8 April at 4 p.m.

460 'echoes' in the first edition.

461 The order was served at Kosi station on 9 April. For a copy of the order, see *CWMG*, vol. 15, pp. 207–08, n. 2.

I was prohibited from entering the boundary of the Punjab, as my presence there was likely to result in a disturbance of the peace. I was asked by the police to get down from the train. I refused to do so saying, 'I want to go to the Punjab in response to a pressing invitation, not to foment unrest, but to allay it. I am therefore sorry that it is not possible for me to comply with this order.'

At last the train reached Palwal. Mahadev was with[462] me. I asked him to proceed to Delhi to convey to Swami Shraddhanandji the news about what had happened and to ask the people to remain calm. He was to *explain why*[M10] I had decided to disobey the order served upon me and suffer the penalty for disobeying it, and *also why*[M11] it would spell victory for our side if we could maintain perfect peace in spite of any punishment that might be inflicted upon me.

At Palwal railway station I was taken out of the train and put under police custody. A train from Delhi came in a short time. I was made to enter a third-class carriage, the police party accompanying. On reaching Mathura, I was taken to the police barracks, but no police official could tell me as to what they proposed to do with me or where I was to be taken next. Early at 4 o'clock the next morning I was waked up and put in a goods train that was going towards Bombay. At noon I was again made to get down at Sawai Madhopur. Mr. Bowring, Inspector of Police, who arrived by the mail train from Lahore, now took charge of me. I was put in a first-class compartment with him. And from an ordinary prisoner I became a 'gentleman'[463] prisoner. The officer commenced a long panegyric of Sir Michael O'Dwyer.[464] Sir Michael had nothing against

M10 tell them that

M11 explain to them how

---

[462] 'accompanying' in the first edition.

[463] 'gentleman' English word in the original.

[464] Sir Michael Francis O'Dwyer (1864–1940), Lt. Governor of the Punjab (1912–19), endorsed General Reginald Dyer's action

me personally, he went on, only he apprehended a disturbance of the peace if I entered the Punjab and so on. In the end he requested me to return to Bombay of my own accord and agree not to cross the frontier of the Punjab. I replied that I could not possibly comply with the order, and that I was not prepared of my own accord to go back. Whereupon the officer, seeing no other course,[465] told me that he would have to enforce the law against me. 'But what do you want to do with me?' I asked him. He replied that he himself did not know, but was awaiting further orders. 'For the present,' he said, 'I am taking you to Bombay.'[466]

We reached Surat. Here I was made over to the charge of another police officer. 'You are now free,' the officer told me when we had reached Bombay. 'It would however be better,' he added, 'if you get down near the Marine Lines where I shall get the train stopped for you. At Colaba there is likely to be a big crowd.' I told him that I would be glad to follow his wish. He was pleased and thanked me for it. Accordingly I alighted at the Marine Lines. The carriage of a friend just happened to be passing by. It took me and left me at Revashankar Jhaveri's place. The friend told me that the news of my arrest had incensed the people and roused them to a pitch of mad frenzy. 'An outbreak is apprehended every minute near Pydhuni, the Magistrate and the police have already arrived there,' he added.

Scarcely had I reached my destination, when Umar Sobani and Anasuyabehn arrived and asked me to motor to Pydhuni at once. 'The people have become impatient, and are very much excited,' they said, 'we cannot pacify them. Your presence alone can do it.'

---

in Jallianwala Bagh, assassinated by Udham Singh on 13 March 1940 in Caxton Hall, London.

[465] 'help' in the first edition.

[466] For details of the arrest, see *CWMG*, vol. 15, pp. 227–28.

I got into the car. Near Pydhuni I saw that a huge crowd had gathered. On seeing me the people went mad with joy. A procession was immediately formed, and the sky was rent with the shouts of *Vande Mataram* and *Allaho Akbar*. At Pydhuni we sighted a body of mounted police. Brickbats were raining down from above. I besought[467] the crowd to be calm, but it seemed as if we should not be able to escape the shower of brickbats. As the procession issued out of Abdur Rahman Street and was about to proceed towards the Crawford Market, it suddenly found itself confronted by a body of the mounted police, who had arrived there to prevent it from proceeding further in the direction of the Fort. The crowd was densely packed. It had almost broken through the police cordon. There was hardly any chance of my voice being heard in that vast concourse.[468] Just then the officer in charge of the mounted police gave the order to disperse the crowd, and at once the mounted party charged upon the crowd brandishing their lances as they went. For a moment I *felt that I would be hurt.*[M12] But my apprehension was groundless, the lances just grazed the car as the lancers swiftly passed by.[469] The ranks of the people were soon broken, and they were thrown into utter confusion, which was soon converted into a rout. Some got trampled underfoot, others were badly mauled and crushed. In that seething mass of humanity[470] there was hardly any room for the horses to pass, nor was there an exit by which the people could disperse. *So the lancers blindly cut their way through the crowd. I hardly imagine they*

[M12] feared that one of the lances might also dispose us of

---

[467] 'beseeched' in the first edition.

[468] 'in that vast concourse' added in the English translation.

[469] 'at the speed of a rail car' to add.

[470] 'In that seething mass of humanity' added in the English translation.

could see what they were doing. The whole thing presented a most dreadful spectacle. The horsemen and the people were mixed together in mad confusion.[M13]

Thus the crowd was dispersed and its progress checked. Our motor was allowed to proceed. I had it stopped before the Commissioner's office, and got down to complain to him about the conduct of the police.

[M13] It was a most dreadful scene. The horsemen and the people seemed like madmen. The mounted police did not see and could not see anything. They bent low on their horses and cut their way. I saw that the time it took them to cut through the crowd of thousands, they could see not a thing before them.

XXXII

THAT MEMORABLE[471] WEEK!–II

So I went to the Commissioner Mr. Griffith's[472] office. All about the staircase leading to the office I saw soldiers[473] armed from top to toe, as though for military action. The verandah was all astir. When I was admitted to the office, I saw Mr. Bowring sitting with Mr. Griffith.

I described to the Commissioner the scenes I had witnessed. He replied briefly: 'I did not want the procession to proceed to the Fort, as a disturbance was inevitable there. And as I saw that the people would not listen to persuasion, I could not help ordering the mounted police to charge through the crowd.'

'But,' said I, 'you knew what the consequences must be. The horses were bound to trample on the people. I think it was quite unnecessary to send that contingent of mounted men.'

'You cannot judge that,' said Mr. Griffith. 'We police officers know better than you the effect of your

---

[471] 'Memorable' added in the English translation.

[472] Sir Francis Charles Griffith (1878–1942), appointed police commissioner of Bombay (1919), inspector-general of Bombay (1922) and later chief constable, New Scotland Yard.

[473] 'soldiers' English word in the original.

teaching on the people. If we did not start with drastic measures, the situation would pass out of our hands. I tell you that the people are sure to go out of your control. Disobedience of law will quickly appeal to them; it is beyond them to understand the duty of keeping peaceful. I have no doubt about your intentions, but the people will not understand them. They will follow their natural instinct.'

'It is there that I join issue with you,' I replied. 'The people are not by nature violent but peaceful.'

And thus we argued at length. Ultimately *Mr. Griffith*[M1] said, 'But suppose you were convinced that your teaching had been lost on the people, what would you do?'

M1 Sahib

'I should suspend civil disobedience if I were so convinced.'

'What do you mean? You told Mr. Bowring that you would proceed to the Punjab the moment you were released.'

'Yes, I wanted to do so by the next available train. But it is out of the question today.'

'If you will be patient, the conviction is sure to grow on you. Do you know what is happening in Ahmedabad? And what has happened in Amritsar? People have everywhere gone nearly mad. I am not yet in possession of all the facts. The telegraph wires have been cut in some places. I put it to you that the responsibility for all these disturbances lies on you.'

'I assure you I should readily take it upon myself wherever I discovered it. But I should be deeply pained and surprised, if I found that there were disturbances in Ahmedabad. I cannot answer for Amritsar. I have never been there, no one knows me there. But even about the Punjab[474] I am certain of this much that, had not the Punjab Government prevented my entry into

---

[474] 'even about the Punjab' added in the English translation.

the Punjab, I should have been considerably helpful in keeping the peace there. By preventing me they gave the people unnecessary provocation.'

And so we argued on and on. It was impossible for us to agree. I told him that I intended to address a meeting on Chaupati and to ask the people to keep the peace, and took leave of him. The meeting was held on the Chaupati sands.[475] I spoke at length on the duty of non-violence and on the limitations of satyagraha, and said: 'Satyagraha is essentially a weapon of the truthful. *A satyagrahi is pledged to non-violence, and, unless people observe it in thought, word and deed, I cannot offer mass satyagraha.*'[M2]

[M2] Unless people remain peaceful I cannot wage the battle of satyagraha.

Anasuyabehn, too, had received news of disturbances in Ahmedabad. Someone had spread a rumour that she also had been arrested. The mill-hands had gone mad over her rumoured arrest, struck work and committed acts of violence, and a sergeant[476] had been done to death.

I proceeded to Ahmedabad. I learnt that an attempt had been made to pull up the rails near the Nadiad railway station, that a Government officer had been murdered in Viramgam, and that Ahmedabad was under martial law. The people were terror-stricken. They had indulged in acts of violence and were being made to pay for them with interest.

A police officer was waiting at the station to escort me to Mr. Pratt, the Commissioner. I found him in a state of rage. I spoke to him gently, and expressed my regret *for the disturbances*[M3]—I suggested that martial law was unnecessary, and declared my readiness to co-operate in all efforts to restore peace. I asked for permission to hold a public meeting on the grounds of the Sabarmati Ashram. The proposal appealed to him,

[M3] over the killings

---

[475] The meeting was held on 11 April 1919.

[476] 'soldier' in the original.

and the meeting was held, I think, on Sunday, the 13th of April,[477] and martial law was withdrawn the same day or the day after. Addressing the meeting,[478] I tried to bring home to the people the sense of their wrong, declared a penitential fast of three days[479] for myself, appealed to the people to go on a similar fast for a day, and suggested to those who had been guilty of acts of violence to confess their guilt.

I saw my duty as clear as daylight. It was unbearable for me to find that the labourers, amongst whom I had spent a good deal of my time, whom I had served, and from whom I had expected better things, had taken part in the riots, and I felt I was a sharer in their guilt.

Just as I suggested to the people to confess their guilt, I suggested to the Government to condone the crimes. Neither accepted my suggestion.[480]

The late Sir[481] Ramanbhai[482] and other citizens of Ahmedabad came to me with an appeal to suspend satyagraha. The appeal was needless, for I had already made up my mind to suspend satyagraha so long as people had not learnt the lesson of peace. The friends went away happy.

There were, however, others who were unhappy over the decision. They felt that, if I expected peace everywhere and regarded it as a condition precedent

---

[477] The meeting was held on Monday, 14 April. See *CWMG*, vol. 15, pp. 220–24.

[478] Vallabhbhai Patel read out MKG's speech.

[479] MKG had commenced the fast on 13 April after his meeting with commissioner Pratt.

[480] 'Neither did the people confess to the crime, nor did the Government condone them.' To add.

[481] 'Sir' added in the English translation.

[482] Sir Ramanbhai Mahipatram Nilkanth (1868–1928), author of the Gujarati classics *Bhadram Bhadra* and *Rai no Parbat*, social reformer, president, Ahmedabad Municipality.

to launching satyagraha, mass satyagraha would be an impossibility. *I was sorry to disagree with them.*[M4] If those amongst whom I worked, and *whom I expected to be prepared for non-violence and self-suffering,*[M5] could not be non-violent, satyagraha was certainly impossible. I was firmly of opinion that those who wanted to lead the people to satyagraha ought to be able to keep the people within the limited non-violence expected of them. I hold the same opinion even today.

[M4] I expressed my disagreement.

[M5] through whom I had expected to offer satyagraha

XXXIII

'A HIMALAYAN[483] MISCALCULATION'

Almost immediately after the Ahmedabad meeting I went to Nadiad.[484] It was here that I first used the expression 'Himalayan miscalculation' which obtained such a wide currency afterwards. Even at Ahmedabad I had begun to have a dim[485] perception of my mistake. *But when I reached Nadiad and saw the actual state of things there and heard reports about a large number of people from Kheda district having been arrested, it suddenly dawned upon me that I had committed a grave error in calling upon the people in the Kheda district and elsewhere to launch upon civil disobedience prematurely, as it now seemed to me.*[M1] I was addressing a public meeting.[486] My confession brought down upon me no small amount of ridicule. *But I have never regretted having made that confession. For I have always*

[M1] Considering the situation in Nadiad, hearing about the arrests of many from Kheda district, during the course of my speech at the public meeting, I suddenly realized that I had, in inviting people from Kheda and elsewhere to offer civil disobedience, committed an error and it appeared to be mountainous.

---

[483] In the original 'mountainous'. Throughout the chapter the word 'mountainous' has been translated as 'Himalayan'.

[484] MKG was in Nadiad on 24 April, having been in Bombay from 18–21 April and in Ahmedabad from 22–23 April.

[485] 'dim' added in the English translation.

[486] 'I was addressing a public meeting.' Added in the English translation.

M2 I have always believed that
we must reduce to a dust
particle the elephantine errors
of others and view our own
errors, small as a mustard
seed, as large as mountains;
only then do we get a relative
estimation of others' and our
own errors.

M3 a good

M4 And if someone were to
advise obedience of such laws,
even persons considered to be
good would not readily agree
to it.

M5 carry head-lights on his
bicycle after dark

M6 acquires the fitness to
distinguish between morality
and immorality

*held that it is only when one sees one's own mistakes with a convex lens, and does just the reverse in the case of others, that one is able to arrive at a just relative estimate of the two.*M2 I further believe that a scrupulous and conscientious observance of this rule is necessary for one who wants to be a satyagrahi.

Let us now see what that Himalayan miscalculation was. Before one can be fit for the practice of civil disobedience one must have rendered a willing and respectful obedience to the State laws. For the most part we obey such laws out of fear of the penalty for their breach, and this holds good particularly in respect of such laws as do not involve a moral principle. For instance, *an honest, respectable*M3 man will not suddenly take to stealing, whether[487] there is a law against stealing or not, but this very man will not feel any remorse for failure to observe the rule about carrying head-lights on bicycles after dark. *Indeed it is doubtful whether he would even accept advice kindly about being more careful in this respect.*M4 But he would *observe any obligatory rule of this kind,*M5 if only to escape the inconvenience of facing a prosecution for a breach of the rule. Such compliance is not, however,[488] the willing and spontaneous obedience that is required of a satyagrahi.[489] A satyagrahi obeys the laws of society intelligently and of his own free will, because he considers it to be his sacred duty to do so. It is only when a person has thus obeyed the laws of society scrupulously that he *is in a position to judge as to which particular rules are good and just and which unjust and iniquitous.*M6 Only then does the right accrue to him of the civil disobedience of certain laws in well-defined circumstances. My error lay in my failure to

---

[487] 'stealing, irrespective of whether' in the first edition.

[488] 'Such compliance will not, however, constitute the' in the first edition.

[489] 'that is required of a satyagrahi' added in the English translation.

observe this necessary limitation.[490] I had called on[491] the people to launch upon civil disobedience before they had thus qualified themselves for it, and this mistake[492] seemed to me of Himalayan magnitude. As soon as I entered the Kheda district, all the old recollections of the Kheda Satyagraha struggle came back to me, and I wondered how I could have failed to perceive what was so obvious. I realized that before a people could be fit for offering civil disobedience, they should thoroughly understand its deeper implications.[493] That being so, before *restarting*[M7] civil disobedience on a mass scale, it would be necessary to create a band of well-tried,[494] pure-hearted volunteers who thoroughly understood *the strict conditions of satyagraha.*[M8] They could explain these to the people, and *by sleepless vigilance keep them on the right path.*[M9]

With these thoughts filling my mind I reached Bombay, raised a corps of satyagrahi volunteers through the Satyagraha Sabha there, and with their help commenced the work of educating the people with regard to the meaning and inner significance of

[M7] initiating

[M8] civil disobedience and its limits

[M9] guide them at every moment

---

[490] 'My error lay in my failure to observe this necessary limitation.' Added in the English translation.

[491] 'upon' in the first edition.

[492] 'mistake of mine' in the first edition.

[493] 'How can those who daily commit breach of law in their thoughts, those who often break laws furtively, recognize civil disobedience all of a sudden? How can they observe its limits? It is easy to understand that such an ideal condition cannot be attained by thousands or hundreds of thousands.' To add. 'But it may be rightly argued: How can a people who are in the habit of frequently evading laws, as most people are, suddenly grasp the significance of civil disobedience, or keep themselves within its strict bounds? I admit, that it is no easy matter for thousands and hundreds of thousands of people to fulfil the ideal conditions mentioned above.' These lines from the first edition were deleted in the 1940 revised edition.

[494] 'well-tried' added in the English translation.

satyagraha. This was principally done by issuing leaflets of an educative character bearing on the subject.[495]

But whilst this work was going on, I could see that *it was a difficult task to interest the people in the peaceful side of satyagraha.*[M10] The volunteers too failed to enlist themselves in large numbers. Nor did all those who actually enlisted take anything like a regular systematic training, and as the days passed by, *the number of fresh recruits began gradually to dwindle instead of to grow. I realized that the progress of the training in civil disobedience was not going to be as rapid as I had at first expected.*[M11]

M10 I could not generate much interest among people

M11 even those who had enlisted began to fall rather than become firmer. I realized that the cart of civil disobedience would move at a pace slower than expected.

XXXIV

'NAVAJIVAN' AND 'YOUNG INDIA'

Thus, whilst this movement for the preservation of non-violence was making steady though slow progress on the one hand, Government's policy of lawless[496] repression was in full career on the other, and was manifesting itself in the Punjab in all its nakedness.[497] *Leaders were put under arrest, martial law, which in other words meant no law, was proclaimed,*[M1] special tribunals were set up. These tribunals were not courts of justice but instruments for carrying out the arbitrary will of an autocrat. Sentences were passed unwarranted by evidence and in flagrant violation of justice. In Amritsar[498] innocent men and women were made to crawl like worms on their bellies.

M1 Martial law was proclaimed, hence there was authoritarian rule. Leaders were arrested.

---

[495] Two leaflets were issued under the title 'Satyagrahi' and twenty-one under 'Satyagraha leaflet'. See *CWMG*, vol. 15.

[496] 'lawless' added in the English translation.

[497] 'in all its nakedness' added in the English translation.

[498] 'In Amritsar' added in the English translation.

Before this outrage[499] the Jallianwala Bagh tragedy[500] paled into insignificance in my eyes, though it was this massacre principally[501] that attracted the attention of the people of India and of the world.

I was pressed to proceed to the Punjab immediately in disregard of consequences. I wrote and also telegraphed to the Viceroy asking for permission to go there, but in vain. If I proceeded without the necessary permission, I should not be allowed to cross the boundary of the Punjab, but left to find what satisfaction I could from civil disobedience. I was thus confronted by a *serious*[M2]   [M2] moral
dilemma. As things stood, to break the order against my entry into the Punjab could, it seemed to me, hardly be classed as civil disobedience, for I did not see around me the kind of peaceful atmosphere that I wanted, and the unbridled repression in the Punjab had further served to aggravate and deepen the feelings of resentment. For me, therefore, to offer civil disobedience at such a time, even if it were possible, would have been like fanning the flame.[502] I therefore decided not to proceed to the Punjab in spite of the suggestion of friends. It was a bitter pill for me to swallow. Tales of rank injustice and oppression came pouring in daily from the Punjab, but all I could do was to sit helplessly by and gnash my teeth.

---

[499] 'procedure' in the first edition.

[500] The Jallianwala Bagh massacre took place on 13 April 1919, when a crowd of non-violent protesters along with Baisakhi pilgrims who had gathered at the Jallianwala Bagh at Amritsar were fired upon by the troops of the British Indian Army under the command of Reginald Dyer. According to the British government, 379 persons died and 1200 were wounded; unofficial figures, including those of the inquiry committee of the Indian National Congress, put the figure of the dead at over 1000.

[501] 'principally' added in the English translation.

[502] 'fanning the flame' translates a colloquial expression which would translate as 'adding ghee to fire'.

Just then Mr. Horniman, in whose hands the *Bombay Chronicle* had become a formidable force, was suddenly spirited away by the authorities.[503] This act of the Government seemed to me to be surrounded by a foulness which still stinks in my nostrils.[504] I know that Mr. Horniman never desired lawlessness. He had not liked my breaking the prohibitory order of the Punjab Government without the permission of the Satyagraha Committee, and had fully endorsed the decision to suspend civil disobedience. I had even received from him a letter advising suspension before I had announced my decision to that effect. Only owing to the distance between Bombay and Ahmedabad I got the letter after the announcement. His sudden deportation therefore caused me as much pain as surprise.

As a result of these developments I was asked by the directors of the *Bombay Chronicle* to take up the responsibility of conducting that paper. Mr. Brelvi[505] was already there on the staff, so not much remained to be done by me, but as usual with my nature, the responsibility *would have become* [M3] an additional tax.

[M3] became

But the Government came as it were to my rescue, for by its order the publication of The Chronicle had to be suspended.[M4]

[M4] But I did not have to bear this responsibility for any length of time. The Government, in its kindness, suspended its publication.

The friends who were directing the management of *The Chronicle*, viz., Messrs Umar Sobani and Shankarlal Banker, were at this time also controlling *Young India*. They suggested that, in view of the suppression of *The Chronicle*, I should now take up the editorship of *Young India*, and that, in order to fill the gap left by the former,

[503] 'while the people slept' to add. The *Bombay Chronicle* was established in 1910 by Sir Pherozeshah Mehta, B G Horniman, Marmaduke Pickthall and Syed Abdullah Brelvi were among its editors, the paper closed down in 1959.

[504] For MKG's immediate reaction to B.G. Horniman's deportation, see *CWMG*, vol. 15, pp. 260–61.

[505] Syed Abdullah Brelvi became the editor of the *Bombay Chronicle* in 1924, remaining in that position till his death in 1942.

Young India should be converted from a weekly into a bi-weekly organ.[506] This was what I felt also. I was anxious to expound the inner meaning of satyagraha to the public, and also hoped that through this effort I should at least be able *to do justice to*[M5] the Punjab situation. For, behind all I wrote, there was *potential*[M6] satyagraha, and the Government knew as much. I therefore readily accepted the suggestion made by these friends.

But how could the general public be trained in satyagraha through the medium of English? My principal field of work lay in Gujarat. Sjt. Indulal Yagnik was at that time associated with the *group of Messrs Sobani and Banker*.[M7] He was conducting the Gujarati monthly *Navajivan* which had the financial backing of these friends. They placed the monthly at my disposal, and further Sjt. Indulal offered to work on it. This monthly was converted into a weekly.[507]

In the meantime *The Chronicle* was resuscitated. *Young India* was therefore restored to its original weekly form. To have published the two weeklies from two different places would have been very inconvenient to me and involved more expenditure. As *Navajivan* was already being published from Ahmedabad *Young India* was also removed there at my suggestion.

There were other reasons besides for this change.[508] I had already learnt from my experience of *Indian Opinion* that such journals needed a press of their own. Moreover the press laws in force in India at that time were such that, if I wanted to express my views untrammelled, the existing printing presses, which were naturally run

M5 offer appropriate criticism of

M6 the power of

M7 same group

---

[506] In *Young India* of 11 June 1919 MKG announced: 'By courtesy of the *Young India* syndicate composed as it is largely of satyagrahis, since the deportation of Mr. Horniman, I have been permitted to supervise the editing of this journal.' *CWMG*, vol. 15, p. 260.

[507] The takeover of *Navajivan* was announced in July 1919. See ibid., pp. 419–21.

[508] 'There were other reasons besides for this change.' Added in the English translation.

for business, would have hesitated to publish them. The need for setting up a press of our own, therefore, became all the more imperative, and since this could be conveniently done only at Ahmedabad, *Young India* too had to be taken there.

Through these journals I now commenced to the best of my ability the work of educating the reading public in satyagraha. Both of them[509] had reached a very wide circulation, which at one time rose to the neighbourhood of forty thousand each. But while the circulation of *Navajivan* went up at a bound, that of *Young India* increased only by slow degrees. After my incarceration the circulation of both these journals fell to a low ebb, and today stands below eight thousand.

From the very start I set my face against taking advertisements in these journals. I do not think that they have lost anything thereby. On the contrary, it is my belief that it has in no small measure helped them to maintain their independence.

Incidentally these journals helped me also to some extent to remain at peace with myself for, whilst immediate resort to civil disobedience was out of the question, they enabled me freely to ventilate my views and to put heart into *the people*.[M8] Thus I feel that both the journals rendered good service to the people in this hour of trial, and did their humble bit towards lightening the tyranny of the martial law.

M8 those who looked towards me for advice and guidance

XXXV

IN THE PUNJAB

Sir Michael O'Dwyer held me responsible for all that had happened in the Punjab, and some irate[510]

---

[509] 'from just a few copies' to add.

[510] 'irate' added in the English translation.

young Punjabis *held me responsible for the martial law.*
They[M1] asserted that, if only I had not suspended civil
disobedience, there would have been no Jallianwala
Bagh massacre.[511] Some of them even went the length
of threatening me with assassination if I went to the
Punjab.

But I felt that my position was so correct and
above question that no intelligent person could
misunderstand it.

I was impatient to go to the Punjab. I had never been
there before, and that made me all the more anxious to
see things for myself. Dr. Satyapal, Dr. Kitchlew and
Pandit Rambhaj Dutt Chowdhari,[512] who had invited
me to the Punjab,[513] were at this time in jail. But I felt
sure that the Government could not dare to keep them
and the other prisoners[514] in prison for long. A large
number of Punjabis used to come and see me whenever
I was in Bombay. I ministered to them a word of cheer
on these occasions, and that would comfort them. My
self-confidence of that time was *infectious.*[M2]

But my going to the Punjab had to be postponed
again and again. The Viceroy would say, 'not yet', every
time I asked for permission to go there, and so the thing
dragged on.[515]

In the meantime the Hunter Committee was
announced to hold an inquiry in connection with the
Punjab Government's doings under the martial law.
Mr. C.F. Andrews[516] had now reached the Punjab.

[M1] did not hesitate even in holding me guilty for the martial law. These irate young men

[M2] plentiful

---

[511] 'and no martial law either' to add.

[512] Rambhaj Dutt Chaudhary (1866–1923), a journalist and a
Congress worker of the Punjab.

[513] 'to the Punjab' added in the English translation.

[514] 'and the other prisoners' added in the English translation.

[515] 'every time I asked for permission to go there, and so the thing
dragged on' added in the English translation.

[516] 'Deenbandhu Andrews' in the original.

M3 suggested

His letters gave a heart-rending description of the state of things there, and *I formed the impression*[M3] that the martial law atrocities were in fact even worse than the Press reports had showed. He pressed me urgently to come and join him. At the same time Malaviyaji sent telegrams asking me to proceed to the Punjab at once. I once more telegraphed to the Viceroy asking whether I could now go to the Punjab. He wired back in reply that I could go there after a certain date. I cannot exactly recollect now, but I think it was 17th of October.[517]

The scene that I witnessed on my arrival at Lahore can never be effaced from my memory. The railway station was from end to end one seething mass of humanity. The entire populace had turned out of doors in eager expectation, as if to meet a dear relation after a long separation, and was delirious with joy. I was put up at the late Pandit Rambhaj Dutt's bungalow, and the burden of entertaining me fell on the shoulders of Shrimati Sarala Devi.[518] A burden it truly was, for even then, as now, the place where I was accommodated became a veritable caravanserai.

Owing to the principal Punjab leaders being in jail, their place, I found, had been properly[519]

---

[517] 15 October 1919. In a telegram dated 3 October 1919, Maffey, the PS to the Viceroy, wrote, 'Orders to which you refer will be withdrawn on October fifteenth.' MKG received the notice withdrawing the orders on 16 October. He reached Lahore on 24 October 1919.

[518] 'with whom I had previous acquaintance' to add. Sarala Devi Chaudharani (1872–1945), poet, nationalist leader, daughter of Jankinath Ghoshal and Swarnakumari Devi, niece of Tagore; MKG's relationship with her underwent intense fluctuations, from a time when he contemplated 'spiritual marriage' with her to cultivated distance. Her son Deepak married Maganlal Gandhi's daughter Rukshmani or Rukhi.

[519] 'properly' added in the English translation.

taken up by Pandit Malaviyaji, Pandit Motilalji[520] and the late Swami Shraddhanandji. Malaviyaji and Shraddhanandji I had known intimately before, but this was the first occasion on which I came in close personal contact with Motilalji. All these leaders, as also such local leaders as had escaped the privilege of going to jail, at once made me feel perfectly at home amongst them, so that I never felt like a stranger in their midst.

How[521] we unanimously decided not to lead evidence before the Hunter Committee[522] is now a matter of history.[523] The reasons for that decision were published at that time, and need not be recapitulated here. Suffice it to say that, looking back upon these events from this distance of time,[524] I still feel that our decision to boycott the Committee was absolutely correct and proper.[525]

---

[520] Pandit Motilal Nehru (1861–1931), nationalist lawyer, twice served as president of the Indian National Congress (1919–20 and 1928–29), founded the English daily *The Leader*, one of the founders of the Swaraj Party and author of the Nehru Report (1928) that envisioned dominion status for India.

[521] 'How' added in the English translation.

[522] Hunter Commission, established to examine the atrocities at Jallianwala Bagh. Lord William Hunter, chairman, Mr. Justice George C. Rankin, Sir Chimanlal Harilal Setalvad, W.F. Rice (member, Home Department), Major General Sir George Barrow, GOC, Peshawar, Pandit Jagat Narayan (member, Legislative Council, United Provinces), Thomas Smith (member, Legislative Council, United Provinces), Sardar Sahibzada Sultan Ahmed Khan (lawyer, Gwalior) were members and H.C. Stokes (member, Home Department) was the secretary of the Commission.

[523] 'is now a matter of history' added in the English translation.

[524] 'Suffice it to say that, looking back upon the events from this distance of time,' added in the English translation.

[525] For the Congress committee's statement, see *CWMG*, vol. 16, pp. 546–50.

As a logical consequence of the boycott of the Hunter Committee, it was decided to appoint a non-official Inquiry Committee, to hold almost a parallel inquiry on behalf of the Congress.[M4] Pandit Motilal Nehru, the late Deshbandhu C.R. Das,[526] Sjt. Abbas Tyabji,[527] Sjt. M.R. Jayakar[528] and myself were appointed to this Committee, virtually[529] by Pandit Malaviyaji. We distributed ourselves over various places for purposes of inquiry. The responsibility for organizing the work of the Committee devolved on me, and as the privilege of conducting the inquiry in the largest number of places fell to my lot, I got a rare opportunity of observing at close quarters the people of the Punjab and the Punjab villages.[530]

In the course of my inquiry I made acquaintance with the women of the Punjab also. It was as if we had known one another for ages. Wherever I went they came flocking, and laid before me their[531] heaps of yarn.[532] My work in connection with the inquiry brought home to me the fact that the Punjab could become a great field for khadi work.

[M4] If the Committee were to be boycotted it was decided to have a Committee on behalf of the people, that is the Congress.

---

[526] Chittaranjan Das (1869–1925), lawyer, pre-eminent leader of the Bengal Congress, president of the Indian National Congress (1921), one of the founders of the Swaraj Party.

[527] Abbas Tayabji (1854–1936), served as the chief justice of Baroda State, appointed as MKG's immediate successor to lead the Salt Satyagraha in case of MKG's arrest, led the raid on the Dharasana Salt Works.

[528] Mukund Ramrao Jayakar (1873–1959), liberal lawyer, member, Bombay Legislative Council and Central Legislative Council, judge, Federal Court of India, member, Privy Council, and member, Constituent Assembly of India.

[529] 'virtually' added in the English translation.

[530] The committee was constituted on 14 November 1919 and began its work on 17 November and submitted its report on 25 March 1920.

[531] 'their' added in the English translation.

[532] 'spun by them' to add.

As I proceeded further and further with my inquiry into the atrocities that had been committed on the people, I came across tales of Government's tyranny[533] and the arbitrary despotism of its officers such as I was hardly prepared for, and they filled me with deep pain. What surprised me then, and what still continues to fill me with surprise, was the fact that a province that had furnished the largest number of soldiers to the British Government during the War,[534] should have taken all these brutal excesses lying down.

The task of drafting the report of this Committee was also entrusted to me. I would recommend a perusal of this report to anyone who wants to have an idea of the kind of atrocities that were perpetrated on the Punjab people.[535] All that I wish to say here about it is that there is not a single conscious exaggeration in it anywhere, and every statement made in it is substantiated by evidence. Moreover, the evidence published was only a fraction of what was in the Committee's possession. Not a single statement, regarding the validity of which there was the slightest room for doubt, was permitted to appear in the report. This report, prepared as it was solely with a view to bringing out the truth and nothing but the truth, will enable the reader to see to what lengths the British Government is capable of going, and what inhumanities and barbarities it is capable of perpetrating in order to maintain its power. So far as I am aware, not a single statement made in this report has ever been disproved.

---

[533] 'tyranny' translates the original term 'Nadirshahi', which refers to the massacre of Delhi after the victory of Nadir Shah of Persia over the Mughal emperor in 1739.

[534] 'during the War' added in the English translation.

[535] See *CWMG*, vol. 17, pp. 114–292.

XXXVI

THE KHILAFAT AGAINST
COW-PROTECTION?

We must now leave for the time being *these dark happenings in*[M1] the Punjab.

The Congress inquiry into Dyerism in the Punjab had just commenced, *when I received a letter of invitation to be present at a joint conference of Hindus and Mussalmans that was to meet at Delhi to deliberate on the Khilafat question. Among the signatories to it were the late Hakim Ajmal Khan Saheb and Mr. Asaf Ali.*[536] *The late Swami Shraddhanandji, it was stated, would be attending and, if I remember aright, he was to be the vice-president of the conference, which, so far as I can recollect, was to be held in the November of that year. The conference was to deliberate on the situation arising out of the Khilafat betrayal, and on the question as to whether the Hindus and Mussalmans should take any part in the peace celebrations.*[M2] The letter of invitation went on to say, among other things, that not only the Khilafat question but the question of cow-protection as well would be discussed at the conference, and it would, therefore, afford a *golden*[M3] opportunity for a settlement of the cow question. I did not like this reference to the cow question. In my letter in reply to the invitation, therefore, whilst promising to do my best to attend, I suggested that the two questions should not be mixed up together or considered in the spirit of a bargain, but should be decided on their own merits and treated separately.

---

[536] Asaf Ali (1888–1953), nationalist, called to the Bar from Lincoln's Inn, played a prominent part in the Quit India agitation (1942), defended Bhagat Singh in his trial and was convenor of the Indian National Army defence team in 1945, served as India's first ambassador to the United States of America. Married Aruna Asaf Ali (née Ganguli).

With these thoughts filling my mind,[537] I went to the conference.[538] It was a very well attended gathering, though it did not present the spectacle of later gatherings that were attended by tens of thousands. I discussed the question referred to above with the late Swami Shraddhanandji, who was present at the conference. He appreciated my argument and left it to me to place it before the conference. I likewise discussed it with the late Hakim Saheb.[539] Before the conference I contended that,[540] if the Khilafat question had a just and legitimate basis, as I believe it had,[541] and if the Government had really committed a gross injustice, the Hindus were bound to stand by the Mussalmans in their demand for the redress of the Khilafat wrong. It would ill become them to bring in the cow question in this connection, or to use the occasion to make terms with the Mussalmans, just as it would ill become the Mussalmans to offer to stop cow slaughter as a price for the Hindus' support on the Khilafat question. But it would be another matter and quite graceful, and reflect great credit on them, if the Mussalmans of their own free will stopped cow-slaughter out of regard for the religious sentiments of the Hindus, and from a sense of duty towards them as neighbours and children of the same soil. To take up such an independent attitude was, I contended, their duty, and would enhance the dignity of their conduct. But if the Mussalmans considered it as their neighbourly duty to stop cow slaughter, they

---

[537] 'With these thoughts filling my mind' added in the English translation.

[538] MKG attended the conference on 23 and 24 November 1919.

[539] 'My contention was that both questions should be examined on their own merit.' To add.

[540] 'Before the conference I contended that' added in the English translation.

[541] 'as I believe it had' added in the English translation.

should do so regardless of whether the Hindus helped them in the Khilafat or not. 'That being so,' I argued, 'the two questions should be discussed independently of each other, and the deliberations of the conference should be confined to the question of the Khilafat only.' My argument appealed to those present and, as a result, the question of cow-protection was not discussed at this conference.[542]

But in spite of my warning Maulana Abdul Bari Saheb said: 'No matter whether the Hindus help us or not, the Mussalmans ought, as the countrymen of the Hindus, out of regard for the latter's susceptibilities, to give up cow slaughter.'[543] And at one time it almost looked as if they would really put an end to it.

There was a suggestion from some quarters that the Punjab question should be tacked on to that of the Khilafat wrong. I opposed the proposal. The Punjab question, I said, was a local affair and could not therefore weigh with us in our decision to participate or not in the peace celebrations.[544] If we mixed up the local question with the Khilafat question, which arose directly out of the peace terms,[545] we should be guilty

---

[542] For MKG's speech at the Khilafat Conference, see *CWMG*, vol. 16, pp. 318–23.

[543] The *Young India* of 20 December 1928, vol. X. no. 51, reads: 'But in spite of my warning the Mussalmans felt called upon at later conferences always to allude to the duty of stopping cow slaughter in grateful recognition of the Hindu's help on the Khilafat question.' *Navajivan* of 16 December 1928 has: 'But in spite of this, the Mussalmans did not stop discussing the issue of cow-protection.' The text of the *Autobiography* was changed in the first edition, vol. 2, pp. 532–33, and the changes were later incorporated in the subsequent Gujarati edition.

[544] 'which concerned the whole Empire' to add.

[545] 'which arose directly out of the peace terms' added in the English translation.

of a serious indiscretion. My argument easily carried conviction.[546]

Maulana Hasrat Mohani[547] was present in this meeting. I had known him even before, but it was only here that I discovered what a fighter he was. We differed from each other *almost from the very beginning*,[M4] and in several matters the differences have persisted.

<small>[M4] at this meeting</small>

Among the numerous resolutions that were passed at this conference, one called upon both Hindus and Mussalmans to take the Swadeshi vow, and as a natural corollary to it, to boycott foreign *goods*.[M5] Khadi had not as yet *found its proper place*.[M6] This was not a resolution that Hasrat Saheb would accept. His object was to wreak vengeance on the British Empire, in case justice was denied in the matter of the Khilafat. Accordingly, he brought in a counter proposal for the boycott purely of British goods so far as practicable. I opposed it on the score of principle, as also of practicability, adducing for it those arguments that have now become pretty familiar. I also put before the conference my view-point of non-violence. I noticed that my arguments made a deep impression on the audience. Before me, Hasrat Mohani's speech had been received with such loud acclamations that I was afraid that mine would only be a cry in the wilderness.[548] I had made bold to speak only because I felt that it would be a dereliction of duty not to lay my views before the conference. But, to my

<small>[M5] cloth</small>

<small>[M6] been reborn</small>

[546] The paragraph 'There was a suggestion from . . . easily carried conviction' was not in *Navajivan* of 16 December 1928 nor in *Young India* of 20 December 1928. This paragraph was added in the first edition, vol. 2, p. 533, and was later incorporated in the subsequent Gujarati edition.

[547] Maulana Hasrat (Syed Fazl-ul-Hasan) Mohani (1875–1951), poet, nationalist, one of the founders of the Communist Party of India.

[548] 'cry in the wilderness' translates '*tuti no avaj*', literally, 'sound of my mouth-organ'.

agreeable surprise,[549] my speech was followed with the closest attention by those present, and evoked a full measure of support among those on the platform,[550] and speaker after speaker rose to deliver speeches in support of my views. The leaders were able to see that not only would the boycott of British goods fail of its purpose, but would, if adopted, make of them a laughing stock. There was hardly a man present in that assembly but had some article of British manufacture on his person. Many of the audience therefore realized that nothing but harm could result from adopting a resolution that even those who voted for it were unable to carry out.

'Mere boycott of foreign cloth cannot satisfy us, for who knows how long it will be, before we shall be able to manufacture Swadeshi cloth in sufficient quantity for our needs, and before we can bring about an effective boycott of foreign cloth? We want something that will produce an immediate effect on the British. Let your boycott of foreign cloth stand, we do not mind it, but give us something quicker, and speedier in addition'— so spoke in effect Maulana Hasrat Mohani.[551] Even as I was listening to him, I felt that something new, over and above boycott of foreign cloth, would be necessary. An immediate boycott of foreign cloth seemed to me also to be a clear impossibility, at that time. I did not then know that we could, if we liked, produce enough khadi for all our clothing requirements; this was only a later discovery. On the other hand, I knew even then that, if we depended on the mills alone for effecting the boycott of foreign cloth, we should be betrayed. I was still in the middle of this dilemma when the Maulana concluded his speech.

---

[549] 'to my agreeable surprise' added in the English translation.

[550] 'platform' English word in the original.

[551] 'Hasrat Mohani' added in the English translation.

I was handicapped for want of suitable Hindi or Urdu words. This was my first occasion for delivering an argumentative speech before an audience especially composed of Mussalmans of the North.[552] I had spoken in Urdu[553] at the Muslim League at Calcutta, but it was only for a few minutes, and the speech was intended only to be a feeling appeal to the audience. *Here, on the contrary, I was faced with a critical, if not hostile, audience, to whom I had to explain and bring home my view-point.*[M7] But I had cast aside all shyness. I was not there to deliver an address in the faultless, polished Urdu of the Delhi Muslims, but to place before the gathering my views in such broken Hindi as I could command. And in this I was successful. This meeting afforded me a direct proof of the fact that Hindi–Urdu alone could become the *lingua franca*[M8] of India. Had I spoken in English, I could not have produced the impression that I did on the audience, and the Maulana might not have felt called upon to deliver his challenge. Nor, if he had delivered it, could I have taken it up effectively.

I could not hit upon a suitable Hindi or Urdu word for the new idea, and that put me out somewhat.[554] *At last I described it by the word 'non-co-operation', an expression that I used for the first time at this meeting.*[M9] As the Maulana was delivering his speech, it seemed to me that it was vain for him to talk about effective resistance to a Government with which he was co-operating in more than one thing. If resort to arms was impossible or undesirable, the only true resistance to the Government, it therefore seemed to me, was to cease to co-operate with it. *Thus I arrived at the word non-co-operation.*[M10] I had

[M7] But here I had to explain to a gathering that held the opposite view.

[M8] national language

[M9] I found the word 'non-cooperation'.

[M10] I made the first use of the word 'non-cooperation' at this meeting. In my address I gave arguments in support of it.

---

[552] 'of the North' added in the English translation.

[553] 'in Urdu' added in the English translation.

[554] 'but, I did respond.' To add.

not then a clear idea of all its manifold implications. I therefore did not enter into details.[555] I simply said:

'The Mussalmans have adopted a very[556] important resolution. If the peace terms are unfavourable to them—which may God forbid—they will stop all co-operation with Government. It is an inalienable right of the people thus to withhold co-operation.[557] We are not bound to retain Government titles and honours, or to continue in Government service. If Government should betray us in a great cause[558] like the Khilafat, we could not do otherwise than non-co-operate. We are therefore entitled to non-co-operate with Government in case of a betrayal.'[559]

But months elapsed before the word non-co-operation became current coin. For the time being it was lost in the proceedings of the conference. Indeed[560] when I supported the co-operation resolution at the Congress which met at Amritsar a month later, I did so in the hope that the betrayal would never come.[561]

---

[555] The paragraph 'I simply said . . . case of a betrayal' was not in the *Navajivan* of 16 December 1928 nor in the *Young India* of 20 December 1928. It was incorporated in the first edition, vol. 2, pp. 538–39, and was later incorporated in the subsequent Gujarati edition.

[556] In the Gujarati, 'another'.

[557] 'thus to withhold co-operation' not in the Gujarati edition.

[558] 'great religious cause' in the Gujarati edition.

[559] 'should the decision on Khilafat go against us' in the Gujarati edition.

[560] The sentence 'Indeed when I supported . . . betrayal would never come' was not in the *Navajivan* of 16 December 1928 or in the *Young India* of 20 December 1928; incorporated in the first edition, vol. 2, p. 538, and later incorporated in the subsequent Gujarati editions.

[561] 'I did so in the hope that Hindus and Mussalmans would have no occasion for non-cooperation.' In the Gujarati edition.

XXXVII

THE AMRITSAR CONGRESS[562]

The Punjab Government could not keep in confinement the hundreds of Punjabis who, under the martial law regime, had been clapped into jail[563] on the strength of the most meagre evidence by tribunals that were courts only in name. There was such an outcry all round against this flagrant piece of injustice that their further incarceration became impossible. Most of the prisoners were released before the Congress opened. Lala Harkishanlal[564] and the other leaders were all released, while the session of the Congress was still in progress.[565] The Ali Brothers too arrived there straight from jail. The people's joy knew no bounds. Pandit Motilal Nehru, who, *at the sacrifice of*[M1] his splendid practice, had made the Punjab his headquarters and had done great service,[566] was the President of the Congress; the late Swami Shraddhanandji was the Chairman of the Reception Committee.

    Up to this time my share in the annual proceedings of the Congress was confined only to the constructive advocacy of Hindi by making my[567] speech in *the national*

[M1] had set aside

---

[562] MKG was in Amritsar from 25 December 1919 to 1 January 1920 and attended the Congress session on 29, 30, 31 December and 1 January.

[563] 'for longer or shorter periods' to add.

[564] Lala Harkishen Lal (1864–1937), studied at Cambridge, prominent businessman of the Punjab, one of the founders and the first honorary secretary of the Punjab National Bank.

[565] 'while the session of the Congress was still in progress' to be placed at the end of the following sentence, instead of this one, as per the original.

[566] 'and had done great service' added in the English translation.

[567] 'little' to add.

M2 Hindi

*language,*M2 and to presenting in that speech the case of the Indians overseas. Nor did I expect to be called upon to do anything more this year. But, as had happened on many a previous occasion, responsible work came to me all of a sudden.

M3 King-Emperor's

M4 not liked by

M5 Royal proclamation

The *King's*M3 announcement on the new reforms[568] had just been issued. It was not wholly satisfactory even to me, and was *unsatisfactory to*M4 everyone else. But I felt at that time that the reforms, though defective, could still be accepted. I felt in the *King's announcement*M5 and its language the hand of Lord Sinha,[569] and it lent a ray of hope. But experienced stalwarts like the late Lokamanya and Deshbandhu Chittaranjan Das shook their heads. Pandit Malaviyaji was neutral.

Pandit Malaviyaji had harboured me in his own room. I had a glimpse of the simplicity of his life on the occasion of the foundation ceremony of the Hindu University,[570] but on this occasion, being in the same room with him, I was able to observe his daily routine in the closest detail, and what I saw filled me with joyful surprise. His room presented the appearance of a free inn for all the poor. You could hardly cross from one

M6 There were people lying around everywhere. It had neither space nor solitude.

end to the other. *It was so crowded.*M6 It was accessible at all odd hours to chance visitors who had the licence to take as much of his time as they liked. In a corner of this crib lay my charpoy in all its dignity.

---

[568] The Montague–Chelmsford Reforms. It became the Government of India Act, 1919, which introduced the system of 'diarchy' and a bicameral legislature by extending the notion of responsible government.

[569] Satyendra Prasanno Sinha, 1st Baron Sinha (1863–1928), president of the Indian National Congress, Advocate General of Bengal (1908), first Indian member of the governor general's Executive Council (1909), first Indian to be appointed parliamentary undersecretary of State for India (1919), elevated to Peerage, first Indian member of the British House of Lords.

[570] See n. 246 in Chapter XVI in Part III.

But I may not occupy this chapter with a description of Malaviyaji's mode of living, and must return to my subject.

I was thus enabled to hold daily discussions with Malaviyaji, who used lovingly to explain to me, like an elder brother, the various viewpoints of the different parties. *I saw that my participation in the deliberations on the resolution on the reforms was inevitable. Having*[M7] had my share of responsibility in the drawing-up of the Congress report on the Punjab wrongs, I felt that all that still remained to be done in that connection must claim my attention.[571] There had to be dealings with Government in that matter. Then similarly there was the Khilafat question. *I further believed at that time that Mr. Montagu would not betray or allow India's cause to be betrayed.*[M8] The release of the Ali Brothers and other prisoners too seemed to me to be an auspicious sign. In the circumstances I felt that a resolution not rejecting but[572] accepting the reforms was the correct thing. Deshbandhu[573] Chittaranjan Das, on the other hand, held firmly to the view that the reforms ought to be rejected as wholly inadequate and unsatisfactory. The late[574] Lokamanya was more or less neutral, but had decided to throw in his weight on the side of any resolution that the Deshbandhu might approve.

The idea of having to differ from such seasoned, well-tried and universally revered leaders was unbearable to me. But on the other hand the voice of conscience[575] was clear. I tried to run away from the Congress and

[M7] I saw that my duty lay in participation during the discussion on the resolution of the reforms. I

[M8] I had also believed that Montague would not allow India to be betrayed.

---

[571] 'I felt that all that still remained to be done in that connection must claim my attention' added in the English translation.

[572] 'not rejecting but' added in the English translation.

[573] 'Deshbandhu' added in the English translation.

[574] 'late' added in the English translation.

[575] '*antarnaad*', literally, 'inner voice', in the original.

M9 were permitted to absent myself

suggested to Pandit Malaviyaji and Motilalji that it would be in the general interest if I *absented myself*[M9] from the Congress for the rest of the session.[576] It would save me from having to make an exhibition of my difference with such esteemed leaders.

But my suggestion found no favour with these two seniors. The news of my proposal was somehow whispered to Lala Harkishanlal. 'This will never do. It will very much hurt the feelings of the Punjabis,' he said. I discussed the matter with Lokamanya, Deshbandhu and Mr. Jinnah, but no way out could be found. Finally I laid bare my distress to Malaviyaji. 'I see no prospect of a compromise,' I told him, 'and if I am to move my resolution, a division will have to be called and votes taken. But I do not find here any arrangements for it. The practice in the open session of the Congress so far has been to take votes by a show of hands with the result that all distinction between visitors and delegates is lost, while, as for taking a count of votes in such vast assemblies, we have no means at all. So it comes to this that, even if I want to call a division, there will be no facility for it, nor meaning in it.' But Lala Harkishanlal came to the rescue and undertook to make the necessary arrangements. 'We will not,' he said, 'permit visitors in the Congress *pandal*[577] on the day on which voting is to take place. And as for taking the count, well, I shall see to that. But you must not absent yourself from the Congress.' I capitulated; I framed my resolution,

M10 with great hesitation

and *in heart trembling*[M10] undertook to move it. Pandit Malaviyaji and Mr. Jinnah were to support it. I could notice that, although our difference of opinion was free from any trace of bitterness, and although our speeches too contained nothing but cold reasoning, the *people*[M11]

M11 assembly

---

[576] 'from the Congress for the rest of the session' added in the English translation.

[577] 'in the Congress *pandal*' added in the English translation.

could not stand the very fact of a difference;[578] it pained them. They wanted unanimity.

Even while speeches were being delivered, efforts to settle the difference were being made on the platform, and notes were being freely exchanged among the leaders for that purpose. Malaviyaji was leaving no stone unturned to bridge the gulf. Just then Jairamdas[579] handed over his amendment to me and pleaded in his own sweet manner to save the delegates from the dilemma of a division. His amendment appealed to me. Malaviyaji's eye was already scanning every quarter for a ray of hope. I told him that Jairamdas's amendment seemed to me to be likely to be acceptable to both the parties. The Lokamanya, to whom it was next shown, said, 'If C.R.[580] Das approves, I will have no objection.' Deshbandhu at last thawed, and cast a look towards Sjt. Bepin Chandra Pal[581] for endorsement. Malaviyaji was filled with hope. He snatched away the slip of paper containing the amendment, and before Deshbandhu had even pronounced a definite 'yes', shouted out, 'Brother delegates, you will be glad to learn that a compromise has been reached.' *What followed beggars description.*[M12] The *pandal* was rent with the clapping of hands, and the erstwhile gloomy faces of the audience lit up with joy.

[M12] What else could be asked for?

It is hardly necessary to deal with the text of the amendment.[582] My object here is only to describe how

---

[578] 'among the leaders' to add.

[579] Jairamdas Doulatram.

[580] 'C.R.' added in the English translation.

[581] Bipin Chandra Pal (1858–1932), along with Lala Lajpat Rai and Bal Gangadhar Tilak were the popular triumvirate Lal, Bal and Pal.

[582] The amendment was to the following effect: 'In the opinion of the Congress, whilst the Reforms Act falls short of the requirement of the situation in India and therefore inadequate and unsatisfactory, the Congress recognizes, it is a definite step towards Responsible Government and without prejudice to its full rights to agitate at

this resolution was undertaken as part of my experiments with which these chapters deal.

The compromise further increased my responsibility.

XXXVIII

CONGRESS INITIATION

M1 That I had to participate in the Congress, I do not regard as my entry into the Congress.

M2 the lowliest of soldiers

M3 one of my capabilities

M4 real work of the Subjects Committee was done

*I must regard my participation in Congress proceedings at Amritsar as my real entrance into the Congress politics.*M1 My attendance at the previous Congresses was nothing more perhaps than an annual renewal of allegiance to the Congress. I never felt on these occasions that I had any other work cut out for me except that of *a mere private,*M2 nor did I desire more.

My experience of Amritsar had shown that *there were one or two things for which perhaps I had some aptitude and which*M3 could be useful to the Congress. I could already see that the late[583] Lokamanya, the Deshbandhu, Pandit Motilalji and other leaders were pleased with my work in connection with the Punjab inquiry. They used to invite me to their informal gatherings where, as I found, *resolutions for the Subjects Committee were conceived.*M4 At these gatherings only those persons were invited who enjoyed the special confidence of the leaders and whose services were needed by them. Interlopers also sometimes found their way to these meetings.

There were, for the coming year, two things which interested me, as I had some aptitude for them. One

the earliest opportunity for remedying the glaring omission in the said Act, it calls upon people to co-operate with the authorities in making the Reforms a success and that this Congress expresses its cordial thanks to Right Hon'ble E.S. Montague and Lord Sinha, for their labours on behalf of India in connection with the constitutional reform.' *CWMG*, vol. 16, pp. 364–65, n. 2.

[583] 'late' added in the English translation.

of these was the memorial of the Jallianwala Bagh massacre. The Congress had passed a resolution for it amid great enthusiasm. A fund of about five lakhs had to be collected for it. I was appointed one of the trustees. *Pandit Malaviyaji enjoyed the reputation of being the prince among beggars for the public cause.*[M5] But I knew that I was not far behind him in that respect. It was whilst I was in South Africa that I discovered my capacity in this direction. *I had not the unrivalled magic of Malaviyaji for commanding princely donations from the potentates of India.*[M6] But I knew that there was no question of approaching the Rajas and Maharajas for donations for the Jallianwala Bagh memorial. The main responsibility for the collection thus fell, as I had expected, on my shoulders.[584] The generous citizens of Bombay subscribed most liberally, and the memorial trust has at present a handsome credit balance in the bank. But the problem that faces the country today is what kind of memorial to erect on the ground, to sanctify which, Hindus, Mussalmans and Sikhs mingled their blood. The three communities,[585] instead of being bound in a bond of amity and love, are, to all appearance, at war with one another, and the nation is at a loss as to how to utilize the memorial fund.[586]

My other aptitude which the Congress could utilize was as a draftsman. The Congress leaders had found that I had a faculty for condensed[587] expression, which I had acquired by long practice. The then existing constitution of the Congress was Gokhale's legacy. He had framed a few rules which served as a basis for running the Congress

[M5] Malaviyaji occupied and continues to do so the first place among those who had tremendous capacity to seek alms for public work.

[M6] I did not have, still do not have, the capacity to garner hundreds of thousands of rupees from princes and kings by bringing them under a magic spell. I have not seen anyone who can compete with Malaviyaji in this regard.

---

[584] 'This I knew when I accepted the position of a Trustee. And so it happened.' To add.

[585] 'or say two' to add.

[586] 'and the nation is at a loss as to how to utilize the memorial fund' added in the English translation.

[587] 'and inoffensive' to add.

machinery. The interesting history of the framing of these rules I had learnt from Gokhale's own lips. But everybody had now come to feel that these rules were no longer adequate for *the ever-increasing business of*[M7] the Congress. The question had been coming up year after year. The Congress at that time had practically no machinery *functioning during the interval between session and session, or for dealing with fresh contingencies that might arise in the course of the year*[M8] The existing rules provided for three secretaries, but as a matter of fact only one of them was a functioning secretary, and even he was not a whole-timer. How was he, single-handed, to run the Congress office, to think of the future, or to discharge during the current year the obligations contracted by the Congress in the past? During that year, therefore, everybody felt that this question would assume all the more importance. *The Congress was too unwieldy a body or the discussion of public affairs.*[M9] There was no limit set to the number of delegates in the Congress or to the number of delegates that each province could return.[588] Some improvement upon the existing chaotic condition[589] was thus felt by everybody to be an imperative necessity. I undertook the responsibility of framing a constitution on one condition. I saw that there were two leaders, viz., the Lokamanya and the Deshbandhu[590] who had the greatest hold on the public. I requested that *they, as the representatives of the people,*[M10] should be associated with me on the Committee for framing the constitution. But since it was obvious that they would not have the time personally to participate in the constitution-making work, I suggested that two

[M7] running

[M8] that enabled it to work through the year or plan for the future

[M9] The Congress had crowds of thousands gathering at its sessions, how was it to do any work of the people?

[M10] their representatives

---

[588] 'Anybody could become a delegate.' To add.

[589] 'upon the existing chaotic condition' added in the English translation.

[590] 'viz., the Lokamanya and the Deshbandhu' added in the English translation.

persons enjoying their confidence should be appointed along with me on the Constitution Committee, and that the number of its personnel should be limited to three. This suggestion was accepted by the late[591] Lokamanya and the late[592] Deshbandhu, who suggested the names of Sjts. Kelkar[593] and I.B. Sen[594] respectively as their proxies. The Constitution Committee could not even once come together, but we were able to consult with each other by correspondence, and in the end presented a unanimous report.[595] I regard this constitution with a certain measure of pride. I hold that, if we could fully work out this constitution, *the mere fact of working it out would bring us swaraj.*[M11] With the assumption of this responsibility I may be said to have made my real entrance into the Congress politics.

[M11] our ship would find the shore. That would happen when it has to.

XXXIX

THE BIRTH OF KHADI

I do not remember to have seen handloom or a spinning-wheel when in 1908[596] I described it in *Hind*

---

[591] 'late' added in the English translation.

[592] 'late' added in the English translation.

[593] Narasimha Chintaman (Tatyasaheb) Kelkar (1872–1947), nationalist leader, literary figure, associate and biographer of Tilak, editor of *The Mahratta*, twice president, Akhil Bharatiya Hindu Mahasabha (1928, 1932).

[594] Indu Bhusan Sen, a 'soil scientist'. Courtesy Ashok Mitra and Uma Dasgupta.

[595] See *CWMG*, vol. 18, pp. 288–90 and 428–31. For the constitution as adopted at the Nagpur session, see *CWMG*, vol. 19, pp. 190–98.

[596] Evident error for 1909. *Hind Swaraj* was composed in November 1909 and published in December that year.

M1 hunger would

Swaraj[597] as the panacea for the growing pauperism of India. In that book I took it as understood that anything that helped India to get rid of *the grinding poverty of her masses would in the same process*[M1] also establish swaraj. Even in 1915, when I returned to India from South Africa, I had not actually seen a spinning-wheel. When the Satyagraha Ashram was founded at Sabarmati,[598] we introduced a few handlooms there. *But no sooner had we done this than we found ourselves up against a difficulty. All of us belonged either to the liberal professions or to business;*[M2] not one of us was an artisan. We needed a weaving expert to teach us to weave before we could work the looms. *One was at last procured from Palanpur,*[M3] but he did not communicate to us the whole of his art. But Maganlal Gandhi was not to be easily baffled. Possessed of a natural talent for mechanics, he was able fully to master the art before long, and one after another several new weavers were trained up in the Ashram.

M2 I had to face great difficulty whilst establishing the loom. We were all ignorant and hence procuring a loom was not the same as running one. All of us could either wield a pen or run a business

M3 A loom was procured from Kathiawad and another from Palanpur and a trainer also arrived

The object that we set before ourselves was to be able to clothe ourselves entirely in cloth manufactured by our own hands.[M4] We therefore forthwith discarded the use of mill-woven cloth, and all the members of the Ashram resolved to wear hand–woven cloth made from Indian[599] yarn only. The adoption of this practice brought us a world of experience. It enabled us to know, from direct contact, the conditions of life among the weavers, the extent of their production, the handicaps in the way of their obtaining their yarn supply, the way in which they were being made victims of fraud, and, lastly, their ever-growing indebtedness. We were not in a position immediately to manufacture all the cloth for our needs. The alternative therefore was to get our cloth supply

M4 We wanted to wear clothes of our own making.

---

[597] 'spinning-wheel till the year 1908 when in *Hind Swaraj*' in the first edition.

[598] 'at Sabarmati' added in the English translation.

[599] 'mill' to add.

from handloom weavers. But readymade cloth from Indian mill-yarn was not easily obtainable either from the cloth-dealers or[600] from the weavers themselves. All the fine cloth woven by the weavers was from foreign yarn, since Indian mills did not spin fine counts. Even today the outturn of higher counts by Indian mills is very limited, whilst highest counts they cannot spin at all. It was after the greatest effort that we were at last able to find some weavers who condescended to weave Swadeshi yarn for us, and only on condition that the Ashram would take up[601] all the cloth that they might produce. By thus adopting cloth woven from mill-yarn as our wear, and propagating it among our friends, we made ourselves *voluntary*[M5] agents of the Indian spinning [M5] unpaid mills. This in its turn brought us into contact with the mills, and enabled us to know something about their management and their handicaps. We saw that the aim of the mills was more and more to weave the yarn spun by them; their co-operation with the handloom weaver was not willing, but unavoidable and temporary.[602] We became impatient to be able to spin our own yarn. It was clear that, until we could do this ourselves, dependence on the mills would remain. We did not feel that we could render any service to the country by continuing as agents of Indian spinning[603] mills.

No end of difficulties again faced us.[604] We could get neither spinning-wheel nor a spinner to teach us how to spin. We were employing some wheels for filling pearns and bobbins for weaving in the Ashram. But we had no

---

[600] 'either from the cloth-dealers or' added in the English translation.

[601] 'take off' in the first edition.

[602] 'and temporary' added in the English translation.

[603] 'Indian spinning' added in the English translation.

[604] 'No end of difficulties again faced us.' Added in the English translation.

idea that these could be used as spinning-wheels. Once Kalidas Jhaveri[605] discovered a woman who, he said, would demonstrate to us how spinning was done. We sent to her a member of the Ashram who was known for his great versatility in learning new things. But even he returned without wresting the secret of the art.

So the time passed on, and my impatience grew with the time. I plied every chance visitor to the Ashram who was likely to possess some information about hand-spinning with questions about the art. But the art being confined to women and having been all but exterminated,[606] if there was some stray spinner still surviving in some obscure corner, only a *member of that sex*[M6] was likely to find out her whereabouts.

^{M6} woman

In the year 1917 I was taken by my Gujarati friends to preside at the Broach Educational Conference. It was here that I discovered that remarkable lady Gangabehn Majmundar. She was a widow, but her enterprising spirit knew no bounds. Her education, in the accepted sense of the term,[607] was not much. But in courage and common sense she easily surpassed the general run of our educated women. She had already got rid of the curse of untouchability, and fearlessly moved among and served the suppressed classes.[608] She had means of her own, and her needs were few. She had a well seasoned constitution, and went about everywhere without an

^{M7} She was prepared to ride on horseback.

escort. *She felt quite at home on horseback.*[M7] I came to know her more intimately at the Godhra Conference.[609]

---

[605] 'Vakil' in the original.

[606] 'and having been all but exterminated' added in the English translation.

[607] 'in the accepted sense of the term' added in the English translation.

[608] 'suppressed classes' translates *Antyaj*.

[609] Between 2 and 5 November 1917 MKG was in Godhra for the Gujarat Political Conference, Social Conference and Antyaj Conference. In his speech at the Antyaj Conference he urged

To her I poured out my grief about the charkha,[610] and she lightened my burden by a promise to prosecute an earnest and incessant search for the spinning-wheel.[611]

XL

FOUND AT LAST!

At last, after no end of wandering in Gujarat, Gangabehn found the spinning-wheel in Vijapur in the Baroda State. Quite a number of people there had spinning-wheels in their homes, but had long since consigned them to the lofts as useless lumber.[612] They expressed to Gangabehn[613] their readiness to resume spinning, if someone promised to provide them with a regular supply of slivers, and to buy the yarn spun by them. *Gangabehn communicated the joyful news to me.*[M1] The providing of slivers was found to be a difficult task. On my mentioning the thing to the late Umar Sobani,[614] he solved the difficulty by immediately undertaking to send a sufficient supply of slivers from his mill. I sent to Gangabehn the slivers received from Umar Sobani,[615] and soon yarn began to pour in at such a rate that it *became quite a problem how to cope with it.*[M2]

[M1] Gangabehn communicated the news to me and my joy knew no bounds.

[M2] tired me out

Gangabehn to teach the Antyaj to read and write. *CWMG*, vol. 14, p. 73.

[610] 'about the charkha' added in the English translation.

[611] 'like Damayanti after Nala' to add.

[612] 'as useless lumber' added in the English translation.

[613] 'to Gangabehn' added in the English translation.

[614] Umar Haji Yusuf Sobani (d. 1926), a millionaire philanthropist of Bombay, owned Elphinstone Mills.

[615] 'received from Umar Sobani' added in the English translation.

M3 I felt hesitant in taking a decision about purchasing the slivers.

M4 He was engaged at a monthly salary of thirty-five rupees or perhaps even higher.

M5 took the responsibility of supplying bales of cotton. Gangabehn expanded her work at once. She brought and settled

M6 spindles

Mr. Umar Sobani's generosity was great, but still one could not go on taking advantage of it forever. *I felt ill at ease, continuously receiving slivers from him.*[M3] Moreover, it seemed to me to be fundamentally wrong to use mill-slivers. If one could use mill-slivers, why not use mill-yarn as well? Surely no mills supplied slivers to the ancients? How did they make their slivers then? With these thoughts in my mind[616] I suggested to Gangabehn to find carders who could supply slivers. She confidently undertook the task. She engaged a carder who was prepared to card cotton. *He demanded thirty-five rupees, if not much more, per month.*[M4] I considered no price too high at the time.[617] She trained a few youngsters to make slivers out of the carded cotton. I begged for cotton in Bombay.[618] Sjt. Yashvantprasad Desai[619] *at once responded. Gangabehn's enterprise thus prospered beyond expectations. She found out*[M5] weavers to weave the yarn that was spun in Vijapur, and soon Vijapur khadi gained a name for itself.

While these developments were taking place in Vijapur,[620] the spinning-wheel gained a rapid footing in the Ashram. Maganlal Gandhi, by bringing to bear all his splendid mechanical talent on the wheel, made many improvements in it, and wheels and *their accessories*[M6] began to be manufactured at the Ashram. The first piece of khadi manufactured in the Ashram cost 17 annas per yard. I did not hesitate to commend this very coarse

---

[616] 'with these thoughts in my mind' added in the English translation.

[617] 'I considered no price too high at the time.' Added in the English translation.

[618] 'in Bombay' added in the English translation.

[619] Yashvantprasad Hariprasad Desai (d. 1933), a mill owner of Bhavnagar, MKG described him as a 'sincere and silent worker' in the Harijan cause.

[620] 'While these developments were taking place in Vijapur' added in the English translation.

khadi at that rate to friends, who willingly paid the price.

I was laid up in bed at Bombay. *But I was fit enough to make searches for the wheel there.*[M7] At last I chanced upon two[621] spinners. They charged one rupee for a seer of yarn, i.e., 28 *tolas* or nearly three quarters of a pound.[622] *I was then ignorant of the economics of khadi. I considered no price too high for securing hand-spun yarn.*[M8] On comparing the rates paid by me with those paid in *Vijapur*[M9] I found that I was being cheated. The spinners refused to agree to any reduction in their rates. So I had to dispense with their services. But they served their purpose. They taught spinning to Shrimatis Avantikabai, Ramibai Kamdar, the widowed[623] mother of Sjt. Shankarlal Banker and Shrimati Vasumatibehn.[624] The wheel began merrily to hum in my room, and I may say without exaggeration that its hum had no small share in restoring me to health. I am prepared to admit that its effect was more psychological than physical. *But*

[M7] But I kept making inquiries.

[M8] I was hitherto completely blind to the science of khadi. I wanted hand-spun yarn and women spinners.

[M9] by Gangabehn

---

[621] 'women' to add.

[622] 'i.e., 28 *tolas* or nearly three quarters of a pound' added in the English translation.

[623] 'widowed' added in the English translation.

[624] MKG later corrected this 'lapse in memory'. He wrote in *Young India* of 31 January 1929, 'Govindbabu of Champapurhat, Utkal, tells me that in "The Story of My Experiments with Truth", I have erroneously mentioned two professional spinners of Bombay as having taught spinning to Shrimati Gangabehn, Avantikabai, and Ramabai and that it was he whom I had deputed to teach these sisters. I am thankful for having had the error pointed out to me. Now that I have taxed my memory, I do remember that I asked Govindbabu to teach many in Bombay who wanted to learn spinning. I have no doubt that in the "Story" there are several such omissions. Only the "Story" has been written not to issue certificates to deserving workers but to relate incidents illustrative of the working of the law of Truth. Those innumerable workers who have helped me in my pursuit must find in service its own reward.' *CWMG*, vol. 38, p. 420. Here, 'Ramabai' refers to 'Ramibai Kamdar' in the *Autobiography*.

then it only shows how powerfully the physical in man reacts to the psychological.[M10] I too set my hand to the wheel, but did not do much with it at the time.

In Bombay, again, the same old problem of obtaining a supply of hand-made slivers presented itself.[M11] A carder twanging his bow used to pass daily by Sjt. Revashankar's residence.[625] I sent for him and learnt that he carded cotton for stuffing mattresses. He agreed to card cotton for slivers, but demanded a stiff price for it, which, however, I paid. The yarn thus prepared I disposed of to some Vaishnava friends for making from it the garlands for the pavitra *Ekadashi*. Sjt. Shivji started a spinning class in Bombay. All these experiments involved considerable expenditure. *But it was willingly defrayed by patriotic friends, lovers of the motherland, who had faith in khadi.*[M12] The money thus spent, in my humble opinion, was not wasted. It brought us a rich store of experience, and *revealed to us the possibilities of the spinning-wheel.*[M13]

I now grew impatient for the exclusive adoption of khadi for my dress. My dhoti was still of Indian mill-cloth. The coarse khadi manufactured in the Ashram and at Vijapur was only 30 inches in width. I gave notice to Gangabehn that, unless she provided me with a khadi dhoti of 45 inches width within a month, I would do with coarse, short khadi dhoti. The ultimatum came upon her as a shock. But she proved equal to the demand made upon her. Well within the month she sent me a pair of khadi dhotis of *45*[M14] inches width, and thus *relieved me from what would then have been a difficult situation for me.*[M15] At about the same time Sjt. Lakshmidas brought Sjt. Ramji, *the weaver,*[M16] with his wife Gangabehn, from Lathi to the Ashram and got *khadi dhotis woven at the Ashram.*[M17] The part played by this couple in the spread of khadi was by no means

[M10] But does the mind contribute any less to making a person healthy or diseased?

[M11] How was I to obtain handmade slivers in here?

[M12] Faithful devotees of the country gave the money and I spent it.

[M13] gave us the measure of our limits

[M14] fifty

[M15] fully met my need

[M16] an Antyaj

[M17] through them khadi of a larger width woven

---

[625] Manibhuvan.

insignificant. They initiated a host of persons in Gujarat and also outside into the art of weaving hand-spun yarn. To see Gangabehn at her loom is a stirring sight.[626] When this unlettered but *self-possessed*[M18] sister plies at her loom, she becomes so lost in it that it is difficult to distract her attention, and much more difficult to draw[627] her eyes off her beloved loom.

[M18] cultured

XLI

AN INSTRUCTIVE[628] DIALOGUE

From its very inception *the khadi movement*,[M1] Swadeshi movement as it was then called, evoked much criticism from the mill-owners. The late Umar Sobani, a capable mill-owner himself, not only gave me the benefit of his own knowledge and experience, but kept me in touch with the opinion of the other mill-owners as well. The argument advanced by one of these deeply impressed him. He pressed me to meet him. I agreed. *Mr. Sobani arranged the interview.*[M2] The mill-owner opened the conversation.

[M1] this activity

[M2] We went to him.

'You know that there has been Swadeshi agitation before now?'

'Yes, I do,' I replied.

'You are also aware that in the days of the Partition[629] we, the mill-owners, fully exploited the Swadeshi

---

[626] 'To see Gangabehn at her loom is a stirring sight.' Added in the English translation.

[627] 'and much less to draw' in the first edition.

[628] 'Instructive' added, 'A Dialogue' in the original.

[629] 'of Bengal' to add. The decision to effect the partition of Bengal in eastern Muslim-majority and western Hindu-majority areas was announced by Viceroy Lord Curzon in July 1905; it came into effect on 16 October 1905 and led to widespread political

movement. When it was at its height, we raised the prices of cloth, and did even worse things.'

'Yes, I have heard something about it, and it has grieved me.'

'I can understand your grief, but I can see no ground for it. We are not conducting our business out of philanthropy. We do it for profit, we have got to satisfy the shareholders. The price of an article is governed by the demand for it. Who can check *the law of demand and supply*?^{M3} The Bengalis should have known that their agitation was bound to send up the price of Swadeshi cloth by stimulating the demand for it.'

M3 this law

I interrupted: 'The Bengalis like me were trustful in their nature. They believed, in the fulness of their faith, that the mill-owners would not be so utterly selfish *and unpatriotic as to betray their country in the hour of its need, and even to go the length, as they did, of fraudulently passing off foreign cloth as Swadeshi.*'^{M4}

M4 , certainly not commit betrayal and would never sell foreign cloth as Swadeshi.

'I knew your believing nature,' he rejoined, 'that is why I put you to the trouble of coming to me, so that I might warn you against falling into the same error as these simple-hearted Bengalis.'

With these words the mill-owner beckoned to his clerk *who was standing by to produce samples of the stuff that was being manufactured in his mill.*^{M5} Pointing to it he said: 'Look at this stuff. This is the latest variety turned out by our mill. It is meeting with a widespread demand. We manufacture it from the waste. Naturally, therefore, it is cheap. We send it *as far North as the valleys of the Himalayas.*^{M6} We have agencies all over the country, even in places where your voice or your agents can never reach. You can thus see that we do not stand in need of *more agents.*^{M7} Besides, you ought to know that India's production of cloth falls far short of its requirements. The

M5 to bring samples. These were samples of blankets manufactured from waste yarn.

M6 to the far North

M7 agents such as you

and cultural protests and the Swadeshi Movement was initiated. The decision was annulled in December 1911.

question of Swadeshi, therefore, largely resolves itself into one of production. The moment we can increase our production sufficiently, and improve its quality to the necessary extent, the import of foreign cloth will automatically cease. My advice to you, therefore, is not to carry on your agitation on its present lines, but to turn your attention to the erection of fresh mills. What we need is not propaganda to inflate demand for our goods, but greater production.'

'Then, surely, you will bless my effort, if I am already engaged in that very thing,' I asked.

'How can that be?' he exclaimed, a bit puzzled, 'but may be, you are thinking of promoting the establishment of new mills, in which case you certainly deserve to be congratulated.'

'I am not doing exactly that,' I explained, 'but I am engaged *in the revival of*[M8] the spinning-wheel.'

[M8] with

'What is that?' he asked, feeling still more at sea.[630] I told him all about the spinning-wheel, and the story of my long quest after it,[631] and added, 'I am entirely of your opinion, it is no use my becoming virtually an agent for the mills. That would do more harm than good to the country.[632] *Our mills will not be in want of custom for a long time to come.*[M9] My work should be, and therefore is, to organize the production of hand-spun cloth, and to find means for the disposal of the khadi thus produced. I am, therefore, concentrating my attention on the production of khadi. I *swear by*[M10] this form of Swadeshi, because through it I can provide work to the semi-starved, semi-employed women of India. My idea is to get these women to spin yarn, and to clothe the people of India with khadi woven out of

[M9] The mill produce does not remain unsold.

[M10] believe in

---

[630] 'feeling still more at sea' added in the English translation.

[631] 'and the story of my long quest after it' added in the English translation.

[632] 'to the country' added in the English translation.

it. I do not know how far this movement is going to succeed; at present it is only in the incipient stage. But I have full faith in it. At any rate it can do no harm. On the contrary to the extent that it can add to the cloth production of the country, be it ever so small,[633] it will represent so much solid gain. You will thus perceive that my movement is free from the evils mentioned by you.'

He replied, *'If you have additional production in view in organizing your movement,*[M11] I have nothing to say against it. Whether the spinning-wheel can make headway in this age of power machinery[634] is another question. But I for one wish you every success.'

M11 If your movement is thus organized

XLII

ITS RISING TIDE[M1]

M1 The Tide of Non-Cooperation

I must not devote any more chapters here to a description of the further progress of khadi. It would be outside the scope of these chapters to give a history of my various activities after they came before the public eye, and *I must not attempt it, if only because to do so would require a treatise on the subject.*[M2] My object in writing these chapters is simply to describe how certain things, as it were spontaneously, presented themselves to me in the course of my experiments with truth.

M2 to do so would be to make a book of these subjects

To resume, then, the story of the non-co-operation movement.[M3] Whilst the powerful Khilafat agitation set up by the Ali Brothers was in full progress, I had long discussions on the subject with the late Maulana Abdul Bari and the other *ulemas*, especially, with regard to the extent to which a Mussalman could observe the

M3 Therefore, it is now time to say something about non-cooperation.

---

[633] 'be it ever so small' added in the English translation.

[634] 'of power machinery' added in the English translation.

rule of non-violence. In the end they all agreed that Islam did not forbid its followers from following non-violence as a policy[635] and further, that, while they were pledged to that policy, they were bound faithfully to carry it out. At last the non-co-operation resolution was moved in the Khilafat conference, and carried after prolonged deliberations. I have a vivid recollection how once at Allahabad a committee sat all night deliberating upon the subject. In the beginning the late Hakim Saheb was sceptical as to the practicability of non-violent non-co-operation. But after his scepticism was overcome he *threw himself into it heart and soul*,[M4] and his help proved invaluable to the movement.

M4 joined in

Next, the non-co-operation resolution was moved by me at the Gujarat Political Conference that was held shortly afterwards.[636] The preliminary contention raised by the opposition was that it was not competent to a provincial conference to adopt a resolution in advance of the Congress. As against this, I suggested that the restriction could apply only to a backward movement; but as for going forward, the subordinate organizations were not only fully competent, but were in duty bound to do so, if they had in them the necessary grit and confidence. *No permission, I argued, was needed to try to enhance the prestige of the parent institution, provided one did it at one's own risk.*[M5] The proposition was then discussed on its merits, the debate being marked by its keenness no less than the atmosphere of 'sweet reasonableness' in which it was conducted. On the ballot being taken the resolution was declared carried by an overwhelming majority. The successful passage of the resolution was

M5 That would enhance the prestige of the main organizations

---

[635] 'to a certain extent' to add.

[636] The conference met in Ahmedabad from 27 to 29 August 1920. For MKG's speech on non-cooperation, see *CWMG*, vol. 18, pp. 200–03.

M6 Abbas Sahib

due not a little to the personality of[637] Sjt. Vallabhbhai and Abbas Tyabji. *The latter*[M6] was the president, and his leanings were all in favour of the non-co-operation resolution.

The All-India Congress Committee resolved to hold a special session of the Congress in September 1920 at Calcutta[638] to deliberate on this question. Preparations were made for it on a large scale. Lala Lajpat Rai was elected President. Congress and Khilafat specials were run to Calcutta from Bombay. At Calcutta there was a mammoth gathering of delegates and visitors.

At the request of Maulana Shaukat Ali I prepared a draft of the non-co-operation resolution in the train. Up to this time I had more or less avoided the use of the word non-violent in my drafts. I invariably made use of this word in my speeches. My vocabulary on the subject was still in process of formation.[639] *I found that I could not bring home my meaning to purely Muslim audiences with the help of the Sanskrit equivalent for non-violent.*[M7] I therefore asked Maulana Abul Kalam Azad[640] to give me some other equivalent for it. He suggested the word *ba-aman*; similarly for non-co-operation he suggested the phrase *tark-i-mavalat*.

M7 I had failed to explain what I needed to through the word 'peaceful' to purely Muslim audiences.

Thus, while I was still busy devising suitable Hindi, Gujarati and Urdu phraseology for non-co-

---

[637] 'not a little to the personality of' added in the English translation. In the original 'due to'.

[638] The special session was held on 7, 8 and 9 September 1920; on the 7th was the meeting of the Subjects Committee.

[639] 'My vocabulary on the subject was still in the process of formation.' Added in the English translation.

[640] Abul Kalam Ghulam Muhiyuddin (1888–1958), erudite scholar of Persian, Arabic and Urdu, president, Indian National Congress (1923, 1940–46), founded the Urdu journals *Al-Hilal* and *Al-Balagh*, first education minister of independent India (1947–58).

operation, I was called upon to frame the non-co-operation resolution for that eventful Congress. In the original draft the word 'non-violent' had been left out by me. I had handed over the draft to Maulana Shaukat Ali who was travelling in the same compartment, without noticing the omission. During the night I discovered the error. In the morning I sent Mahadev with the message that the omission should be made good before the draft was sent to the Press. But I have an impression that the draft was printed before the insertion could be made. The Subjects Committee was to have met the same evening. I had therefore to make the necessary correction in the printed copies of the draft. I afterwards saw that there would have been great difficulty, had I not been ready with my draft.

None the less my plight was pitiable indeed. I was absolutely at sea as to who would support the resolution and who would oppose it. Nor had I any idea as to the attitude that Lalaji would adopt. *I only saw an imposing phalanx of veteran warriors assembled for the fray at Calcutta,*[641] M8 Dr. Besant, Pandit Malaviyaji, Sjt. Vijayaraghavachari, Pandit Motilalji and the Deshbandhu being some of them.

M8 Seasoned fighters had assembled at Calcutta

In my resolution non-co-operation was postulated only with a view to obtaining redress of the Punjab and the Khilafat wrongs. That, however, did not appeal to Sjt. Vijayaraghavachari. 'If non-co-operation was to be declared, why should it be with reference to particular wrongs? The absence of swaraj was the biggest wrong that the country was labouring under; it should be against that that non-co-operation should be directed,' he argued. Pandit Motilalji also wanted the demand for swaraj to be included in the resolution. I readily accepted the suggestion and incorporated the demand

---

[641] 'learned' to add.

for swaraj in my resolution, which was passed after an exhaustive, serious and somewhat stormy discussion.[642]

Motilalji was the first to join the movement. I still remember the sweet discussion that I had with him on the resolution. He suggested some changes in its phraseology which I adopted. He undertook to win the Deshbandhu for the movement. The Deshbandhu's heart was inclined towards it, but he felt sceptical as to the capacity of the people to carry out the programme. It was only at the Nagpur Congress[643] that he and Lalaji accepted it whole-heartedly.

I felt the loss of the late Lokamanya very deeply at the special session. It has been my firm faith to this day that, had the Lokamanya been then alive, he would have given his benedictions to me on that occasion. But even if it had been otherwise, and he had opposed the movement, I should still have esteemed his opposition as a privilege and an education for myself. We had our differences of opinion always, but they never led to bitterness. He always allowed me to believe that the ties between us were of the closest. Even as I write these lines, the circumstances of his death stand forth vividly before my mind's eye. It was about the hour of midnight, when Patwardhan, who was then working with me, conveyed over the telephone the news of his death. I was at that time surrounded by my companions. Spontaneously the exclamation escaped my lips, 'My strongest bulwark is gone.'[644] The non-co-operation movement was then in full swing, and I was eagerly looking forward to *encouragement and inspiration from him*.[M9] What his attitude would have been with regard

[M9] his warmth

----

[642] For MKG's speeches on non-cooperation at the Calcutta session, see *CWMG*, vol. 18, pp. 245–55.

[643] Held in December 1920.

[644] Lokmanya Tilak passed away on 31 July 1920. For MKG's obituary of him, see *CWMG,* vol. 18, pp. 110–11.

to the final phase of non-co-operation will always be a matter of speculation, and an idle one at that. But this much is certain—*that the deep void left by his death weighed heavily upon everybody present at Calcutta. Everyone felt the absence of his counsels in that hour of crisis in the nation's history.*[M10]

[M10] at this critical hour in the nation's history, his absence was felt by everyone

XLIII

AT NAGPUR

The resolutions adopted at the Calcutta special session of the Congress were to be confirmed at its annual session at Nagpur. Here again, as at Calcutta there was a great rush of visitors and delegates. The number of delegates in the Congress had not been limited yet. As a result, so far as I can remember, the figure on this occasion reached about fourteen thousand. Lalaji pressed for a slight amendment to the clause about the boycott of schools, which I accepted. Similarly some amendments were made at the instance of the Deshbandhu, after which the[645] non-co-operation resolution was passed unanimously.[646]

The resolution regarding the revision of the Congress constitution too was to be taken up at this session of the Congress. The sub-committee's draft was presented at the Calcutta special session. The matter had therefore been thoroughly ventilated and thrashed out. At the Nagpur session, where it came up for final disposal,[647] Sjt. C. Vijayaraghavachari was the President.

---

[645] 'non-violent' to add.

[646] For the draft resolution, see *CWMG*, vol. 19, pp. 182–85, and for the resolution as passed, pp. 576–78.

[647] 'where it came up for final disposal' added in the English translation.

The Subjects Committee passed the draft with only one important change. In my draft the number of delegates had been fixed, I think, at 1,500; the Subjects Committee substituted in its place the figure 6,000. In my opinion this increase was the result of hasty judgment, and experience of all these years has only confirmed me in my view. I hold it to be an utter delusion to believe that a large number of delegates is in any way a help to the better conduct of the business, or that it safeguards the principle of democracy. Fifteen hundred delegates, jealous of the interest of the people, broad-minded and truthful, would any day be a better safeguard for democracy than six thousand *irresponsible*[M1] men chosen anyhow. To safeguard democracy the people must have a keen sense of independence, self-respect and their oneness, and should insist upon choosing as their representatives only such persons as are good and true. But obsessed with the idea of numbers as the Subjects Committee was, it would have liked to go even beyond the figure of six thousand. The limit of six thousand was therefore in the nature of a compromise.

The question of the goal of the Congress formed a subject for keen discussion.[M2] In the constitution that I had presented, the goal of the Congress was the attainment of swaraj within the British Empire if possible and without if necessary. A party in the Congress wanted to limit the goal to swaraj within the British Empire only. Its viewpoint was put forth by Pandit Malaviyaji and Mr. Jinnah. But they were not able to get many votes. Again the draft constitution provided that the means for the attainment were to be peaceful and *legitimate*.[M3] This condition too came in for opposition, it being contended that there should be no restriction upon the means to be adopted.[648] But the Congress adopted the

[M1] authoritarian

[M2] The Congress discussed the goal of swaraj.

[M3] truthful

---

[648] 'it being contended that there should be no restriction upon the means to be adopted' added in the English translation.

original draft after an instructive and frank discussion. I
am of opinion that, if this constitution had been worked
out by the people honestly, intelligently and zealously,
it would have become a potent instrument of mass
education, and the very process of working it out would
have brought us swaraj. But a discussion of the theme
would be irrelevant here.

Resolutions about Hindu–Muslim unity, the
removal of untouchability and khadi too were passed in
this Congress, and since then the Hindu members of the
Congress have taken upon themselves the responsibility
of ridding Hinduism of the curse of untouchability,
and the Congress has established a living bond of
relationship with the 'skeletons'[649] of India through
khadi. The adoption of non-co-operation for the sake
of the Khilafat was itself a great practical[650] attempt made
by the Congress to bring about Hindu–Muslim unity.

---

[649] 'skeletons' here refers to emaciated and impoverished Indians.

[650] 'practical' added in the English translation.

FAREWELL

The time has now come to bring these chapters to a close.[651] My life from this point onward has been so public that there is hardly anything about it that people do not know. Moreover, since 1921 I have worked in such close association with the Congress leaders that I can hardly describe[652] any episode in my life since then without referring to my relations with them.[653] For though Shraddhanandji, the Deshbandhu, Hakim Saheb and Lalaji are no more with us today, we have the good luck to have a host of other veteran[654] Congress leaders still living and working in our midst. The history of the Congress, since the great changes in it that I have described above, is still in the making. And my principal

---

[651] In a letter to C.F. Andrews dated 29 November 1928 MKG wrote, 'I have no notion when the whole thing will be finished, even though I am omitting many important events and trying to hurry on to the Non-co-operation days. I want to break off after the special session at Calcutta, because the events are too fresh and there are so many contemporaries whom I must describe if I am to write further. I feel too that it would be advisable for me to stop at the stage for thenceforward my life has been too public. Therefore there is no need for further elucidation. And then of course there is *Young India*, a clear mirror through which anybody who cares can look at me.' *CWMG*, vol. 38, p. 122.

[652] 'meaningfully' to add.

[653] 'These relations are still fresh.' To add.

[654] 'veteran' added in the English translation.

experiments during the past seven years[655] have all been made through the Congress. A reference to my relations with the leaders would therefore be unavoidable, if I set about describing my experiments further. And this I may not do, at any rate for the present, if only from a sense of propriety. Lastly, my conclusions from my current experiments can hardly as yet be regarded as decisive. It therefore seems to me to be my plain[656] duty to close this narrative here. In fact, my pen instinctively refuses to proceed further.

It is not without a wrench that I have to take leave of the reader. I set a high value on my experiments. I do not know whether I have been able to *do justice to them*.[M1] I can only say that I have spared no pains to give a faithful narrative. To describe truth, as it has appeared to me, and in the exact manner in which I have arrived at it, has been my ceaseless effort. *The exercise has given me*[M2] ineffable mental peace, because, it has been my fond hope that it might bring faith in Truth and Ahimsa to *waverers*.[M3]

My uniform experience has convinced me that there is no other God than Truth.[M4] And if every page of these chapters does not proclaim to the reader that the only means for the realization of Truth is Ahimsa, I shall deem all my labour[657] in writing these chapters to have been in vain. *And, even though my efforts in this behalf may prove fruitless, let the readers know that the vehicle, not the great principle, is at fault*.[M5] After all, however sincere my strivings after Ahimsa may have been, they have still been imperfect and inadequate. The little fleeting glimpses, therefore, that I have been able to have of Truth can hardly convey an idea of the indescribable

[M1] describe them truthfully

[M2] While giving these descriptions to the reader I have experienced

[M3] readers

[M4] It has not been my experience that there is a God other than Truth.

[M5] The effort might have been in vain, but the principle is not.

---

[655] 'during the past seven years' added in the English translation.

[656] 'plain' added in the English translation.

[657] 'pains' in the first edition.

lustre of Truth, a million times more intense than that
of the sun we daily see with our eyes. In fact what I
have caught is only the faintest glimmer of that mighty
effulgence. But this much I can say with assurance, as
a result of all my experiments, that a perfect vision of
Truth can only follow a complete realization of Ahimsa.

To see the universal and all-pervading Spirit of
Truth face to face one must be able to love *the meanest*[M6]   [M6] all
of creation as oneself. And a man who aspires after that
cannot afford to keep out of any field of life. That is
why my devotion to Truth has drawn me into the field
of politics; and I can say without the slightest hesitation,
and yet in all humility, that those who say that religion
has nothing to do with politics do not know what
religion means.

Identification with everything that lives is impossible
without self-purification; without self-purification the
observance of the law of Ahimsa *must remain an empty
dream.*[M7] God can never be realized by one who is not   [M7] is an utter impossibility
pure of heart. Self-purification therefore must mean
purification in all the walks of life. *And purification being
highly infectious, purification of oneself necessarily leads to the
purification of one's surroundings.*[M8]

But the path of self-purification is hard and steep.[658]
To attain to perfect purity one has to become absolutely
passion-free in thought, speech and action; to rise above
the opposing currents of love and hatred, attachment
and repulsion. I know that I have not in me as yet that
triple[659] purity, in spite of constant ceaseless striving
for it. That is why the world's praise fails to move
me, indeed it very often stings me. To conquer the
subtle passions seems to me to be harder far than the
physical conquest of the world by the force of arms.
Ever since [M9] my return to India I have had experiences   [M9] Even after

[M8] Such purification is
attainable. The personal and
the universal are so close that
purification of one equals the
purification of many. And the
God of Truth has endowed
everyone, since birth, with the
capacity to strive after self-
purification.

---

[658] 'This I experience at every moment.' To add.

[659] 'triple' added in the English translation.

of the dormant passions lying hidden within me. The knowledge of them has made me feel humiliated though not defeated. *The experiences and experiments have sustained me and given me great joy.*[M10] But I know that I have still before me a difficult path to traverse. I must reduce myself to zero. So long as a man[660] does not of his own free will put himself last among his fellow creatures, there is no salvation for him. Ahimsa is the farthest limit of humility.[661]

In bidding farewell to the reader, for the time being at any rate, I ask him to join with me in prayer to the God of Truth that He may grant me the boon of Ahimsa in mind, word and deed.[M11]

[M10] The experiments with truth have given me great joy, they do so even now.

[M11] Praying for such humility and begging the world to join me in my prayer, I close these chapters, for the present at any rate.

---

[660] 'as one' in the first edition.

[661] 'And it is a fact of experience that without such humility salvation is ever impossible.' To add.

EDITOR'S ACKNOWLEDGEMENTS

To my Ashram colleagues, Kinnari Bhatt and Kartikeya Sarabhai, for making it possible—with all my many limitations—to share the Ashramic space.

Ramachandra Guha, Pratap Bhanu Mehta and Sunil Khilnani, I thank you for reading a draft of the work and for writing an endorsement. Ram with his extraordinary grasp over archival material scattered over three continents has answered my queries. Ajay Skaria reads Gandhi also in Gujarati and I hope that he would hear echoes of our long-distance conversations in this work. Thank you, Ajay. Arindam Chakrabarti, a deep reader of texts, has read the draft of this work and our conversations on the nature of act of reading has shaped my understanding of Gandhi's engagement with philosophical texts and acts.

Harsh Sethi, Malavika and Tejbir Singh have been a source of friendship, warmth, cynical hope and camaraderie. Thank you, *Seminar*.

Rajmohan Gandhi and Gopalkrishna Gandhi have provided the much needed moral compass in times of ignorance and darkness.

The archivists at the Honourable Society of the Inner Temple and the Middle Temple have answered my queries and shared their knowledge.

Richa Burman at Penguin Random House, thank you, for your patient and careful reading. Indrani Dasgupta, thank you.

To Ashis Nandy I owe much. A teacher and guide, he has become a wise elder, teaching me to befriend my daemons, to live with my cultural anxieties. Thank you.

Suhrud, Megha and Katyayani, thank you for your love.

INDEX

773